22

AQA Psychology B

Exclusively endorsed by AQA

A2

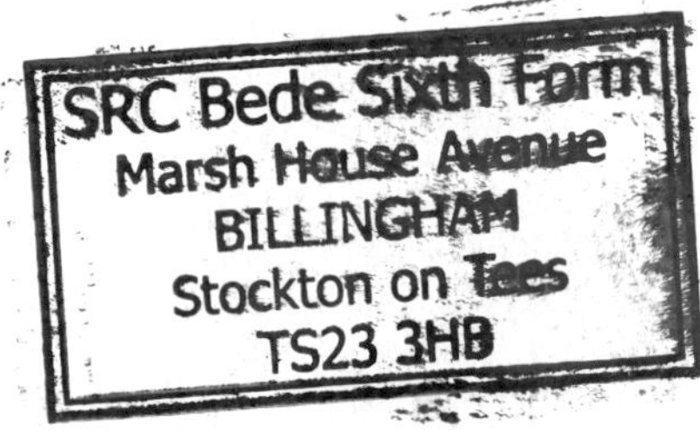

Mark Billingham
Kevin Brewer
Sarah Ladbrook
David Messer
Howard Padley
Sue Standring
Regina Teahan

Nelson Thornes

Published in 2008 by:
Nelson Thornes Ltd
Delta Place
27 Bath Road
CHELTENHAM
GL53 7TH
United Kingdom

08 09 10 11 12 / 10 9 8 7 6 5 4 3 2 1

A catalogue record for this book is available from the British Library

ISBN 978 0 7487 9828 5

Cover photograph by Photolibrary
Illustrations include artwork drawn by Angela Knowles, Peters and Zabransky UK Ltd, Harry Venning and Thomson Digital
Page make-up by Thomson Digital
Printed and bound in Spain by Graphycems

Acknowledgements
The authors and publishers wish to thank the following for permission to use copyright material:

piv: Alamy/Blend images; p3, 4: iStockphoto; p6, Fig. 1: Science Photo Library/Science Source; p7, Fig. 2: Fotolia/nyul; p30: *Psychology of Intelligence* by J. Piaget (1951), published by Routledge and Kegan Paul; p37: *The Origins of Intelligence in Children* by J. Piaget (1952), published by WW Norton and Co.; p48, Fig. 2: Corbis/Hulton Archive; p57, Fig. 4: Barry Donahue/Courtesy of the Harvard Office of News and Pubic Affairs; p59, Fig. 5: adapted figure from 'A Longitudinal Study of Moral Judgement', *Monographs of the Society for Research in Child Development*, Serial No. 200, Vol. 48 (1-2), Colby *et al* (1983), published by the University of Chicago; p71: iStockphoto/Christine Balderas; p72, Fig. 1: Rex Features/Stewart Cook; p73, Fig. 2: iStockphoto; p74, Fig. 3: Rex Features/Matt Baron; Fig. 4: Rex Features; p75, Fig. 5: Rex Features/Matt Baron, Rex Features/Michael Williams; Fig. 6: Rex Features/Paul Grover; p78, Fig. 7: National Archives; Fig. 8: Images supplied courtesy of VisionMetric Ltd; Fig. 9: Dr Charlie Frowd, School of Psychology, University of Central Lancashire, Preston, UK; p82, Fig. 10: PA/Empics; p84, Fig. 11: Alamy/Robert Harding Picture Library; p98: Ron Nickel/Design Pics/PunchStock; p104, Fig. 2: Getty/UHB Trust; p120, Fig. 7: Science Photo Library/Pascal Goetgheluck; p125; Science Photo Library/Will McIntyre; p129, Fig. 12: Science Photo Library/BSIP/Laurent Laeticia; p132: Alamy/Stock Connection Distribution; p133, Fig 1: © Jacky Fleming; p135, Fig. 3: iStockphoto/Alexander Hafemann; p136, Fig. 4: adapted figure from *Advanced Psychology: Health Psychology*, M. Forshaw (2003), published by Hodder and Stoughton; p138, Fig. 7: adapted figure from ORG: *Advanced Psychology Through Diagrams*, Grahame Hill (1998), OUP. Reprinted by permission of Oxford University Press; p139, Fig. 8: adapted figure from *Health Psychology: Biopsychosocial Interactions*, Edward P. Sarafino, (1990), published by John Wiley and Sons, Inc; p159, Fig. 13: *Psychology*, 5th Edition, D. Myers (1998), published by Worth Publishers; p167: Rex Features/Jonathan Hordle; p174: *Forbidden Drugs* by P. Robson (1994), published by Oxford University Press; p183, Fig. 3: *Care of Drug Users in General Practice 2e* by Barry Beaumont ed. (2004), Oxford: Radcliffe Publishing. Reproduced with the permission of the copyright holder; p197, Fig. 1 and p198: Mary Evans Picture Library; p200, Fig. 2: reprinted under Crown Copyright; p201, Fig. 3: reprinted under Crown Copyright; p203, Fig. 5: Professor David Canter; Fig. 6: Rex Features/Photo News Service; p205: *Mapping Murder: The Secrets of Geographical Profiling* by David Canter (2003), published by Virgin Books; p206, Fig. 7: Corbis/Bettman; p207, Fig.8: Mary Evans Picture Library; p223: Science Photo Library/Simon Fraser; p229: *Behaviourism* by J.B. Watson (1924), New York: Norton; p235: *Social Learning Theory* by A. Bandura (1977b), published by General Learning Press; p248: 'Person psychology: Psychoanalytic and humanistic perspectives' by R. Stevens. In *Mapping Psychology* 2, D. Miell, A. Phoenix and K. Thomas (eds) (2002), published by Open University Press; p265: Fotolia/Shocky; p285: 'Psychology as the behaviourist views it' by J.B. Watson (1913), Psychological Review, 20, p158–177, p291: © Alamy/D. Hurst; p307, Fig. 3: Martyn F. Chillmaid.

Every effort has been made to contact the copyright holders and we apologise if any have been overlooked. Should copyright have been unwittingly infringed in this book, the owners should contact the publishers, who will make the corrections at reprint.

Contents

AQA introduction

Nelson Thornes and AQA

Nelson Thornes has worked in collaboration with AQA to ensure that this book offers you the best support for your A Level course and helps you to prepare for your exams. The partnership means that you can be confident that the range of learning, teaching and assessment practice materials has been checked by the senior examining team at AQA before formal approval, and is closely matched to the requirements of your specification.

Blended learning

Printed and electronic resources are blended: this means that links between topics and activities between the book and the electronic resources help you to work in the way that best suits you, and enable extra support to be provided online. For example, you can test yourself online and feedback from the test will direct you back to the relevant parts of the book.

Electronic resources are available in a simple-to-use online platform called Nelson Thornes learning space. If your school or college has a licence to use the service, you will be given a password through which you can access the materials through any internet connection.

Icons in this book indicate where there is material online related to that topic. The following icons are used:

Learning activity

These resources include a variety of interactive and non-interactive activities to support your learning.

Research support

These resources include WebQuests, in which you are assigned a task and provided with a range of web links to use as source material for research.

Audio stimulus

Each chapter has a podcast summarising the important points.

Progress tracking

These resources include a variety of tests that you can use to check your knowledge on particular topics (Test yourself) and a range of resources that enable you to analyse and understand examination questions (On your marks ...).

When you see an icon, go to Nelson Thornes learning space at www.nelsonthornes.com/aqagce, enter your access details and select your course. The materials are arranged in the same order as the sections in the book, so you can easily find the resources you need.

How to use this book

This book covers the specification for your course and is arranged in a sequence approved by AQA.

The book content is divided into two units – Unit 3 and Unit 4 – which match the two units of the AQA Psychology B A2 specification. It is then divided into sections matched to the sections of the specification – Child development; the Applied options: Cognition and law, Schizophrenia and mood disorders, Stress and stress management, Substance abuse, Forensic psychology; Approaches in psychology; Debates in psychology; Methods in psychology. Each section introduction contains a table mapping the section content to the specification so you can see at a glance where to find the information you need. Sections are then further divided into chapters, and then topics, making them clear and easy to use.

The content of the book is designed to meet the requirements of How science works by giving you the necessary skills and information to plan your own psychological investigations.

The features in this book include:

Learning objectives

At the beginning of each topic you will find a list of learning objectives that contain targets linked to the requirements of the specification.

Key terms

Terms that you will need to be able to define and understand.

Hint

Hints to aid your understanding of the content.

Links

This highlights any key areas where sections relate to one another and provides synopticity with the AS book.

Research study

Summaries of important psychological research studies to enhance your knowledge and understanding of a section.

Take it further

This new feature for A2 will help extend your understanding of the subject matter, challenge and inspire you to look at things in a different way and encourage you to develop the skills necessary to achieve higher grades.

End-of-chapter activity

Suggestions for practical investigations you can carry out.

Summary questions

Short questions that test your understanding of the subject and allow you to apply the skills you develop to different scenarios. The final question in each set is designed to be a stretch-and-challenge question and to require more thought. Answers are supplied free at www.nelsonthornes.com/psychology_answers.

Nelson Thornes is responsible for the solution(s) given and they may not constitute the only possible solution(s).

AQA Examiner's tip

Hints from AQA examiners to help you with your study and to prepare for your exam.

AQA Examination-style questions

Questions in the style that you can expect in your exam.

AQA examination questions are reproduced by permission of the Assessment and Qualifications Alliance.

Key points:

A bulleted list at the end of each topic summarising the content in an easy-to-follow way.

Web links in the book

Because Nelson Thornes is not responsible for third-party content online, there may be some changes to this material that are beyond our control. In order for us to ensure that the links referred to in the book are as up to date as possible, the websites provided are usually homepages with supporting instructions on how to reach the relevant pages if necessary.

Please let us know at **webadmin@nelsonthornes.com** if you find a link that doesn't work and we will do our best to correct this at reprint, or to list an alternative site.

Introduction for students

Welcome again to the exciting subject of psychology – the scientific study of mind and behaviour. In the AS textbook for Assessment and Qualifications Alliance (AQA) Psychology B, you were presented with the major **approaches in psychology** and some of the topics representing the **core areas** of social, cognitive, developmental, biological and individual differences. This book is aimed at the more advanced A2 level in your study of psychology and builds on the knowledge and understanding gained at AS. It includes new stimulating topic areas such as 'Forensic psychology' and 'Schizophrenia and mood disorders' and encourages a broader and deeper understanding of the subject as a whole.

The textbook has been designed to prepare you for the AQA Specification B examination. The A2 specification is divided into two units: Unit 3 and Unit 4. Unit 3 covers 'Child development' and 'Applied options' and Unit 4 covers 'Approaches in psychology', 'Debates in psychology' and 'Methods in psychology'. All the information needed for the A2 course is contained in the book. The organisation of the book mirrors the order of topics and approaches within the specification; we hope that this will make following the specification easier for you and will enable you to find information readily when it is needed.

The A2 specification requires you to develop your knowledge from at least two core areas. In Unit 3, there are eight topic areas and you must study three. The only stipulation is that one of these topics is taken from 'Child development' and the other two must be taken from 'Applied options'. Choosing three topics is probably going to be one of the most difficult tasks for your teachers as the topics are all so engaging. There are three topics in the 'Child development' section: 'Social development', 'Cognitive development' and 'Moral development' and, as already stated, you must study one of these.

The chapter on 'Social development' covers the development of attachments and in particular the special bond that develops between an infant and its caregiver. It encompasses theories and research into the consequences for the child of separation from the caregiver, including recent research into Romanian orphan studies. The development of friendship in the older child is also considered. 'Cognitive development' looks at some fascinating work on how children's thinking gradually develops, challenging the old idea that children are simply little adults. An important part of the socialisation process is learning what is 'right' and what is 'wrong'. The topic of 'Moral development' examines some of the psychological theories of how this learning occurs.

You will have to choose at least two topics from 'Applied options'. This section is so named because each topic enables you to understand how psychology is applied to the real world in a variety of contexts.

The first topic, 'Cognition and law' is an application of the topic of 'memory'. The chapter includes theoretical explanations for a familiar everyday problem: recognising a person's face but being unable to identify the face. The chapter also explores the reliability of eyewitness accounts, including the very topical false memory debate.

The approaches studied at AS are applied to the topic of 'Schizophrenia and mood disorders'. The chapter presents theoretical explanations based upon the approaches for these atypical behaviours and evaluates treatments arising from these explanations.

'Stress and stress management' encompasses the biological basis of stress and considers how stress may be linked to illness. Some people seem to suffer from stress more than others, and the chapter explores some of the personal variables that may cause such differences. Finally, the chapter illustrates how psychological knowledge of a health problem can be applied to help manage the problem. The chapter therefore concludes by considering 'stress management'. This is, of course, a highly topical issue in the workplace of today.

The chapter on 'Substance abuse' covers people's use of three of the most common substances: tobacco, alcohol and drugs. It examines some of the psychological explanations for substance abuse and presents a range of psychological treatments and prevention techniques.

The chapter on 'Forensic psychology' deals with some of the problems in both 'measuring and defining crime', gives an overview of 'offender profiling' and examines various theories of offending. These theories are largely based on the psychological approaches. Finally, the chapter considers how psychological knowledge of crime can be applied to the treatment of offenders.

The two main themes of the specification continue to feature in this book. These are **approaches** and **methods** in psychology. In Unit 4, you will revisit the major approaches: biological, behaviourist, social learning theory etc. It may seem odd that you are returning to the same content but there are two differences. First of all, the underpinning knowledge of approaches is elaborated at A2 and, secondly, they are studied at a higher level of analysis, including their contrasting and complementary aspects and application to topic areas. The emphasis at A2 on synoptic assessment, linking the approaches with topic areas, will encourage a more rounded and holistic appreciation of the subject. Debates in psychology also promote an understanding and critical appreciation of the breadth of theory and methods in psychology through debates such as 'free will and determinism' and whether or not psychology is a science. Although you do not need to cover all of the material in the book for Unit 3, all the material for Unit 4 has to be studied.

The AS book introduced you to a range of research methods used by psychologists. You need to continue to be aware of these as you study the new topic areas. Bear in mind that psychology is a practical subject so, as you study each topic, consider how you yourself might investigate aspects of the theory under study. 'How science works' is an important running theme throughout the specification and a key assessment objective. At A2 you will be tested on your knowledge and understanding of methodology: how you might research, analyse and report your work to other people. Because the methods of psychological investigation are so essential to the subject, they are discussed in every chapter and studies are evaluated at a higher level of analysis than at AS. Your knowledge of research skills will be assessed in the 'Child development' section of Unit 3 and in the 'Methods in psychology' section of Unit 4. The numerous studies and 'research studies' in the book draw your attention to the different methods of research, e.g. experiment, observation, case study, etc.

The aims and objectives of the A2 exam are similar to those of the AS exam. You will be required to demonstrate your knowledge and understanding of psychological facts, concepts, theories and studies. Key terms (concepts and specialist vocabulary) are clearly identified and defined; theories are presented in an accessible manner and are both comprehensive and sufficiently detailed. Key research studies are highlighted. Other studies and references to research in the main text serve to add weight to a theory or to challenge it. You do not need to know all of these studies but do try to familiarise yourself with the key studies at least. However, it is useful to remember some of the studies and references to research in the main text too because you can use them in an exam as a discussion point. You will also be expected to analyse, apply and evaluate psychological knowledge. The emphasis on these higher-level skills is greater in the A2 exam than in the AS exam, so discussion, evaluation and application of knowledge carry greater weight. The ability to cope with conflicting theories, which sometimes arise in one area of study, and to evaluate and distinguish between the various theories and approaches to the subject is characteristic of a mature student and something to be aimed for.

The book will help you prepare and develop the skills required for success in the examination. It is designed to put you in control of your own learning. Do not just read it but use the learning objectives to help focus your reading. Learning is enhanced when it is active, so summarise points in your own words and draw diagrams to summarise a topic. Use the questions at the end of each subtopic to assess your knowledge and understanding. Take on board whatever the authors suggest in the examiner's tips. Practical activities in the book will help you remember some of the key aspects of a theory and prepare you for the questions on methods. Remember that a very important ingredient of success at A2 is to demonstrate synopticity. This is where a very valuable feature of the book comes to your assistance in preparing for the exam – the 'links' that draw your attention to links between topic areas in psychology (including those studied at AS) and how these relate to the different approaches, methods and debates. Do not underestimate their value. For those of you who want to extend your understanding of the subject matter, the 'take it further' features provide some direction. Above all, make learning enjoyable!

We hope that you will continue to be engaged and stimulated by the new content areas and by the added depth covered in this book. We are confident that it will be an excellent preparation for a course in higher education, not only in psychology but also in related disciplines, and for careers in which psychology is important, such as teaching, social work, nursing and medicine. Whatever your path beyond the A2 course, we hope that you will find the book helpful and enjoyable. Good luck!

Regina Teahan

Child development

Introduction

The study of child development is a popular and strong area of research in psychology. A number of terms are used to describe this research: 'child development'; 'developmental psychology'; 'child psychology' and 'developmental science'. Each of these gives a slightly different emphasis to the perspectives of the investigators, for example an emphasis on psychology or on the process of development, but all cover a similar set of core issues.

Many questions are asked about children's development: these range from simple ones such as whether a baby looks more like the mother or father (a question about genetics) to those that are difficult or impossible to answer, such as 'what is the best way to bring up a child?' (a question that involves a very large range of complex issues as well as values). Most of us have ideas about which factors influence development and some type of 'theory' about the mechanisms of these processes. However, such theories are usually based on unsystematic observations. Psychologists seek to remedy this situation by providing information about the growth of a whole range of abilities. In addition, they also seek an understanding of the way that this growth takes place. Thus, the psychological study of child development can be characterised by asking two basic questions:

- How does ability change with age?
- How do these changes come about?

Many of the debates about the mechanisms of development have been concerned, in one form or another, with whether development is the result of our inherited abilities or the result of experience. This is often known as the **nature–nurture debate**, or sometimes the debate between **nativists** and **empiricists**.

Many of the same research techniques that are used in psychological investigations of adults are also used with children. However, it is important to be aware that the design of these studies usually differs from those used with adults because of the interest in development and in comparing children's performance at different ages: this involves the use of **cross-sectional** or **longitudinal** studies. Another important consideration in research with children is that they do not always understand the questions in the same way that an adult would, and they may give answers that they think the researcher wants to hear.

This section of the book considers three important areas of research about child development. The section starts with a chapter about social development, this includes issues about the **attachment** of children to their parents, the effect of separation from their parents, and the development of **friendships**.

The second chapter is about cognitive development, the abilities of infants, thinking in childhood, and the role of social experiences in the development of thinking. The last of the three chapters considers the development of children's views about morality, which mostly involves their reasoning about the process.

Key terms

Nature–nurture debate: a debate concerned with the relative contributions of nurture (experience, environment and learning) and nature (inheritance and genetic predisposition) in behaviour.

Nativist: someone who believes that experience plays very little or no role in the development of abilities. This belief is similar to the nature explanation.

Empiricist: someone who believes that knowledge of the world is learned from information acquired through the senses. This belief is similar to the nurture explanation.

Cross-sectional: describes a study where there are two or more groups of different individuals, allowing data to be collected relatively quickly.

Longitudinal: describes a study that takes place over an extended time period; the same individuals are seen at different ages.

Attachment: usually considered by psychologists to be the long-term relationship between a young individual and an adult.

Friendship: a close relationship and trust between two people (Smith, 2003).

Social development

Specification content	Topic content	Page number
Early relationships		
Attachment and the role of caregiver–infant interactions in the development of attachment, including reference to human and animal studies	The role of caregiver–infant interactions in the development of attachment	10
	Animal studies and Bowlby's theory of attachment	5
Function of attachment; secure and insecure attachments; measuring attachment	The function of attachment	11
	Measurement of attachment and identification of types	7
Possible short-term and long-term consequences of privation and deprivation	Privation and deprivation: short- and long-term consequences	13
Romanian orphan studies: effects of institutionalisation, age-related benefits of adoption (Rutter *et al.*, 1998)	Age-related benefits of adoption	17
The work of Bowlby, Schaffer, Ainsworth and van IJzendoorn	Animal studies and Bowlby's theory of attachment	5
	Long-term effects of deprivation	14
	Measurement of attachment and identification of types	7
	The role of caregiver–infant interactions in the development of attachment	10
Later relationships		
The development of friendship in childhood and adolescence; age-related change in friendship; sex differences in children's friendship	The development of friendship	18
Research into the causes and consequences of popularity and rejection	Popularity and rejection	20

Cognitive development

Specification content	Topic content	Page number
Piaget's theory of cognitive development		
Schemas: adaptation, assimilation and accommodation	Important terms relating to Piaget's theory	27
Piaget's stages of intellectual development: characteristics of these stages, including object permanence, conservation, egocentrism, class inclusion	Piaget's stage theory	28
	Infancy: the sensorimotor stage and object permanence	29
	Childhood: Piaget's stages of development	34
Piaget's research, including the three mountains experiment and conservation experiments	Pre-operational stage: 2 to 7 years	34
	Concrete operations: 7 to 12 years	37
	Formal operations: 12 years +	38

Specification content	Topic content	Page number
Alternative approaches to children's cognition		
Vygotsky and cognitive development within a social and cultural context: Vygotsky's zone of proximal development; scaffolding; guided participation in sociocultural activity	Vygotsky: social, cultural and cognitive processes	44
Nativist explanations and early infant abilities, including knowledge of the physical world (Baillargeon)	Nativist explanations and early infant abilities	31
The information processing approach: Siegler's research into problem-solving strategies	Information processing theories How children process information	40 40

Moral development

Specification content	Topic content	Page number
Piaget and Kohlberg		
Piaget's stages of moral development: premoral judgement, moral realism and moral relativism	Piaget's ideas about moral development	52
Kohlberg's preconventional, conventional and postconventional levels: the stages of moral reasoning within these levels	Kohlberg's theory of moral development	57
Ways of investigating moral development including the use of moral comparisons and moral dilemmas	The moral judgement of the child Evaluation of Piaget's explanation of moral development Kohlberg's method of studying moral development Evaluation of Kohlberg's theory	52 55 57 59
Alternatives to Piaget and Kohlberg		
Eisenberg's model of pro-social reasoning, including hedonistic, needs, approval, self-reflective and internalised orientations	Eisenberg's model of pro-social reasoning	64
Gilligan's ethic of care: differences between boys and girls; Gilligan's three levels of moral development	Gilligan's ethic of care: differences between males and females	66
Damon's research into distributive justice	Damon's research into distributive justice	61
Psychodynamic explanations of moral development: the role of the superego	Psychoanalytic perspectives on moral development	48

1 Social development

Early relationships: attachment

Learning objectives:

- define attachment
- explain and evaluate theories about the development of attachment, with particular reference to the work of Bowlby
- explain and evaluate the methods of measuring attachment with the use of the strange situation
- understand the difference between secure and insecure attachments
- explain the development of attachment, in particular, the role of caregiver–infant interactions
- understand the functions of attachment.

Key terms

Infant: a child below about 24 months of age.

Experiment: a method whereby the researcher manipulates an independent variable, whilst controlling other extraneous variables, in order to measure an effect on a dependent variable.

Social relationships are central to human development and are the focus of this chapter. This section starts by showing how our understanding of attachment of children to adults has been influenced by work with animals and by Bowlby's ideas. This is followed by a consideration of the development of attachment in the early years, the role of caregiver–**infant** interaction in that development, and the function of attachment. Following this there is a consideration of the effects of unexpected separations from 'special' people that can cause high levels of distress. There has been a considerable debate about whether such separations, especially prolonged separations, have a negative effect on later development. The chapter ends with a consideration of the development of friendship, as well as issues around popularity and rejection. Here we see that as children become older, social relationships with, and the influence of, other children become increasingly important.

Attachment between children and parents is a significant feature of their lives and is a topic that has been extensively studied by developmental psychologists. Usually, the term 'attachment' is used to refer to the feelings that a baby or child has for an adult. Bonding is often used to refer to the early positive feelings that a mother has for her newborn baby. Attachment can be identified by young children showing distress when someone leaves them and pleasure at reunion. Attachment can occur in both humans and animals.

Animal studies and Bowlby's theory of attachment

Up to the 1950s it was usually thought that rewards were responsible for the development of attachment. Sigmund Freud believed that babies become attached to the people who feed them. From a very different perspective, learning theorists, whose research often involved animals, also explained attachment as a product of feeding. The person who feeds an infant becomes a secondary reinforcer through their association with the primary reinforcement of food.

During the 1950s and 1960s, these assumptions were challenged. An important landmark was an **experiment** by Harlow (1958).

Research study: Harlow (1958)

Aim: Harlow wanted to find out whether infant rhesus monkeys would show attachment to an object that provided food or to an object that provided comfort.

Method: He provided two wire-mesh cylinders. One cylinder contained a nipple so the infant monkey could obtain milk; the other was covered with towelling material (terry cloth). The monkeys were reared without their mothers.

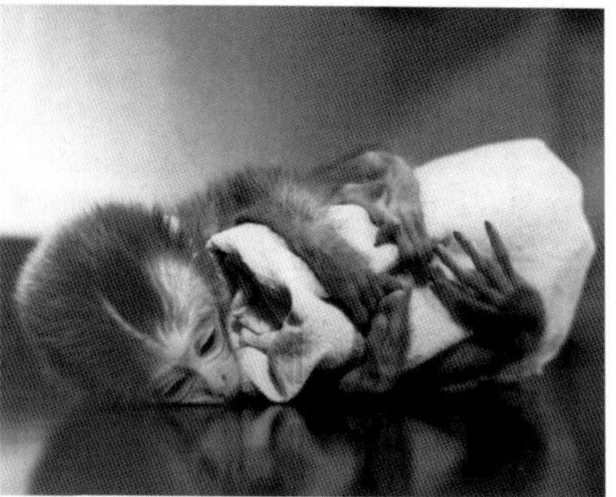

Fig. 1 *Baby Rhesus monkey clings to towelling cylinder for comfort*

Results: The monkeys spent more time on the towelling-covered cylinder and when scared would jump back on to it. They only went on the wire-mesh cylinder when they were feeding.

Conclusion: Reinforcement through the provision of food is not the main determiner of attachment.

Evaluation: The study provided an important finding about attachment, but it raises ethical concerns about the treatment of animals.

Another significant study was conducted by Schaffer and Emerson (1964). They followed up a group of Glaswegian infants and found that infants often formed attachments to people who communicated and played games with them. These relationships would not be predicted by psychoanalytic and learning theories.

At this time John Bowlby, a psychiatrist, was formulating an alternative theory about attachment.

The theory drew on findings from Lorenz and others that some animals are genetically programmed to develop attachments to their mother. This work concerned the process of **imprinting**.

In the wild, the first moving thing a young chick sees is likely to be its mother; imprinting increases the chances of survival as the chicks will stay close to their mother, will seek her when threatened and can be defended by her. In experimental situations, imprinting can occur to any objects that move, even watering cans.

Bowlby believed that attachment in humans is a result of evolutionary pressures. He identified a number of infant behaviours that are part of an innate attachment system: cuddling/clinging; smiling; babbling; following and reaching. He also proposed that adults are likely to respond to these behaviours: for example, crying is a particularly aversive sound for humans. Bowlby also proposed that infants' familiarity and interactions with a particular person would result in attachment.

Bowlby put these ideas together by suggesting that attachment should be seen as part of a **control system**, the purpose of which is to provide a sense of security. The control system works in the following way: if an infant feels insecure, behaviours, such as moving closer to the mother or crying, are produced to increase the sense of security. If an infant feels secure, there is more confidence to explore unfamiliar objects or places. The settings for the security system could change: for example, a child might need more security when tired or ill, or less when older.

Although Bowlby's ideas about attachment have been very influential, one feature has been extensively criticised. This is the concept of **monotropism**; Bowlby believed that the additional attachments that occur after the attachment to the primary caregiver are of less importance. A significant study, which challenged this claim, was conducted by Schaffer and Emerson (1964).

Research study: Schaffer and Emerson (1964)

Aim: To test whether infants first form an attachment to one person (usually the mother).

Method: Sixty infants were observed every month during the first year and again at 18 months, the mothers were interviewed about the infants' responses to separation.

Link

Schaffer and Emerson's study is described below.

Key terms

Imprinting: involves newly born animals becoming attached to the first thing they see that moves. Imprinting is found in some ducks and geese.

Control system: a system with a set point such as the temperature that is set on a central heating system; feelings of security are the set point of the attachment system.

Monotropism: an inbuilt bias to form an initial attachment with one person, usually the mother.

AQA Examiner's tip

It is important to note that Bowlby did not claim that attachment in humans is the same as imprinting in animals.

Take it further

We often assume that if something is present at birth then its origin must be genetic. However, part of the reason for infants' preferences for their mother seems to be familiarity rather than an innate disposition. Newborn infants have already heard their mother's voice when they were in the womb, and this seems to be the reason why they prefer to listen to their mother's voice after they are born.

Results: Nearly a third of the infants had initial attachments to more than one person. At 18 months, only 13 per cent of the infants were attached to just one person. Attachments were formed to people other than the mother and routine activities, such as feeding, did not seem to be relevant to the formation of attachment.

Conclusion: No support was found for Bowlby's idea about monotropism; the findings also showed that feeding was not critical to the formation of attachment.

Evaluation: Because this was a longitudinal study the children's development could be followed overtime. It is widely quoted because it makes two important points about the development of attachment:

- Monotropism is not an accurate description of attachment.
- Social interaction rather than feeding is important for the development of attachments to particular people.

Take it further

Although Bowlby focused on feelings of security, it also is important to remember that attachment will also depend on the infant's cognitive abilities. Schaffer (1996) emphasised the way that cognitive developments, such as the understanding of **object permanence**, can play an essential part in the development of attachment. Schaffer pointed out that at eight months, when object permanence develops, infants also start to show distress at separation from particular people.

The development of attachment in the early years

How does attachment develop? Bowlby (1969) identified four phases in the development of attachment behaviours (see Table 1).

More recent findings suggest that even in the first months of life infants are able to distinguish their mother from other individuals. Babies less than 24 hours old will learn to turn their head in one direction to press a switch so that they can listen to their mother's voice rather than turn in the other direction to listen to the voice of another female (DeCasper and Spence, 1986).

Although newborns show a preference for the characteristics of their mother, psychologists do not consider this to be the same as being attached because the infants do not seem to be any more upset when their mother leaves than when another person leaves them.

Key terms

Object permanence: the understanding that an object or person continues to exist even though it can no longer be perceived (for example when a person leaves a room). Before an infant develops object permanence, something out of sight would be 'out of mind'.

Link

For more on object permanence, see p29 in Chapter 2, Cognitive development.

Table 1 *Stages in the development of attachment (identified by Bowlby)*

Age in months	Stage	Characteristics of stage
0–2	Pre-attachment	No preferences shown for particular adults
2–7	Attachment in the making	Preference for particular adults (such as the mother) in terms of smiling, vocalising and being soothed
7–24	Clear-cut attachment	Protest at separation from particular people, and wariness of strangers
24+	Reciprocal relationships	Understanding that caregivers can have different motives to themselves; behaviour organised to mesh with that of the caregiver

Measurement of attachment and identification of types

For a long time, psychologists were unable to find a satisfactory way to measure the strength of a child's attachment: for example, the amount of crying did not seem to be a good indicator.

A breakthrough in the issue of measurement came with the use of the strange situation (Ainsworth and Bell, 1970). This technique built on Bowlby's ideas by examining the organisation of children's behaviour. The strange situation is described overleaf.

Fig. 2 *A strange situation*

AQA Examiner's tip

Although the strange situation takes place in a 'strange' and unfamiliar place, this does not invalidate the assessment. In fact, some people have argued that the strange situation succeeds because it is unfamiliar and so children show behaviour that would not be seen in less stressful conditions. As the test takes place in a laboratory, it could be thought of as 'unecological', but from the child's point of view this is just one of a number of new and unfamiliar experiences that they have as they grow up.

Hint

Sometimes students spend too long learning every episode of the strange situation. Your time might be better spent making sure that you understand the principles behind the use of these episodes.

Hint

Sometimes the four attachment types are referred to by letters (A, B, C and D). These are provided in the Table so that you will know what is being discussed if these letters are used in other books. It is easier to learn the names of the four attachment types.

Measurement: the strange situation

The strange situation procedure comprises eight episodes, most of which take about three minutes.

Table 2 *Episodes in the strange situation procedure*

Episode	Action
Episode 1	The experimenter takes the caregiver and infant into an unfamiliar room and the caregiver brings the infant to a pile of toys.
Episode 2	The child and caregiver are left alone in the room.
Episode 3	An unfamiliar adult enters the room, sits and reads, then starts to play with the infant.
Episode 4	The caregiver departs, leaving infant with unfamiliar adult.
Episode 5	The caregiver returns, and the unfamiliar adult departs.
Episode 6	The caregiver leaves again and infant is alone in the room.
Episode 7	The unfamiliar adult returns.
Episode 8	The caregiver returns in the reunion episode.

Types of attachment

As you can see, the strange situation is designed to be a complex and stressful experience. Children who take part are usually between 12 and 24 months of age. When the child's behaviours are coded, the important aspect is not the number of behaviours, but rather the overall pattern of responses across the different episodes. Consequently, the strange situation does not measure the **amount** of attachment, but **different types**. A complex coding scheme allows identification of four attachment types (see Table 3), with the behaviour at separation and reunion being particularly important.

Table 3 *Four types of attachment*

Attachment type	Description
Avoidant infants, Type A	During separation there is little sign of distress. The infant does not interact or come close to the caregiver at reunion.
Secure infants, Type B	The infant sometimes shows distress at separation. The infant actively seeks interaction and proximity with the caregiver, especially at reunion, and also shows pleasure at reunion.
Ambivalent infants, Type C	At reunion, the infant shows both contact-seeking and resisting behaviours (e.g. shows pleasure but also turns away or squirms when lifted up).
Disorganised, Type D	No clear pattern is shown across the episodes and bizarre responses to separation and reunion may be shown (introduced by Main *et al.*, 1985).

The following proportions are reported in studies conducted in North America: 67 per cent of infants are secure, 21 per cent are avoidant and 12 per cent are ambivalent. The 'disorganised' attachment type is rare and is associated with infants who are at risk for maltreatment. Sometimes, the term 'insecure attachment' is used to refer to infants who are avoidant or ambivalent.

Evaluation of the strange situation

Limitations

There are several criticisms of the strange situation.

- It focuses on the relationship with one person (usually the mother) and as a result the network of social relationships with other individuals is ignored (e.g. father, **siblings**, grandparents, and so on).
- The strange situation is not appropriate for all cultures. In Japan, Miyake *et al.* (1985) reported that 35 per cent of infants were ambivalent. Takahashi (1990) suggested that Japanese infants may become distressed in the strange situation because they are seldom left alone. Some have argued that this shows that the strange situation is not an appropriate procedure for measuring attachment in non-Western cultures (Rothbaum *et al.*, 2000).
- Kagan (1984) has argued that the strange situation could be assessing temperament rather than attachment. He suggested that avoidant infants behave as they do because they rarely become stressed, while ambivalent infants behave as they do because they are easily stressed.

  If this is true, one would expect an infant to produce similar attachment behaviour with their mother and father. De Wolff and van IJzendoorn (1997) conducted a systematic review of research findings (a **meta-analysis**) and concluded that infants can have a different type of attachment to their mother and father. This provides evidence against Kagan's argument.

Key terms

Sibling: another child in the same family (i.e. a brother or sister).

Meta-analysis: involves a review of a large number of studies about a particular topic, statistical techniques are used to provide a summary of the results from different studies. In this way we can be more confident about the conclusions because they are based on a large number of studies and participants.

Reliability: refers to replicability or consistency.

Adult attachment interview (AAI): a non-experimental method designed to assess the attachment of adults to their parents.

Strengths

Other research has provided support for the use of the strange situation as an assessment of attachment.

- As a measuring instrument, the strange situation has reasonable short-term **reliability** (Thompson, 2000): a child tested at one age is likely to have a similar attachment classification when tested a little while later.
- Attachment type is related to later behaviour and characteristics, as predicated by Bowlby, who supposed that attachment security would become part of the child's internal working model of their world. This involves a set of understandings of how people and things operate, which will guide behaviour. Thus, a secure child would have a more confident approach to new situations than would an insecure child.

  A number of investigators have found support for this idea. Securely attached infants tend to be more cooperative with their mother during problem-solving tasks at 24 months (Matas *et al.*, 1978); they are seen as social leaders by pre-school teachers (Sroufe *et al.*, 1983), to be more positive at reunion with parents at six years of age (Main and Cassidy, 1988), and to have a more positive self-concept at 11 years (Elicker *et al.*, 1992). However, these predictions are by no means perfect and not surprisingly can be affected by the child's life experiences.
- Similar types of attachment have been identified in the strange situation and in the **adult attachment interview (AAI)** (Main *et al.*, 1985). This supports the claim that significant aspects of an individual's relationship are assessed in the strange situation. The AAI involves a semi-structured, one-hour interview. The questions concern early relationships and the way individuals think these have affected them. The concern is not with accuracy, but with coherence and attitudes. The four main attachment types from the AAI are given in Table 4. As you can see, they are similar to the four infant attachment types.

- It has been reported that attachment types identified by the use of the strange situation are moderately related to the AAI classification administered at 20 years (Lewis *et al.*, 2000; Waters *et al.*, 2000). However, as yet, further research needs to be conducted before we can be sure about the nature of this link.

Table 4 *Classification of adult attachment types from the adult attachment interview (AAI)*

Adult attachment type	Description	Links to infant attachment type
Autonomous	Recall of particular events and willingness to see positive and negative features of experiences	Secure
Dismissive	Attachment seen to be of little relevance or importance	Avoidant
Enmeshed	Persons still engaged with issues with their parents	Ambivalent
Unresolved	Often the result of a trauma around the loss of a parent; the issues are still unresolved	Disorganised

Take it further

We have to be careful about over-interpreting findings about a relationship between early attachment and later characteristics. The research is not based on an experimental design. As a result, some other variable could be the cause of the relationship between early attachment and later behaviour. For example, it could be that some children have certain characteristics that enable them to cope well with difficult situations and that these characteristics result in both secure attachment and later behaviours. In this way, having a secure attachment would be just one example of the characteristics of a 'competent' child.

Hint

Because attachment is not the result of reinforcement (Harlow, 1958; Schaffer and Emerson, 1964) this suggests that social interaction can help establish attachment.

The role of caregiver–infant interactions in the development of attachment

What causes different patterns of attachment? Genetics only appear to have a weak role in the development of a child's attachment type (O'Connor and Croft, 2001). Consequently, it seems likely that nurture, in the shape of social experiences, plays an important part. Psychologists have been interested in two issues: the way that caregiver–infant interactions result in attachment to particular people; and the way that caregiver–infant interactions could result in different types of attachment.

Bowlby (1971) suggested that the amount of social interaction with a person will influence the strength of attachment, and he stressed the importance of caregivers responding to infant distress. Similarly, Schaffer (1971) identified caregiver responsiveness to infant signals as the most important determiner of attachment, and, second to this, the amount of interaction with the infant. Five stages in the development of caregiver–infant interaction have been identified by Schaffer (2003).

Table 5 *The nature of caregiver–infant interactions during infancy*

Starting age	Stage	Description
Birth	Biological regulation	Infant's basic biological processes are harmonised with parental requirements (e.g. feeding and sleeping)
2 months	Face-to-face exchanges	Regulation of mutual attention and responsiveness
5 months	Topic sharing	Incorporation of objects into social interactions
8 months	Reciprocity	Initiates actions towards others and develops more flexible and symmetrical relationships
18 months	Symbolic representations	Verbal and other symbolic means of relating to others

(Adapted from Schaffer, 2003)

Caregiver–infant interaction also contains a number of interesting features. For example, even newborn babies can imitate the facial expressions of adults, such as mouth opening and closing, or putting out the tongue (Meltzoff and Moore, 1977). In addition, adults usually speak to infants in a simplified form of speech, which is slow, repetitive and varied in sound patterns. Thus, infants and caregivers have characteristics which seem designed to encourage interaction. Many psychologists believe that social interaction with a limited number of people before eight months is largely responsible for the type of attachment that develops. However, it is very difficult to carry out experiments to identify the key features of interaction that are responsible for infants forming an attachment with a particular person.

Psychologists have recently paid more attention to the relation between caregiver–infant interaction and the types of attachment identified in the strange situation. Ainsworth *et al.* (1978) supposed that caregivers who were responsive to infant distress and demands would have secure infants because the infants would have their needs met; inconsistent responsiveness would result in ambivalent infants; and a low level of response would result in avoidant infants.

However, a review by De Wolff and van IJzendoorn (1997) of 66 investigations indicated that there is only a weak relationship between maternal responsiveness involving the appropriate and prompt response to infants' attachment signals and infants' later attachment type. Another suggestion is that maternal mindmindedness, which can be seen by comments about what an infant is thinking ('Oh, you are grumpy today'), is associated with secure attachments at older ages (Meins *et al.*, 2001). It also appears that interactional synchrony – infant and mother producing similar behaviours – is also associated with secure attachment at older ages (Isabella *et al.*, 1989).

There are indications that childrearing styles in different cultures result in different proportions of the three main attachment types. Grossman *et al.* (1981) reported that 40 to 50 per cent of German infants were avoidant and supposed this might be because of the value placed on independence in that country and that this would influence social interaction and caregiving. However, it should be noted that later studies in Germany have found percentages more similar to those reported in the United States.

Although there has been difficulty identifying precisely the caregiving behaviours that are strongly associated with the different attachment types, it appears that the mother's classification on the AAI is related to the attachment type of her infant (review by van IJzendoorn, 1995). The relation was even found between maternal AAI before the birth of her baby and later attachment types (Fonagy *et al.*, 1991), a finding that is important because it largely eliminates the possibility that birth experiences or characteristics of the infant could have influenced responses in the AAI. Thus, maternal AAI may influence her social and caregiving behaviours, and this has an effect on the infant's security of attachment.

The function of attachment

As has been mentioned, Bowlby believed that attachment is the result of evolutionary pressures. In many young animals, staying close to the mother will provide protection from attack and reduce the chance of becoming lost. This will help ensure that the mother's **genes** are transmitted to future generations.

Take it further

From these findings about the AAI, it would appear that there could be a tendency for cross-generational continuity. However, a study of survivors of the Holocaust illustrates the way that attachment patterns can change across generations (Bar-On *et al.*, 1998). Individuals who had experienced the terrible suffering of the Holocaust (usually their family had been killed) were, not surprisingly, classified as 'unresolved' on the AAI. In the next generation, the percentage of unresolved individuals was only slightly higher than would be expected; and for the following generation there was no difference when compared with a control group. Thus, the devastating psychological effects of the Holocaust did not appear to cause a downward cycle of psychological problems in subsequent generations.

Key terms

Genes: the 70,000 complicated chemicals found on the 23 pairs of chromosomes in most human cells; in interaction with environment and upbringing, genes are responsible for the characteristics of a person.

The discussion of evolutionary pressures on human attachment may seem a bit far fetched, but it is interesting that attachment processes in humans, that involve distress at separation, usually develop at about eight months, an age when babies are starting to crawl and soon will be able to walk.

Belsky *et al.* (1991) have argued that, if resources are limited, an insecure attachment may confer evolutionary advantages. They suggested that insecure attachments would assist in dealing with limited physical and emotional resources and might be associated with early parenting. In contrast, secure attachments would be an advantage in circumstances where there are more resources.

Attachment can also be seen as fulfilling other functions. Bowlby drew attention to the psychological functions of the attachment system because it can provide children with a sense of security. In particular, he proposed that attachment relationships are important for a child's working model of their world. A child who has a secure attachment relationship will have a positive outlook and assume that support will be provided. A child with an ambivalent relationship will be less certain about help and assistance.

Attachment also involves developing a social and communicative relationship with another person. As discussed in Chapter 2 in relation to Vygotsky's work, the help given by adults is a significant factor in the cognitive development of children. In many cultures that do not have a formal education system involving schools, the person who **scaffolds** children's abilities will be a parent or a close relation. Thus, a function of attachment is to provide opportunities for learning.

Key terms

Scaffold: to provide a supportive framework within which a child can develop and learn.

Link

For more about Vygotsky's work and scaffolding, see p44 in Chapter 2, Cognitive development.

Key points:

- The findings of Harlow (1958) and of Schaffer and Emerson (1964) are difficult to explain by learning theory.
- Bowlby's theory about the development of attachment assumes that attachment will help the young of a species survive.
- Schaffer has drawn attention to the role of social and cognitive processes in the development of attachment.
- Four stages in the development of attachment have been identified by Bowlby.
- The strange situation can be used to identify four types of attachment.
- There is debate about cross-cultural differences and about the validity of the strange situation.
- Social interaction and contact appear to be important factors in determining the people to whom infants become attached.
- A number of variables predict children's attachment type, such as maternal AAI and maternal sensitivity.
- A child's attachment type predicts later aspects of development; children's working models of their world may be a reason for these links.

Summary questions

1. What do psychologists mean by the term 'attachment'?
2. Explain one way that young animals become attached to their mother.
3. Describe a study carried out by Schaffer. Indicate why the study was conducted, the procedure used, the results obtained and conclusion drawn.
4. Suggest three behavioural categories that could be used in an observational study of attachment in children aged 16 months.
5. Some pupils in a class were identified as having secure attachments when they were infants; other children in the class were identified as having had insecure attachments. What two differences might you expect between these two groups of children now that they are older?
6. Explain one function of attachment.

Privation and deprivation: short- and long-term consequences

Learning objectives:

- describe the difference between privation and deprivation
- understand and evaluate the short-term and long-term effects of deprivation
- apply research findings about deprivation to issues about separation
- describe the effects of privation
- understand and evaluate the relevance of case studies about privation
- describe and evaluate the effects of institutionalisation
- understand and evaluate the benefits of adoption in relation to the age of a child.

Key terms

Deprivation: in relation to social development, the removal of previous social experiences or person(s) to whom the child is attached.

Privation: in relation to social development, the absence of any meaningful social experiences and/or the absence of any attachment relationship with an adult.

Observation: a non-experimental method that involves recording a participant's behaviour by watching them, often in a natural setting.

AQA Examiner's tip

Try to spell 'separation' correctly – 'seperation' is incorrect.

The terms **deprivation** and **privation** can appear to mean the same thing, but developmental psychologists make an important distinction between them.

Deprivation

After the Second World War, there was both awareness and concern about the effects of children being separated from their parents, because of the evacuation of children, separations in the confusion of war, or because of a parent's death. This stimulated research into the effects of separation and deprivation. In this research a distinction is usually made between the short-term consequences (over days and weeks) and long-term consequences (over years).

Short-term deprivation by separation

Not only was there concern in the post-war period about the effects of deprivation but there was also a growing realisation that the treatment of children in institutions lacked sensitivity. This could involve simple things such as restricted hospital visiting hours or even a complete ban on contact. Because such circumstances were relatively common, research could be conducted into the effects of separation and deprivation that would not be possible today, and the findings from this research helped to provide a basis for changes.

Research study: Robertson and Bowlby (1952)

Aim: To describe the short-term reactions to separation from the child's mother.

Method: Forty-nine children aged between one and four years were observed when separated from their mothers.

Results: The following sequence of reactions was observed:

1 protest, immediate acute distress and crying on separation
2 despair, misery and apathy
3 detachment and apparent recovery, but this sometimes involved rejection of parents.

Conclusion: Acute distress can result from separation and these reactions follow a predictable sequence.

Evaluation: These **observations** have been replicated in a number of other investigations and provide a well-documented description of the way that children cope with these distressing circumstances.

Robertson and Robertson (1971) showed that these acute reactions could be prevented. The Robertsons fostered four children and made sure that each child visited their home before the separation; on separation the children took photographs of their mother, favourite toys and blankets with them and their usual routine was maintained. Another nine children were observed staying in their home with a relative when their mother went into hospital. None of the children showed the acute distress of protest, despair and detachment.

Longer-term effects of deprivation

In his maternal deprivation hypothesis, Bowlby (1953) predicted that there are negative effects on social and cognitive development if children are deprived of contact with their mother when the first attachments are being formed (from about six to 36 months). Bowlby believed that this could result in impairments in the ability to form later relationships and even delinquency.

Bowlby developed this hypothesis in part because of the findings from his study of a group of delinquent boys in London (Bowlby, 1946). When young, these boys had often been separated from their mothers.

Research study: Bowlby (1946)

Aim: To look for a link between separation and emotional maladjustment.

Method: Interviews were carried out with 44 young delinquents (juvenile thieves) attending a clinic. Questions were asked about their behaviour and their earlier childhood. Interviews were also carried out with their families and information was obtained about childhood separations. Bowlby used a control group of non-delinquent young people with emotional problems as a comparison.

Results: Prolonged separation before two years was found to be associated with 'affectionless psychopathology' (an inability to form relationships and a disregard for the feelings of others). Out of 14 individuals who had been labelled as affectionless psychopaths, 12 had been separated from their mothers for a long period of time in the first two years of life. Only five of the delinquents, who were said not to be affectionless psychopaths, had been similarly separated from their mothers at a young age. Out of the control group, only two individuals had been separated for any prolonged period.

Conclusion: Bowlby concluded that prolonged separations resulted in affectionless psychopathology. This conclusion provided a basis for his maternal deprivation hypothesis.

Evaluation: The condition of affectionless psychopathology was diagnosed by Bowlby and so there could have been a researcher bias. Affectionless psychopathology has not been widely recognised as a condition. Cause cannot be established by a natural experiment. Bowlby's methodology has been criticised for the unrepresentative nature of the sample of delinquents, the poor control group, (which was used as a baseline comparison), and the unreliable methods of assessment. Finally, it has been argued that there is no evidence to suggest that psychological damage resulting from early maternal deprivation is irreversible.

Rutter (1972) argued that Bowlby was incorrect in linking antisocial behaviour to the separation of a child from their mother. His own research indicated that the stress and chaotic lifestyles of some families were associated with the long-term negative outcomes (Rutter, 1981, 1987). Thus, according to Rutter, antisocial behaviour is associated with maternal deprivation, not because of the separation itself, but because of the arguments and stress that caused the separation. In addition, Rutter argued, a child's bond with their mother is not necessarily different from their bond with other people.

Research study: Quinton and Rutter (1976)

Aim: To investigate the long-term effects of separations to test Bowlby's ideas about maternal deprivation.

Method: Four hundred and fifty-one children in the UK who had experienced hospital admissions took part. When the children were 10 years old, questionnaires were given to their teachers, and their mothers were interviewed.

Results: Single hospital separations lasting a week or less were not found to be associated with later psychological disturbance. However, if there were repeated separations then children were at increased risk for psychological disturbances, particularly if the children came from disadvantaged families. It also is important to note that around 60 per cent of children who experienced repeated hospitals admissions did not appear to have later emotional disturbances.

Conclusions: No evidence was found to support Bowlby's maternal deprivation hypothesis.

Evaluation: This was an influential and well designed study that undermined Bowlby's ideas about maternal deprivation.

AQA Examiner's tip

If you are writing about 'deprivation', be careful because this term is used in slightly different ways. The term 'maternal deprivation' is usually used in relation to Bowlby's hypothesis, which is no longer widely accepted.

By itself, the term 'deprivation' can be used to describe a child's separation from their mother.

Privation

Harlow's research is relevant to the understanding of privation as infant monkeys were raised in cages without their mother, without any form of caregiving, and in cognitively impoverished conditions (Harlow, 1958). These infant monkeys were terrified when later introduced to other monkeys, often cowering, rocking and biting themselves, sometimes being very aggressive and usually showing no social abilities. Later research revealed that these negative effects could be reduced by housing younger 'therapist' monkeys with the monkey who had been isolated. The two monkeys would cling to one another, and this appeared to help reduce later problems (Suomi and Harlow, 1972). Thus, the effects of privation could be modified by supportive experiences.

There are **case studies** of children who have been abused and kept isolated. These cases provide another form of information about the effects of privation. One of the most famous relatively recent examples concerns a child named Genie who was isolated by her parents in their home; she was only given the minimum of food and there was virtually no communication directed at her. When she was discovered, aged 13 years, she was severely malnourished, could not speak and was in a pitiful state (Curtiss, 1977). Despite the best of efforts, little progress was made in her social or cognitive development. However, we should be cautious about the conclusions we draw from case studies such as these: because it is possible that Genie had learning difficulties before she was isolated, and so it is impossible to know whether the privation caused her difficulties.

In contrast to Genie, other case studies of other children have shown that children suffering physical privation can later recover remarkably if they have a close relationship with another person (overleaf).

Hint

Privation of social experiences is usually associated with lack of food and other physical resources. Privation that only involves social experiences is extremely rare. Thus, it is important to recognise that, when studying the effects of privation, it is difficult to be sure of the cause of children's later difficulties.

Key terms

Case study: a non-experimental method that involves studying one person, group or organisation in detail.

Research study: Koluchova (1976)

Aim: To investigate the recovery of twins who had suffered extreme privation.

Method: This was a case study of identical twins (sometimes known as the 'Koluchova twins') found in Czechoslovakia aged seven years after having been kept together in a small unheated closet or in a cellar. The children's early experiences and their progress after discovery were documented by talking to the twins and other relevant individuals.

Results: The twins' mother died soon after giving birth; the twins were then sent to a children's home for 11 months. They then spent six months with their aunt and after this were returned to their father and his new wife who isolated and maltreated the twins. On discovery, the twins were malnourished and very fearful, and their speech was very poor. However, despite this extreme privation of physical and social resources, the twins made a remarkable recovery and are now apparently well adjusted and cognitively able adults.

Conclusion: There can be remarkable recovery from extreme privation.

Evaluation: These findings are important in showing the resilience of children, but, as this is a case study, it is difficult to be sure about the factors that enabled recovery to take place.

AQA Examiner's tip

Privation can take many forms: privation of the presence of the mother, privation of affection, privation of physical resources. When answering a question on privation, check which of these forms of privation is the focus of the question.

The twins' remarkable recoveries from the effects of privation may have been possible because the isolation they experienced was not total. These children, unlike Genie, were able to relate to, and have basic communication with, another person.

Effects of institutions

It is important to point out that the effects of institutions are variable and, as the study below shows, in some cases do not appear to have an appreciable effect on a child's development.

Research study: Hodges and Tizard (1989)

Aim: To investigate the effects of adoption on children who had been in residential care.

Method: The original sample consisted of 26 children who had been placed in residential care before four months of age. Their care had been impersonal as staff regularly changed and, as a result, these children should, according to Bowlby's hypothesis, have been at risk for later developmental difficulties. The children were adopted when older and seen at six and at 16 years.

Results: Overall, the children were not found to have major difficulties. The only difficulties reported were slight problems with relationships, being overfriendly with strangers and sometimes being seen at school as more aggressive and unpopular. However, most individuals had good relationships with their adopted parents and did not show the severe effects predicted by Bowlby.

Conclusion: Institutional care does not always have an adverse effect on development.

Evaluation: The study appears to show the lack of effects of institutionalisation. However, there have been criticisms: for example, it is possible that families that had difficulties might have dropped out of the study and so the sample could have been biased.

Although many institutions now provide high levels of care for children, even today children who have received institutional care in the UK have higher levels of psychological problems and lower achievements in national examinations. The BBC reported that 11 per cent of young people who were looked after in UK institutions had five good GCSEs, whereas 56 per cent of the general population of pupils achieve this (BBC, 24 April 2006).

Age-related benefits of adoption

Research by Harlow (1958) provides experimental findings showing that the beneficial effects of removing isolated monkeys from very impoverished rearing conditions is dependent on age. Monkeys who were removed from isolation at three months made reasonable recoveries; but, if the removal was delayed until six or 12 months, the monkeys continued to show disturbed behaviours.

Recently, the progress of children who have been adopted into the UK from orphanages in Romania has been investigated. The care levels in the orphanages were extremely low in terms of both physical and psychological resources (O'Connor *et al.*, 2000; Rutter *et al.*, 1998). A comparison was made of children who were adopted before the age of six months and born either in Romania or in the UK. At four years of age, there was no appreciable difference in the development of these two groups. Children who were adopted from Romania after six months of age showed increasing effects of having been left in an institution. Those adopted when aged between six and 24 months had scores about 15 IQ points below the UK comparison group, and those adopted between 24 and 42 months had scores about 25 IQ points below those of another UK comparison group (a deficit of this size would be considered to involve learning disabilities).

Key points:

- Short-term deprivation involves a predictable sequence of distress.
- Acute short-term distress can be avoided if children are supported or remain in a familiar environment.
- Bowlby's hypothesis claimed that maternal deprivation would result in difficulties with later relationships as well as problems such as delinquency.
- Rutter and others found that in some circumstances maternal deprivation does not have long-term negative effects on development; instead, stress and anxiety appear to be the causes of negative long-term effects on development.
- The effects of privation and poorly resourced institutions can be reversed. However, as children become older they are less likely to benefit from transfer to a better-resourced environment.
- Privation and abuse within families are associated with the 'disorganised' attachment.
- Caution is needed when interpreting case studies about the effects of privation; however, there are indications that the presence of another person is associated with later recovery.
- The earlier children can be adopted from privation, the less likely are they to suffer cognitive impairments.

Hint

The AQA specification requires you to know about the work of Bowlby, Schaffer, Ainsworth and van IJzendoorn. Make a table to describe the main research or theory of these investigators.

Child development

Summary questions

7 What is the usual sequence of children's short-term reactions to the unexpected and unsupported separation from their mother?

8 What could you do to help a young child who is going to be separated from their mother?

9 Outline one of Rutter's criticisms of Bowlby's ideas about maternal deprivation.

10 What is meant by the term 'privation'? Illustrate your answer with an example.

11 Children in poorly resourced institutions can make a recovery when they are adopted. Briefly outline the relation between the age of adoption and any recovery that occurs.

12 Privation can affect later development. Why is it difficult to identify whether the absence of social relationships or the low level of resources causes these effects?

Later relationships

Learning objectives:

- understand and evaluate how friendships develop and the age differences in friendship
- describe and discuss differences in friendship between boys and girls
- describe and discuss the techniques used to assess **popularity** and rejection
- understand and evaluate the causes and consequences of popularity and rejection.

The development of friendship

'I like him because we do lots of things together. He lives next to me. He likes the same things as me.'

'We share a lot. We tell each other about secret stuff. I trust her.'

As the descriptions above show, friendship can take a number of different forms.

More than half of three- and four-year-olds have at least one friend, and their friendship lasts at least six months (Howes, 1996). After school entry, at 7 years, children often identify four friends, and 12-year-olds usually say that they have seven friends (Reismann and Shorr, 1978). At all these ages, friends tend to be of the same sex. In addition, friends tend to be similar. Haselager *et al.* (1998) compared nine- to 13-year-olds who were friends and other pupils who were not friends on a range of characteristics. Friends were more likely to have the same characteristics, such as cooperation, shyness, being aggressive and being helpful.

Research study: Selman and Jaquette (1977)

Aim: To investigate opinions about friendship.

Method: Two hundred and twenty-five individuals aged between four and 32 years were interviewed about friendships.

Results: On the basis of the answers, five overlapping stages in the development of friendship were identified; these are shown in Table 6.

Table 6 *Selman and Jaquette's description of the development of friendship patterns*

Approximate age (years)	Features of friendship
3–7	Playing together
4–9	Giving help, but does not include the idea of reciprocity
6–12	Focus on reciprocity
9–15	Intimacy and sharing
12–adult	Interdependence but also autonomy of each person

Conclusion: With increasing age, the nature of friendship changes.

Evaluation: The findings provide information about the way children's friendships develop. However, the study relied on interviews rather than carrying out observations of behaviour between friends.

A slightly different approach was taken by Bigelow and La Gaipa (1980). They asked 960 children from Canada and Scotland who were aged between six and 14 years to write an essay about 'best friends'. The stories were then rated on a number of dimensions by the investigators. From this, three stages in the development of friendship were identified.

Table 7 *Bigelow and La Gaipa's (1980) description of friendship at different ages*

Approximate age (years)	Name of stage	Features of stage and the basis for friendship
7–8	Reward–cost	Common activities, similar expectations, lives nearby
9–10	Normative	Shared values and rules
11–12	Empathic	Understanding, sharing of information about self, shared interest

The two studies differ in the precise description of the development of friendship. However, both studies found that, as children become older, the basis for friendship involves a change from more physical to more psychological processes.

It has been suggested that having friends can be important for later development, and, in particular, one or two friends can make it less likely that rejected or isolated children at older ages experience developmental difficulties. This is shown by the research study by Kupersmidt and Coie (1990) outlined on page 23.

Sex differences in friendship

Waldrop and Halverson (1975) suggested that boys tend to have extensive relationships and to view groups as a network of friendship pairs that engage in joint activities. They suggested that girls, in contrast, have more intensive relationships that focus on the sharing of emotions and information. In the research study described below, boys and girls reported that they would choose a same-sex individual over an opposite-sex individual in relation to play activities.

Research study: Halle (1999)

Aim: To investigate the way in which friendship and gender would influence the choice of a social partner.

Method: One hundred and twenty-two children aged between four and eight years were asked with whom an imaginary child would choose to be in relation to a range of situations. The choices involved same- and opposite-sex **peers**; friends and an unfamiliar peer; same-sex unfamiliar peers and opposite-sex friends.

Results: Children, especially girls and younger children, tended to choose same-sex partners.

Conclusion: Children's choices in an abstract reasoning task appear to be similar to the choices that they make in real situations.

Evaluation: The findings indicate that children carry out activities with same-sex friends.

Key terms

Peer: another child of about the same age and ability.

Research in Brazil has also shown that three- to 10-year-olds usually nominate same-sex individuals as best friends and give higher ratings of liking to same-sex individuals (de Guzman *et al.*, 2004); de Guzman *et al.* also found that girls tend to dislike more individuals than boys do. This is consistent with boys having a wider network of friends than girls, although no evidence was found that there were more intense relations in girls as assessed by the ratings of liking. Interestingly, in this sample of Brazilian children, unlike in the USA, only the middle age group showed a widespread dislike of opposite-sex individuals.

Take it further

When comparing the findings from different studies of friendship, it is important to bear in mind that there are large cultural differences in the amount of time that children spend with others of their age and in the degree to which this time is structured by adults as in nurseries or schools. As a result, we should expect differences between cultures.

For example, in isolated communities social interaction will often be with younger or older children; whereas in communities where there is a higher density of people (e.g. cities) same-age interactions are much more likely to be present. Both factors are likely to affect the development of friendship and the types of friendships that are formed.

Key terms

Popularity: involves being liked by other people or their wanting to carry out activities with the (popular) individual.

Recently, Rose and Rudolph (2006) reviewed over 300 studies that made comparisons between the relationships of boys and girls from pre-school to adolescence; their main conclusions are below:

- By six years, boys tend to play in large groups and engage in rough-and-tumble play; when older they engage in more sports. Boys of pre-school age to adolescence have dense social networks that involve a larger number of relationships, and these relationships tend to have a defined dominance hierarchy. Boys focus more on presenting themselves to the group, and on their place in the hierarchy of the peer group. The pressures and stresses from peers are likely to be in terms of verbal or physical victimisation.
- In contrast, girls have longer social interactions with one other individual, and their relationships involve more pro-social behaviour (being positive and caring). Girls are more concerned about their friendships, have more empathy and more concerns about helping and connecting to others, as well as more concerns about the evaluation of peers. The pressures and stresses they feel from peers involve difficulties with others or problems about social interaction and friendships (e.g. someone stopping talking to you, not having as many friends as you want).

Popularity and rejection

Friendship and **popularity** tend to be associated: a child with friends will usually be popular. However, a child can be unpopular with most children in a class but still have one or two close friends.

A variety of methods have been used to assess children's popularity. The three methods most often used to assess popularity and rejection in children are:

- observation – for example, observations of the duration of play between children, the number of positive or negative behaviours (e.g. smiling, arguing, joint activity)
- adult reports – for example, asking a teacher or parent to identify which children are friends with one another
- child reports – for example, asking children for their opinions; this usually involves questions about each classmate, such as 'Would you like to play a game with X?' (often, photographs are supplied). The actual questions vary from study to study.

Sociometry is a technique used to plot the relationships between people. A sociogram can be used to show which children are friends and which are the children with more friends (see Figure 3). The information in the sociogram can be obtained by, for example, child reports.

Discussions about popularity have usually concerned popular, rejected and neglected children (i.e. children who are identified as popular or as unpopular). However, it is important to recognise that many children do not fit into these three groups. Coie *et al.* (1982) proposed that information should be collected about two dimensions (being liked by others; being disliked by others), from which, they suggested, it is possible to identify five different types of peer ratings (see Table 8).

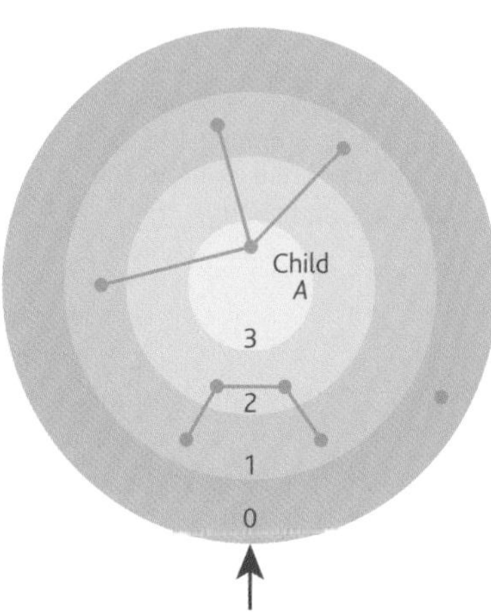

● = 1 Child. Child *A* has 3 friends, and is the only friend of these 3 children.

Fig. 3 *An example of a sociogram*

Table 8 *Responses of peers that identify popular, rejected, neglected, controversial and average children*

Type of child	Liked most often by	Liked least often by
Popular	Many	Few
Rejected	Few	Many
Neglected	Few	Few
Controversial	Many	Many
Average	Average	Average

The causes of popularity and rejection

What are the characteristics of popular, rejected and neglected children? A study that investigated this is described below.

Research study: Dodge (1983)

Aim: To investigate the way in which children joined in play with others and the way that this was related to their popularity.

Method: Observations were made of the way that children with different levels of popularity joined a game being played by two other children. The observations were of five year olds in a playground.

Results: Popular children tended to observe what was going on and then join in by making positive statements about the group; rejected children were likely to interrupt the play and be disruptive, and neglected children tended simply to watch and wait but not get involved.

Conclusion: The rejected and neglected children did not produce socially appropriate behaviour, and their behaviour explains why other children reject or neglect them.

Evaluation: Observational studies are important in helping describe behaviour. However, one limitation of observation is that it does not provide information about cause and effect.

In a study of black South African children between eight and 12 years it was found that popular children and rejected children did not differ in their initiations of contact, but that popular children had more initiations from other children (Bonn and Kruger, 1996).

Using research findings from a number of investigations, Schaffer (2004) has summarised the characteristics of popular, rejected and neglected children (see Table 9). The descriptions below suggest that the characteristics of children influence how they are liked by their peers, in particular, aggressive behaviour results in unpopularity. However, we cannot be sure about this. For example, a child who begins to be unpopular might start to become more aggressive because of the reactions of their peers.

Table 9 *The characteristics of popular, rejected and neglected children*

Popular	Rejected	Neglected
High levels of cooperative play and sharing	Little cooperative play or sharing	Lots of solitary activity
Little aggression	Argumentative and antisocial	Rarely aggressive, little antisocial behaviour
Lots of interaction with another child, ability to sustain an interaction	Much solitary activity	Avoids interaction with a single child, more time in larger groups
Positive disposition, seen as a good leader, physically attractive	Talkative, frequent social approaches, inappropriate and disruptive social behaviours	Shy and unassertive

(Based on Schaffer, 2004)

Investigations in more controlled circumstances can help to understand these issues about cause and effect. Coie *et al.* (1990) assessed children (aged six to eight years) prior to their joining a group that met regularly. None of the children had met any of the other children before. The children's popularity in this group was assessed. It was found that, over time, the children's characteristics identified in the initial assessments were related to their popularity. The effect was most strongly seen in the case of rejected children, where aggression and other characteristics identified at the start of the study appeared to influence the feelings of other children towards the rejected child.

There are indications that rejected children think of themselves as less socially competent and more anxious. They also appear to overestimate their own popularity; having this unrealistic view may mean that they do not see a need to modify their own behaviour (Patterson *et al.*, 1990).

Below is a description of a research study in which young people were asked what makes a person popular.

Research study: Xie *et al.* (2006)

Aim: To find out the characteristics that young people think result in popularity.

Method: Four hundred and eighty-nine African-American students from a high-risk inner city neighbourhood who were 6, 9 and 12 years took part in a semi-structured interview about what makes children popular.

Results: The characteristics and behaviours identified as being important for popularity changed with age. At age 6, positive social behaviours were seen as important; at age 9 and 12 appearance and self-presentation were mentioned the most; and at age 12 deviant behaviours (e.g. aggression, bullying, substance abuse) were mentioned more than at earlier ages, and more for boys than girls.

Conclusion: Age differences were identified. The findings are similar to those in other lower-risk samples and show that deviance does not have a powerful effect on popularity.

Evaluation: There may be limitations in using interview techniques with younger children.

More recent research has examined the relation between sociometric **ratings** of popularity (who do you like to play with the most?) and

perceived popularity (who are the most popular students in your class?). In a **correlational study**, Lease *et al.* (2002) collected both forms of data from a group of 487 pupils aged between 9 and 13 years. There were reasonably strong positive correlations between the two different measures: children with whom others liked to play were also perceived as popular.

The consequences of popularity and rejection

The first point to make is that children tend to remain as popular, rejected or neglected over time, despite changes in class composition and school. Coie and Dodge (1983) report that there is a reasonably high degree of continuity over a period of five years; the study started when the children were either 8 or 10-years-old. Of the different types of children, the rejected children were the most likely to continue to be rated in this way.

Not surprisingly, investigators have paid more attention to the negative outcomes that are associated with rejection, rather than the consequences of popularity. The main issues that have been studied involve school/academic issues, **internalising problems** (e.g. depression, anxiety, stress – problems internal to a person) and **externalising problems** (aggression, truancy, delinquency – problems external to a person).

Parker and Asher (1987) reviewed findings about peer relations and later personal adjustment. They concluded that children who have difficulties with peers, such as rejection, are at risk for later life difficulties. The links were found to be clearest for children who are not accepted by their peers and who are also aggressive; these children were found to be particularly at risk for dropping out of school and for criminality. However, for children who are not accepted by their peers and are shy/withdrawn, Parker and Asher failed to find consistent evidence of later negative outcomes.

Parker and Asher pointed out that these findings might be caused in different ways, and they identified two routes by which peer acceptance might be linked to later negative outcomes, although they suggest that there could be even more complicated models of development:

- **A causal model of peer popularity/rejection**. Aggressive and withdrawn behaviours cause low peer acceptance; this leads to the later negative behaviours. So there are direct causal connections in this sequence (see Figure 4).
- **An incidental model of peer popularity/rejection**. Another possibility is that the aggressiveness results in peer rejection, but peer rejection has no real role to play in causing the later negative outcomes.

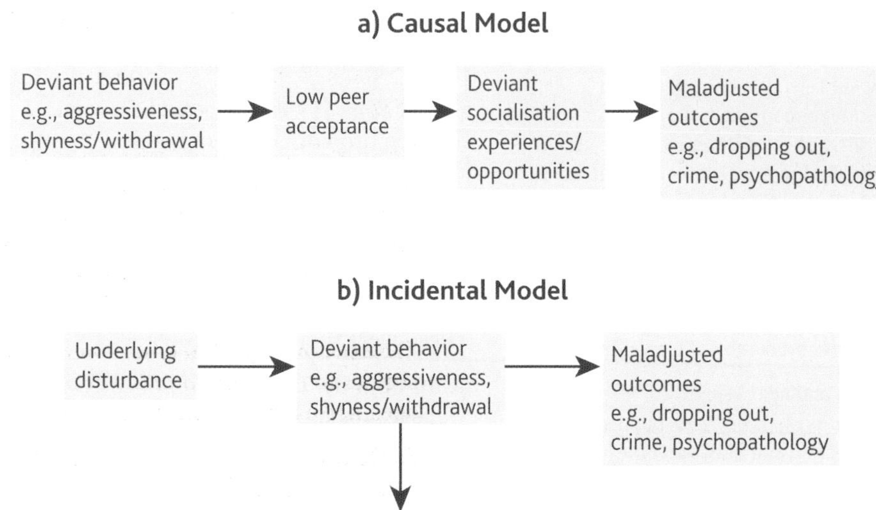

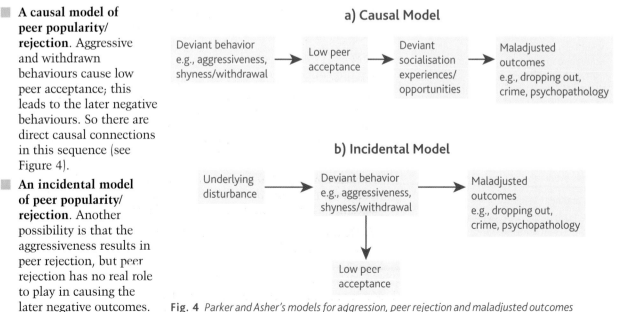

Fig. 4 *Parker and Asher's models for aggression, peer rejection and maladjusted outcomes*

Key terms

Correlational study: involves measuring two naturally occurring variables to establish the relationship between them.

Internalising problems: difficulties originating within a person (e.g. anxiety, stress, depression).

Externalising problems: difficulties in relation to other people or organisations (e.g. aggression, dropping out of school, delinquency).

AQA Examiner's tip

Be careful when answering essay questions about the causes or consequences of popularity, because without experimental findings it is difficult to be sure what is cause and what is consequence. It is much better to write that there are 'links' (e.g. between physical attractiveness and popularity) or use words like 'associated' and 'predicted' (e.g. 'rejection is associated with/predicts later difficulties'; 'rejected children may be at risk for later negative outcomes').

Research study: Kupersmidt and Coie (1990)

Aim: To investigate the characteristics of rejected children when they are older.

Method: A longitudinal study of 112 children in the USA was conducted. Popularity was assessed at 11 years and problems were assessed at 18 years.

Results: Of the young people who had been rejected by their peers at 11 years, around 15 per cent had been suspended or had dropped out of school, and nearly a third had come in contact with the police. In contrast, none of the young people who were popular at 11 years were suspended from school or in trouble with the police. The neglected children had a very similar outcome to the popular children.

Further analyses of the **whole** sample revealed that aggression rather than the rejection was the best predictor of later problems for rejected children. This is consistent with the incidental model that has just been described. However, further analyses on a **subsample** of white children, showed that both rejection and aggression predicted general negative outcomes. This illustrates the complexity of trying to draw clear conclusions from investigations of this topic.

Conclusion: Rejected children are at risk for later negative outcomes. Aggression appears to have a role to play in this process.

Evaluation: Support for the incidental model was obtained for the whole sample, but this model may not be applicable to all individuals.

Take it further

Both peer rejection and aggression tend to occur together (i.e. they are correlated). This raises the question of whether rejection or aggression is the better predictor of later school difficulties. This question can be answered by carrying out advanced statistical analyses which examine the relation between these early characteristics and later behaviour. In a number of investigations these analyses suggest that both peer rejection and aggression independently predict later school difficulties. In other words, rejection by itself predicts later difficulties and aggression by itself predicts later difficulties; however, it also seems to be the case that, if we know about both rejection and aggression, we can make an even better prediction of later difficulties.

The findings of slightly different relationships between popularity/rejection and later outcomes in different studies probably reflects the way that popularity and rejection can mean slightly different things to children depending on the type of school and the way children are taught to treat and accept others.

A large-scale study by Dodge *et al.* (2003) provides the basis for more complex suggestions about the process of development. It was found that, in children who are aggressive at an early age (e.g. five to eight years), their social rejection was related to their later antisocial behaviour. However, in children who are not aggressive, social rejection was not related to later antisocial behaviour.

The findings from several other investigations have indicated that both peer rejection and aggression in childhood make independent contributions to the prediction of later adolescent aggression (Coie *et al.*, 1992; Coie *et al.*, 1995).

Hymel *et al.* (1990) suggested that one of the reasons why rejected children drop out of school is that they associate with others who have low educational expectations and involvement and with those who are at risk of leaving school early. Hymel *et al.* also suggest that the rejected children's difficulties are because they are not part of the school culture and do not support its values.

These and other studies have been reviewed by McDougall *et al.* (2001). These were their conclusions:

- In boys the combination of early aggression and rejection provide the best predictor of later externalising problems.
- In girls, there is no consistency across different studies in findings about the best predictors of later externalising problems.
- For both boys and girls the combination of social withdrawal and peer rejection increases children's risk for later internalising problems. McDougal *et al.* suggest that particularly critical to this process is how the individual feels about their situations; viewing oneself as rejected and lonely puts a child at greater risk for later problems.

Research study: Laursen *et al.* (2007)

Aim: To investigate the hypothesis that friendship reduces the adverse effects of social isolation.

Method: Two hundred and sixty-six Finnish children aged 7 to 9 years took part; the children were seen twice with a gap of 12 months. The children named others (as many or as few other children as they wanted) that they spent 'most time with' to identify pairs of mutual friends and the 'least time with' to identify those children who were 'isolated' in their contact with others. The children's adjustment difficulties were assessed in an interview (e.g. anxiety, depression, aggression, antisocial behaviour).

Results: Examination was made of the relationship between friendship patterns and adjustment difficulties 12 months later. In isolated children who had a mutual friend there was no significant connection between being isolated and later internalising or externalising problems. However, in children without any mutual friends there was a connection between isolation and both types of adjustment at the older age.

Conclusion: The findings were consistent with the hypothesis that the presence of a friend reduces the effects of being an isolated child.

Evaluation: Because this was not an experimental study, we cannot be absolutely sure that friends reduce the effects of isolation.

Dodge *et al.* also suggested that children's beliefs and attitudes have an important role in relation to rejection. The following characteristics were found to make it more likely that children were rejected by their peers: belief that others are hostile; difficulties in resolving conflicts, and inappropriate social responses. Dodge *et al.* believe that rejection increases the strength of these characteristics. This is because rejected children have less social experience with others and they have higher levels of stress. All this increases the levels of aggression in the children. Thus, Dodge *et al.* are proposing a complex set of inter-relations which together can make initial difficulties even worse.

Key points:

- With increasing age, psychological considerations become more important in choice of friends.
- From the pre-school period until adolescence, same-sex friendships are usual; children also tend to make friends with other children who are similar to themselves.
- Friendship groupings of boys and girls are different: boys tend to have large friendship groupings; girls tend to have friendship pairs.
- The activities of friendship groupings of boys and girls tend to be different.
- Because it is very difficult to carry out experimental studies, it is difficult to know why there are these different patterns of friendship. As a result, it is unclear whether these differences are the result of innate characteristics or the result of learning, or a mixture of both.
- Most of the studies have obtained verbal or written views from children about friendships. These may not correspond to what children actually do. Another methodological concern is that young children may have difficulty accurately expressing their ideas.

Summary questions

13 Look at the statements at the beginning of this section; identify the age of these children.

14 Describe two differences between the friendships of boys and girls.

15 Describe two changes in friendship as children become older.

16 Describe one technique of assessing a child's popularity.

17 How would you describe popular and rejected children using the following terms: 'liked', 'disliked', 'by most children' and 'by few children'?

18 Explain two different views about the role of peer rejection in the development of later externalising problems.

Further reading

Davey, G. *et al.* (2008) *Complete Psychology*, 2nd edition. London: Hodder & Stoughton.

Ding, S. and Littleton, K. (2005) *Children's Personal and Social Development*. Oxford: Blackwell.

Slater, A. and Bremner, G. (2003) *An Introduction to Developmental Psychology*. Oxford: Blackwell.

Smith, P.K., Cowie, H. and Blades, M. (2003) *Understanding Children's Development*. Oxford: Blackwell.

- Determining the causes and consequences of popularity and rejection is difficult because experimental studies cannot be conducted for ethical and practical reasons.
- Popularity and rejection tend to persist despite changes in age, class and school.
- Aggression and lack of social competence are associated with rejection.
- Rejection and aggression are associated with later negative outcomes involving externalising behaviours.
- Neglected children are at risk for internalising problems.

End-of-chapter activity 1

Imagine you have been asked to write a short pamphlet for new mothers about attachment and separation. The pamphlet should:

- summarise research findings
- be easy to read
- suggest things to do and things to avoid doing

Remember, the writing should not be in a formal academic style, but it still needs to be clear and understandable.

It is useful to decide the length of the pamphlet, whether to include illustrations, the number of people who work together, how the work is to be divided up in the group and the timetable for the exercise. If this activity is carried out by several groups, it would be useful to have a discussion of the strengths of each pamphlet in a summary session.

End-of-chapter activity 2

This activity is designed to see if the way television presents young people's friendship is similar to the way that psychologists describe these friendships.

First look at what psychologists report are the characteristics of the behaviour between friends. Also look at the way these behaviours change with age. Then devise a recording sheet to note these behaviours. This is an important part of the exercise.

If there is time, apply the coding scheme to examples of young people of the same age who are talking to one another on television. When doing this, try to find examples of young people who are supposed to be friends and young people who are not supposed to be friends.

Look at the recordings to see whether young people who are supposed to be friends show the behaviours that psychologists believe occur between friends.

You could also compare the behaviours of friends and non-friends on the television programme. Are there differences in the behaviours shown by friends and non-friends? If so what are these?

2 Cognitive development

Piaget's theory of cognitive development

Learning objectives:

- define the following terms: 'schema', 'adaptation', 'assimilation' and 'accommodation'
- understand and evaluate Piaget's stage theory of intellectual development and the characteristics of these stages
- discuss and evaluate Piaget's theory of object permanence
- understand and evaluate the alternative nativist ideas of early cognitive development.

Key terms

Cognitive: related to cognition, i.e. to thinking and the processing of information by the brain.

Nature: the argument that (human) behaviour is caused by inherited characteristics.

Nurture: the argument that (human) behaviour is caused by what has been learned from the environment and upbringing.

Schema: a cognitive structure containing information or knowledge that will guide behaviour.

The interest in **cognitive** processes underwent a considerable expansion in the 1950s and 1960s. This expansion can partly be seen as a reaction against the limitations of learning theory and behaviourism particularly because, as internal processes and thinking were not regarded as appropriate topics for scientific study. Psychologists interested in cognitive development wanted to go beyond the description of developmental milestones to explain why new forms of thinking emerge.

Research about cognitive development in the UK and the USA during the 1950s and 1960s was strongly influenced by two people whose work, when translated into English, found a receptive audience. These two people, Jean Piaget and Lev Vygotsky, are key figures in developmental psychology and in this chapter.

This section provides an outline of Piaget's theory and its application to infancy. This is followed by a consideration of alternative ideas. The third section returns to Piaget's theory and his description of cognitive development beyond 2 years of age. Theories that have been developed about information processes make up the next section. The last part of the chapter outlines Vygotsky's ideas and sociocultural viewpoints.

Jean Piaget (1897–1980) was born in Switzerland and originally trained as a biologist. However, his interests changed after working on intelligence tests for children. For the remainder of his life he was concerned with the psychological development of children, and he produced over 200 articles and more than 30 books. Piaget was concerned about the way that children **construct** knowledge about their world. His research and theory was very influential; however, as with any scientific process his ideas have been challenged and in many cases superseded.

Piaget believed that psychological development was the result of both inbuilt processes (**nature**) and experiences (**nurture**). He identified two sets of inherited characteristics that play a part in development: a specific and a general set:

- **Specific** According to Piaget, newborns have primitive reflexes (such as sucking, or startle reactions) which are part of their specific biological inheritance and are the starting point for interacting with the world.
- **General** He also believed that humans possess important, general, inherited ways of thinking (cognitive processes) that enable children eventually to develop a sophisticated understanding of their world.

Important terms relating to Piaget's theory

Important terms used by Piaget are set out below.

- **Schema** Piaget used the term 'schema' to describe a cognitive structure relevant to a set of behaviours (Flavell, 1963).

Hint

Try to think of examples of schemas in young children; identify responses that infants and children produce in relation to objects, people or events in their environment.

Key terms

Adaptation: the process of adjusting behaviour to cope with the environment.

Assimilation: the process whereby a new experience is understood in terms of an existing schema.

Accommodation: the process of modifying an existing schema to fit new experience.

Equilibrium: the state achieved when assimilation and accommodation are in balance.

Stage theory: this type of theory about development has two assumptions: progress through the stages is in a fixed order, and the abilities at each stage have to be achieved before the individual can progress to the next, higher level.

Hint

What are the effects of disequilibrium? Think how you have felt on occasions when you have not understood something.

AQA Examiner's tip

Sometimes in an examination you will be asked to define the terms, 'schemas', 'adaptation', 'assimilation' and 'accommodation'; you might also be asked to give examples of these processes.

A newborn baby will suck most things that are placed in its mouth; this involves a sucking schema. Thus, schemas provide the basis for responses to objects and events, and schemas are changed by experience.

- **Adaptation** Evolutionary theory assumes that living beings are physically adapted to the characteristics of their environment. In the same way, Piaget assumed that schemas become adapted to the child's environment. Adaptation in the case of the sucking schema would involve finding new ways to modify the mouth and lips to the shape of a new nipple.
- **Assimilation** Assimilation is usually thought of as taking in information or experiences and fitting these to an existing schema. A child drinking from an especially large cup recognises that the object is a cup and may at first, when attempting to drink, use existing schemas that are used with smaller cups.
- **Accommodation** This is the process of changing a schema to adapt to the environment. The child's first attempts to drink from the large cup would involve the existing 'drinking from a cup schema', but then the original schema would be accommodated (i.e. slightly changed) as a result of experiences such as spilling some of the drink. Similarly, when a child learns that swans are different from ducks this would be the accommodation of a schema to new experiences and information. It is worth emphasising that Piaget regarded assimilation and accommodation as usually occurring simultaneously. Thus, there is a continuous process of dealing with new experiences and at the same time adapting existing cognitive structures because of these experiences.
- **Equilibrium** When a child is able to respond effectively to an aspect of their environment, the cognitive system is in equilibrium. At this point a child will be able to drink from a large cup, or understand the difference between swans and ducks. Piaget considered that when accommodation has not yet occurred (e.g. a child spills their drink from a large cup) there is disequilibrium, which is a driving force for adaptation.

So to try to put all this together: according to Piaget, children **assimilate** new experiences to existing **schemas**; this results in **accommodation** of the schemas to the new experiences. In other words, the new experiences can change children's thinking. The change involves the **adaptation** of the schema to these new experiences.

Piaget's stage theory

Piaget believed that these general processes occur throughout the life span. However, he also believed that children's thinking changed at certain ages and, as a result, he proposed what is termed a **stage theory**.

Stage theories are useful because they provide a summary of children's abilities over a period of time (see Figure 1). During a stage, children are supposed to be similar; between stages there are supposed to be significant differences.

The stages of cognitive development identified by Piaget are illustrated in Figure 1 and are described in more detail in Table 1. Piaget believed that the stages are universal features of human development, but he also accepted that children varied in the ages at which they reached each stage. Several cross-cultural investigations have identified similar stages in the development of thinking (e.g. Goodnow, 1969).

Table 1 *An outline of Piaget's stages of development*

Approximate age range (years)	Name of stage	Brief description
Birth–2	Sensorimotor	Thinking is based on sensations and motor movements; e.g. by the end of this stage children understand the permanence of objects.
2–7	Pre-operational	There is use of symbolic representations involving language, but reasoning is limited; e.g. children have difficulty understanding what another person can see.
7–12	Concrete operations	Limitations in reasoning are overcome, but children are still better at 'real' (i.e. concrete) tasks than at abstract tasks. Children can understand that there is the same amount of plasticine even when it is shown made into different shapes.
12+	Formal operations	There is the ability to reason abstractly and hypothetically; hypotheses can be made up and tested.

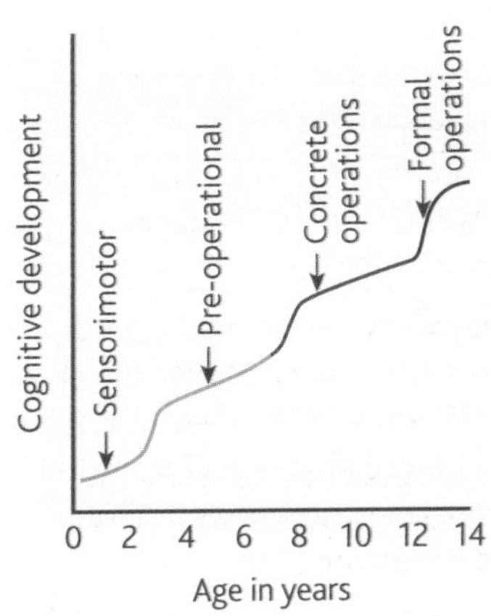

Fig. 1 *A graph showing cognitive development over time*

By proposing a stage theory, Piaget suggested that cognitive development occurs in a step-like manner; however, many investigators have found that development is a more gradual process, especially when there are only small intervals between the observations or assessments.

Researching the stages

Many of Piaget's research studies about the stages of development used the **clinical method**. This involved getting to know the children, and then questioning them about a topic. In an effort to respond to the individual characteristics of the children, the questions and materials were not presented in a standardised way: different questions might be asked of different children (similar to semi-structured interviews). Many of Piaget's books contain the children's answers, and the vividness of his descriptions could have helped to make his ideas so popular with developmental psychologists. Piaget's method contrasted with more usual psychological methods where all children would receive the same questions.

Hint

What do you think might be the advantages and disadvantages of the clinical method?

Infancy: the sensorimotor stage and object permanence

Piaget believed that the sensorimotor stage occurred from birth up to about 24 months. During this period, children do not have full use of speech and so their thinking is unlikely to be based on words; instead, Piaget believed, their thinking is based on sensations and motor movements.

Piaget divided the sensorimotor stage into six substages. The first three of these occur between birth and about nine months. During this time infants develop from only using simple reflex activities (e.g. sucking), to repeating actions which are pleasurable (e.g. learning to move their thumb to their mouth so they can suck it), and then using established schemas to explore new objects (e.g. sucking and shaking an unfamiliar object).

According to Piaget, because infants have only had a limited experience of acting on their world, they only have a limited understanding of it. He

Take it further

Obviously, infants can produce words before 24 months, but for Piaget these words are not symbolic; rather the word is part of the object itself so infants think of the word 'teddy' and the object as being all part of the same sensation and experience.

believed that during most of the first three substages infants do not have an awareness of **object permanence** (i.e. they do not yet understand that an object or person continues to exist even though it is out of sight).

Piaget supposed that for infants who are up to four months old, objects are simply sensations, images that occur; but like the individual frames of a film these images are not connected together, so when the object is no longer present, it has gone from the infant's mind. Piaget suggested that only at around four months do infants start to show an awareness of the permanence of objects by continuing to look at the location where they have seen something that they want to see again.

According to Piaget, from about four until nine months, infants are able to anticipate the future position of moving objects and look to see where an object has fallen. However, when the object cannot immediately be seen, a child will lose interest. Piaget describes how his daughter reached for an object but stopped when he covered the object. Simple observations such as this provided a basis for Piaget to challenge common-sense notions about how infants think about their world.

During the next period of development between 9 and 12 months, infants start to have an understanding of object permanence. At first they are able to retrieve an object that is hidden if they have already started to search for it, and Piaget argued the initiation of retrieval helps the completion of this operation. Soon afterwards infants are able to search for hidden objects, but they do not fully understand that an object should be in the place where it disappeared last. Piaget describes his 10-month-old daughter's reactions (see text on left).

This has become known as the 'A not B error'. Piaget suggested that the A not B error occurs because infants do not yet understand that there is only one object that they see, but probably assume that the object and its location are somehow associated together.

Between 12 and 15 months infants begin to search for objects at the location where they disappeared, but they still do not have a full understanding. This is shown by the following sequence. Someone picks up an object and covers it with their empty hand; the object is placed behind a screen; the person shows their hand to the infant. The infant will search in the hand, but not behind the screen.

In the last stage of sensorimotor development, infants are able to work out that an object is behind the screen. Infants also start to use symbols and these, Piaget believes, are two related developments, having a symbol for something means that one can represent something that is not present.

Take it further

Do you think Piaget was correct? How would you design a study to test his ideas? Think about this and then read Bower and Wishart's study described on p31.

I take her parrot from her hands and hide it twice in succession under the mattress, on her left, in A. Both times Jacqueline looks for the object immediately and grabs it. Then I take it from her hands and move it very slowly before her eyes to the corresponding place on her right, under the mattress, in B. Jacqueline watches this movement very attentively, but the moment when the parrot disappears in B she turns to her left where it was before in A.

(Piaget, 1951, p51)

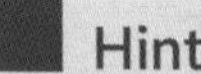

Hint

We might think it strange that infants search in places where an object does not exist, but have you ever gone back again to look for something in the same place when searching for an important object? And have you gone back even though you are almost certain the object is not at that location?

Table 2 *Stages of development of object permanence*

Approximate age (months)	Understanding of object permanence
0–4	No understanding of object permanence
5–9	Position of objects anticipated, but infants will not uncover hidden objects
9–12	Infants will search for/uncover objects, but A not B error occurs
12–15	Success with A not B problems, still failures when objects secretly hidden
15–18	Success with secrete hiding

An evaluation of Piaget's ideas about object permanence

Stage theories can be challenged by findings that children can carry out a task earlier than predicted. However, it is often difficult to know what to make of such findings. Do they mean that the stages should be moved to an earlier age? Or do the findings challenge the overall theory itself? Often, the answer to these questions is a matter of debate.

Research study: Bower and Wishart (1972)

Aim: To investigate whether infants would show an understanding of object permanence before eight to nine months of age.

Method: Sixteen infants, aged 21 weeks, were given a task – to retrieve a toy from under an opaque cup or a transparent cup. In addition, 12 infants, aged 20 weeks, were shown a toy dangling from a string and the lights were turned off before they reached for the toy. The infants' reactions were recorded with an infra-red camera.

Results: The infants could only retrieve an object from under a transparent cup. All the infants reached for the object when the lights were turned off and continued to do so for up to 90 seconds.

Conclusion: The findings showed that there were differences in reactions depending on how the object disappears.

Evaluation: The findings about searching in the dark have been replicated. The findings suggest that Piaget underestimated infants' capabilities because his methods were limited, and this presents a problem for his theory.

Other investigations and theories have concerned the A not B error. It has been suggested that infants simply have a poor memory. Support for this explanation was obtained by Gratch *et al.* (1974) who found fewer search errors at B if the delay was less than one second. Gratch *et al.* suggested that the search is based on postural orientation; they supposed that this information is lost when a delay occurs.

However, the memory explanation has been undermined by Butterworth's findings that B errors occur even when the object is visible, or even if someone else retrieves the object at A (Butterworth, 1974). I will return to these puzzling findings in the next section.

Nativist explanations and early infant abilities

Gibson (1966) has provided an alternative view to Piaget's because he has suggested that infants are able to make use of the rich perceptual information about the world (a nativist view). One of these processes is **direct perception**. However, Gibson also accepted that there will be some learning about perception during development.

If infants directly perceive perceptual characteristics then one would expect them to show evidence of **cross-modal integration**.

The study described below assessed the time that infants spent looking at two objects. Measurements like this of infants' gaze have provided valuable information about their cognitive abilities. The duration of infant gaze provides a useful indication of their interest and can be coded in terms of when the gaze starts and stops. If infants reliably look at one thing rather than another, this shows that they can tell the difference between the two objects and find one of the objects more interesting.

Research study: Meltzoff and Borton (1979)

Aim: To investigate cross-modal integration.

Method: Four-week-old infants sucked for 90 seconds on dummies (pacifiers) that had either a plain or stippled surface. The infants

Key terms

Direct perception: immediate and automatic understanding of a stimulus (such as instantly knowing how far away an object is).

Cross-modal integration: understanding that there is a relationship between different dimensions (e.g. knowing that there is a relation between a sound and the location of that sound).

Link

For more about Gibson's views, see *AQA Psychology B AS*, Chapter 8, Perceptual processes.

Hint

The opposite of a nativist is an empiricist, someone who believes that empirical evidence or experience affects development. Thus, we have two similar contrasts nature–nurture and nativist–empiricist.

were prevented from seeing the dummies before they sucked them. They were then shown both types of dummies.

Results: The infants looked longer at the object they had just sucked.

Conclusion: Cross-modal integration occurs in very young infants. Therefore, either they have an innate understanding that there are relations between different aspects of the physical world or they have learnt this in four weeks.

Evaluation: This challenges Piaget's theory that infants slowly construct knowledge about the world.

Another group of important investigations has concerned infants' visual attention and whether they look longer at events that violate physical laws. Longer looks suggest that infants have seen an event that they did not expect. One of the first of these studies was conducted by Baillargeon *et al.* (1985) who used what is known as the 'violation of expectation' technique.

The violation of expectation technique involves infants being shown an event on a number of occasions so that they become familiar with it. Then some infants are shown an event that is possible and others are shown an event that is impossible. The question is whether infants look longer at the impossible event than at the possible event. If they look longer at the impossible event this suggests that their expectations have been violated.

The infants at first see a rectangular screen that moves back and forth from a position lying flat in front of them, through a vertical position, to a position where the screen is lying flat away from them.

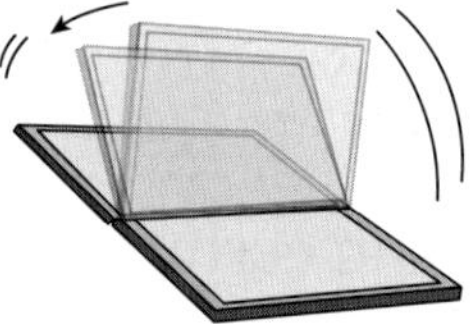

All the infants then see a box placed in the path of the screen.

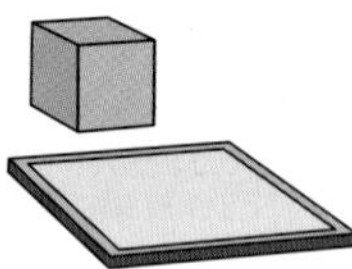

Next, some infants see the box flattened by the screen.

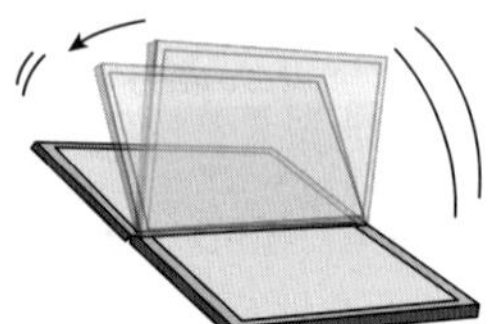

Other infants see the screen coming to rest on the box.

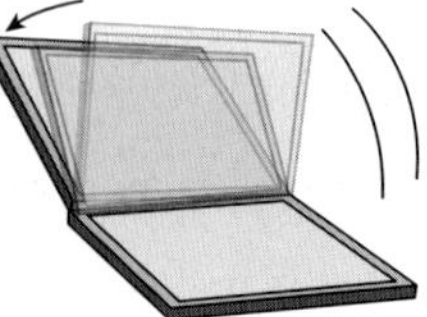

Which group of infants look longer at these two events?

Fig. 2 *The apparatus used by Baillargeon* et al. *(1985)*

Research study: Baillargeon *et al.* (1985)

Aim: To test object permanence by seeing whether infants look longer at 'impossible' events than at 'possible' events.

Method: Twenty-one five-month-old infants sat (one at a time) in front of a screen that was attached by a hinge to a table, rather like a drawbridge that could move through 180 degrees. This arrangement allowed the screen to lie flat in front, be raised to a vertical position and drop down to lie flat, 180 degrees from its starting position (see Figure 2). The infants were familiarised with the screen moving back and forth. Then a cube was placed in the path of the screen, and an infant either saw the screen come to rest on the cube, or saw the screen falling to the ground and by implication flattening the cube. The duration of gaze to these two events was recorded.

Results: Infants looked longer at the screen that fell to the ground and appeared to squash the cube.

Conclusion: This suggests that infants have an understanding of object permanence.

Evaluation: The study was methodologically innovative and challenged Piaget's claim that infants do not understand object permanence. Later, Baillargeon (1987) demonstrated the same effect with 14-week old infants.

Hints

Note: the 'impossible' event in the sequence described above was the same as the familiarisation event. Thus, the longer looks of the infants to the 'impossible' event were not because it was a new sequence. Also note that this is a between-subject design; there was a different group of infants in the two experimental conditions. The dependent variable was the duration of gaze.

It is worth pointing out that, because the study of violation of expectations is very difficult with newborn babies, we do not yet have reliable evidence about whether or not these abilities are present at birth. Such evidence would make nativist claims about the presence of innate abilities more convincing.

Child development

Wilcox *et al.* (1996) used a similar technique to Baillargeon's to investigate the A not B error. Wilcox *et al.* showed infants aged 10 weeks and older an object that disappeared at one location. The object then reappeared in the same location (a possible event) or at another nearby location (an impossible event). The infants looked longer at the impossible event, which suggests that in these circumstances they were not susceptible to the A not B error. The longer looking still occurred after 15 seconds' delay between disappearance and reappearance.

All these findings suggest that before the age of six months, infants have an awareness of object permanence because they look longer at 'impossible' events. However, as we saw in the previous section, infants of this age have difficulty carrying out actions to obtain an object that is hidden.

Recently, it has been suggested that the **perceptual system** of infants is sufficiently developed to distinguish between possible and impossible events. However, when infants need to search for something their **actions** are controlled by a greater range of factors. For example, in the case of the A not B error, infants may go back to familiar routines, or when an object is covered this disrupts planned activities.

Summary questions

1. What did Piaget mean by the term 'schema'? Illustrate your answer using an example.
2. What are the four stages of cognitive development identified by Piaget?
3. Describe one method for assessing object permanence.
4. What do nativists claim about infant abilities?
5. Describe a study that supports nativists' claims about infant abilities.

Key points:

- Piaget described the process of development using terms such as 'schemas', 'adaptation', 'assimilation' and 'accommodation'.
- Although the ideas of accommodation and assimilation seem to capture important characteristics of cognition, the terms are no longer widely used. Instead, one way to understand cognition has been to use more precise descriptions of cognitive processes as given in information processing theories (see p40).
- Piaget identified four stages in children's cognitive development.
- Many investigators believe that Piaget severely underestimated infants' understanding of the physical world and that infants have 'innate core knowledge'.

Childhood: Piaget's stages of development

Learning objectives:

- know and understand the characteristics of the pre-operational, concrete operational and formal operational stages
- be able to describe and evaluate research findings about: conservation, egocentrism and class inclusion
- know and understand Piaget's research including the three mountains task and conservation tasks.

Link

To remind yourself about the stages of development after infancy, look back at Table 1 on p29.

Key terms

Egocentrism: the inability to see or understand something from a viewpoint other than one's own.

Centration: concentrating on one feature and, as a result, failing to see the relevance of another feature.

Piaget tried to show the specific limitations of children's thinking and understanding at each stage of their development. In this section, we return to Piaget's theory of cognitive development and consider the stages of development that he identified at older ages. As we saw earlier (p28), he believed that cognitive development involves universal processes.

Pre-operational stage: 2 to 7 years

The beginning of this stage is marked by the child's use of symbols. A symbol involves the use of sounds, objects or actions to stand for another thing. Examples are a word that represents an object, or a banana that is treated as a telephone in a game. The capacity to use symbols makes humans very different from other species. Piaget used the term 'pre-operational' because children are not yet successful with all mental operations; two important limitations are **egocentrism** and **centration**.

The egocentrism that Piaget described was not deliberate selfishness, rather the tendency to see the world from one's own point of view and not even be aware that one is doing this: for example, a child 'hiding' by covering their eyes but not aware that their body remains visible to others.

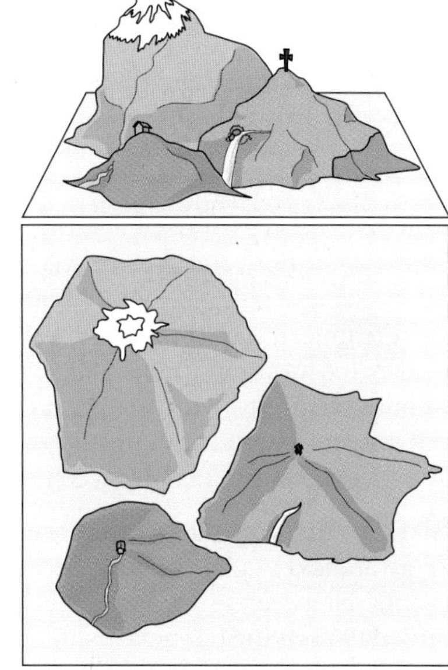

Fig. 3 *Piaget's three mountains problem*

Egocentrism

Piaget believed that the **three mountains task** (see below) illustrated the egocentrism of young children.

Research study: Piaget and Inhelder (1956)

Aim: To follow up previous investigations by testing children's ability to take the visual perspective of another person.

Method: One hundred children aged between four and 12 years were seen. The children were shown a model of three mountains (see Figure 3). They were given three pieces of card shaped and coloured like the mountains and had to arrange the cards to show what could be seen from two different positions in relation to the mountains.

The children also had to pick (from a set of 10) the pictures that were most similar to each of the views seen by a doll when it was seated at several different positions in relation to the mountains. In addition, the children were given pictures and asked where the doll would be sitting to see each picture.

Results: No quantitative data were reported (i.e. the number of different types of response). Instead examples of children's answers were described. From these data it was proposed that the youngest children were unable to distinguish between their own viewpoint and that of a person situated in a different position. However, at around age seven, children started to be able to do this, and children above nine years were much more successful.

Conclusion: Piaget and Inhelder found general support for Piaget's stage theory of development.

Evaluation: This study involves the use of the 'clinical method' and is therefore very different from experimental research. However, Piaget supplied a rich description of children's reasoning and in some respects this is similar to the qualitative approach, which insights gained from the analysis of speech and explanations.

A group of investigators working in Edinburgh devised a series of clever studies that showed that, when given the appropriate circumstances, children could take the perspective of another person. A study relevant to egocentrism is described below.

Research study: Hughes and Donaldson (1979)

Aim: To test children's ability to take another person's point of view in a task that makes more sense to children than the three mountains problem, but made similar cognitive demands.

Method: Thirty children aged between 3 years 6 months and 4 years 11 months took part. Three tasks were used. Only the second task is described here. This involved a model brick wall built in the shape of a cross, and three dolls (a boy and two policemen). The experimenter checked that the children understood the task by asking each child to position the boy so that he could not be seen by one policeman. The children were then asked to hide the boy from two policemen who were positioned at two ends of the walls (see Figure 4). The children did this for four different arrangements of the policemen.

Results: Twenty-seven of the 30 children were successful on three of the tasks; slightly fewer (22 of the 30) were successful on all four tasks.

Conclusion: Young children could successfully accomplish a task which involves the ability to understand what the policemen could see. Hughes and Donaldson (1979) argued that this was possible because the task was very much simpler than the three mountains task and was like a hide-and-seek game, which would be familiar to the children.

Evaluation: The methods are more 'child-friendly' and the findings challenge Piaget's description of development and suggest that he underestimated children's capacities.

Take it further

An important and related area of research has been children's theory of mind (TOM) abilities. Having a TOM involves an understanding that other people can have thoughts and beliefs that differ from yours. The following illustrates this.

Children under four years were given a Smarties tube and asked what was in it. As expected they answered 'Smarties'. However, they were shown that the tube contained pencils. The pencils were put back in the tube and the children were asked, 'What will your friend think is in the Smarties tube when they come in?' Children below four years usually said pencils; children older than four years answered Smarties. Thus, only the older children could work out that their friend would have a different belief from them. Such abilities are important for social interaction and for understanding other people.

Conservation

Conservation involves the ability to understand that, if nothing has been added or taken away from something, then the amount that remains is the same, even when appearances have been changed. For example, a clay ball has the same volume and weight even if rolled into a sausage shape. This may be obvious to us, but Piaget showed that children at the pre-operational stage often give incorrect answers when asked if the amount remains the same. Piaget believed that these children are unable to conserve because of **centration**.

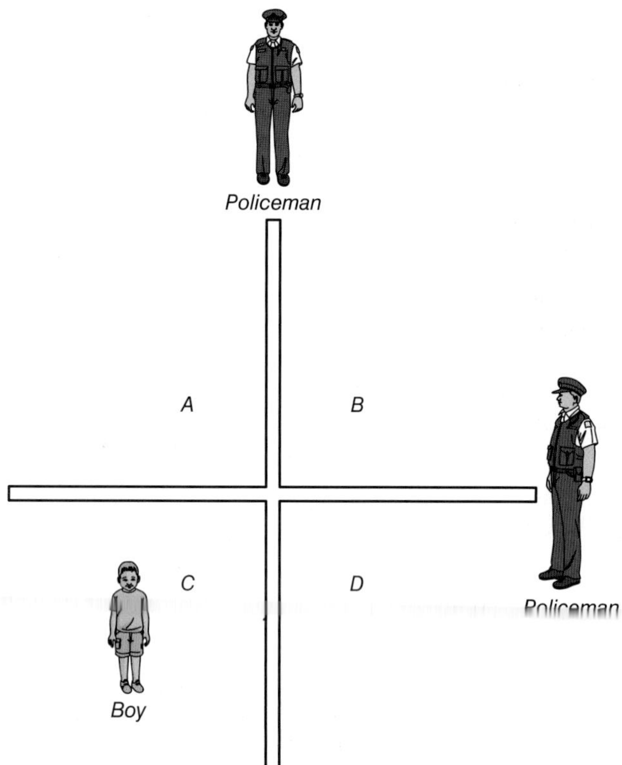

Fig. 4 *Hughes and Donaldson (1979) tried another way of presenting perspective problems to children as an alternative to Piaget's 'three mountains'*

One of Piaget's studies of centration involved setting out a row of sweets and a row of coins, each row having the same number of items, and the objects in each row matching the position of the object in the other row. The experimenter made sure that the children understood there was the same number of items in each row by asking the question, 'Are there the same number in each row?' Then one of the rows was extended to make it longer than the other. Children were asked whether there were more sweets or coins. Usually children younger than six years would reply that there were more items in the longer row. This was taken to show that the children were not able to conserve the number of items. The children appeared to make a mistake due to centration, concentrating on only one aspect of the problem.

The fact that Piaget carefully asked the questions twice, to make sure the child's views had changed, might have affected the answers that children gave. Rose and Blank (1974) showed that young children did better on conservation tasks when they were only asked the second question. This seems to be because adults often ask a second question if a child's answer to the first question is incorrect. As a result, in such circumstances, children adopt a strategy of changing their answers. McGarrigle and Donaldson (1974) carried out a study to investigate this possibility.

Research study: McGarrigle and Donaldson (1974)

Aim: To investigate whether the way that the length of a row of beads was altered had an effect on children's conservation judgements.

Methods: Eighty children aged between four and six years took part in the study. The children were given Piaget's conservation tasks involving length and number.

There were two conditions. In one condition, the alteration was made by the experimenter (e.g. by making one row of beads longer). In the other condition, the alteration appeared as an accident; a toy character, called 'Naughty Teddy', swooped down, 'messed up the game' and made one row longer than the other.

Results: When the experimenter altered the length, 16 per cent of the children showed conservation across all the tasks. When Naughty Teddy altered the length, 62 per cent of children showed conservation across all the tasks.

Conclusion: Children appear to be able to conserve number at younger ages than that suggested by Piaget.

Evaluation: Donaldson admitted that for some young children 'the look of the thing' might influence their answers, so that they are not able to answer the conservation questions correctly. It also is possible that young children do not fully understand what the word 'same' means and may confuse length and numerical correspondence.

Class inclusion

Another task that Piaget used to illustrate the characteristics of children at this stage involves **class inclusion**.

Research study: Piaget (1952)

Aim: To investigate whether children at the pre-operational stage could understand class inclusion.

Method: The total number of children in this investigation was not reported: instead, ages were given with the children's answers. A box with brown wooden beads and two white beads was used. The children were asked questions such as whether the box contained more brown beads or more wooden beads. Sometimes other materials similar to this were used.

Results: Examples of children's answers and reasoning were described. Only children above about six years of age were able to give the correct answers.

Conclusion: The data supported the hypothesis that pre-operational children are unable to understand class inclusion.

Evaluation: This was a descriptive study. The next research study challenges Piaget's conclusion.

Research study: McGarrigle (see Donaldson, 1978)

Aim: To see whether children's responses were affected by the way that questions about class inclusion were asked.

Method: Thirty-five children about six years old took part. Children were shown three black toy cows and one white toy cow. All the cows were put on their sides and the children were told that this was because the cows were sleeping. The children were asked two questions:

1. Are there more black cows or more white cows? (the type of question used by Piaget)
2. Are there more black cows or more sleeping cows?

Results: Question 1 was answered correctly by 25 per cent of the children; question 2 was answered correctly by 48 per cent of the children.

Conclusion: The wording of the question affects children's responses. Giving more emphasis to the whole group by using the adjective 'sleeping' helped children give the correct answer.

Evaluation: It appears that children in the pre-operational stage can solve some class-inclusion problems. This suggests that the questions Piaget used may have influenced the children's answers (i.e. a methodological problem).

Concrete operations: 7 to 12 years

According to Piaget, the thinking of children at the concrete operations stage is no longer affected by egocentrism or centration, and children can carry out reversible operations (e.g. conservation tasks where volume and weight remain the same despite being changed in shape).

Key terms

Class inclusion: the understanding of the relation between a class of objects and subclasses of the objects (e.g. that in a bowl of apples and oranges, there will always be more items of fruit than the individual number of either apples or of oranges).

Take it further

Here is a short example of Piaget's description of Stro aged six years (Piaget, 1952): 'Are there more wooden beads or more brown beads in this box? – *More brown ones* – Why? – *Because there are only two wooden ones.* – But aren't the brown ones made of wood? – *Oh, yes!* – Well then, are there more brown ones or more wooden ones? – *More brown ones.*'

Children at this stage are better at 'concrete' tasks, which are tied to objects or events, rather than abstract tasks.

- An example of a concrete task is the following: 'James is bigger than Adam, and Adam is bigger than John. Is James bigger than John?'
- An example of an abstract task is the following: 'A is bigger than B, and B is bigger than C. Is A bigger than C?'

Research study: Piaget (1952)

Aim: To investigate children's understanding of conservation, which, Piaget argued, is a fundamental aspect of rational thought.

Method: Children were shown two identical cylindrical containers; these had the same amount of liquid in each, as shown by the levels. Each child was asked whether there was the same amount of liquid in both containers. The liquid in one of the cylinders was poured into two smaller identical containers. The children were asked whether there was the same amount of liquid in the larger container as in the two smaller containers. The exact format of the questioning varied from child to child.

Note that, in some conservation experiments, liquid was poured into a differently shaped container.

Results: No quantitative data were reported. Instead the selected examples of children's answers and reasoning were described. Children below seven years were not usually able to conserve volume.

Conclusion: These findings were taken as showing that only when children reach the concrete operations stage are they able to understand reversibility and able to overcome the limitations of centration. In Piaget's terms, they are able to decentre.

Evaluation: What criticisms would you make of this study? If you are not sure, look back at the previous research studies.

Take it further

Piaget suggested that conservation abilities do not occur at the same age for all types of physical properties. Rather, he believed that conservation occurred in the following order: number, quantity, weight and volume. He called the development of the same type of understanding at different ages **'horizontal décalage'**. Piaget believed that this occurs because some physical properties are easier to understand than others: for example, quantity is easier to conserve than weight as the former can be observed directly.

Formal operations: 12 years +

This stage involves the ability to think abstractly, hypothetically and systematically; this is an advance on the concrete operations stage where reasoning is better with 'real' tasks. Piaget did not think that the formal operations stage is reached by everyone.

An example of the formal operations thinking occurs in a task to identify the variables that influence the length of swing of a pendulum. Young people below 12 years tend to evaluate variables like weight of pendulum or length of string in an unsystematic manner. They fail to study the effect of changing one of the variables while holding the others constant. In contrast, systematic strategies are adopted by individuals at the formal operations stage. Thus, formal operations involve the principles of scientific thinking, especially the development and systematic testing of hypotheses.

Evaluation of Piaget's methods

In many (but not all) of Piaget's studies, he used the clinical method. The following problems with this method have been identified.

- The questioning or the tasks were not the same for all children, which could result in unconscious experimenter bias.

- Piaget usually reported examples of conversations rather than statistical analyses. The problem with this is that the examples could have been selected to support his theory. There is, however, no evidence that Piaget did this.
- By being sensitive to the way that questions were asked, investigators have shown that children can perform much better than was suggested by Piaget in his stage theory of development.

All this offers a useful example of how, although descriptive research can provide insights into psychological development, experimental investigations are needed to check the conclusions drawn from descriptive, and more qualitative, research.

Despite these criticisms, Piaget remains one of the most important figures in developmental psychology. One of his most significant legacies has been the emphasis given to **constructivist** views about development: the assumption that knowledge is gradually acquired by building up an understanding of the world and that this occurs through interaction with the world. Piaget's work has had a profound influence on early education and has resulted in emphasis on so-called 'discovery' play, where children find out about the properties of objects through their own exploration and efforts.

Key points:

- Piaget believed that children respond to information according to their stage of cognitive development.
- Piaget described processes involving conservation, egocentrism and class inclusion.
- Piaget's studies involving the three mountains task and conservation supported his stage theory.
- More recent research has challenged Piaget's conclusions about the ages at which children can carry out tasks involving egocentrism, class inclusion and conservation. Children have been shown to be successful on tasks at earlier ages than Piaget assumed.
- The work of Donaldson and her colleagues challenges the age bands associated with the Piagetian stages. Often the age differences are large, making it very difficult to know the best way to adapt Piaget's theory to such findings.
- The methods used by Piaget resulted in his underestimating the abilities of young children. It seems likely that Piaget did not fully appreciate that the abstract nature of the problems made tasks difficult for young children.
- However, Piaget's observations highlighted two important ways in which pre-operational children have a limited ability to process information: egocentrism and centration.
- A more general criticism is that Piaget rarely discussed the way that social processes affect development.
- The criticisms of Piaget illustrate the importance of information processing and the social context in relation to children's thinking.

Link

For an evaluation of qualitative research, see Chapter 11, Methods in psychology.

Hint

It is inaccurate to say that Piaget did not consider social processes. A number of his studies into children of school age were concerned with the way that discussions involving peer interaction could be more beneficial than discussions with adults. He supposed that children would accept the accuracy of adult viewpoints without any accommodation of their schemas because of the status of the adult; in contrast, accommodation of schemas to the views of peers would be more likely.

Summary questions

6. What did Piaget mean by the term 'egocentrism'? Illustrate your answer with an example.
7. Explain two differences between the pre-operational and concrete operational stages.
8. What criticisms can be made of Piaget's method of assessing egocentrism?

Information processing theories

Learning objectives:

- understand and evaluate the information processing approach to cognitive development
- describe and discuss Siegler's research into problem-solving strategies.

Key terms

Information processing theories: theories that attempt to understand the sequence of separate cognitive operations that make up some form of mental activity, such as recalling a face or solving a problem.

Link

For more about the work of Atkinson and Schiffrin (1968) and Baddely (1966), see *AQA Psychology B* AS, Chapter 7, Remembering and forgetting.

Hint

Often information processing theories address the question of what cognitive changes enable children to do something that younger children are unable to do. It is often assumed that younger children have information processing limitations. For example, young children may not notice relevant information or might not be able to remember the information long enough to make use of it.

Information processing theories take a different perspective to cognitive development from that of Piaget but can, in some respects, be seen as growing out of criticisms of his work. The use of information processing theories in developmental psychology can be linked to the use of this approach with adults (e.g. Atkinson and Schiffrin, 1968; Baddeley, 1966).

It is worth noting that there is not 'one' information processing theory, but a collection of theories and models that involve common assumptions.

Piaget was interested in children's knowledge and understanding. He believed that development involves removal of distortions to understanding such as those involving egocentrism and centration. In contrast, information processing theorists are less concerned with knowledge and understanding: instead, they are more interested in how children make use of the information available to them. For example, Piaget's ideas about accommodation, assimilation and centration capture fundamental aspects of our thinking, but it is difficult to go beyond Piaget's descriptions of these processes to understand what precisely happens to the information as it is processed by the brain.

Siegler *et al.* (2003) identified four characteristics of information processing theories:

- the use of task analysis to identify the separate parts of thinking that are needed to complete a task (e.g. perceiving a stimulus, categorising it, forming a short-term memory of an item, and so on)
- consideration of the information processing over time, and the sequence of operations that occur over time
- the similarity between information processing theories and the processes involved in the operation of a computer
- the assumption that children are active problem solvers.

How children process information

Siegler's balance problems

A good example of the information processing approach is Siegler's work on the balance scale (see Figure 5). Children were given different arrangements of weights on the rods and were asked whether the beam would stay level or would go down to the right or to the left.

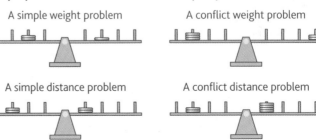

Fig. 5 *Balance scales with arrangements of 'simple' and 'conflict' problems*

Siegler (1976) carried out a task analysis to identify the variables that influence whether or not the scale balances; these variables are weight, distance and the multiplication of weight and distance. Based on this he used different arrangements of weights to gain an understanding of the principles behind children's answers.

Siegler presented children with both 'simple' and 'conflict' problems (see Figure 6). There were two important forms of the simple problems:

- One was a 'simple weight' problem that involved an unequal number of weights either side of the fulcrum. The weights on either side were at the same distance from the fulcrum and, as a result, the side with more weights would go down. Thus, if children gave correct predictions about these weight problems they probably understood the role of weight.
- The other was a 'simple distance' problem. The distance of the weights either side of the fulcrum was unequal, but there were the same number of weights either side of the fulcrum. Thus, if children gave correct answers about these distance problems they probably understood the role of distance.

There were also more difficult arrangements called 'conflict-weight' and 'conflict-distance' problems. These were designed so that children who understand the role of weight would pass the conflict-weight problems, and those that understand the role of distance would pass the conflict-distance problems.

From the children's answers, Siegler identified four 'rules'. These rules relate to children's responses about balance (see Table 3).

Table 3 *Rules identified by Siegler (1976) in relation to children's answers about balance*

Rule	Age usually present (years)	Simple problems	Conflict problems
Rule 1	3–4	Side with more weights is predicted to go down.	Distance does not affect any decisions
Rule 2	9	Weight and distance are each used to make decisions on simple problems and correct answers are given to both types of simple problems	When there is conflict between weight and distance, children predict only on the basis of weight. So they are correct on conflict-weight, but incorrect on conflict-distance problems
Rule 3	13	Same as above	Random responses on conflict problems
Rule 4	Rarely identified	Same as above	Correct responses on all conflict problems

Siegler carried out further research to try to understand why children at Rule 1 failed to take account of distance.

Research study: Siegler (1976)

Aim: To test whether Rule 1 could be explained by a failure at encoding of distance.

Methods: Ten five-year-olds and 10 eight-year-olds took part in the study. The children were shown a balance scale, and weights were put

Take it further

Both Siegler *et al.* (2003) and Brainerd (1983) have outlined three issues, which have been of interest to information processing theorists.

- **Basic processes** (the hardwiring of the system) – these include encoding and speed of processing. The encoding of a stimulus is usually the first stage of information processing where an experience is perceived and processed. Children often fail to encode all of the relevant information (think of the process of centration). An issue facing information processing theories is how children become better at information processing. One possibility is that there is a general increase in capacity due to maturation: for example, more items can be stored in memory or the information can be processed more quickly (Kail and Park, 1990). Another possibility is that children can deal with more information at any one time (Case *et al.*, 1985).
- **Strategies** (the software of the system) – these involve adopting new and better ways of carrying out a task. For example, when children aged between five and eight years are asked to remember something, they will start to repeat the material over to themselves. This is because they know that this helps them to remember something; this involves a **meta-understanding** (the understanding of the processes involved in their own thinking).
- **Content knowledge** (this can probably be best thought of as the memory of a computer) – this increases with experience and teaching. One type of knowledge that has been described is scripts; scripts enable knowledge to be formed about an everyday activity such as going to a fast-food restaurant. Thus, children start to identify different stages in the process (choosing the food, giving the order, receiving the food, etc.) and what happens at each stage.

Hint

In a balance scale, the vertical rods are positioned so that their distance from the fulcrum is either twice, three or four times the distance of the first rod from the fulcrum. As a result, to predict whether the scale will tilt or balance, one needs to calculate for each rod the number of weights on it multiplied by whether the rod is the first, second, third or fourth one from the fulcrum (see Fig. 5). The side with the greater number will go down; if the two calculations give the same number, the beam will stay level.

Take it further

Aspects of the information processing approach have been very helpful with children who have disabilities. For example, research has been conducted on children's ability to identify the separate sounds that are contained in words. From this research, it has been found that children with reading difficulties (dyslexia) have problems with this task and that this appears to be one of the causes of their reading difficulties.

on it. The scale was then hidden and the children were asked to put weights in the same positions on another scale. Different assessments were also carried out to identify which rule each child was using when making predictions about the weights on a balance task.

Results: Almost all of the children were assessed as being at Rule 1. The younger children placed the weights correctly 51 per cent of the time; distances were correct only 16 per cent of the time. The older children placed the weights correctly 73 per cent of the time, and the distances were correct 56 per cent of the time.

Conclusion: Children at Rule 1 are more accurate at encoding weight than distance, but the encoding of both weight and distance improves with age. The findings are consistent with children at Rule 1 paying attention to (encoding) weight and therefore failing to predict correctly the direction of tilt in distance problems.

Evaluation: This is a simple but elegant cross-sectional study which is based around task analysis. The findings indicate there is a relation between encoding difficulties and children's rule use.

Siegler's overlapping waves model

The rule-based description of different types of predictions that children make in relation to a balance scale suggests that children progress from one rule to the next, much like children are supposed to progress through Piaget's stages. However, Siegler now believes that children will try out a range of strategies before they identify the most effective one. He describes development as involving **overlapping waves** with the use of different strategies over time (Siegler, 1996; see Figure 6 and below). It is worth noting that, at some points, the strategies can be less effective so that children's performance becomes worse.

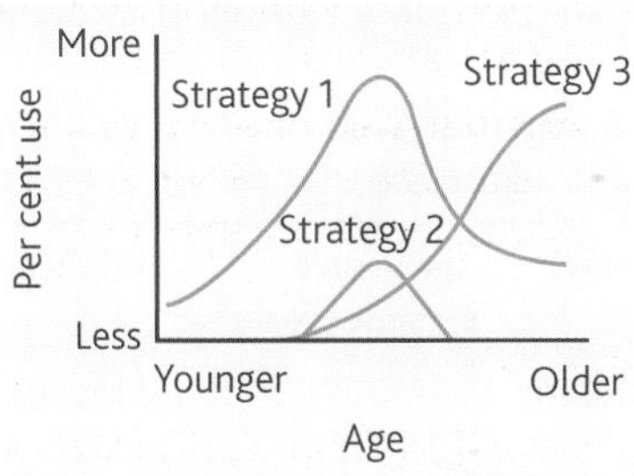

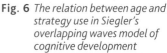

Fig. 6 *The relation between age and strategy use in Siegler's overlapping waves model of cognitive development*

Strategy use involving 'overlapping waves' can be seen in the study of addition described below.

Research study: Siegler and Jenkins (1989)

Aim: To investigate children's use of strategies when adding.

Method: The investigators studied eight children aged between four and five years, who did not yet use the **min** strategy. For a problem like adding up 2 and 5, the min strategy involves identifying the larger number and simply counting up from that to give the answer (e.g. 5 + 1 = 6; 6 + 1 = 7). The children were given these problems three times a week for eight weeks.

Results: From video records and interviews, it was apparent that the children used several strategies. It had been assumed that children would count up from either number they were given and then start to realise that it is more efficient to count up from the larger of the two numbers. However, this does not seem to have been the case. What was discovered was that, when adding 2 and 5, children would use a strategy of simply counting from 1 up to 7 to obtain the correct answer. When they had used this strategy only a few times, they started to use the min strategy. The min strategy was adopted more quickly when the children were given problems like 20 + 2, where the min strategy is especially effective.

Conclusion: Evidence was found that children use a range of strategies before they settle on the most successful one.

Evaluation: The findings support Siegler's overlapping waves model of cognitive development.

Bruner's modes of representation

Information processing theories tend to assume that all stimuli are processed in similar ways. However, a feature of human thinking is that we have different types of representations. Bruner's (1966) ideas provide a good example of this. He described three modes of representation – enactive, iconic and symbolic:

- **Enactive** representations involve actions and experiences (similar to Piaget's sensorimotor stage). These representations can occur at all ages and involve automatic patterns of motor activity (e.g. riding a bicycle).
- **Iconic** representations involve images; according to Bruner these first occur around 12 to 18 months.
- At around six to seven years, Bruner suggested, there is a change to the **symbolic** mode. This enables children to deal with logical relations and reversibility.

Key points:

- Information processing theories have been very useful in providing a description of the cognitive operations involved in particular tasks such as the balance scale.
- The first information processing theories and models have often been tied to particular tasks (e.g. Siegler's rules for the balance scale) and do not have the generality of, for example, Piaget's theory.
- More recent ideas (e.g. Siegler's overlapping waves model) provide a more general theory.
- Information processing theories can be criticised, like Piaget's, for not taking account of social processes and the way that adults help children to learn.

Summary questions

9 Describe three features of the information processing approach to cognitive development.

10 How did Siegler explain the development of children's understandings of the balance scale?

11 Explain Siegler's overlapping waves model of development.

Vygotsky: social, cultural and cognitive processes

Learning objectives:

- understand and evaluate Vygotsky's theory of cognitive development
- understand and evaluate the way in which development occurs in the zone of proximal development
- describe and discuss the processes of scaffolding and guided participation in sociocultural activities.

Take it further

One of Vygotsky's major concerns was the relationship between thought, language and consciousness. In part, this reflected an interest in the private speech that occurs when young children talk to themselves in an apparent effort to help themselves think and reason. Children's use of private speech provided a basis for suggesting that language enables more advanced forms of thinking and reasoning.

Key terms

Zone of proximal development: the area between a child's actual development and the potential level that could be achieved with the help of someone more experienced.

A general criticism of many cognitive theories is that the influence of social processes is neglected, as what we humans learn in social contexts is probably more important than what we learn by ourselves. Lev Vygotsky was the first psychologist to discuss and theorise extensively about the role of speech, social settings and culture in relation to cognitive development.

Although Vygotsky (1896–1934) grew up in Tsarist Russia, his research work was carried out under the communist regime of Stalin. His theorising supported Marxist views, but there was considerable personal danger associated with having independent and challenging views. He died at a young age from tuberculosis. His work only became widely known in the West through translations in the 1960s and 1970s.

In many ways, Vygotsky's exact contribution to developmental psychology is difficult to pin down. Unlike Piaget he did not produce a detailed model of development. Despite this, it is possible to argue that his views have more relevance than Piaget's to current research, this is because of Vygotsky's views about the significance of social and culturally based activities.

Vygotsky stressed the way that thinking is influenced by cultural activities and beliefs (an example was the belief that the world is flat), but he also pointed out that children influence their culture in subtle and important ways. For example, the widespread use today among young people of computer games can be seen as the result of a complex set of influences that involve technical innovation, children's interests and changes in family structure, as well as the wider values and organisation of the culture.

Vygotsky highlighted the way that, in social settings and from the use of language, children learn from others who are more knowledgeable and who support their learning. Vygotsky used the term **zone of proximal development** (ZPD; see Figure 7) when referring to the process, and the idea has had a considerable impact.

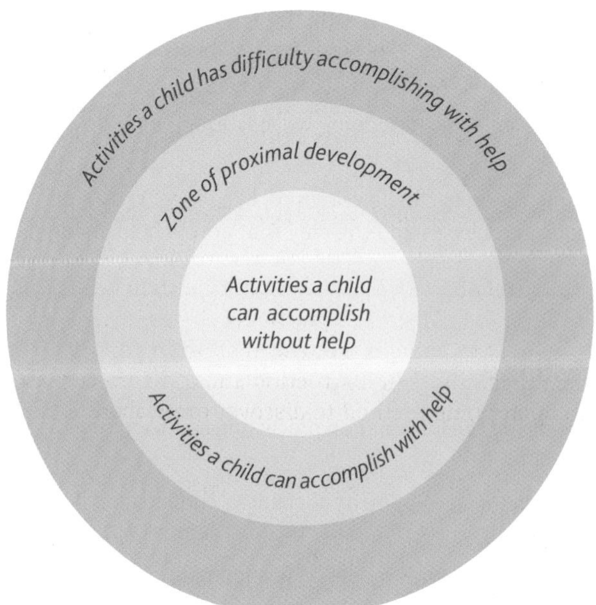

Fig. 7 *A diagram of the zone of proximal development (ZPD)*

The activities a child can accomplish alone form the first 'zone'. Beyond this is the ZPD; here children can accomplish things with help from others (e.g. complete a jigsaw). Beyond the ZPD are activities that a child will find difficult to accomplish even with assistance (e.g. trying to read).

The emphasis Vygotsky gave to the social processes can be seen in his often-quoted statements that any function in development occurs first between people and then within a child. This perspective has given rise to what has become known as **sociocultural theory**.

Key terms

Sociocultural theory: assumptions that social interaction provides the context for the development of human capabilities and functioning and that the social interactions in which learning occurs will be influenced by the cultural context.

In sociocultural theory, emphasis is given to the way cultural tools are involved in learning. These cultural tools can be simple objects, such as a spoon, or complex organisations like the internet. Cultural tools make human development very different from that of animals which act directly on their environment: human actions take place in a cultural environment that has been created by humans. Adults and others assist children in using cultural tools, and, by using cultural tools, children change their own skills and thinking.

Vygotsky's ideas have resulted in analyses of the ways that social settings provide opportunities for learning; but this is not formal teaching, rather the 'tutor' identifies a child's needs and manages the situation so that the child can accomplish parts of the task with assistance. This is an example of what can occur in the ZPD, an important example of which is known as **scaffolding** (i.e. providing a supportive framework within which the child can learn)

Research study: Wood and Middleton (1975)

Aim: To examine interactions between mothers and their children during a problem-solving task.

Method: Twelve mothers and their children, aged three to four years, took part in the study. Their task involved putting 21 wooden blocks together to form a pyramid-like structure. The mothers were shown how to construct the pyramid before the session. At the end, each child tried to build the pyramid without help.

Results: The following types of behaviours were identified: general verbal instruction ('Can you make another one?'); specific verbal instruction ('You need another one with a hole'); drawing attention to the materials ('You need that one there'); preparation (mother prepares blocks ready for putting together); and modelling (providing an example of what to do). The mothers who changed their help on the basis of the child's response were more likely to have a child who later succeeded in the task.

Conclusion: Effective tutorial involves a dynamic, interactive process.

Evaluation: This and related studies have been important in highlighting the way that children's cognitive development can be assisted by adult help. Scaffolding is often seen as an important alternative to more direct forms of instruction and to reinforcement. Observation is an appropriate method to discover more about adult tutoring.

Wood, *et al.* (1976) identified a number of processes that contribute to effective scaffolding:

- recruitment and maintaining the learner's interest in the task
- simplification of the task so that it is not too complicated

Hint

Think about an adult and child putting together a jigsaw. Identify as many types of scaffolding as you can think of. Compare your answers with those of a friend or someone else in the class.

- marking critical features that will help solution
- controlling levels of frustration
- demonstration of the task.

Effective scaffolding involves matching the level of assistance to the children's capabilities, so that the help puts children in a position to accomplish something that they would be unable to do by themselves.

Rogoff (1990, 1995) has been interested in similar processes and has developed a more extensive theory about the relation between social settings and child development. She believes that, as people participate in sociocultural activities, they contribute to community practices that simultaneously contribute to the individual's own development.

Research study: Rogoff *et al.* (1995)

Aim: To describe children's fundraising as a sociocultural activity, in terms of cultural, interpersonal and personal processes.

Method: Two troops of girl scouts, aged 10–11 years, were observed. In one, there was participant observation by a mother. The scouts had tape recorders to record what happened and interviews were carried out. Historical research was also done.

Results: The historical research showed that in the USA fundraising by girl scouts (by selling biscuits) had changed since the 1930s. It had become progressively better organised, but it had also changed from selling door to door to selling to contacts through parental networks because of concerns over safety and because no one was at home during the day. The activity was valued as teaching self-reliance, organisation and dealing with money; it was also valued by former scouts as providing a link between their past and the present generation.

Observations were made of the way that interpersonal activities stretched the capacities of scouts to understand and adjust to others; learning of new techniques occurred with the support of others, such as calculating the costs of the orders.

Conclusions: It was concluded that learning does not simply involve the collection of stored knowledge; activity and events carried out with the support of others transform children's abilities through engagement in shared processes.

Evaluation: The study makes important claims about the way cognitive development occurs. However, the research does not provide quantitative evidence that would convince a sceptic.

Take it further

Related to guided participation are the ideas of **apprenticeship** and **participatory appropriation**:

- Apprenticeship is a relatively straightforward idea that a culturally organised activity with others partly has the purpose of enabling a more mature or advanced participation in the activity (e.g. working with a more expert person such as a qualified plumber or electrician).
- Participatory appropriation refers to how individuals change through their involvement in these activities. For example, the apprentice sees how the expert carries out a task and learns from this.

As you can see, guided participation, apprenticeship and participatory appropriation are not different activities: rather, they are different aspects of the same activity.

Rogoff uses the term **guided participation** not only to include activities such as face-to-face interaction, as in scaffolding, but also for when two individuals work alongside each other or for processes that involve observation. The 'guidance' refers to the influence of cultural and social values. These can be activities as different as tending livestock and selling biscuits as part of a fundraising activity.

Key terms

Guided participation: a wide range of social processes in relation to a culturally meaningful activity.

Key points:

- Vygotsky's sociocultural theory provides a significant contrast to the work of Piaget and even to information processing theories.
- Sociocultural theory emphasises the way that cognitive development occurs in the context of shared social processes and it is argued that significant cognitive developments need to be seen in relation to the features of a child's culture.
- The processes of scaffolding and guided participation provide descriptions of the way that development can occur in the ZPD.
- Sociocultural theory draws attention to the way that learning is part of a social and cultural process. People change through engagement in activities. This is not simply the acquisition of new information or new ways of processing information.

Summary questions

12 Describe what is meant by the 'zone of proximal development'.

13 Outline two differences between the theories of Vygotsky and Piaget.

14 Describe three types of tutorial support that might be given by an adult as a form of scaffolding.

End-of-chapter activity 1

This is a practical task that you can do individually or in a group. Piaget predicted that formal operations can be present in adolescence and adulthood. Carry out the following task to see whether you and/or your fellow students are using formal reasoning.

- **Materials** You will need:
  - strings of various lengths
  - different weights.
- **Procedure** Make a pendulum with strings of various lengths and different weights. See if you can work out what makes the object swing faster or slower when on a pendulum. Record what you change on each attempt. See below for a debriefing.

End-of-chapter activity 2

This activity can be carried out by individuals or groups. Go through the research studies in this chapter (or a selection of these if there is not enough time).

For each of the research studies, decide whether it is a longitudinal, cross-sectional study or another type of study (see index for emboldened page references for links to definitions).

If the study is an experiment:

1 What is the independent variable?

2 What is the dependent variable?

3 Is the design within or between subjects?

4 Is this an experimental or non-experimental study?

Results Debriefing formal operations involves the changing of one variable while keeping the others constant. Thus, if you or your fellow students changed one variable at a time, e.g. the length of the string but not the weight, this would show evidence of formal operational reasoning.

Further reading

Davey, G. *et al.* (2008) *Complete Psychology*, 2nd edition. London: Hodder & Stoughton.

Oates, J., Wood, C. and Grayson, A. (eds) (2005) *Psychological Development and Early Childhood.* Oxford: Blackwell.

Siegler, R.S., DeLaoche, J.S. and Eisenberg, N. (2006) *How Children Develop*, 2nd edition. Basingstoke: Palgrave Macmillan.

Slater, A. and Lewis, M. (eds) (2007). *Introduction to Infant Development*, 2nd edition. Oxford: Oxford University Press.

Smith, P.K., Cowie, H. and Blades, M. (2003) *Understanding Children's Development*. Oxford: Blackwell.

3 Moral development

Psychoanalytic perspectives on moral development

Learning objectives:

- discuss and evaluate psychoanalytic explanations of moral development
- understand the role of the superego in relation to moral development.

In newspapers and television there are frequently discussions about changing morality. Often, it is stated or implied that the present generation of young people is less moral than previous generations, with terms such as 'good' and 'bad' being used to describe behaviour. Articles often focus on 'bad' behaviours, drug use and illegal activities. However, as we will see, morality includes a wider range of behaviours, such as being kind to others, being truthful, being helpful and not being selfish, as well as sexual and illegal behaviour.

Most psychological research about this topic has been concerned with judgements and explanations – an aspect of thinking and cognition. Thinking about morality often has a relation to what people actually do, but many studies have found that there are differences between what people say and what they do.

This section concerns Freud's views about moral development. Later sections examine Piaget's theory and work, this leads on to a consideration of Kohlberg's influential theory and other theories that have involved a wider range of topics. The topics include the way that rewards and resources should be allocated among people, when others should be helped and why, and whether there are differences between males and females in their reasoning about morality. The research on moral development shows the way in which scientific research has progressed. The initial research and the theories of Freud and of Piaget were based on observations or semi-structured interviews. In later research, investigators were much more careful to use procedures that were the same for all participants (e.g. Kohlberg *et al.*, 1983).

Why don't today's adolescents know the difference between right and wrong?

Fig. 1 *Newspaper headlines often focus on morality*

Hint

Discussions and research about morality often include the following topics:

- judgements and explanations about what is right and wrong
- behaviours that can be considered right or wrong.

Freud's explanation of moral development

Sigmund Freud (1856–1939) developed an important theory to explain the way the human mind works. His medical work involved treating adult patients who had a range of psychological and behavioural problems, and his theory grew out of his observations of these patients. Freud's interest was in the way that the more emotional parts of thinking play a role in development. His concern was with the dynamics (i.e. the way that several forces can produce behaviour by interacting with one another) of psychological thinking, hence the term 'psychodynamic'.

Freud was interested in moral development because of its relevance to understanding the psychological problems of some adults. His focus was the psychological processes that resulted in the acquisition in childhood of morality, later psychological work focused more on children's reasoning about moral issues and the way that this changed with age.

Fig. 2 *Sigmund Freud*

Id, ego and superego

Freud identified three components of the self or personality (he used the term 'psychic apparatus') that influence a person's thinking and behaviour. These components are the id, ego and superego; a diagram

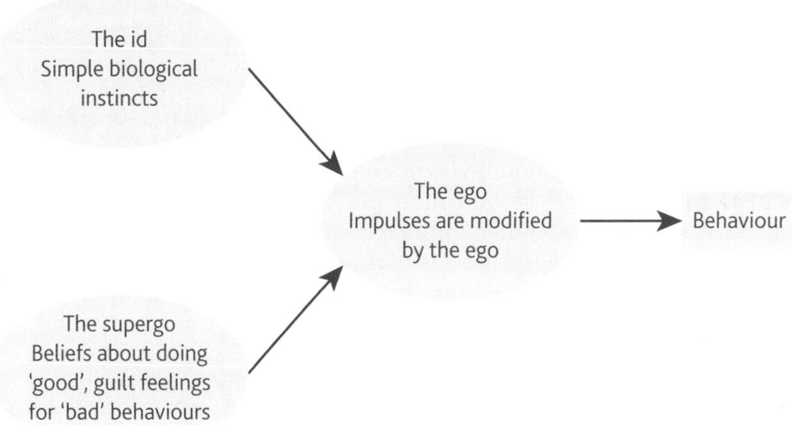

Fig. 3 *The relation between id, ego and superego*

can be created to illustrate their relationship (see Figure 3), much as diagrams have been used by cognitive psychologists to show the flow of information.

However, it is important to recognise that in Freud's theory the connections between the different parts of the mind concern energy rather than information.

The three components are described below:

The **id** is sometimes known as the pleasure principle; it is supposed to be present at birth and 'contains everything that is inherited' (Freud, 1923). Freud considered that the two most important drives were aggression and sex (together these made up the libido). If the id operated by itself then children and people would try to satisfy their biological instincts without any thought for the consequences. Obviously, most people do not operate like this. Consequently, Freud reasoned that thinking is affected by other parts of the mind. He identified two and called these the **ego** and the **superego**.

The **ego** (sometimes termed the reality principle) can 'prevent' the production of immoral behaviour. For example, a child might see some cakes on a table but knows that she will be punished if someone walks in and sees her eating one of the cakes. The dynamics between the 'forces' involved in being hungry and the unpleasantness of the punishment would influence whether or not she took a cake. So if the child was very hungry she would be more likely to take a cake. Freud believed that the ego develops in the first three years of life and, as a result, the id no longer has complete 'control' over thinking and behaviour. Freud described the way that biological needs located in the id would build up pressure or excitation. Without the ego this pressure would result in immediate behaviours relevant to satisfying the instinct. However, the ego can manage or postpone these behaviours.

The **superego** (it is sometimes referred to as the morality principle) was believed by Freud to develop when the child is between four and six years of age. The superego contains two parts. One part is the **ego ideal** which provides a model of the type of behaviour we think we should perform; carrying out these behaviours increases pride and self-esteem. The other part is the conscience which produces feelings of **guilt** when we carry out behaviours that are against the principles of the superego. Freud supposed that the superego and id are often in conflict.

Link

For an example of the type of model that cognitive psychologists use to illustrate information processing theories, see p239 in Chapter 9, Approaches in psychology.

Key terms

Id: in Freud's theory, the source of biologically based drives and motivations (e.g. hunger).

Ego: in Freud's theory, a personality structure that modifies the impulses of the id by taking account of the consequences of an action.

Superego: in Freud's theory, a personality structure that contains ideas about morality.

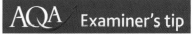

AQA Examiner's tip

Note that Piaget used the term 'egocentric', whereas Freud discusses the 'ego'. Avoid getting these two terms confused and check that you understand the difference between them.

Freud believed that the ego is responsible for the final decision about behaviour. However, he also thought that the person will feel guilty when actions are carried out that are contrary to the principles of the superego.

Freud came to the conclusion that children **identify** with the parent who is of the same sex: boys identify with their father, girls with their mother. Identification involves wanting to be like a particular person and changing to become more like this person; these changes could involve changes in moral principles. Freud also supposed that these changes involved the process of **internalisation**. In this case, internalisation involves using the observed behaviours of a parent as a basis for the principles in the child's own superego. Thus, the actions of others become part of the child's own person and are, therefore, not just superficial changes but ones that are fully incorporated into the child's self.

The Oedipus complex

Many psychologists would accept that identification and internalisation are important processes that have a role to play in various forms of development. However, Freud also developed a broader theory about identification and internalisation that most psychologists do not accept.

Freud proposed that boys experience the Oedipus complex, named after an ancient Greek play in which Oedipus unknowingly kills his father and marries his mother (at the time that Freud was devising his theory, ancient myths and folklore were believed by some to capture universal truths about human nature). Freud argued that, when aged around three to six years, boys are sexually attracted to their mothers. They also unconsciously recognise that this involves rivalry with their father and therefore conflict with him. Freud suggested that, because their father is more powerful and because the rivalry is sexual in nature, boys fear that their father will cut off their penis. This fear is partly based on knowledge that the penis is a source of pleasure and the worry that girls have already been punished in this way. Thus, Freud believed, boys experience two incompatible feelings: sexual desire for the mother together with a fear that the father will punish them for this desire. He proposed that this dilemma is resolved by the young boy wishing to become like the father (identification) and suppressing his desire for his mother. As a result of this identification boys imitate the moral behaviour of the father, internalising these behaviours in the superego.

The Electra complex

Freud supposed that a different and even more complicated process occurred in girls; he termed this the 'Electra complex'. The result is that girls identify with their mother, but Freud believed that this identification is weaker than with the father in boys, and so females have a weaker superego.

Evaluation of Freud's ideas

Strength

Freud's description of the roles of the id, ego and superego captures the dilemmas that many of us feel when deciding to do something, especially if it is something that we think is wrong. Sometimes we feel tempted to do something wrong, but we also feel guilt.

Limitations

However, many of the key aspects of Freud's account of moral development involving the Oedipus and Electra complexes have been challenged or discredited:

- Freud's theory was developed from the explanations of patients about their own experiences and was not based on careful observations of children; this has been a significant criticism made by later researchers.
- Freud's proposals about the Oedipus and Electra complexes are difficult to verify as the processes are unconscious; even so, no investigation has produced generally accepted evidence that supports Freud's theory about these processes.
- Other mechanisms apart from the Oedipus and Electra complexes can be used to explain internalisation: for example, social learning theory and observational learning as demonstrated in the learning of aggressive acts (Bandura *et al.*, 1963).
- The focus of Freud's theory is on two-parent families, and this presents problems when explaining moral development in families where one parent is absent. In addition, it is generally accepted that children's moral development is influenced by factors beyond the family, such as friends, schools and the media.
- Observations and investigations of children by Kohlberg and Piaget suggest that the process of moral development carries on beyond the age of four to six years (see later sections of this chapter).
- In a review of previous research, Hoffman (1975) concluded that there is very little difference between boys and girls in terms of whether or not they would break rules. If anything, girls are less likely to break rules and therefore could be considered to have a stronger superego. Gilligan (1982) pointed out that Freud's work contained Victorian stereotypes about differences between males and females.

Link

For more about social learning theory, observational learning and Bandura's experiments, see Chapter 9, and for more on Gilligan's work see p66.

Key points:

- Freud believed that moral behaviour was the result of dynamic interactions involving the id, ego and superego.
- Freud also believed that moral behaviour was the result of children's identification with the same-sex parent.
- Freud's research methods and his theory about the development of morality have been extensively criticised.

Summary questions

1. Explain what Freud meant by the term 'superego'. Illustrate your answer with an example.
2. Outline a psychodynamic explanation for the development of moral behaviour in girls.
3. Explain three criticisms of psychoanalytic ideas about the development of moral behaviour.

Piaget's ideas about moral development

Learning objectives:

- describe and discuss Piaget's stages of moral development: premoral judgement; moral realism; moral relativism
- discuss ways of investigating moral development including moral comparisons.

Link

For more about the clinical method, see Chapter 2, Cognitive development.

Hint

Piaget's work on moral development was part of his more general theory about cognitive development, so it would be useful to read Chapter 2, Cognitive development. Piaget identified stages of moral development but emphasised that the stages are not closely tied to particular ages; in some cases, he described differences between younger and older children rather than stages of development.

Piaget (1932) carried out the first major investigation of moral development in children using what is termed the 'clinical method', which involved in-depth questioning and discussion with children to understand their thinking and reasoning.

The conclusions and findings were published in his book *The Moral Judgement of the Child* (Piaget, 1932). The book is complex with a series of topics and inter-related issues.

The moral judgement of the child

Piaget begins the book with investigating the rules of children's games. This is not a 'big' moral issue. However, studying this topic helps us to understand children's thinking about rules, which for young children are less abstract and more relevant than, say, the laws of a country.

Research study: Piaget (1932)

Aim: To understand children's thinking and reasoning about the rules of a game.

Method: The children were aged between three and 10 years. Piaget investigated the game of marbles with boys and hide-and-seek with girls. The clinical method was used, using semi-structured interviews. He spent time being around the children; he watched children play the games and played the games with them. He pretended to be ignorant of the rules, asked children to show him the rules of the game and asked them where the rules came from. He made records of children's explanations.

Result: Piaget reported selections of what the children said in response to his questions. From these conversations, Piaget identified different ways of following rules and the understanding of them (see Table 1).

Conclusion: Different forms of thinking were identified in younger and older children.

Evaluation: Piaget's clinical methods allowed him to gain insight into children's thinking. However, it did not involve careful experimentation and he may have underestimated children's thinking by relying on their explanations.

Piaget described four stages in the development of rule use and in the development of explanations of the rules; the ages were based on the sample of children that he interviewed.

Table 1 *Piaget's stages of obeying rules*

Stage and usual age (years)	Description of stage
Stage 1 (before 3)	There is no real use of rules; explanations of play do not concern rules.
Stage 2 (3–5)	Rules are imitated, but usually inaccurately; rules are believed to be unchanging and should not be broken; they originate from higher authority (parents, God).
Stage 3 (7–8)	Rules are employed in a mutually agreed way, but there are often errors in following rules; rules can be changed if others agree.
Stage 4 (11–12 onwards)	Rules are understood and followed by children; there is an interest in rules.

The second chapter of Piaget's book briefly discusses the morality of children below about five or six years of age. The term **premoral stage** has been applied to the morality of these children, in whom Piaget observed several characteristics:

- They sometimes want to carry out rules because they seem to think that the rule has to be obeyed, such as eating up all the food on a plate even when ill and even when adults tell a child that there is no need.
- Children at this age also often believe that they have been naughty if something is accidentally broken, even if reassured by an adult that they are not at fault.

Piaget suggests that these younger children show a form of **moral realism**, but only in their **behaviour**. He suggested that the ability to give verbal explanations of moral realism does not occur until about five or six years. He identified three general characteristics of moral realism:

- **Heteronomous morality** – the rules are usually those of adults. So following rules is seen as 'good', and when rules are disobeyed this is seen as 'bad'. For example, children aged six to seven years have difficulty seeing the difference between saying something which is not true because of a mistaken belief and saying something which is not true and is deliberately a lie.
- The letter rather than the spirit of the law should be followed.
- Acts are evaluated in terms of their consequences rather than their motives or intentions: for example, judging that it is naughtier to steal a large thing for good reasons than to steal a small thing for selfish reasons.

Piaget carried out research into moral realism, by giving children **moral comparisons**.

Key terms

Moral realism: the belief that rules and laws should be followed regardless of the circumstances.

Heteronomous morality: the first stage of moral realism when following rules is the most important aspect of morality.

Moral comparison: a technique that uses pairs of stories to investigate children's thinking about morality.

Research study: Piaget (1932)

Aim: To understand children's ideas about morality.

Method: He used a variety of stories involving moral comparisons such as the one given below.

A little boy who is called John is in his room. He is called to dinner. He goes into the dining room. But behind the door there was a chair, and on the chair was a tray with 15 cups on it. John couldn't have known that there was all this behind the door. He goes in; the door knocks against the tray; bang go the 15 cups and they all get broken.

Once there was a little boy whose name was Henry. One day his mother was out and he tried to get some jam out of a cupboard. He climbed up on to a chair and stretched out his arm. But the jam was too high up and he couldn't reach it and have any. But while he was trying to get it he knocked over a cup. The cup fell down and broke (adapted from Piaget, 1932, p118).

Afterwards the children were asked a range of questions such as, 'Which of these two is naughtier and why?'

Results: The questions and answers are described, but no statistical analyses are included in the descriptions.

e.g. Which was the naughtier? 'Mol (7 years) The second, the one who wanted to take the jam-pot, because he wanted to take something without asking' (p125).

Piaget reports that up to the age of 10 years children give answers that **either** focus on the consequences (e.g. accidentally breaking 15 cups is naughtier than breaking one cup) **or** on the motive alone (e.g. as Mol did). Both of these types of answer were sometimes given by the same child to different stories. The average age for focusing on consequences was seven years and for focusing on intention was nine years. Few children over the age of 10 years focused on the consequences.

Conclusions: Piaget used these types of answers to identify the development of moral realism but admitted that there were not clear-cut stages.

Evaluation: Piaget provided a useful description about differences in children's thinking; however, he did not find clear stages and some children did not always give the same type of reasoning to different questions.

In his third chapter, Piaget discusses what he terms the 'morality of cooperation'. At this level, older children no longer simply obey laws and rules but understand that they are for the general benefit of the group. This has become known as the stage of **moral relativism**.

Key terms

Moral relativism: the belief that rules and laws are for the general benefit of the group and so are not absolutes.

The stage of moral relativism involves several inter-related characteristics (Flavell, 1963):

- Children believe that rules are the result of agreement between people and for the common good.
- Judgements can be influenced by the intentions of a person, and children take account of more than one factor (e.g. intention and consequence).
- Rules are internalised so that children have their own set of beliefs about morality which might not be exactly like those of an external authority.

Piaget and his colleagues presented children with a set of moral comparisons which dealt with issues relevant to moral relativism. The findings are outlined in Table 2.

Piaget suggested that the focus on the amount of damage or harm in the stage of moral realism reflected the way that adults tend to treat children, becoming angrier if more damage is done. He argued that progress to moral relativism was helped by interaction and discussion with other children, as the authority of parents would make challenging their views more difficult. In addition, disagreements and conflicts with other children (peers) allow a child to start to think for themselves; they can disagree with the views of other children and in so doing may develop views of their own, different from those of caregivers.

Table 2 *Moral comparisons: children's judgements about justice and punishment*

Moral realism	Moral relativism	Answers based on samples of 100–160 children reported by Piaget
Belief in **immanent justice** where there is automatic punishment for wrongdoing: e.g. a child does something wrong and then falls into a stream when a small bridge breaks; children believe that this would not have happened if he had been good	Understanding that rules are social in basis and so immanent justice is unlikely	Belief in immanent justice, percentage of sample: 6 years – 86% 9–10 years – 54% 11–12 years – 34%
Belief in **expiatory punishment** where the amount of punishment reflects the seriousness of the wrongdoing, but no account is taken of intentions	Belief in **reciprocal punishment** where the person feels guilt for harming others and punishments are made to suit the wrongdoing (e.g. mending something that is broken)	Belief in reciprocal punishment, percentage of sample: 6–7 years – 29% 8–10 years – 47% 11–12 years – 80%

Evaluation of Piaget's explanation of moral development

Research findings

Research findings have challenged Piaget's claim that young children will follow rules and not question the 'rules' of adults:

- Smetana (1981) found that, in terms of the punishment that should be given, young children aged between two and nine years could distinguish between behaviours that were 'wrong' because of social conventions (e.g. putting a toy in the wrong place) or 'wrong' because of moral conventions (e.g. a child hitting another child). Piaget's work suggested that both types of rules would be judged as equally important.
- Laupa and Turiel (1986) gave six- to 11-year-olds hypothetical stories involving comparisons concerning issues about whom should be obeyed. The children took account of whether the person giving the command was a teacher or a peer who was a monitor and also took account of the nature of the command. Importantly, there was not a simple orientation to authority of adults.

Piaget's methods

Piaget's methods have been shown to be inadequate. There are specific problems related to the presentation of the stories.

- In a study of children aged between four and five years and eight to nine years, Feldman *et al.* (1976) found that moral judgements were influenced by the order in which information was presented. The children's judgements, especially those of the younger children, were largely based on what was heard last, either about intentions or about consequences. Thus, if children were told first about the consequences of an action and then told about the intentions, unlike in Piaget's studies, children based their moral judgements on the intentions of the person in the story. The children tended to forget the information they heard first. This suggests that young children's moral judgements may be influenced by **information processing**, rather than just a focus on consequences of an action.

Key terms

Immanent justice: punishment that follows a misdeed that has gone unpunished or undetected.

Expiatory punishment: punishment where the severity reflects the seriousness of the misdeed but takes no account of intent.

Reciprocal punishment: punishment that makes good the misdeed.

Hint

It is useful to remember that Piaget's studies of moral development occurred in the 1930s, a time when many parents are likely to have had a very different attitude to teaching their children about morality (e.g. immanent justice might have been used as a way to persuade children to be 'good').

Link

For more about information processing, see Chapter 2, Cognitive development.

- The method of presentation has also been shown to be a factor influencing children's moral judgements (see the Evaluation of Piaget on the previous page).
- The moral comparisons used by Piaget (see Turiel, 1998) do not involve a systematic investigation of one variable at a time (the example story about cups involves different intentions and different amounts of damage) and the situations used in the two stories were often different. Thus it would have been better if Piaget had taken more care to ensure that these design issues did not affect the results.
- We have already seen that there have been criticisms of Piaget's reliance on children explaining quite complex ideas through the medium of language (this can be difficult for younger children). Related to this are findings that suggest that young children have difficulty explaining why they made a decision (Karmiloff-Smith, 1992).

Research study: Chandler *et al.* (1973)

Aim: To compare spoken and video presentations of stories involving moral comparisons.

Method: Seven-year-olds took part in the study. The stories about moral comparisons were similar to those used by Piaget.

Results: As with Piaget's findings, moral judgements about the spoken stories took account of consequences and not intentions (i.e. whether the action was an accident or planned to obtain a 'reward'). However, moral judgements about the video presentations took account of intentions. This suggests that moral reasoning does not just depend on the logic of the case, and that children can take account of intentions at a comparatively young age.

Conclusion: The way that the information is presented to children influences the moral judgements that they make.

Evaluation: It would appear that children can show more advanced moral judgements when stories are more realistic and perhaps easier to understand (i.e. child friendly). This is similar to other findings about Piaget's clinical methods.

Link

For further evaluation of Piaget's methods, see Chapter 2, Cognitive development.

Hint

Although both Piaget's and Freud's theories supposed that external viewpoints (e.g. parents) provided the basis of morals, their theories were based on different methodologies and ideas about the process of development; in addition, Piaget considered that moral development continues until a child is at least 11 years old.

Key points:

- Piaget identified three stages in moral development: premoral, moral realism and moral relativism.
- Piaget used moral comparisons as a way of investigating children's opinions.
- Piaget's research has been challenged and criticised because of:
  - findings that young children can distinguish between different types of rule and will not always agree with the views of adults
  - specific methodological problems (order and method of information presentation)
  - general methodological problems (the two stories were not the same in the comparisons and reliance on verbal explanations).

Summary questions

4 A child has been identified as being at Piaget's stage of moral relativism. According to Piaget, what two forms of moral reasoning is this child likely to show?

5 Outline the difference between Piaget's stages of premoral judgement and moral realism.

6 Explain three criticisms of Piaget's methods.

Kohlberg's theory of moral development

Learning objectives:

- describe Kohlberg's levels of moral reasoning
- understand and evaluate the stages of moral reasoning within these levels
- describe and discuss Kohlberg's theory of moral development.

Fig. 4 *Lawrence Kohlberg*

Key terms

Moral dilemma: in Kohlberg's studies, a situation in which a person has to choose between taking an action that most people would think is morally wrong and accepting an undesirable outcome.

Link

Look back at p53, to remind yourself about the use of moral comparisons when investigating moral judgements.

AQA Examiner's tip

One topic in the specification concerns 'Ways of investigating moral development including the use of moral comparisons and moral dilemmas'. So make sure that you know about these methods and can give examples of investigators/investigations that used them.

Link

See the Research study on p58 for a description of the longitudinal investigation by Kohlberg *et al.* (1983).

Following Piaget's pioneering work on moral development in the 1930s, the next major theory was proposed by Lawrence Kohlberg (1927–1987). In many respects, he built on and extended Piaget's work by employing a more careful coding of children's responses to **moral dilemmas**. Kohlberg believed that the stages that he identified were universal.

Kohlberg's method of studying moral development

Piaget had often presented two stories to children and asked them to say who was 'naughtier' and why the person was naughtier. This technique involves a moral comparison. However, as we have seen there are methodological difficulties with these stories. Probably for this reason, Kohlberg chose to present stories which contained a moral dilemma.

The most famous of the stories used by Kohlberg is given below; it involves Heinz. Heinz has to make a choice: either to steal a drug or fail to help his wife who is dying. Both these outcomes are usually considered morally unacceptable. Consequently, the person in the story has the dilemma of choosing the better of two bad alternatives. The stories were read to the participants, and they had to say whether the actions of the person were right, to justify this answer, and to suggest appropriate punishments.

> In Europe, a woman was near death from a very bad disease, a special kind of cancer. There was one drug that the doctors thought might save her. It was a form of radium that a druggist in the same town had recently discovered. The drug was expensive to make, but the druggist was charging ten times what the drug cost him to make. He paid $200 for the radium and charged $2,000 for a small dose of the drug. The sick woman's husband, Heinz, went to everyone he knew to borrow money, but he could get together only about $1,000, which was half of what it cost. He told the druggist that his wife was dying and asked him to sell it cheaper or let him pay later. But the druggist said, 'No, I discovered the drug and I'm going to make money from it.' Heinz got desperate and broke into the man's store to steal the drug for his wife.
>
> ***(Kohlberg**, 1981, p12)*

The participants were asked, 'Should Heinz have done that? Why or why not?'

Kohlberg's findings

Kohlberg *et al.* (1983) identified three **levels of moral reasoning**, each of which was subdivided into two further **stages** (see Table 3).

Table 3 *Kohlberg's stages of moral reasoning*

Level	Stage	Description
Level I Preconventional morality	Stage 1 Heteronomous morality	Avoid breaking rules associated with punishment, obedience for its own sake
	Stage 2 Individualism, instrumental purpose, and exchange	Acting to meet one's own immediate interests and needs and letting others do the same
Level II Conventional morality	Stage 3 Mutual interpersonal expectations, relationships and interpersonal conformity	Living up to what others expect
	Stage 4 Social system and conscience	Fulfilling the duties to which one has agreed. Upholding laws except in extreme cases when they conflict with other fixed social duties. Contributing to society, group or institution
Level III Postconventional morality	Stage 5 Social-contract orientation or individual rights	Being aware that people hold a variety of values and opinions; often, these are relative to the group that holds them and should be upheld as part of a social contract between people. Also a belief that some values and rights, such as life and liberty, should be upheld in any society, regardless of majority opinion
	Stage 6 Universal ethical principles	Following self-chosen universal principles of justice: the equality of human rights and respect for dignity. Judging laws in relation to these principles. When laws violate principles, acting in accordance with the principle

AQA Examiner's tip

Kohlberg's description of moral development is complicated because he has three broad **stages**, each of which is divided into two **levels**. Try to remember to use the correct terms 'stages'/'levels'. The early and later levels are easy: **pre-** and **post**-conventional.

Key terms

Preconventional level: the first level of moral reasoning proposed by Kohlberg. Children keep rules to avoid punishment.

Conventional level: the second level of moral reasoning proposed by Kohlberg. Moral values are influenced by society's rules and norms.

Postconventional level: the third level of moral reasoning proposed by Kohlberg. Moral values are influenced by principles, e.g. equality.

Kohlberg and Colby revised Kohlberg's original assessment procedures to take account of criticisms (Colby and Kohlberg, 1987). When the new system was applied to the original data, it reduced the number of individuals who were at Stage 5 and no one was identified at Stage 6 (Colby *et al.*, 1983, see figure 5).

According to Kohlberg, at the **preconventional level** children's ideas about morality concern rewards and punishment, and an action is often judged in terms of other people's response. Children do not have an overall understanding of conventions or moral codes that govern a range of actions. The first stage of this level is similar to Piaget's stage of moral realism.

The **conventional level** occurs between 13 and 16 years and is based on agreements between people which are to the benefit of the whole group. For example, a law against stealing means that most people's possessions are safer. The **postconventional** level involves the recognition that values are often relative to the group or culture, but there are some values that should be used in any culture (e.g. liberty).

Research study: Kohlberg *et al.* (1983)

Aim: To investigate moral development over 20 years.

Method: Fifty-eight males were seen when they were aged between 10 and 16 years. Interviews were conducted every four years about the same nine imaginary dilemmas. The participants' answers were scored using a standard scoring manual.

Results: Participants progressed through Kohlberg's stages in the predicted order (see Table 3); no one skipped a stage and on only 4 per cent of occasions was there a return to a lower level. Stage scores were related to age, IQ and education.

Conclusion: The findings supported Kohlberg's stage model of moral development.

Evaluation: The longitudinal study is unusual in being conducted over such a long time so the same individuals are seen at different ages and has provided an important set of findings about moral development.

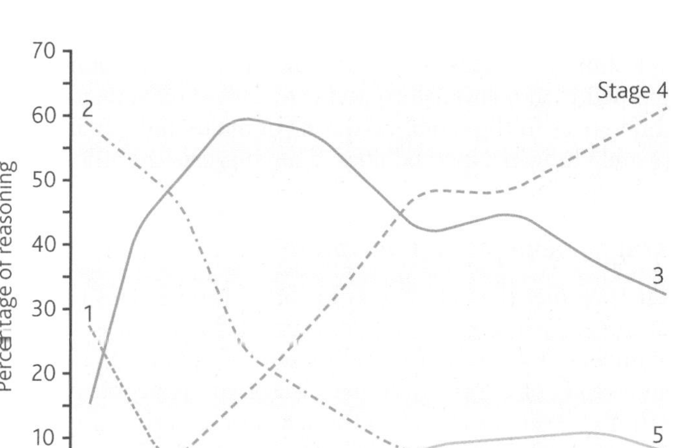

Fig. 5 *Mean percentage of moral reasoning at each stage (Colby* et al.*, 1983)*

Kohlberg believed that young people pass through each of the stages in sequence, and that it is necessary for an individual to have the appropriate level of moral understanding before they are able to pass upwards to the next stage. Kohlberg also believed that progress is a product not only of experience (e.g. instruction and discussion) but also of biological changes that enable young people to think in more advanced ways. In this respect, his theory was a mix of both 'nature' and 'nurture'. In terms of 'nurture', he believed that more advanced thinking would result from growing up in an environment where there was discussion and debate, rather than in one where rules are imposed by authority figures such as parents.

Evaluation of Kohlberg's theory

Methodological criticisms

Although a number of concerns about Kohlberg's methodology and use of moral dilemmas have been raised, further research has usually supported Kohlberg's methods and theory.

The coding scheme constructed by Kohlberg is complicated. However, as different people are able to reach a high level of agreement when coding the explanations given by participants, there is high **inter-rater reliability**.

There have been concerns that some of the moral dilemmas involve situations that a person has never experienced or even talked about before. This means that the stories have low **ecological validity**. However, Walker *et al.* (1987) found that when given Kohlberg's moral dilemmas and another dilemma which was designed to match the

AQA Examiner's tip

How would a person at each of the six stages respond if they were answering the question about Heinz? Make a list of their responses.

AQA Examiner's tip

Remember that methods are an important part of the syllabus/specification concerning moral development.

Key terms

Ecological validity: refers to the degree to which a study is similar to people's usual experiences.

young person's experiences, 66 per cent of the young people were at the same stage of reasoning for Kohlberg's dilemmas as for the 'real life' dilemmas.

Is there a male bias in the stages?

It has been suggested by Damon (1977) that the stories may have different meanings to individuals of different ages: think about the way that the Heinz story might affect a 10-year-old and a 20-year-old. Part of Gilligan's (1977, 1982) criticism of Kohlberg's stages was that the content of Kohlberg's dilemmas did not match female reasoning which is more concerned with relationships and care. However, Walker (1989) did not find differences in the moral reasoning of males and females using Kohlberg's and Gilligan's methodology. This suggests that there is not a male bias in Kohlberg's stages.

Link

See p66 for information about the ethic of care and the Research study on p68 for a description of Walker's (1989) study.

Do the stages have predictive value?

Do the stages predict the behaviour of people? People classified in terms of Kohlberg's stages do not necessarily behave in a way that is always consistent with their moral reasoning. Kohlberg (1975) carried out a study of cheating: 70 per cent of young people at the preconventional level cheated even though they said that this is wrong. There were fewer who were inconsistent at higher levels (55 per cent at the conventional level, 15 per cent at the post-conventional level). However, this is a general issue which concerns the difference between moral reasoning and moral action: a person might understand why something should not be done, but this does not necessarily mean that they will not carry out this action. This is a common problem because verbal reasoning does not always match the actions of a person.

Does moral development always occur in stages?

Kohlberg's stages have been criticised for reflecting Western values of freedom and choice and, as a result, not providing a universal model of cognitive development (a model that applies to all people across the world). Dien (1982) argues that some Asian cultures put a higher value on actions that are of benefit for the group. In a review of 27 cross-cultural studies, Snarey (1985) concluded that most found evidence of Stages 1 to 4, but Stage 5 was rare, suggesting that higher levels of moral reasoning may be related to cultural values. All this suggests that Kohlberg had managed to identify stages in moral development that are usually relevant to other cultures.

Perhaps one of the most serious criticisms has been a general issue about the stages. Turiel (1978, 1983) disagreed with the idea of distinct stages and thought that the process of development is a more continuous one. As, when interviewed, participants often produce responses from at least two different stages, development may be more complex than Kohlberg suggested.

Link

For an evaluation of stage theory, see Chapter 2, Cognitive development.

The other serious criticism is that Kohlberg focused only on certain types of moral reasoning; the next section contains details about the way that morality is relevant to a whole range of issues.

Key points:

- Kohlberg identified the following levels in his theory of moral development: preconventional, conventional and postconventional.
- Within each of these levels two stages of moral development were identified.
- Kohlberg's use of moral dilemmas has advantages over Piaget's use of moral comparisons.
- Although criticisms have been made of Kohlberg's theory in relation to ecological validity, prediction of behaviour, content validity and universality, these criticisms have not been supported by research evidence.
- The research can be criticised for being based on a stage theory that ignores the complexities of development and also for concentrating on one type of moral reasoning.

Summary questions

7 Outline the main characteristics of moral reasoning of a person at Kohlberg's postconventional stage.

8 What are the differences between the preconventional and conventional stages in Kohlberg's theory of moral reasoning?

9 Outline two research findings that support Kohlberg's theory of moral reasoning.

Damon's research into distributive justice

Learning objectives:

- understand and evaluate Damon's research into distributive justice.

Key terms

Distributive justice: making decisions about sharing something, for example possessions or rewards.

Damon (1975) was interested in children's thinking about **distributive justice**, a moral issue that has particular relevance to children who are often concerned with sharing (e.g. sweets). Damon's research gives insight into children's thinking about the topic; his research followed that of Piaget in terms of theory and the age group studied (children between four and 10 years), and he used the clinical method in a similar way.

Piaget (1932) had identified three stages in the development of distributive justice (Flavell, 1963). Piaget proposed that before seven to eight years of age children are in Stage 1 and believe that authority figures are always fair in their decisions; in Stage 2 (when aged 7 to 12 years), children believe that everyone should be treated equally, while in Stage 3, children are prepared to deviate from strict equality to take account of other factors.

Damon presented children with dilemmas about sharing. For example, he used a story about a class of children who make drawings to be sold at a school fair. These drawings earn a lot of money, and the class has to decide how to divide the money. It is explained that some children made more drawings than others; some made better drawings than others, and some children came from poorer backgrounds than others.

Child development

Link

For Piaget's theory of moral development, see p52, and for information on the clinical method, see p29 in Chapter 2, Cognitive development.

Table 4 *Damon's levels of distributive justice*

Level	Description	Typical comment of an individual at this level
Level 0–A	Simple self-interest	'I should get more because that is what I want'
Level 0–B	Self-interest with justification in terms of observable characteristics	'Bigger boys should get more'
Level 1A	Strict equality	'Everyone should have the same'
Level 1B	Distributive calculations	'The person who worked the hardest should get the most'
Level 2A	Compromises about distribution so that there is an attempt to balance different sorts of claims, and to take account of need	
Level 2B	Compromises between equality and reciprocity are considered in relation to situation and what the group is trying to achieve	

(Adapted from ***Damon****, 1980)*

Damon linked his levels of distributive justice to Piaget's general stages of cognitive development. He reported that Level 0 occurred during the pre-operational stage, Level 1 during the concrete operations stage and Level 2 in the transition to formal operations stage. However, Damon also argued that different topics will result in slightly different sets of reasoning which could depend on personal experiences and other factors.

Damon (1980) conducted a longitudinal study over two years to examine development. He found that about 85 per cent of the children showed progress to a higher level during this period.

Enright *et al.* (1980, 1984) constructed what they termed the Distributive Justice Scale (DJS). Unlike Damon's clinical interview, this scale involved using exactly the same procedure with all children. Children were presented with a dilemma about sharing and then they had to choose which of two pictures provided the best way to share something. The choices made by children matched what would have been expected from Damon's description of levels and ages, and occurred in samples from the USA, Sweden and Zaire. In addition, the investigators found that there was higher reasoning when the dilemmas involved family members. It is interesting that this method, which involves children deciding between alternatives, gives findings similar to those obtained using the Piagetian clinical interview.

Research study: McGillicuddy-De Lisa (1994)

Aim: To test the predictions that young children were more likely to be more inflexible than older children when applying the rules of distributive justice, and that girls were more likely than boys to distribute rewards equally (based on Gilligan's arguments about the **ethic of care**).

Method: Ninety-five kindergarten, third-grade and sixth-grade children were presented with two stories about a group of children

Key terms

Ethic of care: a focus on maintaining relationships, responding to the needs of others, and a responsibility not to cause harm.

who made artwork that was subsequently sold at a craft fair. The characters in one story were described as friends, while the characters in the other story were described as strangers. In each story, one character was presented as the oldest in the group, one as the most productive, and one as the poorest. Children were asked to allocate nine dollars to the three characters, give reasons for the distribution, and rate the fairness of the allocation.

Results: The kindergartners' allocations did not vary with the relationship of the characters or their neediness. Older children allocated more money to needy friends than to needy strangers and more to productive strangers than to productive friends. Equality was the most important reason for decisions at all ages. No gender differences were found.

Conclusion: The age differences support Damon's levels of distributive justice; the lack of differences between boys and girls suggests that this aspect of their moral thinking is similar.

Evaluation: The findings support Damon's stages of the development of distributive justice; it might have been interesting to look in greater detail at the reasons for the decisions.

More recently, McGillicuddy-De Lisa *et al.* (2006) have used a very similar method to investigate distributive justice in relation to white and black characters in a set of stories. The younger children did not discriminate between white and black characters; however, the older children's allocations showed evidence of unacknowledged racism.

Key points:

- Damon took Piaget's work further and provided a clearer basis for the description of distributive justice.
- Damon's findings and conclusions about stages have been supported by Enright *et al.* using different methodology and a cross-cultural sample.
- Damon's work can be placed within Piaget's broader theory of cognitive development. This means that some of the criticisms of Piaget's theory and research can also be made about Damon's work.

Summary questions

10 What is meant by 'distributive justice'? Illustrate your answer with an example.

11 Describe one research study which has been concerned with distributive justice.

12 Outline the methods used by Damon to investigate distributive justice.

13 What support is there for Damon's research methods?

Eisenberg's model of pro-social reasoning

Learning objectives:

- understand and evaluate Eisenberg's model of pro-social reasoning
- describe the following stages: hedonistic; needs; approval; self-reflective; internalised orientations.

Key terms

Pro-social reasoning: the principles involved when deciding whether or not to help another person.

Pro-social behaviour concerns positive actions, such as comforting another child. Nancy Eisenberg believed that an important dimension of moral reasoning involves giving help to others, and that this dimension had largely been ignored in the theories of Piaget and Kohlberg. She was particularly interested in **pro-social reasoning**. The distinction between pro-social behaviour and reasoning is similar to the one that we have seen between moral behaviour and moral reasoning.

Eisenberg also supposed that more advanced pro-social reasoning would involve **empathy**, which she defined as an emotional reaction related to another person's feelings in a situation. She also emphasised that her model involves the influence of **feelings** in relation to making decisions about moral issues, whereas Kohlberg stressed the influence of cognitive processes (Eisenberg *et al.*, 2001).

Eisenberg used methods similar to those used by Kohlberg and presented young people with dilemmas. However, in this case, the dilemmas involved reasoning about whether to carry out a positive behaviour when there would be a cost to an individual in carrying out that behaviour. An example is given below.

> One day a girl (boy) named Mary (Eric) was going to a friend's birthday party. On her way she saw a girl (boy) who had fallen down and hurt her leg. The girl asked Mary to go to her house and get her parents so the parents could come and take her to a doctor. But if Mary did run and get the child's parents, she would be late to the birthday party and miss the ice cream, cake and all the games.
>
> What should Mary do? Why?

On the basis of young people's answers to dilemmas such as these, Eisenberg *et al.* (1983) identified five levels of pro-social reasoning. Eisenberg uses the term 'level' rather than 'stage', reflecting her belief that development is less clear cut and more complicated than stage theories would suggest. In addition, she acknowledged that pro-social behaviour varies with culture and will be higher in cultures where such behaviour is rewarded or valued.

Table 5 *Eisenberg's levels of pro-social reasoning*

Approximate age (years)	Level	Description
Up to 7	Hedonistic (self centred)	Helping takes place when it benefits the helper.
7–11	Needs oriented	Helping depends on how much the person needs help, and usually there has to be obvious distress. There is little guilt if help is not given.
11–14	Approval oriented	Helping is motivated by being praised for carrying out the action.
12 and over	Empathic/self-reflective	There is sympathy for others and guilt for not carrying out the action.
	Transitional level	There is partial awareness of duties and principles.
16 and over	Strongly internalised, personal values	Internal values such as responsibility and self-respect are used to justify giving help.

(Adapted from ***Eisenberg*** *et al., 1983)*

Eisenberg carried out a number of longitudinal studies. In the studies of children from pre-school to eight years of age she found changes predicted by her model. Hedonistic reasoning declined with age and there was an increase in Levels 2 and 3 (Eisenberg and Roth, 1980; Eisenberg *et al.*, 1983). However, in adolescence there was an increase in hedonistic reasoning at around 15 to 16 years which, she claimed, is consistent with her view that the levels are neither universal nor occur in only one sequence (Eisenberg *et al.*, 1995).

Despite Eisenberg's rejection of universality, similar levels were identified by Boehnke *et al.* (1989) who collected information from German, Italian and Polish children. In addition, there is evidence that the levels have some relation to children's behaviour. Eisenberg and Hand (1979) compared the amount of sharing by children who were at Levels 1 and 2; there was more sharing in children identified at Level 2. Thus, children's verbal responses corresponded to behaviour they produced when interacting with other children.

Eisenberg emphasised the role of empathy in the development of pro-social reasoning and believed that this emerges at around 12 years, thereby enabling new levels of concern to be achieved. For example, Eisenberg *et al.* (1994) found that, if young people were asked to think about the pain or discomfort of the character in a pro-social dilemma, adolescent participants were more likely than younger ones to suggest that the character is helped. However, Eisenberg's suggestions put the development of empathy at quite a late age. Children who are much younger appear to show empathy with, for example, a child who is crying. In these circumstances, young children will appear concerned and approach the child to comfort them.

Research study: Eisenberg *et al.* (2001)

Aim: To investigate whether emotional and cognitive abilities are related to pro-social reasoning.

Method: One hundred and forty-nine Brazilian adolescents were given pro-social reasoning dilemmas. To assess abilities related to emotional processes the participants were given a questionnaire assessing **sympathy**. To assess abilities related to cognitive processes the participants were given a questionnaire designed to assess the ability to take the **perspective** of another person, which the researchers believed is related to the type of moral reasoning described by Kohlberg. The participants were also given a questionnaire about gender-role orientation (e.g. tender vs assertive styles).

Results: Both sympathy and perspective taking were significantly, but weakly, related to pro-social moral reasoning. In addition, female gender-role orientation was related to both role taking and sympathy.

Conclusion: The findings are consistent with the prediction that both emotional and cognitive processes play a part in pro-social reasoning.

Evaluation: The study investigated the role of cognitive and emotional processes in relation to moral reasoning. The findings support Eisenberg's claim that emotional processes such as empathy and sympathy have a role to play in pro-social reasoning; the findings also support views, such as those of Kohlberg, that cognitive abilities affect moral reasoning. Limitation of the study is that it only involved questionnaire information from the young people and there was no longitudinal perspective.

Key points:

- Although Eisenberg's theory considers a different dimension of moral reasoning from the one studied by Kohlberg, her theory is in many respects similar to his and the research methods are also similar. Looking at Kohlberg's stages and Eisenberg's levels, one can see that there are some similarities in what is being described.
- However, Eisenberg believes that pro-social reasoning is more dependent on culture and context whereas Kohlberg suggested that there are universal stages.
- Research findings broadly support the levels that Eisenberg identified.
- However, because Eisenberg has not put forward a precise stage theory and acknowledges that there will be variation in development, her levels are more descriptive than theoretical.

Summary questions

14 Outline the difference between hedonistic and needs-oriented pro-social reasoning in Eisenberg's model.

15 Give an example of children's reasoning at Eisenberg's level of empathic/self-reflective pro-social reasoning.

16 Explain one similarity and one difference between Eisenberg's and Kohlberg's research.

Gilligan's ethic of care: differences between males and females

Learning objectives:

- understand and evaluate Gilligan's ethic of care
- describe Gilligan's three levels of moral development
- understand and evaluate Gilligan's ideas about the differences between males and females in moral reasoning
- describe and discuss findings about differences between males and females in moral reasoning.

AQA Examiner's tip

Gilligan's work is relevant as a criticism of Kohlberg and is also a topic that could be examined by itself.

Key terms

Ethic of justice: a focus on fairness and equity as assessed in Kohlberg's measures.

Carol Gilligan's ideas have attracted considerable interest. She was named by *Time* magazine in 1996 as one of the top 25 innovative Americans who 'show us the world anew' and who 'educate and entertain us, to change the way we think about ourselves and others' (*Time* 25, 1996, p54). An editorial wrote:

> How likely is it that a single book could change the rule of psychology, change the assumptions of medical research, change the conversation among parents and teachers and developmental professions about the distinction between men and women, boys and girls? (p66)

What attracted this attention? Gilligan argued that there are differences between males and females in moral reasoning and provided supporting evidence, and this linked to debates about the nature of gender differences.

Gilligan (1977, 1982) proposed that males and females reason about moral issues in different ways, each of which is equally valuable. She believed that this difference concerns relationships and caregiving. You may remember that these were some of her criticisms of Kohlberg's theory, which she argued was more concerned with an **ethic of justice** in his sample of males, whereas she suggested that females are more concerned with an ethic of care.

On the basis of a study of women who were considering having abortions, Gilligan identified three levels of care; in later work she also identified three matching levels of justice.

Research study: Gilligan (1977)

Aim: To see if the moral reasoning of women was similar to that described by Kohlberg in his study of males.

Method: Unstructured interviews were conducted with 29 pregnant women who were thinking of having an abortion. The responses were recorded and, from these, three levels of care were identified. In addition, the women were interviewed about three of Kohlberg's dilemmas.

Results: The women's reasoning was at higher levels in relation to abortion than in relation to Kohlberg's dilemmas.

Conclusion: It was possible to identify levels of reasoning in relation to an ethic of care. The women produced higher levels of reasoning about care issues than about Kohlberg's standard moral dilemmas.

Evaluation: Gilligan examined a real-life situation, and this could account for the difference between her findings and those of Kohlberg. A criticism of her study is that it did not involve a comparison of men and women's moral reasoning.

Table 6 *Gilligan's levels of the ethic of care*

Level	Description of care	Equivalent level of justice
Level 1, Self-focused	Making decisions according to what is best for the person	Uphold moral standards and resist lowering of standards
Level 2, Self-sacrifice	Putting others' interests before one's own	People's feelings should be considered, but it is important to uphold principles
Level 3, Non-violence	Avoiding harm and hurt to others	Exceptions can be made, but universal laws are in everyone's best interest

*(Adapted from **Gilligan**, 1977, 1982)*

In a further study, Gilligan compared the reasoning of males and females.

Research study: Gilligan and Attanucci (1988)

Aim: To test the predictions that females would reason at a higher level about care and males would reason at a higher level about justice.

Method: Eighty men and women aged between 14 and 77 were asked about their experiences of moral conflict in an interview lasting about two hours (e.g. 'Have you ever been in a situation where you were not sure what was the right thing to do?', 'Describe the situation', 'What did you do?', 'What do you think was the right thing to do?'). The answers were classified in terms of having a care or justice focus (see Table 6).

Results: 35 per cent of female participants and 2 per cent of male participants showed a focus on care; whereas 29 per cent of the women and 65 per cent of the men showed a focus on justice.

Conclusion: The findings indicate that males and females have different orientations towards morality: women tend to have an ethic of care, whereas men tend to have an ethic of justice.

Evaluation: The findings support Gilligan's argument that men and women reason in a different way about morality. However, it should be noted that interview techniques could allow experimenter biases to be present.

Initially, Gilligan suggested that the levels formed a developmental sequence, but a follow-up of participants after a year failed to find support for the idea of a developmental progression. As a result, she changed her ideas and no longer appears to believe that the levels are a developmental sequence (Gilligan, 1990). Gilligan suggests that the type of thinking provoked by a crisis assists progress to higher levels; however, it is not very clear how and when this would change a person's level of reasoning about care.

Gilligan supposes that the differences between males and females can be traced back to early childcare, when survival requires attachment to an adult. She used Chodorow's work (1978) in developing her ideas. Gilligan proposed that girls identify with their mother, and boys identify with their father. Gilligan followed psychoanalytic theory by arguing that the development of morality was due to boys internalising their father's perspectives and being more concerned with equality and justice, and girls internalising their mother's perspective where there is a greater concern with helping someone in need. Consequently, she rejected the idea that these differences are biologically determined: rather, she thought that behaviour of mothers and fathers affect the development of morality. She also believed that differences in morality between boys and girls will be related to the extent of differences in morality between the adults in their culture.

Gilligan's account of the development of morality has been criticised because issues about justice can be relevant to girls in many family settings where girls may wish to gain equal access to resources (Okin, 1996), and issues about relationships are relevant to many boys, in, for example, teamwork (Turiel, 1998).

Lollis *et al.* (1996) observed mothers' and fathers' interventions in arguments between brothers and sisters aged two to four years over who should have something. Mothers intervened more often and used more care-related reasoning than fathers. Both parents used justice-based reasoning equally often. There was no evidence that girls and boys were treated differently. These are interesting findings and suggest that boys and girls are treated in a similar manner.

However, Gilligan did not argue that morality was related to the way that children are treated. Instead, she argued that boys and girls identify with same-sex parents. This is a subtle difference; it means that the findings reported by Lollis *et al.* do not challenge the core of her theory. However, as has been pointed out in relation to psychoanalytic theories, it is very difficult to investigate and assess identification in young children.

Although Gilligan criticised Kohlberg's work for having a male bias, matching our stereotypes of males and females, many studies have not identified significant differences in the responses of males and females. A number of these studies have been conducted by Walker and his colleagues (e.g. Walker, 1984; Walker *et al.*, 1987).

Research study: Walker (1989)

Aim: To evaluate Kohlberg's stages of moral development in relation to the criticisms of Gilligan about a 'male bias'.

Method: Two hundred and thirty-three participants aged between 10 and 63 years were given the moral dilemmas used by Kohlberg and asked to discuss real-life dilemmas as used by Gilligan. Their responses were coded using the relevant coding schemes. The participants were seen twice with two years between the two interviews.

Results: Walker found no difference in the levels of moral development of males and females. The changes across time were compatible with stage theory as most participants moved up to a higher level of moral reasoning. There was only a weak relation between Kohlberg's stages and Gilligan's levels.

Conclusion: The findings did not support Gilligan's criticism that Kohlberg's stages have a 'male bias'.

Evaluation: This large-scale longitudinal study is a good test of Gilligan's predictions as both Gilligan's moral dilemmas and Kohlberg's moral dilemmas were discussed by the same participants (within-subject design).

A meta-analysis has been carried out by Jaffee and Shibley Hyde (2000) of more than 180 published studies to review whether there are differences between males and females in their ethic of justice and their ethic of care. The review included previous investigations that used interviews, questionnaires or related methods. The overall conclusion was that there is a difference between males and females in the ethic of justice and the ethic of care, but that the difference is only a very small one.

Key points:

- Gilligan's ideas have provoked debate and research.
- Gilligan's work has been important in drawing attention to the possibility of morality involving different dimensions, something that can also be seen in the work of Damon and that of Eisenberg.
- Jaffee and Shibley Hyde's review suggests that there are only small differences between males and females in reasoning about the ethic of justice and reasoning about the ethic of care.
- All this suggests that, like many of the differences between females and males, differences exist but are not particularly large.

Summary questions

17 What did Gilligan mean by the term 'ethic of care'?

18 Gilligan argued that males and females differ in their moral reasoning. Outline these differences.

19 Identify Gilligan's three levels of ethic of care.

20 Briefly explain one criticism of Gilligan's research or theory.

End-of-chapter activity 1

Collect a set of newspapers. Go through the newspapers to identify reports (legal cases are a good bet) or editorials that give opinions about morality. Once these opinions have been identified, decide which of Kohlberg's stages is closest to the opinion of the article. This can be done individually or in groups. It is useful to compare views on the same example, and for there to be a discussion of the difficulties of identifying Kohlberg's stages.

End-of-chapter activity 2

Either individually or in a group think about the different stages or levels of morality identified by the following:

- Damon in his research into distributive justice
- Eisenberg in her model of pro-social reasoning
- Gilligan in her model of the ethic of care.

For each of these models, you should make up an example of the speech or conversation of a young person at each of the levels/stages. If you are working in a group it is useful to carry out the task on an individual basis and then compare, justify and discuss the suggestions that they have made.

Further reading

Eckensberger, L. (1999) Socio-moral development. In D. Messer and S. Millar (eds) *Exploring Developmental Psychology*. London: Arnold.

Slater, A. and Bremner, G. (eds) (2003) *Introduction to Developmental Psychology*. Oxford: Blackwell Publishing Ltd.

Smith, P.K., Cowie, H. and Blades, M. (2003) *Understanding Children's Development*. Oxford: Blackwell Publishing Ltd.

Cognition and law

Introduction

The chapter on cognition and law is concerned with how psychology can be applied in the real world, particularly with respect to the judicial system, and looks particularly at:

- how we can apply the theoretical study of face recognition to real-life events such as identification procedures
- what factors affect eye-witness recall, and how recall can be improved in real-life eye-witness accounts
- the implications of recovering both repressed and false memories.

Recognising faces is an automatic process that we do every day of our lives. Consider the number of familiar people you meet in a day and how quickly you recognise and acknowledge them. Face recognition is a skill we do not often think about, but it is, in fact, a highly complex process. This chapter examines the competing explanations for face recognition, which are of theoretical importance, and then looks at how the knowledge and models of the processes involved in face recognition can have real-life application. For example, knowledge of how faces are recognised can enhance and improve the construction of composites (e.g. a face constructed to form a likeness to the perpetrator of a crime). Such theoretical knowledge has led to the important practical consideration that a more holistic approach to face composition is needed.

The reliability of eye-witness accounts is of the utmost importance because people can be convicted of crimes based partially on eye-witness accounts – which may be fallible. A number of factors have been found to have a significant effect on eye-witness accuracy, including the style of questioning, the presence of weapons, context and the expectations of the eye-witness. The research into eye-witness testimony has had a practical impact on the legal system and has led to techniques such as the **cognitive interview** being used to help the police recover more accurate recollections from witnesses. Of particular interest has been the use of children as witnesses because it is now known that children's retention of an incident can be particularly open to distortion, and children have been found to be less reliable than adult witnesses.

Consider the following scenario:

> **Kate had been feeling depressed for some time and occasionally had suicidal thoughts. It was during a visit to her therapist that Kate first recalled how her uncle had abused her as a child. Her therapist explained that this abuse had been repressed and it was now a 'recovered memory'.**

If such memories are false, and there is evidence that they can be implanted (e.g. by a therapist with a particular belief about the cause of depression) the damage to individuals and families can be very destructive. However, there is also evidence that veridical memories (i.e. those of actual events) can be repressed and later recovered, particularly anxiety-provoking memories. This has led to the '**false memory** debate', which has both ethical and practical implications, some of which are discussed in this chapter.

Key terms

False memory: 'the recollection of an event which did not occur but which the individual subsequently strongly believes did happen' (Brandon *et al.*, 1998).

Specification content	Topic content	Page number
Recognising and remembering faces		
Processes involved in recognition of faces	Processes involved in the recognition of faces	72
Explanations for face recognition, including feature analysis and holistic forms	Explanations for face recognition	72
The construction of likenesses using composite systems	The construction of likenesses using composite systems	77
Identification procedures: simultaneous and sequential line-ups	Identification procedures: simultaneous and sequential line-ups	80
Recalling events		
Factors affecting the reliability of eye-witness accounts and eye-witness; identification, including post-event contamination; improving eye-witness recall, including features of the cognitive interview; children as eye-witnesses; flashbulb memory: memory for shocking events	Factors affecting the reliability of eye-witness accounts	83
	Improving eye-witness recall in the cognitive interview	86
	Flashbulb memory–memory for shocking events	89
The false memory debate: controversy surrounding the recovery of repressed memories; the existence of false memories; evidence relating to repression and false memory; ethical and theoretical implications of the false memory debate.	The recovery of repressed memories	91
	Studying false memories	92
	Theoretical and ethical implications of the false memory debate	94

4 Cognition and law

Recognising and remembering faces

Learning objectives:

- explain the processes involved in face recognition
- describe and evaluate the feature analysis theory of face recognition
- describe and evaluate the holistic theory of face recognition.

Fig. 1 *A familiar face*

Key terms

Configuration: an arrangement of the whole (e.g. the layout of the whole face).

Link

For information on eye-witness recall, see p83–90, and for identification procedures, see p80–82.

Processes involved in the recognition of faces

Face recognition is the process involved when we look at a face and know that we have seen that face before. It is an important skill that we employ each day in many areas of our life. Although the research to be examined in this chapter was largely carried out on the face alone, in real life other cues are present which aid face recognition. For example, a person's voice, mannerisms and the context in which we meet them all assist the recognition process.

Look at Figure 1 and answer the following questions.

1 Do you recognise this face? (see Figure 1)
2 Can you identify the face? (i.e. do you know information about the person? Do you know his name?)
3 Cover the face up and verbally describe the face.

When we recognise a face, a number of processes are involved.

Table 1 *Distinction between three processes*

Process	Description
Face recognition	Recognising the face as one seen before; sometimes a face is recognised but not identified, for example, the name has been forgotten
Face identification	Looking at a face and stating who it is
Face recall	From memory, verbally describing, or drawing, or forming a mental image of the face

(Adapted from ***Cohen****, 1989)*

The processes involved in face recognition are complex and psychologists have attempted to explain these processes by focusing either on the features of the face (feature analysis theory) or on the **configuration** of the face (holistic forms theory).

Face recognition is an area of research that has important practical applications such as when crime victims identify the perpetrator, or eye-witnesses give accounts of an incident.

Explanations for face recognition

Two basic theories attempt to explain the complex processes involved in recognising a human face. Faces, like other objects, may be recognised as a set of different parts (e.g. eyes, nose, mouth) along with the spatial arrangement of those parts; or, alternatively, faces may be recognised more holistically, i.e. as a whole face. Holistic forms theory suggests that faces are processed more as configurations than as independent features.

Feature theory of face recognition

One theory of face recognition proposed that analysing individual features is the most important factor in face recognition. This is known as a 'bottom-up' theory because cues from the stimulus (face) that we are currently looking at will be analysed by the brain, and these visual cues (e.g. the features, textures, light and shade) will be sufficient to enable recognition.

Faces can often be identified from very little information, and research has indicated that just one feature (such as the eyes or the eyebrow) can be enough for recognition of famous faces. Not all facial features are of equal importance when identifying a face. Sadr *et al.* (2003) presented evidence suggesting that the eyebrows might not only be important, but they might well be the most important feature. In their study, participants were asked to identify 50 celebrity face images in three conditions: unaltered image, image lacking eyes, image lacking eyebrows. Performance with the images lacking eyebrows was significantly worse than for both the unaltered images and those lacking eyes. These results suggest that a particular feature – eyebrows – may contribute in an important way to face recognition.

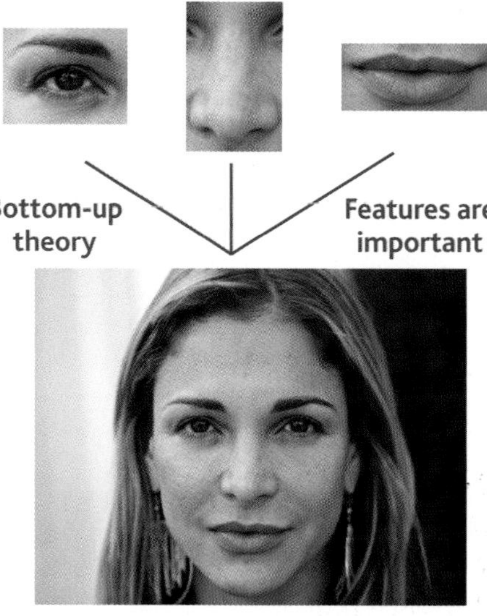

Fig. 2 *Feature analysis theory*

Link

For more on bottom-up theory, see p201 in Chapter 8 of *AQA Psychology B AS*.

Research study: Shepherd, Davies and Ellis (1981)

Aim: To investigate how features are used in the description of unfamiliar faces.

Method: Participants were shown unfamiliar faces for a brief period and were then asked to describe the faces they had been shown.

Results: In the free descriptions, the features most often noted were hair, eyes, nose, mouth, eyebrows, chin and forehead (in that order).

Conclusion: Unfamiliar faces tend to be recalled using the main features. Some of these features seem more important than others.

Evaluation: This study lacks ecological validity because in real life if we are asked to describe a face it would usually be one that we have seen 'live' rather than in a picture.

Ellis *et al.* (1979) noted that with unfamiliar faces we tend to rely on external features (e.g. hair, face shape) whereas with more familiar faces we are more likely to use internal features (e.g. eyes, nose). Although external features are more noticeable, they are also more likely to change (e.g. change of hair style/colour) and so using internal features would be more reliable.

When we describe a face we generally use individual features, such as eyes, nose and mouth, and often give more specific details about these individual features, such as 'blue eyes', 'large nose', etc. It appears that features are certainly important to face recognition and early theories focused on whether the facial features were processed independently. For example, Bradshaw and Wallace (1971) constructed pairs of faces out of **Identikit**, which differed by fixed numbers of features. They found that volunteers were quicker to identify that faces differed if the number of different facial features on the pair of faces was greater, i.e. the more differences there were on the pairs of faces, the quicker the participants could respond. Bradshaw and Wallace concluded that facial features are processed independently and in sequence.

Key terms

Identikit: a set of features used by the police (in the USA) to construct images of faces based on witnesses' accounts.

Sergent (1984) reviewed a number of studies that seemed to come to the same conclusion as Bradshaw and Wallace's: facial features are important and are recognised sequentially. However, Sergent pointed out that there is an alternative interpretation of the findings from such studies. She noted that when faces differed in a number of features the overall configuration also differed, and this too could explain why identification was more difficult. Sergent carried out an important study that showed that facial features are processed interactively and not independently, and, furthermore, she proposed that 'a configuration emerged from a set of features which is more than the sum of its parts'.

Research study: Sergent (1984)

Aim: To investigate if features are processed independently or configuratively.

Method: Participants were shown pairs of faces and the time taken to state if the faces were the same or different was measured. The faces were in pairs and were of four types: the same; differed on one feature only; differed on two features; differed on three features. There were two different chins, two different eye colours, and different internal space (i.e. the eyes and nose were either high or low on the face).

Results: The more features that differed between the face pairs, the faster the 'different' response was made. Also, a difference in chins was the fastest to be detected, and when there was a difference in chin and at least one other difference then differences were detected even quicker, suggesting that features were not processed independently.

Conclusion: Facial features are processed configuratively not independently.

Evaluation: Although this was a well-controlled experiment that did show cause and effect, it is unlikely that we would have to carry out such a contrived comparison in real life, and therefore such results may only tell us about face recognition in a laboratory setting and not how real faces are recognised in real life.

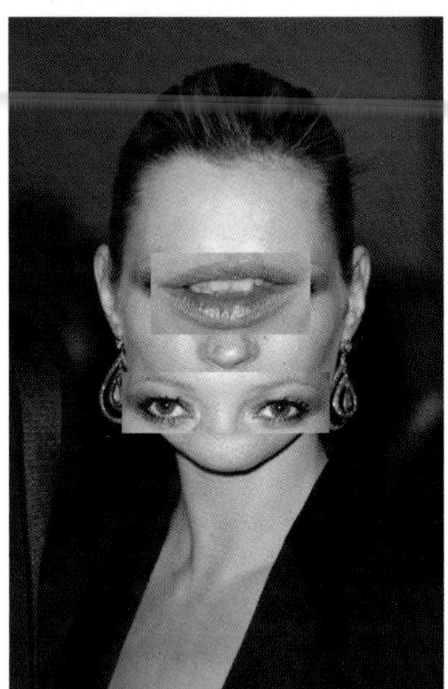

Fig. 3 *Do you recognise this well-known person?*

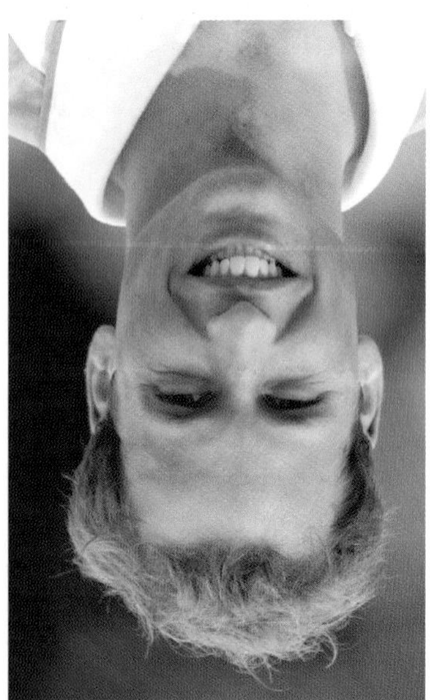

Fig. 4 *How quickly can you identify this face?*

Evaluation of the feature theory of face recognition

There is evidence from a variety of sources that a feature-based model of face recognition is oversimplified.

Scrambled faces

When the configuration of features is altered (e.g. scrambled, see Figure 3), it is more difficult to recognise a well-known face and it takes longer to identify the face (Bruce and Valentine, 1986). Such findings show the importance of configuration to face recognition, because if only features (e.g. eyes) are important it should not matter where those eyes are located.

Inverted faces

Errors are found when attempting to recognise any object that has been inverted, but inverted faces (see Figure 4) produce particular difficulties (Yin, 1969).

Sergent (1984) repeated her experiment with the faces presented upside down. Surprisingly, she found that participants were no quicker on multiple-feature differences than on single-feature differences; these results are consistent with a model of independent feature processing. A number of other studies have suggested that different processing occurs in upright and inverted faces. One explanation for findings from such studies is that faces are normally recognised holistically; therefore, inverting the face makes recognition difficult because the relationship between the features cannot be detected. With inverted faces, the participant may have to resort to independently processing features, which would take longer.

Pairing different halves of faces

Young and Hay (1986) cut pictures of famous faces horizontally and checked that participants could recognise the separate halves. They then combined two halves of different faces together to produce a composite (see Figure 5) and asked participants to name the top and bottom halves. This proved difficult as the composite seemed to produce a new holistic face.

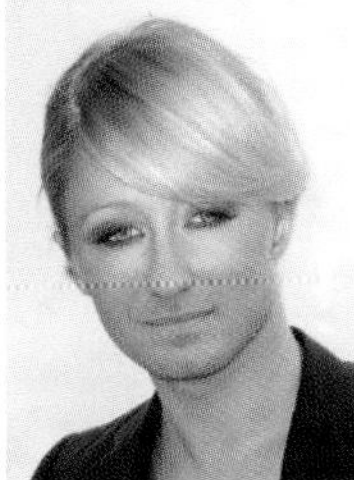

Fig. 5 *Can you name the composite faces?*

Clinical studies

Prosopagnosia is a disorder where patients are unable to recognise familiar faces; in severe cases, they cannot recognise their own face in the mirror. They can recognise individual features on faces (e.g. a nose, mouth, etc.) and feel that they know the person (emotional response), but they have no knowledge of who the person is (no cognitive response).

Capgras syndrome is a delusional disorder where patients think that people they know have been replaced by 'doubles'. Such patients recognise the person (a cognitive response), but they have no emotional response to that individual (believing them to be a 'double').

These specific impairments in face and person recognition suggest that recognising faces is a very complex process. As people suffering from both prosopagnosia and Capgras syndrome have no difficulty in naming and describing individual features of familiar faces, it would seem that face recognition requires more than this. It is much more likely that faces are stored with emotional and semantic information in addition to the features, and a model of face recognition that incorporates a more holistic approach has been proposed by Bruce and Young (1986).

A holistic theory of face recognition

Studies have shown that when the layout of features is altered (e.g. scrambled), it is more difficult to recognise a well-known face. If it is only the individual features that are important in face recognition, why should scrambled faces prove more difficult to recognise? These, and other findings, have led many researchers to investigate a more holistic approach to face recognition. Bruce and Young (1986) have proposed a sequential model for face recognition. Figure 6 is a simplified version of this model, as applied to recognition of familiar faces.

According to the holistic model, when we look at a face we visually encode it; in other words, our sensory system takes in the information from the face. Stored in the brain are **face recognition units** (FRUs) which are like templates of all the faces encountered. If the incoming information matches an FRU then the **person identity node** (PIN) is activated. The PIN stores semantic information about the familiar face, such as where we know the person from, their school or college, their occupation, likes and dislikes, etc. This information may then activate a name, which is generated last and stored separately from other information about the person.

As this model is sequential, one prediction would be that in order to generate a name for a person we must have activated the PIN and therefore must have available other information about that person. This was tested by Young *et al.* (1985).

A holistic model of face recognition

A familiar face

is

Structurally encoded

A representation/description of the face is produced

Activates

Face recognition units (FRUs)

Each face known to the viewer has an FRU containing structural information about that face

Activates

Person identity node (PIN)

Information about the person, e.g. normal context, occupation, interests, etc.

Activates

Name generation

An individual's name is stored separately from other information about them and is accessed last

Fig. 6 *A holistic theory of face recognition*

Research study: Young *et al.* (1985)

Aim: To investigate the difficulties in face recognition experienced in everyday life to find support for a holistic theory of face recognition.

Method: A field study was carried out with 22 volunteers who were asked to keep a diary for eight weeks and record any cases (in the flesh or media) where they failed or had difficulty in recognising someone they knew.

Results: One thousand and eight incidents were recorded and there were no reports of naming an individual without knowing other information about that person. In 190 cases, participants reported knowing information about individuals such as their occupation but being unable to name them. There were 233 reports of participants reporting a feeling of familiarity without being able to access personal identity information or name.

Conclusion: The results support the sequential nature of face recognition proposed by the holistic theory posited by Bruce and Young (1986).

Evaluation: This is a particularly valid study because it was carried out in the real world over a period of time.

Evaluation of the holistic theory of face recognition

- There is converging evidence, not only from diary studies but also from clinical case studies and laboratory research, that the components of the holistic model proposed by Bruce and Young are relevant to the recognition of familiar faces. There is evidence for the sequential nature of processing proposed by the model and to support the theoretical assumptions regarding the order in which information is accessed when we recognise a familiar face.
- Flude *et al.* (1989) presented evidence from a patient with brain damage who could identify the occupations of 85 per cent of the familiar faces presented but could only name 15 per cent, which supports the sequential nature of processing proposed by the holistic model.
- The Bruce and Young model assumes separate processes for familiar and unfamiliar faces. There is evidence that this is the case: Malone *et al.* (1982) described a patient who could recognise famous faces but was very impaired at recognising unfamiliar faces (i.e. faces first encountered in the study). Another patient could match unfamiliar faces perfectly well but had difficulty recognising photographs of famous people, getting only 5 out of 22 correct. This double **dissociation** supports the model.
- The model has been criticised with respect to the explanation for unfamiliar-face recognition, which lacks the detailed evidence that has supported the familiar-face recognition aspect of the model.
- Another problem for the model has been the findings from some patients with prosopagnosia on face-recognition tasks. Although such patients show no overt (conscious) recognition of a familiar face, they do register covert recognition. This has been measured by autonomic responses (e.g. **galvanic skin responses – GSR**) which has found a response to familiar faces (at an unconscious level), where both the FRU and PIN appear to be activated. If conscious familiarity is not available, how can a deeper level of familiarity be available unconsciously? Such findings have led to a modification of the original model, known as the **interactive activation and competition model** (IAC).

Key terms

Dissociation: a disconnection between or separation of processes (in psychology, a demonstration of double dissociation is strong evidence for processes being independent).

Galvanic skin responses (GSR): a measure of changes in the electrical resistance of the skin. (People sweat when the ANS is aroused and moisture increases electrical conductivity.) A method of detecting emotion or stress, GSR is the basis of lie detectors.

Key points:

- The main processes involved in face recognition are face identification, face recognition and face recall.
- The feature analysis theory of face recognition proposes that the most important factors in face recognition are the individual features of the face (e.g. eyes, nose, mouth).
- Altering the configuration of these features (e.g. scrambling faces) results in greater difficulty in recognising the face. Feature analysis theory has difficulty accounting for this, although holistic theory can explain such findings.
- A holistic forms theory of face recognition suggests that it is not simply the individual features but the layout of the whole face that is important to face recognition.
- The holistic model proposed by Bruce and Young (1986) is a sequential model of face recognition that has found support from a number of areas including empirical and clinical studies.

Link

For more on physiological techniques, such as GSR meters, see Chapter 6, Stress and stress management, p141.

AQA Examiner's tip

The two explanations of face recognition (feature analysis and holistic forms) are named in the specification and could be named in an examination paper. Make sure that you can describe and evaluate each separately and are able to compare the two theories. Notice that studies on scrambled faces etc. can be used both to criticise feature theory and to support the holistic theory of face recognition.

Cognition and law

Summary questions

1. Daniel was asked to write down from memory a description of the Prime Minister's face. Which process would this entail: (a), (b) or (c)?
   a Face recognition
   b Face recall
   c Face identification
2. What is meant by: (a) internal features, and (b) external features? Give an example of each.
3. Name four components of the holistic theory of face recognition proposed by Bruce and Young (1986).
4. Explain how 'double dissociation' supports the Bruce and Young model.

The construction of likenesses using composite systems

Learning objectives:

- name the main composite systems used in the UK
- describe and evaluate the named composite systems.

Facial composite systems

A facial composite system enables a visual likeness, usually to the perpetrator of a crime, to be formed. The likeness is known as a **facial composite**. Typically, in a crime investigation, a witness would give a verbal description of the perpetrator, and facial features that match this description would be selected by someone trained in using a composite system. A composite is usually adjusted until the witness agrees that an appropriate facial likeness has been produced.

The most common systems used in the UK to produce composites are E-FIT and EFIT-V. Other systems which have seen use include ProFIT, Sketch and EvoFIT. In the USA, the Identikit system (originally similar to PhotoFIT in which facial features were printed on acetate transparencies) is widely used. The computerised version of PhotoFIT is also used in the US and known as Comphotofit.

Table 2 *The main composite systems*

Photo-FIT	E-FIT	EvoFIT
• This contains 855 features, printed on jigsaw-like pieces that slot into a template. • Features can be enhanced, e.g. by ageing with wrinkles.	• This is a computerised version of Photo-FIT • The composites are more realistic because photographs of features are used.	• Complete faces are generated using a statistical technique known as principal components analysis. • Approximately six faces (from 18) are selected that most resemble the suspect; these become the 'parents'. • The components of the separate faces are then mixed together and the 'offspring' selected. • The offspring are bred together, and this process continues until a good likeness is confirmed and a 'composite' is then saved.
Evaluation • When placed with other distractor faces, composites constructed from Photo-FIT were only identified 12.5% of the time. • Feature demarcation lines seemed to interfere with identification. • Insufficient features were available. • Mac-A-Mug Pro is a computer programme that attempts to deal with some of the problems encountered on the Photo-FIT system; it contains more features and has eliminated feature boundary lines.	**Evaluation** • In a study by Davies et al. (2000) participants were exposed to target faces for one minute and then constructed composites using either E-FIT or Photo-FIT. No significant difference between the two systems was found. • In the Davies study, artistic elaboration was not allowed. Such enhancement is used in police work, which means that the findings from the Davies study cannot be generalised outside the laboratory situation.	**Evaluation** • The EvoFIT system has been produced to fit in with the holistic model of face recognition. • The EvoFIT system allows a composite to evolve from complete faces (i.e. the composite is not constructed from individual features).

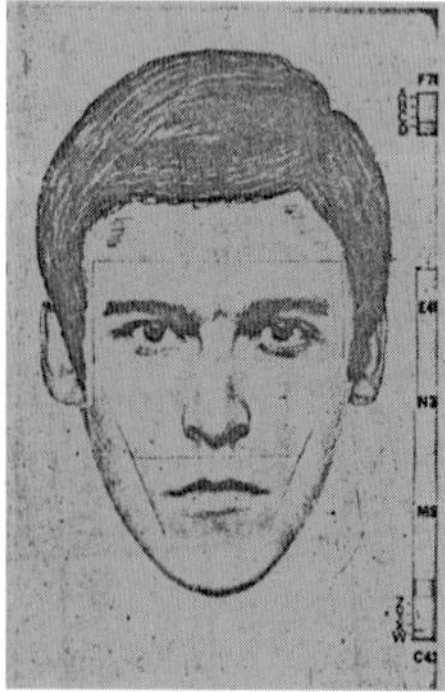

Fig. 7 *The first Photo-FIT used in the UK*

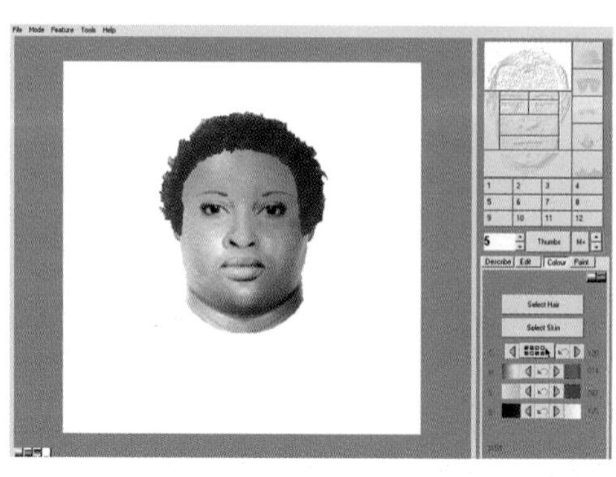

Fig. 8 *Example of an E-FIT*

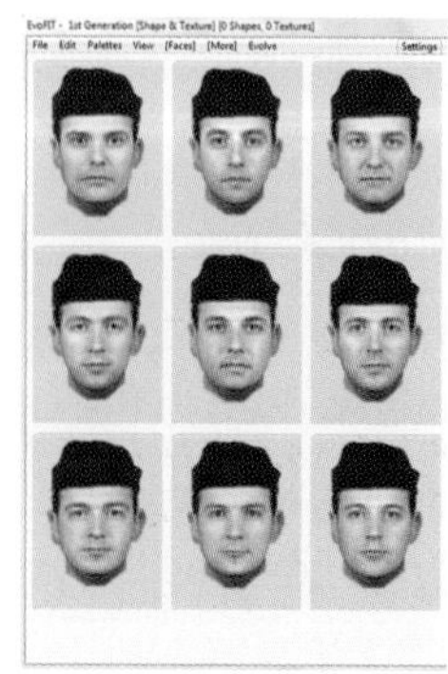

Fig. 9 *A set of faces used to construct a composite using EvoFIT*

Research study: Frowd *et al.* (2005)

Aim: To compare and evaluate the use of five composite systems.

Method: Composites of unfamiliar targets were constructed from memory after a four-hour delay, using experienced operators for each of the composite systems: E-FIT, PROfit, Sketch, Photo-FIT and EvoFIT.

Results: The average naming rate was 10 per cent. PROfit performance was superior except on the more distinctive targets, when E-FIT was superior. Photo-FIT and EvoFIT were the least effective techniques.

Conclusion: The computerised composite constructions techniques (PROfit and E-FIT) appear superior. Facial distinctiveness is an important factor in composite naming tasks.

Evaluation: The contextual information in such studies is minimal and therefore the research in composite studies may lack ecological validity. Under realistic conditions, composites are not used in isolation but accompanied by context information, for example from the crime scene, and this is likely to increase the naming rate in real life.

Evaluation of facial composite systems

- Research into the efficacy of composite systems suggests that 'operator contamination' is likely to have occurred, i.e. when the same person constructs composites of the same target using different techniques there may be a confounding effect. To control for this, Frowd *et al.* (2005) used different (but equally experienced) operators.
- Target familiarity may be a problem on composite studies because, although a witness may state that they do not consciously recognise a target, the target may already be unconsciously familiar, particularly if 'celebrity faces' are used, as in the study by Frowd *et al.*

Key points:

- A facial composite is a visual likeness to a face created by a composite system.
- Composite systems include Photo-FIT, E-FIT, Sketch and EvoFIT.
- E-FIT is a computerised version of the original Photo-FIT.
- EvoFIT is a computerised system that attempts to incorporate a more holistic approach to face composition.
- There is some evidence that the computerised versions are superior to the original manually constructed systems.

Summary questions

5. Briefly describe and evaluate a non-computerised composite system, e.g. Photo-FIT.
6. Name and outline a computerised composite system.
7. Describe a study on composite systems. In your answer, refer to the aim, method, results and conclusion.

Identification procedures: simultaneous and sequential line-ups

Learning objectives:

- understand the basic identification procedures
- explain the difference between simultaneous and sequential line-ups
- evaluate the use of identification procedures.

Link

See p96 for details of the Home Office website, which contains a weblink for the recent update to PACE Code D. Search for PACE within the site and you can look for yourself at the latest versions of the codes of practice for identification procedures.

Link

For information about Video Identification Parade Electronic Recording (VIPER), see p82.

Identification parades and line-ups

Identity parades or line-ups are often used by the police following an eye-witness's description of a perpetrator of a crime. The eye-witness may be a victim or an observer of the event or crime.

The conduct of identity parades and line-ups

All identity parades are carried out with the suspect's consent. The conduct of identification procedures in the UK is governed by Code D of the Police and Criminal Evidence Act 1984 (PACE). Following a review of the PACE Codes of Practice in 2008, changes were made.

Prior to the 2008 review, PACE required the police to attempt to conduct a live identification parade whenever possible. A live parade requires the identification officer (who must be a police officer not involved with the case) to bring together at the same time and place, the suspect (with legal representative), at least eight similar-looking volunteers (the non-suspects or 'distractors') and the witnesses. When the line-up has been assembled, the eye-witness is asked if they can identify the perpetrator from the line-up. Line-ups are often disrupted by the failure of one or more of the party to be present, and this is costly: cancellation of line-ups in the UK costs over £1m each year.

The 2008 review of PACE Code D allows for the use of video line-ups, and these are becoming increasingly popular for a number of reasons discussed below.

Accuracy of eye-witness identification from line-ups

When line-ups are appropriately assembled, eye-witness identification from them is often inaccurate. Valentine *et al.* (2003) report evidence from real-life studies of 640 eye-witnesses who attempted to identify suspects in 314 line-ups. The correct suspect was identified in approximately 40 per cent of cases, with 40 per cent failing to make an identification, and 20 per cent identifying the wrong person.

Wells and Olson (2003) have suggested that the accuracy of eye-witness identification can be influenced by two types of variables: system variables and estimator variables.

System variables

The term 'system variables' refers to the methods or systems employed to try to maximise correct identification; such variables include:

- **pre-line-up instructions** given to the witness, such as explaining that the suspect may not be present
- the **physical characteristics of the 'distractors'** – it is important that the non-suspects are not obviously different from the suspect or the suspect would stand out.

System variables can be controlled by the Criminal Justice System. A meta-analysis of studies carried out where a pre-line-up warning was given that the suspect might not be present found that mistaken identification rates were reduced by over 40 per cent on suspect-absent line-ups, with only a 2 per cent reduction in accurate identification of suspect-present line-ups (Steblay, 1997).

Estimator variables

Estimator variables are other things that affect identification; these were present at the scene and include:

- **use of weapons** – the presence of a weapon during an event can result in 'weapon focus' where the eye-witness may focus on the weapon rather than on the face of the perpetrator and this will affect eye-witness identification
- **conditions at the time of the event** (e.g. poor light, bad weather conditions, etc.).

Estimator variables cannot be controlled by the Criminal Justice System. An interesting finding by Dunning and Perretta (2002) was that witnesses who made a fast decision on the line-up (i.e. in about 10 seconds) were correct nearly 90 per cent of the time, whereas there was only a 50 per cent accuracy with those who took longer to come to a decision.

Simultaneous identification line-up

In a simultaneous identification line-up, the witness views all the line-up members at the same time. In a simultaneous format, false positive choices are more likely because a particular face may be selected on the basis of that individual's familiarity in relation to the others in the line-up. In this procedure **'relative judgements'** are made.

Hint

Simultaneous and Sequential line-ups are named on the specification and you should be able to discuss each of these procedures and compare them.

Sequential identification line-up

In a sequential identification line-up, the witness views each member of the line-up one at a time. Presenting suspects one at a time prevents a relative judgement because having not yet seen the remaining line-up members the eye-witness is not in a position to make a relative judgement. It could be argued that the eye-witness could compare the person currently being viewed with any viewed previously, but the eye-witness cannot be certain that the next person to be viewed will not be an even better likeness to the perpetrator. Sequential identification line-ups encourage **'absolute judgements'** (Lindsay and Wells, 1985).

Evaluation of identity parades and line-ups

- In a meta-analysis of studies using a sequential identification line-up, Steblay *et al.* (2001) concluded that this type of line-up does significantly reduce the rate of false identifications when the real suspect is absent, compared with performance in the simultaneous identification line-up. However, the authors found a slight drop in correct identifications in the sequential identification line-up when the suspect is present.
- Dunning and Stem (1994) asked eye-witnesses to give a verbal description of the process that they used to come to the identification decision. They found that eye-witnesses who used a process of elimination (relative comparisons) were significantly more likely to make a false identification than those who reported a more absolute judgement.

Fig. 10 *A VIPER system*

Video Parade Electronic Recording (VIPER)

Identification line-ups are costly and the necessary personnel are difficult to assemble in one place at the same time. West Yorkshire Police developed the VIPER system in 1996 to provide a solution to the requirement to run a large number of identification parades. This system consists of a centrally held database containing thousands of video sequences. Only the head and shoulders of the person are shown for 20 seconds; the subject is looking directly at the camera and turning to exhibit both profiles. Everything is standardised including the timing, background, movements, etc. When a description of a suspect's appearance has been taken, this is fed into the computer and the database finds a set of 'foils'. The eight most suitable foils are selected to be used in the identification along with the suspect's image. In the VIPER system, sequential identification procedures are used.

Link

Viper is not named on the specification but it is a contemporary example of how sequential identity procedures are used by the police.

Evaluation of VIPER

- Witnesses can view the VIPER images in their own time and at a convenient location.
- In an analysis of 1083 parades that took place in West Yorkshire between 1997 to 1999, Pike *et al.* (2000) found that just over 5 per cent of the 403 VIPER parades were cancelled compared with over 46 per cent of the 680 live parades. The VIPER system is clearly cost effective.
- Because the VIPER parade is sequential, the possibility of false positive identifications is reduced, as relative comparisons are avoided.

Key points:

- Identification line-ups can take the form of a live parade or a video recording.
- There are two distinct techniques used for identification: simultaneous and sequential.
- Studies have found sequential identification procedures to be superior to simultaneous identification.
- VIPER is a video identification system that was developed in 1996 in West Yorkshire and is now being used by a number of police forces in the UK.

Summary questions

8 Distinguish between simultaneous and sequential identification processes.

9 Explain why estimator variables cannot be controlled by the Criminal Justice System.

10 Nick has witnessed an old man being beaten up by two youths and has agreed to help the police with their identification procedures. He gives a description of the appearance of the two suspects to the police and this is fed into a database. Foils are then produced that most closely match the descriptions given. The suspect's image and eight of the most suitable foils are used for the identification process. Nick looks at each 'image' on the computer one at a time.

a Which identification system is being used in this case? Justify your answer.

b Give two advantages of the identification system you have named in part (a).

c Explain why Nick looked at the 'images' one at a time.

Recalling events

Learning objectives:

- describe and discuss the main factors affecting the reliability of eye-witness accounts
- discuss how eye-witness recall can be improved
- explain the research into children as eye-witnesses
- discuss memory for shocking events (flashbulb memories).

Factors affecting the reliability of eye-witness accounts

Accurate eye-witness testimonies are crucially important, not least because decisions based on such accounts can have a huge impact on many lives. If an inaccurate eye-witness testimony is used as evidence towards a conviction, a miscarriage of justice might result. The use of DNA testing by police forces has shown how fallible eye-witness testimonies can be. To date, more than 200 individuals in America have been freed from prison after being falsely detained, on the basis of eye-witness evidence, for a crime that DNA tests have subsequently proved that they could not have committed. As early as 1976, the Devlin Committee in the UK recommended that juries do not convict on a single eye-witness testimony without corroboration, but, as in America, there have recently been a number of convictions quashed on the basis of DNA evidence.

A number of factors have been found to affect the reliability of eye-witness accounts and eye-witness identification; four factors are considered here.

Questioning and post-event contamination

A considerable amount of research carried out by Loftus and others has indicated how eye-witness memories can be influenced by post-event questions, and how misleading information can be inserted into a stored memory of an event. An early study illustrates this.

Research study: Loftus and Palmer (1974)

Aim: To investigate whether the type of questioning affects the reliability of eye-witness recall.

Method Part 1: One hundred and fifty participants were asked to view a one-minute film of a car crash and then (a) describe what had happened, and (b) answer questions about the film. There were three groups: In group A, participants were asked the question 'About how fast were the cars going when they **smashed into** each other?' Group B participants were asked the same question but **'hit'** replaced **'smashed into'**. The third group was not asked the question about car speed (control group).

Results: There was a significant difference in mean estimate of speed: mean for Group A ('smashed' question) was 10.46 mph; mean for Group B ('hit' question) was 8 mph.

Method Part 2: A week later the participants were asked further questions including 'Did you see any broken glass?' There was no broken glass.

Results: Of the participants in the 'Smashed into' group, 32 per cent reported seeing broken glass compared with 14 per cent of the 'Hit' group and 12 per cent of the control group.

Conclusion: The way in which a question is asked influences the answers given, both immediately on estimations of speed, and a week later when information commensurate with the speed is then reported (i.e. broken glass present). Post-event contamination was evident.

Take it further

Recent discussion into post-conviction DNA testing which highlights the vulnerability of eye-witness accounts can be found on a number of websites, e.g: www.cjsonline.gov.uk

Fig. 11 *A car crash*

Evaluation: This study was a laboratory investigation, which means that it was carried out in an artificial environment, and therefore may lack ecological validity. Real-life eye-witness testimonies may be affected in a different manner.

Many studies have been carried out illustrating the reconstructive nature of memory and how individuals draw on information received after the event when describing an incident. Loftus and Zanni (1975) demonstrated how changing a small word in a question, following an incident, led to contamination of memory. They showed participants a film of a car crash and then asked one of two questions: 'Did you see **a** broken headlight?' or 'Did you see **the** broken headlight?' The use of the definite article ('the') affected post-event recall and 17 per cent reported having seen a broken headlight, whilst of those given the question with the indefinite article ('a') only 7 per cent reported having seen a broken headlight.

Evaluation of eye-witness studies

- One criticism of laboratory studies into eye-witness testimony is that participants would not be expecting misinformation to be implanted, and therefore such research lacks ecological validity. However, even when participants are informed about the presence of misleading post-event information, memory is still affected (Eakin *et al.*, 2003).
- Although studies by loftus have concluded that memory is changed by the style of questioning, others have argued that the misinformation presented to witnesses biases the way that they respond to questions and the original memory is in fact intact. This is known as the 'response bias hypothesis'. More recently, Loftus has suggested that there are only limited changes to the original memory and the tendency to accept misleading information increases as memory fades over time.
- Cohen (1993) has argued that the errors evident in eye-witness studies can largely be explained by methodological issues. When questioning eye-witnesses in contrived experiments, closed questions are often used (e.g. *'Was the lady carrying a bag*? **YES/NO**'), whereas, in real-life interviews, open questions are more likely (e.g. *'Tell me what the lady was carrying.'*)

Expectation

A memory for an event can be influenced by the observer's expectations. People hold stereotypes and schemas that can affect memory. When we try to retrieve a memory, say of a crime scene, we reconstruct an account based partly on our surviving memories and on our expectations of what must have happened. The less certain our memory is, the more we are likely to rely on expectations. In criminal cases, it has been found that errors are more likely to occur when the suspect's race is different from the race of the witness. This is possibly due to negative racial stereotypes. Howitt (1991) presented a story to participants who were then asked to recall it; this is a shortened version:

> The time was 5.30 pm in London and the underground train was overcrowded ... Two men of different ethnic origins were standing up facing each other; one had an open double-edged knife and newspaper in his hand. A fight ensued involving a large number of passengers and some people were badly hurt.

Link

Stereotypes and schemas are outlined in the 'Social Cognition' chapter 6 of *AQA Psychology B AS*.

When participants were asked to recall the story, the events were distorted and revealed stereotypical sexist and racist thinking. For example, one report read:

> Five-thirty on a London underground station and there were two black men there. One was carrying a rolled-up newspaper with a knife partly hidden.

Emotion/stress

Studies have found that highly stressful or emotional events can adversely affect memory. Loftus and Burns (1982) showed participants a film of a hold-up and then tested their memory for details. One group saw a violent version of the film where a young boy was shot in the face and fell bleeding to the ground. The control group saw a non-violent version. Participants who saw the violent version had less memory for details prior to the shooting, including the fact that one of the boys had a large number '17' on his jersey. Participants were asked to recall 16 items; those who had seen the violent version of the film did worse on 14 of them. It is likely that witnessing a real-life crime will be even more shocking and that memory following a violent incident may be affected to an even greater extent.

Loftus has used the term **'weapon focus'** to explain how participants may focus on a weapon and not pay attention, therefore, to the face of the perpetrator, resulting in poorer eye-witness recall. Loftus *et al.* (1987) asked participants to watch a short film of either a person pointing a gun at a cashier and receiving cash, or a person handing a cheque to a cashier and receiving cash. The results showed that the participants spent longer looking at the gun than at the cheque (i.e. focused on the weapon), and the memory for details was poorer in the gun condition than in the cheque condition.

Link

See the comments on 'weapon focus' under Estimator variables in this chapter.

However, the effect of emotion or stress on eye-witness recall is not clear cut, as illustrated in the following research study, which concerned a real-life robbery.

Research study: Yuille and Cutshall (1986)

Aim: To investigate eye-witness recall of a real-life incident.

Method: This was a case study of a thief in Vancouver (Canada) who stole a number of guns and some money but was shot six times whilst making his escape and died. The shop owner was shot but survived and was one of 21 witnesses interviewed by the police. Thirteen of the original witnesses were re-interviewed five months later by researchers.

Results: The research team attempted to insert two misleading questions, but these had no effect. In fact, the witnesses had extremely accurate recall of the event even five months after the incident.

Conclusion: In a real-life, highly emotional incident, eye-witness recall was very accurate.

Evaluation: In this study, the insertion of misleading questions did not seem to have the same negative effect that occurs in laboratory research into eye-witness recall. In addition, contrary to Loftus's findings on weapon focus, the use of weapons in this incident did not have an adverse effect on recall; in fact, the most distressed individuals had the most accurate recall.

Yuille and Tollestrup (1990) have proposed a model that can account for the conflicting results of the effect of emotion on eye-witness testimony. They propose that **distinctive** events tend to be rehearsed frequently (these are events that have a great impact and are not normally possible to achieve in a laboratory). During distinctive events, attention may be focused **internally** or **externally**. An internal focus may be on emotions, and therefore few event details are stored; an external focus will be on the event itself, resulting in clearer memories of the event. The extent of memory for details may depend on the emotional focus of the individual.

Context

The context at the time of testimony is usually quite different from the context in which the event was witnessed: for example, a crime is witnessed in the street and a description is given in a police station. Much research on the psychology of memory has indicated that a person's ability to recall information is influenced by the matching of encoding and retrieving contexts: i.e. if a person recalls information in the same context as it was encoded, memory is superior to when the contexts at encoding and retrieval differ. Research on eye-witness testimony has also shown that recreation of context can be an aid to memory. For example, Malpass and Devine (1981) showed participants a film depicting an act of vandalism and interviewed them about the incident five months later. One group was reminded of the day, room and immediate reactions and their recall was significantly better than the control group who were given no contextual cues.

Link

In Chapter 7, 'Remembering and fogetting', *AQA Psychology B AS*, the effect of 'context' on memory is discussed in detail.

A strange real-life incident also testifies to the influence of context on memory. Donald Thomson was a researcher who appeared on Australian television to discuss the unreliability of eye-witness testimony. Whilst the programme was being broadcast, a woman watching the programme was raped in her home. From the woman's description of her assailant the police arrested Thomson and he was picked out in an identity parade as her attacker. Thomson was a victim of **unconscious transference**: the witness recognised the face from the television debate and incorrectly assigned it to the rapist. Fortunately for Thomson, the debate was being broadcast live and a large number of witnesses were therefore able to confirm his whereabouts at that time.

The importance of context to eye-witness recall has been taken into account in the cognitive interview technique, as discussed below.

Improving eye-witness recall – the cognitive interview

Evidence concerning the unreliability of eye-witness testimony has led researchers to devise methods for improving eye-witnesses' retrieval of events. Geiselman *et al.* (1985) developed the cognitive interview as a technique to help the police when interviewing an eye-witness; it is an attempt to maximise the range of retrieval cues. The interviewer would ask the eye-witness to:

1 Recreate the context at the time of the incident, including the environment and emotional state.

2 Report everything; even if it seems irrelevant, the information may prove crucial later.

3 Recount the incident in different orders (e.g. starting from the beginning, middle or end of the incident).

4 Report events from other perspectives, i.e. report what other witnesses would have perceived.

Hint

A discussion on improving eye-witness recall could include the necessity for improvement (due to the evidence factors concerning unreliability), which has led researches to develop new techniques, e.g. cognitive interview.

Points 1 and 2 are related to encoding specificity and attempt to provide as similar a context as possible between encoding and retrieval. Points 3 and 4 are an attempt to retrieve material through different routes.

Research study: Geiselman *et al.* (1985)

Aim: To compare the cognitive interview with two other interviewing techniques.

Method: Participants viewed a violent crime and 48 hours later were interviewed by a police officer. Participants were placed in one of three conditions and three interview techniques were used: standard police interview; interview with hypnotised participants; cognitive interview. The number of accurately recalled facts and the number of errors were recorded.

Results: There was significantly higher recall of accurate statements for the cognitive interview (mean = 41) over the interview under hypnosis (mean = 38) and the standard interview (mean = 29), and there was no significant difference in the number of incorrect responses.

Conclusion: The cognitive interview is superior to other forms of eye-witness interviewing.

Evaluation: There are ethical issues involved when showing violent films to participants. This study was also a laboratory study where the incident was on film rather than real life; this calls into question the ecological validity of the study.

The cognitive interviewing technique has been further refined and Fisher *et al.* (1987) devised the enhanced cognitive interview. In addition to the four points of the basic cognitive interview, there are other recommendations:

- Interviewers should minimise distractions and tailor language to suit the eye-witness.
- The eye-witness should speak slowly, pause, and be encouraged to relax.
- Judgemental comments should be avoided.
- The eye-witness's description of events/people should be reviewed.

In a laboratory study, Fisher *et al.* found that the enhanced cognitive interview produced a higher mean number of correct statements (57.5, compared with 39.6 using the basic cognitive interview); however, the errors also increased with there being 28 per cent more incorrect statements using the enhanced interview. Such a high error rate was not, however, found in a real-life situation, which calls into question the ecological validity of the laboratory research.

Evaluation of the cognitive interview

- The increase in the amount of **incorrect** information as a result of the cognitive interview is a cause for concern.
- The cognitive interview increases recall of peripheral detail rather than central details, and the latter may be of more significance.
- The cognitive interview requires the interview to take place as soon as possible after the incident because at longer intervals retention is adversely affected (Geiselman and Fisher, 1997).
- An important finding from research into the cognitive interview is that it appears to reduce the amount of post-event contamination that can seriously distort memory.

Children as eye-witnesses

Findings from psychological research generally indicate a growth in memory function with age, with the optimum memory function occurring between 20 and 65 years. The use of children as witnesses has, therefore, generated a considerable amount of research.

Research study: Brigham *et al.* (1986)

Aim: To investigate the accuracy of children's eye-witness identifications in a field setting.

Method: Children aged 9, 13 and 17 years were exposed to a staged theft by a target male. They were questioned by an authority figure dressed in a police uniform. Recognition was assessed using a photo line-up of six people including the male suspect. A nine-item, open-ended questionnaire was used to assess recall of the suspect's appearance.

Results: A statistically significant effect of age on reliability of eye-witness testimony was found. Younger children performed significantly less well than older children on the photo line-up and on the recall items.

Conclusion: Young children are less reliable eye-witnesses than adults.

Evaluation: There was a high level of deception involved in this study as the 'theft' was 'staged', and the study could have caused distress to the participants. The study was a field investigation, which would improve the ecological validity.

A number of factors have been found to influence a child witness; these are outlined next.

Misleading questions and false information

Evidence suggests that young children are more vulnerable to misleading questions and false information during interviewing. Ceci *et al.* (1994) investigated the susceptibility of young children to accepting false information during questioning. Children were asked to think about events that had occurred over a 10-week period and were also asked about events that did not occur. The inclusion of 'source monitoring questions' during interviews might, therefore, improve reliability: for example, 'Do you recall that really happening to you or did someone tell you about it?'

Language

Language is also an important factor when interviewing children, because complex language can mislead them. The vocabulary, particularly in a courtroom, can be problematic, as can the length and complexity of questions. Children may be asked to use skills that they have not yet acquired. Goodman and Schaaf (1997) investigated the effect of language in a study of five- to seven-year-old children. One group was asked the question: 'The pirate engaged in blowing bubbles during the course of the puppet show, is that not true?' A second group was asked the question more simply: 'The pirate blew bubbles, didn't he?' There were 10 per cent more errors when the first, more complicated, question was asked.

Link

The cognitive development of children in Chapter 1, and particularly the criticisms of Piaget's research, is relevant here. This research focuses on children having difficulty understanding the language used in, for example, conservation experiment.

Leading questions

Children are also more susceptible to leading questions if they feel intimidated by the interviewer. However, children can be trained to resist misleading questions by, for example:

- explaining to children that it is perfectly acceptable to admit lack of memory or knowledge of an incident
- encouraging children not to acquiesce to adults' suggestions simply to avoid their disapproval or to avoid embarrassment or rejection.

Use of the cognitive interview

A study was carried out by Holliday (2003) on the use of the cognitive interview with children. Children aged 9 to10 years were given a cognitive interview or a standard interview about a real-life event, followed by a written summary of the event containing inaccurate information. Those who had experienced the cognitive interview were significantly less likely to be influenced by the misleading information. It was hypothesised that the reconstruction of memory during the cognitive interview using retrieval cues led to a stronger accurate memory for future recall and less vulnerability to memory distortion.

Flashbulb memory – memory for shocking events

A flashbulb memory is so called because it is like a photographic reproduction of an event. A flashbulb memory leaves a detailed and vivid memory of a public or personal event such as a memory of the attack on the World Trade Centre that took place in the USA on 11 September 2001. Brown and Kulik (1977) argued that flashbulb memories are long lasting and accurate and often include other categories of information in addition to the incident itself, such as where you were, what you were doing and your emotional state at the time you received information of the event. They argued that the brain may process such events differently, i.e. there may be a special mechanism for 'printing' such events as a permanent memory. In addition to being accurate and long lasting, flashbulb memories also typically include:

- information about the people and place
- memory of emotions felt by self and others
- personal consequences of the event.

The notion that there is a special mechanism for the laying down of flashbulb memories is contentious. It may be, for example, that such memories are vivid because they have been rehearsed more frequently. There is evidence from Bohannon (1988) that flashbulb memories are forgotten in the same way as ordinary memories, as he found people's memories for the explosion of the space shuttle *Challenger* fell from 77 per cent at two weeks to 58 per cent after eight months. However, if the explosion on the space shuttle was not perceived as having any personal consequence (considered to be an integral part of the flashbulb memory) then this could account for the fading of the memory.

An explanation of flashbulb memories

According to Conway *et al.* (1994) certain conditions are necessary for a flashbulb memory to occur:

- prior knowledge
- personal importance
- emotional reaction
- rehearsal (an optional process).

Take it further

The emotional-integrative model (Finkenauer *et al.*, 1998) supported the explanation put forward by Conway *et al.* but added two requirements: 'novelty of the event' and 'attitude towards the central person(s)'.

Research study: Winningham *et al.* (2000)

Aim: To investigate the nature of flashbulb memories.

Method: Two groups of participants were questioned about their memory of the acquittal of O.J. Simpson. One group was questioned within five hours of the verdict (the 'immediate group'), whereas the 'delay group' were questioned a week after the acquittal verdict. Eight weeks later both groups were retested. The authors theorised that participants with consistent recollections at the two testing times must have stored a flashbulb memory.

Results: Of the 'delay group', 53 per cent had flashbulb memories, compared with only 23 per cent of the 'immediate group'.

Conclusion: An individual's memory for a dramatic event changes over the first few days due to forgetting and rehearsal.

Evaluation: This study was based on an actual dramatic event and thus was both ecologically valid and had the benefits of a well controlled experiment. The findings challenge the notion that flashbulb memories are formed immediately on exposure to events and led to further research.

Summary questions

11 Read the following text and then answer questions (a) to (e), referring to the text in your answer:

Umar is an 11-year-old boy; he was walking home from school one day when he noticed a man with a gun running out of a shop. The man stopped, looked at Umar and pointed the gun at him, before turning and running down the road. Umar was terrified; he went into the shop and found the shopkeeper lying on the floor with his hands tied behind his back. Umar telephoned the police and waited with the shopkeeper. Umar was taken to the local police station with his father.

a Describe how the investigating officer might conduct a cognitive interview with Umar.

b Outline how emotion/stress might influence the reliability of Umar's account of the incident.

c Outline how one other factor (not emotion/stress) might affect the reliability of Umar's testimony.

d Briefly discuss one important consideration when interviewing a child witness.

e Umar appears to have stored a flashbulb memory of the traumatic incident. Outline what is meant by a 'flashbulb' memory.

Evaluation of flashbulb memories

Talarico and Rubin (2003) carried out a study that also challenged the theory that flashbulb memories have a 'special mechanism'. They assessed students' memories for two things that had occurred on the previous day: (a) the 9/11 terrorist attack and (b) their memory for a recent personal event. The students were tested again 7, 42 or 224 days later. The results showed that both the flashbulb memory and the everyday memory remained strong over the 32-week period.

Finkenauer *et al.* (1998) concluded that, although a particularly efficient encoding takes place for flashbulb memories to be formed, there are no special memory mechanisms involved because all of the processes that they and Conway *et al.* (1994) outlined could be involved in the formation of any memories.

Key points:

- The reliability of eye-witness accounts is of both theoretical and practical importance: many lives can be affected as a consequence of inaccurate testimonies.
- A number of factors have been found to affect the accuracy of eye-witness testimonies, including the use of questions and post-event contamination; expectation; emotion/stress; and context.
- One way of improving eye-witness recall is to use the cognitive interview; this is now used in police forces across the UK. This type of interviewing technique has also proved effective with children.
- Research suggests that children might be particularly likely to give inaccurate eye-witness accounts owing to vulnerability to leading questions and false information.
- A flashbulb memory is a particularly vivid and long-lasting memory for memorable public or personal events.

The false memory debate

Learning objectives:

- explain the term 'repression'
- discuss and evaluate the evidence for the recovery of repressed memories
- discuss and evaluate the evidence for the existence of false memories
- outline the ethical and theoretical implications of the false memory debate.

Key terms

Repress: a memory is pushed below conscious level.

Conscious awareness: anything that we can bring to mind.

Recovered memory: 'the emergence of an apparent childhood recollection of which the individual has no previous knowledge' (Brandon *et al.*, 1998).

Repression: a defence mechanism whereby unpleasant memories, wishes or feelings are forced into the unconscious mind and are not available to consciousness (e.g. a young girl 'forgets' that she has had a termination).

Defence mechanism: an unconscious strategy that protects the ego from unpleasantness.

Link

A full description of the psychoanalytic approach and the nature and function of defence mechanisms, including repression, can be found in *AQA Psychology B AS*, Chapter 3.

The false memory debate concerns three issues:

- whether it is possible to **repress** a memory
- whether traumatic experiences can be repressed out of **conscious awareness** and sometime later be **recovered**
- whether a false event can be implanted such that a person really believes that it did happen.

Sigmund Freud used the term '**repression**' to describe a **defence mechanism** that, he believed, blocks emotionally painful events out of conscious awareness. This concept of repression lies at the centre of the false memory debate. Repression is a difficult concept to examine scientifically; this is largely because the material that is repressed is usually anxiety provoking, and it is not ethical to give participants anxiety-provoking incidents in order to examine the concept of repression.

The recovery of repressed memories

Investigations into the recovery of repressed memories explore the evidence for repression and the extent to which memories that have been repressed, and therefore have become inaccessible, can spontaneously emerge or be recovered.

Experimental studies

An early study by Levinger and Clark (1961) investigated the retention of associations to negative and neutral words. Poorer recall was found for the words associated with emotional cue words than for those associated with neutral cue words and the difficulty in recalling negative word associations may have been due to these being repressed. (For an evaluation of this study see p92.)

Naturalistic studies

Naturalistic studies of repression would typically involve known cases of child abuse, where the abuse may have been repressed but evidence that the abuse took place is well documented and any recovered memory can be compared with the actual records.

Research study: Williams (1994)

Aim: To investigate whether repression was evident in females with a known history of childhood abuse.

Method: One hundred and twenty-nine participants who had been sexually abused between the ages of 10 months and 12 years were interviewed 17 years later. Women were asked during a single interview whether they had been abused.

Results: Thirty-eight per cent denied that they had ever been abused.

Conclusion: The women failed to report the abuse because it had been repressed and was no longer accessible to them.

Evaluation: Repression is only one interpretation of why 38 per cent of the women in this study did not report the abuse. They may have been too embarrassed to talk about it, or felt that it was in the past and they wanted to 'move on' from it.

Key terms

Emotional inhibition: the psychological restraint experienced when attempting to process emotional words.

Arousal: a readiness for action, indicated by level of activity in the brain and nervous system.

Link

A full description of theories of memory can be found in *AQA Psychology B AS*, Chapter 7, Remembering and forgetting.

Evaluation of the concept of repression

- Freud's theories emerged from his case studies, and the concept of repression has not been scientifically substantiated. In fact, Holmes (1990), in his review of 60 years of experimental tests of repression, came to the conclusion that there was no evidence from controlled laboratory studies to support repression.
- The Levinger and Clark study does provide experimental support for Freud's theory that we repress uncomfortable memories. However, the results can be interpreted in a number of ways:
  - The authors themselves did not propose a Freudian explanation for the results but suggested that the findings were due to **emotional inhibition**.
  - An alternative explanation is that the difficulty in recalling the negatively associated words is due to the differing levels of **arousal** caused by emotional and neutral associations. Studies have shown that higher levels of arousal inhibit immediate recall but facilitate longer-term recall (Eysenck, 1982).
- It is difficult to test the concept of repression empirically; however, just because there is limited scientific evidence for repression, it does not mean that repression does not occur.
- A scientifically controlled experiment to investigate repression would be extremely unethical and probably not possible. This is because the fear and threat accompanying a real experience cannot be simulated in laboratory studies.
- Controlled experiments designed to investigate repression have found only limited support for the concept. On the other hand, there is a lot of evidence that people who have suffered traumatic experiences can clearly remember events; no repression seems to have occurred. In one study, Malmquist (1986) investigated 16 children who had witnessed the murder of one of their parents. They all had flashbacks and recurring nightmares about their experiences but there was no evidence of forgetting or repressing the memory.

Studying false memories

One way to systematically study false memory is to employ the procedures first used by Deese (1959), whereby lists of words, all associated with a single non-presented word, are given to participants. For example, participants might be presented with 'cake, pie, gateaux, sponge', followed by a recognition test which included 'dessert'. The non-presented word 'dessert' is usually confidently chosen. However, findings from such studies are limited in so far as they are not personal memories.

Studies have been carried out that show that false autobiographical memories can be implanted.

Research study: Loftus, Feldman and Dashiell (1995)

Aim: To see if people can remember a childhood event as one they actually experienced, even if they did not.

Method: Twenty-four participants aged 18 to 53 were asked to read four short paragraphs, each describing a different childhood event. Three were actual events that had happened to them (as verified with their parents) and a fourth event definitely did not happen but was plausible. For example, 'as a five-year-old you got lost in the supermarket'. Participants were asked to write any additional details about the event that they could remember; they were also asked to write details on two further occasions at weekly intervals.

Results: Of the 24 participants, six reported remembering the false event and provided additional details of the event.

Conclusion: After simply receiving a brief suggestion, people can provide a description in some detail of personal experience of an event that did not happen, but which they clearly believe did.

Evaluation: Further studies have indicated that it is much easier to implant a plausible event such as being lost in a supermarket, than an implausible event.

Evaluation of false memory research

- The research by Loftus *et al.* (1995) has shown how it is possible to implant a false memory, and therefore one could argue that memories of childhood sexual abuse could also be false, perhaps unwittingly implanted during therapy.
- Critics of studies of the type done by Loftus (see above) argue that being lost in a supermarket is such a likely event that results from studies in which the 'memory' of such an event is implanted do not really demonstrate that one could implant a more unlikely false memory, for example of childhood abuse.
- It would be unethical to attempt to implant a false memory of abuse or any other traumatic incident for research purposes; however, an intriguing study was carried out by Pezdek *et al.* (1997) to investigate if people were more likely to accept a suggestion of a childhood religious experience if it was linked to their own religion rather than to an alternative religion. It was found to be significantly easier to implant a plausible event than to implant an implausible one.
- Although the memories are not of a traumatic nature, which would be the case with, for example, childhood sexual abuse, the research does appear to suggest that it is possible to implant a false memory. If a person claims to have recovered a long-lost memory, it might be necessary to seek further corroborative evidence because the memory might be true: on the other hand, it might be false. The debate about whether recovered memories are genuine or false is ongoing.

Theoretical and ethical implications of the false memory debate

When presented with evidence based on a 'recovered' memory in a court of law, the reliability of that memory must be assessed. There have been a number of cases where a 'recovered' memory has led to a conviction, but the conviction has later been found to be unreliable and the memory 'false'. Such cases can have serious implications for the people involved, particularly if a case is concerned with traumatic events such as murder or childhood sexual abuse.

In 1990, in the USA, George Franklin was convicted of the murder of a child (Susan) who was the friend of his own daughter, Eileen, on the basis of his daughter's 'recovered' memory. The memory of her father murdering her best friend emerged 20 years later, when Eileen had her own children. However, on appeal it was shown how the memory of witnessing the murder may have come from the newspaper articles which depicted the crime scene and other details of the crime. Eileen's 'recovered' memory showed a remarkable resemblance to this published information. The conviction was considered unsafe and was overturned on appeal in 1995.

Link

Note that studies of eye-witness reliability have shown how fallible memory can be and how easily information can be inserted into an existing memory (Loftus and Palmer, 1974). For information on factors affecting the reliability of eye-witness accounts, see p80.

Over the last two decades, there has been a steep rise in reports of memories of childhood sexual abuse from adults, who claim that these memories were previously 'unavailable'. Such a claim, often made years later, can cause immense upset not only to the 'victim' but also to family and friends, often leading to complete breakdown of family relationships. The 'repressed' memories sometimes emerge during therapy. The question is, could these memories be false? False memories might be constructed through the process of suggestion (possibly through hypnosis) during therapeutic sessions. Empirical evidence for the creation of false memories in therapy-simulated situations has been presented.

Research study: Mazzoni *et al.* (1999)

Aim: To see if people's beliefs and memories could be changed through dream interpretation.

Method: A life events inventory (LEI) was completed by a group of participants; and a sample was selected on the basis that they had not reported any significant childhood event (e.g. being bullied). Two weeks later, an experimental group completed a dream survey and was then given a 30-minute analysis session during which it was suggested to them that they had either been lost in a crowd or bullied before the age of three. A control group had a non-suggestive dream session. Two weeks later, another LEI was completed.

Results: Half of the experimental group now reported confidently that the critical (false) life event had occurred. The controls reported no changes in their LEI.

Conclusion: It is possible to manipulate memory through dream interpretation in such a way that a false memory can be implanted and confidently be believed to have happened.

Evaluation: Caution is required when interpreting findings from such research. Just because false memories can be implanted during such studies, it does not mean that all recovered memories must be false.

There is ample evidence that false memories can be implanted, and there is growing evidence that, during therapy, suggestions may have been made to some patients that they are victims of childhood sexual abuse. Both in this country and in the USA, societies have been set up to help families who have been wrongly accused of such abuse. The British False Memory Society (BFMS) was established in 1993 and campaigns for falsely accused parents. Since 1993, nearly 1,000 families in Britain have been falsely accused of sexual abuse following the 'recovered' memories of their adult children.

The Brandon Report (Brandon *et al.*, 1998) was first published in the *Journal of British Psychiatry* and was the outcome of a consideration of the issues surrounding recovered memories of childhood sexual abuse. Professor Brandon criticised some of the techniques used by therapists, such as hypnosis and 'truth' drugs, and warned that they are 'powerful and dangerous methods of persuasion'. Points made in the Report include the following:

- **Recovered memory syndrome**, in which childhood abuse is remembered for the first time during psychiatric treatment, is a myth.
- Therapists sometimes use 'questionable' psychological techniques which enable false memories to be implanted and 'recovered' in their clients.
- It is not possible to 'block out' of the mind traumatic events such as sexual abuse, which are then 'recovered' later.
- Memory is 'fallible' and 'open to suggestion'.

Key terms

Recovered memory syndrome: a condition in which an individual becomes obsessed with the memory of a traumatic experience that is false but which the person strongly believes to be true; the condition begins to affect their everyday life.

The Brandon Report has been controversial and many psychiatrists believe that a few recovered memories may be false but many are valid; the Brandon Report may have made it harder for victims of childhood sexual abuse to be heard.

Guidelines for psychologists were set up following the Brandon review (Frankland and Cohen, 1999); the essential features are as follows:

- Child sexual abuse does exist and therapists can uncover memories of events that are real.
- Practitioners should be alerted to the possibility that some memories can be 'literally/historically true or false, or may be partly true, or may derive from fantasy or dream material'.
- Psychologists should avoid suggestion and guard against actively seeking out memories of abuse.

Key points:

- Repression is the blocking from conscious awareness of emotionally painful events.
- There is evidence from both experimental and naturalistic studies that memories can be repressed.
- Evidence suggests that false memories can be implanted.
- There is a debate concerning the extent to which recovered memories might be false.

Summary questions

12 Explain why the concept of 'repression' is important to the false memory debate.

13 Outline and evaluate one study into repression.

14 Outline two ethical implications of the false memory debate.

Further reading

Eysenck, M.W. and Keane, M.T. (2005) *Cognitive Psychology*, 5th edition. Hove and New York: Psychology Press.

Gross, R. (2005) *Psychology: The Science of Mind and Behaviour*, 5th edition. London: Hodder Arnold.

The website for the British False Memory Society provides details of the Brandon Report (1998) and the Society's own work in assisting accused families: www.bfms.org.uk

See the following weblink for the recent update to PACE Code D: http://police.homeoffice.gov.uk/

End-of-chapter activity 1

Find some pictures of famous faces (about eight) – perhaps from the internet or from magazines. On half of the faces, transpose the eyes and mouth so that the faces are scrambled; the remaining four faces are left 'normal'. Use a stopwatch to time how long it takes people to recognise and name the scrambled and normal faces. If the face is not identified after 30 seconds, move to the next one and note down 30 seconds. You should find that the scrambled faces take longer on average to recognise than the normal faces, thus supporting a holistic theory of face recognition. Prior to carrying out the study, think about the design of your study, how you will control any confounding variables and identify the independent and dependent variables. Prepare the necessary materials and a data collection sheet, and analyse your data. Think carefully about the ethical implications of your study.

End-of-chapter activity 2

First, show people a clip from a film. This could be a video of an incident that you have made yourself (e.g. a bag snatch) or a snippet from a film or TV programme. Following exposure to the film, participants should be given a series of questions. Half the participants should receive questions that contain post-event contamination (e.g. a question with the word 'the' instead of 'a'). The other half of the participants should receive the same questions but without the misleading information. Assess the answers to see if the eye-witness accounts have been affected by the misleading questions. Prior to carrying out the study, think about the design of your study, how you will control any confounding variables and identify the independent and dependent variables. Prepare the necessary materials and a data collection sheet, and analyse your data. Think carefully about the ethical implications of your study.

Schizophrenia and mood disorders

Introduction

Schizophrenia and mood disorders are two quite different types of disorders in the field of **abnormal psychology**. The word 'abnormal' literally means 'away from the normal', and thus both schizophrenia and depression are characterised by thoughts and behaviours that are not considered to be 'the norm' in a given society at a particular time. As there is no agreement as to what constitutes 'normality', any discussion of 'abnormality' is fraught with difficulty, but clinicians have had to find workable definitions in order to look for explanations and treatments for disorders.

Schizophrenia is a very serious illness but surprisingly common; many of you will be familiar with some of the symptoms associated with this condition, possibly through personal experience of someone you know, or from the media. It is a disorder of thinking whereby deterioration is evident in recognising reality, making appropriate emotional responses and in communicating. Common symptoms include hallucinations and delusions. Schizophrenia becomes particularly serious when there are adverse social and psychological consequences such as unemployment and a loss of independent living, often resulting in a significant burden to the family of people with schizophrenia. Unfortunately, the general public often misunderstands this illness and, owing partly to selective reporting by the media, a stereotype has developed that people with schizophrenia are disproportionately violent and aggressive. In reality, there is only a slightly increased risk of aggressive behaviour from people with schizophrenia compared with normal individuals, and then it is usually only when under the influence of illicit substances. Psychologists are interested in the causes of, and treatments for, schizophrenia, and these are considered in this chapter.

Mood disorders cover three distinguishable types of depression: unipolar (depressed mood); bipolar (depressed mood with manic episodes); and seasonal affective disorder (recurrent depressive episodes linked to the season of the year). Mood disorders are highly prevalent in the West and the risk of being diagnosed with such a disorder is rising. There is now a more than 1 in 20 lifetime chance of being diagnosed with some form of mood disorder. Sufferers report a variety of symptoms ranging from physical and behavioural to affective and cognitive, and individuals vary in the degree to which they are affected in each of these domains. The word 'depression' is often used in general conversation (e.g. 'the weather is depressing today'), but the type of depression referred to is not the same as clinical depression, which is a very serious illness and can be life threatening. Psychologists are interested in the causes of, and treatments for, depression, and these are considered in this chapter.

Specification content	Topic content	Page number
Schizophrenia		
Classification of schizophrenia, including subtypes; symptoms and diagnosis	Symptoms of schizophrenia Subtypes of schizophrenia	**99** **99**
Explanations, including biological and cognitive; sociocultural explanations, labelling and family dysfunction	Explanations of schizophrenia	**101**
Treatments of schizophrenia, including antipsychotic drugs, behavioural treatments and psychotherapy, and evaluation of these treatments	Treatments for schizophrenia	**111**
Mood disorders		
Unipolar and bipolar depression	Symptoms and diagnosis of unipolar depression Symptoms and diagnosis of bipolar depression	**116** **116**
Seasonal affective disorder (SAD)	Seasonal affective disorder	**128**
Symptoms and diagnosis of mood disorders	Symptoms and diagnosis of mood disorders	**116**
Explanations, including biological, cognitive, behavioural and psychodynamic	Explanations of mood disorders	**118**
Treatments of mood disorders, including biological and cognitive, and evaluation of these treatments	Biological treatments for mood disorders	**124**

5 Schizophrenia and mood disorders

Classification of schizophrenia (including subtypes)

Learning objectives:

- describe the main symptoms associated with schizophrenia
- understand the subtypes associated with schizophrenia
- explain the diagnostic criteria for schizophrenia.

Key terms

Psyche: a term used commonly to refer to the mind.

Hint

With reference to the use of the term 'split', it is a common misconception that schizophrenia means split or multiple personalities; however, multiple personality is a separate disorder, now called 'dissociative identity disorder', and is not associated with schizophrenia.

Symptoms of schizophrenia

Bleuler (1911) first used the term 'schizophrenia' (literally 'split mind') to describe a general class of disorders that are characterised by a number of similar symptoms associated with a split in the **psyche**:

- disorganised thought processes
- a split between the intellect and emotion
- a split between the intellect and external reality.

The main symptoms of schizophrenia

- **Auditory hallucinations** The person 'hears' noises, usually voices in the person's mind, talking to each other or directly to the person.
- **Delusions** These are false beliefs and can take many forms: for example, delusions of grandeur (such as thinking you are God); delusions of persecution (a belief that others are trying to harm you).
- **Disordered thinking** The person feels that their thoughts have been inserted or withdrawn from their mind.
- **Control** The person experiences a lack of self-control, as though they are under the control of an alien power.
- **Emotional and volitional changes** Emotions are 'flat' and the person has little initiative and no energy.
- Wing (1992) has argued for a distinction between **primary impairments**, which are intrinsic to the disorder, and **secondary impairments**, which result from the primary impairments.

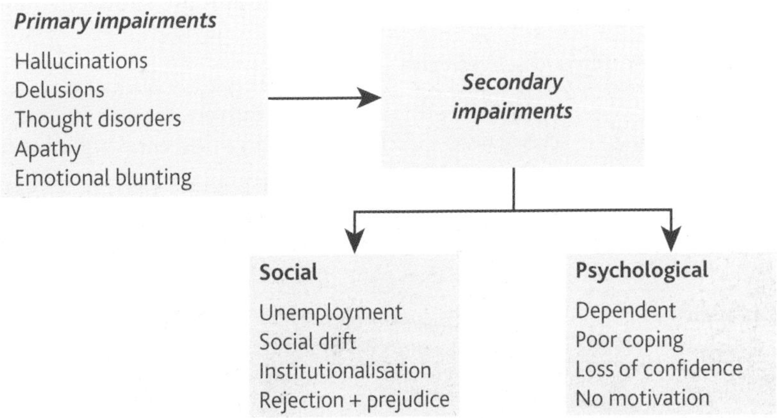

Primary impairments
Hallucinations
Delusions
Thought disorders
Apathy
Emotional blunting

→ ***Secondary impairments***

Social
Unemployment
Social drift
Institutionalisation
Rejection + prejudice

Psychological
Dependent
Poor coping
Loss of confidence
No motivation

Fig. 1 *Primary and secondary impairments in schizophrenia*

Subtypes of schizophrenia

Two general patterns are discernible in schizophrenic symptoms; these are known as 'positive-syndrome schizophrenia' and 'negative-syndrome schizophrenia' (Andreasen *et al.*, 1995). The positive symptoms are

AQA Examiner's tip

There are a number of ways in which the term 'subtypes' can be interpreted with respect to schizophrenia, and a reference to Type I and Type II, and/or the types that appear in the DSM (e.g. paranoid, catatonic) are acceptable in an examination answer.

those that are additional to normal behaviour or experience, such as hallucinations and delusions. With negative-syndrome schizophrenia there is a deficit in normal behaviour patterns, such as lack of communication and emotional expression. Most patients exhibit both positive and negative symptoms, but the prognosis is much poorer where there are more negative symptoms evident.

Related to the positive–negative distinction is the differentiation between Type I and Type II schizophrenia. Type I refers to the positive sub-syndrome and Type II to the negative sub-syndrome. The categorisation by 'type' incorporates a biological element in addition to the symptoms.

Table 1 *Positive and negative symptoms of schizophrenia and Types I and II*

Type I Positive symptoms	Type II Negative symptoms
Responsive to drug treatment	Less responsive to drugs
Limbic system abnormalities	Abnormalities in the frontal lobes and enlarged ventricles

- There is no universal agreement about the simple positive–negative distinction, and some researchers point to a third cluster of symptoms unrelated to the other two, known as 'disorganised schizophrenia' and largely associated with chaotic speech and behaviour.
- The distinction between positive and negative symptoms is not a dichotomy but can be perceived as a continuum with positive and negative at opposite ends.
- The term 'schizophrenia' may be convenient but is also misleading. It is likely that there are several different types of severe mental disorder that we currently call 'schizophrenia' with at least one aspect in common – a loss of contact with reality.

Key terms

DSM-IVR: the *Diagnostic and Statistical Manual*, 4th edition Revised; this is widely used for the diagnosis of abnormalities.

Alogia: speech that is dramatically reduced in content.

Diagnosing schizophrenia

The diagnosis of schizophrenia by health professionals is in response to the symptoms presented. The specific diagnostic criteria currently set out in the **DSM-IVR** are shown in Table 2:

Table 2 *Diagnostic criteria for schizophrenia*

A Characteristic symptoms	Two (or more) of the following, each present for a one-month period: delusions; hallucinations; disorganised speech; grossly disorganised or catatonic behaviour; negative symptoms, e.g. affective flattening, **alogia**.
B Social/occupational dysfunction	For a significant portion of the time since the onset of the disturbance, one or more major areas of functioning such as work, interpersonal relations, or self-care are markedly below the level achieved prior to the onset.
C Duration	Continuous signs of the disturbance persist for at least six months. This six-month period must include at least one month of symptoms (or less if successfully treated) that meet Criterion A.

Types of schizophrenia that appear in the DSM

Paranoid There is a preoccupation with one or more delusions or frequent auditory hallucinations. None of the following is prominent: disorganised speech, disorganised or catatonic behaviour, or flat or inappropriate affect.

Catatonic At least two of the following are present: immobility (including waxy flexibility) or stupor; excessive motor activity; extreme negativism or mutism; posturing; stereotyped movements, prominent mannerisms/ grimacing; **echolalia** or **echopraxia**.

Disorganised All of the following are prominent: disorganised speech; disorganised behaviour; flat affect.

Undifferentiated: Criterion A symptoms are present, but the criteria are not met for the paranoid, disorganised, or catatonic type.

Residual There is absence of prominent delusions, hallucinations, disorganised speech, catatonic behaviour. There are negative symptoms, or two or more symptoms listed in Criterion A in an attenuated form.

Key points:

- The main symptoms of schizophrenia include hallucinations, delusions, thought disorders and emotional flattening.
- The primary impairments above can lead to secondary impairments, both social and psychological.
- Subtypes of schizophrenia include Type I, linked to the positive symptoms, and Type II linked to the negative symptoms.
- Diagnostic criteria for schizophrenia are outlined in the DSM-IVR and include characteristic symptoms, social dysfunction and duration of the disturbance. Diagnosis leads to classification as a particular type of schizophrenia, e.g. paranoid.

Key terms

Echolalia: repetition of a word or phrase.

Echopraxia: the repeating of gestures made by others.

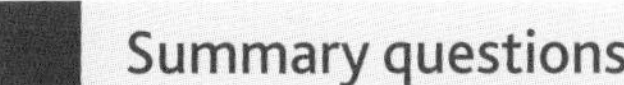

Summary questions

1. Outline three symptoms associated with schizophrenia.
2. Distinguish between two subtypes of schizophrenia.

Explanations of schizophrenia

Learning objectives:

- describe and evaluate biological explanations for schizophrenia
- describe and evaluate cognitive explanations for schizophrenia
- describe and evaluate socio-cultural explanations for schizophrenia.

Biological explanations of schizophrenia

The biological approach is also known as the 'medical model'. This approach sees mental disorders as having physical causes, for example genetics or an abnormality of the brain, and favours the use of biological treatments, such as the use of drugs.

A number of biological explanations for schizophrenia have emerged including genetic, neurochemical and neuroanatomical explanations.

The genetic explanation of schizophrenia

Schizophrenia tends to run in families, and studies have shown that the closer the genetic relatedness the higher is the likely concordance for schizophrenia: i.e. if one family member has schizophrenia, there is an increased risk for other family members. The risk of schizophrenia in the general population is about 1 per cent.

A meta-analysis of early familial studies by Gottesman and Shields (1982) is presented below.

AQA Examiner's tip

There are no named biological explanations on the specification so you could choose to discuss any appropriate theories in an answer. The explanations outlined here are the key biological theories, and you would be advised to learn at least two.

Link

For further information about biopsychology, see Chapter 2, Biopsychology, in *AQA Psychology B AS*; see also Chapter 9, Approaches in psychology, in this book.

Link

If you are unsure what a meta-analysis is, turn back to Chapter 1, Social development, p9, for a definition.

Key terms

Monozygotic (MZ) twins: form when a single egg is fertilised by a single spermatozoon and then splits resulting in two separate same-sex individuals sharing identical genes, sometimes called 'identical' twins.

Dizygotic (DZ) twins: form when two separate eggs are fertilised by two spermatozoa, resulting in twins who share about half their genes (like siblings); also called 'fraternal' or 'non-identical' twins, DZ twins can be of different sexes.

Concordance rate: a numerical value that expresses the degree to which similar traits are shared. When investigating the nature–nurture debate using twins, concordance rates provide an idea of the genetic influence on behaviour by giving the proportion of a random sample of pairs that share a characteristic.

Genotype: the set of genes carried by an individual.

Schizoid: the term for a disorder that resembles schizophrenia but does not have the psychotic symptoms such as 'loss of reality'.

Table 3 *Lifetime risk of schizophrenia in the relatives of people with schizophrenia*

Relative	Percentage of lifetime expectancy
Parent	5.6
Siblings	10.1
Siblings with one parent with schizophrenia	12.9
Child with two parents with schizophrenia	46.3
Grandchildren	3.7

(Adapted from ***Gottesman and Shields****, 1982)*

Family studies have confirmed that schizophrenia does tend to cluster in families. However, the extent to which this is due to genetic or environmental influences is not clear. Twin and adoption studies have attempted to unravel the contribution of nature and nurture in the explanation of schizophrenia.

Twin studies

Monozygotic (MZ) twins have 100 per cent of genes in common, whereas **dizygotic (DZ) twins** have only 50 per cent in common. If schizophrenia is a genetic disorder, one would therefore predict that, where one twin has been diagnosed with schizophrenia, the **concordance rate** for MZ twins should be greater than for DZ twins. Studies have shown this to be the case (see Table 4).

Table 4 *Results from meta-analysis of studies of schizophrenia in MZ and DZ twins*

	Monozygotic concordance (%)	Dizygotic concordance (%)
Average of the concordance rates from five studies (1969–1976)	46	14

(From ***Gottesman and Shields****, 1982)*

Adoption studies

Adoption studies are unique in their ability to separate the environment from genes. Typically, the studies are of children adopted within weeks of birth, from mothers with schizophrenia. Such children have no common genes with the adoptive family that rears them (where no one has schizophrenia), and thus, conveniently, genes and environment are separated. An early adoption study by Heston (1966) of 47 mothers with schizophrenia, whose children were adopted within days by psychiatrically well mothers, found the incidence of schizophrenia in the children to be 16 per cent (well above the 1 per cent chance level).

Evaluation of the genetic explanation

- The 46 per cent concordance rate found for MZ twins suggests a major contribution of **genotype**.
- Concordance for MZ twins is about three times that of DZ twins; nevertheless, although high, there is still a discordance rate of about 40 per cent. However, studies have shown that about half of the discordant group will go on to develop a **schizoid** or similar disorder, and thus, if a broader definition for 'schizophrenia' is adopted, the MZ concordance rate is even higher.
- Owing to the rare incidence of both twins and schizophrenia in the general population, twin studies have, of necessity, contained small samples.

Schizophrenia

- Evidence from normal twin pairs (Lytton, 1977) suggests that MZ twins are reared in a more similar environment than DZ twins, and therefore nurture might partly explain the higher concordance rate found for MZ twins.
- Findings from adoption studies suggest that inheritance does play a part in schizophrenia and that there may be a genetic predisposition to the disorder.

Neurochemical explanations of schizophrenia

Investigation of **neurotransmitters** has been carried out in three ways:

- by looking for evidence of **metabolites** in urine and blood
- through the examination of post-mortem brain tissue
- more recently, through the use of neuroimaging techniques, e.g. positron emission tomography (**PET scan**).

The activity of neurotransmitters, for example dopamine and the enzyme responsible for its metabolism (monoamine oxidase; abbreviation MAO), has been investigated in the search for a neurochemical explanation for schizophrenia.

Dopamine hypothesis

At first it was thought that excessive dopaminergic activity in the brain was the cause of schizophrenic symptoms. Evidence for this theory came from a number of areas:

- When taken by healthy individuals, drugs that increase dopaminergic activity in the brain, such as amphetamines, result in psychotic symptoms like those experienced by people with schizophrenia (e.g. hallucinations).
- Such drugs also exacerbate psychotic symptoms in people with schizophrenia.
- Neuroleptic drugs that block the dopaminergic neurons reduce psychotic symptoms.

However, this early theory that schizophrenia was linked to an overactive dopaminergic circuit in the brain was difficult to support because post-mortem studies did not show consistent evidence for an increased dopamine level in the brains of people with schizophrenia. This led to the theory that the cause was not an increase in dopamine per se: rather, it was the heightened sensitivity of the receptors for dopamine in the brain that led to an abundance of the chemical and to schizophrenic symptoms. Evidence for this comes from a number of areas:

- Post-mortem studies have shown that there are many more D2 (dopamine) receptors in the brains of people with schizophrenia than there are in normal brains.
- Studies using PET scans have reported a substantial increase in D2 receptors in patients with schizophrenia (Pearlson *et al.*, 1993).
- Seeman *et al.* (1993), again using PET, found six times the density of D4 receptors in the brains of people with schizophrenia (D4 is a receptor subtype very similar to D2).

Evaluation of neurochemical explanations

- It is not clear whether the increase in D2 receptors found in the brains of people with schizophrenia at post-mortem is the cause of the pathology or an effect of the neuroleptic drugs taken, as it is known that such drugs are attracted to this particular receptor.

Link

Schizophrenia is an excellent topic to discuss with respect to the nature–nurture debate; see Chapter 10, Debates in psychology.

Key terms

Neurotransmitter: a 'chemical messenger' that enables neurons to communicate with different parts of the brain; there are many types.

Metabolites: substances produced through metabolism. Metabolism refers to the biological processes occurring in an organism that result in growth and energy production.

PET scan: a non-invasive technique of brain imaging that monitors cerebral blood flow in the brain.

Link

For more information on PET and MRI scans, see *AQA Psychology B AS*, Chapter 2, Biopsychology.

- The neuroimaging studies by Pearlson *et al.* (1993) were carried out on patients who had not been exposed to neuroleptic drugs, thus ruling out the cause and effect problem found with post-mortem studies.
- Although it is widely accepted that the major antipsychotic drugs block dopamine receptors, to infer from this that dopamine hyperactivity is the major cause of schizophrenia is to oversimplify. It is now clear that the neurotransmitter systems interact and that the mapping of these cortical pathways is only just being explored.

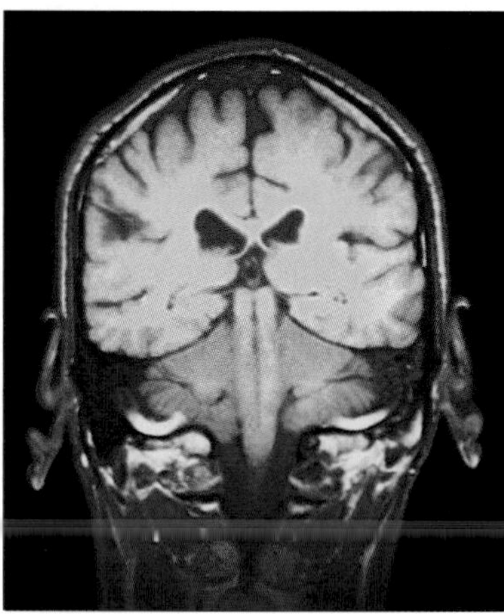

Fig. 2 *The human brain as seen through an MRI scanner*

Link

For more information on the structure and function of the brain and methods of investigation, see *AQA Psychology B AS*, Chapter 2, Biopsychology.

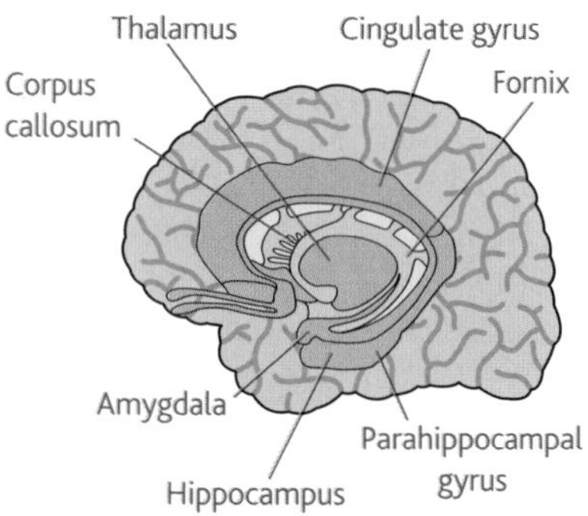

Fig. 3 *The limbic system of the human brain*

Neuroanatomical explanations of schizophrenia

The search for abnormalities in the brain structures of people with schizophrenia has a long history. Typically, the brains of those with schizophrenia are compared with the brains of controls, on various measures such as size of anatomical structure, hemisphere differences and cell counts. Initially, any comparison could only be carried out at post-mortem, even though there are problems of establishing cause and effect with this method. For example, the neuroleptic drugs used to treat schizophrenia may have caused any abnormality found, and this would confound the results. New scanning techniques, for example magnetic resonance imaging (MRI), allow living brain images to be investigated and consistent changes in particular brain areas have been identified.

Structure of the schizophrenic brain

The **limbic system** is a subcortical structure that includes the hippocampus and amygdala. Significant cell loss has been found in structures of the limbic system at post-mortem of patients with schizophrenia, and these findings have been confirmed with more recent imaging studies (Jernigan *et al.*, 1991). There is also evidence of unusual cell connections in the hippocampus.

The **corpus callosum** is a large bundle of fibres and connects the two hemispheres of the brain. Studies have shown that the gender differences in the thickening of these fibres in normal individuals are reversed in people with schizophrenia (Nasrallah *et al.*, 1986).

Abnormal early brain development in the third trimester of pregnancy, when the last stage of the development of the cerebral cortex occurs, is thought to be associated with schizophrenia. It is during this prenatal stage that a disorder in the brain might occur, particularly with the development of neuronal dendrites and organisation of synapses in the cortex. The two hemispheres of the normal brain are asymmetrical, particularly in the tempero-parietal region of the cortex. Both post-mortem and imaging studies have shown that this asymmetry is much less evident in patients with schizophrenia.

Brain imaging studies have found significant differences in both structure and function of the schizophrenic brain.

Studies have shown that people with schizophrenia have reduced brain tissue and enlarged ventricles. A meta-analysis by Raz and Raz (1990) of studies comparing ventricular volume in people with schizophrenia and controls reported a significant increase in size in over half the samples and an overall effect size of 0.6. This is a significant effect and may be linked to major functional abnormalities.

Research study: Suddath *et al.* (1990)

Aim: To investigate discordant twin pairs for structural abnormalities that might account for the incidence of schizophrenia in one of each pair.

Method: Fifteen discordant monozygotic twin pairs, only one of which was diagnosed with schizophrenia, were given MRI scans to determine any differences in brain structures between the twins in each discordant pair.

Results: The co-twin with schizophrenia had a smaller bilateral hippocampus than the twin without schizophrenia in 14 of the 15 pairs, and the co-twin with schizophrenia had larger ventricles (i.e. less brain tissue).

Conclusion: When genotype is controlled for, there is significantly diminished brain volume in the twin with schizophrenia.

Evaluation: It is difficult to establish whether the smaller hippocampus found in the schizophrenic twins is a cause or effect of the schizophrenia.

Functional studies of the schizophrenic brain

Imaging techniques can detect cerebral blood flow (CBF) in parts of the cortex. At rest, people with schizophrenia show evidence of underactivity in the tempero-frontal areas of the cortex compared with controls without schizophrenia. This has become known as 'hypofrontality' and is particularly evident in chronic patients (Liddle, 1996).

Evaluation of neuroanatomical explanations

- Attempts to link the structural changes to particular symptoms have not yet shown consistent findings. For example, Lewis (1990) considered 18 studies and found no significant link between enlarged ventricles and negative symptoms associated with schizophrenia.
- A variety of brain mechanisms seem to be implicated in schizophrenia but, as yet, none is sufficiently understood for researchers to say that it provides a causal link. It might be that changes in structure are caused by the schizophrenia rather than the other way around!
- It is likely that a number of environmental risk factors contribute to the onset of schizophrenia, and it is perhaps more realistic to propose that biological factors contribute towards an individual's liability to develop schizophrenia.

Cognitive explanations of schizophrenia

The cognitive approach is concerned with internal mental processes (known as mediating processes). It is assumed that these mediating processes, the way we think, interpret and perceive ourselves and our environment, can be faulty or biased.

This approach attempts to explain specific symptoms of schizophrenia, in particular the positive symptoms such as hallucinations and delusions.

Hallucinations

Auditory hallucinations are very common in people diagnosed with schizophrenia, with up to 73 per cent reporting experiencing them

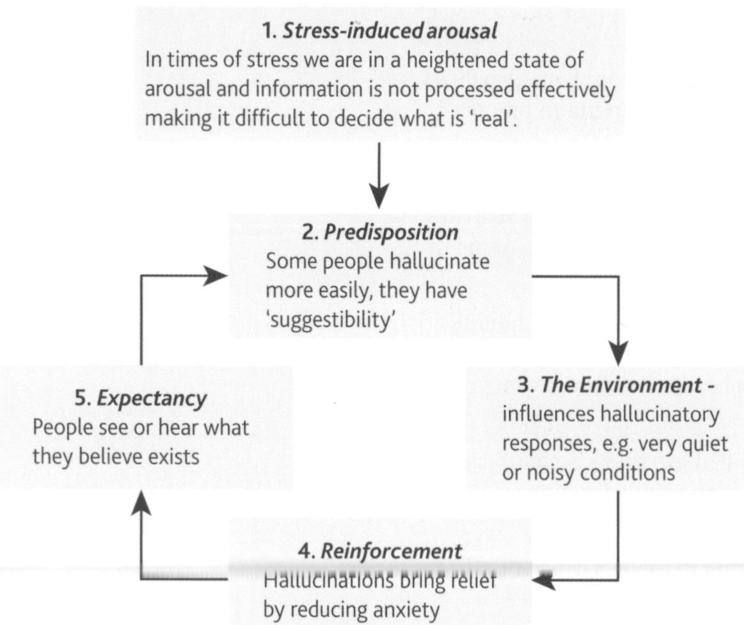

Fig. 4 *The five-factor theory* (**Slade and Bentall**, *1988*)

(WHO, 1973). Bentall (1990) assumes that 'hallucinations occur when people mistake their own internal, mental or private events for external, publicly observable events', i.e. the imaginary is mistaken for the real world.

The five-factor model

Slade and Bentall (1988) have proposed a five-factor theory which, they claim, explains the onset of such schizophrenia-type symptoms as those described by Bentall (1990).

Evaluation of the five-factor model

- According to the five-factor model, sensory deprivation or noise stimulation are conditions associated with hallucinations and this explains why sensory loss in older people makes them more likely to experience hallucinations.
- The five-factor model suggests that hallucinations may be strengthened by reinforcement because the hallucinations bring relief from the anxiety suffered by the individual. However, this is inconsistent with more recent findings that show an increase in anxiety following hallucinations (Close and Garety, 1998).
- According to the five-factor model, people only hallucinate what they already believe to exist; this is supported by cross-cultural studies. In Puerto Rico, for example, individuals who experience hallucinations are visited by spirits, which is considered 'normal'; such individuals are not regarded as mentally ill as may be the case in Western culture (Warner, 1994).

Delusions

Delusions are difficult to define because it is not always possible to differentiate between delusions and other beliefs (e.g. many people believe that God exists). It is probably more appropriate to perceive delusions on a continuum with normality, and the individual's point on that continuum depends on 'the degree of conviction in the belief, and the extent of preoccupation with that belief' (Strauss, 1969). Many of us suffer paranoia occasionally but that does not make us abnormal.

Cognitive theories of delusions

Cognitive theories of delusions are of two types:

- **Delusions are the result of abnormal cognitions in reasoning, attention, memory etc.** Bentall *et al.* (1991) proposed that paranoid and persecutory delusions are a psychological defence against depression and low self-esteem. These defences are maintained by both attention/memory biases and a bias in attributional style; in particular an external bias whereby negative outcomes are attributed to external causes. For example, following a negative event (e.g. losing a job), Bentall argues, we attempt to explain discrepancies between our actual self and ideal self (who we would like to be) in order to maintain our self-esteem. For example, to avoid feeling negative and becoming depressed, a person who has been 'fired' may respond with 'they're just out to get me'.

- **Delusions are the product of abnormal perceptions.** This theory proposes that delusions are an adaptive and rational response to abnormal internal events such as hallucinations. Maher (1974) proposed a model to explain this account:

Maher's Anomalous Experience Model

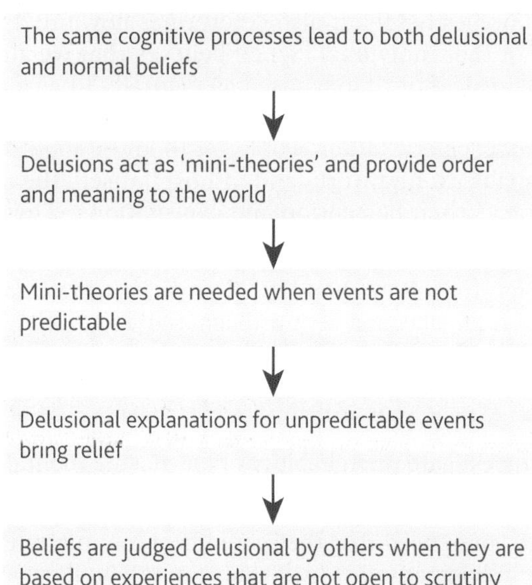

The same cognitive processes lead to both delusional and normal beliefs
Delusions act as 'mini-theories' and provide order and meaning to the world
Mini-theories are needed when events are not predictable
Delusional explanations for unpredictable events bring relief
Beliefs are judged delusional by others when they are based on experiences that are not open to scrutiny

Fig. 5 *The anomalous experience model (**Maher**, 1974)*

Evaluation of cognitive theories

- Studies have shown that delusions occur in a wide range of disorders where no prior history of cognitive impairment is evident (Manschreck, 1979). In addition, when normal individuals undergo abnormal experiences, delusions can occur (Zimbardo *et al.*, 1981). These findings support the idea of a continuum of delusions.
- Maher's model has provided a successful therapeutic model for delusions.
- Cognitive theories point to the importance of attributional and reasoning biases that may contribute to the maintenance of delusions in schizophrenia. However, on their own, these theories are inadequate in explaining the onset of such a complex disorder.

Link

See p114 for information about cognitive therapy for schizophrenia.

Sociocultural explanations of schizophrenia

The sociocultural approach to abnormality looks not within the individual (e.g. at their biology or cognitive processes) but out to the wider social context in which the individual exists. For example, abnormal behaviour is seen as a result of societal or family interactions.

Labelling

Some clinicians have questioned whether schizophrenia actually exists. Thomas Szasz (1979), an American psychiatrist, said that labelling someone with a mental illness, such as schizophrenia, is nothing more than the **'medicalisation of madness'**. He argues that using medical terms such as 'treatment', 'illness' and 'diagnosis' is a form of social

Key terms

Residual rules: rules that are not formalised (e.g. 'Do not steal') but include deviant behaviour in which we might all occasionally engage. Such residual rules are endless (e.g. 'Don't talk to lamp-posts').

Self-fulfilling prophecy: an expectation that someone will behave in a certain way, as a result of which the person's behaviour turns out as expected because they begin to act in a way that will optimise the expected outcome.

DSM-III: the manual for the diagnosis of mental disorders, rewritten in 1980 and in use until DSM-IV was produced in 1996.

control that robs individuals of their liberty. Giving individuals the label 'mental illness' is a way of excluding those individuals who do not conform to our social and cultural norms.

Scheff (1966) has proposed that schizophrenia is a learned social role that is determined by the process of labelling. His **labelling theory** proposes that an individual who breaks one or more **residual rules** is assigned a label 'mentally ill' or 'schizophrenic'. This label not only influences the individual to behave in a manner that fits the label (based on stereotypes held) but also determines how others react to the behaviour of that individual. Scheff believes that we all occasionally break a residual rule, but, if diagnosed as mentally ill as a result, people begin to accept their new social role and find it difficult to fit back into normal society. Other people get to know about their illness; they may be unable to find work; and, if hospitalised, the attention received reinforces their perception and expectations. The diagnosis creates a **self-fulfilling prophecy**.

In a now famous study, Rosenhan (1973) provided an example of how easy it is to receive a label and be 'misdiagnosed' as suffering from schizophrenia.

Research study: Rosenhan (1973)

Aim: To investigate the reliability of diagnosing mental illness.

Method: A group of eight 'pseudo-patients', free from psychological symptoms, pretended that they could hear an unfamiliar voice (auditory hallucination), which said 'empty', 'hollow' and 'thud', in order to gain admission to a variety of hospitals in the USA. All patients were admitted to hospital: seven with the diagnosis 'schizophrenia'. The patients behaved normally once admitted but reported a sense of powerlessness and fear, and their behaviour was interpreted by staff as 'schizophrenic'.

Results: Following admission to hospital the pseudo-patients had difficulty convincing staff that they were sane and they were hospitalised for between 7 and 52 days (an average of 19 days). Indeed, 'normal' behaviour was interpreted as 'abnormal': a patient writing notes was deemed to be showing 'obsessive-compulsive writing behaviour'. Once labelled 'schizophrenic', the label stuck and the patients were discharged with 'schizophrenia in remission'.

Conclusion: The unreliability of diagnosing mental illness was evident, and patients were perceived according to the labels that they had been given.

Evaluation: This study and the follow-up one, helped to improve the reliability of diagnosis of schizophrenia.

Evaluation of labelling theory

- The Rosenhan study helped to improve the reliability of diagnosis with the revision of the diagnostic criteria (**DSM-III**, 1980). The study demonstrated that psychiatric labels tend to become self-fulfilling prophecies, and that we begin to interpret behaviour in a way that 'fits in' with our pre-existing assumptions and beliefs.
- Labelling theory only accounts for how symptoms are maintained; it does not explain the cause, nor does it offer any kind of treatment.

- Labelling theory ignores the compelling genetic evidence.
- Seriously ill individuals with a range of debilitating symptoms exist and require help, and labelling theory has been criticised for trivialising a very serious disorder.

Family dysfunction

Early studies into family patterns and styles

Early studies into family influences and schizophrenia looked at the nature and style of communication. Bateson *et al.* (1956) suggested that communication between parents and offspring was sometimes contradictory; they used the phrase 'double bind'. A parent might be saying one thing, but their body language and tone could be suggesting the opposite. Children experiencing such 'double binds' learn not to trust their own feelings and perceptions, because they cannot trust those of others. They can grow up to mistrust all communications as is shown sometimes by people with paranoid schizophrenia.

According to **family socialisation theory**, families sometimes fail to provide a stable and supportive environment and appropriate role models for the developing child (Lidz *et al.*,1957), and there are two abnormal family structures:

- **Schismatic families** In these families, conflicts between parents result in competition for the affection of family members and a desire to take control and undermine the other parent.
- **Skewed families** In these, one partner is abnormally dominating and the other submissive. The children are encouraged to follow the dominant partner which impairs their cognitive and social development.

In both types of family, parents fail to act in role-appropriate ways, which can cause anxiety, and schizophrenia may be a way of handling the family conflicts.

Evaluation of early studies

Although associations have been found between family patterns and schizophrenia, it is difficult to prove a causal relationship because it is not possible to untangle cause and effect. It may be the parents' reaction to a particularly difficult child that causes the family problems, rather than the family patterns causing the problems in the child.

The expressed emotion explanation

A series of studies into 'expressed emotion' (EE) have investigated family life and the course of schizophrenia. In an early study, Brown *et al.* (1958) found, to their surprise, that people with schizophrenia who were discharged from hospital and returned to parents or spouses fared worse than those returning to lodgings. High face-to-face contact between patient and family was found to increase risk of relapse, and this was attributed to the relatives' 'emotional over-involvement'. Emotional over-involvement was operationalised to include:

- emotion (positive and negative)
- hostility
- critical comments (tone of voice and content).

When these factors are 'high' in a household, i.e. where the EE is high, patients are significantly more likely to relapse than if the patient lived in a family with low EE.

Research study: Bebbington and Kuipers (1994)

Aim: To carry out a meta-analysis of 26 prospective studies of the role of EE as a risk factor for relapse in schizophrenia from a variety of countries including UK, USA, Switzerland and Japan from 1958 to the 1990s.

Method: Data relating to 1,346 patients, obtained from the original authors, were analysed to determine: the proportion of EE families and the average relapse rate for people with schizophrenia returning to high- and low-EE families.

Results: 52 per cent of families were high EE. Relapse in the high-EE families averaged 50 per cent; whilst in the low-EE families it was 21 per cent, a difference that was highly statistically significant.

Conclusion: Expressed emotion is a significant risk factor in relapse rates for schizophrenia.

Evaluation: It is difficult to establish cause and effect (e.g. do families high in expressed emotion cause the relapse in schizophrenics, or do schizophrenics cause families to become high in expressed emotion?).

Summary questions

3 Explain how adoption studies can be used to provide evidence for a genetic link to schizophrenia

4 Outline one strength and one weakness of the dopamine theory of schizophrenia.

5 Brain imaging studies have found differences in both structure and function of the brains of patients with schizophrenia. Explain what is meant by the terms 'structure' and 'function'.

6 Outline one cognitive theory or model that attempts to explain schizophrenic symptoms.

7 Phil is a 19-year-old man with schizophrenia; he has just been allowed out of hospital following a serious psychotic episode that required six weeks' hospitalisation. He is returning to his family home where he is to be cared for by his mother, Elsie. Elsie is a very concerned mother who tries to do her best but doesn't really understand the illness. She is critical of Phil and thinks that he should get a job to take his mind off his illness. When he hears voices, she tells him not to be silly and moans at him for locking himself in his room all day.

With reference to family dysfunction, briefly discuss the implications of Phil's returning to his family home.

Evaluation of the EE explanation

- The ability to predict the relapse rate of people with schizophrenia from the EE measure up to 12 months following discharge is a strong indicator of the predictive validity of EE.
- It is unclear whether EE is a causal agent in relapse rates or just a reaction to the patient's behaviour. If the condition of a person with schizophrenia begins to deteriorate, family involvement is likely to increase, along with family criticism and efforts to control the situation. These all come under the remit of 'expressed emotion' (Kanter *et al.*, 1987).
- Recent studies (e.g. Kavanagh, 1992) have found that high-EE communication patterns are not specific to schizophrenia; they are also found in families with depressive illness and eating disorders. This type of communication pattern is also more evident in Western families (Leff *et al.*, 1990).
- There is a problem with how EE is measured, which is usually via one interview. This might not be sufficient to give an accurate picture of family interaction patterns.

Key points:

- Biological explanations of schizophrenia are drawn from a number of areas including genetic, neurochemical and neuroanatomical paradigms.
- Cognitive explanations are psychological rather than biological and include the five-factor theory proposed by Slade and Bentall, and Maher's anomalous experience model.
- Sociocultural explanations look to the person's environment to explain schizophrenia. Labelling theory suggests that patients are simply responding to a given label in a self-fulfilling manner.
- Families can influence both the onset and maintenance of schizophrenia, the former through socialisation and the latter via patterns of expressed emotion.

Treatments for schizophrenia

Learning objectives:

- describe and evaluate anti-psychotic drug treatment for schizophrenia
- describe and evaluate behavioural treatments for schizophrenia
- describe and evaluate psychotherapy for schizophrenia
- discuss the role of community care.

Link

For the assumptions of the biological approach, see Chapter 9, Approaches in psychology.

Key terms

Akathisia: extreme restlessness and agitation.

Token economy: a person is rewarded for a desirable behaviour by being given tokens. The more a person performs these desirable behaviours, the more tokens they receive. The tokens can then be exchanged for items that the person wants.

AQA Examiner's tip

Recently, behaviourist approaches to the treatment of social skills deficits in patients with schizophrenia have moved away from teaching isolated behavioural skills; many programmes now include cognitive and social perception skills when teaching competent social behaviour. This is essentially a 'cognitive-behavioural' approach and can therefore be included under both 'behavioural treatments' and 'psychotherapeutic treatments' in an examination answer.

Anti-psychotic drug treatment for schizophrenia

In the 1950s, it was discovered that chlorpromazine had a therapeutic effect on agitated patients and, in particular, alleviated hallucinations and delusions. The era of anti-psychotic drugs (referred to as 'neuroleptics') had begun, and these are widely used to treat acute episodes of psychosis and prevent relapse. The control of acute symptoms with neuroleptics is highly effective: a number of double-blind placebo trials of neuroleptic medication for acute psychosis have shown a significant advantage in favour of the active drug. These drugs have been shown to have a specific impact on the positive symptoms (hallucinations, delusions and thought disorders). A small number of patients, however, fail to respond to these drugs: for example, Loebel *et al.* (1992) found that 16 per cent failed to recover within 12 months of the first treatment.

In the last decade, a new range of neuroleptics has been introduced, usually referred to as 'atypical' neuroleptics, e.g. Risperidone. Such drugs have proved effective for those individuals who do not respond to the older neuroleptics. In addition, these newer drugs do not have side effects at normal doses, apart from the occasional reporting of **akathisia**.

Clozapine is also proving to be effective in cases where traditional neuroleptics have failed to shift all the symptoms of psychosis; studies show up to 66 per cent of patients with stubborn symptoms do respond within 12 months (Meltzer, 1999).

Evaluation of drug treatment

- The side effects of neuroleptic medication are distressing, for example muscular spasms, parkinsonism (including tremor and shuffling gait), and tardive dyskinesia (including involuntary movements of the head and tongue).
- Clozapine is associated with potentially fatal lowering of the white blood count and its use requires regular blood monitoring. Other side effects of this drug include sedation, hyper-salivation and weight gain.
- The newer drugs such as Risperidone, do not lead to the distressing side effects found with the original neuroleptic medication at normal doses, but these drugs are not widely used because they are very expensive.
- Neuroleptic medication is best at continual low dosage to control relapse rates, but these drugs only extend the interval between relapses – they do not prevent them.
- The neuroleptics have become popular as bimonthly injections, which ensure adherence to regimes and help to prevent relapse. However, these drugs are a means of controlling, not curing, psychosis.
- There is no evidence that neuroleptic drugs are effective for negative symptoms.

Behavioural treatments for schizophrenia

Behaviour therapy is based on the use of rewards and reinforcements to modify behaviour. In particular, **token economies** are developed as a way of managing behavioural issues such as personal hygiene. Such interventions are useful when medication has reduced psychotic episodes and other behaviours can then be controlled using behaviour therapy. Behaviour therapy can be used to reverse the effects of hospitalisation, and several studies have shown the efficacy of such treatments. For example, a study by Paul and Lentz (1977) found a significant improvement in interpersonal skills and self-care in the 'token economy group' compared with the 'milieu therapy' (a treatment that attempts to control the socio-environment so that it is more conducive to psychological improvement).

Social skills training

Social skills training (SST) is an approach that directly attempts to modify the social behaviour of people with schizophrenia. An important underlying assumption is that people with schizophrenia are not equipped with the behaviours necessary for successful social interactions and interpersonal relationships. Techniques such as modelling, reinforcement and role playing are used to help patients acquire the necessary verbal and non-verbal skills. It is a highly structured form of therapy and a typical programme might include: conversation skills, assertion and conflict management, medication self-management, time use and recreational skills, survival skills and employment skills (Halford and Hayes, 1992). Typically, sessions would be of about an hour's duration up to five times a week. There might be two trainers and 10 patients. Each session would concentrate on a number of key competencies in an area of community functioning; for example, conversation skills might include 'starting a conversation' and 'nonverbal communication'.

Evaluation of SST

- Studies evaluating SST have found it to be effective in increasing patients' ability, comfort and assertiveness in social situations (Birchwood and Spencer, 1999).
- A criticism of SST is that it does not always generalise to real life, as Shepherd (1977) found when assessing social functioning following SST training in a number of naturalistic settings.
- Behaviour therapy alone cannot help with the distress associated with psychotic symptoms, and there has been a move away from discrete behavioural learning of social skills to a more inclusive approach where cognitive and social perception skills are also addressed.

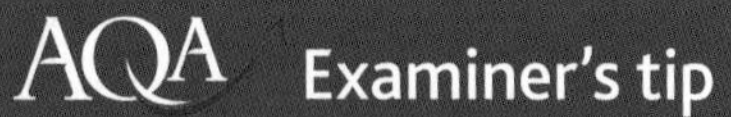

There are no named psychotherapies on the specification and therefore any appropriate therapies can be discussed in an examination answer. Learn at least two, which can be the two named here.

Psychotherapy for schizophrenia

'Psychotherapy' is a generic term that covers a range of therapies such as psychodynamic and cognitive therapies. Psychotherapy is not always effective for individuals with severe schizophrenic symptoms as the therapies often rely on talking and listening. Recently, improvements in the efficacy of cognitive-based treatments for schizophrenic symptoms have been noticeable, and therefore the two therapies to be discussed with respect to schizophrenia are cognitive-behavioural therapies and cognitive therapy.

Cognitive-behavioural therapies for schizophrenia

Cognitive-behavioural therapies have focused on individual symptoms, such as hallucinations and delusions. Patients experience distress with some of the more troublesome psychotic symptoms of schizophrenia and many engage in a variety of coping strategies in response.

Research study: Tarrier (1987)

Aim: To investigate the use of coping strategies during psychotic episodes.

Method: Twenty-five patients with schizophrenia who suffered hallucinations and/or delusions following a psychotic episode were interviewed. Details of psychotic experiences were elicited, including when and where these occurred, the patients' emotional reactions and their use of coping strategies.

Results: One third identified 'triggers' to the symptoms, such as traffic noise or feeling anxious; 75 per cent reported major distress and one third reported disruption to thinking and behaviour. Seventy-five per cent disclosed the use of coping strategies such as distraction, positive self-talk, withdrawal or relaxation.

Conclusion: The use of coping strategies helped patients to cope with their symptoms.

Evaluation: This type of study relies on the client being able to recall and communicate effectively, which is not possible in many cases involving people suffering from schizophrenia.

The study by Tarrier (1987) was groundbreaking and led to the development of a new therapeutic approach; it involves teaching patients new coping strategies based on their own preferred strategy and is known as coping strategy enhancement (CSE). The aim of CSE is to teach the individual how to use coping strategies to reduce the frequency and intensity of psychotic symptoms. Useful strategies already present in the individual are built on and new strategies encouraged. The therapy involves a number of initial steps:

1 **Assess the form and the content** of the psychotic experience, e.g. 'Is there one voice or more?'
2 **Assess the emotional response**, e.g. 'How do the voices make you feel; are you afraid or anxious?'
3 **Assess the person's thoughts** that accompany the emotion, e.g. 'Do you think you are in danger?'
4 **Assess any prior warning** or antecedent, e.g. 'Do you know when the voice will appear?'
5 **Assess the individual's coping strategies**, e.g. 'How do you cope with this?'
6 The individual then **rates each strategy** in terms of its effectiveness.

The therapy then progresses using two components:

- **Education and rapport training** This involves creating an ambience and shared understanding so that therapist and client can work together.
- **Symptom targeting** A symptom is targeted, usually one for which a coping strategy is already in use, and this strategy is then enhanced and practised during the session. For 'homework' the client is asked to assess the use and effectiveness of the strategy and make a record.

Evaluation of CSE

- Tarrier *et al.* (1993) carried out a study investigating the effectiveness of CSE over **problem-solving therapy** in 49 patients taking anti-psychotic medication but who continued to experience hallucinations

Key terms

Problem-solving therapy: an established cognitive-behavioural treatment method, which involves identifying the problem and, as a group, devising the most appropriate solution rather than working on the individual's own natural coping strategies (as occurs in CSE).

and delusions. Patients were randomly allocated to treatment conditions which involved 10 one-hour sessions. Both groups reported a 50 per cent improvement in positive symptoms compared with a control group of patients on a waiting list, and this significant gain was still apparent at the six-month follow-up. Patients receiving CSE, however, also showed a significant improvement in coping skills.

- One of the problems associated with treatment research with patients with schizophrenia is that there is usually a high drop-out rate; in the Tarrier *et al.* (1993) study, 47 per cent dropped out.

Cognitive therapy for schizophrenia

Supporters of cognitive therapy argue that it is beliefs about the self and appraisals of events that are responsible for the negative affect (emotion). The therapy requires thoughts and their associated affects to be elicited and challenged; this might involve putting such thoughts to a 'reality testing'. Up until quite recently, it was thought that this approach would not work with people with schizophrenia because attempting to modify beliefs could end up strengthening them. Two important principles underpinning the present approach are:

- start with the least important belief
- work with evidence for that belief, not the belief itself (Watts *et al.*, 1973).

Cognitive therapy usually includes the following components:

- A verbal challenge of the evidence for the least significant belief is made whereby the therapist questions the client's delusional interpretation and puts forward a more reasonable one (often elicited from the client).
- By challenging the evidence for the belief, a reduction in conviction can occur. Also the client becomes aware of the link between events, beliefs, affect and behaviour.
- Reality testing involves planning and performing an activity to invalidate a belief. This is best explained through an example. Chadwick *et al.* (1996) reported the case of Nigel who claimed to have the special power of knowing what people were going to say before they said it. To test this belief a number of video recorders were put on pause and Nigel had to say what was coming next. Out of over 50 attempts, Nigel did not get one correct, and he concluded that he did not have the power at all.

Evaluation of cognitive therapy

- Research trials using cognitive therapy for delusions have demonstrated a 40 per cent reduction in the severity of psychotic symptoms (Kuipers *et al.*, 1997).
- During a period of acute psychosis, cognitive therapy led to a faster response to treatment in a group of patients with schizophrenia compared with drugs alone, and to improved recovery (Drury *et al.*, 1996).

The role of community care

There has been a move away from hospitalisation and towards caring for, and treating, patients with schizophrenia in the community. The number of hospital beds for the mentally ill has been reduced by approximately two-thirds; there are a number of reasons for this decline:

- The 'antipsychiatry' movement in the 1960s and 1970s led to a rejection of medical concepts of mental illness and a preference

The depressive symptoms are the same as for unipolar disorder, but in addition the individual experiences manic episodes. The symptoms must be causing distress or impaired functioning in social and/or occupational roles.

Table 6 *Diagnostic criteria for bipolar disorder (DSM-IV)*

Three/four or more of the following symptoms at least one of which is elevated/irritable mood	
Unusual talkativeness; rapid speech Distractibility; attention easily diverted Less than usual amount of sleep needed Inflated self-esteem; belief that one has special talents, powers and abilities	Increase in activity level: at work, socially or sexually Flight of ideas/subjective impression that thoughts are racing Excessive involvement in pleasurable activities

Key points:

- Diagnosis of both unipolar and bipolar depression is carried out according to the criteria in diagnostic manuals such as the DSM, which list the symptoms and duration (the requirement is that they impair everyday functioning).
- Symptoms of unipolar depression include depressed mood or loss of interest in normally pleasurable activities, and at least four further symptoms from the list.
- Symptoms of bipolar depression are the same as for unipolar during the depressed state, plus elevated or irritable mood and three other symptoms when in the manic phase.

Summary questions

12 Outline the major symptoms required for diagnosis of (a) unipolar depression; (b) bipolar depression.

13 Distinguish between unipolar and bipolar depression.

Take it further

The BBC screened an award-winning, two-part documentary by Stephen Fry in 2007 called *The Secret Life of the Manic Depressive*, which explores Fry's personal experiences of bipolar disorder (for information, go to the BBC's website and navigate to 'health'; see the section at the end of the chapter, p130, for the website's address).

Woman's Hour (BBC Radio 4): 'Manic Depression' is an excellent insight into the life of a teenage sufferer.

AQA Examiner's tip

Make sure that you can distinguish between the requirements for diagnosis of unipolar and bipolar depression.

Explanations of mood disorders

Learning objectives:

- describe and evaluate biological explanations for mood disorders
- describe and evaluate cognitive explanations for mood disorders
- describe and evaluate behavioural explanations for mood disorders
- describe and evaluate psychodynamic explanations for mood disorders.

AQA Examiner's tip

There are four named approaches on the specification for mood disorders; however, within these approaches no particular theories are identified, so you can choose to discuss any appropriate theories in an answer.

Key terms

Proband: a person with a disorder whose relatives are then investigated to discover genetic transmission of the disorder.

Biological explanations of mood disorders

The genetic explanation

Family studies

Generally, in family studies a **proband** is identified and then information regarding close family relatives of the person diagnosed with a mood disorder is gathered. In a large-scale study (900 patients and controls) by Winokur *et al.* (1995), the rate of unipolar depression was 10.4 per cent in first-degree relatives of the probands, compared with 4.9 per cent of controls' relatives. Children of depressed parents seem to be particularly at risk of developing depression. Studies such as one by Weissman *et al.* (1987) found that approximately 50 per cent of the offspring of depressives display depressive symptoms themselves.

Evaluation of family studies

The results of studies investigating probands cannot be attributed to genetics alone, since psychological factors such as being reared by ill relatives cannot rule out environmental determinants. Offspring studies inevitably mean that children are not only inheriting genes but are also exposed to stressful family environments. It is difficult to draw conclusions specifically about the genetic components of depression from family studies alone and therefore twins have also been investigated.

Twin studies

Monozygotic twins (MZ) share 100 per cent of the same genes. Therefore, if mood disorders are due to genetic inheritance, the concordance in MZ twins should be higher than the concordance found in dizygotic twins (DZ) who share only 50 per cent of their genes.

Research study: McGuffin *et al.* (1996)

Aim: To investigate the genetic component of depression.

Method: The researchers obtained a sample of 214 twin pairs through probands who had been treated as inpatients for depression.

Results: The concordance rate for unipolar depression was 46 per cent for MZ twins and 20 per cent for DZ twins, both substantially higher than the lifetime depression rate in the general population.

Conclusion: Genetic factors play a moderate role in family patterns of depression and may be particularly important in recurrent depression.

Evaluation: DZ twins and normal siblings have the same genetic similarity; therefore, it is difficult for inherited factors alone to explain the much higher concordance rate for DZ twins over normal siblings.

Concordance for bipolar disorder is higher than for unipolar with about 70 per cent concordance for MZ twins reared together or apart, compared with 23 per cent for DZ twin pairs. Egeland *et al.* (1987) claimed to have found

evidence for a genetic link to bipolar disorder in the Amish communities of Pennsylvania. The Amish people show a much higher incidence of the disorder than is found in other populations, and it was thought that the gene responsible for bipolar disorder had been discovered. However, Kelsoe *et al.* (1989) reanalysed the data and found methodological errors.

Evaluation of twin studies

- Twin studies cannot rule out environment altogether as twins are reared in highly similar environments with similar psychosocial experiences.
- Adoption studies would be more convincing as nature and nurture are conveniently separated; however, there is a very limited sample to obtain in this area of study.
- The search for a particular gene responsible for major depression has proved difficult owing to a number of factors: for example, unipolar depression is highly **heterogeneous**.
- Studies that have investigated the interaction of genetic inheritance and environments suggest that rather than cause depression, genes probably influence how susceptible we will be to the effects of life events.

Key terms

Heterogeneous: having many subtypes.

Synaptic cleft: the small space between the pre- and postsynaptic neuron through which neurotransmitters flow.

Link

Mood disorders are an excellent topic to discuss with respect to the nature–nurture debate (see Chapter 10, Debates in psychology). The explanations for mood disorders draw on the assumptions of the major approaches outlined in Chapter 9, Approaches in psychology.

The neurochemical explanation

The area of the brain that is known to play a significant role in emotion is the limbic system; neurotransmitter pathways link the limbic system to other parts of the brain, to the endocrine system and to the autonomic nervous system. In the **synaptic cleft**, neurotransmitters are only active for a short time after which they are destroyed or inactivated or reabsorbed by the cell – known as 'reuptake'. Tricyclic antidepressants (e.g. imipramine) block the synaptic reuptake of amines into the presynaptic neurons, thus increasing their availability. Based on the effects of these drugs, it was claimed that depression results from an insufficiency of neurotransmitters (e.g. noradrenalin and serotonin), while mania results from too much.

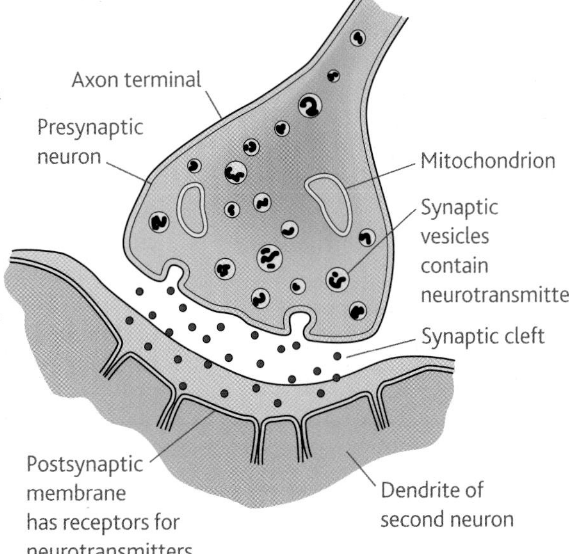

Fig. 6 *Neurotransmitter activity at the synapse between two cells*

Evaluation of the neurochemical explanation

Difficulties began to emerge with this theory in a number of areas:

- Antidepressant medications were discovered that did not have the same effects, i.e. increasing the availability of neurotransmitters.
- Antidepressants immediately increase levels of neurotransmitters but there is a delayed effect on alleviating the symptoms, i.e. it can take several weeks for depression to begin to lift.
- It would appear from the latest evidence that a simple increase in neurotransmitter levels does not explain why the antidepressant drugs alleviate depression. Researchers now believe that an interaction between various neurotransmitters occurs.

Brain structure and functioning in depression

There is some evidence that the limbic system and the frontal lobes are implicated in depression, and this evidence comes from a number of areas:

- Injury or stroke that affects the frontal part of the brain can lead to depression. The frontal lobes are a major regulatory component of the limbic system and this system controls emotion and drives.

Link

For a diagram of the major components of the limbic system in the human brain, see p235 in *AQA Psychology B AS*.

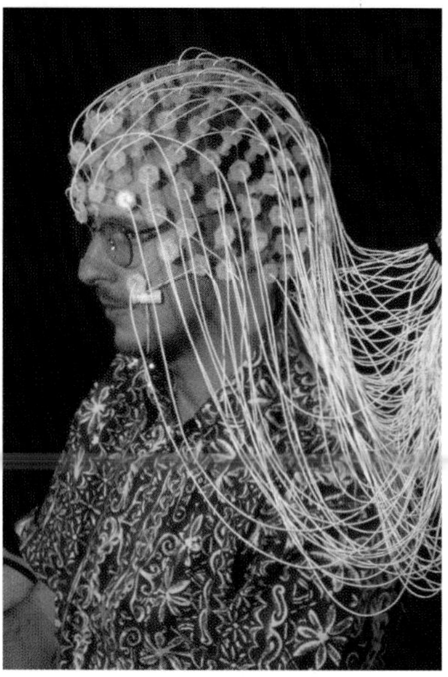

Fig. 7 *EEG recording*

- Neuroimaging studies have found structural abnormalities in the frontal region of the brains of unipolar patients. Using MRI, Coffey *et al.* (1993) demonstrated that depressed patients had lower frontal lobe volume than did controls.
- Using electroencephalographical recording (EEG), Henrique and Davidson (1990) discovered frontal hypoactivation in a sample of 15 unipolar depressed patients. This was not found in the normal controls.

Evaluation

- Findings that show deficits in the brain structures of depressed patients fail to unravel cause and effect. Has the brain abnormality caused the depression, or has the depression caused abnormality in brain regions?
- Henrique and Davidson (1990) proposed a **diathesis-stress model** to explain brain abnormalities found: 'individuals who display frontal EEG asymmetry are more vulnerable to depression, given sufficient environmental stress'.

Key terms

Diathesis-stress model: suggests that disorder is due to an inherited susceptibility combined with a stressful environment.

The Self
'I am hopeless'

The Future
'is bleak'

The World
'will defeat me'

Fig. 8 *The triad of impairments (Beck, 1976)*

Cognitive explanations of mood disorders

Beck's dysfunctional thinking explanation

The cognitive approach is largely associated with the work of Aaron Beck (1967, 1976) who noted the negative thinking patterns of his clients. Having observed that his patients had dysfunctional thoughts, he formulated a cognitive model of depression that had three components:

- the cognitive triad
- faulty information processing
- negative self-schemas.

The term 'cognitive triad' refers to the automatic negative cognitions that individuals prone to depression emphasise about themselves, the world and the future.

According to cognitive theory, defeated, self-critical and hopeless thoughts affect people in a variety of other areas including their mood, behaviour and physiology. In addition to the automatic negative thoughts of themselves, people with such a triad believe that it is futile to attempt to do much as the world and the future are bleak and defeating. Such thinking patterns predispose people to experience depression.

Depressive thinking is distorted in so far as individuals selectively attend to negative interpretations and overgeneralise and magnify adversity. **Information processing** is said to be cognitively biased and this biased way of thinking will ensure that the individual is prone to become depressed and, once depressed, will have increasing difficulty in getting better unless cognitions change. These information processing errors occur because people rely on pre-existing beliefs or schemas.

The third component of Beck's model is the negative **self-schema** (beliefs about self). Schemas allow us to process information selectively and speedily due to 'expectation'. Although a useful cognitive device, these schemas can sometimes lead to our selectively perceiving and interpreting information that fits in with a maladaptive (dysfunctional or inappropriate) way of thinking. If our self-schemas contain negative beliefs, the information we will selectively 'take in' will be that which confirms these negative beliefs, and we will ignore evidence to the contrary. The negative beliefs are probably acquired in childhood as a result of repeated criticism or rejection.

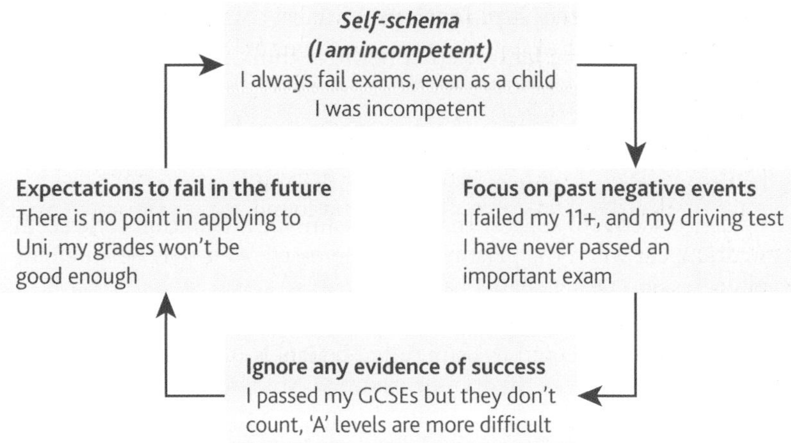

Fig. 9 *A negative self-schema*

Dysfunctional beliefs do not necessarily lead to depression; the individual will become depressed, according to Beck's model, only if they encounter a **critical life event**. This event will then trigger dysfunctional assumptions and biased information processing that will result in symptoms of depression.

The learned helplessness theory of depression

Seligman (1974) first proposed that **learned helplessness** might be a useful model for depression. This was based on his earlier work with animals when he showed that laboratory dogs exposed to uncontrollable shocks later showed an inability to learn in a different situation where they could have controlled the shocks. Indeed, when later put into a situation where shocks could be controlled, the dogs seemed to act passively and had seemingly learned to behave helplessly.

Deficits are said to occur in three areas:

- **Motivation** There is no point trying if you have already learned that you have no control.
- **Cognitive** Learning you have no control results in passive acceptance.
- **Emotional** This passivity is a kind of depression.

Abramson *et al.* (1978) reformulated the helplessness theory and proposed that the types of attributions people make about uncontrollable events are an important element in whether or not they become depressed. The kinds of attributions people make about uncontrollable events can be:

- **internal or external** – caused by something within the individual or the environment
- **global or specific** – will affect all situations, or is just specific to that one
- **stable or unstable** – will always be that way, or can change.

An internal, stable and global attribution reflects a pessimistic attribution style and would leave a person at risk of depression. An example of a pessimistic attribution style would be: 'I am a very stupid person. I have never had any intelligence and I will fail all my examinations and come to nothing in life.'

The more recent **hopelessness theory of depression** (Abramson *et al.*, 1989) proposed that having a pessimistic attributional style coupled with a negative life event can lead to a feeling of hopelessness, which in turn would likely result in depression.

Link

For a brief account of the experimental study of learned helplessness see Chapter 9, Approaches in psychology, p233.

Key terms

Critical life event: an occurrence of major significance in a person's life (e.g. the death of a mother, divorce or the loss of valued employment).

Learned helplessness: in operant conditioning, if punishment is too harsh or escape from punishment too difficult, punishment will not stop a particular response to a stimulus. Individuals continue doing the behaviour and accept their punishment in a fatalistic way.

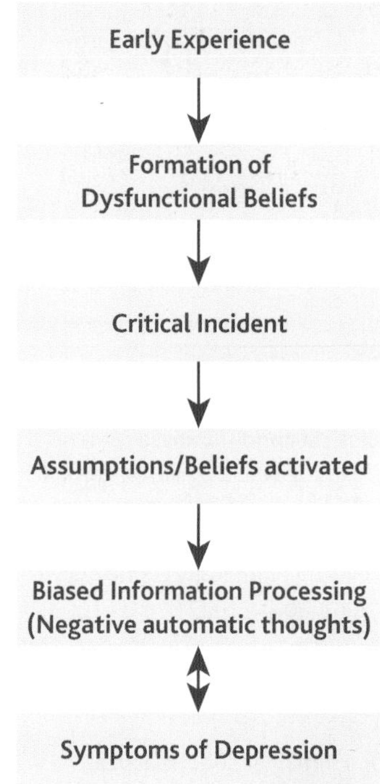

Fig. 10 *Beck's cognitive theory of depression (**Beck**, 1976)*

Evaluation of cognitive explanations

- It is difficult to ascertain whether negative thinking plays a causal role in depression.
- With respect to an information processing bias, Eysenck and Keene (2000) have concluded that there is only mixed evidence for biased information processing in depressed individuals.
- Evidence seems to suggest that the pessimistic attribution style seems to disappear when the person is not depressed, so it may be an **effect** of depression rather than a **cause** of it.
- An ongoing research project on college students with a pessimistic attributional style and dysfunctional beliefs is offering support for the hopelessness theory: for example, students in the 'high risk group' have shown a sevenfold increase in major depression compared with the 'low risk group', after two years (Alloy and Abramson, 1979).
- According to Damasio (2000), neuroimaging techniques have shown that emotional processing can occur before cognitive processing, suggesting that emotions might therefore be controlling cognitions rather than the other way around. If this is the case, Beck's cognitive theory is incomplete, as there seems to be a need to accommodate the influence of emotion in our cognitive responses.
- The focus on internal cognitions also minimises the impact of environmental and social contexts in which people live.

Behavioural explanations of mood disorders

Ferster (1974) has argued that when an individual's responses are no longer positively reinforced then depression can occur. So when a loved one dies, or a relationship ends, our source of reinforcement disappears and this can precipitate depression. Lewinsohn and Gotlib (1995) have also proposed a model of depression that relies on behavioural principles. The failure to receive positive reinforcement leads to a reduction in effort and then to even less reinforcement. A particular area where some people fail to gain reinforcement is social interactions. A person with limited social skills will not interact (e.g. maintain/initiate conversation) and will have few friends, resulting in very little positive reinforcement. The more the person is depressed, the less likely they are to interact socially, and the opportunities to experience reinforcement will gradually decline.

Evaluation of behavioural explanations

- Research does show that depressed people experience fewer positive reinforcements in life than non-depressed individuals. However, only a relationship between depression and positive reinforcement has been demonstrated and this does not mean that depression is caused by the lack of reinforcement.
- More recent behavioural theories emphasise personality and cognitive variables that can mediate responses from the environment and affect the vulnerability to depression.
- Seligman was a behaviourist who investigated the process of **classical conditioning** in dogs. He extrapolated his findings to humans who, he believed, could develop a sense of helplessness (which could lead to depression) owing to past environmental experiences. His theory is a cognitive-behavioural theory of depression.

Key terms

Classical conditioning: a form of learning where a neutral stimulus (NS) begins to produce a response (CR) which was originally produced by a more logically connected stimulus (UCS).

Link

For a reminder about classical conditioning, look at *AQA Psychology B AS*, Chapter 1, Key approaches.

Psychodynamic explanations of mood disorders

Freud believed that the potential for depression was created in childhood, specifically in the oral stage of psychosexual development (which is approximately from birth to two years). During this stage, a child's needs may be overly gratified or not sufficiently gratified; either way, the result will be a person who is orally fixated. One manifestation of this personality type is that the person can suffer from low self-esteem and become overly dependent on other people.

Freud proposed that as a result of the loss of a loved one a person suffers a period of introjection, which is a process of identifying with the loved one. This process results in the person incorporating (taking into themselves) any negative feelings towards the loved one, resenting the desertion by the loved one and feeling guilty. Following the period of introjection is a period of mourning, when memories of the lost one are recalled, which enables a separation to be made. However, in overly dependent individuals (who have become fixated in the oral stage) the emotional bonds cannot be broken and the anger continues to be turned inwards and directed on the self, resulting in depression. Freud also proposed that depression can occur due to imagined or symbolic losses.

Later psychodynamic theorists (e.g. Klein and Bowlby) did not emphasise the notion of regression to an early stage but stressed the importance of the early mother–infant relationship and the link between the nature of that relationship and a susceptibility to depression. Bowlby's attachment theory proposed that if a child is deprived of a warm and loving attachment to a mother figure in the first few years of life, then depression in later life could result.

Evaluation of psychodynamic explanations

- There is evidence that some depressed people are high in dependency (Nietzel and Harris, 1990).
- Depressed individuals often express anger to other people, which is not what one would expect when a theory of depression suggests that anger is turned inwards.
- An important contribution of the psychodynamic approach has been in emphasising the importance of loss to the onset of depression.
- Psychodynamic theories have been criticised for their lack of scientific rigour.

Key points:

- Biological explanations of mood disorders include genetic, neurochemical, and differences in brain structure.
- Cognitive explanations include the theory first proposed by Beck, that depressed people have negative thinking patterns, and the theory of learned helplessness/hopelessness.
- Behavioural explanations rely largely on the theory of operant conditioning which states that if responses are not reinforced they will become extinct.
- Psychodynamic explanations relate depression to anger that is turned inwards and to overly dependent personalities.

Link

The psychosexual theory of development is discussed in *AQA Psychology B AS*, Chapter 3, Gender development, and in Chapter 9, Approaches in psychology, in this book.

AQA Examiner's tip

A common error made by students in examinations is to mix up schizophrenia and mood disorders in their answer. The question should be read carefully and then answered with appropriate material; the disorders are quite distinct.

Summary questions

14 Outline a study that has investigated the genetic explanation for depression. In your answer refer to the aim, method, results and conclusion.

15 Outline one cognitive explanation of mood disorders.

16 Briefly discuss one criticism of the behavioural explanation for mood disorders.

17 Rob's mother died six months ago and he is struggling to come to terms with his loss. His doctor has decided that this is not just a period of mourning but that Rob is suffering from clinical depression. Outline a psychodynamic explanation for Rob's depression.

Treatments for mood disorders

Learning objectives:

- describe and evaluate biological treatments for mood disorders
- describe and evaluate cognitive treatments for mood disorders.

Biological treatments for mood disorders

Antidepressant medications

Antidepressants have become much more widely used owing to the development of newer drugs and the increasing awareness of their usefulness. These drugs were first identified serendipitously when it was discovered that a drug being used for tuberculosis (TB) elevated the mood of patients with TB. It was then discovered that medications known to deplete certain neurotransmitters appeared to cause depression and those that increased specific neurotransmitters reduced depression.

Monoamine oxidase inhibitors

Monoamine oxidase inhibitors (MAOIs) were early drugs that inhibited the activity of monoamine oxidase, an enzyme present in the synaptic cleft that helps to break down the neurotransmitters noradrenalin, dopamine and serotonin. Nowadays, MAOIs are only used in atypical depression when the patient does not respond well to other antidepressants. This is largely due to the multiple side effects, some of which are dangerous, and the fact that they are toxic and require dietary restrictions.

Tricyclic antidepressants

Tricyclic antidepressants (TCAs) were again a fortuitous discovery: imipramine was found to elevate the mood of those people with schizophrenia who are depressed. TCAs operate in a similar way to MAOIs, affecting several different neurotransmitters. They are used to treat severe depressive symptoms, usually for unipolar depression. As with MAOIs, TCAs are toxic (and therefore a risk for suicidal patients) and have side effects such as dry mouth and blurred vision, and, in men, erectile dysfunction.

Selective serotonin reuptake inhibitors

Selective serotonin reuptake inhibitors (SSRIs) are a more recent type of antidepressant and are chemically unrelated to the others. They work by selectively inhibiting the reuptake of serotonin only. SSRIs are now the preferred type of antidepressant as they have fewer side effects and are not fatal in overdose. As with all medications, however, there are some side effects such as nausea, diarrhoea and sexual dysfunction.

Lithium carbonate

Lithium carbonate is the drug used to treat bipolar disorder (sometimes called manic depression). It is not clear how it works but it is effective both during the depressed and the manic phases. It is not effective in the treatment of unipolar depression, suggesting a different aetiology in these two forms of depression. Lithium is usually taken continually, as discontinuation can lead to mania (Suppes *et al.*, 1991). The side effects of this drug are potentially life threatening and early use of this drug led to cases of kidney damage or failure due to the incorrect dosage. Even at lower doses there are side effects, including arrhythmia, blurred vision and lack of coordination.

Evaluation

- The mechanisms of action of all antidepressants are not fully understood. However, it is accepted that it is not as simple as increasing a particular neurotransmitter. If this was the case then results should be rapid, whereas noticeable effects can take three to five weeks.
- Because of the side effects of antidepressants, coupled with the fairly long period before they 'kick in', patients often discontinue before the antidepressant effect is felt.
- There have been some reports that SSRIs (e.g. Seroxat) are associated with suicidal urges (Cole *et al.*, 1990).
- A review of numerous studies comparing antidepressant medications with placebos in controlled blind trials point to the effectiveness of this treatment. Acute depression was lifted in 50 to 70 per cent of cases, which is about 40 per cent higher than in **placebo groups** (Thase and Kupfer, 1996).
- Most depressions arise in response to significant life difficulties and, although medications prove useful in reducing the depressive symptoms, they have little effect on the 'circumstances' or cause. Individuals may require psychotherapeutic intervention to deal with their problems and **exogenous stressors**.
- The efficacy of antidepressants does not mean that there is an underlying biochemical cause for depression. It could be that the depression causes the neurotransmitter imbalance. After all, paracetamol relieves my headache, but I do not suspect that a lack of paracetamol has caused it in the first place!
- A small number of depressed individuals do not respond to antidepressants alone and may require additional treatment (e.g. electroconvulsive therapy; see below) and possibly hospitalisation.

Key terms

Placebo group: a control group that is administered an inactive substance (known as a placebo) so that the active drug effects can be compared over the placebo effect (placebos alone can have up to a 40 per cent therapeutic effect).

Exogenous stressor: something external to a person, such as an event, situation or individual, that causes the person to experience stress.

Electroconvulsive therapy

Electroconvulsive therapy (ECT) is only used on severely depressed patients who do not respond to antidepressants. ECT requires electrical stimulation of the brain so that a seizure is induced. Patients are first given a fast-acting anaesthetic and a muscle relaxant to control potentially damaging physical side effects. Electrodes are attached to the patient's temples (either unilaterally or bilaterally) and a 70- to 150-volt shock is given, lasting for up to one second. The shock produces a convulsion that lasts up to one minute. After treatment the patient is confused, feels nauseous and has a headache. Typically, a course of treatment would be six to nine treatments given over a period of two to three weeks. Lerer *et al.* (1995) recommend no more than two treatments a week to avoid unnecessary cognitive impairments. The exact mechanism underlying the effects of ECT is not well understood, but it is likely that resultant changes in neurotransmitters may be responsible for the antidepressant effects. Nobler *et al.* (1994) have linked ECT to blood flow in the frontal-temporal regions of the brain as they found that successful ECT treatment was generally associated with reduction in blood flow in this region.

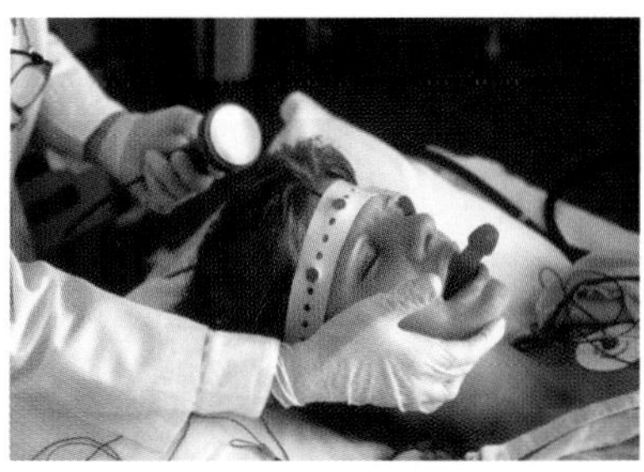

Fig. 11 *ECT treatment*

Evaluation

- ECT is known to affect short-term memory (retrograde amnesia), and it is common to have no recall of events immediately prior to the ECT.
- Animal studies and neuroimaging studies on humans have found no evidence of structural brain change caused by ECT (Devanand *et al.*, 1994).

- Many critics of ECT view it as unethical, particularly as, in extreme cases, it can be administered against the person's will. However, because it has proved effective in cases where other treatments do not work or in life-threatening situations when a rapid response is required, this treatment has not disappeared.
- Weiner and Coffey (1988) reviewed controlled and placebo studies of ECT and found that ECT significantly decreases severe depression.

Cognitive treatment for mood disorders

Cognitive-behavioural therapy

Aaron Beck was a psychoanalytically trained psychiatrist who noticed that his depressed patients were overwhelmed with negative and dysfunctional thinking patterns. He developed a treatment, known as cognitive-behavioural therapy (CBT), which has become widely applied not only for depression but also for a host of other mental disorders. Beck's basic tenet is that when people **think** negatively they will **feel** and **act** depressed, and therefore the therapy attempts to identify the negative beliefs and alter dysfunctional behaviours.

CBT is a brief therapy (e.g. no more than 20 sessions over 16 weeks) which is directive and focuses on current dysfunctional thinking patterns. Homework assignments are set between visits. Typically the treatment includes the following features:

- **Behavioural activation** The client and therapist draw up a list of activities that the client had previously found enjoyable; they then deal with any obstacles to rekindling them. Engagement in such activities should result in a lifting of mood.
- **Graded task assignments** Clients are helped to engage in successively more demanding but rewarding activities.
- **Thought-catching of 'automatic negative thoughts'** This is fundamental to the treatment. Clients are taught to notice the association between thoughts and feelings and note this down (Table 7 shows an example).

Table 7 *A thought-catching report form for an emotion-arousing experience*

Emotion-arousing experience	Automatic negative thought	Challenges to the maladaptive thought
'I asked Kate if she would go on holiday in the summer with me but she declined.'	'She doesn't like me.'	'Kate has already booked her holiday; there is no evidence that she does not like me; in fact, we always go for lunch together.'

Clients are taught to challenge the negative thoughts and replace them with more realistic ones, and this can lead to a change in behaviour. An important part of the therapy is to reduce the recurrence of depression by giving clients coping strategies to deal with any emerging depressive symptoms.

Research study: Elkin *et al.* (1985)

Aim: To investigate the efficacy of different treatments for depression.

Method: Two hundred and fifty outpatients with major depression were randomly assigned to one of four conditions for 16 weeks. The groups were cognitive-behavioural therapy (CBT); interpersonal therapy; drug therapy (imipramine); placebo group. Eighteen months after treatment had ended a follow-up analysis was carried out.

Results: Patients responded equally well to the active treatments, although the most severely depressed initially fared better on medication. Recovery, as defined by a psychiatric rating scale for depression, was 36 per cent for CBT patients, higher than the placebo group but similar to the other treatment conditions. After 18 months, the psychotherapy groups had maintained their improvement above the medication and placebo groups.

Conclusion: There is evidence that CBT is at least as effective as medication, and there are no side effects. Psychotherapy appears to have a long-term advantage over medication.

Evaluation: This is a particularly useful study as it contained a placebo group, who were given no active treatment and therefore acted as a control.

Interpersonal psychotherapy

Interpersonal psychotherapy (IPT) was first proposed by Klerman *et al.* (1984) and is based on the assumption that depressed individuals have difficulties with interpersonal relationships. It attempts to alleviate depressive symptoms and improve interpersonal functioning, particularly with significant others. It does this by 'clarifying, refocusing, and renegotiating the interpersonal context associated with the onset of depression' (Weissman and Klerman, 1990).

IPT is a brief therapy, lasting for 12 to 16 weeks; sessions are usually weekly and one to one. The therapy is focused on the 'here and now' rather than on the historical origins of any problems. There are three phases:

- The **initial phase**, lasting usually a couple of sessions, is for assessment and the formulation of treatment goals. The client is taught the 'sick role', i.e. learns about depression as an illness and, although the client is encouraged to be active, there is no expectation of normal functioning.
- The **second phase** identifies interpersonal problems that are thought to contribute to the depression. Information is gathered in relation to areas commonly associated with depression (including: grief, role disputes and role transitions) and interpersonal deficits.
- The **termination phase** focuses on consolidating learning and on preparing for the use of the skills in future difficulties.

The therapist uses nondirective exploration, through gathering information, insight and role playing to encourage emotional expression and teach more effective methods of communication.

Evaluation of cognitive treatments

- Robinson *et al.* (1990) reviewed 57 studies that had researched the efficacy of a variety of therapies for depression. The meta-analyses identified cognitive-behavioural therapies as being more effective than either other psychotherapies or drug therapy; post-treatment patients' depression levels remained significantly reduced.
- Research into the efficacy of CBT over other forms of therapy has had mixed results, and studies that have been carried out often have methodological shortcomings. However, the study by Elkin *et al.* described above was a large-scale study with excellent controls, and it found similar improvements across different psychotherapies.

Summary questions

18 Name one type of antidepressant and briefly outline how this works.

19 Briefly discuss one criticism of drug therapy for mood disorders.

20 Jack has been treated with medication for major (unipolar) depression for about eight weeks and he is beginning to feel more like his 'old self'. His doctor has suggested that he try a treatment in combination with the drugs and he has an appointment to visit the hospital psychological department where he will receive cognitive therapy. Outline one cognitive approach to the treatment of Jack's mood disorder.

- Cognitive therapies have been criticised on ethical grounds – the therapist decides what thoughts and behaviours are acceptable and then attempts to change the client's beliefs.
- Cognitive therapy is not suitable for bipolar disorder and works best with articulate and motivated individuals.
- IPT is not as well researched as CBT and there is little evidence to evaluate how, or even if, it is effective. Some research (e.g. Frank *et al*., 1990) investigated the use of IPT for the maintenance of gains following medication treatment and found that patients receiving only IPT stayed well for twice as long as those receiving a placebo.

Key points:

- Antidepressant drugs, such as SSRIs and lithium, are widely used in the treatment of mood disorders.
- ECT is still used as a treatment for mood disorders, particularly for severe cases where medication is of no benefit.
- Cognitive treatment for mood disorders includes Beck's CBT, which changes the client's thoughts, feelings and behaviour, and IPT, which aims to improve interpersonal functioning.

Seasonal affective disorder

Learning objectives:

- describe the symptoms of seasonal affective disorder
- describe and evaluate explanations of seasonal affective disorder
- describe and evaluate treatments for seasonal affective disorder.

Symptoms of seasonal affective disorder

Recurrent depressive episodes sometimes show a seasonal pattern, and this has become known as seasonal affective disorder (SAD). The symptoms include feeling miserable, lacking energy, being tired, having low spirits and feeling depressed. Some people also find that their sleep is disturbed; they eat less or more than usual; and they have no sex drive. Symptoms usually start between September and November and almost always disappear spontaneously with the arrival of spring and the longer daylight hours. Unipolar SAD will end at spring and normal functioning returns; however, spring heralds a period of mania for bipolar SAD.

To meet the DSM-IV criteria for recurrent major depression, at least two episodes of depression occurring at the same time over a two-year period (autumn/winter) should be identified, and, in addition, periods of full remission at the same time each year (spring/summer) should be evident. Approximately 2 per cent of the British population suffer from SAD, and 10 per cent endure the milder symptoms of 'winter blues'. Women are three times more likely to be affected than men. Younger people, particularly those between the ages of 18 and 40, are also more likely to suffer from SAD.

Explanations of seasonal affective disorder

Many species have **circannual rhythms** that cover a period of about a year, and these regulate such behaviours as migration and hibernation. It is thought that SAD could be another circannual rhythm and might be under the control of the pineal gland. This gland secretes the hormone melatonin, which in turn influences the production of the neurotransmitter serotonin. Melatonin production is controlled by light; it is produced when it is dark and suppressed when it is light. Owing to the decreasing natural light in winter, there is an increase in the production of melatonin, making people feel drowsy and lethargic.

Occasionally, people suffer from SAD during the summer months, and circannual rhythms cannot explain this. Animal studies have shown that changes in the magnetic fields are correlated with decreased melatonin synthesis and serotonin production. One theory is that geomagnetic storms might be responsible for both summer and winter SAD. Whittell (1995) reports high suicide rates in remote parts of Alaska and argues that this might be due to the northern lights, a source of change in geomagnetism.

Key terms

Circannual rhythm: a biological process that occurs according to seasonal cues at intervals of approximately one year.

Treatments for seasonal affective disorder

Phototherapy

The use of phototherapy or light therapy as a treatment for SAD is based on the assumption that there is diminished exposure to light during winter, when depression occurs. If this is the case, increasing exposure to bright light should reverse the depressive symptoms. The basic procedure is for the depressed individual to sit close to a source of light (at least 2,500 lux) for a period of time (one to two hours) daily. The individual sits two to three feet away from the specially designed light box, wearing a light visor, and allows the light to shine on their eyes. It is not necessary (or advisable) to stare directly at the light during the session.

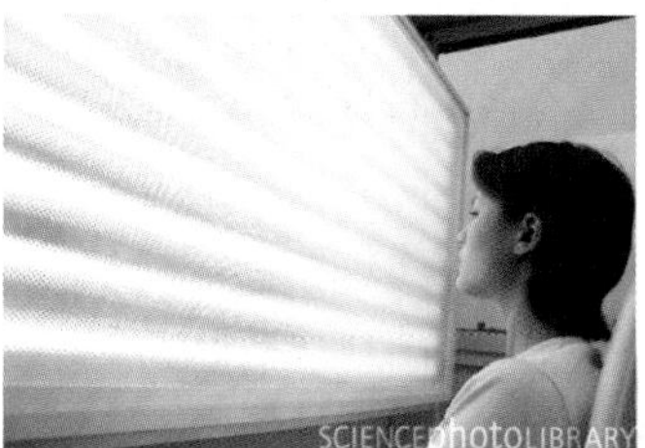

Fig. 12 *Phototherapy lamp*

Medication

Traditional antidepressant drugs such as tricyclics are not usually helpful for SAD as they may exacerbate sleepiness and lethargy. The non-sedative SSRI drugs such as Seroxat and Prozac are effective in helping the depressive symptoms of SAD and combine well with light therapy. One antidepressant, Sertraline, is proving a convenient and effective treatment for SAD. When Sertraline was tested on 200 patients in Britain, Finland, France, Austria and Canada, significant improvements were found in the patients' moods and levels of anxiety. Only 3 per cent dropped out. The drug, taken once a day, works by boosting the effectiveness of serotonin in the brain and leaves patients feeling more positive (Syal, 1997).

Evaluation of treatments for SAD

- Studies have shown phototherapy to be effective with a 70 per cent response rate (Wirz-Justice *et al.*, 1993).
- Although reductions in depression are achieved rapidly with light therapy (usually within three or four days), the positive effect is only temporary and requires continual treatment during low-light months. This makes light therapy inconvenient and costly.
- Exactly how exposure to light affects mood is unclear.
- The antidepressant Sertraline is proving extremely effective in treating patients with winter SAD, and has few side effects.

Summary questions

21 Outline one explanation for seasonal affective disorder.

22 Jade knows that winter must be on its way because she is beginning to feel miserable again. This is the third year running that she has felt lethargic and very depressed. Last year she had four weeks off work in December owing to her low spirits and lack of energy. Now it is October and the same thing is beginning to happen. Last year by March she was beginning to feel much better, and the same pattern had occurred the year before. She is going to visit her doctor again, as she really cannot face going to work on Monday. Briefly discuss whether Jade might be suffering from SAD. Refer to the text in your answer.

Further reading

Birchwood, M. and Jackson, C. (2001) *Schizophrenia*. Hove and New York: Psychology Press.

Gross, R. (2005) *Psychology: The Science of Mind and Behaviour*, 5th edition. London: Hodder Arnold.

Hammen, C. (1997) *Depression*. Hove and New York: Psychology Press.

BBC: www.bbc.co.uk/health

Key points:

- In seasonal affective disorder (SAD), recurrent depressive episodes show a seasonal pattern.
- To be diagnosed with SAD, at least two episodes of depression must have occurred at the same time each year and periods of remission should also occur at the same time each year.
- Current explanations are concerned with excessive amounts of melatonin secretion, either due to decreasing natural light in winter or to changes in magnetic fields.
- The main treatments involve phototherapy and/or medication.

End-of-chapter activity 1

Many people experience feeling more 'down' during the winter months. To investigate the extent of these 'winter blues' a questionnaire could be used. Construct some relevant questions – perhaps both open and closed – and give some consideration to the details required from participants. For example, you might want to analyse any differences in age or sex differences in the experience of 'winter blues', in which case you would need to ask participants to say whether they are 'male or female' and perhaps tick an 'age boundary'. Prior to carrying out the study, think about how you will control any extraneous variables. Prepare the necessary materials and consider how you will analyse your data. Think carefully about the ethical implications of your study.

End-of-chapter activity 2

Make a glossary of the important terms and their meanings for some, or all, of the chosen topic or subtopic. If you are working in pairs or a small group, each person or group could take a subtopic and prepare a small set of cards (about 15).

For example, you could have a set of cards for SAD, and the glossary might include: 'Symptoms of SAD', 'DSM-IV criteria for SAD', 'Phototherapy', etc.

On small cards, write a question on one side and the answer on the other side. When writing the questions, change the terms into questions (e.g. 'What are the main symptoms of SAD?').

The cards can be used in a variety of ways:

- to familiarise yourself with important terms from the specification that can be used in examination questions
- for revision for yourself and your friends
- combined into a class set so that the whole class participates, maybe with competing teams.

Stress and stress management

Introduction

'Stress and stress management' is a topic deserving of study under Applied psychology option for two reasons. Firstly, it is a topic within a burgeoning area of applied psychology – health psychology, and second, 'stress' is recognised as an important topic in its own right. Stress is associated with numerous life events such as work, health and personal relationships. It has received much media attention as a result of growing scientific evidence linking it with a range of physical, mental and behavioural disorders.

Health psychology seeks to understand psychological influences on health and illness. The first reference to the term 'health psychology' was in the title of a book published in 1979 (Stone *et al.*, 1979). However its origins can be traced to early cultures when people believed that illness was caused by evil spirits. Between 500 and 300 BC, Greek philosophers tried to explain sickness by proposing that mind and body are separate entities and that people get sick because of an imbalance in body fluids. During the Middle Ages, when the influence of the Church was dominant, the belief in mystical causes of disease prevailed again. The last three centuries have seen the emergence of the biomedical model as a way of understanding health and illness.

Link

For a discussion of reductionism, see Chapter 10, Debates in psychology.

The biomedical model of health was based on the idea that illness can be explained by the workings of the body such as biochemical imbalances and bacterial or viral infections. It is reductionist, assuming that disease is an affliction of the body and separate from the processes of the mind.

The model enabled researchers to make advances in treating many infectious diseases. However, it was still unable to provide an adequate explanation for what are now the common causes of death e.g. heart disease and cancer. Research has shown that a patient's history, social relationships, life styles, personality and mental processes also need to be taken into account. And so the biopsychosocial model emerged which looks at all levels of explanation from the micro level such as the level of hormones to the macro level such as one's family or culture.

Key terms

Individual differences: the characteristics that vary from one individual to another, such as intelligence, attachment types and anxiety.

Stress and illness can be explained by this model and **stress management** is generally an application of the model. The chapter is divided into four subtopics. The first subtopic, the **physiology of stress**, deals with the biological basis of stress. The second subtopic which covers **individual differences in stress** considers psychological and social factors. A major area of research has been the description of a behaviour syndrome thought to be associated with coronary heart disease. The third subtopic, **coping with stress**, examines the way that people try to deal with stress including the important role of social factors. How people cope has implications for physical and mental health and behaviour. Finally, **techniques of stress management** considers the application of psychological therapies to the management of stress. Health psychology is, after all, an applied discipline that seeks not just to understand psychological influences on health and illness but to promote a state of health.

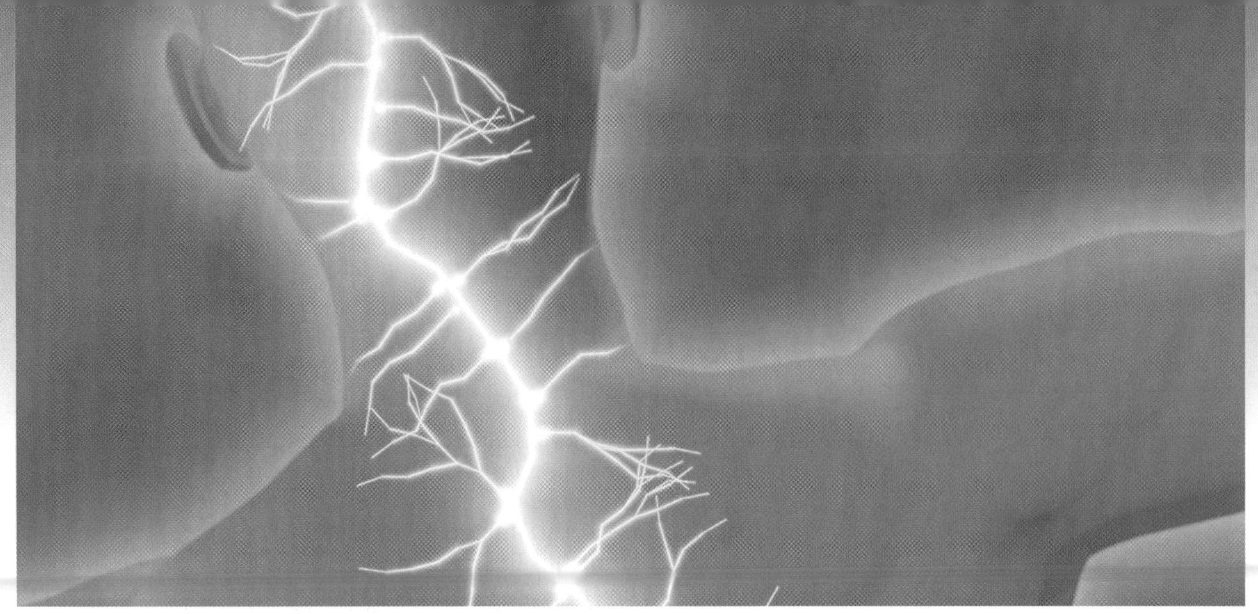

Specification content	Topic content	Page number
Stress and illness		
The role of the autonomic nervous system (ANS) and endocrine system functions in mediating and responding to stress	The physiology of stress Stress and illness	**133** **139**
Ways of measuring stress, including physiological, behavioural and self-report techniques	Measuring stress	**141**
The role of personal variables, including behaviour types A, B and C, locus of control and hardiness in mediating responses to stress	Individual differences in stress	**145**
Stress management		
Problem-focused and emotion-focused strategies; the role of defence mechanisms in coping with stress, including repression, regression, rationalisation and denial	Coping with stress	**151**
Techniques of stress management: behavioural approaches, including biofeedback and systematic desensitisation; cognitive therapy	Techniques of stress management	**158**
The role of social factors in coping with stress: social support, including types of social support	The role of social factors in coping with stress	**155**

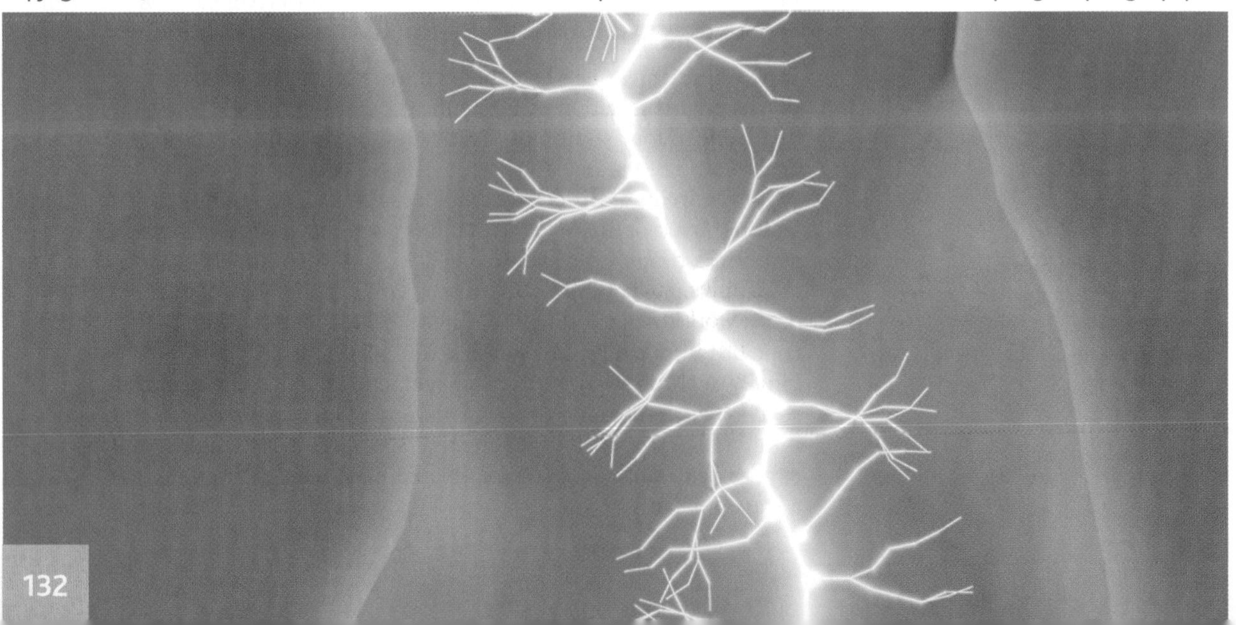

6 Stress and stress management

The physiology of stress

Learning objectives:

- understand what psychologists mean by the term 'stress'
- explain the role of the autonomic nervous system and the endocrine system functions in mediating and responding to stress
- analyse the link between stress and illness.

When we hear others saying that they are 'stressed' we generally have an idea of what this means.

The feelings are familiar, and the situations commonplace, for example:

- the frustration of being stuck in a motorway traffic jam on the way to the airport or to an important meeting with no exit route for miles
- the irritation of being channelled from one menu through to another and subjected to a barrage of loud distasteful music when trying to get through to a human voice on the phone in order to sort out a query
- the feeling of apprehension that the deadline for an assignment is fast approaching but there is still much to do.

The reactions to all these situations (and many more) can neatly be summed up by the word '**stress**'. But what do psychologists mean by the term?

Fig. 1 *Computers – here to make life easier!*

Key terms

Stress: a relationship between the person and the environment that is appraised by the person as taxing or exceeding his or her resources and endangering his or her well-being (Lazarus and Folkman, 1984).

Stressor: a stimulus that is threatening or harmful, causing a stress response.

The nature of stress

Stress has been conceptualised by psychologists in three ways (Baum, 1990; Hobfoll, 1989):

- Stress can be regarded as the stimulus in the environment that causes the stress response. These are the events or circumstances that are perceived as threatening or harmful and that psychologists call **stressors**. Examples are major life events, such as bereavement; daily hassles, such as the car breaking down; and chronic stressors, such as workload or poor housing. External stressors may also be physical stimuli, such as intense noise or extreme temperature. On the other hand, stressors can be internal, for example thoughts and feelings, or physical states such as pain and fatigue.

Hint

Notice that the stress response is (generally) an adaptive reaction that the body makes to the disturbance caused by the stressor. This will become more apparent as you study the topic.

Link

The response to the stressor involves the actions of the autonomic nervous system. The organism is prepared for intense activity whether fighting or running away. For information about the fight or flight response, see Chapter 2, Biopsychology, and Chapter 9, Anxiety disorders, in *AQA Psychology B AS*; see also p135.

Hint

It may help to think of an example for each of the above concepts of stress:

- 'I have a stressful job' (environmental stressor)
- 'I feel stressed out' (internal response or strain)
- 'I have too much to do, too little time and it is making me feel stressed' (interaction between the person and their environment).

Key terms

Strain: the psychological and physiological response to a stressor.

Transactional model of stress: stress is an interaction between the individual's ability to cope and the demands of the environment.

Acute stress: stress caused by time-limited, major or minor events that are harmful or threatening at a particular moment in life or for a relatively short period.

Chronic stress: stress caused by harmful but stable conditions of life and from the stressful roles continually fulfilled at work and in the family.

- Stress can be regarded as a response to a stressor. The response consists of two interrelated parts: psychological and physiological. The psychological part involves behaviour such as running away from the stressor and accompanying emotions such as fear. The physiological part involves heightened body arousal such as a pounding heart and dry mouth. Collectively, the person's psychological and physiological response to a stressor is known as **strain**.
- Stress is not simply a stimulus or a response but also an interaction or transaction between the person and their environment that depends on cognitive appraisal of the situation. According to this view, stress can be regarded as a response that occurs when a person thinks that they cannot cope with the pressures in the environment. This accounts for why the same stimulus may have different effects on different people. For example, two motorists both caught in bad traffic may differ in the amount of strain that they each experience. One person may keep looking at their watch, honking the car horn and getting more and more agitated by the minute. Another motorist, thinking that there is nothing to be achieved by getting angry, remains calm, turns on the radio and listens to a play or some music. What this illustrates is that a person is an active agent who can influence the effect of stressors through behavioural, cognitive and emotional strategies. Moreover, the same individual may react differently to the same stressor on different occasions: for example, heat may be a stressor whilst at work but most enjoyable when on holiday.

The **transactional model of stress** is commonly accepted among psychologists and is the basis of the definition of stress.

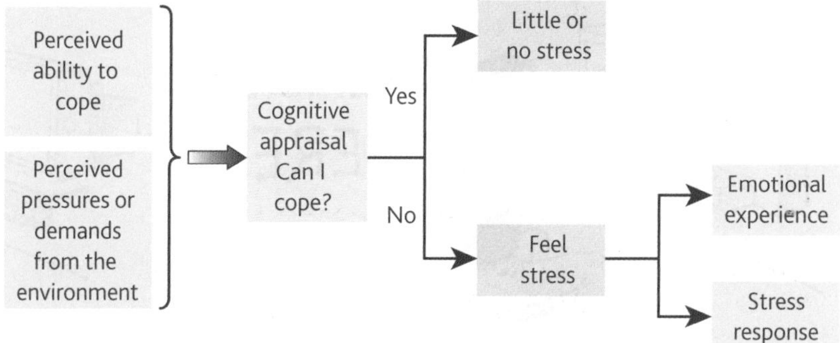

Fig. 2 *The transactional view of stress*

The transactional view is that stress is a complex process with many potential influences: personality factors, the way people appraise the environment, the ways in which they cope and the way in which these influences change. Thus the model sees stress as a shifting process that changes over time and is dependent on how a person appraises the stressors and on their coping mechanisms.

More recently, stress theorists have drawn attention to the distinction between **acute stress** and **chronic stress**. Chronic stress arises from ongoing harmful conditions of life. Typical examples are noisy neighbours, relationship problems, workplace pressures and financial or health worries. Acute stress, on the other hand, is time limited. It can be caused by major events, such as the death of a family member, or minor life events, for example losing the house keys. In either case, the threat can either be perceived or real. Acute stress, however, especially if major, such as a death of a close relative, may create many sources of daily or chronic stress, thereby blurring the distinction between acute and chronic stress.

So far, stress has been presented as negative and by implication bad for the individual (see Table 1 for some of the effects of stress). However, not all stress is bad. Selye (1974) distinguishes between 'distress', which is harmful and damaging, and 'good stress' or **eustress**, which is beneficial. There are several reasons why stress may be beneficial. One is that stress can be motivating: sometimes people need to experience heightened arousal to motivate behaviour. For example, some students get higher grades in their public examinations than would be predicted by their mock examinations because they are under enough stress to perform well. Another reason is that some people thrive in moderately stressful situations and perceive stress as a challenge. Pleasurable emotional responses accompany challenge although it is also possible that the physiological stress response to challenge differs from that of threat (Lazarus and Folkman, 1984). Finally, small amounts of stress can be a form of moderate exercise for the cardiovascular and respiratory systems as heart rate and lung activity are increased.

Table 1 *Some effects of stress*

Type of effect	Effects experienced
Physiological effects	Increased blood pressure and heart rate, expansion of air passages in lungs and as a consequence possible breathing difficulties, release of adrenalin and noradrenalin
Emotional effects	Anxiety, depression, apathy, anger, helplessness
Cognitive effects	Poor concentration, increased distractibility, short-term memory impairment
Behavioural effects	Loss of appetite, restlessness, excessive drinking, disrupted sleep patterns, reduced work performance/absenteeism, confrontation or withdrawal (**fight or flight response**)
Health effects	Fatigue, coronary heart disease, ulcers, headaches and migraines, weakened immune system and lowered resistance to infections

Key terms

Eustress: stress that has positive effects on performance or wellbeing.

Fight or flight response: the response to a stressor that results in a state of physiological arousal so that the individual is prepared to fight or take flight.

Homeostasis: the process of maintaining a constant physiological environment; in terms of stress, homeostasis results in a return to the normal unstressed state. (The term comes from a Greek word meaning 'same state'.)

General adaptation syndrome (GAS): the three-stage sequence of physiological reactions to prolonged and intense stress. The sequence consists of the alarm reaction, the stage of resistance and the stage of exhaustion.

The general adaptation syndrome

What happens to the body under stress? The biologist Hans Selye (1956) viewed the response to stress in physiological terms. He believed that stimuli such as cold or disease seriously threaten the **homeostasis** of the organism and that physiological changes are needed to resist the effects of such threats to homeostasis. In the 1950s, he subjected laboratory rats to a variety of stressors, for example extreme temperatures and harmless injections, and, based on the results, argued that there was a general response to stress. Such a response is necessary for survival and is adaptive.

Selye concluded that the stress response is non-specific (general) and that all animals and humans react to stressors through a three-stage physiological response. This he called the **general adaptation syndrome** (GAS). The GAS involves a complex interaction between the central nervous system (CNS), the autonomic nervous system (ANS) and the endocrine system. These three systems will now be briefly considered.

The central nervous system

The CNS consists of the brain and spinal cord, and its main function is to integrate and coordinate all body functions and behaviour. In relation to the physiological stress response, the most important CNS structure is the hypothalamus. The hypothalamus is situated at the base of the forebrain and is involved in a wide range of different behaviours including

Fig. 3 *Stress can make you depressed*

Hint

'General' means that there is a common response to all stressors: people display the same bodily reactions. In other words, it does not matter if the stressor is starvation, severe weather, a difficult day at work or pneumonia. The body responds in the same way.

Link

The divisions of the nervous system pertinent to an understanding of stress are the central nervous system and the autonomic nervous system. The endocrine system interacts with the nervous system in responding to stress. The topic of stress illustrates the biological basis of behaviour. For more information, see Chapter 2, Biopsychology, in *AQA Psychology B AS*.

Link

In *AQA Psychology B AS*, Chapter 2, Biopsychology, discussion of the central nervous system focused on the cortex and cortical specialisation. The hypothalamus lies under the cortex in the frontal region of the brain. It has connections with the rest of the forebrain and integrates activity of the ANS.

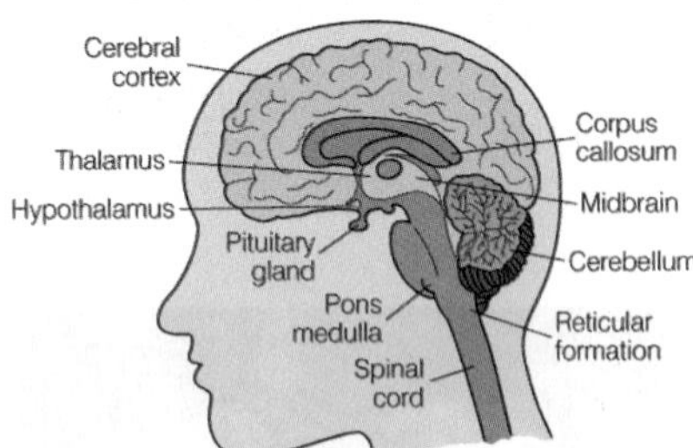

Fig. 5 *The hypothalamus*

Hint

You will notice, as you read on, that the hypothalamus is very important in relation to stress for two reasons:

- It regulates the sympathetic branch of the ANS.
- It controls the pituitary gland, which is the master gland in the endocrine system.

Hint

The autonomic nervous system is so named because many of its functions are self-regulating or autonomous rather than being under the conscious control of the organism. We cannot control our heart beats (although we can behave in ways to reduce stress to the heart).

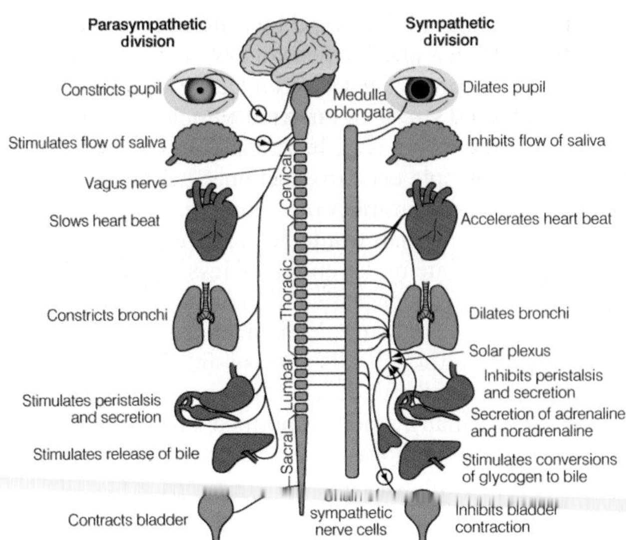

Fig. 4 *The autonomic nervous system*

homeostasis. The cerebral cortex (the surface of the forebrain) sends signals to the hypothalamus when a stressor is perceived, beginning a complex physiological process in response to the stressor.

The autonomic nervous system

The ANS is a branch of the nervous system. Its nerves connect the CNS to the internal organs, glands and muscles over which we have no control, such as the muscles of the stomach and the heart. The main function of the ANS is to regulate the body's involuntary activities and to 'report' to the brain the current state of activity of these organs. The ANS is divided into two branches: the parasympathetic and sympathetic systems. These operate in an antagonistic way to maintain homeostasis. Heart rate, for example, is accelerated by sympathetic activity and slowed down by parasympathetic activity.

The sympathetic system activates the internal organs for vigorous activities, expressing strong emotions and for mobilising the body in an emergency situation. As an illustration, consider the physiological reactions in an emergency situation such as a sudden unexpected noise in the dead of night. The heart pumps at two or three times the normal speed sending a rich supply of blood to the muscles in the arms and legs so that evasive action can be taken. The capillaries under the surface of the skin constrict, which sends the blood pressure soaring, but at least you can sustain a surface wound and not bleed to death. Pupils of the eyes dilate so that you can see well. All the functions of the body not needed for the struggle close down: for example, digestion and intestinal activity are altered, which is why the stomach feels as if it has 'turned over'. This activation of the sympathetic branch has been termed the 'fight or flight' response because it prepares the person (or animal) to respond to the danger either by attacking (fight) or running away (flight) (Cannon, 1929). Although the response happens very quickly it takes time to subside: the state of heightened arousal continues for some time after the 'danger' has passed. For example, having heard a noise the person may find it difficult to sleep and remains in a state of anxiety listening out for every sound.

Cannon proposed that arousal could have both positive and negative effects. The response is adaptive because it mobilises the person to respond quickly to danger, but the state of high arousal if prolonged is detrimental to health.

The role of the parasympathetic branch is to restore the normal body state after arousal. Thus heart beat and heart rate slow down, blood pressure drops, the pupils of the eyes constrict and the usual activity of the digestive system is resumed. The parasympathetic system also carries out the body's maintenance needs, conserves energy and promotes digestion and metabolism. It predominates when we are relaxed or inactive and when an emergency has passed.

It is important to understand that the two systems do not operate in an on/off manner. They generally work in opposition but are also interactive and cooperative. In times of stress, the sympathetic system dominates, but, once the stress passes, the parasympathetic system dominates for some time in order to restore the balance between them.

The endocrine system

The endocrine system is not part of the nervous system but a system of internal glands that often work in close association with the ANS. The nervous system and the endocrine system are linked by connections between the hypothalamus and a gland that lies just below it, the pituitary gland (see Figure 5). These systems share a very important function: communicating with various parts of the body to affect physical states and behaviour. However, each system does this in different ways: the nervous system uses both electrical and chemical messages; whereas the endocrine system communicates only with chemical substances called hormones (powerful chemical messengers) that are released into the bloodstream by endocrine glands (each gland secretes a specific hormone) and distributed to the rest of the body. The secretion of hormones by endocrine glands is controlled by the pituitary gland, which is called the 'master gland'.

Although communication by the bloodstream is much slower than neural communication, the influence of the endocrine system is broad; this is because every cell is directly or indirectly in contact with the bloodstream and hormones can therefore reach every cell.

The hormones enable the body to maintain a steady state. For example, if there is a fall in liquid content in the body, the pituitary gland releases an antidiuretic hormone that controls the extent to which water is reabsorbed into the blood from the kidneys after blood filtration. As a result, less water is excreted into the bladder. The endocrine system and the ANS interact in stressful situations. This is because the sympathetic system causes the adrenal glands to secrete adrenalin into the bloodstream, which increases physiological arousal. Obviously, to maintain a steady state, information must then be fed back to the glands. Thus whenever the required amount of hormone has been secreted the gland is ordered to stop or reduce its activity by a negative feedback loop.

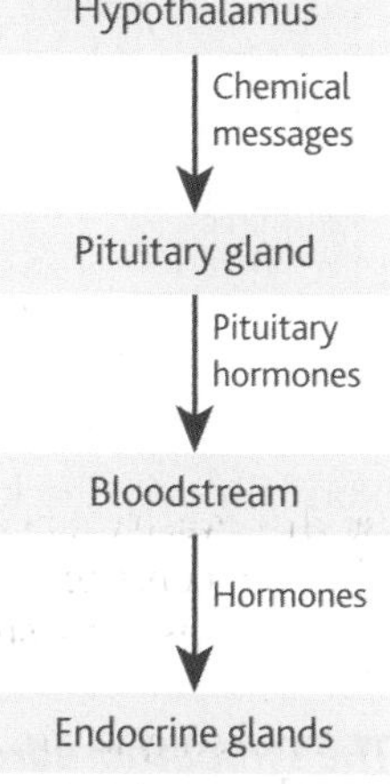

Fig. 6 *The link between the nervous system and endocrine system*

Having looked at the CNS, the ANS and the endocrine systems, let us now consider their role in mediating and responding to stress.

Stage 1 of Selye's GAS: the alarm reaction

This is the immediate reaction to the stressor whereby the body is mobilised for action. It is characterised by two substages. Initially, arousal

Links

Perception of noise becomes accentuated or heightened because we are motivated to respond in an adaptive way to any threat posed. Increased awareness or perceptual accentuation occurs. See Chapter 8, Perceptual processes, in *AQA Psychology B AS*.

The fight or flight response involves the actions of the sympathetic division of the autonomic nervous system. The parasympathetic division restores a state of calm and relaxation. See Chapter 2, Biopsychology in *AQA Psychology B AS*.

Hint

The sympathetic branch acts as a unit (it is connected by a chain of nerve cells). This makes sense as the response involves many organs, which need to work in coordination, yet has to occur quickly. The sympathetic branch involves all the organs working 'in sympathy' or together – hence its name.

Link

Looking at stress from an evolutionary perspective perhaps sheds some light on why it is detrimental to health. In our evolutionary past, when dangers were life threatening, needing quick energetic evasive responses, the fight or flight response was adaptive. For many stress-provoking situations nowadays, such as chronic work stress, it is maladaptive. See Chapter 1, Key approaches, and Chapter 9, Anxiety disorders, in *AQA Psychology B AS*.

Link

The adrenal glands are part of the endocrine system. They produce adrenalin and noradrenalin, both of which are involved in physiological arousal and the fight or flight response. See *AQA Psychology B AS*, Chapter 2, Biopsychology.

Take it further

Why is it that the fight or flight response sometimes occurs when one sits an exam? When standing before an audience, why do some people freeze? Such responses are hardly adaptive. Despite the evolution of societies and cultures, it appears that our physiological mechanisms have not evolved. At one time, when our main stressors were predators or other physical dangers, these responses were highly adaptive. However, many everyday situations that now cause us stress, such as being stuck in a traffic jam, weeks of revision and sitting exams, still elicit the alarm response even though they are not life threatening. Unfortunately for us, the evolution of our physiological mechanisms has not kept up with that of society, resulting in vestigial alarm responses that may be health threatening over time.

drops below normal – this is known as the shock phase. It then very rapidly rises above normal – the countershock phase. The two key players in this substage are the sympathetic branch of the ANS and the endocrine system, although the whole chain of events outlined below begins with the CNS.

The appraisal of whether something is a stressor occurs in the cerebral cortex. If a stressor in the environment is perceived, a signal is sent to the hypothalamus. The hypothalamus starts two simultaneous processes in the body: the first involves the pituitary and adrenal glands and is known as the 'hypothalamic–pituitary–adrenal axis'; the second involves the sympathetic branch of the ANS and is known as the 'sympatho–adrenomedullary axis'.

The hypothalamic–pituitary–adrenal (HPA) axis

The hypothalamus secretes corticotrophic-releasing hormone (CRH). This hormone is vital to rousing the body when a threat presents itself. CRH follows a passageway to the pituitary gland. This in turn releases a hormone called adrenocorticotrophic hormone (ACTH) into the bloodstream. When ACTH reaches the adrenal glands (located just above the kidneys), it stimulates the adrenal cortex (the outer layer of the gland) to release corticosteroids (hormones, e.g. cortisol) which help provide energy by stimulating the liver to release stored sugar. This is why athletes and body builders sometimes take steroids to boost performance. Corticosteroids activate the immune system to fight tissue inflammation and heal wounds.

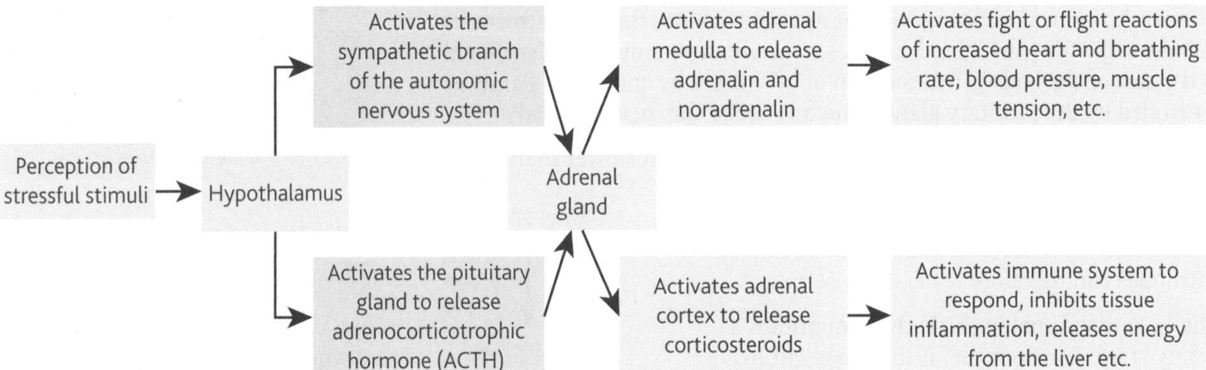

Fig. 7 *The physiological response to stress*

AQA Examiner's tip

Try to remember the names of these axes (pathways) because they neatly summarise the chain of events. It looks impressive in the exam too, and it is really important that you know the role of the ANS and endocrine system functions in mediating and responding to stress. Think up a mnemonic for the first letter of each component (HPA and SAM).

Normally, a feedback loop to the pituitary gland and hypothalamus delivers inhibitory signals keeping hormone manufacture from becoming excessive. If the levels of hormones remain too high, this can have negative consequences including high blood pressure and immune suppression.

The sympatho-adrenomedullary axis

At the same time as the endocrine system is activated, the sympathetic branch of the ANS is also activated. The hypothalamus stimulates the adrenal medulla (the inner core of the adrenal glands) to release adrenalin and noradrenalin (stress hormones) into the bloodstream. The result is increase in heart rate, blood pressure, blood flow, etc. – in other words, the symptoms of the fight or flight response. This rapidly increasing arousal results from the release of the stress hormones by the endocrine system into the bloodstream and, as a result, the body is fully mobilised to resist the stressor. Noradrenalin activates the negative feedback loop to switch off the release of ACTH as the body cannot sustain the alarm reaction for long. If this level of arousal continues, the organism will die within days or even hours.

Stage 2 of Selye's GAS: the stage of resistance

If the stress continues (and is not strong enough to cause death) the body begins to adapt to the stressors to which it is exposed. For example, if the stressor is a shortage of food the person may conserve energy by reducing physical activity, which also maximises the absorption of nutrients from food. Endocrine and sympathetic activities decline a little but, because the body is being subjected to continued stress, higher than normal levels of arousal are required to deal with the situation. A person may appear to be coping but they become increasingly vulnerable to health problems or what Selye termed '**diseases of adaptation**', such as ulcers, high blood pressure and illnesses that result from impaired immune function. People report feeling 'run down' and are less able to resist new stressors. Psychological effects as well as physiological effects have been identified, such as increased irritability and a tendency to be pessimistic.

Stage 3 of Selye's GAS: the stage of exhaustion

Prolonged physiological arousal produced by severe long-term stress or repeated stress is damaging. It weakens the immune system and uses up or 'exhausts' the body's energy reserves. The general pattern of the initial shock phase reappears and alarm signals may return (the higher brain centres override the negative feedback loop and maintain the stress response). Eventually, the body can no longer cope with the stressor. Disease and physiological damage become increasingly likely and eventually death may occur.

Evaluation of the GAS

The GAS model has been very influential in showing that a range of different stressors can trigger the same adaptive response, and it has been supported by scientific research. Increases in the secretion of hormones by the adrenal glands have been found in many studies with a wide variety of stressors (Baum *et al.*, 1982; Ciaranello, 1983). The model has also been very influential in identifying a link between stress and illness.

However, Selye's claim that all stressors produce the same physiological reaction has been challenged. Following extensive studies of various stressors and hormones, Mason (1975) concluded that we 'have not found evidence that any single hormone responds to all stimuli in absolutely non-specific fashion'. Another criticism of the GAS model is that it is based on Selye's work with non-human animals and overlooks the influence of social, cognitive and emotional factors that might mediate between the stressor and the response to the stressor. Such factors would account for why some people do not develop stress-related disorders despite long-term stress.

Finally, although Selye's work is important in showing that severe or prolonged stress can result in disease, stress in moderation can actually increase the ability of a person to cope better with extreme stress. Coaches frequently subject athletes to stressful episodes of physical training in preparation for the much tougher regime before a competition. The stress response is a kind of 'balancing act' in which too little or too much stress carries undesirable consequences (Lovallo, 1997).

Stress and illness

It is believed that stress interferes with the immune system in various ways, reducing its effectiveness. This could explain the link between stress and illness.

Hint

Raised levels of cortisol in the urine are used as an indicator of stress. Cortisol increases blood sugar levels and enhances metabolism, mimicking the activity of the sympathetic nervous system.

Take it further

Recent research from the National Institute of Mental Health in the USA suggests that an over-active HPA may be linked with depression. Antidepressants and electroconvulsive therapy (ECT) treatments used for reducing depression are both known to reduce the high CRH levels commonly found in people with depression. Reduction in these levels is linked with a decrease in depressive symptoms. Although no causal links can be claimed, there does seem to be a link between stress and depression.

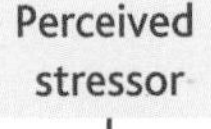

Perceived stressor
Alarm reaction
Body is mobilised to defend against the stressor
Stage of resistance
Arousal remains high, as body tries to defend against and adapt to the stressor
Stage of exhaustion
Resources are very limited, ability to resist may collapse

Fig. 8 *General adaptation syndrome*

Take it further

Owing to the limited space available, only brief coverage can be given to this area. However, several references have already been made to the link between stress and illness; for more on this issue, see Table 1 on p135 and look for 'diseases of adaptation' above.

Research study: Cohen *et al.* (1991)

Aim: To investigate if stress increases vulnerability to infectious disease.

Method: The sample consisted of 154 men and 266 women volunteers. The level of stress in their lives was measured by a life-event scale covering the previous year; a perceived stress scale; and a negative emotion scale, measuring levels of anxiety, fear, depression and irritation.

The combined scores on the three scales produced a Psychological Stress Index (PSI) for each individual.

The volunteers were then exposed either to nasal drops containing respiratory viruses or to a placebo solution and isolated in a hotel for several days. Daily objective (e.g. blood measures) and subjective (e.g. patient **self-reports**) signs and symptoms of illness were monitored while the 'patients' were in isolation.

Results: Participants with a high PSI score developed more colds than those with a low score. The difference was significant. However, participants in the placebo group did not develop the symptoms of a cold regardless of their level of stress.

Conclusion: Stress increases vulnerability to infectious diseases.

Evaluation: This was a highly controlled study. Participants were quarantined to reduce the effect of extraneous variables on the development of the cold. The dependent variable (developing a cold) was measured by objective as well as subjective methods. The inclusion of a placebo group allowed the researchers to eliminate the role of psychological factors in the development of infectious diseases.

Key terms

Self-report: a method, such as an interview or questionnaire, requiring the participants to report on their own thoughts or behaviour.

Several studies have found that people caring for relatives suffering from a chronic condition are subject to high levels of stress and impaired immune function. One such study found that it took nine days longer for wounds to heal in women who cared for relatives with Alzheimer's disease than in a control group of women who had no such responsibility (Kiecolt-Glaser *et al.*, 1995). Another study found that it took longer for wounds to heal following a skin biopsy in people who had to care for relatives with dementia than it did for wounds to heal in a control group (Sweeney, 1995). The production of corticosteroids needed to fight inflammation and heal wounds increases under stress. Although intermittent production has negligible effects on the immune system, unfortunately persistent production impairs its functioning. Of course, in both studies the immune system could have been weakened by other variables apart from stress; poor diet and lack of sleep, owing to the demands of caring, are examples of possible confounding variables. Other researchers have reported lowered immune function without obvious sign of illness for the recently bereaved (Antoni, 1987). Kiecolt-Glaser's group found reductions in immune function in unhappily married women and recently separated women especially if they were unhappy about the separation (Kiecolt-Glaser *et al.*, 1987).

Hint

Immune function can be measured from blood samples although it can also be assessed from salivary samples.

Key points:

- Stress is difficult to define. One view is that stress is a response that occurs when a person thinks that they cannot cope with the pressures in the environment.
- Selye found that non-humans respond to a stressor in a non-specific way. He believed that this physiological response, which is called the 'general adaptation syndrome' (GAS), also applies to humans.
- The first stage of GAS – the alarm reaction – prepares the body for fight or flight. This stage is characterised by the activity of the endocrine system (hypothalamic–pituitary–adrenal axis) and the ANS (sympatho-adrenomedullary axis).
- In the resistance stage, the body continues to draw on its resources although at above normal levels, whereas in the exhaustion stage the stressor can no longer be managed. This results in illness.

Summary questions

1. Identify one way in which stress can be harmful and one way in which it can be beneficial.
2. Briefly explain the role of the hypothalamus in responding to stress.
3. Tony has been suffering from severe headaches for a number of months. He has been increasingly absent from work owing to colds and various infectious diseases. Tony's GP believes that his symptoms are due to chronic stress. Briefly explain the link between Tony's physical symptoms and chronic stress.

Individual differences in stress

Learning objectives:

- know and evaluate the ways in which psychologists measure stress
- explain and evaluate the role of behaviour types A, B and C in mediating responses to stress
- explain and evaluate the role of locus of control and hardiness in mediating responses to stress
- apply personal variables to the differing responses to stressors.

Link

For a definition of galvanic skin responses (GSR), see Chapter 4, Cognition and law, p76.

Early research into stress tended to adopt a simple stimulus–response approach. Researchers looked at the extent to which stressors such as long working hours predict an outcome for, for example, cardiovascular disease. Such an approach, however, ignored intervening 'person' variables in the response, and results proved inconclusive. Health psychologists have therefore become increasingly interested in looking at how factors in the individual (their personality) or the interaction between the individual and their environment (involving social support, for example) interact to determine the level of strain experienced. However, before looking at the role of some of these intervening variables in mediating responses to stress, we need first to examine how researchers measure stress.

Measuring stress

Health psychologists typically use two types of measures:

- measures of environmental events or situations, such as life events and daily hassles; these of course are the stressors
- measures of strain such as physical symptoms and behaviour.

Physiological techniques

Stressors bring about physiological arousal which is reflected by physical symptoms. These symptoms can be measured in several ways using electrical or mechanical equipment. Blood pressure, heart rate, respiration rate and galvanic skin responses (GSR) are all indexes of arousal which can be measured separately, for example by using a heart-rate monitor to measure heart rate, or simultaneously using a **polygraph**. Samples of blood or urine can also be analysed to assess the level of hormones secreted by the adrenal glands, mainly cortisol, adrenalin and noradrenalin. These levels can be monitored to determine both immediate reactions to stress and long-term reactions to stress.

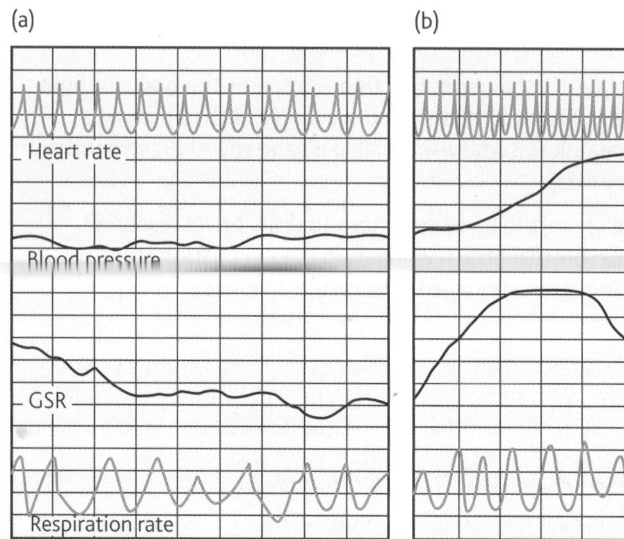

Fig. 9 *Graphical record of indexes of arousal measured and recorded simultaneously by a polygraph showing differences between someone who is calm (a) and someone who is under stress (b)*

Advantages of using physiological techniques

- Physiological techniques measure the body's response to a stressor. These physical symptoms of stress produce measures that are objective, easily quantified and reliable.
- Measures of physiological arousal can be taken relatively easily. Miniature versions of polygraphs are available with recording units so that assessments of stress may be taken in everyday settings: at home, at work, or in any other 'stressful' situation of research interest. For example, using polygraphs researchers have shown that paramedics' blood pressure is higher during ambulance runs and at the hospital than during other work situations (Goldstein *et al.*, 1992).

Disadvantages of using physiological techniques

- Some physiological techniques raise ethical and methodological issues. Attaching electrical devices, such as the polygraph, to a person's body or taking blood samples may be stressful in itself.
- Physiological arousal is a general response. It is not possible to know the type of stress being experienced from measures of physiological arousal alone. Is the arousal due to the anxiety of having too many things to do or is it due to the exhilaration of having just passed a driving test? In other words, the researcher has to rely on other information, such as the context in which the behaviour occurs or self-reports. Unfortunately, physiological measurements are often not consistent with self-reports. McGrath and Beehr (1990) suggest that this may be because each measure may relate to a different time. A blood test may still contain the residue of the previous day's stress, whereas self-reports may be based on the experience of the current situation or thinking about a future stressor.

Hint

To 'mediate' means to 'come in between'. In looking at the various personal variables in mediating responses to stress, we are looking at factors that come in between the stressor and the response to the stressor (e.g. the personality of that person, characteristics of their behaviour, etc.) and affect the stress response. These mediating variables account for some of the individual differences in stress.

Link

In science, theory and measurement go together. In order to develop theories about the various aspects of stress, health psychologists must use reliable and valid measuring tools. See Chapter 10, Debates in psychology, for the features and principles of the scientific approach, and Chapter 11, Research methods in psychology, for a discussion of reliability and validity.

Key terms

Polygraph: an electromechanical device that assesses the body's arousal by measuring and recording several physiological indexes (e.g. blood pressure and heart rate) simultaneously.

Hint

The terms 'corticosteroids' and 'catecholamines' are frequently used to refer to two categories of hormones secreted by the adrenal glands. Cortisol belongs to the former category and adrenalin and noradrenalin to the latter.

Link

Although physiological arousal happens internally, it does in fact produce 'overt' behaviour. Blood pressure, GSR, etc. is open, available and detectable by whoever observes it. Overt behaviour is amenable to scientific research. See Chapter 11, Research methods in psychology.

- It may be difficult to control some of the variables that affect measures of physiological arousal (Jex and Beehr, 1991). These include stable factors (e.g. gender and age) and 'passing' factors (e.g. the person may have just run up several flights of stairs or had a cup of coffee).

Behavioural techniques

Behavioural techniques involve observations and measurements of overt behaviour considered by psychologists to be indicators of stress. Examples are facial expression, rate of speech and body posture. People talk more quickly when stressed and the content of what they are saying may lack coherence. They may frown, tense their body and engage in nervous repetitive behaviour, such as nail biting. Other signs of stress may be drinking, smoking and aggressive behaviour. Of course, none of these behaviours on its own is informative. To get an indication of stress, the researcher needs to know how the person usually behaves.

Advantages of using behavioural techniques

Measures of behaviours such as rate of speech, facial expressions, etc. are, like measures of physiological arousal, considered to be objective. Behaviour can be recorded accurately, is easily quantified and reliable. For example, the researcher could measure the number of words spoken per minute.

Disadvantages of using behavioural techniques

Information about a person's usual behaviour is needed. A person may habitually bite their nails so, on its own, nail biting cannot be taken as a measure of stress. For the same reason, any experimental research taking a behavioural measure of stress requires a control condition. Additionally, the person may be aware of being observed and may behave differently – a phenomenon called 'reactivity'.

Self-report techniques

An obvious way of finding out if people are stressed is simply to ask them. This sounds easy enough to do and demands little of the researcher or the respondent. All the researcher has to do is ask. All the respondent has to do is to report on whether or not they feel stressed or how stressed they feel: literally, self-report. But of course reality is not that simple. Stress must be measured as objectively and precisely as possible. With these aims in mind, a number of different scales have been developed to measure people's stress.

The Social Readjustment Rating Scale

The Social Readjustment Rating Scale (SRRS) (Holmes and Rahe, 1967) considers the stress caused by major life events. These are events considered difficult to deal with, requiring a degree of psychological readjustment and associated with the onset of illness.

The scale was compiled by analysing approximately 5,000 patients' records. Any major life events that had occurred before the person became ill were noted. In total, 43 life events, such as divorce, pregnancy and trouble with the boss, were identified. Hundreds of men and women of various ages and backgrounds were then asked to rate the amount of adjustment each event would require. This was based on their own personal experience and observations of others' experiences. The researchers used the ratings to assign values (known as 'life change units' or LCUs) to each event and construct the scale. The higher the LCU value, the greater the readjustment required and the more stressful the event. A sample of the scale is shown in Figure 10.

Link

One of the problems with the scientific approach is that when taking part in an experiment or observation the participants' behaviour might alter. Reactivity may occur: i.e. a participant may change their behaviour (e.g. showing off, trying harder or showing evaluation apprehension). The advantage of physiological techniques is that they measure responses not under the control of the participant although they can be affected by the stress of participation. See Chapter 11, Research methods in psychology.

Hint

Think of how one might recognise the signs of stress in one's self or others as such signs are also behavioural measures of stress:

- insomnia
- forgetfulness and making mistakes
- avoidance of stressful situations such as absenteeism.

AQA Examiner's tip

Behavioural measures such as insomnia, forgetfulness and avoidance of stress are usually recorded as a diary. So as well as observations and measurements of overt behaviour psychologists study stress through a diary record of behaviour. Consider here the strengths and weaknesses of qualitative and quantitative data.

AQA Examiner's tip

As you consider the rest of this topic, take note of how stress has been measured in each research study. It may be useful to keep a record of these studies and your observations. This should prove useful for answering a question on 'measuring stress'.

Hint

Notice that a person is not asked to report whether or not they feel stressed or how stressed they feel. It is the stressors that provide the measure of stress; the LCU score is a number corresponding to the amount of change that a person has had to face and adjust to.

Rank	Life event	Mean value
1	Death of spouse	100
2	Divorce	73
3	Marital separation	65
4	Jail term	63
5	Death of close family member	63
6	Personal injury or illness	53
7	Marriage	50
8	Fired at work	47
10	Retirement	45
11	Change in health of family member	44
12	Pregnancy	40
13	Sex difficulties	39
16	Change in financial state	38
17	Death of close friend	37
18	Change to different line of work	36
23	Son or daughter leaving home	29
27	Begin or end school	26
38	Change in sleeping habits	16
42	Christmas	12
43	Minor violations of the law	11

Fig. 10 *A selection of life events from the Social Readjustment Rating Scale*

To measure the amount of stress experienced, people have to check off the events that happened to them during a given period of time, usually the past 24 months. The LCU values are then summed to give a total stress score.

One of the main uses of the scale has been to assess the link between stress and subsequent illness or injury. Although some studies have shown a link between high ratings and subsequent illness (Johnson, 1986; Rahe and Arthur, 1978), the relationship is actually quite weak (only about 0.30). This could be because there are reasons other than stress for why people become ill and have accidents. Another reason is that the SRRS has several weaknesses. Nevertheless, Holmes and Rahe believed that stress could be measured objectively as an LCU score, which in turn predicts the person's chance of becoming ill or having an accident or injury.

Link

Post-traumatic stress disorder (PTSD) is an example of how major life events can be linked to illness. It is an anxiety disorder caused by extreme life events such as a life-threatening accident. It is characterised by flashbacks and dreams of the traumatic event as well as the usual severe anxiety. You can read about anxiety disorders in *AQA Psychology B AS*, Chapter 9.

Evaluation of the SRRS: strengths

- The SRRS includes a wide range of events that many people find stressful. These conform to everyday notions of the effect of these events; people talk of being 'shattered' as a result of bereavement or suffering from depression following marital separation.
- The values assigned to each event were carefully determined from the ratings of a broad sample of adults and provide an estimate of the relative impact of each event on an individual.
- The SRRS is quick to administer.

Evaluation of the SRRS: weaknesses

- The scale does not discriminate between positive and negative events. 'Marriage' though stressful is viewed by many as something positive whereas marital separation is, generally, a negative experience. Studies have found that, although negative life events are correlated with illness, desirable events are not (Sarason *et al.*, 1985). This point is important to bear in mind when looking at the additive and quantitative nature of the scale. Can the LCUs of Christmas (12) plus Marriage (50) reasonably equate with death of a close family member or a term in prison (63)?
- The SRRS ignores individual differences: the differing significance of life events to people with varying priorities, motivations and coping

Link

Here we have an example of using quantitative data to try to convey feelings probably better expressed by qualitative data. However, the added problem with the SRRS is that qualitatively different experiences, i.e. positive and negative life events, are given equivalence by using the same quantitative scale. For more about qualitative and quantitative data, see Chapter 11, Methods in psychology.

styles (Lazarus, 1990). The death of a close but terminally ill family member may be expected and thus have a different effect on a person than if a death is totally unexpected. A pregnancy may be highly desirable for one person but may get in the way of a career for another.

- The SRRS relies on people's retrospective memories. The reliability and validity of these reports has been questioned. Rahe (1974) has found that estimates of **test-retest reliability** vary widely, depending on the time interval between administrations of the questionnaires. Brown (1974) has suggested that people may need to find a reason for their illnesses, leading them to report more life events than those who have no illnesses. In support of this claim, he cites a study (Polani *et al.*, 1960) that found that parents of children with Down's syndrome reported significantly more 'shocks' during early pregnancy (a hypothesis now rejected) than a group of controls. He suggested that this is because parents were seeking an explanation for the disorder.
- The final problem with the SRRS is that it ignores daily events; although more 'minor' than life events, these are more frequent. Major life events are quite rare – in fact, many people score close to zero on the SRRS. Kanner *et al.* (1981) believe that it is the minor stressors and pleasures of everyday life that have a more significant effect on heath than the major life events.

The Hassles and Uplifts Scale

This scale, developed by Kanner *et al.* (1981), included 117 daily hassles such as losing objects, traffic jams and financial concerns. It is unlike the SRRS in that respondents indicate which hassles occurred in the last month and rate their severity from 'somewhat' to 'extremely severe'. As the researchers believed that having desirable experiences makes hassles more bearable and reduces their impact on health, they designed the 'uplifts' scale, which lists 135 events that bring satisfaction and joy (e.g. completing a task or eating out). In a study of 100 men and women over a nine-month period, Kanner confirmed that hassles were both correlated with, and a predictor of, psychological health. In another study, hassle scores and life events scores were correlated with health – both correlations were weak although hassles were more strongly associated with health than were life events. Uplifts scores had virtually no association with health (DeLongis *et al.*, 1982). Other studies generally support these findings regarding the relationship of hassles and uplifts to health.

Individual differences in stress

Behaviour types A, B and C

Cardiologists Friedman and Rosenman (1974) were studying dietary differences between male heart disease victims and their wives when one of the wives exclaimed, 'If you really want to know what is giving our husbands heart attacks, I'll tell you. It's stress, the stress they receive in their work' (Sarafino, 1994). This prompted the researchers to focus on possible links between stress, behaviour and illness. They compared the stress-related behaviours of heart disease patients with those of similar, 'healthy' people and found that the patients were more likely than non-patients to display a pattern of behaviour known as **Type A**. This behaviour pattern describes someone who is impatient, competitive, time pressured, hostile and angry.

In contrast, the **Type B behaviour pattern** is characterised by low levels of competitiveness, time urgency and hostility. Type B people take life as it comes and are more easy going.

Key terms

Test-retest reliability: the external consistency of a measuring instrument, such as a questionnaire, which is assessed by giving the same test twice to the same set of participants and correlating their results.

Type A behaviour pattern: a behavioural style characterised by high levels of competitiveness, time urgency and anger or hostility.

Type B behaviour pattern: a behavioural style characterised by low levels of competitiveness, time urgency and anger or hostility.

Link

Any correlation between stress and illness cannot provide information about cause and effect. Stress may be a precursor of illness but people may be more aware of stress in their lives as a result of illness. The relationship between life events and illness could result from a third variable (e.g. anxiety – highly anxious people may be more prone to illness and more diligent in reporting life events). For more on correlation studies, see Chapter 4, Research methods, in *AQA Psychology B AS*.

Link

'Individual differences' are characteristics that vary from one person to another. The nomothetic approach, upon which many psychological theories are based, assumes that people are the same. For more on the nomothetic approach, see Chapter 10, Debates in psychology.

Hint

When evaluating a theory or a piece of research in psychology, think about 'individual differences'. People differ not only in their responses to the same stressors but also in terms of their intelligence, genetic make-up, emotions and life experiences, etc. Some of these variables are, of course, linked.

AQA Examiner's tip

Try to use the term 'behaviour pattern' when referring to Types A and B (rather than using 'personality'). Sometimes text books and articles use the latter term but, in fact, the terms describe behaviours. In the original article, the authors used the term 'behaviour pattern' rather than personality type.

Type A and B behaviour patterns are measured either by interview or by questionnaire. The most widely used method is the structured interview, a standard procedure in which a trained interviewer asks a series of questions about behaviour patterns (see Figure 11): in particular, characteristics such as competitiveness, impatience and hostility. The interviewer also records how the interviewee behaves during the interview, such as frequency of sighing and whether or not they fidget. Deliberate attempts are made to annoy the interviewee, for example by prolonged pauses or interruptions, to see how they respond to frustration. The sessions are audiotaped or videotaped and then scored by trained independent researchers who determine the classification into Type A or B. Type A classification derived from structured interviews has been associated quite consistently with ill health outcomes, particularly heart disease.

The alternative to an interview is a questionnaire; some of the questions in the structured interview have been adapted to construct self-report questionnaires.

Link

The issue of the comparative strengths and weaknesses of questionnaires and interviews applies here. The structured interview is time consuming. Questionnaires are more time and cost efficient. Both methods can be biased by socially desirable responses to questions but the structured interview has the added benefit of allowing observation of the interviewee's behaviour as an aid to classification. Hence, researchers generally favour the structured interview approach. To remind yourself about the two methods, see Chapter 4, Research methods, in *AQA Psychology B AS*.

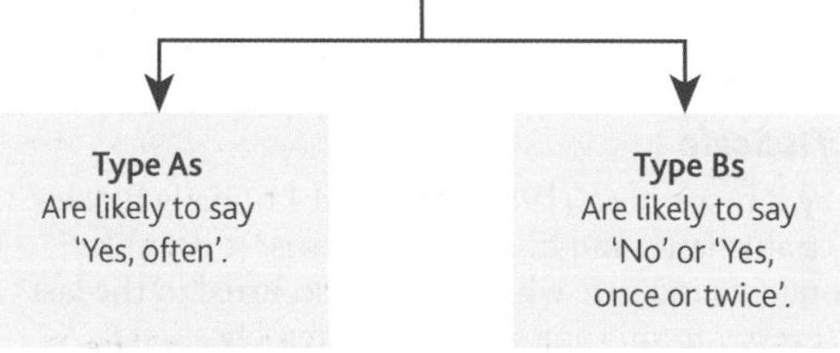

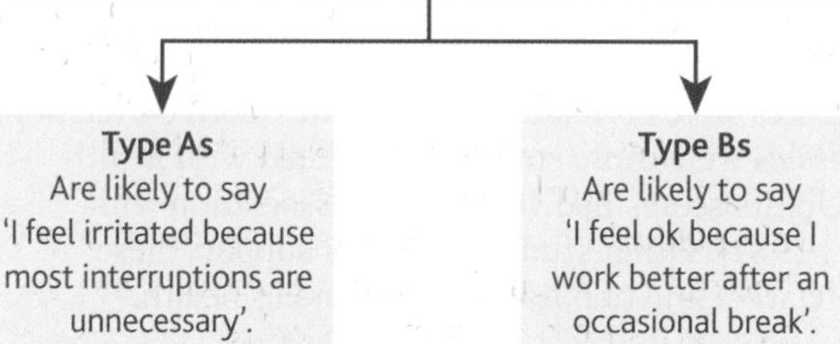

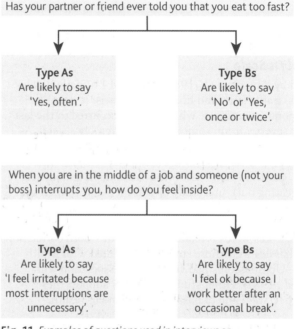

Fig. 11 *Examples of questions used in interviews or questionnaires to classify behaviour into Types A and B*

Hints

Type As in this study were described as competitive, hard driving, impatient, time conscious, super motivated, verbally aggressive and easily angered. These behaviours were either observed or picked up by the questionnaire component of the structured interview.

CHD covers illnesses that result from the narrowing or blocking of coronary arteries; these are arteries which supply blood to the heart muscles. The illnesses include angina, arteriosclerosis, and myocardial infarction (heart attack).

Much research has been carried out into the relationship between Type A behaviour and stress-related illnesses, in particular coronary heart disease (CHD). Several studies have confirmed these links.

A 12-year longitudinal study reported by Friedman and Rosenman (1974) involved over 3,500 healthy, employed, middle-aged men. People with Type A behaviour pattern (determined by the structured interview) were twice as likely to develop and die of CHD as people with Type B behaviour patterns. By the time the study was complete, 257 men had suffered heart attacks, 69 per cent of whom were Type A. Because of these and similar results, Type A has been called 'coronary-prone behaviour' (the researchers took account of various variables associated with heart disease such as obesity and smoking). Furthermore, different kinds of Type A behaviour correlate with different kinds of heart disease. Angina sufferers tended to be impatient and intolerant with others; those with heart failure tend to be hurried and rushed, inflicting pressures on themselves (Banyard, 1996).

However, not all research supports the relationship between behaviour and health. In a study of men who were already coronary patients, those with Type A behaviour pattern had a lower mortality rate from CHD over a 12-year period than those with Type B (Ragland and Brand, 1988). Perhaps people who display Type A behaviour respond to heart attacks by changing their lifestyle, and perhaps people with Type B behaviour patterns don't. Another possible explanation is that Type A patients may have been misclassified as Type B if they were taking medication. Whatever the reason, the link between health and behaviour is not that straightforward.

More recently, a **Type C behaviour pattern** has been identified. People who show Type C behaviour are characterised as mild mannered, easy going, industrious and conventional. They may not react well to stress and find it difficult to express emotions especially negative emotions such as anger. According to Temoshok (1987), they are cancer prone. Some research suggests that the experience of a major stressful event is a significant predictor of breast cancer, particularly in women who did not express anger (Cooper and Faragher, 1993).

The link between Type C and cancer is unclear. Although Greer and Morris (1975) found that women diagnosed with breast cancer showed significantly more emotional suppression than those with benign breast disease, other research suggests that emotional suppression may only influence the progression of cancer (Weinman, 1995).

Locus of control

It is an undeniable fact that life is full of stressors. Although we often cannot control the causes of stress, we can to some extent modify the effects of stress. According to Rotter (1966), the perceived **locus of control** can affect how stressed people feel.

Some people are described as having an **internal locus of control**. Such people believe that they have control over what happens to them. It is they who are responsible for their behaviour. Imagine a person who has a very stressful job, which involves long hours. Stress could be reduced by taking control: delegating some work to others, getting help at home to free up time and planning ahead to ensure that a holiday is possible. Conversely, people who believe that their lives are controlled by forces outside themselves, such as luck or circumstance, are described as having an **external locus of control**. Such a person may just let the work take control and the stress mount. People who have a strong sense of control in dealing with the demands of a stressful situation are better able to cope. This sense of control reduces the strain from stressors (Suls and Mullen, 1981). Giving birth is stressful, but women who attend natural childbirth classes learn techniques that enhance their personal control in the birth process, reducing the stress during labour.

A study by Glass and Singer (1972) demonstrates quite vividly that a sense of control can reduce stress. A group of participants were deceived into believing that they could control a loud noise by pressing a button. They showed a lowered level of arousal compared with a control group who were also exposed to the same noise but who were not given any control over the noise. This effect occurred even though the participants in the experimental group never actually used the button! This suggests that if people believe that they are in control, even if they are not, they are likely to be less stressed.

Take it further

Why might Type A behaviour pattern be linked to stress and to CHD? One interesting finding is that people with Type A behaviour show a greater physiological response or 'reactivity' to stress. In other words, they respond more quickly and strongly to stress than Types B do. They are also more likely to interpret stress as a threat to their personal control (Carver *et al.*, 1985). These findings suggest that reactive Type A individuals are more often 'combat ready'. Type A behaviour may increase the person's chances of encountering stress, through seeking out demanding situations. Other research suggests that Type A behaviour pattern may in part be **caused** by the physiological reactivity. Krantz *et al.* (1982) found that patients classified as Type A and then prescribed beta-blockers (drugs that dampen the activity of the sympathetic nervous system) showed less Type A behaviour in the structured interview than a control group not prescribed beta-blockers. Frequent episodes of high arousal lead to wear and tear of the cardiovascular system. Research has shown that chronically high levels of adrenalin and noradrenalin can injure heart and blood vessels and that high blood pressure strains the heart and arteries.

Key terms

Type C behaviour pattern: a behavioural style characterised by repressed emotional reactions and helplessness in the face of stress. Types C are further characterised as mild mannered, easy going, industrious and conventional.

Locus of control: the perceived source of control over one's behaviour. People with an internal locus of control tend to take responsibility for their actions and to view themselves as having control over their own destinies. People with an external locus of control tend to perceive control as being caused by external influences or luck.

Hint

Be careful not to confuse the two meanings of 'reactivity'. One meaning of the term is 'the physiological response to stress'. The other meaning is 'the participants' reaction to the presence of an observer resulting in a change in behaviour'.

AQA Examiner's tip

In any question on the role of Types A, B and C in mediating responses to stress, take care not to oversimplify the facts. Typologies may give an indication of risk but these are only relative. The vast majority of Types A do not develop CHD and many Types B do. The vast majority of Types C do not develop cancer. Health is too complex to be reduced to two or three simple behaviour patterns.

Hints

The extreme opposite of internal locus of control might be helplessness. Faced with repeated traumatic events over which one has no control and repeated levels of stress, a person may come to feel helpless and depressed. A worker who just cannot please their boss, a student who fails exams time and time again, a patient who just cannot relieve pain – each of these examples describes a situation that can produce apathy, helplessness and ill health.

Locus of control is not about whether control **is** internal or external but how the individual **perceives** it. Moreover it is not the case that people assume that everything in their lives is under their control. It is the degree to which they attribute control and responsibility to themselves rather than to external influences that determines their locus of control.

Hint

Remember that the level of arousal is an indicator of stress. High levels of arousal suggest that the person is stressed. In Glass and Singer's study (1972), stress was measured by the GSR.

Stress

Research study: Frankenhaeuser (1975)

Aim: To investigate the link between stress and perceived control among workers in a Swedish sawmill. The workers had no control over their work which was repetitive and dull.

Method: The biochemical effects of stress, i.e. levels of adrenalin and noradrenalin (catecholamines), were measured. Additionally, self-report measures of headaches and digestive problems as well as blood pressure levels were recorded.

Results: Significantly higher than normal levels of catecholamines were found. These are commonly regarded as the stress hormones. The workers also showed more than average signs of stress for hypertension, headaches and digestive problems

Conclusion: The workers had no control over their work, and the higher than normal levels of stress were attributed to the nature of the work.

Evaluation: The strength of the study is that it was carried out in the working environment and not in an artificially controlled laboratory setting. However, the sample was biased as it consisted only of sawmill workers and there was no control condition of similar workers who did have some control over their work. It is therefore not possible to come to any firm conclusions about cause and effect.

Perceived lack of control is associated with health problems. Marmot *et al.* (1997) found that men and women in clerical and office-support jobs were at a higher risk of developing cardiovascular disease than people in executive positions. Marmot investigated several possible contributory factors but low job control emerged as the biggest factor. Studies have found that, when animals or humans feel unable to control their environment, cortisol levels rise and immune responses drop (Rodin, 1986). In a classic study by Weiss (1972), two rats received electric shocks simultaneously. One of the rats could turn a wheel to stop the shocks (the 'executive rat'); the other one could not. Therefore, the only difference was control over the shock. The rat that had no control over what was happening showed lowered immunity to disease. Captive animals also experience more stress and are more vulnerable to disease than wild animals (Roberts, 1988).

However, greater control is not necessarily stress free. Being in control can be stressful because with control comes responsibility. High-profile jobs give a person control and autonomy but also responsibility and stress. Being responsible for what happens is very stressful, especially when things go wrong (Schaubroeck, 2001).

In reality, most people have moderate beliefs about the influence they have on their lives, with locus of control falling midway between highly internal or highly external. Nevertheless, the research shows that, in situations of stress, a sense of lack of personal control intensifies the feelings of stress and harms health.

Hardiness

According to Kobasa (1979), individual differences in personal control are only part of the reason why some people under stress become ill whilst others do not. There are other personality characteristics that,

together with personal control, make up the personality trait known as **hardiness**.

Hardiness includes three characteristics:

- **Control** This is a person's belief that they can influence events in their lives – a sense of personal control. A person strong in control wants to keep trying even if situations are difficult. This is, of course, what Rotter means by 'internal locus of control'.
- **Commitment** This is a person's sense of purpose or involvement in life including other people. People with a strong sense of commitment are deeply involved in whatever they do. A person strong in commitment believes in staying involved with people and events, even under stress.
- **Challenge** This is a person's tendency to view changes as normal and an opportunity for growth and development rather than as a threat to security.

According to Kobasa, hardy people with a strong sense of control, commitment and challenge will remain healthier than people who are less hardy. A hardy person shows resilience in the face of stress and is able to deal with stressors effectively, reducing the anxiety and arousal and the consequent risk of ill health.

Research study: Kobasa (1979)

Aim: To investigate if hardiness was the differentiating factor between people with high illness and people with low illness in a group of highly stressed executives.

Method: Kobasa tested several hundred executives in a large American corporation. She used a questionnaire to divide the executives into two groups. One group had experienced high levels of stress and illness. The other also experienced high levels of stress but little illness. A questionnaire was used to assess hardiness.

Results: The 'low illness' group appeared to be hardier than the 'high illness' group: they reported a greater sense of control, commitment and challenge.

Conclusion: The results suggest that hardiness plays a role in mediating responses to stress.

Evaluation: Hardiness was not manipulated but deduced as a possible contributory factor in the difference between the groups of ill and not-so-ill executives. Consequently, other possible variables may be involved and cause and effect cannot be assumed. Another interpretation is that people who are ill find it harder to be hardy. A strength, however, is that the study was based on a large sample of workers and those workers were experiencing authentic work-related stress.

Evaluation

How might hardiness affect health? One possibility considered by Kobasa is that hardy people are better able to deal with stress by working through problems or transforming them into positive ones. Turning a stressor into something positive is known as 'positive reappraisal'. For example, redundancy from work could be seen as a benefit rather than as a problem: an opportunity to gain further qualifications and a better

Link

There are parallels here with internal and external attributions – assumptions about causes of behaviour. Internal attributions locate the cause of behaviour within a person (e.g. their personality). This type of attribution assumes freedom of choice, control and that the individual is responsible for the action. Conversely, external attributions locate the cause of behaviour in the situation: the behaviour was not freely chosen and the person cannot claim responsibility. For more about attribution, see Chapter 6, Social cognition, in *AQA Psychology B AS*.

Key terms

Hardiness: a group of personal characteristics that enable individuals to cope with stress and resist illness. Hardiness is characterised by the '3 Cs' of control, commitment and challenge.

Hint

To help you remember and understand 'hardiness', think of some of the common expressions used about people to convey resilience to stress:

- 'She can cope with anything'.
- 'He's a survivor'.
- 'She'll bounce back'.
- 'He can take it'.

job. Another possibility is that hardiness affects health indirectly through social support. Researchers have found that hardiness and social support are correlated (Blaney and Ganellen, 1990). However, it is not clear if hardiness causes an individual to turn to others in times of stress or if hardiness is encouraged because of having a social support network.

Relating personal qualities to stress does make intuitive sense, and there is certainly some evidence that hardiness can play an important role in maintaining health. Several studies of nurses in stressful settings, such as hospital operating theatres and hospices, have found a negative correlation between the nurses' hardiness levels and the number of days off sick. Another study of business consultants showed that those high in hardiness invoiced their clients for more hours worked than consultants low in hardiness (reported by Maddi and Khoshaba, 2005).

However, the concept and research are not without criticism. The three characteristics are not always found together in the same person and do not correlate very highly with each other. Only control and commitment have consistently been associated with health: challenge has not (Gentry and Kobasa, 1984).

Research into hardiness has generally been carried out on white, professional, middle-aged American men. It is not known if hardiness has different effects for women and people of other ages, ethnic and occupational groups.

Key points:

- Psychologists measure stress in three ways: measures of physiological arousal, observation and measures of people's behaviour, the use of self-report techniques such as the SRRS.
- There are several person variables mediating responses to stress. One such factor is people's tendency towards either Type A or Type B behaviour patterns. Type A is associated with CHD. More recently Type C has been associated with cancer.
- Another factor is the individual's sense of personal control over events. A lack of personal control intensifies the feelings of stress and harms health.
- Hardiness is also a modifier of stress. Hardy individuals have a strong sense of control, commitment and challenge and tend to remain healthier when under stress than individuals who are less hardy.

Summary questions

4 Outline one criticism of the SRRS.

5 Explain the difference between behaviour patterns A and B.

6 'Stress for one individual may be a challenge for another.' Explain how such individual differences may affect health.

Coping with stress

Learning objectives:

- explain the use of defence mechanisms in coping with stress
- understand the difference between problem- and emotion-focused strategies in coping with stress
- evaluate the use of problem- and emotion-focused strategies in coping with stress
- analyse the role of social support in coping with stress.

Hint

Coping methods do not necessarily lead to a solution of the problem. They may be used to alter a person's perception of the discrepancy, to escape or avoid the situation or simply to accept the threat.

Key terms

Repression: a defence mechanism whereby unpleasant memories, wishes or feelings are forced into the unconscious mind and are not available to consciousness (e.g. a young girl 'forgets' that she has had a termination).

Regression: a defence mechanism whereby the individual flees from reality into a more infantile state (to an earlier stage of development) to escape stress or anxiety; the familiar is a defence against uncertainties (e.g. a troubled student quits college and returns to the safety of home).

Hint

Defence mechanisms are a form of emotion-focused coping.

According to Lazarus's transactional approach (p134), stress occurs when there is a perceived discrepancy between the demands of a situation and the resources of the person. Lazarus and Folkman (1984) suggest that an individual first appraises the situation (primary appraisal) – does the stressor or event pose a threat? – and next considers whether or not they have the ability or resources to deal with the stressor (secondary appraisal). If, as a result of the secondary appraisal, a person perceives a gap between the demands of the situation and their resources to deal with that situation, stress occurs.

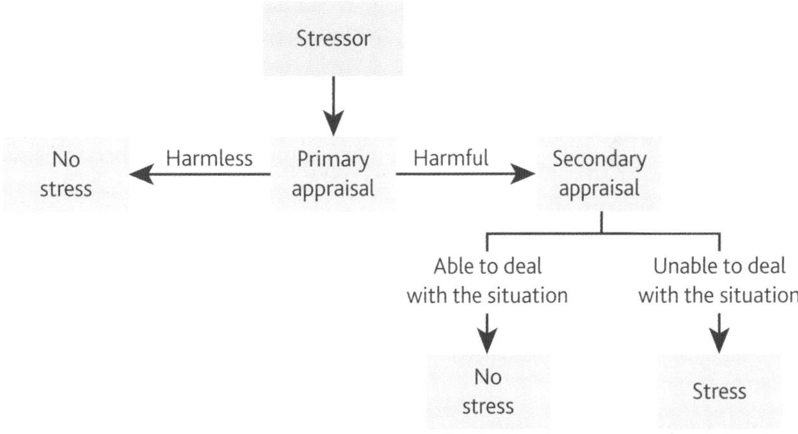

Fig. 12 *Stages of appraisal in determining stress*

The emotional and physical strain that accompanies stress is uncomfortable, motivating people to take action to reduce their stress. In other words, people try to 'cope' with stress. Coping activities are geared towards decreasing the person's appraisal of the discrepancy or lessening the emotional impact of the stress. A variety of psychological coping methods are used:

- defence mechanisms
- strategies aimed at either changing the situation that is creating the problem or managing the distress; these are known as problem-focused strategies and emotion-focused strategies, respectively
- social support from family and friends.

The use of defence mechanisms to cope with stress

The concept of coping can be traced back to the work of Freud at the end of the 19th century. Freud's theory focused on the ways in which individuals deal with anxieties either by **repressing** them or by using other defence mechanisms. These include, among others, **regression,**

AQA Examiner's tip

You will notice that the research has focused almost exclusively on what is done as a reaction to stress rather than what can be done to avoid stress. You can consider this point if asked to evaluate coping strategies.

Link

Freud's theory has had an enormous influence in psychology; the topic of stress is just one illustration of the scope of Freudian theory. For an evaluation of the psychodynamic approach, see Chapter 9, Approaches in psychology.

Key terms

Rationalisation: a defence mechanism whereby an acceptable rational explanation is given for what is in fact an unacceptable behaviour or situation (e.g. justifying a vicious attack on a child by saying that 'children need to be taught discipline').

Denial: a defence mechanism that involves protecting oneself from painful reality by an unconscious refusal to recognise some aspect of reality (e.g. a widow continues to lay the table for her recently deceased husband).

Repressors: individuals who react to anxiety by using an avoidant style of coping, which includes repression, denial and rationalisation.

Sensitisers: individuals who react to anxiety by attempting to reduce anxiety by approaching or controlling the threats, such as by seeking information or using the defence mechanism of intellectualisation.

Intellectualisation: a defence mechanism used to mask stress or anxiety by discussing the problem in a detached, intellectual manner. Such a defence mechanism is often used by people who must deal with life and death matters in their daily job.

rationalisation and **denial**. Defence mechanisms operate in the unconscious mind and involve some degree of distortion of reality and self-deception.

The defence mechanisms listed above are known as avoidance strategies because they operate by avoiding the problem. They do not alter the stressful situation but simply change the way in which the person perceives the situation. Coping strategies that face rather than avoid the problem (such as in problem-focused strategies discussed below) are known as approach strategies (Roth and Cohen, 1986).

Both avoidance and approach strategies can be beneficial but under different circumstances. Seriously ill or injured people sometimes use avoidance strategies. Defence mechanisms, such as denial, may provide hope, can be an incentive to keep trying and may also give the person time to face the truth. In this sense, denial can be adaptive. Servicemen who have faced combat have reported that denying the possibility of death helped them function (Atkinson *et al.*, 1993). But denial can also be maladaptive as when people postpone seeking medical help for a lump which may well be malignant. Thus denial may be beneficial when there is little that can be done about the problem but not if there is something that can and should be done. Denial can also be maladaptive when taken to an extreme as seen in some cases of amnesia. When a person has so many troubles that life becomes unbearable, one solution is to deny one's identity.

Suls and Fletcher (1985) pooled the results of a large number of studies in a meta-analysis to clarify the effects of approach and avoidance strategies and drew the following conclusions:

- Avoidance can be helpful in the short run such as in the early stage of a prolonged stress experience. This would apply to individuals diagnosed with a serious illness. As a rule, the effectiveness of avoidance strategies seems to be limited to the first couple of weeks of a prolonged stress experience.
- As time goes by, approach strategies become more effective than avoidance in the process of coping.

A dispositional view of coping

According to Roth and Cohen (1986) people have a natural predisposition to use different coping strategies. Byrne (1961, 1964) draws a distinction between **repressors** and **sensitisers**. One of the key issues for psychologists is whether or not these different dispositional tendencies are linked to different health outcomes. Field *et al.* (1988) investigated the use of approach and avoidance strategies by hospitalised children; the children were undergoing surgical procedures and were observed for the two styles of coping. Sensitisers (those who asked questions, protested and observed what was happening) made quicker recoveries than repressors (who asked few questions, made little protest and shied away from what was happening).

Confronting the problem may be stressful at the time but may be beneficial in the long run. It may also be that sensitisers are using another defence mechanism: **intellectualisation**.

Evaluation of the use of defence mechanisms in coping with stress

- Many psychologists are critical of psychodynamic ideas and reject any links with a theoretical approach that is seen as fundamentally untestable. However, the idea that defence mechanisms are used when coping with stress has influenced modern psychological theories, one of which suggests that there are avoidant versus approach ways of dealing with stressors. A study that examined the coping strategies of women after they had undergone mastectomies for breast cancer found that patients who avoided thinking about the problem and minimised the impact of their illness showed less evidence of distress than those who did not (Meyerowitz, 1983)

- Most defence mechanisms are seen as unhealthy processes creating emotional problems and self-defeating behaviour. But some can be helpful and constructive, for example intellectualisation. As a general rule, however, as a solution to stress, defence mechanisms may be desirable in the short term but unhealthy and undesirable in the long term. As Savickas (1995) aptly summarises: 'coping improves fit between the individual and the environment while defence maintains misfit while reducing perceived stress.'

Problem- and emotion-focused strategies

According to Cohen and Lazarus (1979), coping can serve two main functions. It can alter the problem causing the stress or it can manage the distress – the emotional response to the problem. Folkman *et al.* (1986) identified eight coping strategies classifying them as either **problem-focused coping** or **emotion-focused coping**. When dealing with a stressful situation, most people use both.

Problem-focused strategies

Planful problem solving

Making a plan of action and following it. If, as a result of secondary appraisal, a person realises that the deadline for a piece of work is too close for comfort, they will feel stressed. By making a plan of action, for example cutting out all social activities until they reach a certain target or doubling efforts, stress will be reduced. Although this sounds like an obvious strategy, it is surprising that a lot of people do not use this approach, preferring instead to avoid the problem (Forshaw, 2003).

Confronting

This involves dealing with the problem or source of the problem 'head on'. If a teacher or employer has set an unreasonable deadline, the issue could be discussed with them face to face. It may involve standing one's ground for what is reasonable or even expressing anger to the person perceived to be causing the problem.

Emotion-focused strategies

Distancing

The problem is 'put at a distance', for example making a joke of it, forgetting about it or carrying on as if it did not exist.

Self-controlling

With this strategy, feelings are kept under control ('bottled up'). Others may not know that stress is being experienced.

Seeking social support

Unlike self-controlling, the person may prefer to get things off their chest and this may involve seeking social support. Sharing problems may make the person feel better – 'a problem shared is a problem halved'.

Link

In psychodynamic theory, ego defence mechanisms are the strategies used by the ego to defend itself against anxiety. These defences are unconscious and are a key dynamic of the personality. See *AQA Psychology B AS*, Chapter 3, Gender development.

Hint

Denial and repression can easily be confused. Denial involves unconscious exclusion of present events or future uncertainties whereas repression is concerned mainly with the inhibition of memories of past events. Repression is not the same as the defence mechanism of suppression. Suppression involves deliberate self-control (e.g. deliberately not thinking about something stressful, like an overdrawn bank account). A person is aware of suppressed thoughts but not of repressed impulses or memories.

Link

To what extent are these 'natural' predispositions in coping styles 'nurtured' by the environment? Sensitisers may have received attention or reinforcement for such inquisitive behaviour or learned to question and watch what was happening to them by observing such characteristics in their parents. For a discussion of the nature–nurture issue, see Chapter 10, Debates in psychology.

Hint

Intellectualisation is a useful response at one level (a person may deal with the diagnosis of a terminal illness by reading medical books on the disorder). However, emotional issues are ignored and may be displaced elsewhere.

Key terms

Problem-focused coping: strategies people use to reduce the discrepancy between their resources and the demands of the situation.

Emotion-focused coping: strategies people use for managing the emotional response to the stressor.

Take it further

Why might repression and avoidance coping styles be linked with poorer health outcomes? In a one-year study, participants who experienced a high degree of stress and who reported a greater tendency to use avoidance strategies suffered from more psychosomatic symptoms, for example headaches (Holahan and Moos, 1986). Research has linked repression with a range of negative outcomes such as poorer immune functioning (O'Leary, 1990), poorer outcome among cancer patients (Jensen, 1987) and increased coronary disease risk factors such as high cholesterol (Niaura *et al.*, 1992). Repression may be linked to poorer health outcomes because repressing thoughts may be physically taxing. Freud believed that repression is seldom completely successful – the repressed impulses and fears threaten to break into consciousness. The individual becomes anxious (although unaware of the reason), using several other defence mechanisms to keep the repressed impulses from awareness. Repressing thoughts and monitoring whether or not the thoughts are returning may require physical energy and may lead to chronic arousal which damages the body (Atkinson *et al.*, 1993).

Take it further

Repression is an unconscious strategy, so how can it be measured using self-report measures? One approach (Byrne, 1961) was to assume that a repressor would report low anxiety in response to stress. In reality though, such a person may indeed not be anxious. One way of overcoming this problem is to use more than one method of data collection – there is some evidence that interviews may be more appropriate (Myers, 2000). According to another approach (Weinberger *et al.*, 1979), to be classified as a repressor, one has to produce two measures: a low score on a scale of anxiety and a high score on a scale of defensiveness. For more on scientific methods, see Chapter 11, Methods in psychology.

Accepting responsibility

This can be a healthy approach because by accepting responsibility for their actions, the person may avoid similar situations in the future. However, accepting responsibility when one is not to blame may be harmful, as it may lower self-esteem or give rise to negative feelings.

Escape-avoidance

The problem can be avoided by thinking about or doing other things, throwing oneself into one's work, relaxing, taking exercise, drinking, sleeping or fantasising.

Positive appraisal

Experiences are reappraised so that something 'good' emerges from the problem: for example, on losing a prestigious job one might say, 'I rediscovered what really matters in life'.

Research study: Billings and Moos (1981)

Aim: To investigate the extent to which people use problem-focused and emotion-focused strategies to cope with stress.

Method: Two hundred married couples were asked to fill out a survey. The participants first described a recent personal crisis or negative life event that had happened to them and then answered questions about how they had coped, such as whether or not they had talked with a friend or relative about the problem or got busy with other things to keep their mind off the problem.

Results: Both husbands and wives used more problem-focused than emotion-focused strategies to cope with the stressful event. Wives used more emotion-focused strategies than their husbands. The better-educated participants and those in the higher income brackets reported greater use of problem-focused strategies. All participants used fewer problem-focused strategies when the stress involved death in the family than when it involved other kinds of problems such as illness.

Conclusion: The use of emotion-focused and problem-focused strategies varies according to gender, background and the type of stress experienced.

Evaluation: By using a survey, the researchers were able to extract a considerable amount of information about the two strategies and how they are related to different variables. However, the data collected are not accessible through direct observation so there is no way of knowing the impact of social desirability bias.

Evaluation

- People have many ways of coping so categorising coping strategies is useful in making sense of their relative effectiveness. Thus planful problem solving, accepting responsibility and confrontative strategies are particularly useful when a person can actually do something about the stress but not when there is little or nothing that can be done (Forshaw, 2003). Billings and Moos (1981) believed that all types of strategies seem to be 'equally successful or unsuccessful' and that each person has to develop a style of coping suited to them as a person and to the event.

- People who tend to use problem-focused coping in stressful situations show lower levels of depression both during and after the stressful situation (Billings and Moos, 1984). This could of course be because people who are less depressed find it easier to use problem-focused coping. However, longitudinal studies show that problem-focused coping leads to shorter periods of depression even when people's initial levels of depression are taken into account. Interestingly, people can be taught to use problem-focused strategies, and this can be effective in helping them to overcome their depressions and react more adaptively to stressors (Nezu *et al.*, 1989).
- Categorising coping strategies does not, however, mean that coping behaviour falls neatly into one category only. Parents coping with a child's illness may research the illness and as a result become experts, advising others and setting up self-help groups. These behaviours may span several categories: distancing, positive reappraisal, confronting, planning, social support and accepting responsibility for their child's wellbeing.

The role of social factors in coping with stress

A key social factor in coping with stress is social support. Social support refers to the perceived comfort, caring, esteem or help that a person receives from other people or groups (Sarafino, 1994). It can come from various sources, for example family, friends, co-workers and the community. The degree of support varies depending on factors such as age, gender, culture and the social networks and organisations to which a person belongs. Old age, for example, is a time when social support sometimes declines. Women seem to use their social networks of support more effectively than men do.

The types of social support also vary and psychologists have tried to classify these. Classifications suggest that there are five types of social support (Stroebe, 2000).

Types of social support

Emotional support

This involves the expression of empathy, caring and concern towards the person at a time of stress. It can bring comfort and reassurance. It can also provide a feeling of membership in a group that shares common interests and activities. During the intensive bombing of London during the Second World War, there was a significant reduction in the number of people who needed help with their emotional problems. People were supporting one another and working together against a common enemy. Individual anxieties, often faced alone, were forgotten.

Esteem support

This is given when other people boost a person's self-esteem and make them feel valued. It is particularly useful during the appraisal of stress when a person assesses whether the demands exceed their personal resources. Esteem support occurs through positive regard for the person, positive comparisons with others and encouragement or agreement with their feelings or ideas.

Instrumental support

This involves direct assistance such as helping with jobs or lending money in times of stress. It is the material help offered when people say, 'Let me know if there is anything I can do to help'.

AQA Examiner's tip

If asked to discuss the role of defence mechanisms, a discussion could include:

- appropriateness/effectiveness in different situations
- comparisons with alternative ways of coping (e.g. social support, problem-focused strategies)
- psychodynamic roots and implications
- empirical validation of concepts
- usefulness of emotion-focused strategies in general.

Hint

Confronting does not mean 'confrontation' or aggression. In this sense, 'confronting' means coming face to face with the problem. Some 'confronting' may be emotionally charged but not necessarily.

Link

The defence mechanism of denial is an emotion-focused strategy. Some 'distancing' behaviours are essentially like denial but, unlike the defence mechanism, these are conscious, as when a person might say, 'I don't want to be reminded' or 'don't talk about it'. For more information on defence mechanisms, see *AQA Psychology B AS*, Chapter 3, Gender development.

AQA Examiner's tip

Seeking social support can also be a problem-focused strategy because it can be a way of obtaining advice about a problem or finding out more. So you can use this strategy if asked to outline/describe an emotion-focused or a problem-focused strategy. It can also be used in a discussion pointing out the problems of classification.

Take it further

Many studies suggest that aerobic exercise can reduce stress, depression and anxiety. McCann and Holmes (1984) randomly allocated one-third of mildly depressed women to a programme of aerobic exercise and one-third to a treatment of relaxation exercise; one-third, the control group, received no treatment. Ten weeks later, the women in the aerobic exercise programme reported the greatest decrease in depression. 'Many of them had literally run away from their troubles' (Myers, 1998). Numerous other studies confirm the benefits of exercise on stress, depression and anxiety. Even a 10-minute walk stimulates two hours of wellbeing by raising energy levels and lowering tension (Thayer, 1987, 1993).

But apart from 'escape' why might aerobic exercise alleviate the effects of stress and negative emotions? It is known that exercise strengthens the heart and lowers blood pressure. It also increases the production of mood-boosting neurotransmitters. Perhaps increased body arousal, warmth and a sense of wellbeing enhance a person's emotional state.

Hint

People engage in emotion-focused coping:

- to prevent being overwhelmed by negative emotions
- to prevent them from engaging in actions to solve their problems
- when the problem is uncontrollable.

Hint

Distancing as used in the example of researching an illness is similar to the defence mechanism of intellectualisation. Intellectualisation is frequently used by the medical profession. By reading books on the disorder, emotion is removed from a stressful situation and the illness is dealt with in an abstract intellectual way. Both distancing and intellectualisation involve a detached view of an illness.

Stress

Informational support

This refers to the useful information a person may get from social contacts. As well as knowledge, this form of support also includes receiving advice, suggestions and feedback.

Appraisal support

With this type of support, a person is enabled or encouraged to understand and evaluate their own 'stress state' and to put their stressors into context, for example through the provision of information.

Research findings suggest that social support is associated with reduced stress.

Research study: La Rocco *et al.* (1980)

Aim: To investigate the link between work stress and social support.

Method: Two thousand men in a variety of jobs were asked to complete a questionnaire. The two variables assessed were job stress and social support. The measures of social support included items about emotional and instrumental support. Social support from three sources was examined: the employee's boss; co-workers; and support from outside work, i.e. wife, family and friends.

Results: Analysis revealed a negative correlation between the social support available to the employees and the psychological strain reported. Although lower job stress was linked to social support from home, it was more strongly linked to the support that the employees received from their bosses and co-workers.

Conclusion: Social support (particularly from work) and work stress are related.

Evaluation: One of the study's strengths is that it was based on a large sample; however, because of its gender bias, application does not extend to work stress in women. The study also took account of various types of social support, separating social support at work from that outside work. However, correlation does not inform about causation. There could be a third factor involved. If a person is unsociable they may not attract social support **and** may also be more susceptible to stress. Nevertheless, similar associations have been found in other studies (Constable and Russell, 1986; Cottington and House, 1987), strengthening the validity of the findings.

Evaluation

Fleming *et al.* (1982) investigated the influence of social support on stress experienced by residents in the area of a damaged nuclear plant. Those residents with high levels of emotional support showed less strain and cognitive harm than those with low levels of support. Lynch (1990) found that widowed, divorced and single people have far higher death rates from heart disease than married people do. He argued that being lonely is a risk factor for heart disease. Waxler-Morrison *et al.* (1991) studied 133 women after they received a diagnosis of breast cancer. Although the key factor in survival was how developed the disease was, social support also had an effect. Longer survival was associated with having more and deeper friendships and working outside the home.

Theoretical explanations of the link between social support and wellbeing

Psychologists have proposed two theories.

Buffering hypothesis

Social support affects health by protecting the person against the negative effects of high stress. There are two ways in which this happens:

- One is cognitive appraisal. Individuals with a high level of social support will be less likely to appraise the situation as stressful. Knowing that there is someone to help will make the person feel that they can meet the demands of the situation.
- Secondly, social support can modify a person's response to a stressor once they have appraised the situation as highly stressful. For example, someone in the social network might provide a solution to the problem or help re-appraise the situation as 'it's not that bad after all'.

Direct effects hypothesis

Social support is beneficial to wellbeing regardless of the amount of stress. Social support affects mental health, which in itself has a direct effect on physical health (e.g. making individuals more resistant to infection). Some studies show that social support calms the cardiovascular system and lowers stress hormones (Uchino *et al.*, 1996). Social relationships may also enhance health through promoting healthy behaviours and a positive outlook on life.

Evaluation of the role of social factors in coping with stress

- People vary in the way that they both find and evaluate social support. Some people are inherently better able to create supportive social networks in times of great stress and to perceive such support as helpful (Kessler *et al.*, 1992). People from caring families and who have good relations with peers learn the social skills needed to seek (and give) help when it is needed (Sarafino, 1994).
- People may not necessarily perceive help as supportive if the help offered does not match their needs. Cutrona and Russell (1990) have suggested that instrumental support is valuable when stressful events are controllable whereas emotional support is more helpful when the stressor is uncontrollable. Of course, the picture is more complicated than this. Other types of support may be needed: for example, a person experiencing the uncontrollable event of losing their job may benefit from esteem and instrumental support. Sometimes, people do not perceive help as supportive because they are too emotionally upset or do not want it.
- Social ties may be harmful to an individual's attempts to cope with stress. The social support offered may be damaging to an individual's wellbeing. Health-damaging behaviours, such as excessive drinking or smoking, occur within a social environment. Sometimes, family and friends can increase stress. Following an illness, for example, families may be overprotective, discouraging a person from returning to work or becoming active again. This could result in the person becoming increasingly dependent, thus increasing stress. Minimising the seriousness of a problem or simply saying that everything will be all right may actually create more stress than giving no help at all. For example, a parent who says, 'Of course you will pass the exam' presents the student with an additional stressor – that of not disappointing the parent.

Hint

According to the buffering hypothesis:

- social support blunts the effects of stress
- social support is effective only when the person encounters a strong stressor.

Hint

The direct effects theory is also known as 'the main effect model'. According to this theory:

- social support is always beneficial, both mentally and physically
- social support is effective regardless of any stressors experienced.

AQA Examiner's tip

In discussing social support, use the appropriate terminology. You could say that, if a person is seriously ill, informational and emotional support may be particularly important, but when the illness is less serious, though chronic, appraisal support may be more appropriate.

AQA Examiner's tip

It is useful to know the scope of research into social support and stress. All of the studies referred to indicate a link between social support and wellbeing. But do remember that none of these studies are experimental, so all that they can do is point to an association between social support and wellbeing. Cause and effect cannot be implied.

Link

Individual differences in whether or not people receive social support when it is needed could be explained by both inherent tendencies and learning. For discussion of the nature–nurture debate, see Chapter 10, Debates in psychology.

Link

It is generally considered that perceived support is a more useful measure of predicting wellbeing than is real support. Of course, real support is easier to access; it can be gathered from observations or from records such as membership lists of organisations. This relates to the problem of the subject matter of psychology: overt behaviour versus subjective private experience. For further discussion, see Chapter 10, Debates in psychology, and Chapter 11, Methods in psychology.

Key points:

- There are several ways in which people cope with stress: defence mechanisms, problem- and emotion-focused strategies, and using and seeking social support.
- Defence mechanisms are generally seen as unhealthy processes creating emotional problems and self-defeating behaviour. However, they may sometimes be helpful and constructive, particularly in very stressful situations.
- People tend to use problem-focused coping when they believe that they can change the situation and emotion-focused coping when they believe that they cannot change the stressful conditions.
- Emotion-focused coping regulates the emotional response to stress whereas problem-focused coping reduces the discrepancy between the demands of the stressor and the person's resources.
- Psychologists have identified five types of social support in coping with stress. Social support is generally associated with stress reduction.

Summary questions

7 Why are defence mechanisms unlikely to reduce stress in the long term?

8 Identify one type of problem-focused strategy and one type of emotion-focused strategy. Using an example of a stressful situation, illustrate how each might be used in coping with stress.

9 Anna is a six-month-old baby who suffers from epilepsy as a result of a brain injury. Anna's parents have found it very stressful coping with the demands of the situation and have requested help from social services. Using your knowledge of the role of social factors in coping with stress, explain why help should be provided.

Techniques of stress management

Learning objectives:

- understand and evaluate behavioural and cognitive techniques of stress management
- explain the use of stress management techniques

Everybody is exposed to stressful situations. Stress is a basic element in the lives of all organisms and plays an important role in survival. However, as research has shown, stress can have negative effects on both physical and emotional health; furthermore, research into personal variables has shown how some people are at a disadvantage compared with others in coping with stress. But the good news for all is that it is possible to bring stress under control – to make stress more manageable or tolerable. So how can stress be managed?

Some of these **stress management** techniques focus mainly on the person's behaviour and some focus on the person's thinking processes. Techniques based on behavioural and cognitive approaches will now be considered.

Behavioural approaches

Biofeedback and **systematic desensitisation** are two well-known behavioural stress management techniques. Behavioural techniques involve changing people's behaviour or responses. The physiological response to stress is arousal so the aim of the behavioural approach is to change that response. The opposite of arousal is relaxation. According to the notion of **reciprocal inhibition**, you cannot simultaneously be anxious (aroused) and relaxed; relaxation is therefore a key feature of both biofeedback and systematic desensitisation.

Biofeedback

In the 1960s, the psychologist Neal Miller began using the technique of operant conditioning to control the activity of parts of the autonomic nervous system in rats. Miller found that rats could modify their heart beat if given reinforcement in the form of pleasurable brain stimulation when their heart beat increased or decreased. Such research by Miller and others (e.g. Miller and DiCara, 1968) led to the development of biofeedback.

The basic rationale for biofeedback is that if a person is aware of their physiological functioning they can gain some control over physiological or bodily responses. Usually, people are largely unaware of most bodily responses, such as blood pressure, and are therefore unable to control them. Biofeedback aims to give an individual some direct feedback about bodily responses, enabling them to take control of the response.

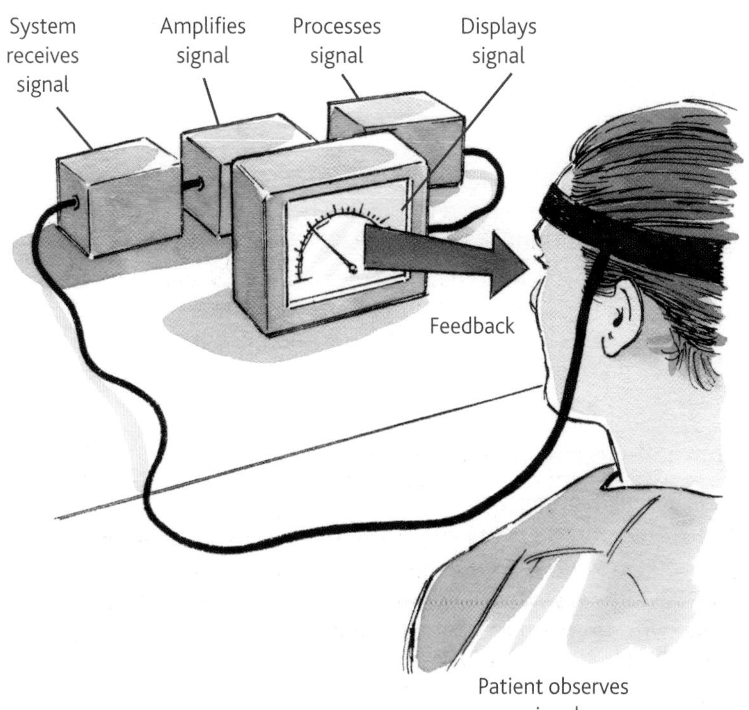

Fig. 13 *Biofeedback – a system for electronically recording, amplifying and feeding back information about changes in bodily responses*

Monitoring devices are used to track a person's physiological responses (e.g. heart rate, blood pressure, muscle tension, the pattern of the brain

Key terms

Stress management: a range of psychological techniques used in a deliberate way, usually in a professional setting, to help people reduce their stress levels.

Biofeedback: a technique of stress management for humans based on the principle of controlling involuntary (autonomic) physiological responses by receiving information or feedback about those responses as they occur.

Systematic desensitisation: a form of behaviour therapy designed to reduce the anxiety that an individual feels in the presence of an anxiety-provoking situation or object. The client is gradually exposed to the anxiety-provoking situation or object, first by using the imagination and then in actual physical situations, and conditioned to associate relaxation not fear with the object.

Reciprocal inhibition: the inhibition of the action of one response by another. It is impossible to maintain two opposing responses at the same time (e.g. anxiety and relaxation).

Link

The theoretical basis of operant conditioning is that the consequences of a response determine the probability of its reoccurring in the future. Thus responses can be controlled, resulting in numerous applications to behaviour. For further discussion, see Chapter 9, Approaches in psychology.

Link

Biofeedback is based on the behaviourist approach. Feedback in the form of information about physiological responses enables the person to gain voluntary control over these responses using operant conditioning. The feedback acts as reinforcement, strengthening the response. For further discussion, see Chapter 9, Approaches in psychology.

Hint

You may come across some of the following terms and abbreviations when reading about biofeedback:

- electromyography (EMG) – a graphic record of muscle tension
- electroencephalograph (EEG) – a record of changes in the electrical activity of the brain
- galvanic skin response (GSR) meter – measures the change in the electrical resistance of the skin.

Link

Heart rate, blood pressure, etc., are all involuntary and controlled by the autonomic nervous system (ANS). It was not thought possible to bring these functions of the ANS under voluntary control. For more on the ANS, see *AQA Psychology B AS*, Chapter 2, Biopsychology.

AQA Examiner's tip

If you are asked to discuss biofeedback or any example of a behavioural approach to managing stress, you will gain credit for discussing relevant points relating to the approach in general, such as:

- the scientific basis of the behaviourist approach
- measurable behavioural outcomes
- the problem of extrapolating from animal studies
- treatment of behaviour and not the cause
- mechanistic and reductionist approach.

Hint

Two key features of biofeedback are:

- relaxation
- feedback about current physiological responses.

activity, skin conductance and temperature). These devices provide the person with feedback, usually in the form of the onset of a light or tone whenever they change the response in the required direction. The light or tone acts as reinforcement, indicating that their efforts are causing the desired change in the physiological response. For example, if the person is trying to reduce neck-muscle tension and the device reports that the tension has decreased then the feedback reinforces whatever efforts the individual made to cause this decrease. With practice, a person learns to control all sorts of bodily functions mainly through relaxation.

Evaluation of biofeedback

The findings about the usefulness of biofeedback are quite mixed:

- According to some studies, biofeedback has been used successfully in treating stress-related health problems. An experiment was carried out with patients suffering from tension headaches (Budzynski *et al.*, 1973). Patients given training in deep-muscle relaxation and biofeedback for muscle tension in their foreheads later showed less tension in those muscles and reported fewer headaches than those in control groups who received no biofeedback. These benefits were still evident at a check-up three months later.
- Biofeedback has been used to treat patients with high blood pressure. Combined with relaxation training, biofeedback has proved effective in lowering blood pressure for some individuals (Tarler-Benlolo, 1978). In a typical procedure, patients are shown a graph of their blood pressure whilst it is being monitored and are taught to relax various groups of muscles. In so doing, patients learn to modify muscular tension.
- Because relaxation training is often given along with biofeedback, it is hard to tell whether it is the 'feedback' aspect of biofeedback or the relaxation training that is more effective. Some research has found that relaxation techniques alone are just as effective for reducing stress as relaxation plus biofeedback (Hatch *et al.*, 1982). Nevertheless, the usefulness of relaxation training alone seems to depend on the individual. Some learn to relax faster when they receive biofeedback. Others learn to relax equally well when they receive training in muscle relaxation without any biofeedback. It is not known exactly how biofeedback works: it may lead to benefits by producing a sense of control rather than through physiological mechanisms.
- A major problem with biofeedback is that a person learns the techniques in a laboratory or at home and usually in a comfortable, relaxed, stress-free environment. But stress occurs in the 'real world': at work, when driving or shopping. So the skills learned do not easily generalise to times when the stressors are present.

Systematic desensitisation

Systematic desensitisation is a form of behaviour therapy. It is based on the belief that anxiety is learned by classical conditioning whereby an association is made between a situation or object and an unpleasant event. For example, if a young child is made to cry in school by an older child, the young child may very quickly associate school with anxiety. The young child becomes 'sensitised' to school and in extreme cases may even become school phobic and avoid going to school.

According to behaviourists, a person suffering from anxiety has learned an inappropriate stimulus–response association. For example, school (stimulus) is associated with anxiety (response). Desensitisation is a classical conditioning procedure that reverses the learning. The sufferer gradually learns to pair the anxiety-provoking object or situation with relaxation rather than with anxiety. In the case of the young child described above, school (stimulus) would become associated with feeling calm (response), and the child becomes 'desensitised' to school.

The technique uses a stimulus hierarchy. Each step of the hierarchy (usually about 10 to 15 steps) brings the person closer to the anxiety-provoking situation or object.

An outline of the technique follows:

- The client learns deep muscle relaxation.
- With the help of the therapist, the client draws up a hierarchy of increasingly threatening situations. For example, the child anxious about school may find that imagining animals at school in a story may be only mildly threatening. Actually being in the school playground may be the most frightening situation. Seeing other children going to school may lie somewhere in the middle of the hierarchy of steps.
- Each step in the hierarchy is presented individually whilst the client is calm, relaxed and comfortable. So the child in our example will, in the first session, listen to a story in which animals attend school and will be told to imagine the scene whilst feeling and remaining relaxed. The steps follow a sequence from the least to the most threatening for the individual. If at any time the client feels anxious, they are encouraged to relax and the procedure is only continued once 'calm' is restored.

Evaluation of systematic desensitisation

The technique can certainly boast of some success. In one study with dental-phobic adults, who imagined each step in the hierarchy, the procedure reduced their fear in six sessions, each of one and a half hours' duration (Gatchel, 1980).

However, although the fear response may be similar to the stress response, stress and fear are not the same. Fear can be sensed but stress involves a cognitive component – the individual perceives a gap between the demands of a situation and their resources. Thus a major problem with systematic desensitisation is that the technique is only treating the behaviour – the fear or anxiety response. It makes no attempt to achieve insight into the underlying cause of the stress or anxiety or into how the client perceives the situation. For that reason, a technique involving a cognitive component may be better suited to stress management.

Another problem, when systematic desensitisation is applied to stress, is how well the technique generalises to everyday minor hassles or major life events. Gradually exposing an individual to a stressor by using the imagination – or even real life – in the controlled therapeutic environment, may be effective but maintaining a calm and anxiety-free state at school, work or in a stressful home environment may be more difficult.

Cognitive approaches

Stress results from cognitive appraisals that are often based on faulty thinking. Hence, some cognitive therapies guide people towards what Lazarus (1971) terms **cognitive restructuring**. One such therapy is called **rational emotive therapy (RET)**. The therapy attempts to change the way people think about their life situations and themselves in order to change their emotional responses and behaviour.

Link

Classical conditioning is a simple form of associative learning. According to behaviourist theory, all learning can be explained by observable events and without reference to mental events. For more on classical conditioning, see Chapter 1, Key approaches, in *AQA Psychology B AS*, and Chapter 9, Approaches in psychology, in this book.

Hints

If you want to use behaviourist terminology, notice that the anxiety-provoking situation or object is the 'conditioned stimulus'. The response to the stimulus is anxiety (conditioned response), which has been learned.

Systematic desensitisation is also known as 'exposure therapy' because the client is gradually brought face to face with the anxiety-provoking stimulus.

Key features of systematic desensitisation are:

- relaxation
- stimulus hierarchy
- gradually confronting the threatening situation.

Key terms

Cognitive restructuring: a process by which stress-provoking thoughts or beliefs are replaced with ones that reduce the person's appraisal of threat or harm. These thoughts and beliefs are more constructive.

Rational emotive therapy (RET): a cognitive therapy for replacing irrational thought patterns that provoke stress with thought patterns that are more realistic.

Take it further

There are other techniques that come under the umbrella of 'behavioural approaches'. Modelling is one such technique. Because people learn stressful reactions by observing these behaviours in others, modelling can be used to reverse this learning. The method used is similar to that of desensitisation: the person relaxes while watching a model (on film, video or in real life) perform a series of activities arranged as a stimulus hierarchy. Melamed *et al.* (1983) have shown that modelling procedures can reduce stress experienced by hospitalised children and improve their recovery from surgery.

Exercise is also a behavioural method as it involves people changing their behaviour and exercising. Numerous studies have shown a relationship between taking exercise (aerobic exercise in particular) and coping with stress. Studies in the USA have found that American adults who exercise regularly cope better with stressful events (and display more self-confidence and are less depressed) than those who exercise less (Brown, 1991).

Link

The cognitive approach to therapy features in several other topic areas (see *AQA Psychology B AS*, Chapter 9, Anxiety disorders, and Chapter 5, Schizophrenia and mood disorders, in this book). All cognitive therapies are based on the assumptions that people's emotions and behaviours are influenced by the way they think about their experiences and that changing the way they think will help people overcome their problems.

Hint

RET is also known as rational emotive behaviour therapy (REBT). Notice the use of the term 'behaviour'. This is because the therapy is based on the assumption that maladaptive behaviour is due to faulty thinking. Therefore, in order to change behaviour, the therapist must change the thinking.

Rational emotive therapy

RET was developed by Ellis (1962) and is the most widely known of the approaches that focus on cognitive restructuring. Ellis believed that faulty or irrational ways of thinking affect stress appraisal processes and increase the appraisal of threat or harm. According to Ellis, some commonly used irrational ways of thinking include:

- 'awfulising' (e.g. 'It is awful if I don't get things right the first time')
- 'can't-stand-its' (e.g. 'I can't stand not passing an exam')
- catastrophising (e.g. 'The soup I have made for the dinner party is salty; the whole evening will be ruined').

The procedure used in RET focuses on the A–B–C–D–E framework for restructuring thoughts. This is a confrontational therapy whereby the therapist bluntly and even aggressively challenges the client to examine their belief systems to realise how irrational and damaging they are. Table 2 illustrates the application of the framework in a hypothetical situation. Jane has applied for promotion and feels worthless, depressed and anxious because she has not been successful.

Table 2 *Illustration of Ellis's A–B–C–D–E framework for RET as applied to a hypothetical situation*

A	This is the **activating** experience that creates the stress: e.g. Jane has failed to be promoted at work.
B	This refers to the thoughts and **beliefs** that go through Jane's mind in response to A. The thoughts might be quite rational, such as 'I suppose I did not have as much experience as other applicants', or unnecessarily negative, such as 'I am a failure'. Jane focuses on the negative/irrational thoughts.
C	This refers to the emotional and behavioural **consequences** of A and B. These could be positive, like deciding to go on a course, but Jane feels depressed, ashamed and helpless and has not attempted to broaden her experience or apply for another promotion.
D	This refers to **disputing** irrational beliefs and is part of the therapeutic process. With the help of the therapist, Jane will be made to discriminate between rational beliefs, such as 'I wish I had been better qualified', and irrational ones, such as 'I am a failure'. Irrational thoughts are critically and logically examined in RET – a form of hypothesis testing – so that they can be disproved.
E	This stands for the therapy's **effect**, which consists of a restructured belief system. Instead of thinking 'I am a failure' Jane will accept that 'I will fail some promotion panels but will succeed in others' and 'this kind of thing happens to everyone now and then'. With this effect Jane should be able to apply for promotion without fear of being a failure.

An important aspect of RET is that it involves 'homework' assignments, such as reading about irrational beliefs, doing desensitisation exercises and applying constructive ways of thinking to everyday life.

Evaluation of rational emotive therapy

Some research into the effectiveness of RET has found that it is successful in treating anxiety and depression (Di Guiseppe and Miller, 1977). However, the evidence is far from conclusive. Many questions still remain as to why the therapy works and whether improvements persist (Patterson, 1986). Arnkoff and Glass (1982) believe that faulty thinking processes are not simply a product of irrational beliefs but are a reflection of a personality structure – one that is 'closed-minded'; thus, it is an oversimplification to believe that cognitive restructuring can address maladaptive thinking.

Nevertheless, unlike behavioural therapies, RET attempts to treat the cause of the behaviour and not just the behaviour. For this reason, it is potentially more effective in the long term. Given the role of cognitive appraisal in stress, a strength of RET is that it examines and attempts to change a person's belief systems.

Stress-inoculation training

Another well-known cognitive technique, **stress-inoculation therapy (SIT)** (also known as self-instructional training), is designed to teach people skills for reducing stress and achieving personal goals.

SIT was developed by Meichenbaum (1977) and involves three stages.

Conceptualisation

This is the cognitive preparation stage. The therapist talks with the client about their stress responses and explores ways in which stressful situations are thought about and dealt with. The client learns to identify and express feelings and fears and is educated about stress and its effects.

Skill acquisition and rehearsal

The client learns some basic behavioural and cognitive skills useful for coping with stressful situations: for example, the client may be taught how to relax or may be required to observe a model. They may also be taught positive coping statements or 'preparation statements', such as 'just think about what you can do about it; that's better than getting anxious' and 'when fear comes, just pause'. Some skills may depend on the individual's personal circumstances: for example, the person may be taught parenting or study skills that they then practise under supervision.

Application and follow-through

This phase involves preparing for transition to the real world. The therapist guides the client through progressively more threatening situations (a bit like the hierarchy of needs in systematic desensitisation). The client is given a wide range of possible stressors to prepare them for real-life situations. Follow-up sessions are held periodically during the year.

Evaluation of stress inoculation training

As with RET, the evidence for SIT's effectiveness is inconclusive. Meichenbaum (1977) found that the technique works well for short-term stressors, such as public speaking, and longer-term stressors, such as work-related stress. SIT has been used in sports with some effect. A study of cross-country runners showed that stress inoculation was useful not only in reducing stress but also in improving performance in running (Zeigler *et al.*, 1982).

SIT prepares a person for stress in real-life situations. Most of the other techniques are reactive: in other words, they try to reduce stress once it has occurred.

However, SIT like RET only suits a particular type of individual. The procedure is lengthy, requiring commitment, effort and motivation.

A final general point to consider is that stress is complex, often involving many factors, so one particular technique alone may not be sufficient, and each case has therefore to be considered individually. An effective approach may require both behavioural and cognitive approaches and even the use of medication. SIT uses a variety of techniques, for example cognitive coping strategies, relaxation, desensitisation and modelling.

Hints

Key features of RET are:

- addressing irrational beliefs
- cognitive restructuring – replacing irrational beliefs with more realistic and constructive beliefs.

The hypothesis-testing process of RET casts the client as a scientist.

Key terms

Stress-inoculation therapy (SIT): a cognitive approach to stress management that teaches people skills for reducing stress and achieving personal goals.

AQA Examiner's tip

If asked to evaluate or discuss cognitive approaches to managing stress, you could include other general points:

- The therapies require client motivation and participation. This can of course be a limitation as well as a strength.
- Cognitive therapies give clients a sense of control; the client is an active agent.

Hints

Inoculations are used as medical treatments. A person is given a weak version of a disease so that the body can develop defences against the full-blown disease. The rationale behind SIT is the same. The individual is prepared for stress by developing coping skills.

Key features of SIT are:

- training people in new skills
- practising the new skills
- applying these skills to stressful everyday situations.

Take it further

Because the body's response to a stressor involves physiological arousal and feelings of anxiety, drugs that can reduce these symptoms are used to manage stress. Two main types are benzodiazepines and beta-blockers. Both types reduce physiological arousal and feelings of anxiety but work in different ways. The neurotransmitter GABA, a natural form of anxiety relief, is normally produced in times of stress, stopping other neurons responding to anxiety. Benzodiazepines (e.g. Valium and Librium) work by enhancing the activity of GABA. Beta-blockers (e.g. Inderal), block the activity of the sympathetic neurons in the peripheral nervous system (PNS) that are stimulated by adrenalin and noradrenalin. Because beta-blockers act on the PNS, they cause less drowsiness than benzodiazepines which work on the central nervous system. Using drugs to manage stress is generally a short-term measure, used, for example, during an acute crisis. Although drugs are quick, effective and easy to prescribe and use, like behavioural approaches they only treat the symptoms not the underlying causes. They can also have side effects such as dizziness or tiredness.

Key points:

- Stress management techniques are used in a deliberate way to help people manage their stress.
- There are two main categories of psychological stress management techniques: behavioural and cognitive.
- Biofeedback, which is based on operant conditioning principles, and systematic desensitisation, which is based on classical conditioning, are examples of techniques that adopt a behavioural approach.
- Cognitive techniques include rational emotive therapy and stress inoculation therapy.
- Both approaches have strengths and weaknesses. One major advantage of cognitive approaches over behavioural approaches is that they consider the underlying causes of stress.

Summary questions

10 Identify two features of biofeedback and two features of systematic desensitisation.

11 Outline one way in which RET and SIT are similar and one way in which RET and SIT are different.

12 Melissa is feeling very stressed because she has to do a presentation. She does not think that she is good at public speaking. Identify one psychological stress management technique that might help reduce Melissa's stress. Explain your answer.

End-of-chapter activity 1

Investigate gender differences in coping with stress. Work in small groups. Brainstorm as many ways of dealing with stress as you can think of. Categorise each coping strategy until you have six examples of emotion-focused strategies (e.g. go out for a drink) and six examples of problem- focused strategies (e.g. write out a plan of action to deal with the stressor).

Don't forget to consider ethical issues, such as consent, the right to withdraw and confidentiality.

Give the list of 12 strategies to about 20 males and 20 females and ask each to tick three 'preferred' coping strategies (i.e. ones that they typically use to deal with stress). As each participant can only select three strategies, at least two will be either emotion focused or problem focused. This will be their preferred coping style. Draw up a table (example below) and count the number of males who preferred emotion-focused strategies and the number of males who preferred problem-focused strategies. Do the same for females and fill in the table.

Table 3 *A table to show the preferred coping strategies of males and females*

	Preferred coping strategy	
	Emotion-focused	**Problem-focused**
Males		
Females		

The data collected (the number of males and the number of females who use each type of coping strategy) are frequency data. The level of measurement is nominal. It would be appropriate to use the chi-square test.

Having completed the group activity, write out a summary of the aim, method, results and conclusion of your study. Consider how you addressed the ethical issues in this study and include a statistical test to indicate the significance of the results.

End-of-chapter activity 2

Investigate the external reliability of a 'hassles scale' (a non-experimental self-report method).

In groups of three, write a list of everyday 'student hassles'. The scale should consist of about 20 items such as 'the library is too noisy', 'parents ask too many questions', 'always short of money'. Each item should be written on a separate line with a small box next to it so that participants can enter one of three numbers in the box to indicate how often each item irritates them (0 = 'almost never'; 5 = 'sometimes'; 10 = 'frequently').

Present about 20 students with a copy of the scale and ask them to fill it in. Keep a record of the total score for each participant but make absolutely sure that you keep this information confidential (you may think of some coding system). About two weeks later, ask each participant to repeat the exercise. You will now have two scores for each participant. Plot a scattergram to display the relationship between first and second testing (test–retest) for all participants and carry out a statistical test to find out the strength of the correlation and the significance of the results. (Test–retest is a way of testing external reliability or reliability over time. Spearman's rank order correlation could be used to assess the strength of the correlation and the significance of the results.)

Having completed the group activity, interpret the results and evaluate your study. Consider how you addressed the ethical issues in this study. Discuss the problems, such as writing the scale, whether or not the scale is reliable, implications for validity and how the study could be improved.

Further reading

Banyard, P. (1996) *Applying Psychology to Health*. London: Hodder & Stoughton.

Bartlett, D. (1998) *Stress: Perspectives and Processes*. Buckingham: Open University Press.

Jones, F. and Bright, J. (2001) *Stress. Myth, Theory and Research*. Harlow: Pearson Education Ltd.

Ogden, J. (2000) *Health Psychology: A Textbook*. Buckingham: Open University Press.

Sarafino, E.P. (1994) *Health Psychology*, 2nd edition. New York: John Wiley & Sons.

Substance abuse

Introduction

Key terms

Drug: a chemical substance that has a physiological or psychological effect on a person's body or behaviour.

Abuse: the use of drugs outside the boundaries of medical intervention or social convention in a way that may harm the individual and society.

'Dad gave son heroin overdose.' 'Alcohol misuse causes 22,000 premature deaths every year.' We see headlines like these in newspapers, and on TV. They seem to demonstrate that '**drug**-taking' is both common and potentially dangerous to the user and to society at large.

Substance **abuse** may involve alcohol, smoking, heroin, cannabis, solvents and other substances. Alcohol has been used for thousands of years. Columbus brought tobacco leaf smoking from the Americas to Europe in the late 15th century. LSD began to be used in the 1960s as a manufactured drug to change the perception of reality.

Early uses of these substances did not cause alarm. It took widespread excessive use and better knowledge of the long-term health problems to prompt concern and legal action to restrict use. For example, cigarette smoking was admired and reached its high point in the 1960s. This coincided with an increasing awareness of the long-term health problems of lung cancer and heart disease. In the last 50 years, in the UK, taxation, advertising and legal restrictions have been used to attempt to restrict cigarette smoking.

Research methods

From 1960 onwards there has been a huge growth in the study of substance abuse, as the adverse effects have become more apparent and interest in the effectiveness of treatment and prevention has grown. Few experiments have been conducted because of the ethical implications of inviting participants to use potentially harmful substances. Instead, many correlational studies have been conducted using data from interviews, questionnaires and medical and other records. These studies often show a positive correlation between variables, but this does not necessarily show that they have a cause-and-effect relationship. There are problems with the collection of data by 'self-report' methods, such as interviews; factors such as lack of honesty by the participants and lapses in memory for past events may make them unreliable.

However, many studies are also prospective. That is, they involve a group of people in a longitudinal study where predictions are made at the start and tested over a long time period, such as 20 years. In this way the scientific test of 'falsifiability' can be applied to explanations and predictions.

The key questions

What are the substances involved in drug misuse? What effects do they have on the human body? Why do individuals abuse substances? How can they be treated? How can abuse be prevented? These are the kinds of questions that psychologists and other scientists have researched. In this topic you will be able to study their findings and explanations for them.

7 Substance abuse

Use and abuse: substances and responses to them

Learning objectives:

- understand the effects that the abuse of different substances have on the body
- understand biological explanations of the effects of substance abuse, such as dependence, withdrawal and tolerance
- understand the distinctions between addiction, physical dependence and psychological dependence.

Some abused substances

The substances alcohol, nicotine, cocaine, heroin, cannabis and solvents will be used as the main examples in this chapter. Some of these can be used clinically: for example, heroin/diamorphine is used to ease severe pain. Others can be used recreationally, for example alcohol to produce a sense of relaxation and social confidence. However, all of them can be abused.

Alcoholic drinks are used by over 90 per cent of the UK population and about 25 per cent absorb nicotine through smoking cigarettes. Cocaine has been used by some high-profile celebrities. Fatal heroin overdoses are reported quite often. Cannabis is the most commonly used of the legally classified substances and is often regarded as a 'gateway drug', i.e. one that can lead a person into using more damaging ones. Solvents are readily available in the average home, in about 30 products such as hairspray and adhesives. Their use accounts for over 70 deaths each year, some involving first-time users.

The use of any of these substances has legal restrictions. Heroin and cocaine are Class A drugs. Cannabis was 'downgraded' to Class C during 2004 but reclassified as Class B in 2008, owing to worries about the increased strength of the drug. Under-18s may not buy alcohol. It is illegal for shopkeepers to sell tobacco products to anyone under 18, or products containing solvents to anyone under 18 who, they suspect, may want to inhale them.

Hint

Cannabis is not mentioned in the specification, but you may find it a useful example to illustrate your exam answers. It is the most commonly used 'illegal' drug in the UK.

How abused substances may affect the user

These substances are **psychoactive**. Alcohol users expect to feel more relaxed after a few drinks. In the 1960s, LSD users were looking for mystical 'trips', to inspire more intense music and poetry.

Terms used for the effects of the substances on the body include **stimulant**, **depressant** and **hallucinogen**. Heroin and alcohol usually act as depressants; cocaine and nicotine as stimulants. Cannabis and solvents can act as depressants or hallucinogens.

Key terms

Psychoactive: a term used about drugs, such as LSD, that have an effect on the brain or nervous system and, therefore, on a person's behaviour.

Stimulant: a substance, such as cocaine, that stimulates the central nervous system and tends to produce a sense of energy and wakefulness.

Depressant: a substance, such as alcohol, that slows down the activity of the central nervous system and tends to produce a sense of relaxation and contentment.

Hallucinogen: a substance, such as LSD, that alters the perception of reality and may produce hallucinations.

Some biological explanations for the effects of abused substances

The brain responds to sensory inputs, such as sound and light, and passes messages back to muscles. These messages travel along neurons as electrical signals. In the gaps between neurons, which are called synapses, the messages are carried by chemicals called neurotransmitters. The brain uses about 30 of these (dopamine is an example); they are released by one neuron and stimulate specific receptors to activate the next neuron.

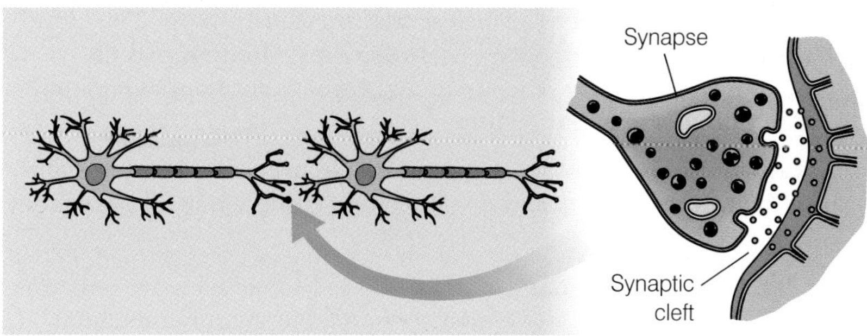

Fig. 1 *Brain cell, synapse and the role of neurotransmitters*

Psychoactive drugs affect how neurons work by copying the action of the neurotransmitters or combining with the receptors. The production of neurotransmitters in the brain is determined by sensitive 'feedback' from neurons. One possible consequence of the prolonged use of psychoactive drugs is that the brain adjusts to the high levels of the drugs and accepts this situation as 'normal'. To maintain this new 'normality', the brain reduces its own production of neurotransmitters.

The person using the drug is probably unaware of this until their drug use is abruptly stopped, for example in a rehabilitation programme. The sudden decrease in the levels of the drug may cause unpleasant physical symptoms for several days, until the brain is able to restore neurotransmitter production to its previous rate. This provides one explanation for the painful **withdrawal symptoms** that occur when people 'come off' drugs, such as heroin, on which they are physically dependent.

Tolerance is another outcome of these mechanisms. The first ever alcoholic drink can produce quite powerful effects. However, after several years of steady drinking, the first drink of the day would produce almost no behavioural change; to repeat the initial powerful effects would now require several drinks.

Psychological effects also play a part in tolerance and dependence. In 1988, Shepard Siegel, of McMaster University in Canada, put forward the idea that tolerance is also linked to classical (Pavlovian) conditioning. He suggested that environmental cues associated with the substance abuse stimulate a **drug compensatory response** to counteract the effects of the drug. Typical cues could be the pub for alcohol or the place where heroin is usually injected. In familiar locations the body prepares itself, for example for the **pain-killing** effects of heroin by becoming **more** sensitive to pain. Continued use of the substance produces a stronger compensatory response so that large doses are needed to achieve the same effects. This could explain why many units of alcohol may cause less intoxication in a pub than they would do if consumed at home. Sadly, it could also partly explain why a person's 'usual' dose of heroin has proved fatal when administered in a different location. Siegel demonstrated the importance of environmental cues in a study of rats.

Research study: Siegel *et al.* (1982)

Aim: To find out how rats' tolerance to heroin is affected by environmental cues.

Method: One group of rats was given increasingly larger heroin injections, in the same cage and room, every two days over a two-week period. Another group was given placebo injections with the same schedule. At the end, each rat was given a single large dose

Take it further

Legal classification of drugs

- Class A (heroin, cocaine, LSD): possession carries penalties of up to seven years' imprisonment and an unlimited fine.
- Class B (amphetamines, cannabis, codeine): possession carries penalties of up to five years' imprisonment and an unlimited fine.
- Class C (steroids, tranquillisers): possession carries penalties of up to two years' imprisonment and an unlimited fine.

Note:

- These penalties don't apply to drugs prescribed for personal therapeutic use.
- The penalties for supplying and trafficking are more severe.

Link

For a more detailed explanation of synaptic transmission, re-read Chapter 2, Biopsychology, in *AQA Psychology B AS*.

Key terms

Withdrawal symptoms: painful physical effects, such as cramps, sweating and restlessness, that occur when a person suddenly stops using some psychoactive drugs.

Tolerance: a situation where, through prolonged use, the user needs larger doses of the substance to repeat the original effects. This happens because the body and brain have adapted so that the presence of the substance has become the 'normal' state.

Drug compensatory response: an opposite, counteracting response in the body, prompted by environmental cues, when a substance such as heroin is about to be used.

of heroin, about twice the largest dose previously given. The 'prior exposure' rats were divided into two groups: Group A had the final injection in the same room and cage, while group B had the injection in a different setting.

Results: Of the 'placebo' group of rats, 96 per cent died as a result of their injection, whereas 64 per cent of group B and 32 per cent of group A died.

Conclusion: Both groups A and B showed some tolerance to heroin. Group A showed greater tolerance than group B. Environmental cues do stimulate tolerance. An exclusively biological explanation of tolerance would predict that both groups A and B would show similar death rates.

Evaluation: This research would probably not be sanctioned in the UK at the present time, owing to the obvious harm to the rats.

Link

Re-read Chapter 1, Key approaches, in *AQA Psychology B AS*, to refresh your memory about classical conditioning. This will also be helpful for the section on treatments later in this chapter.

Addiction and dependence

Although descriptions such as 'she's a heroin addict' and 'it's an addiction with him' are in common use, '**addiction**' and 'addict' are becoming less popular terms with professionals in the field of substance abuse. This is because there are a variety of definitions for the terms and their tone tends to be negative. Most uses of the words refer to compulsive behaviours carried out in search of pleasure. This 'pleasure' may come from stimulation of the brain's reward system and involve increased levels of the neurotransmitter, dopamine. The 'pleasure' provides a motivation to repeat the behaviour and will reinforce it.

'**Physical dependence**' is an easier term to apply. For example, suppose a person has used heroin to the point where unpleasant withdrawal symptoms are experienced if regular use is interrupted. The compulsion to use heroin again may now be less concerned with 'seeking pleasure' than with avoiding physical discomfort.

There is also '**psychological dependence**', which applies, for example, if someone's life is centred on alcoholic drinks to the point where alcohol is needed to face social situations, and cravings and discomfort are experienced if it is not available.

Abuse of substances such as heroin, nicotine and alcohol may result from a combination of both kinds of dependence. For example, heroin users soon become physically dependent on it but living through the period of withdrawal symptoms does not guarantee that the user will be 'cured'. Psychological dependence, linked to lifestyle, social groups and expectations, may cause the ex-user to **relapse**.

Key terms

Addiction: compulsive behaviour, with potentially harmful consequences, in search of pleasure.

Physical dependence: a state in which the body and brain have adapted to the presence of a drug so that the drug is needed for normal functioning. Compulsive use continues to prevent the unpleasant withdrawal symptoms that occur if the drug use is stopped suddenly.

Psychological dependence: a situation in which a person's life is focused on a substance to enable them to 'feel good' and cope socially. Compulsive use continues to maintain a normal state of mind and avoid withdrawal symptoms such as irritability and depression.

Relapse: a return to using the problem substance, for example drinking alcohol or smoking, after successful treatment.

AQA Examiner's tip

Addiction' and 'dependence' can be difficult terms to define and distinguish. Learn the definitions carefully and, to illustrate them, link them to good examples.

Key points:

- Prolonged use of substances such as heroin, cocaine, alcohol, nicotine and solvents can lead to harmful effects for both the user and society at large.
- Legal restrictions apply to the sale, purchase and use of many substances that can be abused.
- The effects of substances can be summed up by terms such as 'depressant', 'stimulant' and 'hallucinogen'.
- Heroin and alcohol are depressants; cocaine and nicotine are stimulants; solvents can produce hallucinations.

- Most abused substances are psychoactive drugs that influence the transfer of messages between neurons in the brain.
- Abuse of substances may involve tolerance to them, physical and/or psychological dependence on them and withdrawal symptoms when their use is abruptly stopped.
- The term 'addiction' is less widely used these days but can also apply to substance abuse.

Summary questions

1 For each of the following types of drug, state one example:
  a stimulant
  b depressant
  c hallucinogen.

2 Distinguish between the terms 'depressant' and 'stimulant' as applied to drugs.

3 Jane has been drinking alcohol for many years. She has developed a tolerance to it. Phil has been using heroin for a while and is physically dependent on it.
  a What is meant by 'tolerance' in this context? How might Jane's experience and behaviour demonstrate a tolerance to alcohol?
  b What is meant by 'physically dependent' in this context? Describe one effect that might happen because of Phil's physical dependence on heroin.

Explanations for substance abuse

Learning objectives:

- understand, explain and evaluate the effect of hereditary factors on substance abuse
- understand, explain and evaluate the effect of personality characteristics and disorders on substance abuse
- understand, explain and evaluate the effects of peer influences, social norms and role models on substance abuse.

Substance abuse is widespread. Reasons given for why a character in a TV 'soap' has a heroin problem or for why an acquaintance smokes a lot may include stress, family background, or peer pressure. This section looks at the role played by hereditary factors, personality characteristics and social influences. Alcohol, heroin and tobacco are used as examples, but the same principles apply to many abused substances.

Hereditary factors

People say, 'They all drink heavily in that family' or 'She smokes a lot, just like her mother'. One explanation is the 'nurture' argument. This suggests that a person's attitude and behaviour towards, for example, alcohol, was learned from parents and older siblings. On the other hand, there is also the 'nature' argument, which suggests that people inherit characteristics that make them more likely to be involved in abusing substances. How can these two suggestions be tested separately?

Inherited characteristics are passed on at conception. The child receives a random selection of 50 per cent of the genes of each parent. The

AQA Examiner's tip

Questions about the explanations for substance abuse may be phrased in several ways, for example, 'factors affecting ...', 'explanations for ...', 'reasons why some people are a greater risk of ...'. These questions should all be answered using the factors identified in this section although the material may have to be used in slightly different ways.

Hint

Most behaviour is considered to be a result of interaction between nature (inherited characteristics) and nurture (the environment and upbringing). For example, our intelligence is partly a consequence of the genes we received from our parents and partly a consequence of the learning we have done at home, school, etc.

Links

For definitions of MZ and DZ twins, see p102 in Chapter 5, Schizophrenia and mood disorders.

The nature–nurture debate is considered in some detail in Chapter 10, Debates in psychology. Alcohol abuse is an example that you could use to illustrate the importance of both nature and nurture in causing behaviour.

Key terms

Type 1 alcoholism: a type of alcoholism that starts in later life, involves psychological dependence and occurs in both men and women who have not been involved in antisocial or criminal behaviour.

Type 2 alcoholism: a type of alcoholism that may start at an earlier age and occurs in men who have been involved in antisocial or criminal behaviour.

influence of heredity has been studied where there are clear genetic relationships between the participants, for example children and parents, pairs of MZ (identical) and DZ (fraternal) twins, and in wider family circles. Studies of children adopted at birth are also interesting because the children have some genes in common with the biological parents (nature) but are brought up in an environment with different parents (nurture).

Robert Cloninger, a psychiatrist at Washington University, carried out a study of male children in Sweden who were adopted at an early age. The research involved both **Type 1** and **Type 2** alcoholism.

Research study: Cloninger (1987)

Aim: To find out the effect of inherited characteristics, from both Type 1 and Type 2 alcoholic fathers, on alcohol abuse shown by the sons.

Method: The participants were 1,724 Swedish males, adopted at an early age between 1930 and 1947. Medical, criminal and insurance records were used to identify alcohol abuse in the biological fathers and in the sons, who were aged between 23 and 43. The social class of the adoptive father was used as a rough guide to the likely exposure of the adopted son to heavy drinking. It was assumed that the lower social class would have more exposure; and higher classes, less. The researchers calculated the percentages of adopted sons involved in alcohol abuse from combinations of abusing and non-abusing biological fathers and higher- and lower-class adoptive fathers for both Type 1 and Type 2 alcoholism.

Results: For both types of alcoholism, a higher percentage of the sons of 'abuser' biological fathers became 'abusers'. For example, in Type 2 alcoholism, 17 to 18 per cent of the sons of men who abused alcohol did so too. Only 2 to 4 per cent of the sons of non-abusers did.

Conclusion: For both Type 1 and Type 2 alcoholism, the sons were more likely to be alcohol 'abusers' if their biological fathers were. This applied whether or not their adoptive fathers abused alcohol. This suggests that inherited characteristics have an influence on alcohol abuse behaviour.

Evaluation: For both types of alcoholism the largest percentage of sons were alcohol 'abusers' when both the natural and adoptive fathers were heavy drinkers. This shows that the environment in which the boys were brought up also had an influence on their potential for abuse.

When Cloninger studied female adoptees, he found that Type 1 alcoholism was influenced by heredity, but Type 2 was not, so the latter may be 'male-limited'.

Twins, both MZ and DZ, have been extensively studied in the Minnesota Twin Family Study, which began in 1989, at the University of Minnesota. The research aims to study the development of psychological traits, such as personality, and the origin of behaviours. The findings of the research into substance abuse are outlined below.

Research study: McGue *et al.* (1992)

Aim: To find out the extent of similarities between male MZ and DZ twins in DSM-III diagnoses of alcohol abuse or dependence.

Method: Many pairs of male MZ and DZ twins were interviewed about their alcohol use, particularly about the features of the DSM-III criteria.

Results: The following alcohol abuse concordance rates were found: male MZ twins – 77 per cent; male DZ twins – 54 per cent.

Conclusion: The male MZ twins showed greater similarity in their alcohol abuse than the male DZ twins. The MZ twins have 100 per cent of their genes in common; the DZ twins about 50 per cent. This suggests that heredity has an influence on alcohol abuse.

Evaluation: MZ twins are likely to experience environmental influences that are more similar than those experienced by DZ twins. For example, parents may treat 'identical' twins in more similar ways than they treat DZ twins, so similarities in alcohol abuse may partly be explained by environmental, 'nurture' influences.

Link

A 77 per cent concordance rate for alcohol abuse among DZ twins would mean that 77 per cent of the pairs shared the same level of alcohol abuse (e.g. 'no abuse' or 'high level of abuse'). See p102 in Chapter 5, Schizophrenia and mood disorders, for a definition of concordance rate.

The concordance rates for female twins were found to be 39 per cent for MZ twins and 42 per cent for DZ twins, which suggests that heredity has more influence on alcohol abuse in males than in females (McGue *et al.*, 1992).

Explanation

Inherited characteristics could affect the way in which alcohol is metabolised in the body. Alcohol (ethanol) turns into acetaldehyde (ethanal), which causes nausea, and is further oxidised to carbon dioxide and water. A build-up of acetaldehyde in the body of a person with a slower metabolism causes more nausea and less appetite for alcohol. The person with a faster metabolism can drink more alcohol without immediate unpleasant affects and so is at greater risk of alcohol abuse.

A specific genetically based enzyme deficiency is found among many Asian people. It causes a delay in alcohol metabolism, which causes facial flushing and nausea after drinking small amounts of alcohol.

A different inherited characteristic could be sensitivity to alcohol, i.e. how intoxicated a person becomes when they drink. A person with lower sensitivity might drink more alcohol and so be more prone to abuse. Dr Marc A. Schuckit of the University of California, San Diego, has studied this effect.

Research study: Schuckit (1985)

Aim: To find out how sensitivity to alcohol varies between sons of alcoholic and non-alcoholic fathers, and whether there is a link to future alcoholism.

Method: The participants (454 men, aged about 20) were invited to take part in an 'alcohol challenge' where they consumed three to five drinks and reported on their level of intoxication. The men were followed up about 10 years later with interviews, comment from close relatives and evidence from urine samples and medical records.

Results: About 40 per cent of the sons of alcoholic fathers showed low sensitivity to alcohol and reported low levels of intoxication compared with 10 per cent of the non-alcoholics' sons. Ten years later, alcoholism was found in 43 per cent of those who showed the least response to alcohol and in only 11 per cent of those who showed the most response.

Conclusion: A low sensitivity to alcohol is one factor that makes alcoholism more likely. This low sensitivity is partly inherited.

Evaluation: This research method is expensive, time consuming, ethically suspect and inappropriate with active or recovering alcoholics.

Schuckit's research team has found similar results for women. Recently, they have abandoned the 'alcohol challenge' and used a 12-item 'Self Rating of the Effects of Alcohol' measure instead, with similar results. This followed ethical concerns about the 'alcohol challenge', especially where the participants had an alcohol abuse problem or were recovering from it.

Other research has found that smoking and alcohol dependence frequently occur together. For example, alcohol-dependent people are 4.7 times more likely to smoke than those who are non-alcohol-dependent. Habitual smoking, too, may partly have a genetic origin. Continuing research into the human genome and the DNA of deceased alcoholics has begun to show potentially significant genes such as the dopamine D2 receptor gene, which is found more commonly in alcoholics than non-alcoholics. However, there may not be such a strong genetic link to other kinds of substance abuse.

It is unlikely that heredity, alone, causes people to abuse substances. Cloninger's research showed that a combination of a heavy-drinking biological father and adopting father was linked to the greatest likelihood of the son being a heavy drinker. This demonstrates the importance of interaction between inherited (nature) and environmental (nurture) influences.

Schuckit's research has also shown that a significant proportion of alcoholics show symptoms of personality disorders, such as **antisocial personality disorder** (APD).

Key terms

Antisocial personality disorder: one of the most common personality disorders associated with little regard for the rights of others, lack of concern for rules, deceitfulness, lack of responsibility, impulsive behaviour, irritability, law breaking and aggression.

Personality characteristics

Is there an addictive personality? Common personality characteristics do not strongly influence substance abuse, but, according to Robson (1994):

> For what it is worth, the typical drug-user-to-be is likely to possess at least some of the following characteristics: ... nonconformity to conventional values ... a relative lack of ambition and commitment to school work or career building; independent mindedness ... impulsivity; preoccupation with pleasure seeking and risk-taking; a history of physical or mental illness ... or consistently low self-esteem.

Many adolescents explain their experiments with drugs in terms of 'buzz, fun and curiosity'.

There are also **personality disorders**: psychiatric conditions marked by chronic behaviour patterns that cause serious problems with relationships and work. The treatment of people who abuse substances often includes a personality assessment by means of interviews and the completion of personality tests, such as the Minnesota Multiphasic Personality Inventory. This reveals 10 psychiatric conditions, such as **psychopathic deviance** (Pd).

Berzins *et al.* (1974) studied over 1,200 heroin addicts who were patients at the Lexington Public Health Hospital. Many of these showed characteristics of antisocial personality disorder and **psychopathy**. A similar study on people who abuse alcohol is outlined below.

Research study: Morgernstern *et al.* (1997)

Aim: To investigate the extent to which personality disorders are found in people who abuse alcohol.

Method: Three hundred and sixty-six people who abuse alcohol were studied; they were patients at a variety of sites. They were given structured diagnostic interviews and other measures to assess their personality characteristics and levels of alcohol abuse at least 14 days after their treatment started.

Results: Personality disorders were common among the patients. APD was one of the disorders particularly associated with severe symptoms of alcoholism.

Conclusion: Many people who abuse alcohol have personality disorders and APD is one of the most prominent.

Evaluation: This link is a correlation, so does **not** show that APD **causes** alcohol abuse.

Studies on people who abuse cocaine show similar results. The overall pattern is that some common personality characteristics and some personality disorders correlate positively with abuse of a range of substances.

Evaluation

The links between substance abuse and personality characteristics and disorders are correlational. Therefore, they do not necessarily show that the characteristic or disorder is the **cause** of the substance abuse. It is also true that prolonged substance abuse can lead to changes in personality. The person abusing the substance could become more aggressive, antisocial, and less sensitive to moral sense.

The research work has often focused exclusively on the abusers of the substance and their personalities and has not compared them with matching 'control' groups. For example, we notice that many people who abuse alcohol show symptoms of APD. APD is thought to be the most common personality disorder, affecting about 3 per cent of the population. Is alcohol abuse found widely among this group? Fabrega *et al.* (1991) found that 40 per cent of those seeking therapy for APD also had substance abuse problems.

The influences of heredity and personality on substance abuse are difficult to separate. Many studies show that children of alcoholic

Take it further

'Personality' can be difficult to define. The root of the word is the Latin 'persona', which means a mask. The term includes the 'personas' which we project to others and also inner parts of psychological experience, which we call 'self'. We can get a simple idea of our personality by writing a series of honest 'I ...' statements about ourselves. Students were asked to do this in research into 'self-concept' by Kuhn (1960).

Key terms

Psychopathic deviance/ psychopathy: a personality disorder involving a lack of conscience and feeling for others, violation of social norms, and the use of charm, intimidation or violence to control others and satisfy needs.

parents not only have an increased risk of experiencing substance abuse problems but also are at increased risk of conduct and personality disorders (e.g. Merikangas and Avenevoli, 2000). This suggests that these disorders may also be partly the result of heredity.

Social influences

Key terms

Social norm: the expected and accepted behaviour within a particular society.

In a poll of UK residents, about drug use, conducted by ICM Research and published in the *Observer* in April 2002, 28 per cent admitted 'taking an illegal drug'. The reasons stated were curiosity (75 per cent); peer pressure (22 per cent); desire to emulate heroes (3 per cent). Findings like these show the importance of social influences in starting and continuing problem drug use. Research work has focused on family influences, peer influences and **social norms**.

Family and parental influences

The family provides a setting where the principles of social learning theory can apply, as proposed by Bandura and Walters (1963). For example, a child may observe parents and older siblings using alcohol for pleasure and seek to imitate these respected role models. The child's use of alcohol may then be reinforced by the models' approving comments.

The studies of twins and adopted children, described on p173, attempted to separate out the influence of nature and nurture in relation to heavy drinking. Research with 'ordinary' biological families cannot easily do this. A typical example is the longitudinal study by White *et al.* (2000) which included the effects of parental smoking and drinking on these behaviours in their offspring. On four occasions, data were collected from the parents and their children (age range 15 to 28 years). The results showed that parental modelling, particularly by the mother, affected the offspring's drinking but had less influence on their smoking. Brook *et al.* (1999) showed that peer and personality influences were more likely to affect initiation into marijuana use.

Evaluation

It appears that parental modelling may be more influential with respect to alcohol use than for other substances.

Peer influences

Peer groups provide a setting where conformity to group norms can happen. A teenager may be part of a group of friends who experiment with smoking and may feel pressure to fit in with this group behaviour (an example of normative conformity). Some of the most influential research into the factors affecting group conformity was conducted by Asch (1951).

The study by Brook *et al.* (1999), mentioned above, showed that the onset of marijuana use in people from the age of nine to the early 20s was affected by peer influences. A typical study, which shows the role of peer influences, is outlined below.

Research study: Garnier and Stein (2002)

Aim: To find out which peer and family influences are the best predictors of problem behaviours, such as substance abuse, in adolescence.

Method: One hundred and ninety-eight children, from conventional and non-conventional families, were studied up to the age of 18, in a longitudinal study. The pregnant mothers and, later, their teenage children were interviewed and filled in questionnaires. Data were gathered about the family situation, childhood and teenage peer relationships and behavioural and substance abuse problems.

Results: The best predictor of teenage substance abuse problems was similar behaviour by peers.

Conclusion: Peer pressure and a desire to fit in with group norms have a significant influence on teenage substance abuse.

Evaluation: This link is a correlation so it does **not** show that peer pressure **causes** substance abuse.

Link

To refresh your memory about 'social norms', 'group norms', 'conformity' and 'peer pressure', re-read Chapter 5, Social Influence, in *AQA Psychology B AS*.

Evaluation

Peer influences, too, have a limited effect. Reed and Rountree (1997) studied the effect of group pressure and social selection on entry to and exit from substance abuse. They found that social selection was more influential than group pressure. In other words, teenagers who are at risk of involvement in substance abuse may seek out and actively join peer groups of those already involved.

The relative influence of parents and peers also changes as children pass through the teenage years. This study on smoking habits illustrates this.

Research study: Bricker *et al.* (2006)

Aim: To study the influence of parents' and peers' smoking on teenagers' smoking habits.

Method: In a longitudinal study, 6,006 10-year-olds were studied until the age of 17. The researchers examined 'smoking transitions': from never smoking to trying; from trying smoking to monthly smoking; and from monthly to daily smoking. These were related to whether or not the parents and close friends were smokers.

Results: At all the studied ages, peer smoking was most influential on 'trying smoking' while parental smoking became more influential on the transition from monthly to daily smoking as the teenager got older.

Conclusion: Different levels of smoking may be influenced in different ways by parents and peers.

Evaluation: This study had an impressively large number of participants, which makes its findings more reliable.

Social norms

Generalisations about '**societies**' – such as 'university students are heavy drinkers' and 'the French have a much more sensible attitude to drinking alcohol than the British' – are examples of apparent social norms. Such norms have an influence on behaviour as people often feel that they want to 'fit in' and 'do what everybody else does'.

Key terms

Society: a national population or a more specific group, such as 'university students'.

Alcohol consumption and its effects show wide variations throughout different cultures. Muslim cultures prohibit its use. In Britain, heavy drinking is often associated with aggressive and antisocial behaviour while drinking the same number of units in Italy or France leads to pleasant relaxation and sociability.

The relationship between social norms and alcohol-related problems is evident in the countries of Taiwan and Korea (Helzer *et al.*, 1990). Both countries have a Confucian moral ethic and have experienced significant technological and industrial progress in recent years. However, alcohol-related problems are much more common in Korea than in Taiwan. The reason is linked to the social norms in these countries. In Korea, alcohol consumption is encouraged and public displays of drinking are associated with male mastery and domination. In Taiwan, alcohol is used with meals and on ceremonial occasions; drunkenness is disapproved of and seen as a sign of degeneration and weakness.

Evaluation

People may overestimate the peer use of a wide variety of abused substances, for example alcohol, tobacco and marijuana. A study of over 76,000 American college students showed that there was consistent overestimation of the quantity of alcohol drunk by their peers (Perkins *et al.*, 2005). This finding applied whether the actual norm was for light, moderate or heavy drinking. There is often a difference between the 'perceived norm', which is based on what people think their peers are doing, and the actual norm. It is possible that people try to 'fit in' with a perceived norm which describes a more extreme behaviour than the actual norm. Student drinking may also be affected by 'self-selection' where, rather than conforming to an actual or perceived norm, the heavy-drinking student selects peers who also drink heavily. As a result, the perceived norm for these students will be of 'heavy drinking'.

Social influences have more effect on some people than others. Bandura (1994) coined the term 'self-efficacy' to describe people's beliefs about the extent to which they influence and control their lives. A person with high self-efficacy would be less affected by social influences and be more resistant to peer pressure to abuse substances.

Key points:

- Some people are at greater risk of becoming involved in substance abuse than others.
- This may be because of heredity, personality characteristics and disorders or social influences.
- Important inherited characteristics include sensitivity to substances, such as alcohol, or personality characteristics, such as impulsivity.
- Studies of the influence of heredity have been done with MZ and DZ twins, adopted children and their biological and adopting parents, and families with high and low levels of abuse.
- The risk of experiencing substance abuse has a positive correlation with personality characteristics, such as rebelliousness and pre-occupation with pleasure seeking, and with personality disorders, such as APD.
- Social influences linked to peer groups, families and social norms can increase the risk of involvement in smoking or abuse of substances such as alcohol.

Summary questions

4 People may be at greater risk of involvement in substance abuse owing to heredity, personality or social influence:

a State one inherited characteristic that may make alcohol abuse more likely.

b State one personality characteristic that may make substance abuse more likely.

c State one personality disorder that may make alcohol abuse more likely.

d State one kind of social influence that may make teenagers more likely to experiment with smoking cigarettes.

5 Tom had his first drink of alcohol, at the age of 10, at a football club social event. He was encouraged to 'down a pint' by his elder brother Jack, whom he admired and respected. As a teenager, Tom began to drink heavily with his own group of friends. On leaving school, he was unemployed and bored. His daily activity began to be focused on alcohol. After a conviction for criminal damage, he spent a spell in prison; he joined Alcoholics Anonymous on his release, to see if he could overcome his drinking problem.

a State and explain the social influence that was involved in Tom's first experience of drinking alcohol.

b Many teenagers would say, 'It was peer pressure that caused me to start drinking.' Evaluate this explanation.

6 Several researchers have found a significant positive correlation between heroin abuse and personality disorders involving psychopathic deviance.

a Explain what is meant by a 'positive correlation' in this example.

b Identify one limitation of correlation studies.

c Discuss the link between heroin abuse and personality disorders

Treatments for people who abuse substances

Learning objectives:

- describe and explain the use of aversion therapy in treating people who abuse substances
- describe and explain the use of self-management strategies in treating people who abuse substances
- evaluate the effectiveness of these treatments.

Key terms

Aversion therapy: a type of behaviour therapy in which an unpleasant stimulus (e.g. a noxious smell) is associated, through classical conditioning, with addicted substances or behaviours, with the aim of conditioning a negative response to the addiction substances or behaviours.

Detoxification: a process that involves stopping the use of the 'problem' substance, while being helped through the withdrawal process, perhaps with the aid of medication.

Maintenance: a programme involving prescribing the substance, or an alternative, to stabilise the level of use while the user considers further treatment.

Harm reduction: policies, programmes, services and actions that work to reduce the health, social and economic harms to individuals, communities and society that are associated with the use of drugs.

Emetic: a substance, such as salty water, that causes nausea and vomiting.

Detoxification and harm reduction

When they first wish to change their behaviour, people with a drug problem are not always ready for psychological treatments, such as **aversion therapy** and self-management strategies. Some may undergo **detoxification**; others will begin a programme of **maintenance** or **harm reduction**. The latter might involve providing clean needles to reduce the risk of contracting infections or prescription of oral medications, for example methadone and buprenorphine (subutex), in place of heroin to avoid street crime.

Aversion therapies

These therapies are based on behaviourist principles of classical conditioning. The treatments have been used with substance problems involving alcohol and smoking and also with behavioural disorders. The abused substance and its use are paired with an unpleasant stimulus so that the behaviour is no longer enjoyed but linked to unpleasant outcomes. With alcohol, for example, all parts of the process of drinking, opening the bottle, smelling the contents, swirling the glass and tasting the drink are paired with an **emetic**, such as an injection of emetine or a drink of salty water, so that the drinker experiences nausea and vomiting. This treatment typically takes place, on alternate days, during a 10-day stay in a hospital or clinic. Between these sessions the person may have soft drinks, tea and coffee without the emetic so that it is only **alcohol** that is associated with vomiting, not merely drinking.

The following diagram illustrates this process of classical conditioning and is a reminder of the usual vocabulary associated with it:

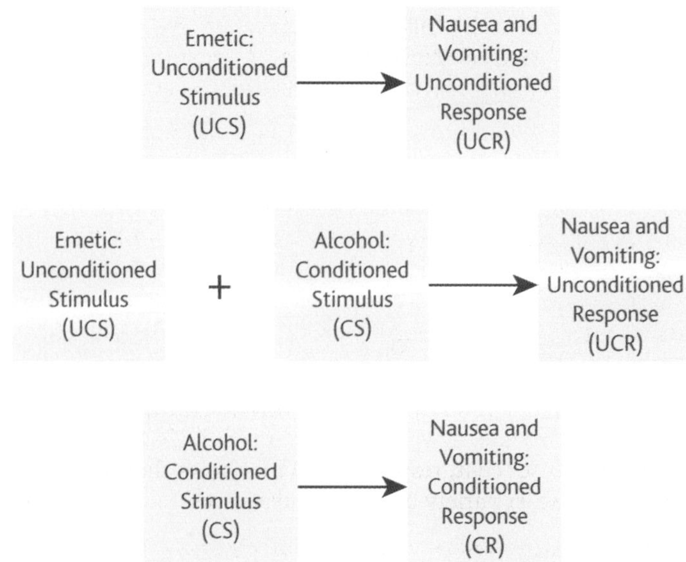

Fig. 2 *The process of aversion therapy in treating alcohol abuse*

An electric shock can be used as alternative unpleasant stimulus. This is given to the wrist through electrodes in a cuff and adjusted to be as painful as the participant can bear. This treatment has advantages compared with using an emetic, as the effect of the emetic is uncertain and there could be dangerous side effects. The shock is more reliably unpleasant and can be self-administered.

Most aversive therapy is carried out in private institutions, not least because of the high cost. Hospitals such as Schick-Shadel in Seattle have used independent research groups to assess the success of their treatments. An example of such a study is shown below.

Research study: Smith and Frawley (1993)

Aim: To find out the level of success in **abstaining** from alcohol, in treated participants, at least one year after in-patient aversion therapy.

Method: An independent research organisation randomly selected 600 previous patients and attempted to contact them by telephone for a structured interview, between 12 and 20 months after their treatment. Most of the patients had received 'emetic' therapy; a few had the 'shock' when the other treatment was unsuitable. The interview was designed to see if the participants had abstained from alcohol and other drugs that they had previously used, during the period since treatment. Four hundred and twenty-seven patients were contacted. Verification interviews were carried out with 40 per cent of the participants.

Results: Sixty-five per cent of the participants reported abstaining from alcohol for 12 months after treatment.

Conclusion: Aversion therapy has a high success rate in causing patients with an alcohol problem to abstain for 12 months after treatment.

Evaluation: The interviews involve the participants in 'self-report', which may make their statements unreliable. However, attempts were made to verify the data.

The best evidence from clinical trials is from RCTs (randomised controlled trials) where matched groups of, for example, people who abuse alcohol receive different kinds of treatment or no treatment so that comparisons of success rates can be made.

The results of this study are consistent with many others. Meyer and Chesser (1970) reported a 50 per cent abstinence rate 12 months after treatment and Elkins (1991) a 60 per cent rate. In the study by Smith and Frawley (1993), the participants were also asked, 'Did the treatment help you lose the urge to drink?' About 80 per cent reported diminished 'urges' or 'cravings'. Those who chose 'lost all urges' showed the highest abstinence rates.

Some of the people in the study also had aversive treatment for cocaine and cannabis use. They reported 12-month abstinence rates of 84 per cent and 70 per cent, respectively. This shows that the treatment can be used for a wider variety of abused substances.

Aversion to cigarette smoking can also be created by a 'quick puff' technique, where rapid puffs produce a hot and unpleasant feeling in the mouth and 'satiation', where participants are required to smoke at several times the usual rate to produce nausea. Smith (1988) reported on graduates of the Schick-Shadel hospital programme: of 327 participants, 52 per cent abstained from smoking for 12 months after the treatment.

Take it further

You may like to find out more about detoxification and harm reduction, although these issues are not immediately related to the earning of exam marks. You could use the internet to find out what a course of detoxification consists of and what it costs. You could find out some of the harm-reduction tactics that are used with heroin, smoking, etc.

Key terms

Abstaining: (abstinence) not using a substance, for example alcohol, at all for a period of time.

AQA Examiner's tip

Detoxification and harm reduction strategies are **not** psychological treatments. They should not be written about when the question refers to 'psychological treatments'. They have been included so that you get a fuller picture of the scope of drug treatment.

Link

To refresh your memory about classical conditioning, reread Chapter 1, Key approaches, in *AQA Psychology B AS*.

Hint

The behaviourist models of classical and operant conditioning can be applied to explanations for substance abuse and the treatment of people who abuse substances. Make sure that you don't confuse the two models. Remind yourself what the terms mean by rereading Chapter 1, Key approaches, in *AQA Psychology B AS*, or reading Chapter 9, Approaches in psychology, in this book.

Evaluation

Schuckit (1998) reported that aversion therapy made up only about 1 per cent of treatments for substance abuse in the USA. The report of the UK's National Treatment Agency (NTA) on the effectiveness of treatments for alcohol problems states that 'aversion therapy is not recommended' for treating alcohol problems; although it is effective, it is expensive (Heather *et al.*, 2007).

Schuckit also points out that aversive conditioning weakens with time. Schick-Shadel hospital offers 'reinforcement' treatments. People who took advantage of two of these during the first year after treatment were more likely to be abstinent (69 per cent) after 12 months than those who had no reinforcement (29 per cent). The 'shock' therapy for smoking provided an ingenious reinforcement in the form of a tight rubber band worn around the wrist. The person could 'ping' the rubber band to provide a sharp pain like an electric shock if the urge to smoke recurred.

The results of the studies show that up to 40 per cent of those treated by aversion therapy relapse in the first 12 months. In the 'smoking' study referred to earlier 86 per cent of the men who came from a 'non-smoking' household abstained for 12 months, but only 14 per cent of the men from 'smoking' households did so. It is evident that other factors, such as social norms and 'triggers' (environmental cues), can influence return to 'problem' behaviour. It may be a conditioned response. Effective treatments using aversion therapy must therefore also involve other therapies. For example, the alcohol programme referred to earlier gave the participants inpatient counselling during the treatment and the opportunity to join support groups or Alcoholics Anonymous when they were discharged.

The emetic and electric shock are clearly unpleasant, which raises ethical concerns. Participants might be unwilling to continue with treatment, leading to a high drop-out rate. However, many participants reported that they found the treatment less unpleasant than the personal disclosures involved in other kinds of therapy.

Take it further

Aversion therapy: classical or operant conditioning?

Different writers may talk about 'aversion therapy' either in terms of classical conditioning, as is the case in this chapter, or in terms of 'punishments' that make a behaviour less likely, which is a feature of operant conditioning. Can you explain aversion therapy in terms of operant conditioning?

Link

You will find the key ideas for operant conditioning in Chapter 1, Key approaches, in *AQA Psychology B AS*, and in Chapter 9, Approaches in psychology, in this book.

Covert sensitisation

Covert sensitisation is one response to the unpleasant nature of aversion therapy. In this case, the conditioning to abstain from a substance comes from vivid imagination and graphic descriptions. For example, in treating alcohol problems, the therapist takes the participant through a detailed story of vomiting, lack of coordination and subsequent hangover that is designed to cause nausea and anxiety. The participant is encouraged to imagine the scene and to repeat the process when they feel an urge to use the substance. Cautela (1970) recommends that the unpleasant outcomes should be associated with the **intention** to drink, rather than being associated with the **action**, so that the conditioning acts at an earlier stage in the process. He also advocates the use of smells and sounds to enhance the story.

Evaluation

The effectiveness of covert sensitisation is hard to evaluate because the treatment is usually combined with others, and some researchers, for example Barrett and Sachs (1974), suggest that success may partly be the result of raised motivation in the participants. Where covert sensitisation has been compared with other treatments the evidence is contradictory. Olsen *et al.* (1981) found that this treatment led to 70 per cent six-month abstinence rates, but Telch *et al.* (1984) raised questions about the value of covert sensitisation for outpatients as supportive group therapy proved more effective.

Self-management strategies

These are 'talking' therapies, which give the person who abuses substances greater responsibility for the process and the outcome. These therapies use principles from the cognitive, humanistic and behaviourist approaches and are the most common kinds of treatment offered in the UK.

Current practice in the UK is guided by *Tackling Drugs to Build a Better Britain*, a government strategy document, which was updated in 2002. There is a four-point focus on education, the availability of drugs, drug-related crime and getting more problem users into treatment. In response, local authorities have set up, Drug and Alcohol Action Teams (DAATs), involving agencies such as education, police and treatment services. *Models of Care* (NTA, 2002) sets out four tiers of provision for the 'problem drug user', ranging from the general medical services at the local surgery to residential settings. In many cases, the first approach is to the GP as there is less of a stigma than in going to a specialist treatment agency. Government intends that at least 30 per cent of GPs should specialise in offering care to drug users.

Take it further

You may like to find out more about your local DAAT. If you use 'Drug and Alcohol Action Teams' as the key words in a search engine, you will be able to access many websites around the UK and see how these local teams respond to the strategy document.

Theoretical models of behaviour change

Treatments for substance abuse aim to promote changes in behaviour. Self-management strategies are based on well-supported explanations for this. These include the **stages of change** model applied to substance abuse by Prochaska *et al.* (1992), the **health belief** model put forward by Rosenstock (1966) and the **theory of reasoned action** (TRA) proposed by Ajzen and Fishbein (1980).

The stages of change model

This model can be represented as a wheel or a spiral. It incorporates the idea that relapse will happen and the cycle of change will occur several times before permanently changed maintenance behaviour is achieved. The stages are:

- **pre-contemplation** – not thinking about changing behaviour
- **contemplation** – thinking about changing behaviour in the near future
- **decision/preparation** – making a plan to change behaviour
- **action** – implementing the plan to change behaviour
- **maintenance** – continuation of behaviour change
- **relapse** – returning to original behaviour.

With support, the cycle of change may start again.

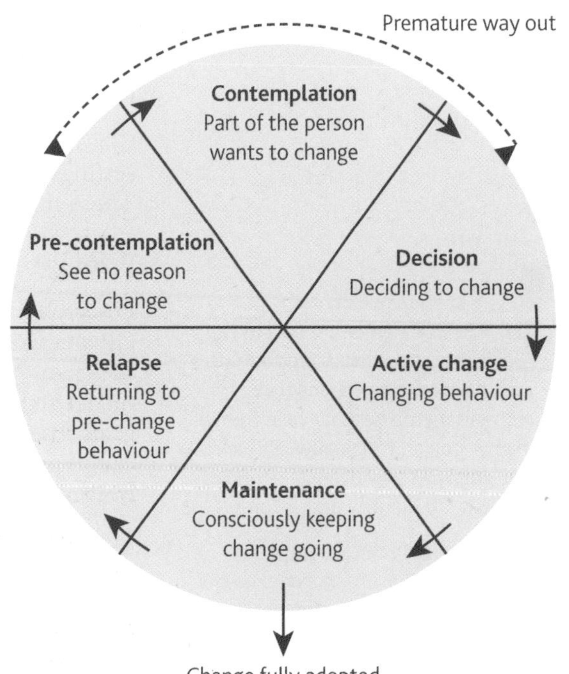

Fig. 3 *The stages of change model (**Prochaska** et al., 1992)*

The health belief model

The health belief model concerns how a person will respond to a threat to health. The likelihood of action depends on how the threat is rated and the costs–benefits of action. For example, a 30-year-old woman smokes 40 cigarettes per day. She is aware of the danger to her health and that various health problems have been experienced by older family members who smoke, so the threat is rated highly. She sees that stopping smoking will be difficult and may cause her to gain weight but will save money and make serious illness less likely (the costs and benefits). So, she is likely to act to stop smoking.

The theory of reasoned action

The theory of reasoned action suggests that behaviour is based on intentions that are influenced by a person's attitude to the behaviour and the likely response of others to it (subjective norms). For example, a 30-year-old man may see that he is drinking too much alcohol and that drinking less would be a benefit (his attitudes to the behaviour). His wife and family have encouraged him to drink less and their opinion is important to him (the subjective norms). His intention will be to drink less, which may lead to a change in behaviour.

Therapeutic techniques

These broadly belong under the umbrella title of **cognitive-behavioural therapy** (CBT), a psychotherapy based on modifying cognitions, assumptions, beliefs and behaviours. Some of the main features of these strategies involve the individual in:

- keeping a record of their substance use and where it happens
- becoming aware of the causes of problem drug use for themselves and others
- becoming more informed about the consequences of substance abuse for themselves and others
- learning skills to resist substance use in social situations
- learning what to do when they relapse.

There are a wide range of techniques, several of which may be used together.

Contingency contracting

The therapist and client draw up a contract about goals for behaviour and substance use for the coming week. Progress is reviewed in the next session. Token punishments or rewards may be applied.

Stimulus control/response substitution/cue exposure and response prevention

Classical conditioning may prompt the use of substances in certain settings (e.g. alcohol in the pub, with friends, before a football match). These treatments aim to weaken or avoid this conditioned response.

Brief interventions/motivational interviews

Research within the NHS has found that a few sessions with a specialist GP are cost effective in reducing problems linked to alcohol, especially if the client has motivation to change. The interviews use Prochaska *et al.*'s model and the health belief model: the GP and client discuss the client's goals, their plans to achieve these and the support they will have. The client gives a progress report to the GP at a later date and the process can continue, perhaps setting more challenging goals.

12-step programmes

These started with Alcoholics Anonymous (AA) in the 1930s. Problem drinkers formed self-help groups without professional input. AA claims that up to 75 per cent who 'are really serious' become abstinent. Claims are difficult to test as the membership is anonymous. A comparison of outcomes

Take it further

The '12 steps', which are part of the Alcoholics Anonymous programme, include admitting dependence, recognising the need for help from a 'higher power' (originally God) and working with a recovering alcoholic 'sponsor' to identify past errors.

You may like to find out more by visiting the AA website. For example, how might the AA 12-step programme operate for a 20-year-old unemployed male with an alcohol problem?

for court referrals to different kinds of treatment or none (Brandsma *et al.*, 1980) showed that treatment led to greater improvement but that the AA treatment was less successful than the others. The programme has also been applied to other drugs. Strengths of this approach include honest confession, public commitment, group support and the sponsor system.

Relapse prevention

The positive behavioural changes achieved by participating in a treatment programme may be lost, through relapse, when the person returns to their normal lifestyle. Relapse prevention focuses on identifying particular high-risk situations, the learning of coping styles, such as how to say 'no', and increasing a person's sense of self-control. It has been used successfully with alcohol, smoking and cocaine problems.

Evaluation

There is general agreement that all the treatments individually lead to reductions in the use of problem drugs and that combinations of treatments, a 'multi-modal' approach, can be particularly successful.

One of the issues with relevant research studies is that it is difficult to identify exactly why a person has changed their behaviour. Was it because of the specific treatment, or the 'professional health-oriented' setting or the quality of care, support and interest shown by a professional?

Another issue has been variation in, or lack of, agreed measures of the beneficial outcomes of treatment. The NTA developed a Treatment Outcome Profile (TOP) in 2007, to use with problem drug users when their situation is reviewed. This will allow fair comparisons of different kinds of treatments and of progress over time. The TOP includes questions about level of drug use, housing and whether the user is in education or employment.

A typical piece of research, on adolescents in the USA, is outlined below.

Research study: Hser *et al.* (2002)

Aim: To examine how successful a variety of treatment programmes are in reducing drug use and associated problem behaviour in adolescents in the USA.

Method: The participants were 1,167 adolescents, aged 11 to 18, associated with four centres. They were studied before treatment and one year after. Participants were involved in either residential, short inpatient, or outpatient 'drug-free' treatment designed for adolescents. The treatments included individual and group counselling, 12-step programmes, family therapy and skills training. The participants were interviewed, about drug use, education and criminal activity, before and after treatment by an independent research organisation. The drug use of a random sample was checked by urine testing.

Results: Weekly marijuana use declined from 80 per cent to 44 per cent; the percentage with average or better school grades went up from 53 per cent to 80 per cent; and the number involved in any illegal act went down from 76 per cent to 53 per cent. Participants reported higher self-esteem and fewer thoughts of suicide. Cocaine and hallucinogen use showed little change.

Conclusion: A variety of different treatment styles are effective in reducing adolescent drug use and crime and in improving educational achievement.

Take it further

You may like to illustrate the techniques that are briefly described in this section. For example:

- What might contingency contracting involve for a 25-year-old female who smokes 40 cigarettes a day?
- What might stimulus control to combat conditioning involve for a 40-year-old man who regularly drinks too much alcohol?

Hints

There are a lot of 'talking' therapies with their own acronyms, CBT, MET, BCST, etc. It would be wise to focus on the theories of behaviour change and the general features of self-management strategies.

The theoretical models of behaviour change can apply either to changes of behaviour, for those engaged in problem drug use, or to changes of attitude by those who have never used drugs or do not yet have a problem. The same models would therefore apply to strategies used to prevent substance abuse.

AQA Examiner's tip

The section on self-management strategies has a lot of diverse material. It would be helpful to write out an exam-type answer containing the key points that earn marks in exams. For example, what self-management strategies are; some key features that apply to them; theories of behaviour change that they use; one detailed example of how a method might be used with a named substance, e.g. alcohol; evaluation of the treatment by using evidence and comparing the treatment with aversion therapies; problems of relapse; and the idea that a mixture of treatments is often more effective than any single one.

Take it further

If you would like to know more about the various 'talking therapies' used in treating problem drug users, conduct some internet research on CBT, MET, BCST, MI, etc. Try to identify aspects of the therapies that reflect the assumptions and practices of the behaviourist, cognitive and humanistic approaches.

Evaluation: Adolescence is a period during which drug use may be expected to increase so this research indicates the value of treatments targeted at that age range.

Key points

- Psychological treatments for people who abuse substances include aversion therapy and the use of self-management strategies.
- Aversion therapy is based on the behaviourist model of classical conditioning.
- Self-management strategies make the person who abuses substances responsible for the outcome of the treatment and could involve cognitive, behaviourist, humanistic and psychodynamic therapies.
- Aversion therapies have had some success in helping people who abuse alcohol and smoking to stop, but people may find the treatments unpleasant and drop out of them.
- Aversive conditioning weakens over time and people may relapse when they return to familiar settings.
- Self-management strategies have had some success in reducing early-stage substance abuse but are no more successful than other treatments.
- Treatments tend to be most successful when several different approaches are used at the same time.

Summary questions

7 What do the following terms mean?

a Aversion therapy

b Covert sensitisation

c 12-step programme

d Self-management strategy

8 Tom is a heavy smoker but pays little attention to those who tell him that smoking is a threat to his health. Jill has been drinking heavily for several years. She has lost her job and fallen out with her family. She has begun to make plans to cut out most of her drinking.

a Which of Prochaska's stages is Tom in?

b Describe one tactic that a specialist GP might use with Tom to move him on towards reducing his smoking.

c Which of Prochaska's stages is Jill in?

d Describe one tactic that a specialist GP might use, in a motivational interview with Jill, to make her more likely to reduce her level of drinking.

9 Describe and evaluate the effectiveness of one self-management strategy.

Substance abuse

Prevention of substance abuse

Learning objectives:

- understand and illustrate the idea of 'at-risk groups' and the value of targeting prevention techniques to them
- understand and illustrate the idea of different levels of prevention technique
- describe, explain and illustrate the use of fear-arousal appeals in preventing substance abuse
- evaluate the effectiveness of fear-arousal appeals in preventing substance abuse
- understand and evaluate the idea of social inoculation.

Key terms

At-risk groups: people who are more likely than others to be involved in problem drug use, owing to heredity, personality, homelessness, criminal activity, social influences, etc.

Social inoculation: programmes for young people to help them develop the knowledge, attitudes and skills needed to resist social influences to become involved in substance abuse.

Take it further

Khat leaves contain at least two Class C drugs, cathine and cathinone, although khat, itself, is not classified as a 'dangerous drug'. Users show some dependence, loss of appetite and sleeplessness. There may be a link to psychotic episodes.

A brief history of preventive measures

Attempts by governments and private agencies to reduce or prevent substance abuse have a long history. Legislation has included the 1971 Act, which introduced the current Class A, B, C system for drugs. Public campaigns have included 'Just say No' in the USA and, in 1995, the UK 'Sorted' crusade, led by Leah Betts's parents, after her MDMA-related death. In 2002, the current policy document, *Tackling Drugs to Build a Better Britain*, was launched.

The social, criminal and financial costs linked to problem drug use are huge. One focus in *Tackling Drugs to Build a Better Britain* is 'preventing young people from using drugs through education'. Prevention could involve TV adverts, poster campaigns, progressive teaching programmes in schools and activities with targeted **at-risk groups**. These activities could include fear arousal and **social inoculation**, which are dealt with in this section, and health promotion or education. These approaches overlap.

Identifying and targeting at-risk groups

Influences on problem drug use include the law, availability and price and potentially apply to everyone. Persuasive communications, designed to change the attitudes and behaviour of potential and actual users can be most effective when at-risk groups are targeted. Targeting may be achieved through age groups, for example teenagers in secondary schools; through locations, for example clubs, GP surgeries and Job Centres; through lifestyle, for example adverts on the internet; or with cultural groups.

According to the British Crime Survey for 2005–2006, the highest levels of recent drug use were reported among those aged 16 to 24 years, with the behaviour moderated or abandoned in the next few years. This identifies teenagers as a broad at-risk group. The same survey showed that teenagers who have been 'looked after' (formerly known as being 'in care'), homeless, truanted, excluded from school or involved in serious or frequent offending, such as prostitution, were even more at risk.

The section 'Explanations for substance abuse' (on p171) discussed factors such as heredity, personality, social influence and social norms that may make a person more at risk of problem drug use. Some targeting may be possible. For example, GPs may deal with members of families in which there is heavy drinking and be able to provide preventive advice; psychiatrists meet patients with APD who are at greater risk of alcohol abuse.

Cultural factors can also be important. The chewing of khat (leaves of a shrub that grows in the Horn of Africa) is common among the Somali, Ethiopian and Yemeni communities in cities such as London and Bristol. The leaves are stimulants and produce euphoria and wakefulness. Members of the communities defend the use of khat as a cultural practice that holds the community together.

Link

The composition of at-risk groups is partly linked to the factors which were dealt with in the section 'Explanations for substance abuse' (pp171–178). Read that section again.

Levels of prevention activity

This helpful analysis of prevention activities matches them to people in three different categories based on their experience of drug problems. For example, an eight-year-old boy who thinks that 'taking drugs is awful and I never would' would not benefit from the same kinds of activities as a 25-year-old woman who has been drinking for several years and is on the verge of becoming a problem drinker. This analysis was first applied to disease prevention (Gordon, 1987) and then to substance abuse (Kumpfer *et al.*, 1997). Table 1 shows the three levels and their broad aim.

Table 1 *Classification of different types of substance abuse prevention activity*

Type of prevention activity	Broad aim
Primary (universal)	To prevent the start of problem drug use, for example among children under the age of 11
Secondary (selective)	To prevent or reduce experimentation with substances among at-risk groups, for example teenagers, and especially those with extra risk factors such as truancy or a history of offending
Tertiary (indicated)	To reduce or eliminate problem drug use among those who are already involved, for example heavy drinkers or smokers who visit their GP

Key terms

Fear-arousal appeal: a presentation about the consequences of substance abuse that is designed to scare the audience and produce changes in attitude and behaviour.

Cognitive dissonance: a state of tension brought about by holding conflicting beliefs.

Fear-arousal appeals

'I'd show them some pictures of tar-laden lungs from a person who died of lung cancer. That would put them off smoking for good.' Remarks like this illustrate the popular belief that it is possible to scare people into changing their attitudes and behaviour. The suggestion is an example of a **fear-arousal appeal**.

Anti-smoking adverts have shown graveyards and tombstones. The 'Sorted' crusade led by Leah Betts's parents showed an image of her as she lay dying in bed after using Ecstasy tablets for the first time. In 2007, a TV campaign showed a young man dressed as Superman jumping from scaffolding, to serious injury or death, after a heavy drinking bout.

Studies of the effects of fear arousal began in the 1950s; researchers investigated how the level of fear arousal affected peoples' interest, attitudes and behaviour. Explanations of attitude change, such as Festinger's (1957) theory of **cognitive dissonance**, suggested that presenting the frightening consequences of a particular behaviour would create a negative drive state for those involved. A change of attitude would happen to reduce this uncomfortable tension. This led researchers to wonder if a greater level of fear would cause more change. Laboratory experiments on fear arousal could cause psychological harm to the participants. Because of this ethical concern, the classic study described below was based on dental health.

Research study: Janis and Feshbach (1953)

Aim: To find out the effect on interest, attitudes and behaviour of different levels of fear arousal concerning the consequences of poor dental hygiene.

Method: The whole 'freshmen' class of males and females in a large Connecticut high school were given a questionnaire on dental hygiene. They were randomly divided into four groups who received different 15-minute illustrated lectures as follows:

- A (high fear) – 71 references to the unpleasant outcomes of poor dental care, e.g. toothache, gum disease, etc.

- B (moderate fear) – 49 references
- C (low fear) – 18 references
- D (control group) – a similar lecture on 'eye care'.

Immediately after the lectures, the participants filled in a questionnaire about the effects of the lecture on their attitudes. One week later they filled in a third questionnaire about their oral-hygiene behaviour.

Results: The 'high fear' group showed the most anxiety and interest immediately after the lecture. The 'low fear' group showed the most change in dental hygiene one week later.

Conclusion: Some fear arousal is helpful in producing changes in attitudes but high levels of fear are ineffective in changing behaviour. Janis and Feshbach suggested that participants will tend to ignore the high level of fear and minimise the threat to health if the presentation does not provide a feasible course of remedial action.

Evaluation: Many audience and message factors influence the effectiveness of fear arousal presentations. Hovland *et al.* (1953) pointed out that the complexity of the message and whether it is one-sided or two-sided should be matched to the audience. Also, some people are more sensitive to 'fear' because of differing levels of anxiety and self-esteem

---

Janis and Terwilliger (1962) carried out a study on two groups of **smokers**. One group was given apparently medical information about a form of lung cancer that could be avoided by a reduction in smoking. The other, higher-fear, group also received details of the life-threatening nature of the cancer. The 'higher-fear' participants were more frightened but also more likely to reject the information provided and therefore less likely to change their attitude to smoking. Results such as these led to the **inverted U theory**, i.e. that a moderate level of fear arousal is more effective in causing change than either a high level or none at all. The inverted U is thought to apply to the relationship between performance and arousal, with optimal performance occurring when arousal is moderate. Some researchers thought that the same shape could apply to arousal and attitude or behaviour change, which would be at a maximum when arousal was moderate.

Key terms

Inverted U theory: the theory that the relationship between arousal and attitude or behaviour change would be depicted on a graph as an inverted U shape.

Insko *et al.* (1965) carried out a study with non-smoking junior high school students, in which the 'higher fear' group had less intention of starting smoking or becoming regular smokers. These participants did not need to reject the 'fear' message as it did not apply directly to them.

A classic anti-smoking poster from The American Cancer Society showed three images side by side. The first, of a healthy lung, the second, a smoker's lung with a cancerous tumor and the third, a smoker's lung with emphysema. The poster depicted a high level of fear with no suggestion of remedial action. It should, therefore, deter non-smokers but have less influence on those who already smoke.

The inverted U theory suggests that shock tactics do not work. However, a meta-analysis of 35 studies (Sutton, 1982) showed that increases in

Key terms

Efficacy: the extent to which people feel that they can deal with a threat to their health. This depends on whether they think that the preventive action will work and whether they think they are capable of doing it.

Link

If you are unsure what a meta-analysis is, turn back to Chapter 1, Social development, p5, for a definition.

Link

Look back to the section on 'Explanations for substance abuse' on p171, to remind yourself about the influence of peers, families and social norms.

fear consistently led to greater attitude change. Many of these studies investigated other factors, such as **efficacy**.

A more convincing explanation of the effects of fear arousal is the **extended parallel process model** (Witte, 1992), which takes account of both level of fear and efficacy. For example, a poster warning a pregnant woman that smoking can damage her baby presents a high level of threat. If it also carries the message that stopping smoking during pregnancy will leave the baby unharmed and offers advice and help on how to quit, there may be high efficacy: under these circumstances, the woman may well stop smoking. This is called 'danger control'. However, posters such as the one illustrated in Figure 4 show a high threat but no 'way out', so efficacy is low. Under these conditions, a person is unlikely to change and will tend to deny or argue against the threat. This is called 'fear control'.

Social inoculation

Teenagers often refer to 'peer pressure' as an explanation for experimenting with drugs. The idea that young people could be 'immunised' against these social pressures emerged in the 1960s (McGuire, 1968) and led to the development of social inoculation theory.

The key features of effective social inoculation programmes are:

- providing accurate information about the short- and long-term consequences of using drugs, for example smell from smoking, lack of control when drinking alcohol and health risks
- training in resisting pressure to use drugs (from media, peers and family members), for example developing a more critical attitude to media messages and practising 'resistance skills' through role play
- providing information about norms for substance use and why adolescents use substances, with the aim of developing 'non-use' norms and expectations; teenagers may be encouraged to make public commitments to abstain from drugs in a school assembly
- development of skills in problem solving, decision making and stress management and activities designed to raise self-esteem.

Education authorities in the UK and across the world oblige schools to have a 'drug policy' and to provide social inoculation activities. Reviews of the programmes consistently show positive effects, particularly a short-term reduction in substance use. A typical piece of research, from Holland, is outlined below. About 70 per cent of Dutch schools, involving 350,000 students, are involved in the Healthy School and Drugs project.

Research study: Cuijpers *et al.* (2002)

Aim: To evaluate the short- and long-term effectiveness of the Healthy School and Drugs project, in Dutch schools, in reducing problem drug use.

Method: The study compared 1,156 students from nine schools that use the programme with 774 students from three schools that don't. Participants were surveyed before the programme and one, two and three years later. They self-reported on the use of tobacco, alcohol and cannabis, their knowledge about them, their attitude towards them and their sense of efficacy in resisting drug use.

Results: The programme led to an increase in knowledge about the substances and some reduction in their use. This reduction was less obvious after two years but was still significant for alcohol. The programme had little effect on attitudes or sense of efficacy.

Conclusion: The Healthy School and Drugs project led to some reduction in drug use, particularly in the short term.

Evaluation: Later studies (2006) suggest less impact from the programme and little effect on later dependence. The most effective programmes are those which involve the features mentioned earlier.

Evaluation

The evidence for a link between social influences and drug use comes from correlational studies. Unlike experiments, these do not show that the social influence causes the drug use. In the case of peer pressure, for example, teenagers may actively seek groups that smoke because they want to join in with that behaviour. Learning to resist social pressure would have little effect on this behaviour.

Social inoculation programmes often use peer trainers or mentors, for example older school students, as they are a credible and attractive source of information and skills. However, the effectiveness of their influence may be reduced precisely because the younger students are developing peer resistance.

The effects of social inoculation on teenagers often wear off during the one to two years that follow the programme (Flay, 1985); regular 'refreshers' are therefore needed to maintain the original effects.

Key points:

- Groups of people, such as teenagers or those with a family history of alcoholism, are at greater risk of being involved in problem drug use and may be targeted with preventive activities.
- There are three levels of preventive technique linked to a person's experience of problem drug use.
- Fear-arousal appeals are used as a preventive technique and have some success, particularly if they provide a person with a credible 'way out' or increased efficacy.
- Social inoculation can be used to enable at-risk groups to resist social pressures to use drugs. It can reduce short-term substance use among school students but the effects diminish over time.

Summary questions

10 What do the following terms mean?

a At-risk group

b Fear-arousal appeal

c Social inoculation

d Efficacy

11 Fear-arousal appeals have been used to prevent substance abuse. Describe and explain the circumstances in which they are effective.

12 A school is designing a social inoculation programme to encourage its 15-year-old students to reduce or eliminate their drinking of alcohol. Outline and justify two features that might be used in the programme.

Substance abuse

Health promotion and education in the treatment and prevention of substance abuse

Learning objectives:

- describe, explain and illustrate the use of health promotion and education in the treatment and prevention of substance abuse
- evaluate the effectiveness of health promotion and education
- use theories, examples and studies from the sections on models of lifestyle change (e.g. Prochaska's), fear arousal and social inoculation to develop a full understanding of health promotion and education.

AQA Examiner's tip

Good exam answers about health promotion and education can involve material from the sections on models of lifestyle change, fear arousal and social inoculation. These can be used as components within health promotion and education or as a comparison or contrast with it. It would be a good idea to produce a sample answer on health promotion, which includes these features, so as to practise drawing material together to produce a coherent answer.

Link

Look back to the section on 'Theoretical models of behaviour change' on p183, to remind yourself about the three theories described there.

'Scare and shock tactics' have popular appeal for changing potentially harmful behaviour. There is also much support for the value of 'education'. Problem drug use causes a threat to health. Most people feel that 'prevention is better than cure'. This is the background to the growth of health promotion and education initiatives since the 1970s. In the UK, the NHS, with its traditional focus on treating illness, has seen an increasing emphasis on promoting health through exercise, diet and reduction in drinking and smoking. Schools, the Youth Service and the media are also involved. The broad aim of health promotion is to enable people to take greater control over their own health and so improve it. Clearly, this is most likely to succeed if begun at an early age, so schools have a vital role.

Programmes for employees

Some employers have seen the potential benefits of health promotion among their employees. In the USA, programmes such as Johnson and Johnson's Live for Life have been used by thousands of workers. They provide health screening, action groups, for example on quitting smoking, and a work environment offering opportunities for exercise. Where companies offered this programme, there were greater health improvements, for example less smoking (Fielding, 1990).

Programmes for young people

Health promotion programmes have developed out of psychological theory about why 'unhealthy' behaviour happens and why people make lifestyle changes. There are many possible explanations for substance abuse. Programmes with school students have concentrated on cognitive, behavioural and psychosocial factors, such as expectation, conditioning, peer pressure and social norms. Explanations of lifestyle change such as the health belief model, theory of reasoned action and Prochaska's model of change are used.

So, programmes involve the threat to health, the implications of preventive action and attitudes to drugs, social norms and skills training to enable progress through a gradual cycle of change. Characteristics of persuasive communication are also important. The source, for example the teacher, must be credible and expert and the message must be appropriate for the age and experience of the audience.

DARE

One of the earliest programmes in widespread use in schools was the Drugs Abuse Resistance Education project (DARE) produced by the Los Angeles Police and Schools District in 1983. The original course was delivered to students at the end of the elementary school, that is when they were 10 to 11 years old, and consisted of 17 weekly lessons of one hour led by a police officer trained in its use. The course has since been extended to an older age range. The key elements of the course were:

- providing information about drugs
- teaching decision-making skills
- building self-esteem
- considering healthy alternatives to drug use.

The teaching methods involved lectures, discussion, question-and-answer sessions, audiovisual material, workbook exercises and role playing. There have been many studies of the effectiveness of the DARE project and of other teaching programmes that could be classified as more or less interactive. Details of a meta-analysis of several of these are given below.

Research study: Ennett *et al.* (1994)

Aim: To compare the effectiveness of DARE projects in school with the effectiveness of more or less interactive ones, in terms of knowledge, attitudes, social skills, self-esteem, involvement with the police and drug use.

Method: Evaluations of eight DARE projects were compared with evaluations of 25 projects of a more or less interactive nature, in terms of knowledge, attitudes, social skills, self-esteem, involvement with the police and drug use.

Results: The DARE projects had most effect on knowledge and social skills and least on drug use. The biggest changes were shown for tobacco: DARE was more effective than the non-interactive programmes and less than the interactive ones.

Conclusion: DARE projects have positive effects on substance abuse but the effects are less than those achieved by more interactive programmes.

Evaluation: DARE projects were always taught by police officers whereas the other programmes were taught by teachers. The police officers clearly had expert authority but may have been less skilled in delivering the teaching programme. The DARE teaching also relied heavily on traditional, formal methods, which may be less successful in engaging the students.

The DARE curriculum was amended more recently to include more interactive features. In the UK, DARE is a charity which offers teaching programmes to primary school children and the 11 to 13 age range. It also has a short course for parents and carers, which recognises the role of families and local communities in drug use. A later meta-analysis of 37 teaching programmes in the USA (Tobler *et al.*, 1999) showed that interactive programmes involving the development of social skills were more effective than non-interactive, lecture-oriented programmes involving knowledge and emotional development in reducing the use of cannabis.

Take it further

You may like to find out more about the DARE programme in the UK. You will find more information about DARE on its website (see end of chapter, p196).

The current practice in English and Welsh schools is governed by *Drugs: Guidance for Schools*, a document published by the Department for Education and Skills in February 2004, in response to the strategy document *Tackling Drugs to Build a Better Britain*, which was updated by the government in 2002. One of the four points of focus was 'preventing young people from using drugs through education'. The aims for this education are to:

- increase pupils' knowledge and to clarify their misconceptions about drugs and their use
- develop pupils' self-esteem and personal and social skills to keep themselves safe and healthy through resisting pressure
- enable pupils to explore their own and other people's attitudes towards drugs and drug users, including challenging stereotypes and exploring media and other influences.

Based on the evidence of research studies, the document makes recommendations; it notes that drug education is most effective when:

- it is addressed by the whole school and wider community
- it is consistent with the values and ethos of the school and is delivered in a supportive environment where pupils feel able to engage in open discussion and are confident about asking for help if necessary
- it is mostly provided by teachers, with help from visiting experts and health professionals
- it is integrated into respected parts of the curriculum, such as PSHE and science
- it is part of the curriculum for all students from five to 16 and progresses from year to year in line with the age and experience of the students
- it takes account of local drug issues
- the special needs of at-risk groups, such as students who are looked after or involved in exclusion, are met.

Project Charlie

A typical programme is Project Charlie, which has been used throughout England. 'Charlie' stands for **Ch**emical **A**buse **R**esistance **L**ies **I**n **E**ducation. It is used with children in primary schools and the early years of secondary school. The course consists of 14 lessons, which focus on helping young people explore their knowledge about drug use and misuse, providing accurate factual information on different legal and illegal drugs, exploring the consequences of using drugs and understanding the roles of peers, society and media pressure. Various interactive teaching methods are used to encourage active learning. It is suggested that there is a feedback discussion for reflection at the end of each lesson. Communication with parents and carers is seen as vital both before and during the drug education sessions. A 1996 study of Project Charlie followed up children who had received this drug prevention programme in primary schools in 1992; the results showed less experimentation with tobacco and drugs compared with a control group that had not had the programme.

Hint

You will notice a lot of overlap between the features of the DARE programme and the advice given to UK schools by the Department for Education and Skills. This should not be a surprise! Make sure that you can list the key features, explain what they mean and give examples to show how they might be used in practice with a particular age range.

Take it further

Schools for pupils aged 11 to 18 will have a drugs policy and scheme of work about drugs. If you attend an 11 to 18 school, it would be interesting to analyse the school's policies in the light of the advice to schools. You could write a report that, for example, answers the following questions:

- Which substances are dealt with in each age range?
- Which teaching methods are used? Are they different for different age ranges, key stages?
- To what extent are the policy guidelines followed?
- What are the strengths and weaknesses of the policy and scheme of work in the light of government advice?

Evaluation

There is an annual survey of drinking, smoking and drug use among 11 to 15-year-olds in England. The 2006 survey by the Drug Education Forum (Brown, 2006) asked students about their drug education and its effect on them. Between 55 and 60 per cent of the students recalled having a lesson on smoking, drinking and drugs during the past year. Most of these students stated that the lessons had increased their knowledge and helped them to refuse drugs. Many students overestimated the proportion of their peers who smoked and drank: a reminder that perceived social norms are often different from the real ones! Ninety-six per cent of the schools reported that they had a drugs policy; in over 60 per cent of these, students had helped with its development.

A study of Scottish drug education (Coggans *et al.*, 1991), involving nearly 1,200 students, reported improvements in drug-related knowledge but no change in attitudes or behaviour.

There is a growing involvement of peer educators or peer mentors in drug education. This is interesting as one of drug education's aims is to enable teenagers to resist peer pressure. However, peers can act as positive role models for social learning and have obvious credibility as communicators.

They can also help to dispel false stereotypes and perceived social norms that 'everybody does it'.

Health promotion involves more than teaching programmes, which tend to focus on particular groups of people. Posters, leaflets and TV adverts are available to all. They will be effective only if they put into practice well-researched ideas (see pp188–190). A survey of 31 public health leaflets in the UK designed to encourage sensible drinking, found that they used fear arousal about the negative physical consequences of heavy drinking (Abraham *et al.*, 2007). However, none encouraged the readers to believe that abstinence or moderate drinking was possible. That is, efficacy was ignored, and the leaflets are therefore unlikely to produce change in behaviour.

Key points:

- Health promotion and education programmes are provided in schools and companies to enable people to take more control over their own health and so improve it.
- Preventing substance abuse is a key feature of health promotion, especially for school-age people.
- Health promotion can include elements of fear arousal and social inoculation. It will also make use of explanations for lifestyle change, the health belief model, the theory of reasoned action and Prochaska's model.
- Effective drug education involves developing knowledge and understanding, looking at attitudes, learning social and problem-solving skills and developing self-esteem.
- Drug education has been successful in increasing knowledge but much less successful in reducing long-term drug use.
- Interactive teaching methods are more effective than non-interactive ones.

End-of-chapter activity 1

The aim of this activity is to find out how news about drugs features in the local and national press. It will help to apply the vocabulary and ideas from the topic so that you become more confident in using them. The preparation stage will involve cutting out extracts that mention problem drug use (alcohol, smoking, heroin, cannabis, cocaine, etc.) from newspapers or magazines. These are likely to include court reports and items about police raids; personal stories, perhaps of celebrities; and issues to do with prevention. Once there is enough material, you could try some of these suggestions, on your own or in groups:

- Highlight names of substances, key vocabulary and key ideas on each extract.
- 'Tell the story' of one of your extracts to the class, in your own words.
- Categorise the pieces under such headings as 'drugs and the law', 'personal stories', 'prevention issues', etc.
- Carry out **content analysis** on one of the groups of extracts. This would involve making a table to analyse the contents of the extracts, and, perhaps, testing a hypothesis. For example, the 'drugs and the law' extracts could be analysed for substance, sex of offender, age of offender, nature of sentence, etc. You could test a hypothesis such as 'Males are more likely to be convicted of drugs offences than females'. You could write this up briefly in terms of variables, kind of sampling, conclusions, limitations, etc.
- Make a personal or group presentation to the rest of the class to show what you have found out.

Summary questions

13 What do the following terms mean?

a Health promotion

b Interactive teaching

c Peer pressure

14 Describe three key features of an effective drug education programme.

15 Evaluate the effectiveness of health promotion in preventing young people from using drugs.

AQA Examiner's tip

The final parts of A2 questions often begin 'Discuss'. This implies that there are more marks available for analysis, evaluation, examples, comparisons and the use of evidence than for details and description. You should plan this part of the answer to make sure that these marks are gained.

The final parts of A2 questions don't always mention 'evidence' or 'comparison'. There will always be marks available for using psychological evidence to support or refute an idea or technique. There will also be marks available for comparing different techniques for the same purpose, for example fear arousal and health promotion or aversion therapy and self-management strategies. There are opportunities to put this into practice in the section containing examination-style questions.

Key terms

Content analysis: a non-experimental method that involves analysing secondary material in order to give insight into human thought or behaviour.

End-of-chapter activity 2

The aim of this activity is to become more confident in the ideas linked to preventing substance abuse. The class may be able to work in groups, on slightly different projects, producing a poster or making a presentation to the rest of the class. Here is an outline of a possible activity:

- Choose an age group to focus on, e.g. 9 to 11-year-olds at the end of the primary school or 16 to 18-year-olds doing A Levels.
- Choose an appropriate substance to focus on, one that is appropriate to the age group, e.g. alcohol for the 16 to 18-year-olds.
- Re-read the chapter sections on fear arousal, social inoculation and health promotion.
- Apply the key ideas to producing a series of preventive posters or detailed planning for a lesson or lessons about the chosen substance and appropriate to the age range.
- When your posters or plans are complete, swap with another group. Your task, now, is to write a critique of the other group's plans or posters. How effective are they likely to be? Which good ideas have they included? Which have they missed out? What improvements can you suggest?
- You may like to amend your work in the light of the comments of the other group.
- You could then make a presentation of your ideas to the rest of the class.

Further reading

Gerada, C. (2005) *RCGP Guide to the Management of Substance Misuse in Primary Care*. Glasgow: Bell and Bain.

Oltmann, T.F. and Emery, R.E. (2006) *Abnormal Psychology*. New Jersey, USA: Prentice Hall.

Sarafino, E. (2005) *Health Psychology: Biopsychosocial Interactions*. USA: John Wiley & Sons.

Schuckit, M.A. (1998) *Educating Yourself about Alcohol and Drugs: A People's Primer*. Reading, MA: Perseus Books.

Alcoholics Anonymous(UK): www.alcoholics-anonymous.org.uk

ASH UK (Action on Smoking and Health): www.newash.org.uk

DARE UK (Drug Abuse Resistance Education): www.dare.uk.com

Release: www.release.org.uk

National Treatment Agency for Substance Misuse (NTA): www.nta.nhs.uk

Talk to Frank: www.talktofrank.com

Forensic psychology

Introduction

Fig. 1 *After meeting the Ripper in the street, women were lured to their violent deaths in the Whitechapel alleyways*

One of the most famous historical cases of interest to any student of forensic psychology dates back to the late 1800s and is often referred to as the 'Jack the Ripper' murders. Between 1888 and 1891, Jack the Ripper was regarded with terror by the residents of London's East End as the man who murdered and savagely mutilated prostitutes. Although the Ripper was not the first serial killer, he was probably acknowledged as the first owing to the influence of the media, which were at the time becoming a strong force for social and political change. It is not certain just how many women the Ripper killed. Various writers have estimated somewhere between four and nine. It is generally accepted, however, that he killed five women. It was left to the police officers of Scotland Yard to apprehend the fearsome killer. Despite every effort and inquiry, Jack the Ripper was never found and his full identity is shrouded in mystery even today.

In the late 1800s, London's Metropolitan Police force had no methods of forensic analysis such as fingerprinting and blood analysis, which we have today. There were no crime laboratories at Scotland Yard until the 1930s and even taking photographs of victims at the crime scene was not considered usual practice. Today the police, working alongside forensic psychologists and psychiatrists, have developed an elaborate profiling technique in order to understand and help identify murderers, rapists, arsonists and sexual psychopaths such as Jack the Ripper (see 'Offender profiling' on p202).

What is forensic psychology?

Forensic psychology is concerned with the collection, analysis and presentation of evidence to the judiciary in order to assist in the apprehension of criminals. The term 'forensic' comes from the Latin word '*forens*', which literally means 'forum' where the first Roman courts were held. Forensic psychologists initially provided evidence to criminal courts in cases such as rape and murder and to civil courts, in the assessment of custody cases, for example. Today, forensic psychologists apply psychological theory, research methods and statistical analysis to understand the psychological problems associated with criminal behaviour, and in the assessment and treatment of offenders. Treatment programmes may involve developing rehabilitation programmes such as anger management, social skills training and various treatments for drug and/or alcohol dependency. Other tasks also undertaken by forensic psychologists include giving evidence in court on such matters as fitness to plead by the defendant and the defendant's mental state, advising parole boards and mental health professionals, helping police and prison officers to cope with stress and understanding bullying, as well as working with victims to deal with the effects of crime. Forensic psychologists are mainly employed by Her Majesty's Prison Service, but they can also work in the health service (secure hospitals), police force, probation service, government departments and in universities, doing research and lecturing to students.

Specification content	Topic content	Page number
Offending behaviour		
Problems in defining crime; measuring crime, including official statistics and alternatives (victim surveys and self-report measures)	What is a crime? Ways of measuring crime	**199** **199**
Offender profiling, including typology and geographical approaches	Offender profiling	**202**
Theories of offending: physiological approaches – atavistic form and somatotype theories; biological explanations, including genetic transmission; psychodynamic and learning theory explanations, including social learning; Eysenck's theory of the criminal personality	Physiological explanations of offending Biological explanations of offending Psychodynamic explanations of offending Learning theory explanations of offending Social learning theory Eysenck's theory of the criminal personality	**206** **208** **209** **211** **211** **212**
Treatment of offenders		
The role of custodial sentencing; effectiveness of custodial sentencing, including recidivism; alternatives to custodial sentencing	The aims of sentencing The effectiveness of custodial sentencing Alternatives to custodial sentencing	**213** **214** **215**
Treatment programmes: behaviour modification; social skills training and anger management; evaluation of these treatment programmes	Behaviour modification Social skills training Anger management	**217** **219** **218**

8 Forensic psychology

Defining and measuring crime

Learning objectives:

- explain problems involved in defining crime
- describe and evaluate ways in which crime can be measured including official statistics and alternatives (victim surveys and self-report measures).

Hint

An effective way of explaining the difficulties with defining crime is to use examples in your answer.

What is a crime?

Crime is the breach of a rule or law for which a punishment is given by legal enforcement agencies such as the courts. But what exactly is a crime? *The Oxford English Dictionary* defines crime as: 'An act punishable by law, as being forbidden by statute or injurious to the public welfare … An evil or injurious act; an offence, sin; esp. of a grave character.'

The problem with *The Oxford English Dictionary*'s definition is that it raises more questions. For example, does the law cover all acts that are injurious to public welfare? For an orthodox Muslim, drinking alcohol is a sin, but it is not a crime under UK law if the individual is over 18 years of age. Is it always against the law to take another person's life? Consider the Iraq war: are the soldiers murderers or merely defending the Queen's peace? What these questions highlight is that there is more than one way of perceiving what is meant by a crime. On the one hand, crimes can be seen as acts that break the law – the legal definition of crime. On the other hand, crimes are acts that can cause offence to moral norms or values held by society such as religious beliefs – the normative definition of crime. However, these two perceptions of crime cannot operate together. Some legally defined crimes might not be acceptable when judged against the norms of socially acceptable behaviour. Keeping small amounts of money that we find on the pavement is good luck, surely? Who is going to report the small amount of money lost to the police anyway? A crime is therefore dependent on whether it is viewed from a legal or a normative perspective. The meaning of crime cannot be isolated from the various meanings attached to it. Social scientists would therefore describe the meaning of crime as a **social construction**.

Ways of measuring crime

Every year the Home Office publishes the latest crime statistics and trends for England and Wales. These are based on two sources of data: the British Crime Survey (BCS) and official statistics recorded by the police.

Official statistics

The official crime figures for 2005–2006 suggest that crime has remained stable over the last few years although there has been an increase in some violent crimes, for example gun related. The government claim that, despite a peak in 1995, the incidence of crime has fallen by 44 per cent in the last 10 years. Rose (2006) analysed Home Office figures and found that the government failed to report the significant drop in conviction rates. In 1997, for example, the number of recorded rapes in England and Wales was 6,281. This figure rose to 12,867 between 2004 and 2005. The conviction rates, however, dropped from 9.2 per cent to 5.5 per cent. The media tend to hide this issue by, instead, reporting the increasing number of people in prison. This is not the correct picture being portrayed to society: the figures actually reflect the longer sentences being passed by the courts rather than

Take it further

Hollin (1989) outlines three main approaches to defining crime:

- **Consensus view** Society's laws are based on an agreement, or consensus, among its citizens as to what behaviour is considered intolerable and should therefore receive punishment. The aim of a legal system is a means of maintaining a stable society that is more or less of equal benefit for all.
- **Conflict view** This view is sociological in that its underlying principles are based on Marxist philosophy. This view states that the law benefits some individuals far more than others. Criminal law seeks to protect and benefit the powerful from the rest of the population.
- **Interactionist view** This view is in between the opposing consensus and conflict views. It states that there are no values of right or wrong because these depend on the meanings that individuals give to them. For example, in the UK, euthanasia is considered an illegal act, which some people would like to see decriminalised (see the arguments presented in the legal case of *R* v. *Pretty* [2001]). The interactionist view is concerned with the way in which legal rules adapt to changing moral values.

AQA Examiner's tip

You will not be expected to relay the exact figures of crime (e.g. government statistics) in your answer. Instead, focus on what the different methods tell us about the incidence of crime and the strengths and limitations of these methods.

Link

For more on 'reliability' and 'validity', see Chapter 11, Methods in psychology.

Hint

The British Crime Survey is only one example of victim surveys.

the number of convictions. In 2004, the Crime and Society Foundation published a report claiming that official statistics do not show a valid picture of crime (cited on the British Crime Survey website). The only purpose official statistics have is to provide the government with a false set of figures whereby they can claim success in reducing the rate of crime in England and Wales. The Statistics Commission (2006) has suggested that the public doubts the reliability of crime data and so the Home Office should therefore distance itself from the production of these criminal statistics in order to win back public confidence.

The British Crime Survey

The British Crime Survey (BCS) is an example of a **victim survey**. The BCS measures the amount of crime in England and Wales by asking 50,000 people about the incidence of crime they have experienced in the past year and whether or not they have reported this crime to the police. Figure 2 shows the number of crimes estimated by the BCS throughout the 1980s and 1990s and up to 2006. The trend shows a peak of 19 million crimes in 1995 although the levels have decreased and stabilised during the years 2005 and 2006. The number of crimes recorded by the police has risen over this period due largely to changes to the rules governing the measure for crime, police recording practices and the actual reporting of crime by the public.

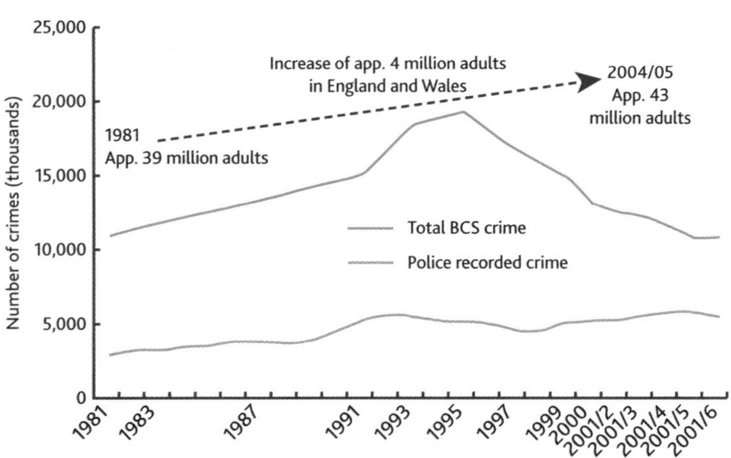

Crime in England and Wales 2006/06 (**Walker, Kershaw and Nicholas**, *2006*)
Fig. 2 *Trends in BCS and police recorded crime, 1981 to 2005–2006*

The British Crime Survey provides a more accurate picture of the incidence of crime compared with official statistics as it includes crimes that have not been reported to the police and, so, are not recorded. The amount of unreported and undiscovered crime is known as the **dark figure of crime** (see Figure 3). This figure refers to the gap between the official level of crime recorded and the amount of crime that actually occurs in communities.

There are many reasons why crimes are not reported to the police:

- The general public regards the crime as too trivial, for example the theft of a £5 note.
- Individuals may be unaware that they are actually victims of crime, for example in cases of fraud.
- Individuals may fear a revenge attack if they name the offender.
- Individuals may lack confidence in the police: for example, 'the police are too busy trying to control more serious crimes so why would they bother with a more trivial crime?'

Some crimes are much more likely than others to be reported and recorded:

- Individuals are more likely to make a fraudulent claim on their insurance for household goods.
- More serious crimes, for example the theft of a car, are more likely to be reported than trivial crimes such as theft of a garden spade.
- Media campaigns can highlight the incidence of particular crimes to the general public and, in doing so, create a **moral panic**. This causes the public to become more vigilant to this type of crime and so they report it more. This is known as **deviance amplification**.

Levels of recorded and unrecorded crime, 1981 and 2005/06 BCS

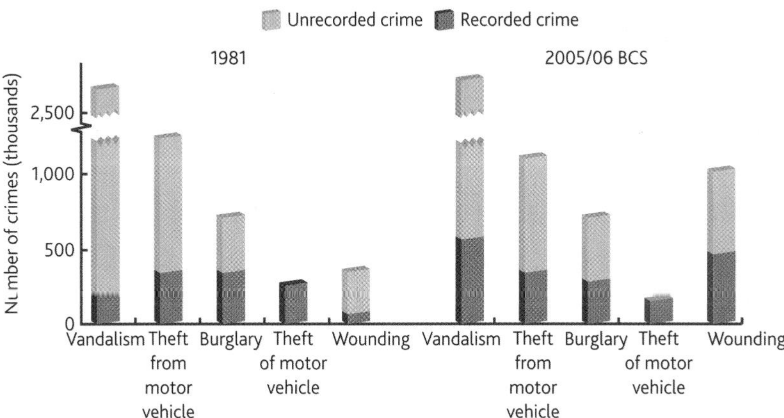

Hough and Mayhew (1983), Crime in England and Wales 2005/06 (Walker, Kershaw and Nicholas, 2006)

Fig. 3 *Levels of recorded and unrecorded crime, 1981 and 2005–2006 (BCS)*

Self-report studies

A self-report study is a type of research method used to determine the extent of crime and deviant behaviour. Most self-report studies involve the use of questionnaires where the individual has voluntarily to record whether or not they have committed any of the listed offences. The data are then compared with the official number of convictions recorded in order to measure which types of offenders are most likely to be convicted. Self-report studies are more likely than official statistics to identify the different types of offender. However, a number of problems are associated with self-report studies:

- **Unreliable answers** The respondents may exaggerate, may be too embarrassed or may be unable to remember what happened.
- **Biased selection of offences** Studies may ignore middle-class crime, may uncover trivial offences rather than the more serious.
- **Biased selection of interviewees** Researchers may not be able to interview the more dangerous offenders; business executives who are rich and powerful may exclude the researchers from investigating certain areas of crime such as corporate crime.

Summary questions

1. What is meant by a 'crime'?
2. Explain one limitation of using self-report studies to measure crime.
3. What is meant by a 'dark figure of crime'? Give an example in your answer.
4. Compare the effectiveness of official statistics and victim surveys as measures of crime.

Key terms

Moral panic: exaggerated and sensationalised reporting by the media of a certain action or social group. This action or group is then seen as a threat by the rest of society.

Key points:

- A crime is the breach of a rule or law for which a punishment is given.
- Crimes may be classified according to their legal definition or their normative definition.
- Official statistics are published annually by the Home Office and show the crime rates in England and Wales.
- The British Crime Survey is an example of a victim survey, which measures the number of crimes reported to the police.
- The 'dark figure of crime' is the gap between the official level of crime recorded and the amount of crime that actually occurs.
- Self-report studies measure whether or not offenders have committed a crime. These figures are then compared with the official statistics.

Offender profiling

Learning objectives:

- describe the FBI approach to offender profiling
- explain the principles of investigative psychology
- describe the method of geographical profiling
- evaluate the use of offender profiling.

Key terms

Offender profiling: the collection of empirical data in order to build up a picture of the characteristics of those involved in a certain type of crime.

Link

For more on 'hypothesis testing', see Chapter 11, Methods in psychology.

Link

For more on the scientific versus common sense debate, refer to Chapter 1, Key Approaches, in *AS Psychology B AS* and to Chapter 10, Debates in psychology, in this book.

AQA Examiner's tip

Some of the literature refers to the comparisons between the two approaches to offender profiling as being either 'bottom-up' or 'top-down'. This is rather outdated. It is better to focus your answers on more sophisticated comparisons between the FBI approach and the investigative approach to offender profiling.

The origins of **offender profiling** date back to Jack the Ripper in the 19th century (see p197). Our fascination with offender profiling has had a long history, for example with Jodie Foster's character in *Silence of the Lambs* and, more recently, television programmes such as *Waking the Dead*. Offender profiling is much more than what we see on television, however. It involves painstaking analysis of the crime scene supported by hours of statistical analysis. In Britain we follow an investigative approach to offender profiling (see p203) whereas in America, offender profiling is based more on the actual information recorded by the Federal Bureau of Investigation (FBI), and crimes are then categorised as either 'organised' or 'disorganised'.

The FBI approach to offender profiling

Offender profiling, which had its origins in the Behavioural Science Unit during the 1970s, was developed by the FBI. Profiling techniques known as **crime scene analysis** were eventually developed and formed the basis for establishing whether offences had been committed by 'organised' or 'disorganised' offenders. Hazelwood (1987) states that an **organised offender** usually has above average IQ, is sexually and socially competent, usually lives with a partner and experiences anger or depression at the time of the attack. The crime scene will show signs of careful planning and control with the victim usually being a targeted stranger. A **disorganised offender** usually lives alone and near to the crime scene, is sexually and socially inadequate, has severe forms of mental illness, has been physically and/or sexually abused and is frightened or confused at the time of the attack. The crime scene will show no planning; whatever weapon can be found at the scene (e.g. a rock) will be used in the attack. The victim will usually have been randomly selected, and the attack will be quick and brutal.

There are four main stages in the construction of an FBI profile (see Figure 4).

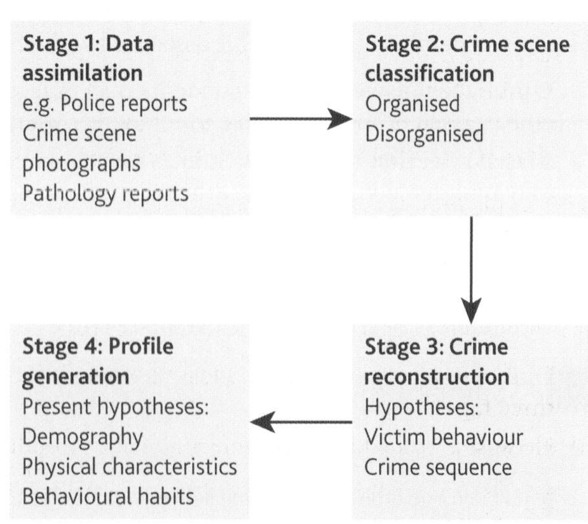

Fig. 4 *The four stages of FBI crime scene profiling*

Owing to its emphasis on intuition, the FBI approach to offender profiling has been criticised for lacking scientific evidence and evaluation. It is therefore disregarded as a science and considered more as art. Alison and Barrett (2004) state that the approach is over-reliant on dated theories of personality and contains 'many erroneous lay beliefs about the consistency of human behaviour and the ability to classify individuals into discrete types'.

Forensic psychology

The investigative approach to offender profiling

Fig. 5 *David Canter is widely known as the pioneer of offender profiling and established the Centre for Investigative Psychology in 1994*

In the UK, offender profiling is more associated with **investigative psychology** and the work of Professor David Canter (see Figure 5) who prepared a psychological profile that led to the capture of the 'Railway Rapist' and serial killer, John Duffy, in 1986 (see Figure 6).

Key terms

Investigative psychology: the scientific discipline concerned with the psychological principles, theories and empirical findings that may be applied to investigations and the legal process.

The case of the 'Railway Rapist'

Between 1982 and 1986, the Metropolitan Police investigated 24 sexual attacks that took place near railways in North London. Between 1985 and 1986, three murders were also committed, again near railways. As the victims' bodies had been burnt, the forensic evidence was minimal. However, the method of attack seemed to be a link between the rapes and murders. The Metropolitan Police invited David Canter to assist in the investigation and compile a psychological profile. Canter suggested the following about the offender:

- lived near to where the sexual assaults took place in 1983, possibly arrested, with a wife or girlfriend, probably no children
- mid to late 20s, right-handed and approximately 5′ 9″
- skilled or semi-skilled job, weekend work
- a quiet person, some close male friends, little contact with women at work, detailed knowledge of railways
- previous criminal record, engaged in sexual activity prior to the attacks, probably aggressive attacks whilst under the influence of alcohol.

The profile narrowed down the list of suspects and finally led the police to arrest John Duffy, who was convicted of two murders and five rapes. Duffy was given seven life sentences. The police had had little to go on in this case until Canter applied psychological principles to the police data. It is quite remarkable just how accurate this profile was:

- Duffy lived in North London close to where he committed the first three rapes.
- He was separated from his wife and had no children.
- He was in his late 20s, right-handed and worked as a carpenter for British Rail.

The victims' bodies were burned in a deliberate move to conceal forensic evidence, which was a tip that Duffy picked up from the police when his

Fig. 6 *John Duffy*

house was searched after the rape of his wife. In 2001, Duffy's accomplice, John Mulcahy, was convicted of seven rapes, three murders and five counts of conspiracy. He was eventually arrested and subsequently prosecuted after Duffy officially named him as an accomplice.

Techniques of the investigative approach

The focus of investigative psychology is still on the crime scene but the aim is to identify a pattern of characteristics through the use of statistical techniques. These techniques are then used to identify how likely it is that some characteristics will co-exist with others at the crime scene, thereby establishing a baseline. For example, if a series of rape cases shows a certain pattern where the offender always apologises to the victim, then it is likely that the offender may display the same behaviour in all other rape cases. Data analysis can identify the statistical chances of this behaviour occurring again and may also identify other key features of the offender.

Assessment of the crime scene involves analysis of the behaviour and social interactions shown by the offender and the victim. Canter (1994) suggested that certain psychological principles can assist profiling in the following ways:

- **Interpersonal coherence** The actions displayed by the offender will be the norm to him or her. For example, the choice of victim will be significant.
- **Significance of time and place** The offender needs to feel in control and so will choose a specific location.
- **Criminal characteristics** Analysis of crimes and the offenders will assist in classifying categories and identifying patterns of behaviour.
- **Criminal career** This is influential in the number of repeated crimes the offender commits. These crimes may increase as the offender's confidence grows.
- **Forensic awareness** Offenders who have been in contact previously with the police will cover their tracks in order to mislead investigators.

Canter believes that, in comparison with the FBI approach to offender profiling, the principles of investigative psychology are more scientific and are potentially more useful to investigators in actually catching the offender than crime scene analysis. Nevertheless, the use of psychological profiles has been much criticised. Copson (1995), in a survey of detectives working with offender profiling, found that the profile only succeeds in catching the offender in 3 per cent of cases. This is due to a lack of consistency between psychologists and psychiatrists in their own individualistic ways of establishing psychological profiles. As Ainsworth (2000) states, the reputation of offender profiling in the UK is at stake owing to, for example, the public disagreement between Canter and another high-profile criminal psychologist, Paul Britton, who argues for a different approach to profiling; this can only serve to exacerbate the problem of a lack of consistency in the UK's approach to profiling compared with the FBI's more consistent approach in the USA.

The geographical approach to offender profiling

Geographical profiling is one of the fastest growing fields of investigative psychology and consists of three key areas:

- studies of criminal spatial behaviour
- development of decision-support tools that incorporate research findings
- exploring the effectiveness of these support tools in helping police investigations.

The pioneer of geographical profiling is Kim Rossmo who focused on one key question: what does the location of a crime say about where the offender might live?

How does geographical profiling work?

Geographical profiling focuses on how the location of a crime scene can provide the police with vital clues about the offender. It assesses and predicts the most likely area in which the offender might live, place of work, areas where the offender might choose to socialise, certain routes travelled, and so on.

In preparing a geographical profile, a number of procedures are carried out:

- examination of the case file such as autopsy reports, witness statements and psychological reports
- analysis of the crime scene
- meetings with the crime investigators and key police personnel
- analysis of **demographic** data and local crime scene statistics
- study of rapid transit, zoning and street maps
- overall analysis and submission of the report to lead investigators.

The geographical technique uses a computer system called Criminal Geographic Targeting (CGT). Spatial data, which are data relating to the distance, movement and time to and from the crime scene, are analysed to produce a three-dimensional model known as a **jeopardy surface**.

This jeopardy surface contains colour and height probability codes, which are superimposed on to a map where the crimes have taken place. This provides the investigation team with an indication of where the offender might live and their place of work. This computer software is invaluable as a tool for aiding police and law enforcement agencies. It also assists in the research into spatial behaviour of offending populations and analysis of patterns and trends in data in relation to crime.

Does offender profiling work?

Campbell (1976) suggested that 'there is no clear evidence that psychologists are any better than bartenders at the remote diagnosis of killers'. The police, however, tend to regard profiling as an invaluable tool in assisting arrest. Alison *et al.* (2003) gave police officers two psychological profiles that were very different from each other. The police had to evaluate the accuracy of the profile in comparison with the facts given by the offender. Both groups of police officers felt happy with the profiles despite the fact that they were very different. It seems that the police just selected out the facts that most closely related to the offender and ignored the inaccuracies in the profile.

Overall, all forms of offender profiling must be subject to a thorough evaluation, although it is clear that applying psychological principles to the investigation of a crime is positive, in terms of resources and strategies. Offender profiling can only serve to enhance the productive and realistic working relationship between forensic psychologists and the police and legal personnel.

Key terms

Demography: the study of the statistics of births, deaths, disease, etc., as illustrating the conditions of life in communities.

Take it further

Fred West (29, September 1941–1 January 1995) was a serial killer who, together with his wife Rosemary West, was responsible for the murder of 12 young women (including the couple's daughter), mainly at the couple's home at 25 Cromwell Street in Gloucester, England.

In his book *Mapping Murder*, Professor David Canter explores the underlying psychological processes of Fred West's behaviour, untangling the mind of a serial killer through analysis of West's personal memoirs. Note in the following extract West's poor literacy skills:

> I Was Loved By an angel. Ana. I Met ana in Glasgow in Scotland she Was the children Nanny. She Work for My Wife, Rean I had Nothing to do With. Ana has she Was a young Girl. She always Made Me a cup of Tea When I came in and My Dinner.

(Excerpt from the memoirs of Fred West, in **Canter**, *2004)*

You can read the details of the case of Rosemary West (*R* v. *West* [1996]) online (see end of chapter, p221, for the website). What do you think was the role of the forensic psychologist in this case? What psychological profile was made of Rosemary West?

Summary questions

5 What is meant by investigative psychology?

6 Identify the four stages of the FBI's approach to offender profiling. Illustrate your answer with an example of each stage.

7 Compare the FBI approach and the investigative approach to offender profiling.

Key points:

- Offender profiling involves the use of empirical data in order to build up a picture of the characteristics of an offender.
- The FBI approach categorises information recorded as either an organised or disorganised crime.
- Investigative psychology concerns the application of psychological theories, principles and empirical findings to criminal investigations.
- Geographical profiling focuses on how the location of a crime can provide the police with vital clues about the offender.

Theories of offending

Learning objectives:

- describe physiological and biological explanations of offending
- describe psychodynamic and learning theory explanations of offending
- describe Eysenck's theory of the criminal personality
- evaluate explanations of offending.

Link

For more on the nature versus nurture debate, see Chapter 10, Debates in psychology.

Link

It would be useful to look at 'Evolution and behaviour' in *AQA Psychology B AS*, Chapter 1, p5.

Key terms

Atavism: reverting to or suggesting the characteristics of a remote ancestor or primitive type.

Are criminals born or are they made? This is one of the fundamental questions psychologists and biological theorists have continued to debate for many years. Consider some of the most serious crimes committed over the last century. Between 1963 and 1965, for example, Ian Brady and Myra Hindley, who were lovers at the time, committed severe acts of sexual brutality and the murder of three young children and two teenagers. Brady and Hindley buried the children's bodies on Saddleworth Moor. At their trial, Mr Justice Fenton Atkinson described Brady and Hindley as 'two sadistic killers of the utmost depravity'. He also described Brady as being 'wicked beyond belief'. The question therefore remains to this day: were Ian Brady and Myra Hindley born criminals or were they influenced in any way by society?

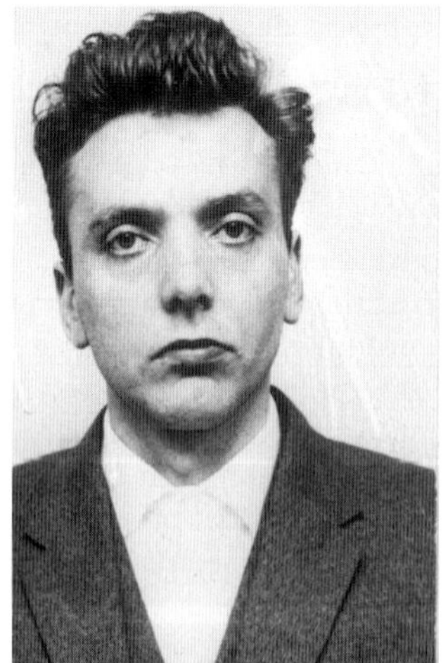

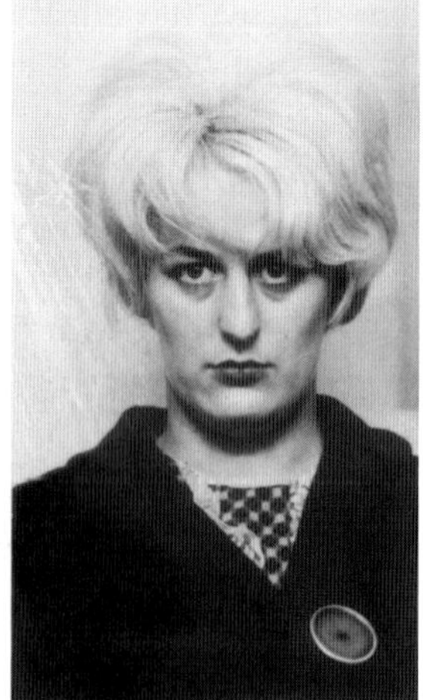

Fig. 7 *The police mug shots of Ian Brady and Myra Hindley when they were arrested in October 1965*

Physiological explanations of offending

Atavistic form

The concept of **atavism** was put forward by the Italian criminologist Cesare Lombroso in the 1870s (Lombroso, 1876). Lombroso argued that criminals had different physical features (which he labelled as 'atavistic') compared with non-criminals and that this difference demonstrated a more primitive evolutionary stage of development. For Lombroso, the physical characteristics of a criminal were a narrow sloping brow, strong prominent jaw, extra nipples, toes and fingers, high cheekbones, large ears, etc. Lombroso suggested that different subtypes of criminal could be identified through their physical characteristics: for example, murderers were said to have bloodshot eyes, curly hair and a prominent jaw. Lombroso claimed that these characteristics were heritable and therefore suggested that criminals were 'born' and not 'made'. In his later writings, however, Lombroso was less dogmatic and suggested that only about one-third of criminals directly inherited their criminal behaviour. The rest, he claimed, had become criminals owing to a number of other environmental factors, such as a poor education.

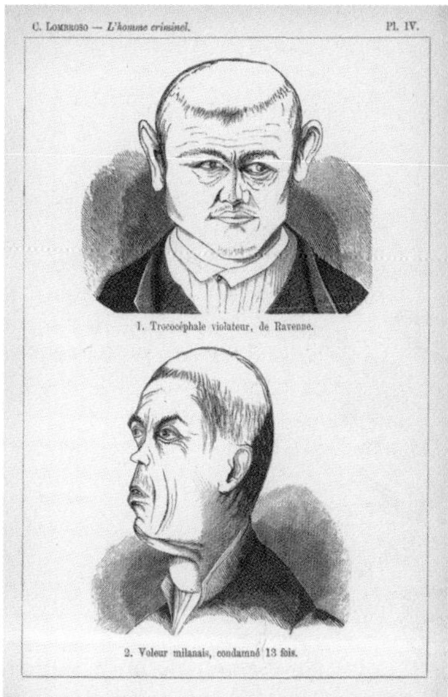

Fig. 8 *Lombroso claimed that criminals displayed primitive characteristics such as a strong jaw and heavy brow*

Evaluation

There have been a number of criticisms of Lombroso's methodology. First, he did not compare criminals with non-criminals so there was no comparative measure of whether or not the physical features associated with criminals were found in non-criminals. Secondly, his sample consisted of individuals with psychological disorders so perhaps Lombroso confused criminality with psychopathology. There was also strong debate between Lombroso and some of his contemporaries as to the nature of criminal behaviour. Charles Goring (1913/1972), conducted a study comparing the physical features of 3,000 English criminals with 3,000 non-criminals and found no significant difference in the physical features. Although Goring's research methods were themselves criticised, his findings were far less dubious than Lombroso's. Despite the fact that Lombroso has received criticism, he was responsible for moving the explanation of criminality away from 'wickedness' and more into the scientific realm. He is regarded by many researchers as 'the father of modern criminology' (Schafer, 1976).

Somatotype theory

William Sheldon (1949) proposed a more scientific explanation for aggressive and criminal behaviour based on physical appearance. For Sheldon, individuals were said to have one of three body types:

- endomorph – fat and soft
- ectomorph – thin and fragile
- mesomorph – muscular and hard.

Sheldon stated that endomorphs tended to have a relaxed, loving nature and enjoy the company of other people. Ectomorphs are more solitary, introverted and self-conscious individuals. Mesomorphs are characterised as criminals, being aggressive, callous and mindless of other people's feelings. Sheldon stated that it was rare, however, for individuals to be pure somatotypes; instead, each individual would display a combination of each of the three personality traits according to their own particular somatotype.

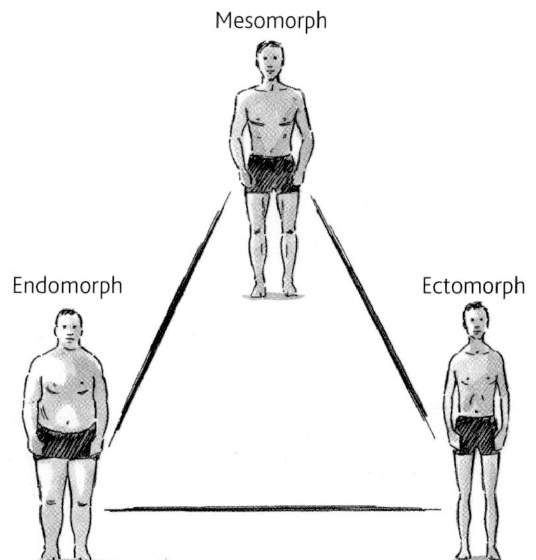

Fig. 9 *Sheldon stated that criminals have a mesomorphic body type*

In a study of 200 college students and 200 male delinquents, Sheldon rated a full-length picture of the participants according to each of the three body types. The pictures were given scores out of 7 (see Table 1).

Table 1 *The results of Sheldon's comparison of the body types in two samples: students and criminals*

Body build	Students	Criminal delinquents
Endomorph	3.2	3.4
Ectomorph	3.4	1.8
Mesomorph	3.8	5.4

Sheldon found that male criminal delinquents had a mesomorphic body type. The results showed that students, on average, had the same body type whereas the criminal delinquent group were significantly more mesomorphic thus supporting Sheldon's theory that those with a muscular and hard physique were more prone to criminality.

Link

For more on research methods, see Chapter 11, Methods in psychology.

Evaluation

Despite this finding, Sheldon's study has been much criticised. Cortes and Gatti (1972) argued that Sheldon's classification of the somatotypes was unreliable. Sutherland (1951) criticised the way that Sheldon selected his sample of delinquents (he did not use legal criteria in defining 'delinquent'). When the data were re-analysed using legal criteria for delinquency, Sutherland found that the association between delinquency and a mesomorphic body type was no longer present, thereby refuting Sheldon's theory and research findings.

Even though some research has shown a link between mesomorphy and criminal behaviour, there are other explanations for such anti-social behaviour. First, it may be that individuals who have a muscular build learn from an early age that the only way to get what they want is to behave in an aggressive and dominant way. Secondly, a muscular body type might be attractive to gang members who entice the mesomorphic individual to join them in committing criminal acts because they may be perceived to be more successful at crime. Other criticisms have come from large-scale studies, such as the British National Survey (cited on the British Crime Survey website), which found that delinquents who were guilty of serious offences were not strong and muscular but actually smaller in body type compared with the average person.

Link

See *AQA Psychology B AS*, Chapter 2, Biopsychology, for information about the use of twin and adoption studies.

Biological explanations of offending

Genetic transmission

Recent genetic research has moved away from the more simple theories put forward by Lombroso and Sheldon and instead focuses on genetic contributions to criminal behaviour. The main research areas include twin and adoption studies.

AQA Examiner's tip

Make sure that you understand the meaning of concordance. Candidates often make the mistake of assuming a clear genetic basis of behaviour in studies that really show low concordance (35 per cent) between MZ twins, for example.

Twin studies

The rationale underlying the use of twins in explaining criminal behaviour is that if one monozygotic (MZ) twin displays aggressive and criminal tendencies and so does the other twin, then that behaviour must be innate. However, if one MZ twin displays aggressive and criminal tendencies but the other twin does not, then the environment may be more responsible. The expression of the degree of similarity in twin pairs is by concordance rate.

Link

For a definition of concordance rate, see Chapter 5, Schizophrenia and mood disorders, p102, where you will also be able to remind yourself about MZ and DZ twins.

One of the earliest twin studies was reported by the German physician Johannes Lange (1929). He found that MZ twins showed a much higher degree of concordance than dizygotic (DZ) twins for criminal behaviour.

Christiansen (1977) studied 3,586 twin pairs from the Danish islands and found concordance rates of 35 per cent (MZ) and 13 per cent (DZ) for male twins and 21 per cent (MZ) and 8 per cent (DZ) for female twins. Similarly, Dalgaard and Kringlen (1976) in a Norwegian study found concordance rates of 26 per cent (MZ) and 15 per cent (DZ).

Evaluation

Whilst these studies seem to suggest that criminal tendencies are inherited, a number of important points must be considered. First, the concordance rates in these studies are low, indicating that environment has a substantial influence. Secondly, a more plausible explanation for the concordance rates in MZ twins is that they share a similar and close environment, where they may be treated more alike because they look similar, whereas DZ twins tend not to.

Adoption studies

The rationale underlying the use of adoption studies in explaining criminal behaviour is the comparison of criminals with both their biological and adoptive parents. If, in criminal behaviour, the child is more similar to their biological parents than to their adoptive parents, with whom they share the same environment, a genetic basis of criminality may be suggested. Conversely, if the child is more similar to their adoptive parents than to their biological parents, an environmental argument for criminality is favoured. Almost 50 per cent of children in a sample of adopted children whose biological mothers had a criminal record had a criminal record themselves by the age of 18 (Crowe, 1972). In a matched control group of children whose biological mothers did not have a criminal record, only 5 per cent of the adopted children had been convicted of a criminal offence. Hutchings and Mednick (1975) found that, if both biological and adoptive fathers had a criminal record, 36.2 per cent of sons also became criminals. When only the biological father was the criminal, 21.4 per cent of sons were criminal. When only the adoptive father was the criminal, 11.5 per cent of the sons were criminal. When neither the biological nor the adoptive father had a criminal record, only 10.5 per cent of the sons went on to have a criminal record. The findings of Hutchings and Mednick's study show that, whilst genetic factors clearly play a role in influencing criminal behaviour, environmental influences cannot be neglected. Finally, Stott (1982) argues that the prenatal environment influences how the child develops. A high degree of stress on the mother, particularly if she is from a low socio-economic class where criminal conviction rates are high, can result in a variety of developmental disorders. If the adopted child shows criminal tendencies as an adult, this may be because of problems incurred during pregnancy and not as a result of the environment.

Evaluation

As with twin studies, adoption studies have a number of limitations. First, children who are adopted tend to be placed in environments that are very similar to those of their biological parents. Secondly, some children are adopted at a far later age – months or even years after birth. It may be that their early life experiences are the cause of their criminal behaviour.

Psychodynamic explanations of offending

The id, ego and superego

The id, governed by the **pleasure principle**, seeks instant gratification of biological urges such as food, warmth and sex. If the id is prevented from fulfilling these urges, aggressive tendencies emerge. Freud stated that

Link

For the assumptions of the psychodynamic approach, see *AQA Psychology B AS*, Chapter 1, Key approaches; see also Chapter 9, Approaches in psychology, in this book.

Link

For more on the role of the superego, see Chapter 3, Moral development.

Hint

Remember that the superego develops at around the age of four to five years. This will have a bearing on your answers to scenario questions where the age of the child may only be two, for example.

Links

Bowlby's work on attachment and maternal deprivation is discussed in Chapter 1, Social development.

Bowlby's study of 44 teenage thieves is described and evaluated in Chapter 1 (see p14).

AQA Examiner's tip

Make sure that you learn the findings and conclusions of research studies covered at A2. It is essential that you understand the implications of these studies and incorporate these clearly in your answers.

humans tend to be antisocial beings driven by their own needs and urges even if these conflict with other people in society. The ego, governed by the **reality principle**, seeks consciously to fulfil the demands of the id in relation to the constraints and rules imposed by society. Finally, the superego, governed by the **morality principle**, develops at around the age of four to five years during the phallic stage of psychosexual development. The superego comprises two subsystems: the conscience and the ego-ideal. The conscience comprises moral rules and the ego-ideal is what the individual aspires to be. Thus, the superego provides the ego with a set of goals and values.

According to psychoanalytic theory, children have no concept of morality until the superego is fully formed. Therefore, when young children do as they are told by their parents, it is more out of fear of punishment than from an understanding of right and wrong. This lack of morality changes, however, around the age of four or five when the boy experiences the Oedipus complex. Freud theorised that the boy experiences strong sexual urges for his mother, and, fearful that his father will find out and castrate him, the boy resolves this conflict by identifying with his father and taking on board his morals and values. As a result of this process of identification, the superego is established. If, however, a father figure is weak or absent, then the Oedipus complex cannot be fully resolved and so the superego is weak. Conversely, if the father is overly strict, the superego becomes so strong that it overpowers the id.

The experience for girls is, according to Freud, very different. During the Electra complex, girls fear losing their mother's love and believe that they have already been punished by castration and so they repress their urges and identify with their same-sex parent: the mother. Since girls do not have a penis, they are unable to develop a conscience in the same way as boys. Freud claimed that the female superego is therefore weaker than the male superego and, as a result, females are morally inferior.

According to psychodynamic theorists, having a harsh, deviant or weak superego leads to an imbalance between the three components of the personality; a harsh superego can result in immense feelings of guilt and obsession when the id attempts to get satisfaction. People with strong superegos tend to be law abiding although they do, at times, commit anti-social behaviours and strange deviant behaviours. For example, it is suggested that when sexual urges from the id become so overwhelming, the person feels guilty and so commits a crime such as flashing towards another person so as to be punished. More commonly, crime tends to arise from a weak and underdeveloped superego. Here, the individual is oblivious to other people's feelings and is led by the demands of the id. The inability to develop a fully functioning superego is thought to be as a result of having unloving or absent parents. This formed the basis of John Bowlby's maternal deprivation hypothesis. Bowlby (1946) undertook a study to see if teenage thieves who displayed affectionless psychopathy were more likely to have experienced early maternal deprivation compared with those who did not. From his findings he concluded that delinquency is linked to maternal deprivation in childhood.

Evaluation

The psychodynamic explanation of crime has several limitations:

- Freud theorised that females have a weaker superego compared with males. If this is the case, surely females would commit more criminal acts than males? However, Hoffman (1977) suggests that females show a much stronger moral orientation compared with males, which refutes Freud's theory of the weak female superego.

- The theory does not explain all types of crime: for example, many white-collar crimes, such as fraud, require careful planning and execution rather than impulsively acting on an irrational thought process.

Learning theory explanations of offending

The learning theory explanation of crime relates to the principles of both classical and operant conditioning: we learn to behave in a criminal manner in the same way as we learn other behaviours. Classical conditioning involves learning to associate a neutral stimulus with a new, conditioned response. For example, a child may learn to associate stealing sweets from a shop with a feeling of excitement. Operant conditioning focuses on the consequences of the child's actions; if the child is punished for stealing sweets, this behaviour will decline in the future. However, if the child is praised and rewarded by its peers for stealing the sweets, then this behaviour is likely to be repeated as the praise given by the peers is a form of positive reinforcement.

Social learning theory

Social learning theory acknowledges the role of mediating cognitive variables that lie in between stimulus and response. These mediating variables help to shape our behaviour by making us think about the consequences of our actions. Bandura *et al.* (1963) stated that the main influences on an individual's behaviour are from observations of role models in the individual's environment. Whether or not an individual chooses to imitate the role model depends on a number of variables such as the model's status in society and the consequences of their actions: if the model is positively reinforced for their behaviour, the individual is more likely to imitate them through a process known as **vicarious reinforcement**.

Vicarious reinforcement is an indirect form of reinforcement and involves learning by observing others rather than directly receiving rewards or punishments oneself (see Figure 10). For example, if Child A observes Child B steal a toy from Child C and start playing with it without being told off by an adult, Child A may regard the behaviour as being acceptable and is therefore likely to replicate it in the future. Conversely, if the adult told Child B off and made the child give back the toy to Child C, Child A is unlikely to replicate the behaviour in the future as they do not wish to receive the same punishment.

Link

For the assumptions of social learning theory, see *AQA Psychology B AS*, Chapter 1, Key approaches; see also Chapter 9, Approaches in psychology, in this book.

Key terms

Vicarious reinforcement: reward (or punishment) given to another and experienced second hand by the observer. Learning is not a result of direct reinforcement or experience but rather comes from an individual's observation of another person's experience.

Evaluation

One of the major strengths of social learning theory is that it explains why some individuals commit the same crime but for different reasons. This is because the individual's motivations and expectations are dependent on who their role models are and their own individual learning experiences. However, some limitations of social learning theory involve its reliance on laboratory studies (for example, Bandura, 1986) which lack both ecological validity and generalisability. Finally, social learning theory as an explanation of offending is rather deterministic. It states than an individual's criminal behaviour is as a result of their learning experiences and observations of role models that surround their environment. The theory fails to acknowledge the importance of free will.

Fig. 10 *Children learn appropriate behaviour through vicarious reinforcement*

Sutherland's differential association theory

Sutherland's (1939) theory of differential association is a sociological one, which states that criminal behaviour is learned through exposure to criminal norms. Crime occurs because of two factors: learned attitudes

AQA Examiner's tip

Sutherland proposes nine principles in the differential association theory. It is not necessary to learn all of these; just focus on the general features of the theory.

and imitation of specific acts. Sutherland states that criminal activity is as a result of an individual expressing their needs (e.g. for money). However, the need for money is learned and it therefore cannot be used to explain all criminal behaviour. Sutherland states that an individual is exposed to the values and attitudes of the people who surround them in their environment. For example, a child learns the needs and values of their parents by observing their attitudes towards the law. Some of the parents' attitudes towards the law may be favourable and others, unfavourable. If, as a result of learning, the child acquires more favourable attitudes towards crime, then they too may become a criminal like their parents. Sutherland states that there may also be variations in individuals' attitudes towards crime. For example, a person's attitude may be that stealing from others is unacceptable and yet the same person may feel that it is acceptable to make a false claim for state benefits.

Evaluation

Some of the limitations of this theory concern its vague and untestable definitions. For example, it is difficult to see how the number of unfavourable attitudes a person has towards crime can be accurately measured. Also, just how many unfavourable attitudes does an individual need to be classed as a 'criminal'? The theory does not explain crimes of passion and other more impulsive crimes such as stealing underwear from a washing line; these crimes are not as a result of an individual having been raised to have deviant values.

Eysenck's theory of the criminal personality

Eysenck's theory of criminal behaviour (Eysenck, 1977) suggests that crime arises from certain personality traits, which are biological in origin (see Figure 11). Originally, Eysenck stated that an individual's personality traits could be reduced to just two dimensions: neuroticism (N) and extroversion (E). An individual with high neuroticism is prone to depression, anxiety and variable moods, whereas an individual who is low in neuroticism tends to be more emotionally stable. The extroversion dimension relates to the amount of stimulation an individual receives from their environment. Individuals who require large amounts of stimulation are said to be high on the extroversion dimension, whereas individuals who require little environmental stimulation are low on the extroversion dimension. Eysenck devised the Eysenck Personality Questionnaire or EPQ to measure these personality traits, which, in the majority of the population, are normally distributed.

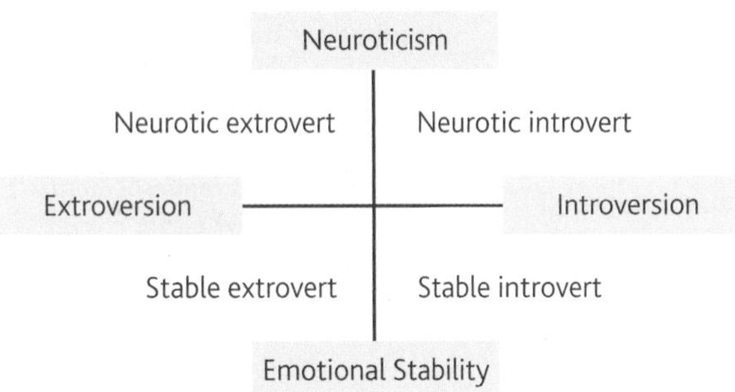

Fig. 11 *Eysenck stated that criminal behaviours were associated with people who scored high on the extroversion–neuroticism scale*

Eysenck stated that the personality traits of extroversion and neuroticism related to the central nervous system. Extroversion is associated with autonomic arousal; the lower this is, the more stimulation a person seeks from their environment. Neuroticism relates to the stability of the individual's central nervous system: a high neuroticism score shows that an individual has high anxiety levels – their nervous system reacts strongly to aversive stimuli. Eysenck stated that these individuals find it difficult to learn socially appropriate behaviours, for example not behaving aggressively towards others.

Link

For more on normal distributions see *AQA Psychology B AS*, Chapter 4, Research methods; see also Chapter 11, Methods in psychology, in this book.

Eysenck theorised that criminal behaviour is associated with individuals who scored high on both the extroversion and neuroticism dimensions. The combination of these two traits means that the individual would constantly seek stimulation (high on extroversion) but does not learn from their punishments (high on neuroticism). Later, Eysenck suggested a third personality dimension: psychoticism (P). Individuals who are high in psychoticism are uncaring, aggressive and solitary. He stated that individuals who are extreme in their dimension of psychoticism are also likely to engage in criminal behaviour.

Evaluation

In a study of prisoners, Farrington *et al*. (1982) found that where the participants tended to score high on psychoticism, they did not on extroversion or neuroticism. Other research has found inconsistencies between criminal activity and extroversion with some research showing criminals to have higher extroversion compared with controls; other criminals to be lower in extroversion compared with controls; and some criminals having the same level of extroversion as controls. Finally, Zuckerman (1969) suggests that the environmental stimulation sought by individuals is not necessarily related to extroversion. It may simply be as a result of boredom, which arises from increased rather than decreased arousal.

Key points:

- Lombroso stated that criminals could be identified by their atavistic features such as a narrow, sloping brow and prominent jaw.
- Sheldon theorised that individuals who have a mesomorphic body type are more prone to criminal behaviour.
- Twin and adoption studies have provided evidence of a genetic contribution to criminal behaviour.
- Psychodynamic theorists have pointed to a harsh, weak or deviant superego as an explanation for offending.
- Social learning theorists state that individuals learn appropriate or inappropriate behaviours as a result of modelling, imitation and vicarious reinforcement.
- Eysenck stated that individuals high on the extroversion and neurotic dimensions are more prone to criminal behaviour.

Summary questions

8 Briefly discuss one limitation of the psychodynamic approach to explaining criminal behaviour.

9 Outline two features of Eysenck's theory of the criminal personality.

10 John and his friend Ian go to the local shop. Ian watches as John steals a bag of sweets and puts them in his pocket. John leaves the shop and shares his sweets with Ian. The next day, Ian goes into the same shop and steals a bag of sweets. Suggest how social learning theorists would explain why Ian stole some sweets.

Custodial sentencing

Learning objectives:

- describe the four aims of sentencing
- evaluate the effectiveness of custodial sentencing
- suggest alternatives to custodial sentencing.

The aims of sentencing

There are four main aims of sentencing.

Retribution

This term simply means punishment. In an objective way, the offender who has broken a rule will be punished. The offender will receive a punishment that will reflect the seriousness of the crime and the level of moral fault.

Forensic psychology

Fig. 12 Custodial sentencing can be effective in reducing rates of recidivism

Key terms

Recidivism: persistent committing of crime or reoffending. If someone is always getting into trouble with the police, they may be described as a recidivist.

Hint

Make sure you know some of the factors affecting recidivism.

Deterrence

The purpose here is to deter others from committing crime. **Individual deterrence** is to prevent the offender from committing the same crime in the future. **General deterrence** aims to deter the rest of the population from committing the same crime. However, Home Office figures on **recidivism** show that 70 per cent of offenders who receive custodial sentences go on to reoffend within two years of release. This suggests that deterrence is unlikely to reduce the amount of crime in general or prevent the individual from reoffending in the future.

Rehabilitation (or reform)

The aim is to cure the offender from the 'deviance' for example drugs, which caused the offender to commit the crime in the first place. Effective counselling and educational programmes are required in prisons to treat drug offenders so as to reduce recidivism.

Protection of society

Serious offenders, such as those who commit rape or murder, should be imprisoned to protect other people in society from becoming victims. The Criminal Justice Act 1991 focused on the rights of citizens to feel protected in their society. In 2002, the Chief Justice (CJ) Lord Woolf also reiterated this view in the Court of Appeal when he called for all those who steal mobile phones to be given an immediate custodial sentence!

The effectiveness of custodial sentencing

The psychological effects of imprisonment

For many offenders, imprisonment can be brutal, demeaning and generally devastating (Bartol, 1995). It is very difficult to generalise the psychological effects of imprisonment as prison regimes can vary from one prison to another, individuals cope with prison life in different ways, and there is also a lack of controlled longitudinal studies in this area. Nevertheless, a common initial reaction to imprisonment is one of depression, guilt and anxiety. Bukshel and Kilmann (1980) found that symptoms such as restlessness, anxiety and sleeplessness tend to occur at the beginning of the term of imprisonment where adjustment to prison life has to be made. Perhaps one of the most famous experimental studies of the psychological effects of 'imprisonment' is Philip Zimbardo's Stanford Prison Study (1971).

Research study: Zimbardo (1971)

Aim: To investigate the situational rather than dispositional causes of negative behaviour and thought patterns in prison settings with 'normal' participants playing the role of guards and prisoners.

Method: A basement corridor in Stanford University was converted to represent a 'mock prison' for the two-week experiment. Twenty-two male participants were randomly allocated to the role of 'guard' or 'prisoner'. Each participant had previously volunteered to take part in the experiment knowing that some of their human rights would be violated. Guards were given a prison uniform including mirrored sunglasses. Prisoners were given their 'uniform', including identification numbers, and a lock and chain around the ankle. The prisoners remained in the prison 24 hours a day and followed a strict regime. The prison guards were given no specific instructions by

Zimbardo other than to 'maintain a reasonable degree of order within the prison necessary for its effective functioning' and a clear ban on the use of all forms of physical violence. Zimbardo and his colleagues observed the guards and prisoners via video cameras and audiotape.

Results: The experiment had to be stopped after six days because of the extreme and abnormal reactions by both the prisoners and the guards. The prisoners showed disbelief that they had actually been imprisoned, followed by extreme rebellion. The prisoners began to show negative emotions such as depression, crying, fits of anger – nearly all of them had to be released early. The guards, on the other hand, showed pleasure at the power that had been given to them. They dehumanised the prisoners by only allowing them to eat as a privilege, made the prisoners stand in one position for hours at a time and verbally insulted the prisoners until they begged for forgiveness.

Conclusion: This experiment clearly supports situational attributions of behaviour. It was the prison situation itself that caused the participants' behaviour, rather than their own, innate individual personalities.

Evaluation (ethical): the experiment was ethically approved and all of the participants had received and signed an informed consent document beforehand. The participants knew that they were taking part in an experiment but may not have been aware just how realistic their term of imprisonment would be. Zimbardo stopped the experiment early but made sure that debriefing and assessment of all the participants took place, weeks, months and even years afterwards.

Evaluation (methodological): Zimbardo's role-play prison situation lacks ecological validity. The experimenters themselves admitted that factors such as the length of sentence and lack of physical violence had an effect on the guards' and prisoners' behaviour and, hence, the overall results.

Link

See *AQA Psychology B AS*, Chapter 5, Social influence.

AQA Examiner's tip

Whilst it is tempting to convey to the examiner your knowledge of Zimbardo's prison experiment, remember that your examiner already knows what occurred in this study! Focus your answers instead on what the **implications** of this study are and the evaluative points that can be made.

Research evidence suggests that, for many offenders, a period of time spent in prison is effective in reducing rates of recidivism. However, Glaser (1983) suggests that perhaps community sentencing is a better option as prisons can often reinforce criminal behaviour particularly for 'low risk' offenders, i.e. those in the early stages of offending. Because the offender is among other offenders 24 hours a day and seven days a week, prisons have often been called 'universities of crime'. The length of custodial sentences given does not necessarily have an effect on reducing recidivism. Walker and Farrington (1981) found that length of sentence made little difference to whether or not the offender went on to reoffend. Davies and Raymond (2000) are heavily critical of the four aims of sentencing described above. They argue that prison sentences are often given in response to public demand rather than as a means of reducing recidivism. They go on to point out that prisons are not necessarily effective as a deterrent – it is unlikely to deter an offender who committed a 'crime of passion' when they lost emotional control.

Alternatives to custodial sentencing

Absolute or conditional discharge

The offender is not necessarily given a 'sentence' per se, but if the discharge is conditional, they will be sentenced by the judge for the original offence if another offence of the same type is committed within a specified period. This period may not exceed three years.

Fines

Fines are a sum of money that the offender is ordered to pay to the State. This is, by far, the most common form of non-custodial sentencing and is often imposed for motoring offences, for example. In *R* v. *Baldwin* [2002], Lord Woolf CJ, commented that:

> bearing in mind the stress in our prisons today from overcrowding, if there are good prospects that an offender is not going to prey upon the public again, there are advantages in using the penalty of a fine rather than sentencing someone to a further period of imprisonment.

Community orders

One of the most radical changes made by the Criminal Justice Act 2003 was to improve the community sentencing regime and produce a more flexible and responsive approach to sentencing.

Community rehabilitation order

This sentence applies to offenders over the age of 16. The offender is placed under the supervision of a probation officer. The period of the order is not less than six months and not more than three years. The order may contain special requirements such as treatment for drug and alcohol dependency, curfews, exclusions, and so on.

Community punishment order

This sentence applies to offenders over the age of 16. The offender has to carry out unpaid work for the benefit of the community, for example education projects, garden projects and charity work. The National Probation Service undertakes the organisation of such work. The work should be completed within a year and last between 40 and 240 hours.

Community punishment and rehabilitation order

This sentence applies to offenders over the age of 16. This sentence is a combination of a community rehabilitation order and a community punishment order. The offender is supervised by a probation officer for between one and three years as well as undertaking community work for between 40 and 100 hours.

Key points:

- The four aims of sentencing are retribution, deterrence, rehabilitation (or reform) and protection of society.
- Some of the psychological effects of imprisonment are restlessness, anxiety, sleeplessness, suicide and self-mutilation.
- The Stanford Prison Study (1971) showed how situational factors, i.e. the prison itself, caused extreme distress in some of the participants.
- The effectiveness of custodial sentencing in reducing rates of recidivism is questionable.
- The main alternatives to custodial sentencing are absolute or conditional discharge, fines and community orders.

Take it further

The aim of the Criminal Justice Act 2003 was to improve community sentencing programmes. Consider the different community orders given in this section. For each, assess how effective this type of order has been in reducing rates of recidivism. Compare your findings with those for the other community orders. Are some more effective than others? If so, why do you think this is? What do you think could be done to improve the community orders that are considered to be the least effective?

Summary questions

11 What are the four aims of sentencing?

12 Outline some of the psychological effects of imprisonment.

13 Evaluate Zimbardo's Stanford Prison Study.

14 Compare the effectiveness of custodial and non-custodial sentences.

Treatment programmes

Learning objectives:

- describe behaviour modification, anger management and social skills training programmes
- evaluate the use of these treatment programmes.

Link

For more on operant conditioning, see *AQA Psychology B AS*, Chapter 1, Key approaches.

For the use of token economies in the treatment of schizophrenia, see Chapter 5, Schizophrenia and mood disorders, in this book.

It is becoming increasingly clear that much of the work done within the prison service helps to reduce the likelihood of reoffending. In recent years, there has been a more consistent attempt by the prison service to offer effective treatment programmes to prisoners in an attempt to reduce recidivism.

Behaviour modification

Behaviour modification, also known as behavioural therapy, refers to the techniques that are based on the principles of **operant conditioning**. Ayllon and Azrin (1968) developed this programme in order to build up desirable behaviour, i.e. increase the occurrence of certain behaviours and decrease the occurrence of others.

Many behaviour modification programmes rely on using a **token economy** to modify behaviour. This is where appropriate and desirable behaviour is rewarded with a token that may later be exchanged for material goods. This form of reward system acts as a **positive reinforcer** and so the likelihood of the person displaying the same desirable behaviour again in the future is increased.

In relation to crime, the idea behind the token economy is that, if criminal behaviour is learned in the same way as any other behaviour (i.e. through Skinner's principles of **reinforcement** and **punishment**), these inappropriate behaviours can be 'unlearned' in the same way. Token economy programmes began to be used with offenders in the 1960s after success in treating the mentally ill. In implementing the programme for an offender, the institution will create a list of desirable behaviours that the offender must acquire. These might include complying with prison rules, completing chores such as the laundry and positive relationships both with the prison officers and other prisoners. When the offender behaves in a positive way, they are given a token. These tokens may then be exchanged for **primary reinforcers** such as sweets, money and cigarettes. Through **selective reinforcement**, therefore, desirable behaviours are learned and undesirable behaviours are **extinguished**. However, if the offender chooses not to comply with the list of desirable behaviours and is aggressive or non-compliant, then they may have privileges taken away (e.g. watching television or going into the exercise yard). The removal of such privileges is a form of **negative reinforcement**.

Evaluation

Token economy programmes tend to be effective in the short term. Hobbs and Holt (1976) investigated the effects of the introduction of a token economy programme to young offenders in three different institutions compared with a fourth institution which acted as a control group. Tokens were given for compliance with rules, cooperation with staff and other young offenders, and appropriate social interaction. These tokens were then exchanged for soft drinks, leisure time and visits home. The researchers found a significant increase in desirable behaviours compared with the one institution that acted as a control. Ayllon and Millan (1979) found that this form of token economy programme also worked equally well with adult offenders. Despite the obvious benefits in increasing desirable behaviour in individuals, the long-term effects of token economy programmes are not so favourable. Rice *et al.* (1990)

failed to find any long-term benefits of the token economy programme in a follow-up of offenders who had received this form of treatment whilst in an institution. Likewise, other research has found that once this type of positive reinforcement is discontinued, i.e. when the offender is released from prison, the desirable behaviours tend to disappear.

Overall, the effectiveness of behaviour modification programmes is that they are successful in changing targeted behaviours under carefully controlled conditions such as prisons. As this type of programme requires little training, it is economical and can be carried out by virtually anyone; there is no need for a trained clinical psychologist to administer this type of treatment. The disadvantages, however, rest in the fact that a high degree of commitment and time is needed for continual implementation. The effectiveness of the treatment programme can be extremely difficult to measure in a prison situation where rewards and punishments may come from other sources such as the prisoners themselves. Finally, there are ethical issues associated with this type of treatment programme in relation to the violation of human rights. One of the major problems here is the removal of food, drink, etc. as a form of negative reinforcement; some argue that these are actually a right of the offender, not a privilege dependent on behaving in a certain way.

Anger management

Anger management programmes are based on the concept that an individual's anger was the primary cause of their criminal act and that, if the individual can learn to control this anger, rates of recidivism will decrease. Anger management is a cognitive-behavioural technique whereby the individual still experiences the emotion of anger but does so in a more controlled way. The technique involves learning skills such as self-control and self-monitoring of behaviour and emotions, conflict resolution, and so on. According to Ainsworth (2000), anger management programmes involve three stages:

1 **Cognitive preparation** – offenders are asked to analyse their own anger and to identify the particular situations that make them angry. They then attempt to analyse their own thought processes during this situation and to recognise why their anger may be perceived to be irrational.
2 **Skill acquisition** – offenders are taught the skills necessary to help them avoid anger-provoking situations or to help the offender deal with these situations more effectively. Skills, such as relaxation in order to avoid becoming excessively aroused, assertiveness to help the offender to communicate their point without becoming angry, and other skills, such as resolving conflicts, are taught.
3 **Application practice** – offenders are given the opportunity to apply their newly learnt skills to role-play situations. This involves the offender acting out the scenario which, in the past, would have made them violent. The offender then uses their skills to help deal with the situation more effectively. The offender receives feedback from the group counsellor and the other group members on their performance.

Evaluation

Feindler *et al.* (1984) found that, in a group of young offenders, anger management programmes were effective in instilling problem solving and self-control as methods of reducing aggressive behaviour. Ainsworth (2000) states that anger management programmes are effective in reducing anger within prisons but only if these programmes are well managed and supported. In terms of the long-term benefits, Law (1997) found that only one individual who had completed an eight-session course showed any benefits compared with the rest of the group.

Social skills training

Social skills are skills that we learn as children, such as turn-taking in a conversation, standing a comfortable distance from someone, making eye contact with the person you are talking to, and so on. When we come across a person who lacks certain social skills, this can make us feel quite uncomfortable. For example, imagine talking to a person standing in front of you: whilst you are talking, the person does not look at you at all. This makes you feel uncomfortable because it seems as if they are not interested in what you have to say, which actually may not be the case. The person lacks the social skills necessary to put you at ease and make you feel that what you have to say is valued. Many offenders are said to lack social skills and so the aim of these training programmes is to help offenders acquire these skills so that they may lead a 'normal' life when released from prison and, hence, reduce recidivism.

Social skills training is a cognitive-behavioural treatment programme based on the assumption that violent offenders lack social skills. Many violent offenders behave in such an aggressive way because they lack social skills and, hence, appropriate ways of dealing with challenging situations. Through the training, the offenders are given the necessary social skills, and they are less likely to reoffend in the future. A typical social skills training programme might involve focusing on what are known as **micro skills**, such as appropriate eye contact and proximity to others during a conversation, as well as **macro skills**, such as negotiating and assertiveness. Social skills training varies between programmes but they are all largely based on the principles of **modelling** (observation and imitation of others) as well as role plays, during which the participant is given instructions and feedback from the group counsellor about their performance.

Link

Social skills training is also discussed in Chapter 5, Schizophrenia and mood disorders.

Evaluation

Goldstein (1986) reviewed 30 studies of social skills training used with aggressive and delinquent teenagers and found that various skills such as negotiation with their probation officer and appropriate eye contact had been learned. Other social skills training programmes have shown an improvement in an offender's self-esteem and a far greater sense of control over their lives. However, individuals in a control group who received no social skills training, but instead shared their problems through discussion with others, showed an equivalent improvement in self-esteem, thereby casting doubt on the effectiveness of social skills training programmes alone. Piliavin and Briar (1964) suggest that both the appearance of the suspected offender and their overall manner can affect the likelihood of whether the police detain them for questioning. Therefore, a criticism of social skills training programmes nowadays is that perhaps we are training offenders to communicate more effectively with the police and, as a result, they are less likely to be arrested. That said, Aiken *et al*. (1977) suggested that social skills training can be used to provide teenagers with the social skills necessary to resist peer pressure and so lessen the likelihood that they will become involved in crime. Overall, it is clear that there are short-term benefits from social skills training programmes but what are uncertain are the long-term benefits or how they can be generalised to real-life situations.

Hollin (1999) provides three general conclusions regarding the effectiveness of treatment programmes as a whole:

- There is a 10 per cent reduction in recidivism for offenders who have received treatment compared with a control group. (This figure does not take into account, however, the variability between different treatment programmes.)

Summary questions

15 Explain the three stages involved in anger management programmes.

16 What is meant by 'token economy'? Explain how this method increases the occurrence of desirable behaviours.

17 In social skills training programmes, counsellors attempt to improve both micro skills and macro skills. Give two examples of each skill.

18 Briefly discuss the effectiveness of one treatment programme in reducing recidivism.

Link

See *AQA Psychology B AS*, Chapter 4, Research methods, for non-experimental methods and ethical issues in psychological research.

Link

See *AQA Psychology B AS*, Chapter 4, Research methods.

- The treatment programmes offered are more effective with medium- to high-risk offenders.
- Treatment programmes offered to offenders whilst they still live in the community are more effective in reducing recidivism compared with treatment programmes offered in residential establishments.

Key points:

- Behaviour modification programmes are based on the principles of operant conditioning.
- Token economy programmes reward desirable behaviours with tokens, which then act as positive reinforcement and so increase desirable behaviour.
- Anger management programmes involve three stages: cognitive preparation, skill acquisition and application practice.
- Social skills training programmes aim to improve micro skills, such as maintaining eye contact, and macro skills, such as assertiveness.
- Hollin states that treatment programmes are more effective in reducing recidivism compared with controls.

End-of-chapter activity 1

Conduct an interview with different members of your family (e.g. your parents, grandparents, etc.). The purpose of the interview is to investigate possible reasons for the 'dark figure' of crime. Design a structured interview. You should write between 10 and 15 questions. Some of the questions should be closed, where your participants have to choose from pre-determined answers, and some of the questions should be open, where your participants can state their own opinions. Consider the ethical issues that might arise when conducting the interview. How will you overcome these ethical issues (e.g. brief, consent form, debrief)? Plan how you will record and analyse the data from your interview. How will you display your data in an appropriate graphical form? Explain the findings from your research. What are the common reasons given by your participants for why there is a 'dark figure' of crime? You should also evaluate the design of your investigation (e.g. were any of your questions ambiguous? If so, how would you improve the clarity of these questions if you were to carry out the interview again?). Finally, evaluate the use of the structured interview as a method of psychological research.

End-of-chapter activity 2

Choose one newspaper. The purpose of this activity is to convert qualitative data into quantitative data by analysing the different types and characteristics of crime reported by the media. Before you read the newspaper, design a record sheet in order to keep a tally of the different types and characteristics of each crime. You might like to consider headings such as 'Burglary', 'Stabbing', 'Motoring Offence', etc. Carefully read each page of the newspaper. For each crime that is reported, consider the following. What type of crime is it? What are the characteristics of this crime (e.g. number of victims, age of victim(s), characteristics of the offender, area in which the crime took place, etc.)?

When you have completed this part of the activity, consider how to present your data in graphical form. What conclusions can you draw from your research?

For the next part of the activity, do exactly the same task as above, but with a different type of newspaper. For example, if you initially chose a broadsheet, now choose a tabloid. What are the similarities and differences between the newspapers in the types of crime reported? Do both newspapers report the same crimes? If so, are there any differences in the reported characteristics of each crime?

Further reading

Adler, J. (ed.) (2004) Forensic Psychology: Concepts, Debates and Practice. Cullompton: Willan Publishing.

Ainsworth, P.B. (1998) *Psychology, Law and Eyewitness Testimony*. Chichester: Wiley.

Ainsworth, P.B. (2000) *Psychology and Crime: Myths and Reality*. Harlow: Longman.

Ainsworth, P.B. (2001) *Offender Profiling and Crime Analysis*. Cullompton: Willan Publishing.

Alison, L.J. (2005) *The Forensic Psychologist's Casebook: Psychological Profiling and Criminal Investigation*. Cullompton: Willan Publishing.

Canter, D. (1995) *Criminal Shadows: Inside the Mind of the Serial Killer*. London: HarperCollins Publishers.

Canter, D. (2007) *Mapping Murder: The Secrets of Geographical Profiling*. London: Virgin.

Carson, D. and Bull, R. (eds) (2003) *Handbook of Psychology in Legal Contexts*. Chichester: Wiley.

Harrower, J. (2001) *Psychology in Practice: Crime*. London: Hodder and Stoughton.

Howitt, D. (2006) *Forensic and Criminal Psychology*, 2nd edition. Pearson: Prentice Hall.

Kapardis, A. (2003) *Psychology and the Law: A Critical Introduction*. Cambridge: Cambridge University Press.

Maguire, M., Morgan, R. and Reiner, R. (2007) *The Oxford Handbook of Criminology*, 4th edition. Oxford: Oxford University Press.

Ormerod, D. (2005) *Smith and Hogan Criminal Law*, 11th edition. Oxford: Oxford University Press.

Towl, G. (ed.) (2006) *Psychological Research in Prisons*. Oxford: Blackwell.

www.a-level-law.com/caselibrary (for the details of *R* v. *West* [1996])

crimeinfo: www.crimeinfo.org.uk

Home Office: www.homeoffice.gov.uk (search for the British Crime Survey)

Smart Justice: www.smartjustice.org

All About Forensic Psychology: www.all-about-forensic-psychology.com

The International Academy for Investigative Psychology: www.ia-ip.org

tru TV CRIME LIBRARY: www.crimelibrary.com

Centre for Investigative Psychology: www.i-psy.com

www.investigativepsych.com

University of Liverpool: www.liv.ac.uk (search for 'psychology')

Approaches in psychology

Introduction

'Since psychology is concerned with the full range of what makes us human, it is not surprising that the scope of the discipline is extensive' (Phoenix and Thomas, 2002, p7).

Psychology can be called the scientific study of behaviour. Although this is a good, precise definition, it hides the diversity within psychology. Throughout the history of psychology, there have been varying theoretical viewpoints, called 'approaches', that have underpinned the study of behaviour. Each approach produced a different way of looking at behaviour.

For example, Wilhelm Wundt, who established the first research laboratory in psychology at the University of Leipzig, Germany, in 1879, was a structuralist. He was classed as a structuralist because he focused upon the structure of conscious experience using **introspection**. Structuralism made the assumption that conscious experience can only be studied by the individual themselves. It declined by the 1920s because of the growth of other approaches, and the limitations of introspection.

Today, there are many different approaches to psychology, but the most important are the biological, behaviourist, cognitive, psychodynamic, humanistic and social learning theory. They each vary in a number of ways:

- **Underlying assumptions about behaviour** Each approach has a set of assumptions that are taken for granted about behaviour: for example, all behaviour has an unconscious cause (psychodynamic approach) or it is learnt (behaviourist approach).
- **What is deemed the appropriate subject matter for psychology** Approaches differ as to which areas of behaviour are considered suitable for study. For example, the humanistic approach is to concentrate on the subjective experience of the individual, while those adopting the behaviourist approach believe that only observable behaviour should be studied (particularly in non-human animals).
- **The methods used to study behaviour** The approaches may vary in the methods used to study behaviour: for example, the experiment (biological and behaviourist approaches) or case studies (psychodynamic approach). The methods used will determine the knowledge collected about behaviour. This is known technically as epistemology: 'the form which our understanding or knowledge takes, the assumptions which underlie it and the methods we use to establish it' (Stevens, 1996a, p77).
- **The position taken in the debates in psychology** Debates include nature–nurture and **free will–determinism**.
- **The role of psychology in the world** Approaches with a scientific basis, like the biological and behaviourist, see the role of psychology as discovering knowledge about the causes and effects of behaviour. On the other hand, the aim of the humanistic approach is to improve the lives of individuals and encourage their personal growth. Another area of disagreement here is whether theory or application (e.g. therapy) is more important.

Key terms

Introspection: the process by which a person looks into their own mental experiences and reports on their conscious experience.

Free will: the ability to make decisions and choose behaviours freely; behaviour is under the control of the volition (will) of an individual rather than other forces.

Determinism: a belief that all behaviour is caused by prior events, external or internal factors; determinism leaves no room for alternatives.

AQA Examiner's tip

A good way to compare the approaches in this chapter is to make a table summarising the key assumptions of each approach.

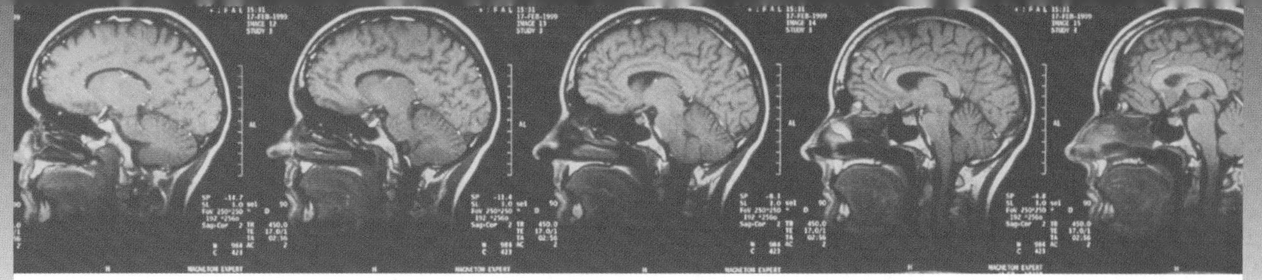

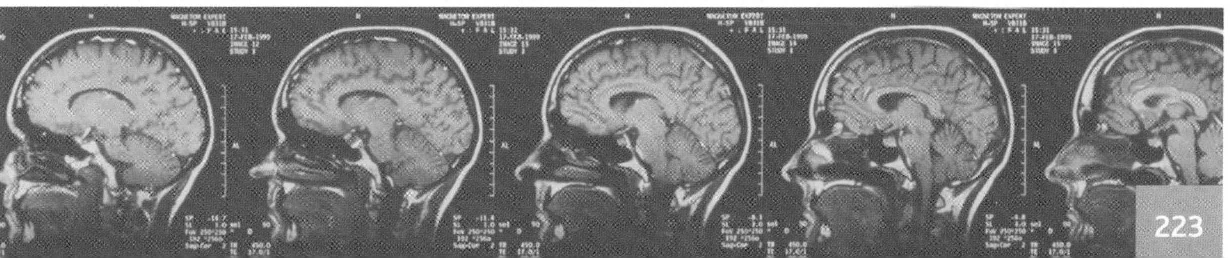

9 Approaches in psychology

The biological approach

Learning objectives:

- understand what is meant by the biological approach to psychology
- distinguish between causal and functional levels of analysis
- evaluate the biological approach in psychology.

> It hardly needs saying that our experience of being a person in a social world reflects the fact that we are biological beings, commonly assumed to be the product of a process of evolution
>
> ***(Toates**, 1996, p37)*

The biological approach applies the principles of biology to psychology. This means that the starting point for understanding and explaining behaviour is the individual's biology. If you ask a biological psychologist why a person is aggressive, for example, they will answer with reference to physiological explanations (e.g. too much of certain hormones) and genetic/evolutionary explanations. Physiological explanations are known as the causal level of analysis, and evolutionary explanations are the functional level.

It should also be noted that human beings are seen as no different from other animals because we share the same basic biology.

Hint

Assumptions of this approach

- All behaviour has a biological basis which is the focus of this approach.
- The causal level of analysis concentrates on the physiological processes underlying behaviour.
- The functional level of analysis is the evolutionary basis of behaviour including genetics.

Link

In *AQA Psychology B AS*, see Chapter 1, Key approaches, for an introduction to the biological approach, and Chapter 2, Biopsychology, for an introduction to biopsychology.

Link

For more about the ANS, see Chapter 6, Stress and stress management.

Causal level of analysis

As human beings, we are embodied, i.e. we exist in a physical form. This physical form (or physiology) of the human body comprises millions of cells that communicate by minute electrical and chemical signals. In biological language, we are electrochemical machines.

Behaviour is controlled by the nervous system (see Figure 1). The central nervous system is the brain and the spinal cord, and the peripheral nervous system, which consists of all nerves radiating from the central nervous system. The latter also includes the autonomic nervous system (ANS), which controls the automatic processes in the body, like heart rate and blood pressure (see below), and the somatic nervous system, which controls muscles related to movement.

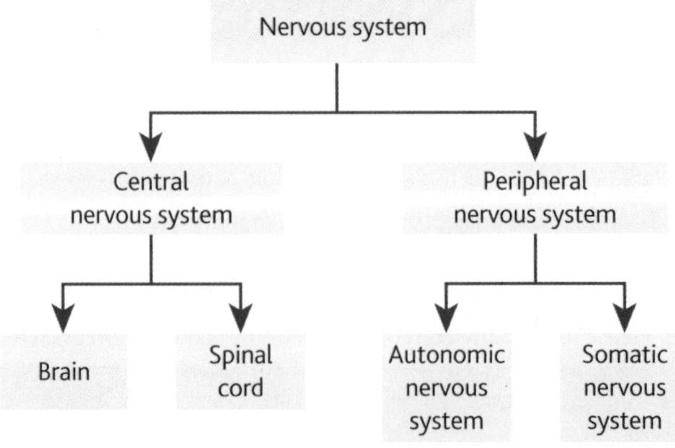

Fig. 1 *Main divisions of the nervous system*

The following are key functions of the ANS:

- heart rate
- blood pressure
- respiration
- body temperature
- 'fight or flight syndrome'.

In the central nervous system, specific cells called neurons communicate with each other chemically at their junctions known as synapses. The chemicals are known as neurotransmitters. They tend to act between neurons, while hormones, another chemical messenger, act throughout the body travelling in the bloodstream (Table 1).

Table 1 *Examples of chemical messengers in the body*

Main neurotransmitters	Key hormones
Acetylcholine	Adrenalin
Adrenalin	Noradrenalin
Noradrenalin	Corticosteroids
Dopamine	Thyroxin
Serotonin	Oestrogen
	Progesterone

Functional level of analysis

The biological approach also focuses upon the evolutionary and genetic basis of behaviour. Originating from Charles Darwin's work in the 19th century, evolutionary theory sees survival and the ability to reproduce as key to behaviour in all species.

Darwin proposed two concepts central to evolution: natural selection and sexual selection.

Natural selection

This is the idea that, within a species, those animals that will survive have particular traits that give them an advantage compared with the others. This behaviour is 'adapted', and is well suited to the environment in which the animal lives. These 'fit' animals will survive and leave more offspring, facilitating the spread of 'adaptive traits' in that species. For example, running faster is an adaptive trait for prey that is chased by fast predators.

More formally, natural selection depends on three principles (Dowling, 1994):

- **Principle of diversity** There are a large number of variant forms of the same species (known as members of the population).
- **Principle of interaction** These variant forms interact with the environment to see which 'fit' (e.g. animals that breathe air will not 'fit' a permanent underwater environment).
- **Principle of differential amplification** The variants that 'fit' will spread at the expense of those who don't 'fit' (i.e. will have more offspring).

Sexual selection

The best strategy for passing the genes on to the next generation differs between the male and female of the species. The male is able to produce many sperm and so can theoretically have as many offspring as the mates found can produce. But the female is restricted by giving birth to the offspring. Thus, she has more invested in its survival (Table 2).

Table 2 *Sexual selection and strategies for males and females (in this example, the male mates with 10 females, who have one offspring each in the breeding season)*

	Offspring	Strategy
Male	10 fathered; can afford some not to survive	Find many female mates, i.e. indiscriminate; little concern for post-natal care
Female	Each female has one offspring and thus survival is important	Female invests time and effort in survival but must exercise choosiness about male, i.e. only mate with male who has 'best genes'

Brewer, K. (2002) Comparative Psychology By Animal: Lions No. 1. Orsett: Orsett Psychology Services

Darwin's ideas about evolution are based upon the survival of the individual. But Dawkins (1976) suggested that it is the survival of the genes that matter. For example, a mother who sacrifices herself for her three offspring will guarantee that three copies of half of her genes survive, which has an evolutionary advantage over the survival of the mother at the expense of her offspring. This idea has led to the focus on 'inclusive fitness' (the survival of the individual and their biological relatives).

Within the biological approach, sociobiologists and evolutionary psychologists, in particular, have argued that all human behaviour can be explained by evolution. Thus behaviour exists because there is an evolutionary advantage now or there was one when humans first appeared approximately 200,000 years ago (Laland and Brown, 2002).

Genes

The process of evolution occurs through the inheritance of genes from the biological parents. Small mutations in the genetic material lead to changes in the next generation.

Each cell in the body contains a complete set of chromosomes. Chromosomes are spread in two ways.

- The first process of cell division is known as **mitosis**. The new cell contains the exact duplication of pairs of chromosomes as the original.
- While in the process of **meiosis**, the gametes (matured sex cells, i.e. sperm or egg) receive half the pair of chromosomes of the parent. Thus, during reproduction the pair of chromosomes is reformed from the mother's and father's gametes.

However, one chromosome does not follow these rules: the sex chromosome, of which there are two forms, X and Y. Pairing of the sex chromosomes results in either XX (which determines a female) or XY (for a male).

The chromosome complement is known as a **karotype**, which for humans is 46: 22 pairs (known as autosomes) which are the same for either sex, and then XX or XY.

Chromosomes are made up of genes, which consist of a sequence of DNA (deoxyribonucleic acid). DNA is made up of four bases: adenine (A), guanine (G), cytosine (C) and thymine (T). These are ordered around two chains wrapped together as the double helix.

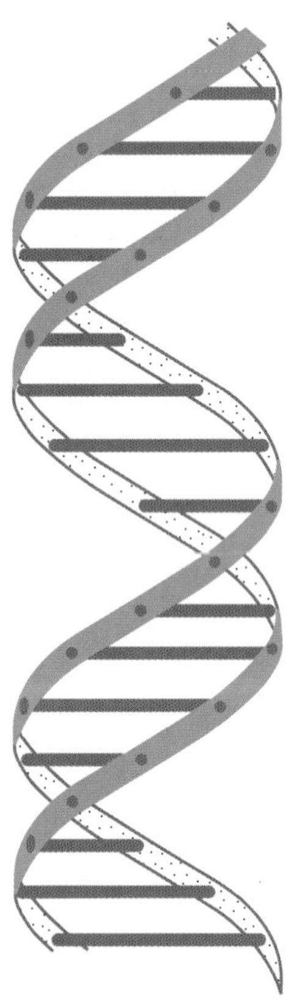

Fig. 2 *The double helix*

Genes produce a phenotype (manifestation of behaviour or characteristics based on genetic make-up and environment) and are viewed as dominant

or recessive. For the behaviour or characteristic to show in the phenotype, only one copy of a dominant gene is required (this can come from either parent), but, in the case of recessive genes, both copies are needed. Individuals with one copy of a recessive gene are known as carriers.

Evaluation of the biological approach

Strengths

- It is a scientific approach. The principles of the biological approach have always been based upon using scientific methods. Experiments have been used to establish the cause-and-effect relationships of physiology and behaviour.
- There is consequently a lot of good evidence for the biological basis of behaviour, and for the nature side of the nature–nurture debate. Throughout the last 150 years, famous experiments have told us more about the biological basis of behaviour. Examples are Karl Lashley's attempts to localise memory in the brain in the 1920s and Hubel and Wiesel's work in the 1950s and 1960s, when they recorded single-cell activity in the brain (Kandel and Squire, 2000).
- Measurement of physiology can be done objectively. With the development of technology, different aspects of an individual's physiology can be accurately measured by machines that are not open to subjectivity. Brain activity can be measured by scanning (e.g. PET scans) and recording with an electroencephalogram (EEG). Techniques that quantify galvanic skin response (GSR) measure the underlying arousal of an individual.
- The biological approach makes sense because, as human beings, we are embodied. We live in a physical body and this influences our behaviour, especially if the physical body is damaged in some way. The study of damaged physical bodies has also been useful, particularly with patients with brain injury (such as HM).
- Findings from the study of physiology can be used to help people. For example, the knowledge of neurotransmitters has led to the development of psychotropic drugs, such as antidepressants, to help those with mental disorders.

Limitations

- The biological approach is deterministic. It sees people as determined by their physiology (physiological determinism), genes (genetic determinism), evolution (evolutionary determinism), or a combination of all three (biological determinism). This means that free will is an illusion.

  Biological determinism can also mean that individuals could claim that they are not responsible for their actions. If this is applied to criminal behaviour, for example, it could be argued that offenders should not be punished because they cannot stop themselves. This type of defence has occasionally been used in court cases. In the USA, Stephen Mobley was unsuccessful when, in order to avoid the death penalty after being convicted of murder in 1991, he cited as a defence the inheritance of violence. His family had four generations of serious behavioural disorders (Denno, 2006). The existence or not of genes for aggression is very controversial and evidence is limited.
- The biological approach is reductionist and dehumanising. It reduces all human behaviour to biological processes and presents humans as 'biological machines'. Everything is seen as due to biology, and thereby humanity is robbed of its uniqueness. Francis Crick (1994, p3)

Link

The biological approach is applied to schizophrenia and mood disorders in Chapter 5, Schizophrenia and mood disorders, and to offending behaviour in Chapter 8, Forensic psychology.

AQA Examiner's tip

At AS Level, you were introduced to the biological approach. However, A2 Level requires more detail and places more emphasis on evaluating the approach rather than just describing it. This is applicable to all of the approaches in this chapter.

Link

To remind yourself about HM, see *AQA Psychology B AS*, Chapter 7, Remembering and forgetting, p181.

AQA Examiner's tip

One approach can be evaluated by comparing it with another approach. For example, the behaviourist approach is very different from the biological approach.

summed up the biological view: 'that "You", your joys and your sorrows, your memories and your ambitions, your sense of personal identity and free will, are in fact no more than the behaviour of a vast assembly of nerve cells and their associated molecules.' Advocates of the humanistic approach are the strongest critics here.

The biological approach is also reductionist because it sees humans as no different from other animals. The biology of all animals is the same, but this ignores the differences in the human brain leading to language, culture and technological development.

- The biological approach ignores many aspects of behaviour. First, it ignores the role of nurture (in the form of the environment, society, upbringing and learning in behaviour). There is a biological basis to behaviour, but it interacts with experiences. Some researchers accept a combination of both nature and nurture; this is known as bio-social theory.

  Secondly, the biological approach ignores subjective experience and individual meaning. The physiology of a kiss is nothing compared with the subjective experience and meaning of it, for example. Ignoring subjective experience is a problem with science generally.

- There are methodological problems. Technically, physiological measures are only correlated with behaviour. It may seem that the changes in the brain during scanning are causing thinking, but we can only talk about a correlation between them.

  Physiological processes are difficult to measure and thus must take place in a laboratory environment. For example, brain scans are made in artificial situations and cannot be made of real-life events.

- In terms of evolution, the biological approach is better at explaining behaviour after the event (i.e. the reason that this behaviour exists today is because it has evolved). Evolutionary theory is not that good at predicting what will happen. Prediction is a criterion of good science.

  Evolutionary theory also involves a lot of speculation about what humans were like when they first evolved, and this is subjective. In fact, the most vocal critics see evolutionary psychology as 'pseudo-science' (Rose and Rose, 2000).

Table 3 *Strengths and limitations of the biological approach*

Strengths	Limitations
Scientific approach	Deterministic
Good evidence to support	Reductionist
Objective measurement	Ignores nurture
Makes sense as we are embodied	Methodological problems with measuring physiology
Findings can be used to help people	Criticisms of evolutionary theory

Link

Determinism, reductionism and the nomothetic method are described in detail in Chapter 10, Debates in psychology.

Key points:

- The focus is upon the biological basis to all behaviour.
- Behaviour is caused by evolution and genes (functional level) and physiology (causal level).
- Physiology and behaviour, not subjective experience and individual meanings, are the area of study.
- This approach is scientific.
- This approach is deterministic, reductionist and nomothetic.

Summary questions

1. What is the key assumption of the biological approach?
2. Distinguish between the causal and functional levels of analysis.
3. Is the biological approach a scientific approach? Explain your answer.

The behaviourist approach

Learning objectives:

- understand what is meant by the behaviourist approach in psychology
- distinguish between classical and operant conditioning
- evaluate the behaviourist approach in psychology.

Hint

Assumptions of this approach

- All behaviour is learnt through the processes of conditioning, past experiences and the environment.
- Classical conditioning is learning through association.
- Operant conditioning is learning due to past reinforcements and punishments.

Link

The behaviourist approach is introduced in *AQA Psychology B AS*, in Chapter 1, Key approaches.

Key terms

Neo-behaviourism: the inclusion of social learning theory as part of the behaviourist approach.

The behaviourist approach (or behaviourism) developed at the beginning of the 20th century and dominated psychology for a large part of that century. It began as a reaction to ideas of the time (e.g. introspection and psychoanalysis) that concentrated on the mind.

In 1913, J.B. Watson wrote an article entitled 'Psychology as the behaviourist views it' in which he stated that psychologists should 'never use the terms consciousness, mental states, introspectively verify, imagery and like'. This established a key principle of behaviourism: studying only visible and observable behaviour. This is classic behaviourism.

Watson wished psychology to be a science comparable to biology or chemistry. He also attacked the idea of innate or instinctive factors (i.e. inherited characteristics).

Behaviourism is concerned with the learning of all behaviour, which occurs through conditioning (classical and operant). Watson (1924) summarised the view on learning:

> Give me a dozen healthy infants ... and I'll guarantee to take any one at random, and train him to become any type of specialist I might select ... regardless of his talents, penchants, tendencies, abilities, vocations, and race of his ancestors.
>
> ***(Watson**, 1924, p104)*

Classical conditioning is associated with the work of Ivan Pavlov and Watson; operant conditioning is associated with B.F. Skinner. Skinner's ideas are sometimes classed as radical behaviourism because he argued for the control of human society through behaviourist principles. This can be seen in his books *Science and Human Behaviour* (1953) and *Beyond Freedom and Dignity* (1971).

For behaviourists, there is 'no dividing line between man and brute. The behaviour of man, with all of its refinement and complexity, forms only a part of the behaviourist's total scheme of investigation' (Watson, 1913, p158). Studying non-human animals makes sense if we (humans and animals) are all the same.

Radical behaviourism presented human behaviour as entirely determined by past experiences and conditioning. In 1956, Skinner debated with Carl Rogers (a proponent of the humanistic approach) about the nature of free will (Rogers and Skinner, 1956).

Skinner developed his ideas further in the science-fiction book *Walden Two* (1966; originally written in 1945 and published in 1948). He presented a 'behaviourally engineered' utopia where operant conditioning was used to control society. Through applying the principles of reward and punishment, everybody had food, clothing and shelter, worked four hours a day, and lived peacefully together.

Other forms of behaviourism are methodological behaviourism and **neo-behaviourism**. Methodological behaviourism takes the view that all approaches in psychology use some aspects of behaviourism, and neo-behaviourism (e.g. social learning theory) attempts to include cognitive processes and ideas (Eysenck and Flanagan, 2001).

Approaches

Key terms

Extinction: in classical conditioning, the conditioned response (CR) will cease if the unconditioned stimulus (UCS) does not appear after the conditioned stimulus (CS).

Discrimination: in classical conditioning, the conditioned response (CR) is elicited by only the original conditioned stimulus (CS).

Generalisation: in classical conditioning, other stimuli similar to the original conditioned stimulus (CS) produce a conditioned response (CR).

Before conditioning

Food (UCS) → Saliva (UCR)
Bell (NS) No response

During conditioning

Bell + Food → Saliva

After conditioning

Bell (CS) → Saliva (CR)

Fig. 3 *Stages of classical conditioning*

Link

Behaviour therapies for anxiety disorders are introduced in Chapter 9, Anxiety disorders, in *AQA Psychology B AS*. Systematic desensitisation and aversion therapy are discussed in Chapters 6 and 7, respectively, in this book.

Classical conditioning

In the context of classical conditioning, Ivan Pavlov's work with dogs is the most quoted (summarised in Pavlov, 1927). It is an important series of studies. Pavlov was, however, a physiologist and his interest was in the secretion of juices during the digestion of food. The process of secretion is a reflex: the presence of food in the mouth (stimulus) causes salivation to occur (response). No conscious processing is involved: the stimulus automatically elicits the response.

During this research, Pavlov noted that the dogs would sometimes salivate (produce saliva) at the appearance of a particular scientist. Pavlov called these 'psychic secretions' and saw them as contaminating his study of reflexes (Littleton *et al.*, 2002); he set about testing these 'psychic secretions'.

Presenting a neutral stimulus (NS; e.g. bell ring) to the dogs just before food was given caused the dogs to salivate (unconditioned response, UCR). The neutral stimulus and the food (unconditioned stimulus, UCS) became paired together over time. Eventually, the ringing of the bell (now the conditioned stimulus, CS) elicited salivation (now called the conditioned response, CR). The learning of a reflexive response to a neutral stimulus in this way is known as classical or 'Pavlovian conditioning' (Figure 3).

But if the bell is rung and then no food appears, the dog will stop salivating at the sound of the bell. This is known as **extinction**. The dog can be taught to make the CR to specific tones of bell (known as **discrimination**) or spontaneously transfer the CR to similar objects, for example bell-like noises (known as **generalisation**).

In one of his many experiments, Pavlov conditioned the dogs to salivate to the sound of a tuning fork of 500 Hz rung before the food arrived. After conditioning, this sound produced an average of 50 drops of saliva in 30 seconds. Then Pavlov used tuning forks of different frequencies, for example, 600 Hz produced 25 drops of saliva. Response to other frequencies is generalisation, while only responding to 500 Hz is discrimination.

Watson took up the principles of classical conditioning developed by Pavlov, and tested them on a child, 'Albert B', known as 'Little Albert' (Watson and Rayner, 1920). This research aimed to show that a child could be conditioned to fear a specific object. Albert was allowed to play with a white rat and showed no fear. Then, as he was playing with the rat, the researchers made a loud noise which scared Albert. The noise was paired with the rat a number of times. Eventually, Albert showed a fear reaction at the appearance of the rat.

> The instant the rat was shown, the baby began to cry. Almost instantly he turned sharply to the left, fell over on left side, raised himself on all fours and began to crawl away so rapidly that he was caught with difficulty before reaching the edge of the table.
>
> *(Watson and Rayner, 1920)*

So powerful was the effect that the fear generalised and Albert was afraid of a rabbit, cotton wool and a fur coat.

Classical conditioning is used in the form of behaviour therapy to condition individuals to stop abnormal behaviours. **Systematic desensitisation**, for example, conditions positive associations with feared objects in phobias, while **aversion therapy** conditions negative associations with addictions. It is argued that individuals have learnt these abnormal behaviours, and it is a question of learning new associations.

Operant conditioning

Another form of conditioning is known as operant or instrumental conditioning. Pioneered by the work of B.F. Skinner, operant conditioning focused on learning that occurs as a result of feedback about the consequences of behaviour.

Edward Thorndike (1898) originally coined the law of effect: 'if a certain response has pleasant consequences, it is more likely than other responses to occur again in the same circumstances'. For example, if a rat by chance presses a lever and receives a food pellet, then the lever-pressing behaviour will continue. This process is positive reinforcement. However, if next time the lever is pressed there is a mild electric shock, the behaviour will stop. This is punishment.

These are the basic principles of operant conditioning, which Skinner developed through his years of work with rats and pigeons. Behaviourists distinguish between positive and negative reinforcement; positive and negative punishment; and continuous and partial reinforcement (Table 4).

Table 4 *Schedules of reinforcement*

Type of schedule	Description
Continuous reinforcement	Reinforcement after every correct response
Partial reinforcement	Fixed ratio reinforcement (FR) – 1 reinforcer every fixed number of correct responses (e.g. FR3 = 1 reinforcer after every 3 correct responses)
Fixed interval reinforcement (FI)	1 reinforcer given after fixed period of time provided that at least 1 correct response has been made during that time (e.g. FI10 = 1 reinforcer every 10 seconds provided that at least 1 correct response occurred during that time)
Variable ratio reinforcement (VR)	1 reinforcer given after an average number of correct responses (e.g. VR3 = 1 reinforcer after average of 3 correct responses)
Variable interval reinforcement (VI)	1 reinforcement given after average time interval provided at least one correct response has been made during that time (e.g. VR10 = 1 reinforcement after average 10 seconds provided 1 correct response occurred during that time

Hint

It may be useful to make a table comparing classical and operant conditioning.

Operant conditioning, in the form of behaviour modification, has been used to control behaviour. This technique was applied in the case of Sophie, a 10-year-old with a severe learning disability who deliberately injured herself (Colsey and Hatton, 1994). Table 5 shows the series of steps.

Table 5 *Table showing the steps taken to modify Sophie's behaviour*

Step	Actions
Step 1	Specify behaviour to change, e.g. throwing herself to the floor, biting herself, screaming, hitting herself and others, and throwing objects.
Step 2	Set goal to achieve – stopping the behaviours in Step 1.
Step 3	Set baseline of maladaptive behaviour – number of times per hour of each behaviour.
Step 4	Develop strategy to achieve goal – use of Jaffa Cakes as reinforcer for not showing behaviour in Step 1.
Step 5	Plan reinforcement schedule – Jaffa cake every time Sophie does not perform the behaviours in Step 1.
Step 6	Apply treatment – over 20 days of programme, undesired behaviour removed.

In an example known as token economy (Allyon and Azrin, 1968), individuals are rewarded with plastic tokens for acts of good behaviour, and punished with the removal of tokens for bad behaviour. The tokens can be exchanged later for something desirable. This is known as secondary reinforcement.

Link

For a discussion of the behaviourist approach as applied to treatment of offenders, see Chapter 8, Forensic psychology; for its application in substance abuse, see Chapter 7, Substance abuse; and for applications in stress management, see Chapter 6, Stress and stress management.

Evaluation of the behaviourist approach

Strengths

- Behaviourism has been a driving force in the development of psychology as a science. In the early 20th century, psychology was dominated by approaches that focused on the mind. These approaches used methods like introspection, where the individual describes their thought processes. There is no way of verifying the accuracy of what is said, and ultimately the development of psychology is limited. At the time of Watson's writing in 1913, psychology was the 'science of the phenomena of consciousness'.

  By concentrating on observable behaviour (and using the experimental method), behaviourism allowed psychology to develop as a science with objective, verifiable facts about behaviour.
- The experimental method is rigorous, controlled and replicable. The experiment allows the researcher control over variables, and the findings can then be replicated by other researchers. The use of the experiment has also produced 'universal principles of learning that apply across situations and species' (Littleton *et al.*, 2002).
- Evidence for the principles of conditioning comes from studies with non-human animals. Many of the behaviourists' findings come from work with rats and pigeons, as these can be studied in detail in a way that humans could not. Because conditioning occurs in the same way in all animals, what is learnt from how a rat behaves in a maze in response to rewards and punishments can be applied to human behaviour.
- Behaviour therapy focuses on the now and deals with resolving the individual's problem. For example, if a person has a fear of leaving their house, the therapist 'trains' the individual to overcome this problem. There is a clear definition of cure and measures of improvement. Other therapies, such as psychoanalysis, concentrate on the past, and sometimes show slow progress.
- Behaviour modification has proved to be effective in reducing problem behaviour. Goals and the steps by which these will be achieved are set out clearly, and the method is safer than drug treatment because drugs can have side effects.

Limitations

- The behaviourist approach is deterministic. It sees all behaviour as determined by past experiences that have been conditioned. Free will is an illusion.

  It can also be called 'environmental determinism' because behaviour is determined by the stimuli in the environment around.
- The approach is reductionist and mechanistic. It reduces all behaviour to stimulus–response units. A stimulus occurs and, because of conditioning, a certain response is given. The individual is treated as a machine where stimulus produces response (as when pressing a button on a machine produces a given response). This is what is meant by 'mechanistic'. Littleton *et al.* (2002, p180) wrote that, 'To portray humans as little more than glorified banks of available responses to be selected by the environment is seen as not only degrading but also scientifically inaccurate.'

Human beings can have conscious insight into their behaviour, and can actively change it.

Albert Bandura (1977a), a social learning theorist, believed that, if operant conditioning was right, 'people would behave like weather vanes, constantly shifting in radically different directions'. But individuals are generally consistent in their behaviour.

- The assumption is made that conditioned animal behaviour is the same as human behaviour. But this ignores the role of cognitive processes, even with non-human animals. For example, a pet cat learns through classical conditioning that the sound of a tin being opened signals food. But the cat has not just formed a reflex to respond to the sound; there is a notion of expectancy. There is the acquisition of the knowledge that the sound of the tin opening signals that the food is being put out. Expectancy is a cognitive process, and it is also not directly observable by the researcher. So even classical conditioning involves cognitive processes.

  Tolman (1932) suggested that rats form cognitive maps when running through a maze. Rather than just finding the shortest route through the maze to the food, rats pick up a picture of the maze, which they store in their memories.

  The cognitive approach emphasises that humans are making sense of the world and are not just stimulus–response machines. However, some of the ideas within the cognitive approach have been built on the work of behaviourism.
- There is evidence to contradict the principles of conditioning; an example is the concept of **learned helplessness**. Overmeier and Seligman (1967) gave dogs mild electric shocks to motivate them to jump back and forth over a low fence. After a while, the dogs gave up jumping back and forth, and lay down and accepted the punishment. According to operant conditioning principles, behaviour should change to avoid punishment. But where punishment is constant and unavoidable, individuals give up and accept the punishment. This behavioural response continues later even when there is no punishment.
- Behaviour therapy and behaviour modification do not seek the underlying reasons for problem behaviour, reasons that may cause it to reoccur in the future. Furthermore, problems, such as phobias, may not necessarily be learnt by conditioning; they could occur because of genetics or observational learning.

  Some forms of behaviour therapy can also be unpleasant for the participant: for example, flooding therapy forces the person to face their object of fear and learn a non-fear reaction to it. James (2000) reported the case of Debbie Holden, a person with anorexia nervosa. She was left in a hospital room with nothing, and only given her belongings back and privileges (reinforcement) when she ate food.

Table 6 *Strengths and limitations of the behaviourist approach*

Strengths	Limitations
Driving force in development of psychology as science	Deterministic
Use of experimental method	Reductionist
Evidence from animal studies	Assumption that animal behaviour and learning are same as human
Benefits of behaviour therapy	Contradictory evidence to principles of conditioning
Behaviour modification effective with problem behaviour	Problems with behaviour therapy and behaviour modification

Link

The learned helplessness theory of depression is discussed in Chapter 5, Stress and Schizophrenia and mood disorders.

Key points:

- Behaviour is learnt through conditioning.
- There are two types of conditioning: classical and operant.
- This approach uses experiments, often with non-human animals.
- It is deterministic, reductionist, nomothetic, and on the nurture side of the nature–nurture debate.
- The principles of conditioning are applied in behaviour therapy and in behaviour modification programmes.

Summary questions

4. What is the key difference between the behaviourist approach and the biological approach?
5. Name two differences between classical and operant conditioning.
6. Why does the behaviourist approach study non-human animals?

Social learning theory

Learning objectives:

- understand how social learning theory is a bridge between traditional behaviourism and the cognitive approach
- understand what is meant by social learning theory in psychology
- evaluate social learning theory in psychology.

Hint

Assumptions of this approach

- Behaviour is learnt from a combination of observation of others' behaviour and expectation of reinforcement or punishment for copying what is seen.
- It combines principles from the behaviourist and cognitive approaches.
- Imitation of others' behaviour is a key idea.

Link

Social learning theory is introduced in *AQA Psychology B AS*, Chapter 1, Key approaches.

AQA Examiner's tip

SLT is introduced at AS Level but at A2 there needs to be more evaluation, including the role of SLT as a bridge between behaviourism and the cognitive approach.

Link

The terms used in SLT such as 'observational learning', 'imitation' and 'identification' are covered in more detail in *AQA Psychology B AS* in Chapter 3, Gender development.

SLT as a bridge between behaviourism and the cognitive approach

Social learning theory (SLT) is seen by some not as a separate approach but as part of the behaviourist approach (neo-behaviourism) or as part of the cognitive approach. SLT is treated as a separate approach here because historically it attempted to build upon the ideas of behaviourism and bridge the gap to the cognitive approach. These approaches have many ideas in common (Table 7).

Table 7 *Similarities and differences between SLT and the behaviourist and cognitive approaches*

	Behaviourist approach	Cognitive approach
Similarities to SLT	Role of reinforcement Behaviour learnt	Role of cognitive processes Focus on human behaviour rather than animals
Differences from SLT	Importance of expectancy SLT looks forward while behaviourism looks backwards Distinction between learning and performance in SLT, while they are the same for behaviourism Animals not seen as same as humans in SLT	Observational learning not part of cognitive approach Cognitive approach concentrates more on cognitive processes, e.g. schemas SLT still tends to focus on external behaviour, while cognitive approach interested in internal processes

Principles of SLT

Albert Bandura developed SLT in the 1960s to explain human behaviour and learning in a more complex way than the stimulus–response of the behaviourist approach. He made the observation that:

> Learning would be exceeding laborious, not to mention hazardous, if people had to rely solely on the effects of their own actions to inform them what to do [and so] from observing others one forms an idea of how new behaviours are performed, and on later occasions this coded information serves as a guide of action.
>
> *(**Bandura**, 1977b, p22)*

Playing down classical conditioning and reflexes, Bandura emphasised two parts to learning:

- **Observational learning** This is learning of behaviour from observing the behaviour of others and then imitating it, or, in the case of children, learning through identification. However, imitation is not automatic.
- **Expectancy** Behaviour will only be copied if there is an expectancy of reinforcement for doing so. A child, for example, watches an aggressive adult winning a fight. This sets in the child's mind the expectancy of winning by using aggression and the child copies the aggression for this reason. This means that cognitive processes are involved in the SLT.

The cognitive processes involved are:

- attention – concentrating on the model and relevant behaviour
- retention – keeping what is seen stored in the memory
- reproduction – being able to reproduce the behaviour seen
- motivation – the presence of reinforcement (or punishment) motivates the individual to reproduce the observed behaviour (or not).

Not all models are copied, and identification with a model depends upon certain characteristics, the likelihood being increased by:

- appropriateness of the model's behaviour, particularly in relation to gender behaviour
- relevance of the model's behaviour (e.g. boys imitate male models)
- similarity of the model to observer
- warmth and friendliness (warm and friendly adults are imitated more than unfriendly ones)
- the model having power
- the model being admired
- the consistency of the model's behaviour.

There are a number of key differences between SLT and operant conditioning:

- Although they both talk about reinforcement, the process has a different place in the two approaches. For Bandura (1977b) 'reinforcement serves principally as an informative and motivational operation rather than as a mechanical response strengthener'. He argued that reinforcement has a role not only in the later imitation of the behaviour but also in focusing the attention on the model, while in behaviourism reinforcement determines behaviour. Thus, SLT is less deterministic than behaviourism.
- In behaviourism, the focus is working backwards from the behaviour, i.e. the feedback after the behaviour occurs. In SLT, it is about working forwards: after observing the behaviour the individual thinks ahead about the expected feedback if the behaviour is imitated.
- Behaviourism dismisses cognitive processes, but in SLT individuals must memorise the observed behaviour and store it until needed (i.e. an appropriate situation arises in which to imitate it). Thus, there is a difference between learning (from observation) and performance of the behaviour. In the behaviourist approach, no such difference is made.

The 'Bobo' doll experiments

Albert Bandura is famous for the series of experiments that he did at Stanford University, California, using the 'Bobo' doll to test for the imitation of aggressive behaviour by young children. The original study was reported as Bandura *et al.* (1961), with key developments reported later (Bandura *et al.*, 1963; Bandura 1965).

Research study: Bandura *et al.* (1961)

Aim: To investigate the imitation of aggression in children.

Method: This study involved 36 boys and 36 girls with an average age of 52 months. They were divided into eight experimental groups of six, and one control group of 24 children. Each group was matched on pre-experiment aggression ratings made by teachers and observers.

The basic design of the experiment was to place the children alone in a playroom for 10 minutes with an adult acting as the model. The nine groups in the experiment were divided into three types:

'Aggressive conditions': the adult hit the five-foot high 'Bobo' doll, and performed distinct acts of aggression, such as sitting on the doll, throwing it in the air, or hitting it with a wooden mallet. Distinct phrases like 'Sock him in the nose' were spoken. There were four 'aggressive conditions': aggressive female model with female participants; aggressive male model with male participants; aggressive female model with male participants; aggressive male model with female participants.

'Non-aggressive conditions': the adult spent the time playing alone with the toys, and ignored the 'Bobo' doll and the child. There were four 'non-aggressive conditions': non-aggressive female model with female participants; non-aggressive male model with male participants; non-aggressive female model with male participants; non-aggressive male model with female participants.

Control group: the child was alone in the playroom with no adult model.

The child was deliberately frustrated by the experimenters. They showed the child new toys, got them excited about playing with the new toys for two minutes, and then stopped the child from doing so. Then the child was left in the playroom for 20 minutes with a selection of other toys, including a three-foot high 'Bobo' doll.

The child's aggressive behaviour was observed through a one-way mirror, and by an adult sitting in the corner of the playroom.

The 20-minute observation period was divided into five-second intervals to give a total of 240 response units. For each unit of time, the participants were scored on three measures of 'direct imitation': physical aggression towards the 'Bobo' doll, verbal aggression and verbal non-aggression towards it.

Results: This experiment made a number of findings about aggression and imitation:

- There were significantly more aggressive acts towards the 'Bobo' doll in the 'aggressive conditions' than in the 'non-aggressive' or control conditions. For example, the mean physical aggression score was 51 in the 'aggressive conditions' compared with 4 in 'non-aggressive conditions'.
- Boys had significantly higher physical aggression scores towards the 'Bobo' doll than the girls, but not for verbal aggression.
- There was a significantly higher aggression score for imitation of the adult male model for physical aggression by both sexes.
- Children in the 'non-aggressive conditions' obtained lower aggression scores than the children in the control condition.

Conclusion: The children learned the aggressive acts from watching the models, but other factors also affected their learning.

Evaluation: The experiments took place in a laboratory environment and were artificial. They had low ecological validity.

Bandura used this same basic experimental design in future experiments.

In the study by Bandura *et al.* (1963), the experiment compared the amount of imitation of aggression and non-aggression between live adult models and filmed ones. There was greater imitation for the filmed models.

In another study (Bandura, 1965), the children were shown a film of adult models. There were three possible endings to the film:

- The adult was aggressive towards the 'Bobo' doll (control condition).
- The adult was aggressive towards the 'Bobo' doll and was then rewarded by another adult with sweets and lemonade to restore their energy ('reward condition').
- After the aggression, the adult was punished ('punishment condition').

When left in the playroom, the children in the first and second conditions were equally aggressive towards the 'Bobo' doll (mean number of imitated aggressive responses = 2.5) compared with the children in the 'punishment condition' (mean = 1.5 acts).

Later the children were **asked** to copy the behaviour they had seen on the film. In all three conditions, the children were equally as aggressive (mean = 3.5 acts). This research made the distinction between learning the behaviour and performance of the behaviour based on expectation of reward or punishment.

AQA Examiner's tip

It is important to know the similarities and differences between the SLT and behaviourist and SLT and cognitive approaches.

Evaluation of SLT

Strengths

- SLT adds to the principles of behaviourism by stressing the existence of cognitive processes. Human behaviour is learnt in a different way from other animals' behaviour because:
  - humans have the ability to store what they have seen
  - humans are able to think ahead as to when to copy a behaviour.
- The principles of SLT are based on Bandura's laboratory experiments. The experiment is the most rigorous method in psychology and the best by which to establish cause-and-effect relationships.
- SLT is less deterministic and reductionist than the behaviourist approach. Bandura (1977a) talked more of an interaction between behaviour and the environment; he called this 'reciprocal determinism': 'Behaviour partly creates the environment and the resultant environment, in turn influences the behaviour.'
- In terms of child development, SLT is good at explaining specific imitation of behaviour, such as when a little girl copies her mother who is cooking.

  Also learning by trial and error, as in operant conditioning, can be dangerous for survival. Bandura wrote that 'most people would never survive their formative years because mistakes often result in fatal consequences' (Bandura, 1973, p68).
- SLT is able to explain the development of culture and complex behaviours, especially in technologically developed societies. Children can learn behaviour from observing the media rather than just individuals around them, and this can explain the widespread development of cultural behaviours. The behaviourist approach is not really able to do this, because using the principles of conditioning the whole process would take far too long to achieve.

Link

SLT is applied to offending behaviour in Chapter 8, Forensic psychology.

Limitations

- Although there is some reference to cognitive processes in SLT, the theory does not specify how the observed behaviour is stored or reproduced. The cognitive approach concentrates more on explaining the internal processes.
- In fact, SLT still places most of its emphasis on the external (observable) behaviour. Thus, it ignores subjective experience.
- The experiments performed by Bandura took place in a laboratory environment and were therefore artificial. They have low ecological validity as well as other weaknesses that apply to the experimental method generally.
- There are specific criticisms of Bandura's experiments about aggression. For example, Cumberbatch (1992) noted experimental weaknesses that encouraged the children to be aggressive towards the 'Bobo' doll:
  - Demand characteristics of the experiment made it clear to the children what was expected.
  - The 'Bobo' doll is pleasant to hit because it always bounces back up.
  - The novelty of the 'Bobo' doll would increase aggression scores.
  - The film lasted over three minutes and contained only aggressive acts towards the 'Bobo' doll.
- SLT is not very good at explaining the learning of abstract ideas, such as the moral principles of justice and fairness; these are hard to learn simply by observing another's behaviour and copying it.

Link

For a review of the weaknesses of the experimental method, see Chapter 11, Methods in psychology.

Table 8 *Strengths and limitations of social learning theory*

Strengths	Limitations
Adds cognitive processes to behaviourist principles Based on laboratory experiments Less deterministic and reductionist Good at explaining specific imitated behaviour Explains development of culture and complex behaviours	Does not explain how cognitive processes work Still concentrates mostly on external behaviour Laboratory experiments are artificial Criticisms of 'Bobo' doll studies Not good at explaining learning of abstract ideas

Summary questions

7 Identify one key similarity and one key difference between the behaviourist approach and social learning theory.

8 Describe two criticisms of Bandura's experiments with the 'Bobo' doll.

9 How is vicarious reinforcement different from direct reinforcement?

Key points:

- SLT is a bridge between the behaviourist and cognitive approaches.
- Learning involves observation of behaviour and then copying because of the expectation of reinforcement.
- SLT involves cognitive processes, for example expectancy.
- SLT is based upon experimental work by Albert Bandura.
- SLT is less deterministic than the behaviourist approach.

The cognitive approach

Learning objectives:

- understand what is meant by the cognitive approach in psychology
- understand the idea that thoughts influence behaviour
- evaluate the cognitive approach in psychology.

Hint

Assumptions of the cognitive approach

- This approach focuses upon the cognitive processes of the individual.
- Human beings are seen as information processors.
- Individuals are not automatically responding to stimuli (S–R), but are trying to make sense of the world (S–O–R).

Link

- The cognitive approach is introduced in *AQA Psychology B AS*, in Chapter 1, Key approaches.
- Chapter 4, Cognition and law, explores the cognitive processes related to eye-witness testimony.

Computer

Input ➔ Storage ➔ Retrieval ➔ Output

Human

Stimulus ➔ Attention ➔ Memory ➔ Response

Fig. 4 *The information processing approach applied to human behaviour*

Link

Episodic memory is covered in *AQA Psychology B AS*, in Chapter 7, Remembering and forgetting.

The cognitive approach developed in the 1960s as a reaction to the behaviourists ignoring what was happening inside the head. Although proponents of the cognitive approach agreed with many of the ideas of behaviourism, they were unhappy to see humans as simple stimulus–response machines. So the cognitive approach moved the focus to cognitive processes (the 'organism' in the formula stimulus–organism–response; S–O–R). The stimulus occurs; the individual makes sense of it and then responds. Thus, the same stimulus can produce different responses in individuals depending on how each one makes sense of the situation.

Humans as information processors

The cognitive approach is underwritten by the concept of information processing, which sees cognitive processes as like those of a computer. The information processing approach holds that 'information is assumed to be received via the senses, further processed or transformed, and then used to guide action and behaviour' (Littleton *et al.*, 2002, p187). There are a series of stages in information processing including attention and memory (Figure 4).

The cognitive approach is involved with processes in the mind rather than with the physiology of the brain (as in the biological approach).

Making sense of the world

A key part of how we make sense of the world is the way in which information is stored in the brain, via, it is thought, categories, concepts and schemas, which are ways of organising information about the world into similar groupings.

Knowledge of the world that is stored as schemas is not in the form of single concepts but a cluster of relevant ideas including individual past experiences. So an individual's schema about restaurants contains factual information about restaurants, how to behave in them (cognitive scripts), and personal experiences of restaurants (episodic memory).

When an event happens (a stimulus), we retrieve information from the appropriate schema, and this guides our response. For example, if a passing stranger stands on your foot in a crowded room, you will try to make sense of why this happened. Was it an accident or a deliberate act of provocation? Based on past information, you will usually make the attribution that it was accidental because of the situation. However, certain individuals always perceive such events as deliberate provocation. These individuals make sense of the world through the hostile attribution bias (Dodge, 1986); this is the tendency to view the world as a hostile and threatening place, the appropriate response to which is aggression. For such individuals, ambiguous stimuli lead to an aggressive response, which leads to problems. Cognitive-behavioural therapy (CBT) would help to change such attributions.

Mischel (1973) distinguished five variables that influence the response to a stimulus:

- competencies – the individual's unique set of abilities
- encodings – how individuals categorise the world

Link

CBT is covered in Chapter 5, Schizophrenia and mood disorders.

AQA Examiner's tip

Make a list of the different cognitive processes, like memory, that influence behaviour, and say how they influence behaviour.

- expectancies – how the individual expects the world to be
- values
- plans.

Together these variables influence the attribution process and, consequently, behaviour. Take the example of a job interview (stimulus) and the response of two candidates: one confident and the other nervous. The nervous candidate expects the interview to be hard and categorises the event as stressful. The confident candidate sees the interview as an opportunity to talk about their skills and expects that the questions asked will facilitate this. The same event produces different responses based on how the individual makes sense of the world.

The study of cognitive development is concerned with how individuals learn categories, concepts and schemas about the world; social cognition is interested in the ways in which individuals make attributions about the reasons for other people's behaviour.

Evaluation of the cognitive approach

Strengths

- The cognitive approach builds on the work of the behaviourists by including cognitive processes between stimulus and response. Cognitive processes are the focus of human behaviour: humans make sense of the stimulus before responding; we are not simply responding in an unthinking way to a stimulus.
- The cognitive approach is less deterministic than other approaches. It allows for individuals to think before responding to the stimulus. But individuals do not have complete autonomy (as proposed by the humanistic approach); they are limited by the way in which cognitive processes work.

  For example, the visual system is primed to look at moving objects (as opposed to stationary ones), but you can choose whether or not to pay further attention to the object. A lot of Premiership football grounds have moving advertisements around the pitch. The eye is automatically attracted to movement, but then you can choose to look back at the game. Allowing autonomy within certain limits is classed as 'soft determinism'.
- This approach takes a middle position in the nature–nurture debate. How the cognitive processes work are inherited (nature), but the content on which the processes operate is learnt (nurture). The process of category formation in cognitive development is innate, but the actual categories stored in memory are learnt.
- This approach uses rigorous methods of study with, first and foremost, the experiment, but also computer modelling of cognitive processes.
- Knowledge about cognitive processes has been applied to help individuals in cognitive-behavioural therapy (CBT). For example, Clark (1989) proposed a cognitive approach to panic attacks. Clark believed that individuals misinterpret bodily sensations (e.g. a racing pulse) as a sign of a catastrophe, such as a heart attack, and this begins a panic attack. CBT helps the individual to reinterpret the bodily sensations as non-catastrophic and stop the panic reaction. CBT has been found to be more effective than drug treatment in reducing panic attacks (Clark *et al.*, 1994).

Link

For applications of CBT, see Chapter 5, Schizophrenia and mood disorders, and Chapter 8, Forensic psychology.

Limitations

- It is not possible to see the cognitive processes at work, only the behaviour that results from them. Thus, it is assumed, from the way the person behaves, that attributions, for example, have taken place in the 'black box' of the brain.
- The cognitive approach is good at describing the cognitive processes involved in behaviour, but it is less able to explain why they happen. For example, when attributing the behaviour of others, individuals often make the fundamental attribution error. This is the tendency to make a dispositional attribution (it is the individual's fault) rather than a situational attribution (it is the fault of the situation) despite the evidence. The cognitive approach is not very good at explaining why the fundamental attribution error occurs.
- The cognitive approach is reductionist: it reduces human cognitive processes to those of a computer. In doing so, it is also mechanistic because it treats the cognitive processes as those of a machine. Some supporters of the cognitive approach say that the computer is an analogy, others that the brain is a 'flesh computer'. The latter view is more reductionist and mechanistic.
- There is too much emphasis on the information-processing approach that sees the brain as a computer. 'This metaphor is limited, however, because it does not acknowledge that human beings are biological organisms that have evolved for life on Earth' (Medin *et al.*, 2001, pp8–9).

  Because of this overemphasis on the computer analogy, it is assumed that cognitive processes are rational, and, therefore, if they are not rational, there is an error. But humans are different from computers because of emotions that are intertwined with all aspects of behaviour. For example, memories are not simply stored facts (semantic memory): episodic memory contains our personal, emotional autobiography. It is triggered by emotions, includes emotions and can be altered by them. False memory is a product of emotions and computers do not suffer from it.
- There are limitations with using experimental methods to study cognitive processes. For example, experimental studies of memory use lists of words (sometimes even nonsense syllables) in an artificial recall task. In some studies, individuals are given forced-choice questions. Qualitative methods focus on individuals talking about their everyday use of memory and would allow a deeper insight into the cognitive processes.

Table 9 *Strengths and limitations of the cognitive approach*

Strengths	Limitations
Adds cognitive processes to behaviourist ideas	Not possible to see cognitive processes at work
Less deterministic than other approaches	Not good at explaining why cognitive processes happen as they do
Takes middle position in nature–nurture debate	Reductionist
Uses rigorous methods, e.g. experiment	Too much emphasis on brain as computer
Ideas applied in cognitive-behavioural therapy	Limitations of using experiment

Link

For information about the false memory debate, see Chapter 4, Cognition and law.

Key points:

- The focus is on cognitive processes, which underpin all behaviour.
- The cognitive approach sees cognitive processing as similar to how a computer operates.
- The individual's cognitive processes mediate between stimulus and response, producing S–O–R.
- Methods used include experiments and computer models.
- The approach holds the middle position in some debates: weak (or soft) determinism; and nature–nurture debate.

Summary questions

10 How is the S–O–R idea of the cognitive approach different from the behaviourist approach?

11 How does the attribution of other people's behaviour influence our own behaviour?

12 Name one problem with using a computer analogy for the human brain and behaviour.

The psychodynamic approach

Learning objectives:

- understand what is meant by the psychodynamic approach in psychology
- understand Freud's theory of personality structure and development
- evaluate the psychodynamic approach in psychology.

Hint

Assumptions of this approach

- Early childhood experiences determine adult behaviour and personality.
- The focus of this approach is the unconscious mind.
- The personality is made up of different elements (id, ego and superego) in conflict.

Link

- The psychodynamic approach is introduced in *AQA Psychology B AS*, in Chapter 1, Key approaches.
- Bowlby's views and subsequent criticism are discussed in Chapter 1, Social development.
- The case study method is evaluated in Chapter 11, Methods in psychology.

The psychodynamic approach covers the ideas of Sigmund Freud and those who developed his ideas, for example Erik Erikson and Melanie Klein. Technically, the term 'psychoanalytic' refers only to Sigmund Freud and his work (Thomas, 1996).

Basic assumptions

Despite the differences in the individual theories within psychodynamics, there are basic assumptions common to psychodynamics (Thomas, 1996):

- Human behaviour and personality are largely determined by unconscious motives. Our behaviour is caused by the unconscious mind, which we cannot consciously access. Thus 'our ordinary accounts, to ourselves and others (including psychologists) of what we do, what we feel and what happens to us are at best limited and most of the time are likely to be inaccurate' (Thomas, 1996, p286).
- Our understanding of ourselves is distorted by defence mechanisms. What little insight we have into our conscious mind does not provide an accurate picture of who we are. Through defence mechanisms, such as repression and projection, we distort reality to avoid the psychological pain of the truth. But these defence mechanisms originate in the unconscious mind, so we do not know that we are doing it.
- Experiences and relationships in the first few years of life set the pattern for what is in the unconscious mind, and thus the individual's personality and behaviour in adulthood. For example, John Bowlby said that an infant who does not form a secure attachment to the mother in the first year of life will, without fail, have problems in later life. The lack of an attachment sets patterns of behaviour in the unconscious mind and these determine adult behaviour, such as an inability to form close relationships.
- The best way to study humans is through the case study method. This allows the individual to be studied in detail, and what is said and done can be interpreted by the analyst for the underlying unconscious motives.

Sigmund Freud (1856–1939)

Freud was writing about the individuals whom he studied as patients in analysis. His writings span a period of nearly 50 years. Freud's theory, which was developed during the process of treating and writing about his patients, was not described in a simple, coherent way. In fact, there are places where his writings contradict each other, and he did not make it clear when new ideas superseded old ones. However, three main areas of Freud's theory can be drawn out; these relate to the structure of personality, the structure of the mind, and the stages of psychosexual development.

The structure of the personality

Freud described the personality as comprising three parts: the id, the ego and the superego. The id, which exists in the unconscious mind, is concerned with instant gratification and is dominated by the instinctual forces. The id is present at birth, while the other two parts of the personality develop in the early years of life. The superego, which develops during the phallic stage of psychosexual development, is the moral part of the personality and includes the conscience. The id and the superego are in conflict, and the ego must maintain equilibrium between them and with the realities of society.

The ego may use defence mechanisms to protect the conscious mind from discovering what is in the id. For example, repression is motivated forgetting where unpleasant memories are forced deep into the unconscious mind so that they cannot be consciously recalled. The only signs that the memories exist are manifested in, for example, phobias. In analysis, the therapist uses 'clues' like this to discover what is hidden in the unconscious mind.

The structure of the mind

The mind also comprises three parts: unconscious, conscious and pre-conscious. The majority of the mind is the unconscious (or, technically, the dynamic unconscious). Like an iceberg, only a small part is visible above the surface, and this comprises the conscious and pre-conscious parts of the mind. The conscious mind is what we are aware of, and the pre-conscious is what we can become aware of if we switch our attention.

The psychosexual stages of development

According to Freud, much of who we are as adults is established in the first five years of life during three key stages of psychosexual development. Freud was interested in describing where the libido (an instinctive energy) was focused in the child's body.

In the first year of life, the libido is focused around the mouth; this is the oral stage of psychosexual development. The child gains pleasure from sucking and then biting when the teeth appear. Too much or too little pleasure can lead to fixation. It is almost as if the individual becomes trapped in this stage in their unconscious mind. Freud believed that oral fixation manifests itself as overeating, thumb-sucking as an adult, or smoking.

The second stage of psychosexual development (when the child is two to three years old) is the anal stage. Now the focus of pleasure for the child is control of the bowels, and the process of toilet training can cause conflict. Failure to develop properly here can lead to an anal-retentive personality. Someone with this type of personality keeps everything in, including emotion, and is characterised as being mean with money or obstinate. The opposite is an anal-expulsive personality: someone who is too generous, always giving out. These fixations are again concentrated in the unconscious mind, so the individual will not consciously know why they are being mean or generous.

The third stage of psychosexual development occurs when the child is three to five years old and is termed the phallic stage; this stage is different for boys and girls. Most of what Freud wrote about this stage concerned boys and the Oedipus complex. Boys develop sexual interest for their mothers as the libido is now focused in the genitals. But the child is also concerned about his father finding out about these desires. This causes the boy to feel castration anxiety (the fear that the father will castrate him). To overcome such a powerful fear, the child identifies with the father. It is through this process of identification that the superego (an internalisation of the punishing father) develops and there is appropriate gender development.

The experience of girls during the phallic stage has been described as the Electra complex. Freud was less clear about the details. Because of her sexual attention towards her father, the girl comes into conflict with her

Approaches

Link

For the implications for moral development, see Chapter 3, Moral development, pp 48–51.

AQA Examiner's tip

The psychodynamic approach appears at AS Level, but A2 Level requires more sophisticated knowledge, including more evaluation and discussion of developments by post-Freudians.

mother. Not only does the girl experience penis envy of the father but she also believes that her mother has castrated herself and her daughter. To resolve this conflict the girl identifies with the mother, leading to the development of the superego and appropriate gender development.

Freud also described two other stages of psychosexual development, but these were of limited importance to him; these are the latency stage (six years to puberty) and the genital stage (puberty to adulthood).

The post-Freudians

Psychodynamics has been described as 'either an argument with him [Freud] or a self-conscious tidying up of loose ends' (Billig, 1999).

Those who developed Freud's ideas are known as post-Freudians or neo-Freudians. There are many of them, and how their ideas developed depended to some extent on when and where they worked (e.g. Germany, Britain or the USA).

Note that, because Carl Jung broke with Freud in 1913, there is some dispute as to whether he is a post-Freudian or whether he set up his own separate branch of psychology (known as analytical psychology).

Table 10 *Main distinctions between post-Freudians and Sigmund Freud*

Paid less attention to:	Paid more attention to:
id	ego
psychosexual stages	development throughout lifespan
instincts	role of culture and society

Erik Erikson (1902–1994)

Erikson followed Freud's ideas of stages of development, but expanded them to cover the whole lifespan rather than just childhood. Erikson devised eight stages that individuals pass through during their lives; a ninth was added, after his death, by his wife (Erikson, 1997). At each stage, conflict arises that centres around two possible outcomes (Table 11).

Table 11 *Erikson's eight stages of psychosocial development*

Stage	Age (years)	Name	Conflict
1	0–1	Basic trust vs basic mistrust	Trust vs suspicious, insecurity
2	1–3	Autonomy vs shame and doubt	Sense of autonomy/self-esteem vs shame and self-doubt
3	3–5/6	Initiative vs guilt	Initiate activities vs fear of punishment, guilt about feelings
4	7 12	Industry vs inferiority	Sense of competence and achievement, self-confidence vs feelings of inadequacy and inferiority
5	12–18	Identity vs role confusion	Strong person identity vs confusion
6	20s	Intimacy vs isolation	Ability to experience love vs isolation
7	20s–60s	Generativity vs stagnation	Wider outlook vs lack of growth, boredom and self involvement
8	60s+	Integrity vs despair	Sense of satisfaction, acceptance of death vs regret, fear of death

In the ninth stage (80 to 90s), the individual reflects upon all the other stages and experiences growing frailty and loss of ability. The positive outcome is gerotranscendence (a wider cosmic understanding and sense of peace towards death).

Similarities between Erikson's ideas and Freud's

- Erikson accepted Freud's ideas about the three parts of the personality, and three parts of the mind.
- Erikson also agreed that the stages of development were genetically determined.
- Both argued that there is a conflict to be resolved at each stage of development

Key differences between Erikson's ideas and Freud's

- Erikson placed more emphasis on social factors than Freud, and he talked of psychosocial development rather than psychosexual development. He was also more interested in the development of the ego.
- Erikson believed that there are stages of development throughout life not just in childhood.
- Although both argued that there is a conflict to be resolved at each stage of development, for Freud the conflict was related to the family, whereas, for Erikson, the early stages involve conflicts related to the family, but conflicts in later stages of childhood relate to school and peers.
- Erikson placed more emphasis on the development of the ego, whereas Freud was interested in the id.
- Erikson used a wide range of research methods, including anthropological studies of Native American groups and **psychobiography** of famous historical figures (e.g. Martin Luther and Gandhi). Erikson also studied children and adolescents.

Evaluation of the psychodynamic approach

Strengths

- The psychodynamic approach gives the first detailed theory of the human condition. No one individual has written as much as Sigmund Freud about human behaviour, personality and motivations. Other approaches do not explain behaviour as fully as this one.
- Because it involves listening to what is said, the case study method, as used in this approach, provides a comprehensive account of individuals' experiences. However, what is said is then interpreted by the analyst for the underlying meaning in the unconscious.
- The use of the case study method allows detailed, qualitative data to be collected. More information can be collected about the individual's whole life, whereas the experimental method is just concerned with what happens during the experiment.

  The psychodynamic approach involves the study of individuals rather than groups of people, and each individual matters rather than being a number or a representative of the population as a whole.
- The psychodynamic approach highlighted that things are not always what they seem. There are hidden reasons for people's behaviour and problems in their unconscious and/or in their past. Seeking the hidden origins of problems in childhood has become accepted as normal in today's society, and it shows how Freud's ideas have influenced society.

  The approach can also explain why people behave in an apparently irrational way, or say one thing and do another.

Take it further

Melanie Klein (1882–1960) pioneered close observation and interpretation of children's play.

Key differences between Klein and Freud.

- Klein studied young children and adults.
- Klein emphasised first 2–3 years as most important. Development of the superego through a form of Oedipus complex occurs here, which is younger than Freud said.
- The superego is an introjection of the punishing mother and the punishing father for Klein.

British Object Relations School believed infants have an innate drive to attachment with people and that the child's need to feel loved by the primary carer is as important as the drive for pleasure described by Freud. These ideas influenced John Bowlby (1907–1990) in his work on maternal deprivation. Other British Object Relations theorists included Donald Winnicott (1896–1971) and W.Ronald Fairbairn (1889–1964).

Key terms

Psychobiography: a study of the life of an individual and the interpretation of their behaviour using psychoanalytic principles.

Link

Attachment is covered in more detail in Chapter 1, Social development.

AQA Examiner's tip

Make a table showing the similarities and differences between Freud and individual post-Freudians to help you remember them for exam questions.

Link

Case studies as a method appear in Chapter 1, Key approaches, and Chapter 4, Research methods, in *AQA Psychology B AS* and in more detail in Chapter 11 of this book, Methods in psychology.

- The psychodynamic approach takes a middle position in many of the debates in psychology. It is idiographic because it concentrates on the individual but also nomothetic because of the general principles of the theory. It is holistic because it concentrates on the individual's life but reductionist because all behaviour is reduced to unconscious motives. Finally, in relation to the nature side of the nature–nurture debate, it emphasises that some behaviour is instinctive (e.g. the stages of psychosexual development), but it adopts the nurture position when stressing that how parents interact with the child matters (e.g. toilet training and strictness).

Limitations

- The psychoanalytic approach is based upon hypothetical constructs, such as the id and the ego, which cannot be seen and tested. This has led to the criticism that it is not science (Eysenck, 1985). Also, it does not allow for predictions that can be proved or disproved, known as the scientific principle of falsification (Popper, 1959).

  But defenders of Freud have argued that, by the principles of his day, Freud's work was 'science' in the sense of making systematic and careful observation of patients (Ashfield, 2000).

- The use of the case study method has limitations. It is not possible to generalise the findings to others, yet Freud based his universal theory on case studies of a small number of patients. For example, the Oedipus complex may be found in a particular kind of family structure where the father is dominant yet distant as in the Jewish patriarchal family in which Freud grew up (Stevens, 2002).

  Furthermore, it is not possible to establish cause and effect using this method. Establishing a causal relationship is only possible with the experimental method. Yet Freud talked about causes of problems in childhood and their effects in adult behaviour.

- The psychodynamic approach is doubly deterministic. It explains our behaviour as determined by early childhood experiences and thus what is in the id and unconscious mind. Any free will we think we have is an illusion.

- Because most of the mind is made up of the unconscious to which we have no access, it means that any conscious ideas we have about our behaviour are also an illusion. If things are not what they seem, the reasons we give for our behaviour cannot be right.

  Furthermore, it means that every behaviour has a hidden meaning, and there are no accidents. According to Freud, this is shown in Freudian slips (such as slips of the tongue): the true meaning in the unconscious comes out in such mistakes. Freud gave the example of a doctor who accidentally untied the bow of a female patient's dressing gown as he was leaving. Freud saw this as evidence of the erotic desire in the unconscious. Reason (2000) re-analysed this from the viewpoint of cognitive psychology as an 'action slip'. This is an automatic behaviour taking over when consciously distracted. The doctor often untied gowns to examine patients (automatic behaviour) and this behaviour took over because he was distracted as he was leaving.

- Freud has been criticised because he mainly studied aristocratic Viennese women and no children, yet much of his theory is about child development.

  The only recorded case study of Freud's that involved a child was of five-year-old 'Little Hans'. Freud met the child between 1908 and

1909, but most of the analysis took place through questions and answers in letters between Freud and Hans's father. This study is quoted as the main evidence for the Oedipus complex. Post-Freudians have, however, studied children.

Freud is also criticised by Wood (1990) who quoted evidence that the reported case studies were distorted to fit the theories.

Table 12 *Strengths and limitations of the psychodynamic approach*

Strengths	Limitations
Detailed theory of human condition	Hypothetical constructs that are not testable
Listens to individuals talking about their experiences	Limitations of case study method
Use of case study method	Deterministic
Things are not always what they seem in behaviour	Too much emphasis on unconscious
Middle position in many debates in psychology	Freud's limited sample of patients

Key points:

- The psychodynamic approach emphasises the importance of early experience and unconscious processes in explaining behaviour.
- Much of our conscious experience and understanding is an illusion.
- Method used is case study.
- Post-Freudians both expanded on and changed some of Sigmund Freud's work.
- Position in debates: deterministic; some reductionism; some idiographic.

Summary questions

13 Which two aspects of Freud's theory are used to suggest that free will and choice are an illusion?

14 What is the evidence that Freud used to support his theory?

15 Name one idea of Freud's that a post-Freudian developed further and one idea that was contradicted.

The humanistic approach

Learning objectives:

- understand what is meant by the humanistic approach in psychology
- understand an alternative to the scientific view of psychology
- evaluate the humanistic approach in psychology.

In the history of psychology, the humanistic approach is classed as the 'third force' because it developed in the 1950s and 1960s as a reaction to the dominance of the behaviourist and psychodynamic approaches. The key figures are Abraham Maslow and Carl Rogers. They and others set up the Association for Humanistic Psychology because it was felt that behaviourism ignored subjective experience and psychodynamics marginalised our conscious awareness.

Principles of the humanistic approach

The humanistic approach takes a stand against scientific psychology arguing that such an approach is dehumanising. Heather (1976) said that 'psychologists have attempted to squeeze the study of human life into a lab situation where it becomes unrecognizably different from its naturally

Approaches

Hint

Assumptions of this approach

- Individuals are free to choose their behaviour.
- The focus is on the individual's subjective experience and conscious awareness.
- Personal growth is a key concept.

Link

- The humanistic approach is introduced in Chapter 1, Key approaches, in *AQA Psychology B AS*.
- The strengths and limitations of scientific psychology appear in Chapter 10, Debates in psychology, subtopic Psychology and science.

Key terms

Holism: the belief that the emphasis should be on the whole person, whole system, whole of behaviour or whole experience rather than on the components.

Reductionism: the belief that complex phenomena (things) can be explained by breaking them down into separate, simpler components.

Link

- Autonomy vs determinism and holism vs reductionism are discussed in more detail in Chapter 10, Debates in psychology.
- For an illustration of Maslow's hierarchy of needs, see *AQA Psychology B AS*, Chapter 1, Key approaches.

occurring form', and science regards the individual 'as something passive and inert, propelled into motion only by the action of some force, either external or internal upon him.'

The humanistic approach places great emphasis on conscious awareness and our ability consciously to choose our behaviour. In the free will–determinism debate, this approach is the only one of the six that supports the free will side. In all situations, we have autonomy – we can choose our behaviour in small ways (e.g. putting down this book and doing something else), or in major ways (e.g. our career choices). The ability to choose leads to personal growth (becoming the best we can). According to the humanistic approach, individuals are potentially good and, left to themselves, they will become better people.

However, we are not totally free but have 'situated freedom'. This means that we are always constrained in some way, whether by society or by our physical body. We cannot choose when to be born or to whom we are born, for example.

In the **holism–reductionism** debate, the humanistic approach differs from the others in being holistic. It concentrates on the whole person rather than on specific neurons or behaviours.

The core of the humanistic approach is conscious experience or, more precisely, the 'flow of conscious awareness':

> Moving inexorably through time, sometimes lagging, sometimes so fleeting that we are aware of awareness in retrospect, the ever-changing kaleidoscope of conscious is marked by changes in quality – from drowsiness to the freshness of waking, from the grey mists of depression to the excitement of expectation.
>
> *(Stevens, 2002, p195)*

This is also sometimes called reflexive awareness.

Our conscious or subjective experience is meaningful to us. This is very different from the view held by the behaviourists, who ignore meanings and see humans as just products of stimulus–response. According to the humanistic approach, understanding the meanings is to understand the individual. To know why people perform certain behaviours, it is necessary to know about their subjective world and meanings.

Abraham Maslow

Maslow studied conscious awareness, and, in particular, one type called 'peak experiences'. These are occasional experiences characterised by 'a sense of delight, wholeness, meaningfulness and abundant energy' (Stevens, 2002). These special spontaneous experiences can occur in many different situations – from looking at the sunset to being in the middle of an intense sporting competition. It is almost as if the individual is 'at one with the universe' for those short moments of the peak experience.

The problem is that these experiences are unique to each individual and thus difficult to study, especially because, often, they cannot be put into words.

Maslow was also interested in motivation; he proposed that individuals have a hierarchy of needs that can be envisaged as a pyramid. At the highest level is the need for self-actualisation, which is rarely achieved; this is the need 'to become everything that one is capable of becoming' (Maslow, 1987, p22), i.e. to reach our full potential.

Maslow (1973) researched self-actualisation by studying famous 'self-actualisers' (e.g. Albert Einstein). These individuals had a number of characteristics in common, including doing something they loved, being creative, spontaneous, accepting of others and themselves, having intimate relationships but being happy alone, being slightly unconventional, viewing the world in original ways; also they reported peak experiences. Maslow (1987) later accepted that there may be a negative side to being a self-actualiser, including a tendency to be stubborn, vain and anxious.

Approaches

Carl Rogers

Carl Rogers is the most famous proponent of the humanistic approach. Three key concepts underpin his work (Stevens, 2002):

- **The 'fundamental predominance of the subjective'** This means that each individual lives in their own subjective world. They are the centre of their world of experiences.
- **The importance of personal growth** Individuals are motivated towards personal growth (i.e. developing their potential), and problems arise when this process is inhibited by society or by the demands of others.
- **The self is composed of subjective experience and the evaluation of others** Problems can occur if the evaluation of others, particularly parents, is conditional. A child comes to believe that they are loved (evaluated positively) when they do certain things, such as get good grades at school. The love is seen as conditional on good grades, and working for good grades may come into conflict with subjective experience, which does not enjoy this, producing incongruence.

Rogers developed client-centred therapy (CCT) to help overcome incongruence. An important aspect of CCT is that the therapist gives the client unconditional positive regard (positive evaluation of the client whatever they choose to do).

> **Hint**
> CCT is also referred to as PCT or person-centred therapy.

Evaluation of the humanistic approach

Strengths

- The humanistic approach emphasises our autonomy and free will in choosing our behaviour, which is the opposite of deterministic approaches.
- The humanistic approach seeks an alternative to scientific psychology. It concentrates on subjective experience and meanings, which cannot be studied in experiments.
- It is the only one of the six approaches to place the individual's subjective experience and meanings at the centre. The psychodynamic approach listens to what people say about their experiences but then interprets that for unconscious meanings. The humanistic approach listens to what the person says about their experiences because only the individual themselves is the expert on their personal world.
- It is not reductionist: the individual is not seen as the product of neurons firing or past stimulus–response links. The humanistic approach is holistic and concentrates on the whole individual, putting the person in context. If there is a problem, then all aspects of the individual (e.g. thoughts, feelings, beliefs) and their surroundings are relevant to understanding the underlying reason.
- CCT is supportive of individuals with problems and treats them with respect. It is a non-directive form of therapy, as the therapist does not

tell the client what to do. The therapist's task is to help the client to find their own solution to problems.

Limitations

- The humanistic approach is too positive about human nature. It assumes that individuals are intrinsically good and will choose positive paths for their lives. It is too idealistic to assume that individuals are basically good. (If they are, why are there so many bad things in the world?)

  Furthermore, the possibility of free will and choice is limited for many people. The notions of free will and choice reflect the thinking of the rich, Western world. Individuals living in poverty in the Third World have few choices. Individuals struggling to survive are not concerned about personal growth, but about where the next meal is coming from.
- There is too much emphasis on subjective experience. This is personal and difficult to communicate to others, which makes it very hard to study.
- The approach is not scientific: it does not use rigorous, objective methods and does not make predictions that it is possible to prove or disprove.
- The emphasis on conscious awareness limits the scope of the humanistic approach. There are times when individuals do things and do not know why; the psychodynamic approach is able to explain such a situation using the concept of unconscious motivation. Many of the automatic workings of the body are outside conscious awareness (e.g. release of hormones, digestion).
- CCT is of limited help for individuals with complex or severe problems or those who need direct help. Leaving individuals to find their own solutions may not be the best way: there are times when individuals would benefit from direction and guidance; other people can sometimes see the solutions more clearly than the individual themselves can.

AQA Examiner's tip

The humanistic approach is different from the other approaches. Make a table showing one difference between the humanistic approach and each of the other approaches to help you remember the features for the exam.

Table 13 *Strengths and limitations of the humanistic approach*

Strengths	Limitations
Emphasises autonomy	Too positive about human nature
Alternative to scientific psychology	Too much emphasis on subjective experience
Places subjective experience and meaning at centre	Not scientific
Holistic	Ignores anything outside conscious awareness
CCT is supportive	CCT limited in whom it can help

Key points:

- The humanistic approach is person centred – individuals live in subjective and personal worlds.
- Individuals are free to choose their behaviour.
- According to the humanistic approach, the scientific study of human behaviour is dehumanising and artificial.
- This is the only approach to take the position of autonomy/free will and holism.
- According to the humanistic approach, the role of psychology is to help individuals to grow personally and achieve their potential.

Summary questions

16 Name one aspect of the humanistic approach that makes it different from scientific psychology.

17 Why is personal growth important to the humanistic approach?

18 What is the chosen method used by this approach?

Comparison of approaches

Learning objectives:

- understand about taking an eclectic approach in psychology
- compare the different approaches in psychology.

Stevens (1996b, p45) admitted that 'one of the problems facing anyone attempting to study social behaviour and experience is the multiplicity of approaches and theories ... The impact of this can be overwhelming and confusing.'

Adopting an eclectic approach

One way to deal with this multiplicity is to adopt an eclectic approach and combine different approaches rather than stick rigidly to one. The idea is to use the different approaches in a 'pick and mix' way to help understand behaviour, and different approaches may be used in different situations. The eclectic approach is more common in applied psychology (e.g. therapy).

The eclectic approach can take different forms:

- theoretical eclecticism – the combination of different theoretical ideas and approaches
- methodological eclecticism – the combination of different research methods
- epistemological eclecticism – the combination of different positions in the debates in psychology (e.g. nature and nurture)
- applied eclecticism – the use of combinations of approaches in applied psychology (e.g. using drugs and cognitive-behavioural therapy to treat depression)
- selective eclecticism – the use of different ideas alone or together in different situations (e.g. explaining depression with biological ideas but using psychodynamic and cognitive theories to explain anorexia).

Trimodal theory

Stevens (1996a) has proposed a model for combining different approaches in psychology. According to the model there are three modes of understanding behaviour (hence 'trimodal'). The primary mode concentrates on the biological basis of behaviour; the secondary mode focuses on symbolic processes (meanings); the tertiary mode focuses on reflexive awareness (Table 14).

Table 14 *Using trimodal theory to combine approaches*

Mode	Primary	Secondary	Tertiary
Focus	Biological processes e.g. genes, hormones	Symbolic processes (meanings/learning)	Reflexive awareness (ability to think about behaviour and change)
Approaches	Biological	Behaviourist, cognitive, social learning theory, psychodynamic	Humanistic

Let us use trimodal theory to explain gender development. The primary mode focuses upon the biological sex of the individual (usually male or female) and the hormones released in the body (biological approach). The secondary mode focuses on the meanings of society (usually masculinity and femininity): in other words, the learning of appropriate gender behaviours (behaviourist approach and social learning theory). Finally, the tertiary mode: the individual has the choice of whether or not to perform the appropriate gender behaviour (humanistic approach).

Limitations of trimodal theory

There are two main problems with this model. First, it places too much emphasis on the tertiary mode and the humanistic approach (allowing individuals to reflect upon their behaviour and choose to change).

Secondly, the model is limited by the direct contradictions between modes. For example, the biological approach argues for the biological determinism of behaviour and denies our ability to choose. Nevertheless, this model is an attempt to show eclecticism in practice.

Evaluation of the eclectic approach

Strengths

- There are examples of overlap and complementarity between the approaches and this approach takes the best part of all approaches and combines them to give a better understanding of behaviour.
- In therapy, the approach most appropriate to a particular problem is used because what matters most is helping the client.
- Human behaviour is too complex and varied to be completely explained by just one approach.
- Approaches develop and build on one another, and thus there is plenty of overlap between them.
- Too much emphasis on one approach may mean that relevant information from other approaches is missed.
- Being eclectic may also involve being multi-disciplinary and looking to subjects other than psychology for more information to explain behaviour (e.g. sociology, anthropology, medical subjects).
- Individual approaches can be insular and only interested in their own debates. For example, advocates of the psychodynamic approach have written vast amounts about defence mechanisms and the Oedipus complex.

Limitations

- There are irreconcilable differences; some approaches are directly contradictory and cannot be combined. For example, the humanistic approach argues that we consciously choose our behaviour, while the psychodynamic approach sees our behaviour as caused by unconscious forces (hidden from our conscious awareness). This level of disagreement has led some people to talk about the existence of 'psychologies' rather than psychology.
- It is not clear how the different approaches are combined in practice.
- Being eclectic may mean that there is no theoretical basis to psychology. Scientific psychology, in particular, emphasises the importance of underlying theory when explaining behaviour and to drive applications.
- A 'pick and mix' of approaches can produce a watered down version that is no better than common sense.
- It is difficult to know when to combine approaches or use one approach in one situation and another in another situation.

- Being eclectic can gloss over the real differences between approaches and their researchers.
- Using many different approaches can lead a therapist to become a 'jack of all trades and master of none'. It is very hard to know all the approaches equally well.

The way forward

In 2005, the British Psychological Society (BPS) set up the Dialoguing across Divisions in UK Social Psychology group to encourage psychologists from very different approaches to come together. Reicher and Taylor (2005, p549) noted that from the meetings came 'a mutual sense of respect and a realisation that the biggest threat to intellectual progress is not arguing with each other' but 'ignoring and being ignorant of each other'.

Comparison of approaches

Table 15 *Examples of similarities and differences between approaches*

Overlap/Complementarity between approaches	Irreconcilable differences/contradictions between approaches
Focuses on learning of behaviour (behaviourist and social learning theory)	Individuals can choose their behaviour (humanistic) vs cannot (biological, behaviourist, psychodynamic)
Uses scientific methods (behaviourist and biological)	Scientific research methods (biological, behaviourist) vs non-scientific (humanistic, psychodynamic)
Listens to individual describing their experiences (humanistic and psychodynamic)	Biology (biological) vs learning (behaviourist) as cause of behaviour
Stresses importance of cognitive processes (cognitive and social learning theory)	Study subjective experience (humanistic) vs observable behaviour (behaviourist)
Studies animals to understand human behaviour (biological and behaviourist)	Importance of theory (biological, behaviourist) vs application (humanistic, psychodynamic)
Treats mental illness, e.g. drugs and CBT (biological and cognitive)	Different types of determinism, e.g. physiological, genetic (biological) vs unconscious (psychodynamic)
Regards application of ideas to helping people as most important (humanistic and psychodynamic)	Position in debates, e.g. nature (biological) vs nurture (behaviourist)

Table 16 *Summary of six main approaches in psychology*

Approaches	Key assumption about behaviour	Main research methods used	Areas of psychology
Biological	Behaviour has biological basis	Experiments, physiological measures (e.g. EEG), genetic studies	Biopsychology, genetic basis to mental illness and personality
Behaviourist	Behaviour learnt from conditioning/past experiences	Experiments, particularly with non-human animals	Behaviour therapy, behaviour modification, stress management
Social learning theory	Behaviour learnt from observing others and reinforcement when copied	Experiments	Aggression, moral behaviour, gender development
Cognitive	How individuals make sense of world influences their behaviour	Experiments, computer modelling, questionnaires	Cognitive psychology, social cognition, cognitive-behavioural therapy (CBT)
Psychodynamic	Early experiences and unconscious processes cause behaviour	Case studies	Psychoanalysis, gender development, personality development
Humanistic	Individuals are free to choose their behaviour	Q-sorts, unstructured interviews	Client-centred therapy (CCT), self concept, motivation

Key points:

- The eclectic approach combines ideas from the different approaches in psychology.
- Some approaches are compatible but others are not.

Summary questions

19 Name two approaches that are compatible.

20 Name two approaches that are not compatible.

Further reading

Two classic psychology textbooks:

Glassman, W.E. and Hadad, M. (2008) *Approaches to Psychology*, 5th edition. Maidenhead: Open University Press.

Tavris, C. and Wade, C. (2000) *Psychology in Perspective*, 3rd edition. Upper Saddle River, NJ: Prentice Hall.

For discussion of debates and approaches:

Valentine, E. (1992) *Conceptual Issues in Psychology*, 2nd edition. London: Routledge.

Provides an overview of the history of psychology:

Fancher, R.E. (1994) Historical backgrounds of psychology. In Coleman, A.M. (ed.) *Companion Encyclopaedia of Psychology*, Vol. 1. London: Routledge.

Offprints of classic works at: http://psychclassics.yorku.ca

Vanguard University: www.vanguard.edu (search for *Classics in the History of Psychology*: an electronic resource developed by Christopher D. Green at York University, Toronto, Canada includes Freud, Maslow, Pavlov, Rogers, Skinner and Watson).

Association for Humanistic Psychology: www.ahpweb.org

End-of-chapter activity 1

Here is an extract from a brief psychological assessment made by a psychiatrist:

'K' is a 30-year-old man who has a long history of violence. He was most recently arrested (for the fifth time) for an attack on another man in a crowded pub. 'K' claimed that the man had knocked over his drink and laughed about it.

At the time of arrest, 'K' was found to have abnormally high levels of testosterone (as well as high blood alcohol level).

He reported many experiences of seeing his father being aggressive and suffered himself in the form of beatings. 'K' said little about his mother, who appeared to have often been absent during this time, although this did not seem to be a concern for 'K'. 'K' was excluded from school on many occasions for bullying other children.

If 'K' had a philosophy of life, it came from his father, and it was 'never show weakness to others'.

I recommend further detailed psychological assessment.

The task is to analyse the case of 'K' using six different approaches. The class can be divided into six groups, with each group allocated one of the approaches and given the following questions to answer:

- How would the approach explain the causes of 'K's behaviour?
- What methods would psychologists using the approach use to assess 'K'?
- What therapeutic strategies or treatment would be advocated by psychologists using the approach?

End-of-chapter activity 2

Many psychologists prefer to be eclectic, and combine the different approaches in their work. Whether or not this is possible depends upon the area of practice.

Here are 10 situations in which psychologists could be involved; your task is to decide which approach alone is best to use or whether to be eclectic (and, if so, which approaches to combine).

- Studying the genetic causes of schizophrenia
- Treating the thoughts and behaviours associated with major depressive disorder
- Teaching animals to do tricks for a television programme
- Investigating the role of choice in risky health behaviours
- Setting up an experiment to investigate if seeing cartoon characters eating healthy food influences children's choices at lunch
- Developing team bonding at a rugby club
- Developing an anger management programme around what individuals think before they become aggressive
- Finding out what motivates successful businesswomen
- Investigating whether there is a link between interest in horror films as an adult and attachment type as a child
- Studying the experience of having an eating disorder as a teenage boy

Debates in psychology

Introduction

Chapter 10 considers some of the major issues and controversies within the field of psychology as a whole. It is therefore no coincidence that the chapter is presented at the end of the book and follows Approaches in Psychology. An underpinning knowledge of topics and approaches is required both to appreciate and engage in these debates.

'Psychology' is derived from two Greek words: *'psyche'*, meaning soul or mind, and *'logos'*, meaning word or study. So psychology began as the analysis of the mind or soul and like many other academic disciplines is rooted in philosophy. However, just over 100 years ago, Wundt established the first psychology laboratory in Leipzig, a significant event for two reasons. Firstly, it marked the beginning of psychology as a discipline in its own right and, secondly, it signalled a new method of enquiry into the study of human mental activity and behaviour. Gone was the philosophical method of rational enquiry and the scientific method became the order of the day. However psychology still continues to be provoked by some deep philosophical issues.

The **free will and determinism** debate occupied philosophers for centuries and continues to be of fundamental importance within psychology as it is concerned with the causes of human behaviour. Philosophers such as Descartes rationalised that humans in contrast to animals, possess a 'soul', reasoning ability and free will. The philosophical ideas of existentialism also emphasise free will and personal responsibility, a basic tenet of the humanistic approach. On the other hand determinism, with its emphasis on causal laws, is the basis of science and the majority of approaches in psychology adopt a strict deterministic view of human behaviour. This division is partly the basis of another controversy – **psychology and science**. Is psychology really a science or, even more fundamentally, should it aspire to be a science? Further debates follow. If psychology is a science then **nomothetic** research is necessary. However, if one assumes that each individual is unique then the **idiographic** approach is more appropriate. Another debate closely linked with psychology and science is **holism and reductionism**. Reductionism works on the scientific principle that complex phenomena should be explained by the simplest underlying principles possible, although amongst psychologists this view is contentious.

Finally, the **nature–nurture** debate (known as the **nativism–empiricism** controversy in philosophy) is a long-standing debate over the relative contributions of experience and inheritance to the make-up of an individual. Locke is often associated with this debate the empiricist position that the newborn baby's mind at birth is a 'tabula rasa' or blank slate upon which experience will write. Empiricism also applies to the scientific method of conducting research through direct experience and was one of the influences on early behaviourism.

The differing beliefs and approaches held by psychologists affect the view of human behaviour and how research should be carried out.

Key terms

Nativism: a philosophical theory that stresses inborn or inherited influences on behaviour over experience and acquired influences.

Empiricism: the belief that all knowledge should be derived from sensory experience and learning as opposed to being inherited. In an extreme form, the mind at birth is seen as a 'blank slate'. Empirical methods conduct research through direct experience, preferably the experiment.

Specification content	Topic content	Page number
Free will and determinism: hard determinism and soft determinism; biological, environmental and psychic determinism; the scientific emphasis on causal explanations	Free will and determinism	257
The nature–nurture debate: the relative importance of heredity and environment in determining behaviour; an interactionist approach	The nature–nurture debate	263
Holism and reductionism: the strengths and limitations of reductionist and holistic explanations; an interactionist approach	Holism and reductionism	270
Idiographic and nomothetic approaches: the strengths and limitations of idiographic versus nomothetic research	Idiographic and nomothetic approaches	276
Psychology and science: the features and principles of the scientific approach – a paradigm; the role of theory; hypothesis testing; empirical methods and replication; generalisation; the subject matter of psychology – overt behaviour versus subjective, private experience; the role of peer review in validating research	Psychology and science	280
Strengths and limitations of the scientific approach in psychology	Strengths and limitations of the scientific approach in psychology	286

10 Debates in psychology

Free will and determinism

Learning objectives:

- understand what psychologists mean by the terms 'free will' and 'determinism'
- analyse the free will and determinism debate and appreciate its importance to psychology
- apply the free will and determinism debate to the different approaches and topic areas in psychology
- explain how the free will and determinism debate relates to how science works in psychology.

Link

The terms 'free will' and 'determinism' are defined on p222, in Chapter 9, Approaches in psychology.

Key terms

Internal determinism: belief in the internal causes of behaviour; e.g. internal biological factors and mental processes are seen as causes of behaviour.

Biological determinism: the belief that all behaviour and thought is caused by the action of the nervous system and genetic factors.

The free will and determinism debate is one that applies not only to psychology but also to everyday situations. It can be illustrated by the many excuses people make for behaviour. For example, 'I smoke because I need to. My body needs nicotine'; 'I had to go to the party. If I hadn't, she'd never speak to me again.' It can also be seen in the explanations or attributions that people make of others' behaviour, such as 'No wonder he drinks. You never see his father without a glass in his hand.' Each of these examples implies that the behaviour is not of the individual's own choosing or 'free will'. Of course, not everyone would accept such an explanation of behaviour, hence the debate. Essentially, if the belief is that people can make choices about their behaviour, that they can behave differently given the same circumstances and are the agents of their behaviour then they have free will. If not, then their actions must come from forces beyond their control; psychologists say that their behaviour is determined. To put it simply, could an individual's behaviour in a given situation have been different if they had willed it? Supporters of determinism would respond with 'no'; those who advocate free will would respond with 'yes'.

Internal and external determinism

Biological determinism

Internal determinism is associated with **biological determinism**. It includes a number of aspects, such as our instinctive needs to eat, sleep and drink; the role that the different parts of the brain play in controlling behaviour; our hormonal system; evolutionary forces; and of course our genes. We will briefly consider each of these in turn:

- **Instinctive needs** Although we can, to a certain extent, choose when to eat, drink and sleep, what to eat and drink and how much to sleep, we cannot avoid the fact that each of these behaviours is essential to our survival. We have no choice; these behaviours are determined.
- **The controlling role of the different parts of the brain** The hypothalamus (a small structure at the base of the forebrain) controls many aspects of behaviour, such as water and food intake and aggressive responses. Language functions are predominantly located in the left hemisphere of the brain; Broca's area is involved in speech production and Wernicke's area in the understanding of speech. No amount of willing can help someone with damage to either of these areas overcome the devastating effect on language.
- **Hormonal system** Some research has implicated the synthetic form of oestrogen in sexual preference and behaviour. Seven out of 30 adult women whose mothers had taken the synthetic hormone to prevent miscarriage reported some degree of same-sex or bisexual interest. In a control group of 30 women whose

Debates

Link

All these examples of behaviour make external attributions where the cause is 'outside' the person. A person is not seen as being responsible for their behaviour. This links back to social cognition, the topic covered by Chapter 6 in *AQA Psychology B AS*.

AQA Examiner's tip

In the exam, you will be required to explain how the debate relates to different topics in psychology. Think of these as you go through the text and gather notes in preparation. Note that in the first paragraph of this section, two examples of topics are used: 'substance abuse' and 'social influence'.

Hint

To remember the essential elements of 'free will', it may help to think that:

- 'free' means a person or behaviour is independent of any cause
- 'will' is the idea that people can make choices.

Key terms

Psychic determinism: the belief that all thought and behaviour is caused by unconscious forces associated with the life and death instincts.

Overdetermination: the belief that a single observed effect is determined by multiple causes at once, any of which, alone, might be enough to account for the effect.

Link

The case study of Little Hans illustrates the role of unconscious mental processes on behaviour. Hans's fear of horses was symbolic of his unconscious fear of castration by his father as a result of the Oedipus complex. See Chapter 3, Gender development, in *AQA Psychology B AS*.

mothers had not taken synthetic oestrogen when pregnant, only one woman reported same-sex interest. This study suggests that sexual preference may not necessarily be the result of free choice (Meyer-Bahlburg *et al.*, 1995).

- **Evolutionary forces** The fight or flight response by which animals and humans prepare themselves to deal with environmental demands can be explained from an evolutionary perspective. A sequence of activity prepares the body for either flight (escape) or fight (defending or attacking). In some situations the individual responds by freezing or even fainting. Whilst this was arguably an adaptive response in our evolutionary past, it is questionable how useful the response is today. However, the point is that these behaviours are determined: we do not choose to freeze in front of an audience or during an exam.
- **Genes** Numerous twin studies have pointed towards a genetic predisposition in behaviours such as depression and schizophrenia. Biological determinism is often advanced as an argument for the absence of free will in schizophrenia.

Biological determinism also places limits on behaviours that are beyond the capabilities of the human body. One may wish to fly at will or live under water but without wings and gills, this is not possible.

Although the biological approach stresses the biological causes of behaviour, it is incorrect to speak purely of 'biological determinism'. The biological approach considers the interaction of biology and the environment (behaviour after all occurs within an environment). So people are doubly determined: biologically and environmentally. For example, introverted people inherit an over-aroused nervous system. This biological predisposition influences choice of environment (peace and quiet), which depresses levels of arousal (Gale, 1979). There are no choices. What appears to be freely chosen behaviour is determined by biological factors interacting with the environment.

Psychic determinism

Another aspect of internal determinism is **psychic determinism**, a view represented by psychoanalytic theory. Humans are depicted as biologically determined by strong inherent instincts of sex and aggression and by repressed conflicts, childhood experiences, wishes and memories within the unconscious mind. Mental activity and behaviour is thus the result of unconscious mental processes. For Freud, there were no accidents; he believed that, no matter how apparently random or irrational behaviour may appear to be, unconscious causes can always account for them. Because the causes of behaviour are unconscious, people believe that they are free but, in Freud's view, free will is an illusion. Furthermore, the Freudian concept of psychic determinism proposed that much of our behaviour, thoughts and feelings have multiple causes. This was termed **overdetermination**. In *The Interpretation of Dreams*, Freud (1900) wrote that many features of dreams were overdetermined. By this he meant that a dream was caused by many factors in the life of the dreamer such as the 'residue of the day' (superficial memories), deeply repressed conflicts, unconscious wishes, etc. This had implications in psychoanalysis because one had always to search beyond the first unconscious causes. Freud favoured interpretations that accounted for such features not only once but many times.

Environmental determinism

Environmental determinism or **external determinism** is the idea that our behaviour occurs because there is a cause in the environment. Unlike internal determinism, which focuses on internal biological or mental processes, environmental determinism considers factors external to (outside) the individual. Research into social influence (Asch, 1955; Milgram, 1963) demonstrates the power of the situation and how social factors can have a strong causal effect on behaviour.

The behaviourist approach represents the extreme in environmental determinism. Behaviour is regarded as the product of prior reinforcements (positive and negative) and punishment. Skinner is well known for his assertion that free will is an illusion. It must be remembered, however, that the theoretical basis of behaviourism lies in laboratory research involving animals. Humans are considered to be qualitatively different (consciousness is often regarded as distinguishing human beings from other animals) and mechanistic laboratory behaviour is far removed from the everyday behaviour, decisions and choices facing humans. Even so, Skinner claimed that, in human society, inconsistent and uncontrolled reinforcement contingencies give an illusion of free will. According to Skinner, the successful conditioning of behaviour does not require any element of free will but consistent reinforcement. If a child is badly behaved in class then its behaviour can be changed for the better if the teacher consistently reinforces the child's good behaviour (and ignores the bad behaviour!). Appealing to the child's 'will' is not necessary. Rather, behaviour is moulded by agents of socialisation: parents, teachers, peers and society in general. There is no such thing as personal freedom; the causes of behaviour are often hidden in the environment.

Evaluation

The ideas of determinism are compatible with the scientific method, giving psychology the esteemed status of 'a science'. Determinism assumes that all behaviour has a cause, is orderly and obeys laws. Current behaviour is a result of what went before and a cause of what will happen next. Therefore, one can predict and ultimately control behaviour. A student may well predict that, if an essay is not handed in on time without good reason, the teacher will inform the student's parents. Knowing this, the student can think of an acceptable 'excuse'. Thus, the student has some control over the teacher's behaviour. However, it is a false assumption that accurate predictions are possible. There are numerous influences on any behaviour and uncertainty does not just apply to human behaviour. Even physicists have to build uncertainty factors into their laws.

It is ironic, however, that determinism, although compatible with the scientific approach, is in itself unfalsifiable. The reasoning is that if a cause cannot be found for behaviour that is because it has yet to be found.

An important issue raised by explanations of behaviour based on determinism is that of moral responsibility. If behaviour is 'caused' irrespective of whether the cause is internal or external, the individual is not responsible. There is no need for blame, praise or prison to punish the individual. However, this is not how most people or societies view behaviour. When a crime is committed, the justice system looks for a **culprit** deemed **responsible** and deserving of **punishment**. Hence, a common plea of defendants – that the cause of their behaviour is temporary insanity. This removes all responsibility and choice from the individual: the cause is their internal mental state and not their will. In

Key terms

Environmental determinism: the belief that all behaviour is under the control of environmental stimuli and external forces of reward and punishment.

External determinism: the belief that behaviour occurs because there is a cause in the environment. The behaviourist approach represents the extreme in external determinism.

Hint

'Psychic' generally means relating to the mind or that which is mental. According to psychoanalytic theory, behaviour and conscious thought are determined by internal processes – the unconscious mind – hence, psychic determinism.

AQA Examiner's tip

In discussion, remember that ego-psychologists such as Erikson have challenged Freud's extreme deterministic view. Erikson stressed the more rational conscious ego processes in behaviour, believed that the goal of analysis was ego-strengthening and that the individual is more in control of their behaviour. Freud saw the extent of change as a result of analysis as limited.

Link

Research into social influence, e.g. by Asch (1955) and Milgram (1963), attributes causes of conformity and obedience to environmental factors. Milgram's research in particular provoked a debate as to whether or not participants were responsible for their behaviour. For more on Asch's and Milgram's work, see Chapter 5, Social influence, in *AQA Psychology B AS*.

the war crimes trials of Nazis after the Second World War, defendants used external factors as a reason for obedience to a destructive authority: 'I was only obeying orders.'

The problem of free will

Free will is associated with the writings of a number of philosophers. Descartes, in particular, argued that humans are unique among living things because they can plan and make choices and have moral responsibility. However, there are several problems with 'free will'.

What do we mean by the term 'free will'?

Precision in definition of terminology is a goal of any science. It is important to avoid ambiguity, to be certain that the meaning of something is clear. However, it is difficult to specify what the 'will' or 'self' that does the choosing consists of. So an immediate problem is how to define 'free will'. The *Penguin Dictionary of Psychology* (2001) defines free will as 'a hypothetical and often reified internal agency that functions independently of externally imposed forces'. A problem with this definition will be discussed in the next section. Logically, free will might also be defined as the opposite of determinism. This would imply that behaviour has no cause and is entirely unpredictable and random. However, everyday experience does not support this view. Even freely chosen behaviour has a cause and is predictable. For example, someone setting off on a holiday may ask a friend to give them a lift to the airport. The friend has a choice whether or not to agree to the lift and is therefore exercising free will. If they are a helpful person (and assuming that it is convenient) then one can predict that they will help. So their behaviour though freely chosen has a cause: it is determined by their personality. The position adopted by William James, who used the term rather than 'free will', is that of **soft determinism**: where there is a consistency between a person's wishes and actions there is an element of free will. If actions are voluntary and in line with a person's conscious desired goals (in the above example, to be helpful to others) then they are free.

Whilst a person can choose between a number of behaviours, there is only free will (soft determinism) if there is no coercion (compulsion or force). In the above example, giving a lift is caused by the friend's generous nature and is in line with what they want to do. However, if the friend only agrees because they are part of a social group and are conforming to some group norm, their behaviour is again caused or determined but not by their free will but by coercion (an 'external force'). The term **hard determinism** has been used to distinguish true determinism from soft determinism.

How can 'free will' be tested?

The lack of an operational definition means that 'free will' or 'soft determinism' cannot meet the rigours of scientific testing. Abstract and hypothetical concepts such as 'free will' should be defined in terms of measurable and observable operations. An example will make this clearer. 'Hunger' is an abstract concept: it does not exist in material form – it is not 'real' but is a 'state' that results from food deprivation. However, even though hunger is an abstract concept it can be measured by the number of hours since food was last consumed. So it can be operationally defined and scientifically tested. But what set of operations defines free will so that it can be measured and tested? We would need to

AQA Examiner's tip

Do not confuse determinism with fatalism. Fatalism is a philosophical view that all events are predetermined and subject to fate, a deity, the stars, etc. (i.e. 'What will be, will be'). Determinism stresses that all events have preceding causes.

From studying operant conditioning, you will probably recall that the behaviour is 'voluntary' (e.g. pressing a lever). However, do not mistake voluntary behaviour for free will. Even though the behaviour is voluntary (as opposed to involuntary such as salivation to food), it is not freely chosen. It is the consequence of the behaviour that determines the probability of its occurring again – not free will.

Hint

When discussing the behaviourist approach, it may be useful to refer to Skinner's work with rats and pigeons and applications to therapy, such as token economies, to illustrate how behaviour is controlled by the consequences of behaviour.

Key terms

Soft determinism: the belief that behaviour is determined or caused by a person's own character, wishes or conscious desired goals. Behaviour is free from coercion (force) but not free from causation.

Hard determinism: the belief that behaviour is caused by events outside one's personal control. Free will is an illusion; behaviour is totally predictable and determined.

know what type of behaviour we were suggesting that free will affected and how we would measure it. Without precise definitions, research is vague and **replication** is impossible.

The evidence for the existence of free will is mostly subjective; people will insist – and genuinely believe – that they have freely chosen a certain lifestyle, certain friends, or to support a particular charity. However, where objective studies have been conducted, the results have proved surprisingly counter-intuitive.

Research study: Libet (1985)

Aim: To investigate if the brain activity involved in an action began before or after the decision to act.

Method: Participants were asked to hold out their arms in front of them and then, when they were ready, to flex their wrists. This occurred over several trials. Libet measured: the start of the wrist-flexing movement (electrodes on the wrist were used); the start of 'readiness to act' (electrodes on the scalp were used); the actual decision to flex their wrists (for this a clock face was used with a revolving spot; participants had to say where the spot was on the clock face when they made the decision to flex their wrists).

Results: The activity in the brain began half a second **before** the participant reported the decision (choosing to flex their wrists).

Conclusion: This suggests that the conscious decision was not the cause of behaviour (wrist flexing) but a consequence of brain activity.

Evaluation: This was an objective attempt (albeit indirectly) at investigating the existence of 'free will'. The use of the revolving spot on the clock face has been found in other studies to be an accurate measure for timing external stimuli. There is no reason why people should be less accurate with their own private decisions. However, critics claim that the voluntary wrist action in the experiment cannot be compared with the everyday spontaneous decisions that people have to make in real life. Sceptics uncomfortable with the whole notion of free will argue that the results of the study are not surprising and to believe that some sort of force acts on brain matter is like believing in magic.

Evaluation

One cannot overestimate the significant problem with belief in free will: it is inconsistent with the assumptions of science. The scientific emphasis is on causal explanations. Although soft determinism does bring causality into the equation, nevertheless a problem still remains. How can something non-physical (the will) have an effect on the physical world in the form of behaviour? This is further complicated by the uncertainty about what is meant by free will. Nevertheless, most people feel morally responsible for their actions and hold others responsible for theirs. In other words people believe that there are choices and that free will operates. Brehm (1966) argued that **psychological reactance** occurs if people believe that their freedom is threatened and try to regain or reassert their freedom. A common response is to do the opposite behaviour (bloody-mindedness).

The humanistic approach is the best example of an approach that emphasises free will. The theories of Maslow and Rogers both stress free will and the power of individuals to direct their lives according to their

Key terms

Replication: refers to whether the findings of a study can be repeated (the results will be the same or similar) when following the same procedure with different people and on different occasions.

Psychological reactance: reaction against attempts to restrict or control one's choices and decisions. When an individual perceives strong pressure from others to force a decision or an attitude, a 'contrary' behaviour is likely to be selected.

Take it further

Heisenberg's uncertainty principle (1927) states that it is impossible to know both the exact position and the exact velocity of an object at the same time. The effect is so tiny that it can only be noticed on a subatomic scale. However, the point is that up to the beginning of the 20th century the deterministic model for describing the behaviour of physical systems had been applied but Heisenberg's uncertainty principle placed a limit on that level of certainty. More recent developments in physics have shown that uncertainties are not limited to the atomic level. Chaos theory has shown that uncertainties in behaviour can also be applied to larger systems, defying the deterministic explanation that can be applied to the overall behaviour of the system. Chaos theory is the study of events that look like they are random but actually have a hidden order or way of acting. All it would take is something new to come into the system or pattern, and almost everything changes. Scientists call this the 'butterfly effect' because it is now possible to imagine that even a butterfly flapping its little wings somewhere could cause, or stop, a storm somewhere else.

Link

Replication is discussed in more detail on p284.

self-chosen goals. The approach as a whole is well known for its rejection of science that is based on determinism. However, Rogers did not exclude determinism outright. In his later writings, he seemed to suggest that whilst people choose their behaviour it is at the same time being determined. According to Rogers (Rogers, 1983, quoted in Morea, 1990), the healthy, fully functioning person 'not only experiences, but utilises, the most absolute freedom when he spontaneously, freely and voluntarily chooses and wills that which is absolutely determined.' Another aspect of free will is seen in humanistic therapies: client-centred therapies that emphasise the freedom of the individual to solve their own problems.

The cognitive approach and social learning theory are more complex. When people face new events they experience both freedom of decision and limits on their behaviour. Information processing serves as a typical example. People select information out of the environment to attend to, thus exercising freedom of choice. They also interpret information but these interpretations are bounded by the schemas they use.

Key points:

- The free will and determinism debate is a debate about the extent to which an individual is in control of their own behaviour. The free will view regards people as exercising choice whereas determinism is the view that actions come from forces over which people have no control.
- There are two main categories of determinism: internal and external. The biological and psychodynamic approaches are both examples of internal determinism. Behaviourism is an example of external or environmental determinism.
- The humanistic approach is the nearest one can get to free will in psychology.
- 'Soft determinism' is a term used to convey the idea that free will is not freedom from causation but from coercion. Hard determinism is more extreme and embodies the idea that all behaviour is predictable and caused by forces outside of the person's control.
- The ideas of determinism are compatible with the scientific method.
- Free will and determinism overlap. Humanistic psychologists lean towards free will but also accept constraints on behaviour, and determinists accept the existence of 'uncertainty factors'.

Summary questions

1 Distinguish between hard and soft determinism.

2 Outline two problems of 'free will' in psychology.

3 Explain why determinism is compatible with the scientific approach. Use an example of a psychological approach to illustrate your answer.

AQA Examiner's tip

It is important to understand terminology such as 'hard' and 'soft' determinism and to be able to use it appropriately in an exam. Practise by thinking up your own examples and explaining these. Use the terms where appropriate in revision questions.

Link

Libet's study raises the question of ecological validity and demonstrates the need for objective studies as opposed to subjective evidence. See Chapter 4, Research methods, in *AQA Psychology B AS*, and Chapter 11, Methods in psychology, in this book.

Take it further

The 'mind–body' problem or debate is closely linked to the free will and determinism debate. Essentially, it is another philosophical question, looking at how the conscious mind is related to the physical brain. How can something non-physical/ non-material influence or produce changes in something that is physical (the brain/body)? The classic example given by philosophers to illustrate the problem is the act of deciding to lift one's arm. Can a non-physical mind cause a physical event? From a strictly scientific perspective this kind of causation should be impossible. However, our subjective experiences tell us that our minds do affect behaviour and that consciousness does have causal properties. (Lift your arm.) Several theories have been advanced and one hinted at by the above study is that mental processes are purely physical processes.

Link

Belief in free will has implications for behaviour. People with an external locus of control suffer more from the effects of stress than do people with an internal locus of control (Rotter, 1966). There is more about locus of control in Chapter 6, Stress and stress management.

The nature–nurture debate

Learning objectives:

- understand what psychologists mean by the 'nature–nurture' debate in psychology
- explain what is meant by an 'interactionist' approach in the context of the nature–nurture debate
- analyse the methodological problems in investigating the contributions of nature and nurture to behaviour
- apply the nature–nurture debate to the different approaches and topic areas in psychology.

Link

The Gestalt psychologists believed that the basic principles of perceptual organisation are innate (see Chapter 8, Perceptual processes, in *AQA Psychology B AS*). Empiricism was sustained in conditioning theories (see Chapter 1, Key approaches, in *AQA Psychology B AS*, and Chapter 9, Approaches in psychology, in this book).

Hint

The nature–nurture debate is also known by other terms, such as the heredity–environment debate/controversy and the nativism–empiricism controversy.

Most people would agree that we are all influenced by genes and experience. The question is how important each is. For physical features such as eye colour the question poses little controversy: the genetic factor predominates. For psychological characteristics, however, the question is more controversial and the answer less obvious.

For many years, psychologists considering this question have fallen into two camps, espousing two philosophical ideas: nativism and empiricism. The nativists emphasised nature: genes and inborn characteristics in behaviour. The French philosopher Descartes (1596–1650) believed that certain human characteristics and even aspects of knowledge are innate. On the other hand, the empiricists focused on nurture in the form of learning and experience. The British philosopher John Locke believed that at birth the human mind is simply a blank slate (tabula rasa) that is gradually filled in by experience and learning from the environment. The nature–nurture debate is focused on the roles of heredity and environment in determining behaviour. At the heart of the debate lies the question of the relative contributions of nature and nurture.

Changes in the emphasis of the nature–nurture debate

Nowadays, psychologists do not adopt an extreme position of **either** heredity **or** environment as an explanation of behaviour. Such a position is illogical. Heredity is, after all, expressed in an environment. For example, genes for walking on two legs and using lungs to breathe in oxygen influence the type of environment inhabited: for the human species, this is land as opposed to water. Both nature and nurture are essential for any behaviour, and it cannot be said that a particular behaviour **is** genetic and another **is** environmental. Nor can it be said that a particular behaviour comprises a percentage of each. Aside from the impossibility of separating the two influences, this position is also illogical as nature and nurture do not operate in a separate and additive way but **interact** in a complex manner. Each individual is a 'unique genetic mosaic' (Tavris and Wade, 1995) with unique experiences and history. Thus genius at violin playing could largely be a result of inherited musical talent or coming from a musical family of violin players or inspiration from going to an opera at an early age or a combination of all three. But it is not possible to say how much each influence might contribute or to separate these influences. For one person, genes may make a big difference; for another, the environment could be more important.

Although we cannot say that a specific behaviour in any given individual is mostly due to heredity or mostly environmental, what we can say is that the **difference** between two people's behaviour (or any physical characteristic) is mostly due to heredity or is mostly environmental in origin. Differences in eye colour, for example, are attributed to genetic differences although both genes and environment are needed for the development of eye colour. Differences in language between peoples are ascribed to the environment although both environment and heredity are required for the development of language. Thus the thrust of the debate and research is aimed at trying to investigate the relative contributions of nature and nurture in **individual differences** (i.e. the characteristics that vary from one individual to another, such as intelligence, attachment types and anxiety) and to understand the interactions between them.

Methods of investigating the relative contributions of nature and nurture

Twin studies

Twin studies are the main method of assessing the relative contributions of heredity and environment to differences in behaviour.

The term 'twin studies' refers collectively to a large number of studies carried out on monozygotic (MZ) and dizygotic (DZ) twins reared together or apart from each other. The object of these studies is to separate out the relative contributions of heredity and environment to human behaviour, for example as displayed in scores on intelligence (IQ) tests. Because an individual's behaviour results from an interaction of environmental and inherited factors, twin studies cannot tackle the logical impossibility of saying which is more important in the case of an individual. Twin studies are simply designed to produce a **heritability estimate**. If the heritability estimate for IQ in this country was 90 per cent, it would mean that 90 per cent of the differences between people's IQ scores were due to inherited factors (the remaining 10 per cent of the variation would be due to environmental factors).

MZ twins share the same genes. In contrast, DZ twins are no more alike than any other two siblings and may be of different sexes. If MZ twins reared together (same genes and same environment) are more alike than DZ twins reared together (different genes, same environment) any increased similarity must be genetic. The degree of agreement is expressed as a **concordance rate**. If 20 pairs of twins were studied and 16 pairs had identical or near identical intelligence, this would produce a concordance rate of 16/20 or 0.8 which is very high agreement. Obviously, if there was perfect agreement then the concordance rate would be 1.

Perhaps, however, the environments shared by MZ twins differ from those shared by DZ twins. Investigators have therefore studied MZ twins who were separated early in life and reared apart (same genes, different environments). Any similarity between them in spite of the separation should primarily be genetic.

In some studies of intelligence (Bouchard and McGue, 1981; Erlenmeyer-Kimling and Jarvik, 1963), pairs of MZ and DZ twins have been compared when reared apart and when reared together. Typically, such studies have found the highest concordance rate for MZ twins. Even when MZ twins brought up in different environments have been compared with DZ twins reared in the same environment, concordance rates have been higher for MZ twins. Such findings point to a clear genetic influence.

Adoption studies

Adoption studies are another method used to investigate heritability. If adopted individuals are found to be more similar to their biological parents, for example on a measure of intelligence, than to their adoptive parents then this suggests that genes are more influential than environment. Such studies have been used to support the role of genetic factors in a variety of disorders including depression, alcoholism and schizophrenia.

Hint

A useful analogy is to consider the area of a rectangle. This is determined by both length and breadth. Without length or breadth the rectangle does not exist so it is illogical to ask how much each contributes. However, if one rectangle is considerably longer than another and both are of similar breadths, it can be said that the difference between the two rectangles is mainly due to the differences in their lengths.

Link

Twin studies are used to investigate the genetic basis of behaviour such as schizophrenia and mood disorders. See Chapter 5, Schizophrenia and mood disorders. You will find definitions of MZ and DZ on p102.

Key terms

Heritability estimate: a statistical estimate of the proportion of the total variance in some trait within a group that is attributable to genetic differences among individuals within the group.

Link

For a definition of the term 'concordance rate', see p102, in Chapter 5.

Hint

MZ twins are identical twins with the same genetic make-up. DZ twins are non-identical and share only 50 per cent.

Implications

The nature–nurture debate is not purely of academic interest. Findings from studies of intelligence, schizophrenia and aggression do have implications. If genes are largely implicated in differences between the intelligence of individuals, this raises the question of whether it is worth investing time and resources into enrichment programmes. If nurture or the environment is implicated in schizophrenia, this could lay the burden of blame on the family. If aggression is considered to be largely under the influence of the environment, this places the burden for the control of behaviour on society.

The different types of environmental influence

The environment is commonly thought of as:

- external to the individual
- post-natal
- acting on a passive individual.

Such a view is, however, oversimplified and inaccurate.

Levels of the environment

Lerner (1986) talks of different levels of the environment. The environment can be internal and pre-natal (as well as external and post-natal). Moreover, the influence of the environment can be quite narrow, such as the pre-natal environment in the womb, or more general, such as the sociocultural environment.

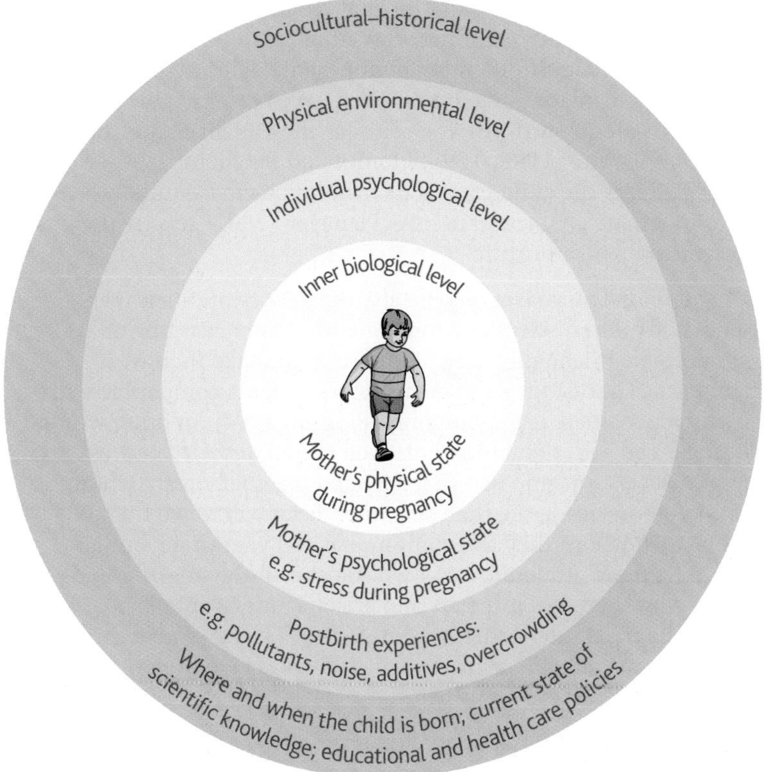

Fig. 1 *Levels of the environment*

AQA Examiner's tip

How science works: notice the difficulties faced by researchers in trying to tease out the separate contributions of nature and nurture to individual differences in behaviour.

- Twin studies are a form of natural experiment – genetic relatedness and environmental conditions are not controlled by the experimenter.
- It is very difficult to identify a cause-and-effect relationship.

AQA Examiner's tip

Be absolutely clear about the meaning of 'heritability'. Heritability estimates do not apply to individuals, only to variations within a group. Journalistic accounts of behavioural genetics research overlook this fact. In a *Time* article on the heritability of intelligence (12 January, 1987), a passage read: 'How much of any individual's personality is due to heredity? The ... answer: about half.' Such a statement is clearly misleading.

AQA Examiner's tip

Exam questions may require you to discuss examples of topic areas in the context of the nature–nurture debate. Have ready at your fingertips topics that illustrate the debate. Possible topic areas to consider are perception, theories of cognitive development, gender, anxiety and mood disorders, theories of offending and substance abuse.

Take it further

The inner-biological level

This *in utero* environment is both internal and pre-natal. Any influence exerted by the genes can be modified by the physiological state of the mother. The critical factors are the 'three D's': disease, drugs and diet. Immediate examples that spring to mind are rubella, alcohol and malnutrition. Rubella is most dangerous if transmitted during the first month of gestation. The organs most likely to be affected are the ears, eyes and heart. Deafness is a common outcome. In the early 1970s, fetal alcohol syndrome (FAS) was identified in some children born to alcoholic mothers (Jones *et al.*, 1973). Infants with FAS are generally smaller than normal with smaller brains, heart defects and low IQ scores. Indeed, FAS is considered the leading known cause of intellectual retardation in the USA. The mother's diet is also important. If she is severely malnourished, there are increased risks of stillbirth, low birth weight and infant death during the first year. Girls born to malnourished mothers continue to have stunted growth patterns throughout childhood and are more likely to bear low-birth-weight babies even if during pregnancy their nutrition was adequate (Werner, 1979). Rose (1976) claimed that malnutrition in a female rat in infancy may affect the condition in her womb (even if she is well fed later in life) so that offspring themselves will be in a deprived pre-natal environment. He believes that this could be a contributor to the apparently genetic factor in the development of intelligence in humans. What appears to be a genetic effect is in fact environmental.

Key terms

Constructivism: the view that human experience is a construction of reality. Individuals shape and actively create their own experiences.

Shared and unshared environments

The findings that even MZ twins reared together (same genes, same environment) do not yield perfect concordance rates have prompted psychologists to search for a possible explanation. As a result, psychologists have begun to focus on the unshared environments of siblings. It does not follow that just because two children are brought up in the same home they share the same environment. Individuals from the same home may have different experiences, friends, teachers, hobbies, etc. Furthermore, the same experience may have differing effects on each person thus creating different environments. For example, a parent may become unemployed when one child is 13 years old but the other is only a toddler. The same experience may have a different effect on each child because of their age. Elder (1974) found that paternal unemployment during the Great Depression had different effects on a child depending on the age and sex of the child. Chance factors such as accidents and illnesses are further examples of 'unshared nurture'.

Interaction of heredity and environment

A possible reason why unshared environmental influences were neglected until recently is that they interact so closely with genetic factors as not to be easily recognised. An individual's innate characteristics may elicit particular responses from people. For example, a baby genetically predisposed to be sociable and easygoing will attract more affectionate and stimulating care than a more 'difficult' baby. Thus the environments of the two babies will differ. Belsky and Rovine (1987) have suggested that children with different temperaments present different challenges to their caregivers; these determine the caregiver's responses to them, and these responses change the environment for that child. So two children brought up in the same home and seemingly the same environment may in fact create their own uniquely different environments. This helps explain why some MZ twins reared in different families have been known to report their adoptive parents' warmth as so similar they might almost be the same parents (Plomin, 1988, 1994; Plomin and Bergman, 1991; Plomin *et al.*, 1977). Thus the child creates its own 'microenvironment', which is related to its innate characteristics. As Flanagan (2002) succinctly puts it 'nature creates its own nurture'.

According to **constructivism**, people also actively create their own experiences. 'Children select environments that are rewarding or at least comfortable; niche-picking ... Children can make their own environments. That is, they can create environments compatible with their own propensities; niche-building' (Plomin, 1994). In other words, people shape and select environments well suited to their 'natures'. As an example, let us imagine two sisters reared together, one of whom is 'naturally' more academic than the other. Each will make friends with those with whom they feel comfortable and who share similar interests. The more academic sister will most probably make friends with those who share her interests and are of a similar intellectual level and whom she finds intellectually stimulating. The other sister may feel uncomfortable in such an 'environment' and will make friends with those who share her interests.

The point that Plomin is making is important: it is not possible to define the environment independently of the person. People may be seen as making their own environments – attaching their own meaning to events and experiences. This runs contrary to the behaviourist approach that views the individual as a passive recipient of environmental influences.

Even the seemingly purely biological 'ripening' of the nervous system turns out on closer investigation to involve the environment.

Research study: Blakemore and Cooper (1970)

Aim: To investigate the effects on perceptual processing of being reared in a restricted visual environment.

Method: Newborn kittens were placed in drums that had either vertical or horizontal lines on the walls; the floor was made of glass reflecting the pattern of stripes (see Figure 2). The kittens were fitted with collars around their necks so that they could not see their own bodies. At five months, the kittens were tested for line recognition.

Results: Those who had been brought up in the 'vertical world' acted as if blind to a horizontal world: for example, they would trip over ropes. Conversely, those brought up in a 'horizontal world' acted as if blind to a vertical world: for example, they would walk into chair legs. This behavioural blindness was mirrored by physiological blindness. Microelectrode recordings confirmed that the cells in the visual area of the brain only showed an electrical response to the orientation experienced by the kitten.

Conclusion: Such findings suggest that the environment is important to the development of innate systems.

Evaluation: The study has been criticised on ethical grounds.

Fig. 2 *The vertical world – Blakemore and Cooper's (1970) experiment*

Phenylketonuria (PKU) is an inherited disorder and a classic example of the interaction between heredity and environment. People with PKU are unable to metabolise phenylalanine (a protein contained in many everyday foods). In people with PKU, phenylalanine is broken down into a substance that is poisonous to the developing nervous system, resulting in brain damage and intellectual retardation. Genetic factors are strongly implicated as the problem can be traced to a pair of defective genes. However, if the disorder is detected soon after birth and the child is raised

Hint

This illustrates why it is not possible to say that individual personalities are 'x' per cent genes and 'y' per cent experience as the gene-experience effect is so intertwined.

Link

Friendships are based on shared mutual interests and mutual understanding. One explanation for same-sex preferences in most children's friendships is that boys and girls prefer different activities. See Chapter 1, Social development.

Take it further

The works of R.D. Laing, the so-called 'anti-psychiatrist' guru, stress environmental factors in the origin of schizophrenia. He claimed that it was the micro-environment of the person's family that might be responsible for the patient's condition. *Sanity, Madness and the Family* (Laing and Esterton, 1970), presents reports on interviews with 11 people with schizophrenia. These reports present the families as 'schizogenic' (families with poor communication systems and high conflict). According to Laing, schizophrenia is an understandable response if looked at from the sufferer's perspective; a way of coping with the mad things that go on in the immediate family. Perhaps more contentious was the proposal that the concepts of 'normality' and mental 'illness' are social constructions in the first place and that a sufferer's distress is made worse by the attempts at 'culturing out' any thoughts, feelings and behaviours that might be unacceptable to society (Bell, 2002). Present-day psychiatry is on the whole sceptical about these claims, not least because no control group of 'healthy' families was used to check whether or not 'mad things' went on in all families. Additionally, twin studies (e.g. Shields, 1978) tend to support the genetic link for schizophrenia.

on a phenylalanine-free diet, development is normal. So, although PKU is hereditary, it is not possible to separate nature and nurture. It is not possible to say that genetic factors caused low intelligence. Neither can it be claimed that the environment caused the low intelligence.

The different approaches and the nature–nurture debate

Although both nature and nurture interact and have a role in shaping behaviour, the different approaches tend to stress different ends of the nature–nurture dimension. Below is a summary of the approaches' positions in relation to the nature–nurture debate.

The psychoanalytic approach

Freud stressed the biological nature of human beings. The focus of this approach is on the instinctual drives of sex and aggression, which are expressed within the restrictions imposed by society. The reactions of significant others to the child's attempts to gratify biological urges and the consequent frustration or satisfaction can produce long-term effects on the child's personality, such as fixation at particular stages of development. However, although Freud acknowledged the influence of the environment in terms of the different experiences as the child passes through the psychosexual stages, nurture is always secondary.

The behaviourist approach

Behaviourists such as Skinner and Watson put forward an extreme viewpoint: environmental determinism. They saw the role of nurture as of paramount importance. Behaviour was seen as being directly shaped and controlled through associative learning and the consequences of behaviour. In human society, the micro-environments of the home, school and work and the sociocultural and political macro-environments are the determining factors in a person's behaviour. The behaviourists' commitment to the nurture extreme of the nature–nurture dimension is absolute.

Social learning theory

Social learning theorists stress the role of the environment on a person's behaviour. Little attention is paid to the biological determinants of behaviour: inherently, we are neither good nor bad, neither clever nor dull; our behaviour is modifiable by environmental factors in our personal histories and contemporary situational circumstances. However, social learning theorists differ from radical behaviourists in acknowledging that environmental factors are not the only influence on behaviour. Higher-level cognitive processes, such as the individual's appraisal of the situation, also have an effect on behaviour. Thus social learning approaches differ from behaviourism by considering the interaction between the individual and their environment. Individuals and situations influence each other reciprocally.

The cognitive approach

Cognitive psychologists are interactionist in their approach. Their focus is on innate information processing abilities that are constantly refined by experience. For example, Piaget has proposed that the stages of cognitive development are determined by nature: the order is invariant and roughly age related. Innate schemas develop and expand through continuous interaction with the external world.

Link

Disorders in which there appears to be an inherited susceptibility are a good example of the interaction between heredity and environment. The disorder will only appear under certain environmental conditions. Two people with the same genotype could be influenced quite differently by different environments. See Chapter 5, Schizophrenia and mood disorders.

Link

Personality is shaped as the biological drives are modified by different conflicts at the different stages of psychosexual development. See Chapter 9, Approaches in psychology.

Link

The behaviourist approach argues that essentially all behaviour is acquired from the environment through classical and operant conditioning. Two people differ from one another because of the different environments to which they have been exposed and not because of differences they have inherited. See Chapter 9, Approaches in psychology.

Link

Social learning theory emphasises the rewards (or punishments) that a child receives for sex-appropriate (or sex-inappropriate) behaviour and a process of identification with the same-sex adults based on observational learning. See Chapter 3, Gender development, in *AQA Psychology B AS*, and Chapter 9, Approaches in psychology, in this book.

Link

The child constructs his or her own knowledge and understanding of the world through interaction with the environment. However development is always limited by biological maturation. Piagetian followers and other developmental psychologists are interested in examining ways in which improved environments can maximise children's potential for psychological development.

The humanistic approach

According to humanistic psychologists, life's main motive, the need to self-actualise is innate. However, humans are significantly influenced by environmental variables. If a person is provided with unconditional positive regard and conditions are favourable then progress toward fulfilment will occur. For humanistic psychologists, both nature and nurture have roles in determining behaviour and setting the boundaries within which one is free to develop.

The biological approach

According to the biological approach, there is continuing interaction between nature and nurture. Although the focus of the approach is on heredity, the interaction with the environment is nevertheless acknowledged. For example, the study by Blakemore and Cooper (1970) illustrates the plasticity of the visual cortex (see p267). Nature interacts with nurture.

Key points:

- The nature–nurture debate concerns the role of genes and environment in determining behaviour.
- The emphasis in the debate has changed. It is now recognised that genes and environment interact with one another and that both are needed in any explanation of behaviour.
- Twin studies and adoption studies are used to estimate the heritability of behaviours.
- The complexity of the debate is emphasised by Lerner (1986) who describes different levels of the environment.
- More recently, psychologists have considered unshared environments as part of the explanation for sibling differences.
- Innate characteristics shape the environment. People actively construct their experiences consistent with their genetic tendencies.

Summary questions

4 Give one reason why the nature–nurture debate in psychology does not ask which of the two, heredity or environment, is responsible for behaviour.

5 What is meant by an 'unshared environment'? Explain why this is an important concept in the nature–nurture debate.

6 Briefly compare two approaches in the context of the nature–nurture debate.

Link

Maslow refers to 'favourable' conditions for self-actualisation. The fact that few people reach the pinnacle of the hierarchy of needs illustrates the powerful force of 'nurture'. Similarly few people experience unconditional acceptance from others as described by Rogers. See Chapter 1, Key approaches, in *AQA Psychology B AS*, for Maslow's hierarchy of needs, and see Chapter 9, Approaches in psychology, in this book, for Rogers' views.

AQA Examiner's tip

It is incorrect to say (as candidates sometimes do) that 'nature is determinism' and 'nurture is free will'. In cases of aggression, for example, genetic evidence is rarely accepted as a defence where a crime is committed. Skinner totally rejects the role of free will in behaviour and talks of environmental determinism.

Holism and reductionism

Learning objectives:

- understand what is meant by 'holism' and 'reductionism' in psychology
- evaluate reductionist and holistic explanations of behaviour
- apply reductionism to topic areas in psychology
- in the context of the holism and reductionism debate, explain what is meant by an interactionist approach.

Link

For definitions of 'holism' and 'reductionism', see Chapter 9, Approaches in psychology, p248.

Hint

'Component' quite simply means a 'part'. In the context of the 'class', each person in the class is a 'component' or 'part'. In reductionism, explanations of behaviour lie in reducing behaviour to the **simplest** parts.

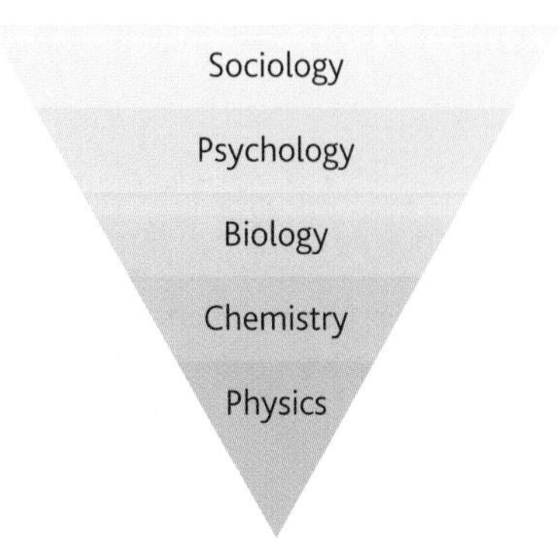

Fig. 3 *A reductionist hierarchy of explanation*

What is meant by 'reductionism' and 'holism?

Imagine a person displaying symptoms of depression and consulting a general practitioner (GP) for help. How might the GP respond to the patient? There are, broadly speaking, two approaches. One is to confirm the diagnosis, prescribe drugs designed to control the activity of brain neurotransmitters and send the patient home. The other approach is to try to find out more about the patient and the background to the problem. This could be by looking into their family background, recent life events, physical health in general, employment, etc. The latter approach takes time and may involve further consultations and talking to other people such as family members.

If the GP decides to give the patient drugs this means they are looking at the condition of the patient from a **reductionist** point of view. The patient is seen as a biological organism with an organic illness – most probably decreased levels of the neurotransmitter serotonin – that simply requires drugs to redress the balance. The explanation for the disorder can be 'reduced down' to the level of brain neurotransmitters. No other explanation is required. However, if 'the bigger picture' is considered, such as the patient's family background, recent life events, employment record and the patient's own subjective view of the world, then the condition is looked at from a **holistic** point of view.

Before considering examples of reductionism, it is important first to clarify two ways in which the term 'reductionism' is used in psychology and to consider a related concept; 'levels of explanation'.

Reduction to separate components

Complex phenomena can be explained by breaking them down into separate, simpler components. For example, the behaviour of a class of pupils can be explained as the result of the behaviours of all the individuals within it. When the class is taught, by whom, the nature of the subject matter and class dynamics are not relevant to an explanation of the class's behaviour.

Reduction to a lower level

This use of the term is closely linked with the first. This version of reductionism places psychology in a hierarchy of sciences between the social sciences and the physical sciences. The less precise and more general sciences are at the top of the hierarchy and the more narrowly focused and precise physical sciences are at the bottom. Ultimately, psychological explanations may be replaced by explanations in terms of the physical sciences, such as biology, or even in terms of physics and chemistry.

Reductionism and levels of explanation

Reductionism when applied to psychology results in different levels of explanation. These overlap with sociology (higher-level explanations) and biology (lower-level explanations).

The table below outlines these levels and illustrates how they might be applied to explain the behaviour of signing a cheque.

Table 1 *Levels of explanation*

Level of explanation	Description	As applied to the signing of a cheque	Holistic/Reductionist
Societal/sociological/ political level	Cultural context	Explanation at the level of the context in which one lives: e.g. in order to transfer money, it is necessary to sign a cheque	**Holistic**
Social-psychological	Interactions/ relationships between people	Explanation at the level of the person as a social animal: e.g. I am making a gift to a relative. Much observable behaviour has social implications	
Psychological	Aspects internal to the person: cognitive processes; personality; emotions	Explanation at the level of what is going on in the writer's 'head' whilst signing the cheque: e.g. resentment at having to pay a bill	
Physical/muscular	Central and peripheral nervous system	Explanation at the level of **overt behaviour**: e.g. movement of the writer's arm	
Physiological units	Parts of the brain	Explanation at the level of hand–eye coordination: visual cortex and cerebellum	
Neurological	Neurons and their interconnections	Explanation at the level of the pathways in the brain needed to write the signature	**Reductionist**

(Adapted from ***Rose****, 1976)*

To what level should psychologists reduce descriptions in order to provide the 'best' explanation of behaviour? That is the question that concerns psychologists. Is greater insight into the underlying nature of a phenomenon achieved by the sum of its components and explanations at a basic level? Or does reductionism lead to an oversimplification of explanations of behaviour?

Reductionist explanations of behaviour

Biological reductionism

Biological reductionism is the attempt to explain all behaviour in terms of neurophysiology, biochemistry or genes. It is argued that, because we are made up of biological 'components' (neurons, chemicals, genes, etc.), all behaviour can be reduced to a biological level and explained at that level, and other levels are unimportant. Thus, the simple act of shaking hands with a friend can be reduced to neural and muscular activities.

Evaluation

Biological reductionism has been applied to topics such as schizophrenia, addiction, depression, crime and forgetting. The obvious advantage of biological reductionism is that behaviour can be described in precise and concise terms. It is much easier to understand and explain schizophrenia as being due to over-activity of the neurotransmitter dopamine or the action of genes than to consider social and environmental explanations. Higher-level explanations are not readily observable nor easily defined or measured. Similarly, it is easier to understand and explain depression as being due to decreased levels of the neurotransmitter serotonin than to use vague psychological terms such as 'the need for self-actualisation'. Biological reductionism therefore fits in with scientific psychology.

However, although there does seem to be a biological basis to some disorders and behaviours, few would accept biological reductionism as an adequate explanation of behaviour. There are biological explanations

Key terms

Overt behaviour: behaviour that is open, available and detectable by whoever observes it. It is what the strict behaviourist argues should be the subject matter of psychology although more recently technology has made that which was covert open for observation.

Hint

The higher levels are more 'holistic' and involve the 'bigger picture'; they are further removed from simpler explanations. The lower the level, the more reductionist the explanation.

Link

Early attempts to explain perception reduced perception to elementary sensations. Perception is an example of a complex phenomenon; see Chapter 8, Perceptual processes, in *AQA Psychology B AS*.

Debates

for schizophrenia but equally there are explanations at a higher socio-cultural level. Thus, it is not accepted that biological processes alone can provide an adequate explanation of the disorder.

Research into addiction (Alexander *et al.*, 1978) suggests that more is involved than simply biological factors such as a genetic predisposition or a lack of naturally occurring pain-relieving chemicals.

Research study: Alexander *et al.* (1978)

Aim: To investigate the role of social and environmental factors in addiction.

Method: This was an independent groups design. One group of rats was kept in isolated and cramped conditions. Another group of rats was kept in roomy conditions and in the company of other rats. The independent variable was whether the rat was raised in a social and roomy environment or in an isolated and cramped environment. For both groups of rats the only liquid available for drinking was a solution of morphine. Once the rats were habituated to (familiarised with) the morphine, a series of test trials began. The rats were given a choice between the morphine solution and water.

Results: The dependent variable was measured by the amount of morphine solution consumed. Rats raised in cramped, isolated conditions drank significantly more of the morphine solution than those raised in roomy and social conditions.

Conclusion: The process of addiction is influenced not just by biological factors but also by social and environmental factors.

Evaluation: The strength of this study is its simple manipulation of the two conditions of the experiment. This was made possible by the use of animals in the study. The many causes of addiction were reduced to a manageable number in the smaller world of a laboratory. But this results in another form of reductionism – experimental reductionism – and the ensuing question of ecological validity. The main weaknesses of the study are the questionable extrapolation of results from animal research to humans and the ethical issue of creating morphine dependency in rats.

Behaviourism

Reductionism is one of the main criticisms levelled at the behaviourist approach. A basic assumption of this approach is that only overt behaviour should be the data for psychology (the physical/muscular level). The lower levels are dismissed as being the concern of the biological sciences and not psychology and the higher levels as dealing with aspects not readily observable. The behaviourist approach is only concerned with openly observed behaviour and maintains that the appropriate unit of analysis is the simple stimulus and response association (S–R links) strengthened by reinforcement. Complex behaviour is simply a series of S–R links. **Radical behaviourism** maintained that all psychological phenomena are in fact behaviours and that to understand these there was no need to refer to cognitive factors. For example, Watson termed thinking 'sub-vocal' speech or 'events beneath the skin' that can be measured by electrical activity in the larynx. In other words, thinking can be reduced to overt behaviour: quiet speaking. His theory was refuted by Smith (Smith *et al.*, 1947) who very bravely took a curare derivative (curare is a poison), which paralysed all his muscles including those in his larynx (an artificial respirator was used to

AQA Examiner's tip

Take care not to confuse the issue in this debate. The argument is not concerned with whether these biological processes play a role in behaviour but whether they **alone** can provide insight into complex behaviour.

To prepare for the exam, consider reductionist attempts to explain behaviour in the topics you have studied at AS and are studying at A2. Make a note of the strengths and weaknesses of such reductionist explanations.

Link

Sociocultural explanations of schizophrenia are labelling and family dysfunction. These are higher-level and more holistic explanations then the lower-level biological explanations. See Chapter 5, Schizophrenia and mood disorders.

AQA Examiner's tip

It is important to be aware of 'how science works' in all the debates. The reductionist approach unlike the holistic approach fulfils the aims of science: **prediction, understanding** and **control** of behaviour. Prepare for the exam by writing a short paragraph to explain this. Refer to a topic to illustrate your answer.

Key terms

Radical behaviourism: the view that there may be mental events but these are not relevant to any explanation of behaviour. This was Skinner's position: any reference to internal mental processes was rejected.

keep him alive). According to behaviourists, he would not be able to think owing to the paralysis of the larynx. However, Smith was able to understand what was going on around him and what people were saying and to think about these events even though the muscles in the larynx were paralysed.

Evaluation

Given the emphasis on overt behaviour and the implication the study of overt behaviour has for measurement and objectivity, behaviourism can claim to be a highly scientific approach. However, as behaviourists believed that humans and animals are related both physiologically and behaviourally, their research into learning was carried out on animals. It was argued that complex high-level functioning of humans can be understood at the level of S–R links studied in rats and other animals. This view is certainly not shared by all psychologists:

- Humanistic psychologists would argue that the human condition is unique: humans are both qualitatively and quantitatively different from animals.
- Gestalt psychologists believed that learning was not an association between stimuli and responses but a restructuring or reorganising of the whole situation (see p274).

Strengths of a reductionist approach

- Reductionism is consistent with a scientific approach to psychology and links psychology to respected scientific disciplines such as biology and neuroscience. By breaking phenomena down into smaller simple components these can be more easily tested and theories falsified.
- Reductionism simplifies behaviour and makes it easier for behaviour to be explained in concrete and concise terms. A principle that lies at the heart of the reductionist approach was suggested by Morgan (1852–1936). Morgan's law of parsimony states that there is no need to explain behaviour in terms of complex psychological processes when it can adequately be explained in terms of much simpler ones. Scientific methods seek explanations that are as parsimonious as possible. A good parsimonious explanation does not go beyond the available evidence. The behaviourist approach, which focuses on overt behaviour, is parsimonious: the psychoanalytic approach, which focuses on the unconscious mind, conflicts, Oedipus complex, etc., is not.

Weaknesses of a reductionist approach

- The complexity of behaviour is missed. In the example of signing a cheque referred to earlier, the real importance of a cheque is its social psychological meaning. After all the vast majority of actions derive their meaning from their relevance to interactions with others. Explaining the behaviour at the level of neural and muscular activities leaves out the psychological reasons for signing the cheque (e.g. is it a gift or repaying a debt?). The meaning of the action, the 'why' of behaviour is often gained from the situation or cultural context, not its underlying physiological description. Furthermore, the psychological dimension of an experience is crucial to an understanding of behaviour. The feeling of depression is not describable or explicable in terms of neurotransmitters.
- Reductionist explanations may distract attention from other levels of explanation. Research has shown that people who feel that they can do nothing to influence what happens to them develop a sense of 'learned helplessness' (Seligman, 1974). Eventually this can lead to depression. Research has also found that, although this happens to men

Key terms

Sociobiology: a branch of biology that focuses on the biological basis of social behaviour.

Take it further

Sociobiology, closely allied to genetic explanations of behaviour, is a reductionist approach to the study of social behaviour. All social behaviour is explained in terms of evolutionary processes and the motive for all behaviour is assumed to be the continuation of one's own genes. For example, altruism, (putting the interests of others first) may result in an individual's death but may allow for the survival of a relative such as an offspring. So, in helping biological relatives with whom genes are shared, the individual increases the survival of their own genetic code.

Hint

Do not confuse sociobiology with the theory of evolution. In sociobiology, it is the gene rather than the individual that is the basic unit of evolution.

Link

The biological approach discusses behaviour at the physical level; behaviourists also reduce all behaviour to S–R links, ignoring mental processes. For both approaches, the problem of lack of predictability of humans and the potential for free will can be conveniently put to one side and scientific status claimed. For more on the free will and determinism debate see pp257–262.

Hint

'Parsimony' in this context means being economical with explanations. It is a scientific principle which states that if there are two opposing theories and both are equally possible, the simpler one is preferred.

Take it further

Reductionism and the mind–body problem

This philosophical issue is concerned with the relationship between mind (awareness) and the body. Behaviourists used the term 'black box' to refer to the mind, which was considered totally irrelevant to any understanding of behaviour. To behaviourists, the mind was reduced to an epiphenomenon: a secondary process which arises simply from the existence of the brain (rather like 'dreams' arising from biochemical and neurological events during sleeping). It does not influence behaviour and is not required to explain behaviour.

and women, the latter are more vulnerable to depression. This could be because of women's status in society relative to men. Women also are in greater need of approval from others and depend on others for their feelings of self-worth. This is a social-psychological explanation of depression which does not point to treatment by physiological means yet drug therapy continues as does the research into biological explanations.

Holistic explanations of behaviour

Reductionism is often contrasted with holism. Holism is any approach that emphasises the whole person, whole system, whole of behaviour or whole experience rather than the component parts. Two examples in psychology are Gestalt psychology and the humanistic approach.

Gestalt psychology

Gestalt psychologists working in the period 1915–1945 argued that, when studying any aspect of human functioning, it is essential to look at unified wholes, complete structures and totalities. The nature of an experience or behaviour is not revealed simply by analysing the several parts that make up the whole. In other words, 'the whole of behaviour and experience is more than the sum of its parts'. Gestalt psychologists applied their beliefs mainly to the study of perception. The rule of closure illustrates how by dividing up phenomena we can destroy their character. When shown the figure (Figure 4) and asked to describe the experience, people report seeing a rectangle (the object as a whole) – not a rectangle with a bit missing or a figure comprising four lines joined at right angles, one of which is shorter than the others, and so on. Similarly, when asked to read the following extract people do not report being unable to read it.

> I cdnuolt blveiee taht I cluod aulaclty uesdnatnrd waht I was rdanieg The phaonmneal pweor of the hmuan mnid. It deosn't mttaer in waht oredr the ltteers in a wrod are, the olny iprmoatnt tihng is taht the frist and lsat ltteer be in the rghit pclae. The rset can be a taotl mses and you can sitll raed it wouthit a porbelm. This is bcuseae the huamn mnid deos not raed ervey lteter by istlef, but the wrod as a wlohe.

The explanation is in the text! Additionally, the context in which a 'word' is placed is part of the 'whole' experience.

Key terms

Gestalt: a German word meaning 'whole configuration'. Members of the Gestalt school of thought argued that a behaviour can only be understood in terms of its whole rather than by being broken down into component parts.

Insight learning: a cognitive view of learning whereby a new behaviour is acquired simply through the process of insight rather than by trial and error. It is the sudden solution to a problem.

Insight learning is a Gestalt view of learning and opposed to the reductionist S–R approach. Kohler (1925), a leading Gestalt psychologist, demonstrated insight learning in chimpanzees. A banana was placed outside the cage, well out of reach of a hungry chimpanzee. A long stick was also placed outside the cage but within reach. After unsuccessfully trying to grasp the banana with its hand (by extending its arm), the chimpanzee suddenly reached for the stick and raked in the banana. Insight learning happens when all the parts (in this study, the stick, the arm, the distances involved) are seen in relationship to each other, forming a meaningful whole. It is the 'sudden reorganisation or restructuring of the pattern … allowing one to grasp the relationships relevant to the solution' (*Penguin Dictionary of Psychology*, 2001).

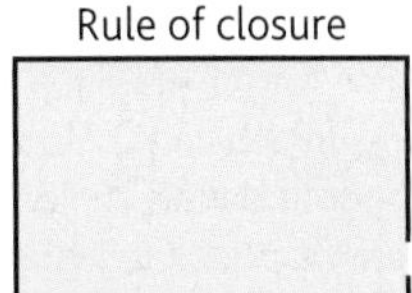

Fig. 4 *Rule of closure – we tend to see the figure as a whole although it is incomplete*

The humanistic approach

The humanistic approach investigates all aspects of an individual. According to humanistic psychologists, any attempt to analyse personality in terms of simple responses to stimuli is not only futile but is 'disrespect for the unique quality of the human spirit' (Matson, 1971). Humanistic psychologists believe that a person can only be understood as a whole (body and mind) and cannot be reduced to laws of conditioning or to biochemical processes in the brain. According to humanistic theory, the drive for self-actualisation gives purpose and unity to the whole of the person. This is reflected in the therapies and theories of both Rogers and Maslow. In Rogers' client-centred therapy, the individual is encouraged to develop a sense of the 'whole person'. Maslow studied healthy individuals from a holistic perspective; for Maslow, peaks of experience give people a sense of unity, wholeness and a sense of fulfilment.

An interactionist approach

An **interactionist approach** considers several levels of explanation to explain phenomena. Attempts by psychologists to explain abnormal behaviour provide a good example of this approach. In explaining schizophrenia, for example, biological, psychological and social factors are considered both within the person's immediate social group and within society as a whole. It is only by taking account of all these factors that psychologists can achieve a better understanding of the problem.

Strengths of anti-reductionist approaches

- Holistic and interactionist approaches provide a more complete picture of behaviour and experience than reductionist approaches.
- Higher-level explanations do not ignore the complexity of behaviour and can therefore be more meaningful.

Weaknesses of anti-reductionist approaches

- There is difficulty in integrating and in investigating explanations from different levels.
- Holistic explanations are more hypothetical than lower-level reductionist explanations and so lack the predictive power of a scientific explanation.

Cohen (1977) sums up the debate neatly:

- Behaviour is variable and determined by many factors so to look for a single causal explanation is not helpful.
- Sometimes lower-level explanations are helpful. For example, in some cases, memory failure may be due to trace decay, which is a biological explanation, but, if a psychologist wanted to predict how people would vote in a forthcoming election, a detailed biochemical and physiological examination of their brains would not be of value and a high-level explanation will be required.
- Sometimes more than one level will be necessary (e.g. biological, psychological and social factors in mental disorders).

Key points:

- Reductionism works on the scientific assumptions that complex phenomena should be explained by the simplest underlying principles.
- The biological and behaviourist approaches in psychology are typical examples of reductionism.
- The issue in reductionism is whether or not reductionist explanations adequately explain behaviour.
- One alternative to reductionism is holism, which considers higher-level explanations. Examples are the Gestalt approach and humanistic approach.
- Another alternative to reductionism is an interactionist approach, which looks at the interaction between several levels of explanation.

Key terms

Interactionist approach: explanations of human behaviour in terms of links or interactions between different levels of explanations.

Links

According to the holistic theory of face recognition, a face is recognised as a whole including the layout of the features, emotional information and the context in which the face is seen. A face is not recognised simply by reducing it to its component features.

Illusions show that people perceive more than the sum of sensations on the retina. In the Muller-Lyer illusion, the perceived length of two lines of equal length differs depending on the shape of the fins at the end of the lines. See Chapter 8, Perceptual processes, in *AQA Psychology B AS*.

Hint

Insight learning is the 'eureka' experience attributed to Archimedes. He is said to have experienced this as he got into a bath and saw the water level rising. This flash of insight – that an object displaces its own volume in water – was the solution to a problem.

Take it further

If you want to explore the philosophical aspects of this debate, you may be interested in the philosopher J.S. Mill's argument for 'emergence'. This means that events can only be described and explained at one level. To reduce them to another level is impossible because the explanatory terms do not apply. To take an example from chemistry, salt (NaCl) has emergent properties. Its texture and appearance are not predictable from any combination of the properties of sodium (Na), a metal, and chlorine (Cl), a gas. A psychological example is 'beauty' contained in a person's face. Beauty is not found in the individual features but the way they come together, expressions, grace, etc.

Link

Humanistic psychologists adopt an idiographic approach and look at people as individuals in a holistic way. This has implications for methods of research. See below.

Hint

Even though they are both anti-reductionist, there is a subtle difference between an interactionist approach and holism. Holism considers a higher-level explanation; whereas an interactionist approach considers interactions between different levels of explanation, such as in the diathesis stress model of schizophrenia.

Summary questions

7 Name two types of reductionism and provide examples of each.

8 Outline two alternatives to reductionism. For each alternative, state why it might provide a better explanation.

9 Explain why reductionism is compatible with the idea of psychology as a science. Refer to examples in psychology.

Idiographic and nomothetic approaches

Learning objectives:

- understand what is meant by the idiographic and nomothetic approaches
- evaluate the idiographic and nomothetic approaches
- apply the idiographic and nomothetic approaches to topic areas in psychology
- explain why the idiographic and nomothetic approaches can be seen as complementary.

Key terms

Idiographic approach: an approach or method in psychology that is concerned with understanding behaviour through studying individual cases.

Nomothetic approach: an approach or method in psychology that is concerned with developing general laws of behaviour that apply to all people.

One of the major differences between the approaches in psychology is the degree of attention paid to the individual. This issue is highlighted in the debate between the **idiographic** and **nomothetic approaches**:

- An idiographic view takes the position that everyone is unique and therefore everyone must be studied in an individual way to capture the richness of human individuality. It emphasises laws for the individual; no general laws are possible because of chance, free will and the uniqueness of individuals. The humanistic approach in psychology takes an idiographic view.
- A nomothetic view focuses on general laws of behaviour, typified by behaviourism. It involves studying a large number of people, trying to understand why they behave in similar ways in certain situations. The debate as to which is more appropriate, however, is not just restricted to the types of laws about behaviour that should be developed. It is fundamental in psychology because of the implications for how psychologists should carry out research and how it affects psychology's standing as a scientific discipline. An extreme nomothetic view takes the position that scientists are concerned not with the uniqueness of the individual but with the development of general laws that apply to all people. This view is captured in the following statement by Eysenck (1951), 'Science is not interested in the unique event; the unique belongs to history and not to science'.

The idiographic approach

Features and methods of investigation

The key feature of the approach is the individual and the recognition of their uniqueness. This includes numerous aspects of individuality: for example, private, subjective and conscious experiences; feelings; beliefs and values. This approach also involves investigating individuals in a personal and detailed way. Methods of investigation tend to be qualitative.

The case study method, which can provide a complete and global understanding of the individual, is favoured. Other methods include unstructured interviews as well as the less mainstream methods such as self-report, introspection and reflection and the use of autobiographies and personal documents such as diaries and letters. In psychoanalysis, free association and dream analysis are acceptable investigating tools. However, it is important to note that numerical measurement is not excluded in the idiographic approach: it is just that the main form of data collected is description rather than measurement.

The nomothetic approach

Features and methods of investigation

The defining features of this approach are similarities between people and laws that govern behaviour. Unlike the idiographic approach, which emphasises laws for the individual, the nomothetic approach emphasises general laws of behaviour that can be applied to large populations of people. For example, research on moral development highlights the way that men, on the whole, and women, on the whole, differ from one another in their moral reasoning.

According to Radford and Kirby (1975), these general laws can be of three kinds:

- **Classifying people into various groups** An example is the *Diagnostic and Statistical Manual of Mental Disorders* (DSM-IV), which provides a means of classifying more than 200 types of disorders. Classification is based on a person's symptoms.
- **Establishing principles of behaviour that can be applied to people in general** The principles or laws of learning apply in a similar way to all people. Research in social psychology, such as the findings from conformity and obedience experiments, has resulted in general principles of behaviour that apply to all people.
- **Establishing dimensions on which people can be placed and compared** For example, intelligence quotient (IQ) scales measure people's intelligence, resulting in scores that allow for comparisons between people.

Nomothetic research uses scientific and quantitative methods of investigation, usually experiments. Theories generate hypotheses that are then tested under controlled experimental conditions. The findings of experiments and other quantitative methods, such as observations, are provided by a large number of people. Numerical data of group averages are produced; these data can be statistically analysed and predictions made about people in general. The scientific method is applied in the same way as it is used in the natural sciences. An example of nomothetic research comes from Schuckit (1985).

Research study: Schuckit (1985)

Aim: To investigate how heredity might affect alcohol abuse. (Twin and adoption studies have shown that heredity is linked to alcohol abuse.)

Method: Male participants were categorised as either 'high risk' or 'low risk' for becoming alcoholic, depending on whether or not they had close relatives who abused alcohol. This was a matched

AQA Examiner's tip

Do not think of the approaches as simply holding conflicting positions as how best to study people.
The approaches can be seen as complementary to each other and as both being necessary to the study of behaviour. Keep these points in mind as you study the approaches.

Hints

Idiographic comes from the Greek word '*idios*', which means 'personal'. It is the root of the word 'idiosyncrasy', meaning 'a mannerism that is unique or peculiar to an individual'.

The term 'nomothetic' comes for the Greek word '*nomos*', which means 'law'.

Links

'Quantitative' means to measure on some numerical basis and 'qualitative' emphasises meanings and experiences, often verbally described. Qualitative data can be later quantified to some extent. See Chapter 11, Methods in psychology.

Piaget (1953) studied cognitive development. He carried out longitudinal studies on his three children over a period of several years keeping frequent notes of his observations and a flexible method of interviewing children (the clinical interview). In so doing he gained rich and detailed information about the development of his children's thinking. See Chapter 2, Cognitive development.

Freud (1909) used the clinical case study method to gain information about his patients. They were seen frequently and Freud kept detailed notes of his interpretations. His techniques (e.g. free association) were deliberately unstructured to allow for spontaneity and free expression of patients' thoughts. See Chapter 3, Moral development.

Hint

Although 'qualitative methods' or 'research' are commonly used terms, strictly speaking it is the data or information collected is that is 'qualitative'. The same applies to 'quantitative methods/research'.

Link

Using DSM-IV, people are classified along with others suffering from a similar type of disorder such as anxiety, schizophrenia and depression. Classification has implications for clinical settings, helping practitioners with diagnosis and selection of the appropriate treatments. See Chapter 5, Schizophrenia and mood disorders.

Key terms

Generalisation: in research methodology, the application of findings from a sample to the population from which it was drawn.

Link

- The behaviourists believed that the laws of learning (reinforcement and punishment) are universal. Experiments were usually conducted on animals, such as rats or pigeons, but their laws were applied to many aspects of human behaviour, e.g. moral development and behavioural disorders. See Chapter 9, Approaches in psychology.
- Eysenck's personality inventory aims to measure personality dimensions (extroversion/ introversion and neuroticism/ stability). According to Eysenck, criminal personalities are more likely to score high in both extroversion and neuroticism than non-criminals. See Chapter 8, Forensic psychology.

pairs design; participants were matched on the basis of important variables such as age, amount of alcohol consumed per week, race and education.

All participants received either a placebo or a strong alcoholic drink. The placebo looked, smelt and tasted like the alcoholic drink. One hour after taking the drink all participants had to rate their feeling of drunkenness.

All participants were tested during the late adolescent or early adult years before any of them had developed a drinking problem.

Results: Participants in the 'high risk' group who had taken the alcoholic drink gave lower ratings of drunkenness levels than those in the 'low risk' group. In the placebo group, all participants reported lower levels of drunkenness.

Conclusion: People who are genetically prone to becoming problem drinkers may have an impaired ability to perceive the effects of alcohol and fail to notice the symptoms of drunkenness early enough to stop drinking.

Evaluation: This study has many features of the nomothetic approach. It isolated a major variable: the risk for alcoholism (participants were identified as either high or low on this dimension). The study was well controlled: participants were matched on important variables and a placebo was used. The data could be analysed in terms of group scores. The findings could be statistically analysed and be generalisable to others who differ in their risk for alcoholism, allowing predictions to be made for people who differ on the 'high–low risk alcohol' dimension. However, the conclusions are in general terms only. They cannot predict the outcome for a particular individual.

Strengths and limitations of the idiographic approach

The main problem with the idiographic approach is that **generalisations** cannot reasonably be made to a wider population. This is one of the criticisms levelled at Freud. His case study method is clearly idiographic, yet he provided a theory of personality that, he argued, is applicable to all humans.

The methods of research tend to be subjective, flexible and unstandardised, making replication of research findings, prediction and control of behaviour very difficult. The use of statistical analysis is problematic in small-scale research using mainly qualitative data. Therefore, the idiographic approach is regarded as 'unscientific'.

However, the goals of science are not simply prediction and control of behaviour. Other goals are to describe and understand behaviour, and these are best served by the idiographic approach. In fulfilling these criteria, it could be argued that the idiographic approach complements the nomothetic approach, satisfying some of the aims of science. Thus, some scientific principles can be applied to the study of the individual. Furthermore, Allport (1937) claimed that the idiographic approach could make predictions for a single individual.

The idiographic approach also provides a global and more complete understanding of the individual than the nomothetic approach. For example, Freud's case study of Little Hans provides a detailed account of the origin and development of Hans's unconscious fear. The study illustrates the application of two of Freud's more contentious concepts to behaviour: castration anxiety and the Oedipus complex. In addition, because the idiographic approach investigates individuals, it is possible to explore naturally occurring but unusual cases. These can shed further light on general laws of behaviour. In developmental psychology, Koluchova's (1972) study of a pair of Czechoslovakian twins suggested that (contrary to Bowlby's theory and research) extreme maternal privation is not irreversible. Blakemore's (1988) case study of Clive Wearing gives a very rich account of the effects of selective impairments to memory function as a result of damage to certain parts of the brain.

A further strength of the idiographic approach is that findings can serve as a source of ideas or hypotheses for later study: 'the single pebble which starts an avalanche' in terms of advances in theory (Dukes, 1965). The findings from Piaget's work with his own children, for example, became a source of inspiration for further research into cognitive development.

Strengths and limitations of the nomothetic approach

The main criticism of the nomothetic approach is that, although predictions can be made of group results, these may not apply to any one individual's behaviour. For this reason, the nomothetic approach has been accused of losing the 'whole person'. Being told that there is a one in 100 chance of becoming an alcoholic is of little help to the person who wants to be able to predict their own behaviour. The nomothetic approach also gives a very superficial understanding of a person: two people may both be classified as extrovert but they may have arrived at the same score by scoring on completely different items from each other. However, in defence of the nomothetic approach Radford and Kirby claim that, although such tests of personality or general laws of behaviour may not be precise, they are a close psychological fit.

The main strength of the nomothetic approach is that it is in tune with scientific psychology. The emphasis is on precise measurement, prediction and control of behaviour. Investigations involve large groups of people using objective and controlled methods that allow for replicability and generalisability.

Idiographic and nomothetic approaches: complementary or conflicting?

There is a tendency when considering any debate to take a conflicting 'either/or' position. However, as Kluckhohn and Murray (1953) have stated, 'every man is in certain respects like all other men, like some other men, and like no other men'. Thus both approaches have a role in psychology. The relative value of the two approaches depends on the purpose of the research. If one wants to understand general aspects of behaviour, such as the features and processes of short-term memory in general, then it makes sense to use the nomothetic approach and study a large sample of people. However, if one wants to understand and predict a particular person's ability to apply short-term memory to learning a long series of digits then an in-depth investigation using an idiographic approach may be preferable.

AQA Examiner's tip

Consider the approaches in relation to the debate. The behaviourist, cognitive (including social learning theory) and biological approaches seek to establish general principles of behaviour and can be described as nomothetic. The humanistic approach, which focuses on uniqueness, is clearly idiographic. The psychoanalytic approach is less easy to categorise.

Take it further

Freud tried to validate his work using various triangulation techniques. Triangulation involves corroborative research, such as interviewing the client's family members and medical practitioners to back up the client's history and biological and anthropological evidence. Freud also used evidence from cultural artefacts, such as stories, jokes and myths (Sachs, 1991). For these reasons, Freud maintained that his theories are generalisable.

AQA Examiner's tip

Most case studies are sources rather than test of hypotheses. You must be extremely cautious not to present case studies as evidence.

Take it further

Koluchova (1972) studied identical twins that had spent much of their first seven years of life locked in a cellar. When eventually found, they were in poor physical condition and could not understand language or talk. They were fostered and by the age of 14 were essentially normal. Such research could not have been manipulated 'experimentally' both for practical and ethical reasons but the finding that extreme maternal privation is not irreversible is extremely important. This case highlights a strength of the idiographic approach; an unusual finding can challenge an accepted theory – in this case Bowlby's theory of maternal deprivation.

The two approaches can also be complementary. In the Koluchova example quoted above, an idiographic approach shed further light on a general law of behaviour – Bowlby's maternal deprivation theory – established through a nomothetic approach. In the Piaget example, individual case studies unearthed issues that could be explored for their wider applicability using a nomothetic approach.

Key points:

- The idiographic approach is associated with qualitative methods of research and the nomothetic approach with quantitative methods of research.
- Of central interest for the idiographic approach are the unique, subjective aspects of an individual. For the nomothetic approach, similarities between people and laws that govern behaviour are of central interest.
- The main strength of the idiographic approach is that it can provide a more complete and global understanding of an individual. However, it is not possible to make generalisations from single case studies and the approach is seen as unscientific.
- The main strength of the nomothetic approach is that it deals with the general rather than the particular which makes the approach more scientific. However, the main drawback of the approach is the loss of the 'whole person'.
- The approaches are not necessarily conflicting but can be seen as complementary.

Link

Koluchova's (1972) study is described in more detail in Chapter 1, Social development.

AQA Examiner's tip

Prepare to 'discuss' the idiographic and nomothetic approaches as 'complementary'. Notice that there are several examples of 'complementarity' of approaches: the reference to Dukes (1965); the points about the Koluchova study; and that both approaches are part of the scientific method.

Summary questions

10 Identify two features of the idiographic approach.

11 Briefly explain one strength of the nomothetic approach.

12 Some psychologists would suggest that the argument over which approach is better is not productive because both approaches are needed. Give a reason in support of this claim.

Psychology and science

Learning objectives:

- explain what is meant by the 'scientific approach'
- discuss whether or not psychology is a science
- apply the scientific approach to the different approaches and topic areas in psychology
- evaluate the use of the scientific approach in psychology.

When people talk of science they often mean subjects such as physics, chemistry and biology. There is a popular belief that psychology is not a science; that it is 'all common sense', lacks precision in its procedures and cannot boast of a definable subject matter. In order to assess the controversial question of whether or not psychology is a science, it is necessary to examine the features and principles of the scientific approach and to consider how psychology measures up to these.

The features and principles of the scientific approach

- There must be a definable and agreed-upon subject matter or **paradigm**. The subject matter is what the science is about.
- There must be theory construction from which hypotheses are derived and tested.
- Empirical methods of investigation are used to gather information.
- Science should attempt to discover general laws or principles. In the case of psychology, these are universal laws that govern behaviour.

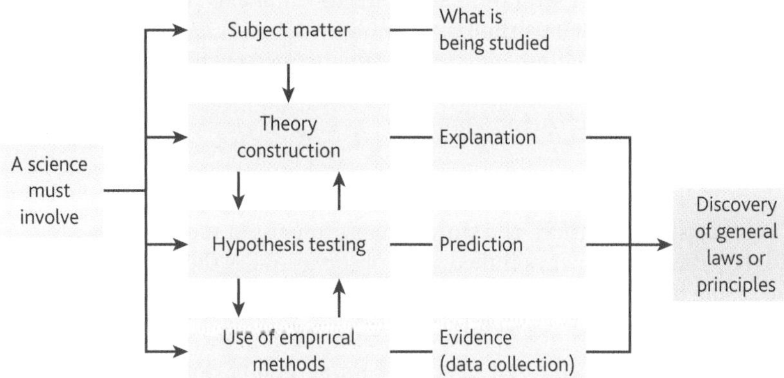

Fig. 5 *The key features of the scientific approach*

Paradigm

Kuhn (1970), a philosopher of science, believes that a subject can only be called a science if the majority of its workers agree with and work within a common 'global' theory or paradigm. In biology, nearly all biologists accept the theory of evolution and this is what unites their field and defines their work. So biology does have a paradigm.

Kuhn describes three historical stages in the development of science: pre-science, normal science and revolution. In pre-science the subject has no paradigm. It only becomes a science when someone proposes a perspective or theory that seems to explain all the facts and unites the field. Once a paradigm has been established, a settled state of normal science follows and researchers dedicate themselves to exploring the paradigm. However, a point is reached in almost all sciences where so much evidence conflicts with the paradigm that it is rejected and replaced by one that can accommodate the conflicting findings. This stage is known as 'revolution' and is relatively brief. Einstein, for example, revolutionised Newtonian physics with the theory of relativity. When such a 'paradigm-shift' occurs, there is a return to normal science.

A question now arises: does psychology fit the criterion of a 'science'? Kuhn believes that psychology is not at present characterised by a paradigm: that is, it is still a pre-science. There are too many conflicting theoretical approaches and methods of enquiry and no one global unifying theory. For example, cognitive psychologists focus on the study of mental processes whereas behaviourists believe that behaviour alone should form the object of study. The humanistic and psychodynamic approaches base their theories largely on evidence from case studies. By contrast, the other three approaches primarily use experimental methods of enquiry to inform their theories.

Key terms

Paradigm: a collective set of theoretical assumptions about a subject and its methods of enquiry. These form the generally accepted perspective of a particular subject at a point in time.

Hint

The word 'paradigm' comes from the Greek word '*paradeigma*' which means pattern. A paradigm is like a pattern or a set of shared (agreed) assumptions about something – in this case, the subject matter of psychology.

Link

Behaviourists explain depression and anxiety as a result of faulty learning; cognitive psychologists see them as due to irrational ideas and beliefs, and psychodynamic psychologists as due to unresolved and unconscious conflicts. Humanistic psychologists take the view that it is the inability to express one's true nature that is the root of the problem and biological psychologists look at genetic and organic causes. See Chapter 5, Schizophrenia and mood disorders, and Chapter 9, Approaches in psychology.

When considering such topics in psychology as depression and anxiety, explanations of behaviour illustrate the lack of shared general assumptions by the major approaches in psychology. Although each theoretical approach may be of value, unless there is a coming together of these different approaches, psychology by Kuhn's definition cannot legitimately claim scientific status.

However, not all philosophers and psychologists take the view that psychology is still at the pre-science stage. For instance, most psychologists accept the definition of psychology as the study of mind and behaviour so there is broad agreement about the overall subject matter. Palermo (1971) argues that psychology has already gone through several paradigm shifts: from structuralism, with its emphasis on identifying the elements of conscious thoughts and feelings, to behaviourism, with its emphasis on behaviour, and now finally back to cognitive psychology, which has once again replaced behaviour with the 'mind' and is probably the dominant research area today.

The role of theory and hypothesis testing

In everyday conversation, the word 'theory' means 'a mere hunch'. In science, 'theory' is always linked with observation. A theory explains observable behaviours and events using an integrated set of general principles and predicts observations.

Theories are a necessary part of science for several reasons:

- All scientists share the belief that events in the world are not random but ordered. Theories provide understanding by organising facts, finding regularities and patterns and condensing these to a short list of general principles. For example, a good theory of depression will organise countless observations concerning depression into a much shorter list of principles. Observations that depressed people describe themselves, their past, present and future in gloomy terms may lead to a theory that low self-esteem contributes to depression. The self-esteem principle neatly summarises a long list of facts about depressed people. Theories therefore satisfy a key principle of science: order.
- On basis of a theory, it is possible to make a prediction or hypothesis that can be tested. A theory is essential to research; there is no point carrying out research just in the hope of finding out something. Furthermore, an essential characteristic of a scientific theory is that it is amenable to scientific testing. In other words a scientific theory must generate testable hypotheses. Returning to the example about self-esteem and depression, a number of hypotheses can be put forward (e.g. that people with depression will be less likely to apply for a promotion than people who do not show depression) See figure b. The process of deriving new hypotheses from the theory is known as **deduction**. Deducing testable hypotheses from a theory is known as the hypothetico-deductive method.

If the predictions are not confirmed when tested, the theory is not supported and has to be reconsidered. However, if the predictions are confirmed this does not prove the theory correct. Just because some predictions are confirmed does not mean that all future predictions will also be confirmed.

Popper (1959), a scientific philosopher, believed that a theory should be falsifiable and subjected to attempts at refutation. This means that

Take it further

Wundt founded the school of structuralism. He and his associates believed that psychology should concern itself with the processes of conscious experience. The structure of conscious experience could be broken down into basic elements in the same way as in chemistry one describes the structure of water. The elements of conscious experience identified by Wundt were sensations (e.g. smell and sights), feelings (e.g. love and joy) and images (e.g. memories). An experience such as meeting a friend in a street was thought to be composed of all these elements and combined together by the mind. Wundt studied the elements of consciousness using a technique known as introspection. This involved participants reporting on their own mental processes as they experienced an object or an event under highly controlled conditions. Hence, structuralism represented an early attempt to analyse the conscious mind using the 'scientific' technique of introspection. Introspection, however, was rejected by the behaviourists as too subjective and not open to validation by others. Today, proponents of the cognitive approach, whilst recognising that cognitive processes can only be inferred from observable behaviour, believe that the processes can be studied using experimental techniques.

AQA Examiner's tip

Never write that a theory is 'proven', 'correct' or 'true', only that it is 'supported'. Hundreds of accurate predictions cannot prove a theory to be true but one inaccurate prediction disconfirms the theory. The theory could yet prove to be false.

Key terms

Deduction: the process of moving from reasoning about the general to reasoning about the particular.

the researcher should be able to imagine some occurrence that would contradict it. The 18th-century belief that drawing blood from a patient would be a cure for every illness could not be falsified. If the doctor drew blood and the patient got better, the theory was supported. If the patient died, the explanation was that it was too late to help. No possible outcome was taken as evidence against the theory.

It has been established that a theory should be based on observable data, should be a source of new hypotheses and be testable and falsifiable. But a theory should also be parsimonious; it should account for all the known facts in as economical a way as possible and not go beyond the available

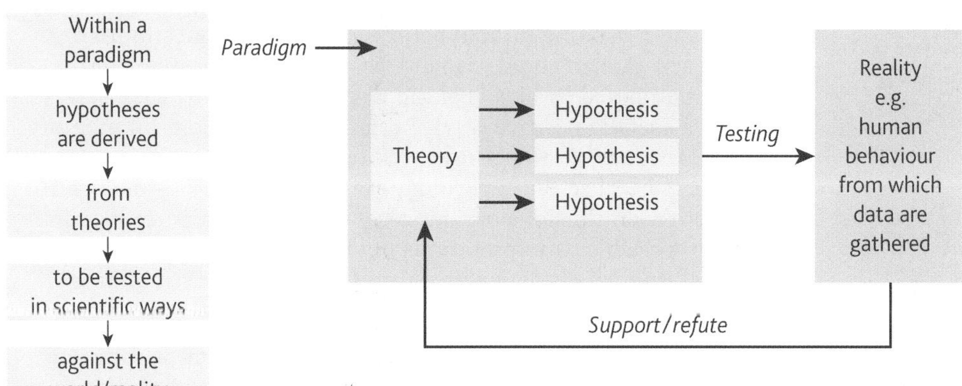

Fig. 6 *The scientific method*

empirical evidence. Predictions from theories should also have useful and practical implications such as solving problems and improving the human condition.

Empirical methods and replication

Empiricism is another principle of the scientific approach. The word derives from the Greek word meaning experience. The scientific method is empirical, that is to say that it is based on the collection of data through direct sensory experience, i.e. through observation and experiment. It does not rely on argument, belief, ideas, hearsay or faith. Experiments and observations are carried out rigorously and reported in detail so that other investigators can repeat and attempt to verify the work.

All scientific theories must at some point be subjected to empirical investigation. Any theory or idea that remains untested cannot claim to be scientific. The findings from the classic experiment by Milgram (1963) were very different from those that people predicted based on their everyday observations and beliefs. The study illustrates that common sense is of little use in understanding and predicting human behaviour and that the best way of achieving these goals is by experiment and the other empirical methods available to the researcher.

Because the term 'empirical' relates to factual and verifiable information, a corollary is that empirical methods must be **objective**. Generally speaking, methods that have the greatest control and structure, especially the experiment, can be said to be reasonably objective.

AQA Examiner's tip

Remember that a scientific theory not only explains a particular body of knowledge but is also amenable to rigorous testing. In its simplest form, a theory might just explain but strictly speaking it would fail the test of a true 'scientific theory'.

Link

Theories provide laws to predict the future but this can only occur if a deterministic/nomothetic view is taken. If there is order in events, it makes sense to assume that events happen for a reason and are determined. Determinism is another principle of science. See Chapter 9, Debates in psychology.

Key terms

Empiricism: the belief that all knowledge should be derived from sensory experience. Empirical methods refer to methods of conducting research through direct experience, preferably the experiment.

Objective: relating to that which is real or physical, publicly verifiable and externally observable. Objective data consist of facts uncoloured by the researcher's feelings or opinions. The laboratory experiment is regarded as the most objective method, whereas unstructured methods (e.g. participant observation and psychoanalysis) are not regarded as objective.

Hint

Notice that a theory can generate numerous hypotheses or predictions. It is impossible to test the whole theory. It is only possible to test aspects of the theory.

Hint

A theory offers a useful summary and brings order. Theory construction is like solving a dot-to-dot puzzle. As lines are drawn connecting the dots, a coherent picture emerges even before all the dots are connected.

Hint

A falsifiable theory means one that is capable of being 'shown to be wrong'. Freud's psychodynamic theory has been accused of being incapable of being shown to be wrong. Whatever the findings, Freudian theory can offer an explanation.

Link

Scientists propose a null hypothesis because science advances through refutation rather than support. Researchers try to falsify the null hypothesis – to demonstrate that it is false or wrong. See Chapter 4, Research methods, in *AQA Psychology B AS*, and Chapter 11, Methods in psychology, in this book.

Hint

Generalisation nearly always involves a process of induction; it is derived from a limited number of observations of participants and extended to people in general and situations in general.

However, it is unrealistic to talk of any observation as being totally objective and value free. Popper (1972) claims that observation is always pre-structured and directed and this is as true of physics as it is of psychology. He demonstrated this by asking a group of physics students to take some paper and a pencil, observe, and write down what they observed. The students (not surprisingly) asked what they were to observe, thereby showing that undirected observation cannot be followed. This disproves the idea that a scientist sees all and is equally prepared for all observations.

Nevertheless, objectivity in psychology is harder to achieve than in other sciences. This is because the subject matter in physics and chemistry is inert matter whereas psychology deals with living, conscious and reasoning human beings. A score on a questionnaire measuring self-esteem could arguably be classed as objective but it will be contaminated by bias (e.g. the respondent putting themselves forward in a socially positive way). Even in an experiment on memory, the participant may try to perform well to impress the experimenter or underperform because the experimenter reminds them of someone they do not like. Visual illusions provide clear evidence that true objectivity is not really possible. Interpretations of visual information involve expectations and beliefs about the stimulus – what the stimulus is likely to represent.

It has already been mentioned that an aspect of the scientific approach involves replication. Experiments and observations are carried out rigorously and reported in detail so that other investigators can repeat and attempt to verify the work.

Replicability of findings is an important feature of science for several reasons:

- Confidence in results is increased when investigations can be replicated.
- If similar results are found, a theory is strengthened.
- Replication confirms the validity of the finding.
- It is not possible to generalise from the findings of one study only. Participant variables such as culture may bias the findings.
- Replicable findings improve the practical value of theories.

Replication is harder to achieve in psychology than in other sciences because of the subject matter: human behaviour.

Generalisation

Generalisation refers to the ability of the researcher to make a justified extension of their conclusions, applying them to other members of the target population and other situations.

For the findings to be generalisable, the sample must be representative of the target population. One problem concerns the use of volunteers in psychological research. Given the practical and ethical constraints within which psychologists must work, volunteer bias is an ongoing problem in psychological research. There is evidence that volunteers may not be typical of a non-volunteering population. Volunteers tend to be insecure, dependent upon and influenced by others, aggressive and introverted (Ora, 1965). Thus it is not legitimate to generalise results from a volunteer sample to a wider population. Another problem relates to ecological validity; the degree to which the results of an investigation can be generalised beyond the immediate setting to other settings.

It has already been said that a feature of science is to discover general laws or principles. In the case of psychology, researchers aim to discover general laws of behaviour. A theory cannot be 'closed' and settled by the testing of one or two predictions that support it. This could happen by chance and, besides, any one study can only investigate a fragment of the whole theory. The scientist's theory is always open to challenge and further testing so that general laws can be more firmly established. Thus generalisation is linked with replication of findings.

Overt behaviour and subjective private experience

Psychology is sometimes defined as 'the scientific study of behaviour and experience'. Distinctions that have been made between behaviour and experience are that behaviour is external or **overt** and amenable to scientific enquiry whereas experience is internal, subjective and not open to scientific enquiry. These distinctions are in fact misleading. The work of biological psychologists who study internal events using 'scientific' techniques such as EEG recordings can be classified as behavioural. Cognitive psychologists attempt to investigate thought processes, memory, perception and attention. These are part of internal, private and conscious experience yet are amenable to scientific enquiry. Insights into these mental processes may be inferred from an individual's observable response.

Certainly cognitive processes such as memory constitute part of what psychologists mean by conscious experience but not what is meant by **private subjective experience**. Perhaps a more helpful distinction is the criterion of accessibility. Behaviour, whether external or 'under the skin', can be directly observed by a researcher or at least inferred using empirical methods, whereas private subjective experience cannot.

The philosopher William James (1890) spoke of a 'stream of consciousnesses' – a kind of internal monologue that is always present, unique, private and accessible only to the individual. People are aware of external events through the combined information from all the senses but this second-by-second awareness cannot be fully verbalised as it is fleeting and there is too much to report. Private subjective experience cannot therefore be fully accessed or replicated. James pointed out that people can never perceive the same event twice because on the second occasion the event is a different experience.

Ironically, the first branch of scientific psychology to emerge concentrated on experience. Wundt and his colleagues at Leipzig in the 1880s and 1890s trained participants in structured introspection to turn inwards into their world of mental experience and report what went through their mind whilst carrying out some action. Despite the laboratory setting, the 'science of mental life' as it was called could not be regarded as scientific. Introspective reports could not be verified, were subjective and accessible only to the individual reporting the experience. Only those processes of which the participant was aware could be reported. In 1913, Watson published a paper that changed the focal point of psychology from experience to behaviour. He stated:

> Psychology as the behaviorist views it is a purely experimental branch of natural science. Its theoretical goal is the prediction and control of behavior. Introspection forms no essential part of its methods, nor is the scientific value of its data dependent upon the readiness with which they lend themselves to interpretation in terms of consciousness.
>
> ***(Watson**, 1913)*

Take it further

Popper (1972) argued that is too easy to look for support for ideas: 'once your eyes were ... opened [to the belief] you saw confirming instances everywhere: the world was full of verifications of the theory. Whatever happened always confirmed it.' Science must be more demanding and this is why Popper's solution is to look for refuting evidence rather than verifications. He said, 'observations and ... statements of experimental results are always interpretations of the facts observed; they are interpretations in the light of theories.' This is one of the main reasons why it is always deceptively easy to find verifications of a theory, and why scientists have to adopt a highly critical and rigorous attitude towards theories if they do not wish to argue in circles: the attitude of trying to falsify them. Repeated failure to falsify a theory provides more and more confidence that a theory is likely to be true. For Popper, refutation is an essential feature of the scientific approach. This can be achieved through bold and precise hypotheses which can be empirically tested as in a laboratory experiment.

Key terms

Private subjective experience: personal subjective phenomena and unique to the individual. Private subjective experiences are not easily investigated using scientific procedures.

Hint

A good scientific theory:

- fits known facts
- generates several hypotheses
- is falsifiable
- is parsimonious.

Key terms

Phenomenology: the study of an individual's subjective and contemporary experience or unique perception of the world. The emphasis is on understanding events from the person's point of view rather than focusing on behaviour.

AQA Examiner's tip

You need to be aware of 'how science works' in the context of the role of the scientific community in validating new knowledge and ensuring integrity. The objectivity and rigour involved is a fundamental feature of the scientific approach.

AQA Examiner's tip

Consider the psychodynamic and behaviourist approaches. Are they based on 'scientific' theories? Use the checklist of what makes 'a good scientific theory' to guide your thinking.

AQA Examiner's tip

From topic areas in psychology, list some examples of studies that lack ecological validity. Research into memory, for example, has often been criticised for lack of ecological validity owing to the stimulus material tested (nonsense syllables or lists of words) and the artificial laboratory settings. Explain why such studies lack ecological validity.

Hint

- Think of private experience as meaning 'what is going on in the head'.
- Think of a 'stream of consciousness' as constantly changing like a river or a stream.

A good deal of recent psychology is characterised by **phenomenology**. Thus, psychology is turning back to subjective experience as part of its subject matter. Some psychologists argue that the hard-line scientific and deterministic approach of the behaviourists should not have allowed psychologists to turn away from the subject's true subject matter – mental life. This is debatable, but the fact remains that the study of subjective experience fits far less comfortably (than the study of behaviour) into a traditional model of science.

The role of peer review in validating research

Communication of psychological ideas occurs through journals, books, conference proceedings and monographs. Peer review plays a crucial role in:

- validating the quality and relevance of these ideas
- evaluating proposals to funding bodies for financial support for future work.

When work is submitted for publication, peer review involves specialists in the relevant field reading the article or book and assessing the quality of work. Their role is to ensure that appropriate methodology was used; this includes the statistical tests used to analyse the data. The reviewers will assess the quality of the work and the conclusion drawn and comment on the manuscript in a constructive way. Comments are fed back to the authors, and this may lead to minor revisions of the work before it is accepted for publication. Reviewers may suggest that a piece of writing is inappropriate for publication; perhaps because of a weak experimental design, inappropriate hypothesis or a poorly written manuscript. Generally, two or three independent psychologists will review a piece for publication. It is important that they are objective and unknown to the author. The peer review process will be managed by a supervisor such as the editor of a journal or the commissioning editor of a publishing house. When a book is published, an initial proposal will also have been peer reviewed.

Psychologists applying for money to support a piece of work that may later be published go through a similar process. This time, the peer review process will be supervised by the grant awarding team that is seeking to identify proposals most worthy of support. The team will be looking for a well-designed project that has technical merit, feasibility and relevance.

Strengths and limitations of the scientific approach in psychology

Strengths

- By applying the scientific approach to the study of behaviour, psychology earns the credibility afforded to 'scientific status'. Without the rigour of the scientific approach, people would probably believe a lot of things that are false.
- The scientific approach strives for objectivity. It provides accurate, reliable and generalisable results.
- The scientific approach involves theories that provide hypotheses to be tested. Theories allow psychology to progress as a science and provide general laws of behaviour fulfilling the aims of science – understanding, prediction and control.

- The scientific approach has provided many applications to improve people's lives and solve problems. The validity of these applications rests on the ability of the scientific method to understand the causes of behaviour and predict certain patterns of behaviour.

Limitations

The main problem for psychologists in using the scientific approach lies in applying empirical methods of enquiry, in particular the experimental method, to the subject matter – humans. It is not possible completely to prevent participants from exerting their influence on findings of research, and researchers can also exert an influence on the findings without being aware that this is happening. This leads to several sources of bias:

- The experimental situation can alter the participant's behaviour in many ways. Participants try to guess what the experiment is about and then try deliberately to do or not do what is expected of them. Thus the participant's behaviour is not a true reflection of 'normal' behaviour and the findings may be of little value. Orne and Evans (1965) found that out of 18 participants, 15 were prepared to pick up a 'poisonous' snake and throw 'acid' into the face of the experimenter. Neither of these actions would have been likely outside the experimental situation. Additionally, in many experiments participants are volunteers so there is the added problem of volunteer bias. Volunteers are usually more highly motivated than randomly selected participants.
- Rosenthal (1969) has conducted research into the influence of the experimenter on research results. He found that the physical characteristics of the experimenter, such as age and sex and psychosocial factors, could have differing outcomes. Additionally, experimenter expectancy effects may distort results. This is not because expectations are correct but because expectations cause alterations in behaviour. The communication of such expectations is quite subtle. As described in *Pygmalion in the Classroom* (Rosenthal and Jacobson, 1968), teachers were told that a group of randomly selected children would do well over the school year. These children did in fact do better in intelligence tests a year later than children who had no predictions made about them. Thus, the expectations of the teachers were realised.
- Ethical restrictions apply to psychological research. Although ethical issues feature in all the sciences, in psychology they pose more of a problem because of the nature of the subject matter – human and animal behaviour. As a result, certain studies, such as those causing fear, anxiety and loss of self-esteem, stress or guilt, may have to be adapted or abandoned even though they may be of scientific value and interest.
- Scientific methods strive for objectivity and control. This results in several problems:

  The more control imposed over variables, the more artificial the study: this has implications for the generalisability of findings.

  The inability to control all variables that underlie human behaviour means that accurate prediction and control is impossible.

  Although total objectivity is never possible in science, it is particularly difficult in psychology as researchers and participants are members of the same species. This makes it difficult for researchers to keep a 'distanced' perspective. Related to this is the problem of reactivity. Atoms, stars and elements do not usually react and change their behaviour when they are observed, but humans are highly reactive.

Link

The behaviourist approach has been criticised as being mechanistic and ignoring many of psychology's greatest concerns. Without it, though, it is doubtful if psychology would be as well established scientifically. Although the behaviourists imposed limitations on the subject matter by choosing to deny any reference to mental experience, there is no doubt that they established methods that have benefited psychology. It is easier to justify behavioural psychology as being scientific than to make out a case for a science of experience.

The methods and subject matter of the behaviourist approach were a reaction to Wundt's introspection and concentration upon the 'inner world'. 'Experience' was replaced by 'behaviour' which is open, observable and can be accurately measured with a precisely specified response such as pressing a lever. For more on behaviourist psychology, see Chapter 9, Approaches in psychology.

AQA Examiner's tip

Do not confuse the scientific approach with the experimental method. The scientific approach covers the scientific method and empirical methods of enquiry. However, although the preferred method of gaining information about behaviour is the experiment, other methods such as observations are also empirical.

Hints

Experimenter bias is known by a variety of other names such as 'expectancy effect', 'experimenter expectancy effect' and 'the Rosenthal effect'.

Psychosocial factors are to do with the experimenter's social skills. Participants may feel at ease with a friendly experimenter but may be put off by one that is overly friendly.

Because people know that their behaviour is being investigated, they may change it, for example by showing off, trying harder or showing evaluation apprehension.

- The scientific approach is deterministic and reductionist. People's behaviour is seen as controllable, predictable and reducible to general laws of behaviour. Humanistic psychologists argue that such a mechanical and reductionist view ignores the role of free will in behaviour and destroys the 'totality' of human experience and behaviour.
- Scientific laws are generalisable across time and space. However, psychological explanations are often restricted to particular places and times.
- Much of the subject matter of psychology is unobservable. Hence, it cannot be accurately measured and is inferential.

Link

The psychoanalytic approach, for example, is concerned with the unconscious mind. Unconscious mental processes exist only as an inferred construct created and described by the analyst. In cognitive psychology, there is a gap between the actual data obtained in research (e.g. the number of words recalled from the middle of a list of words) and the explanation put forward – displacement. For more on the cognitive approach, see Chapter 9, Approaches in psychology.

Whether or not the scientific approach is the best route for understanding human behaviour and experience is clearly debatable. Many people believe that, even without formal training in psychology, they understand human nature. However, this 'common-sense' psychology tends to be vague and contradictory, leading to false conclusions and ineffective actions. Without the systematic scientific approach, one will never know whether an intuitive understanding is right.

Key points:

- The philosopher Kuhn (1962) claims that psychology lacks a uniting paradigm, an essential characteristic of a mature science.
- Scientific theories generate several hypotheses, are falsifiable and parsimonious. Not all psychological theories meet these criteria.
- Scientific theories must be empirically tested. Replicability and generalisability of findings are also essential features of the scientific approach.
- The study of subjective experience fits far less comfortably into a traditional model of science than the study of behaviour.
- The special nature of the subject matter and the researcher's relationship to it creates difficulties in conducting research objectively.
- The scientific approach is advantageous to psychology. It provides understanding, prediction and control of behaviour.

Summary questions

13 Identify two features of the scientific approach.

14 Explain why Kuhn believes that psychology is not a science.

15 Outline the importance of a theory in the scientific approach.

16 'Science is not the route to all knowledge.' Explain why some psychologists might regard the study of subjective experience as the best way to gain knowledge about people. Refer to two approaches in psychology.

End-of-chapter activity 1

Consider the following scenario.

A psychologist goes on holiday to a remote island. He soon notices that several of the people living there are frightened of him when he wears his sunglasses and decides to investigate the matter. He carries out a case study on one of the island people (without his glasses!) interviewing him, his family and acquaintances. He observes him in a variety of different settings and carries out some psychological tests. He gathers a mass of rich and detailed information.

On returning to the UK, the psychologist discovers that some research has already been carried out into hyalophobia (the fear of glass). He examines the research carefully in an effort to identify common factors or experiences. A cause is suspected. He sends out a structured questionnaire to several hundred people to test his hypothesis.

In small groups consider the following questions:

1. Which aspect of his investigation (case study or structured questionnaire) is more scientific and why?
2. What are the advantages of each approach? Give reasons for your answers.
3. Compare the type of data collected by each approach.
4. How might the psychologist investigate if there is a genetic basis to hyalophobia?

Link

- Nature–nurture: several of the island people suffer from the phobia. Could this be nature, nurture or an interaction between the two? See p263.
- Idiographic and nomothetic approaches: the idiographic approach focuses more on the individual case as a means of understanding behaviour whereas the nomothetic approach involves the study of a large number of people and then seeks to make generalisations about them. The two approaches are complementary. See p279.
- Qualitative and quantitative data: the case study is based on qualitative data and the data generated by the structured questionnaire will be mainly quantitative. See Chapter 11, Methods in psychology.

Debates

End-of-chapter activity 2

This activity requires four 'actors':

- Miss Marple: the accused
- a prosecuting lawyer
- a defence lawyer
- a judge.

The rest of the class can make up the jury.

Before the court scene begins, arrange the seating so that all members of the jury can hear and get a good view of the trial

Miss Marple has committed grievous bodily harm (GBH). She was heard screaming at her boyfriend by neighbours and caught standing over him, brandishing a knife.

The accused, Miss Marple, must create a story and share this with her defence lawyer before the trial.

The role of the defence lawyer is to put forward the case either for mitigating circumstances (e.g. domestic violence, lack of fidelity, provocation) or for diminished responsibility on the grounds of mental illness.

The role of the prosecuting lawyer is to convince the judge and jury that Miss Marple is sane and responsible and therefore guilty.

The judge and jury must decide whether or not Miss Marple is responsible for her behaviour and therefore guilty of GBH.

Following the 'trial' work in small groups:

- Summarise the arguments for free will and those for determinism emerging from the 'trial'.
- Make a list of topic areas in psychology where the debate is relevant.

Link

- Free will and determinism: clearly the debate does not just concern psychologists. Free will has implications for responsibility and behaviour in everyday situations. See p257–262.
- Reductionism and holism: the reasons for crime can be complex. Mental 'illness' is a deterministic and reductionist explanation. See p270–273.

Further reading

Bell, A. (2002) *Debates in Psychology*. Hove: Taylor & Francis.

Eysenck, M. (1994) *Perspectives on Psychology*. Hove: Lawrence Erlbaum Associates Ltd.

Gross, R. (1999) *Themes, Issues and Debates in Psychology*. London: Hodder & Stoughton.

Malim, T., Birch, A. and Wadeley, A. (1992) *Perspectives in Psychology*. London: The Macmillan Press.

Medcof, J. and Roth, J. (1979) *Approaches to Psychology*. Milton Keynes: Open University Press.

Methods in psychology

Introduction

It is easy to be an 'armchair psychologist' and come up with theories from the comfort of our living rooms! However, professional psychologists have to get up and get out there and provide evidence for their theories. Not surprisingly, the public want 'proof' that a theory is correct (or valid), and evidence provides this proof.

Strictly speaking, it is virtually impossible to prove a theory. This is not just a problem for psychology, but for all sciences. To prove a theory, a researcher should be 100 per cent certain about their findings. In psychology's case, this could mean that a theory of behaviour should apply to all humans in all situations. Of course, we can rarely be sure that a theory does apply to everybody to whom it is supposed to apply – generally it is not feasible to study everybody that you would want to. Therefore, theories are tested by seeing how much they apply or how certain we can be about them. This is essentially testing reliability.

Since it is virtually impossible to prove a theory, researchers tend to seek to disprove theories – even their own! This is actually easier because you only need 'one exception to the rule' to disprove a theory. For example, if a psychologist theorises that nobody can recall more than nine items from short-term memory, then it only takes one person to recall 10 items (from short-term memory) to disprove that theory. And, of course, if a theory is hard to disprove then it would suggest that it is quite a reliable theory.

Imagine a researcher who has a series of findings that support her theory and none of them disputes it. Does she therefore have reliable evidence? Most psychologists would not make this judgement themselves because it is open to bias. Instead, they tend to rely on statistical analyses, which provide an objective measure of the reliability of data. Statistical analysis asks questions such as the following:

- Has the same finding occurred enough times for us to be confident in it?
- What is the chance of getting that finding again and again without it being true?
- Is the difference between results from two conditions a significant difference?

Basically, statistical analyses operate according to the law of probability: they can suggest that a set of results and their associated theory are probably valid. However, they cannot say that they are definitely valid. This is the problem with all research – how can we ever be absolutely sure that anything is true? Perhaps we should just go back to our armchairs …

Specification content	Topic content	Page number
Statistical inference		
The concepts of probability and levels of significance	Identifying a critical value	310
Hypothesis testing: null and alternative (experimental or research) hypothesis	Selecting a test	303
One- and two-tailed tests	Selecting a test	303
Type I and Type II errors	Identifying a critical value	310
Positive, negative and zero correlation	Selecting a test	303
Limitations of sampling techniques and generalisation of results	Selecting a sampling technique	299
Statistical tests		
Use of non-parametric and parametric tests: statistical tests of difference – the sign test; Wilcoxon signed ranks test; Mann-Whitney; related (repeated measures) and independent t tests; statistical tests of association – Spearman's rank order correlation; Pearson's product moment correlation; the chi-square test	Analysing data using inferential statistics	314
Factors affecting the choice of statistical test, including levels of measurement, type of experimental design	Selecting a test	303
Criteria for parametric testing: interval data; normal distribution; homogeneity of variance	Selecting a test	303
Issues in research		
Strengths and limitations of different methods of research: strengths and limitations of qualitative and quantitative data	Selecting a method of investigation Quantitative data vs qualitative data	292 300
Reliability and validity applied generally across all methods of investigation; types of reliability and validity; ways of assessing reliability and validity	Selecting a method of investigation	292
Critical understanding of the importance of ethical considerations within the social and cultural environment; ethical considerations in the design and conduct of psychological studies and within psychology as a whole	Ethical considerations in investigating psychology	323

Methods in psychology

Selecting a method of investigation

Learning objectives:

- outline different methods of investigation and their relative strengths and weaknesses
- discuss the issue of reliability in relation to different methods of investigation
- consider different ways in which reliability can be assessed
- discuss the issue of validity in relation to different methods of investigation
- consider different ways in which validity can be assessed.

Link

For more detailed coverage of research methods see *AQA Psychology B AS*, Chapter 4, Research methods.

AQA Examiner's tip

Make sure that you can **explain** the strengths and limitations of different methods rather than just stating them.

Key terms

Construct validity: the extent to which a construct is assessed to give a true or accurate measure.

Observer bias: when a researcher sees something from their own point of view rather than objectively.

Observer effect: when participants behave differently from normal because they are aware of being watched.

Methods of investigation

There are a number of methods of investigation that psychologists can use to collect evidence to support or refute their theories. The main methods are listed below:

- experiment – a method in which the researcher manipulates an independent variable, whilst controlling other extraneous variables, in order to measure an effect on a dependent variable
- self-report – a method, such as an interview or questionnaire, where participants report on their own thoughts or behaviour
- observation – recording a participant's behaviour by watching them, often in a natural setting
- correlation – measuring two naturally occurring variables to establish the relationship between them
- case study – studying one person, group or organisation in detail
- content analysis – analysing secondary material in order to give insight into human thought or behaviour.

Evaluating different methods of investigation

Table 1 *Summary of the relative strengths and limitations of different methods of investigation*

Method	Strengths	Limitations
Experiment	Only method that can reliably establish cause and effect Very objective because the researcher cannot easily bias the results	Low levels of ecological validity and **construct validity** Open to demand characteristics because participants are more aware of the research process
Self-report	Allows access to participants' thoughts and feelings Can discover what participants would do in certain situations without having to set that situation up	An unreliable method if participants are dishonest, inarticulate, lack confidence, lack insight, or have poor memories Participants may be unfairly influenced by the researcher's questioning
Observation	Possible for researchers to directly observe participants' behaviour rather than relying on self-reports High ecological validity as natural situations are normally observed	Not possible to make reliable observations of thoughts and feelings Observations may be invalid due to **observer bias** and **observer effect**

Method	Strengths	Limitations
Correlation	Allows researchers to make reliable measurements of the strength and direction of a relationship between two variables Can statistically analyse naturally occurring phenomena which would not be open to manipulation (for ethical and practical reasons)	Cannot reliably establish the cause and effect between variables (only the relationship) Variables have to be quantified to be measured and this can affect the construct validity of findings
Case study	High in validity as research offers detailed insight into a naturally occurring phenomenon An efficient method as it only takes one case study to disprove a theory	Difficult to generalise from findings as samples are small and often unusual Researchers can become too involved with this method and lose their ability to be objective
Content analysis	Allows researchers to investigate people it may be difficult or impossible to access directly Few ethical problems because studying material rather than people	Because there is no direct contact with people, their thoughts and behaviour may be misinterpreted through analysis Qualitative content analysis produces findings that are potentially subjective whereas quantitative content analysis produces findings that may lack construct validity

The issue of reliability

As Table 1 shows, reliability is a key issue when evaluating different research methods.

A reliable method is one that is easy to replicate, and the concept therefore applies to methods that are highly structured. For example, a questionnaire is easy to replicate because the questions (and possibly answers) are pre-set and it requires little personal input from the researcher to carry out a survey. A different researcher can repeat the same survey as long as it is clear how the questionnaire was administered and to whom. If an investigation is replicated and produces similar results each time, then the findings are also described as reliable.

It is important that findings are reliable because that suggests that the findings can be trusted. For example, if one survey shows that 20 per cent of respondents have taken antidepressants and three other separate surveys quote similar percentages, this would make the research reliable. If something keeps happening, then the law of probability suggests that is likely to be true (or valid).

Methods, such as the case study, tend to be less reliable. This is because two researchers could carry out a case study of the same person (e.g. a serial killer) but come to different conclusions about their personality and the reasons for their crimes. The results from a case study are much more open to interpretation owing to the qualitative nature of its evidence. Two researchers may investigate the same person differently by asking different types of questions, which could illicit different kinds of information. In other words, it is not really possible to carry out a case study in the same

Hint

To help you understand the concept of reliability, think about how it is used in real life. For example, an unreliable car is one that breaks down a lot – it cannot be trusted; on the other hand, a reliable student turns up to every lesson and meets deadlines – they are consistent.

way as another researcher would; if nothing else, time would have moved on and this will change the individual under investigation and therefore what can be observed. This not only makes the method unreliable but also the findings; these only reflect one person's opinion of a certain situation at a certain point in time that will not occur again.

Clearly, some methods are more reliable than others, as Table 2 shows.

Table 2 *Levels of reliability for the different methods of investigation*

Method	Level of reliability	Explanation
Experiment	High	Experiments involve high levels of control so are easy to replicate by following procedures that are clearly set out.
Correlation	High	Correlations rely on statistical analysis of scores so variables under investigation need to be quantified. This involves using clear measures of behaviour that are easy to scrutinise and use again.
Self-report	Variable	Questionnaires and structured interviews are easy to replicate because questions are pre-set and available to be asked again (although the context and interview style may affect reliability). Unstructured interviews are more difficult to repeat because the questions depend on the answers that an individual gives at the time.
Observation	Variable	Structured observations are more reliable because they use coding systems, which other researchers can use to conduct an observation of the same or similar participants in the same or similar situation. However, qualitative observations involve simply recording what is seen at any one point in time – which also depends partly on the observer's own interpretation.
Content analysis	Variable	Quantitative content analyses are more reliable because they use numerical coding systems, which other researchers can use to analyse the same or similar material. However, qualitative content analyses involve interpreting material through description and this is much more open to interpretation and therefore difficult to replicate (e.g. two researchers may see something different in the drawings of a person with schizophrenia).
Case study	Low	Case studies involve high levels of involvement and interpretation on the part of the researcher. This makes it difficult for another researcher to carry out the research in the same way to achieve the same results.

Methods

Types of reliability

At this point it might be useful to distinguish between **external reliability** and **internal reliability**:

- **External reliability** refers to the extent that a measuring instrument is consistent across different times and situations. For example, a ruler has high external reliability because, if someone measured the height of the same person in two different situations, a ruler would give them the same reading. For a psychological instrument (e.g. an observation) to have external reliability, it would have to give the same results in different contexts.
- **Internal reliability** refers to the extent that a measuring instrument is consistent within itself, i.e. measures the same construct throughout. For example, a stop-clock has high internal reliability because it consistently measures time and each second takes the same measure of time. For a psychological instrument (e.g. a questionnaire) to have internal reliability, each item (e.g. question) would have to measure the same construct at the same level as the other items.

Key terms

External reliability: consistency between measures.

Internal reliability: consistency within measures.

AQA Examiner's tip

Note that the different types of reliability are **not** listed explicitly in the specification. This means that they cannot be asked about directly. However, you can demonstrate your understanding of reliability by distinguishing between external and internal reliability in a relevant answer.

Ways of assessing reliability

The test–retest method

The external reliability of an instrument can be assessed using the test–retest method. This simply involves using the same instrument on two different occasions to see if it gives the same or similar results. Ideally, in the case of psychology, the instrument should be used on the same person (or people) each time.

Table 3 shows the data collected so that the reliability of a questionnaire measuring an individual's criminal personality could be assessed using the test–retest method. Just by looking at the table, we can see that each participant scores similarly on the two occasions that they are tested. This suggests that the questionnaire has external reliability. Indeed, if the scores are statistically analysed, they give a very high **correlation coefficient** of +0.997.

Table 3 *Participants' scores for a test of criminal personality taken on two occasions*

Participant	Criminal personality score (Test 1)	Criminal personality score (Retest)
1	23	24
2	36	34
3	37	37
4	12	15
5	45	44
6	22	20
7	20	20
8	9	8
9	30	26
10	39	42

Of course, if the tests are close together, the results may be similar because the individual completes the second test from memory. Depending on what is being measured, the results may even improve through practice or get worse through fatigue. This may imply that the method is unreliable when it is not. A solution would be to do the retest after a period of time, normally an interval of at least two weeks. However, then there is the problem that the results may change due to extraneous variables, such as a change in level of maturity or social situation.

Measuring inter-rater reliability

Another way of assessing external reliability, particularly where rating scales are being used, is by comparing the measures of two or more researchers. If there is a high level of agreement in their ratings, there is high **inter-rater reliability**. For example, two researchers may be scoring a group of pre-school children for their level of interaction. They may check their scores with each other to ensure that their rating scale and therefore their findings are reliable. If there are high levels of disagreement then the findings should not be trusted. Of course, where there are high levels of agreement, it would be wrong to assume that this automatically means that the findings are reliable. A number of researchers work closely together and may therefore be using the same biases in their judgements.

The split half method

The internal reliability of an instrument can be assessed using the **split half method**. This simply means splitting a test in half to check that the scores for each half are approximately half of the total measure given. For example, if a questionnaire had 30 items, a researcher may look at the total score for the odd-numbered items and compare it with the total

Key terms

Correlation coefficient: a measure of the strength (closeness to 1 or −1) and direction (positive or negative) of the relationship between two variables.

Inter-rater reliability: consistency between the recordings of two or more researchers.

Split half method: a method of comparing two sets of scores from a test or measure after dividing the test or measure into two equal sections or parts.

Link

To see how a correlation coefficient is calculated (as in a test–retest), see the Spearman's rank order correlation test on p320 or the Pearson's product moment correlation on p321.

Take it further

Locate a psychological test (e.g. an IQ test from the internet) and assess its external reliability by carrying out the test–retest method, using a small sample of participants. Think carefully about the time span that you will need to leave between the two tests.

You should use Spearman's rank order correlation to carry out the test (see p320 for method).

Hint

Sometimes candidates forget which test assesses what type of reliability. To help you remember, notice that the test for external reliability has 'e's in it – test–retest. Meanwhile, the test for internal reliability has the letter 'i' in it – split half.

score for the even-numbered items. If the scores for one half of a test are very different from the scores for the other half, this would imply that the test is unreliable and not measuring a concept in a consistent way. Of course, this would be carried out a number of times, using different people's scores. The final step would be to correlate pairs of scores to check for a significant relationship.

Table 4 shows the individual scores of a person taking a psychological test to measure his levels of stress.

Table 4 *An individual's scores on a test measuring levels of stress*

Question	Q1	Q2	Q3	Q4	Q5	Q6	Q7	Q8	Q9	Q10	**Total**
Score	3	3	4	5	3	1	6	2	4	5	36
Question	Q11	Q12	Q13	Q14	Q15	Q16	Q17	Q18	Q19	Q20	
Score	4	5	4	4	4	3	3	2	5	4	38
										Total	74

His total score is 74. If we apply the split half method by calculating his score on the first 10 items and then his score on the second 10 items, the two scores are very similar (36 and 38, respectively), suggesting that the test is internally reliable

Table 5 shows the mean speed at which a group of participants recognised 12 faces. It is easy to see that the scores are quite different for the first six faces than for the second six. It would seem that the first six faces are generally easier to recognise that the other six. This would suggest that the test is unreliable if each item is supposed to measure face recognition in the same way.

Table 5 *The mean speed of face recognition for a set of 12 faces*

Face	1	2	3	4	5	6	7	8	9	10	11	12
Mean recognition time (secs)	1.05	1.10	0.88	1.23	1.08	0.99	1.45	2.00	1.57	1.74	1.75	1.27

AQA Examiner's tip

Note that the different ways of assessing reliability are **not** listed explicitly in the specification. This means that they cannot be asked about directly. However, you can demonstrate your understanding of testing reliability by referring specifically to them in a relevant answer.

One problem with the split half method is that an instrument may appear reliable (or unreliable) just by chance, especially if a researcher carries out the technique only once. A statistical test known as Cronbach's alpha is a solution to this, as it essentially calculates all possible ways of splitting a test and gives the average from doing so.

The issue of validity

Validity, like reliability, is a key issue when evaluating method. Indeed, for many psychologists, the two are linked. If something keeps happening (i.e. it is reliable) then it is likely to be the truth (i.e. valid). However, researchers should be cautious. An experiment may show the same results each time (i.e. reliable results) but if the setting is artificial each time then the findings are not necessarily true to life (i.e. valid). This shows how reliability (consistency) and validity (truth) are different concepts.

A valid method is one that gives valid findings, i.e. discovers the truth. In this sense, all methods aim to be valid because otherwise there would be no point in doing research! There is an argument, however, that some methods offer more validity than others.

Key terms

Validity: the extent to which an instrument accurately or truly measures what it is supposed to or a concept stands up to testing.

Types of validity

It is quite difficult to discuss the validity of a method in broad terms so psychologists find it useful to refer to different types of validity. These include ecological validity, **external validity**, **content validity** and **predictive validity**.

Methods with ecological validity allow research to be carried out in a real-life setting or a good simulation of it. Methods that can be used in naturally occurring environments (such as observations) tend to have ecological validity. Methods with artificial settings (such as laboratory experiments) do not.

Methods with construct validity allow researchers to measure constructs as they occur in real life. Qualitative methods (such as case studies) tend to have higher levels of construct validity because they describe behaviours as they occur. Quantitative methods (such as experiments) tend to have low levels because they tend to take narrow measures of behaviour and distort them by scoring them. For example, in an experiment, a participant may not be very successful at identifying celebrity faces by name under timed conditions. However, is this person usually poor at recognising faces?

Methods with external validity produce findings that are generalisable to other people, in other situations, at other points in time. This is largely to do with the make-up of the sample but methods that allow for large samples (e.g. questionnaires and some experiments) may have greater external validity.

Ways of assessing validity

It is clearly difficult to assess whether something reflects the truth or not – especially when there is a debate about what counts as the truth in the first place! However, there are established ways of testing the truth.

Testing for content validity

To test for content validity is simple: results are analysed to see if they look like they reflect what people assume or expect to be true. This can be done quite rigorously by experts, or simply be a check for **face validity** by laypeople. Of course, this is still essentially a subjective exercise and is based on someone else's perception of the truth.

Testing for predictive validity

This is where a method is tested for validity by seeing if it can predict the truth. For example, if a questionnaire is devised to identify people prone to depression, its validity can be tested by investigating how many of those people end up being diagnosed with clinical depression. Of course, because of the self-fulfilling prophecy, people participating in an investigation may end up behaving as predicted.

Testing for concurrent validity

When testing for concurrent validity, results are checked against those from an established test. For example, imagine that a new test has been devised to measure a person's level of moral development. The scores from this can be correlated against an existing test that has already demonstrated predictive validity. If a person scores similarly on both tests, this would suggest that the new one has concurrent validity and is providing an accurate measure of moral development. Of course, this is only reliable if the existing test is indeed valid!

Hints

To help you distinguish between reliability and validity, consider the following example. If a teacher gives you a low mark for a piece of work that you think is very good, then you may question the **validity** of the score. If three other teachers agree on the mark, this makes it more **reliable** and therefore more likely to be right (valid). However, all of the teachers could be marking it too strictly. So although they are being consistent (reliable), the mark is not necessarily a fair or valid one!

To help you understand the concept of validity, think about how it is used in real life. For example, an invalid password is one that is not right or accurate. Or a valid argument is one that stands up or holds true.

Key terms

External validity: the extent to which findings are generalisable beyond the research itself.

Content validity: the extent to which a concept appears to be true and accurate.

Predictive validity: the extent to which a measure accurately predicts something.

Face validity: a test to see whether something looks valid 'on the face of it'.

Link

For a definition of ecological validity, see p59.

AQA Examiner's tip

Note that the different types of validity are **not** listed explicitly in the specification. This means that they cannot be asked about directly. However, you can demonstrate your understanding of validity by making reference to the different types in a relevant answer.

Link

The term 'self-fulfilling prophecy' is defined in Chapter 5, Schizophrenia and mood disorders, p108.

AQA Examiner's tip

Note that the different ways of assessing validity are **not** listed explicitly in the specification. This means that they cannot be asked about directly. However, you can demonstrate your understanding of testing validity by referring specifically to them in a relevant answer.

Key points:

- There are a range of methods of investigation used by psychologists and all have strengths and limitations.
- Reliability is a key strength of a number of methods: they can be easily replicated to investigate the consistency of findings.
- Reliability can be assessed through the test–retest method, inter-rater observations and the split half method.
- Validity is a key strength of any method as it means that it has produced findings that are true and accurate.
- Validity can be assessed through testing content validity, predictive validity and concurrent validity.

Summary questions

1. Outline the difference between the test–retest method and the split half method as tests of reliability.
2. Explain why self-report methods are generally more reliable than observational methods.
3. Explain why reliable findings are not necessarily valid findings.
4. Imagine that a psychologist has devised a new test for measuring leadership skills. She has to convince people that her test is a valid measure of leadership and that they should invest in it. Describe how the psychologist could use content validity, predictive validity and concurrent validity to assess the validity of her test.

Methods

Selecting a sampling technique

Learning objectives:

- outline different sampling techniques
- evaluate different sampling techniques, with particular reference to generalisation.

Key terms

Random sampling: a sampling technique that gives each individual in the target population an equal chance of being selected for the sample (e.g. drawing names from a hat).

Systematic sampling: a sampling technique where the sample is made up of every *n*th (e.g. every 5th) individual from the target population.

Stratified sampling: a sampling technique in which the target population is first divided (or stratified) into different groups (e.g. by sex, age, personality). Secondly, participants are randomly selected from each group in numbers that reflect their occurrence in the target population.

Opportunity sampling: a sampling technique where participants are selected for a sample for their convenience (e.g. they are in the locality, they are known to the researcher). The sample is made up of individuals who are willing and available.

Target population: the group of people to whom research findings should generally apply.

Link

For more detailed coverage of sampling techniques, see *AQA Psychology B AS*, Chapter 4, Research methods.

Link

The issue of generalisation is discussed in Chapter 10, Debates in psychology.

Once a researcher has selected a method, they also need to decide on whom it will be used, i.e. the sample. There are a number of sampling techniques open to psychologists. Some of the key ones are:

- **random sampling**
- **systematic sampling**
- **stratified sampling**
- **opportunity sampling**.

When choosing a sample, researchers will normally be aware of the issue of generalisation. A representative sample contains a good cross-section of the **target population** (e.g. a range of ages, different personality types) and it is therefore possible to generalise. This means that the researcher can assume that the results from the sample would also apply to the wider population (e.g. if 15 per cent of the sample have committed a violent crime in the last year then approximately the same percentage of the population will have done so). However, if the sample is biased towards certain types of groups of people then it is unrepresentative. For example, if a sample contains mainly young people this may over-exaggerate the extent of criminal behaviour and a researcher would have to be cautious about generalising to a wider age group.

Stratified sampling tends to offer the most representative samples as a conscious effort is made to include all key groups of people. For example, if different age groups are identified first (or different personality types), this guarantees a better range of participants. On average, random sampling and systematic sampling provide representative samples. Laws of chance (on which they are based) tend to give a wide selection of people. However, there is also a chance of a freak sample. The least representative samples tend to come from opportunity sampling as available people often represent narrow groups (e.g. because they come from the same locality, or the same social group as the researcher).

If opportunity samples are so difficult to generalise from then why do psychologists still use them? The reality is that, compared with the other methods, this sampling technique is relatively quick to plan and administer and is therefore more efficient and cost effective.

Key points:

- There are many ways of selecting a sample including randomly, systematically, using stratification or by opportunity.
- Different sampling techniques have different strengths and weaknesses. There is generally a trade-off between how much effort a sampling technique requires and how generalisable the findings will be.

Summary questions

5 Explain why it is possible to generalise from a representative sample.

6 Explain why a random sample from a prison would not necessarily give a representative sample of criminals.

Quantitative data versus qualitative data

Learning objectives:

- distinguish between quantitative and qualitative methods of investigation
- consider the relative strengths and weaknesses of quantitative and qualitative data.

Key terms

Quantitative data: data in numerical form.

Qualitative data: data in descriptive form.

Structured observation: an observation with pre-determined categories to look for and to be scored in some way.

Take it further

Find detailed descriptions of key studies, for example by accessing the journals in which they were originally published. When reading the description of the methods, try to identify whether quantitative or qualitative data (or both) were collected. Justify your decision in each case.

AQA Examiner's tip

Even if you are not explicitly asked for the strengths and weaknesses of different types of data, you can still discuss them if you are evaluating a method. However, don't just say a strength of a method (e.g. an experiment) is that it produces quantitative data – explain **why** this is a strength, i.e. what is good about quantitative data. Alternatively, you may want to explain what is bad about it – in which case, it becomes a disadvantage. The same advice applies to qualitative data.

As well as selecting a method and a sample, psychologists also need to make a choice about the type of data they wish to collect. To some extent, this is dictated by the method they choose. Certain methods are more likely to give **quantitative data** whereas others are more likely to give **qualitative data**. Quantitative methods **measure** constructs whereas qualitative methods **describe** constructs.

Quantitative methods include:

- experiments where variables are strictly measured for high levels of control
- self-reports using closed questions, where it is possible to count the number of responses chosen for each question
- **structured observations** where behaviours may be counted or rated
- correlations, which measure the strength and relationship between two sets of scores
- quantitative content analyses where content may be tallied or coded.

Qualitative methods include:

- self-reports using open questions where answers can be summarised or transcribed in written form
- qualitative observations where researchers describe or visually record what they see
- case studies, which offer a detailed description of the person, group or situation under investigation
- qualitative content analyses where content is described rather than scored in some way.

One strength of quantitative data is that they are more reliable and objective, whereas qualitative data are more open to interpretation. For example, it is easier to agree on a score rather than a description of how stressful someone's occupation is. Another strength is that it is possible for quantitative data to be analysed statistically to identify trends. This helps psychology achieve its goal of describing **patterns** in thought and behaviour.

One strength of qualitative data is that they are high in construct validity, whereas quantitative data tend to give narrow measures of complex phenomena. For example, in reality we would describe someone's depressive behaviour rather than simply scoring it. Another strength is that qualitative data are richer in detail, offering more insight into whatever is being investigated.

Key points:

- Quantitative methods produce numerical data whereas qualitative methods produce descriptive data.
- Quantitative data are more reliable because they are more objective and easier to analyse for patterns. Qualitative data, meanwhile, are richer and have higher construct validity.

Summary questions

7 State whether the following examples would give quantitative or qualitative data:

a the mean number of faces recognised in two minutes

b the heart rate of an individual before and after being put in a stressful situation

c notes written down during an interview with an individual suffering from schizophrenia

d video recording of a child attempting a conservation task.

8 Outline the arguments for and against using quantitative data to measure fear of crime.

The use of inferential statistics

Learning objectives:

- understand the use of descriptive statistics
- understand the use of inferential statistics.

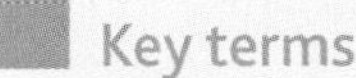

Key terms

Descriptive statistics: techniques for describing or demonstrating the patterns in data without actually statistically analysing these patterns for significance.

Link

For more detailed coverage of descriptive statistics, see *AQA Psychology B AS*, Chapter 4, Research methods.

AQA Examiner's tip

In an exam, you should not suggest that descriptive statistics can be used to see if there is a **significant** difference (or correlation) within a set of data. They can describe differences (or correlations) but it would be wrong to assume that they tell you whether these are **significant** differences (or correlations).

Let us assume that a psychologist has collected quantitative rather than qualitative data. We have already suggested that such data can be analysed for patterns or trends. But how is this done?

There are many types of statistics that allow psychologists to analyse data. One set comprises **descriptive statistics** and includes techniques such as calculating percentages, constructing graphs and using measures of central tendency (mode, median, mean) and measures of dispersion (range, standard deviation).

Take the example of a mean. Table 6 shows how this measure of central tendency can be used to summarise and therefore analyse a set of data. The table clearly demonstrates that participants are much better at recognising faces presented the right way up rather than inverted.

Table 6 *The number of faces identified by participants in two conditions (right way up and inverted)*

Participant	Faces right way up	Faces inverted
1	12	7
2	14	6
3	16	6
4	16	8
5	18	4
6	13	2
7	14	6
8	10	7
9	11	10
10	17	9
Mean	14.1	6.5

Now look at the data in Table 7, which is from a similar experiment.

Table 7 *Summary results from another inverted face recognition experiment*

	Faces right way up	Faces inverted
Mean	12.2	10.1

The researcher conducting this experiment had formulated a **hypothesis** that predicted that participants would identify significantly more faces presented the right way up than they would when the faces are inverted. Should she reject or retain her hypothesis?

This is a difficult question to answer as, in this case, there is some evidence that participants do recognise more faces when they are presented the right way up, but whether it is **significantly** more is in question. If the difference is not a significant one, it is not likely to be a reliable finding. To be sure that it is easier to recognise faces in their normal configuration, the researcher would want many more faces to be identified in the first condition. Does 2.1 more, on average, constitute 'many more'?

Some researchers may look at the data and argue that a difference of 2.1 faces is significant. But this is not good enough. The difference needs to be tested statistically and this is where inferential statistics are useful.

Inferential statistics describe a range of statistical tests that have been devised to analyse sets of data to measure if there actually is a significant difference (or correlation) between them. So rather than guessing whether two means are significantly different, a researcher can reliably test this by applying an inferential test.

Key points:

- Descriptive statistics demonstrate patterns in data.
- Inferential statistics analyse the significance of patterns in data.

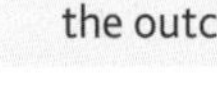

Key terms

Hypothesis: a statement predicting the outcome of an investigation.

Hint

To help you understand the idea of a significant difference, it may help to consider it from a personal point of view. If two schools achieved average pass rates of 57 per cent and 61 per cent, respectively, you probably wouldn't care which school you were at. Their results are similar and not that different. However, if one school's average was 57 per cent and the other's was 71 per cent, you may well consider this difference significant. In other words, it would indicate a consistent and substantial difference between the schools.

AQA Examiner's tip

If you are asked in the exam to suggest how a researcher may test to see whether a difference (or correlation) is significant then you have to refer to inferential tests. Only inferential tests measure statistical significance.

Summary questions

9 Give three examples of descriptive statistics.

10 Explain the distinction between 'two conditions having different scores in a task' and 'two conditions having significantly different scores in a task'.

Selecting a test

Learning objectives:

- understand the criteria for choosing an inferential test
- describe different types of hypotheses, designs and data
- know what test to use under which conditions
- understand the significance of parametric assumptions in choosing a test.

The criteria for selecting a test

As mentioned previously, there are many inferential tests that can be used to analyse data from an investigation. The test used depends on a number of criteria:

- what the **hypothesis** predicts
- the type of **experimental design** used to obtain data
- the **level of data** collected.

Hypothesis – what does it predict?

Every investigation begins with a hypothesis, where the researcher predicts what the results will be.

Hypotheses can predict a difference. For example:

> H_1: There is a significant difference in the percentage of men and the percentage of women who have knowingly broken the law.

Alternatively, hypotheses can predict an association or correlation. For example:

> H_1: There will be significant relationship between the age of an infant and the length of time they spend searching for an object.

When a hypothesis predicts a difference or correlation it is known as a **research hypothesis** (or H_1). If the investigation uses the experimental method, the H_1 can be called the **experimental hypothesis**.

As well as research hypotheses, there are **null hypotheses** (H_0) which predict no significant difference or no significant correlation. Every investigation should have an H_0 as well as an H_1.

For example:

> H_0: There is no significant difference in the percentage of men and the percentage of women who have knowingly broken the law: any difference is due to chance.

In other words, this null hypothesis is saying that both sexes are equally likely (or unlikely) to commit crimes.

> H_0: There will be no significant relationship between the age of an infant and the length of time they spend searching for an object; any relationship is due to chance.

In other words, this null hypothesis is predicting a **zero correlation** between age of infant and time spent searching for an object.

Some researchers do start with H_0 and predict no difference or no correlation between variables. In this case, the H_1 becomes known as the **alternative hypothesis**. Increasingly, researchers start by predicting no difference (or correlation) – not necessarily because it is what they want or expect. It has become good scientific practice to seek to support the opposing hypothesis. The theory is that if a researcher goes out of their way to disprove a hypothesis, yet it is still retained, then it must be a reliable prediction.

Key terms

Experimental design: a process for allocating participants to conditions.

Level of data: the nature and detail of information provided by data.

Research hypothesis: a statement predicting a significant difference or correlation.

Experimental hypothesis: a research hypothesis used in an experiment.

Null hypothesis: a statement predicting no significant difference or correlation.

Zero correlation: there is no relationship between variables.

Alternative hypothesis: a statement predicting a significant difference or correlation as an alternative to a null hypothesis which predicts none.

Link

For more detailed coverage of experimental designs see *AQA Psychology B AS*, Chapter 4, Research methods.

Whatever the outcome of an investigation, H_1 or H_0 cannot both be true as they are 'opposites' of each other. Researchers retain the hypothesis that is supported and reject the one that is refuted. They make this decision by carrying out an inferential test.

It is the nature of the research hypothesis that is the first factor in determining which inferential test is chosen.

If H_1 predicts a difference, this requires one sort of test. However, if H_1 predicts a correlation (or association), this requires a different sort of test.

Experimental design – related or unrelated?

The second factor that determines the sort of inferential test to be used is the type of experimental design used in the investigation. There are three types of experimental designs: **repeated measures**, **matched pairs** and **independent groups**.

However, when choosing a test, researchers just distinguish between **related** and **unrelated designs**. Repeated measures is a related design because the participants in one condition are related to the participants in the other condition(s), i.e. they are the same people. Matched pairs is also classed as a related design because each person in one condition is paired with somebody like them (i.e. someone they are 'related' to) in the other condition. Independent groups, meanwhile, is an unrelated design because the participants in one condition have no connection to the participants in other conditions – they are separate people who have normally been randomly allocated to conditions.

Experimental designs, perhaps obviously, are only used in experiments. They are used when a hypothesis predicts a difference (between conditions). This is why different groups of participants need to be tested in more than one condition, or why the same participants need to be tested more than once.

It is not possible to investigate a correlation by using an experiment, so a correlational study is used instead. Here, the design is straightforward. It has to be a related design. There would be no point in looking for a relationship between two measures taken from two different people. For example, a researcher would not expect child X's numeracy score to correlate with child Y's logic score. However, the researcher might reasonably expect to correlate two scores taken from the **same** child. In short, correlational studies always use a related design – each participant is tested twice on a different variable each time.

Level of data – nominal, ordinal or interval

For the purposes of statistical analysis, there are different types, or levels, of data. On this basis, different inferential tests work on different levels of data.

If you are asked in the exam to suggest how a researcher may test to see whether a difference (or correlation) is significant then you have to refer to inferential tests. Only inferential tests measure statistical significance

Data can be collected on three levels: **nominal**, **ordinal** and **interval**.

To decide what level of data they have, researchers need to ask what they know about any one individual participant. If a researcher has categorised a participant in some way then it is nominal data. However, if each participant has some kind of score then the researcher has ordinal or interval data. Table 8 contains nominal data. Remember, just because the table contains numbers, it does not mean that the data are ordinal or interval. The point is that for each respondent we know whether they strongly agreed, agreed, disagreed or strongly disagreed with the statement – in other words we have

Key terms

Repeated measures: a design in which participants are used in all conditions of the independent variable.

Matched pairs: a design in which different participants are used in each condition of the independent variable, but they are matched on one or more key characteristics.

Independent groups: a design in which a different group of participants is used for each condition of the independent variable; participants are normally randomly allocated to these conditions, i.e. not matched up.

Related design: a design in which participants are the same or similar across conditions.

Unrelated design: a design in which participants are different and not matched across conditions.

Nominal data: data in the form of categories.

Ordinal data: data in the form of scores, but not necessarily taken from a scale with equal intervals.

Interval data: data in the form of scores, taken from a standardised scale with equal intervals.

AQA Examiner's tip

You may find other sources refer to ratio data, which is a fourth level of data that is higher than interval data. However, you do not have to worry about this as it is not covered by the specification. Strictly speaking, measures such as distance and time are ratio data (which means that they have a scale that starts at zero). However, measures like these are still **at least** interval data and will be referred to as such in this chapter.

a category for them, not a score. Table 9, on the other hand, shows a score for each participant so would be at least ordinal data.

Table 8 *The distribution of respondents' answers to the statement 'More criminals should be treated through rehabilitation rather than imprisonment'*

Strongly agree	12
Agree	27
Disagree	33
Strongly disagree	15

Table 9 *Participants' raw scores in a test of memory*

Participant	Score
1	11
2	9
3	11
4	15
5	7
6	11
7	13
8	4

Nominal data

Nominal data are in categories. If a person was categorised as 'tall' or 'short', this would give us nominal data on them. Other examples of nominal data include classifying people as introvert or extrovert; identifying people as high, moderate or low achievers; observing whether people did or did not stop at traffic lights.

Essay grades can be nominal data. By deciding whether a student has passed or failed an essay, teachers are putting their performance into a category. This also illustrates why nominal data is the lowest level of data – because it gives us limited information on the variable being measured. In the case of an essay, the variable is a student's understanding of a particular topic. A 'pass' would suggest a good level of understanding. But how good? Did the student just pass, or were they well over the boundary? Of course, this question would be easy to answer if we knew the actual score that the essay achieved. If a student is given a score for an essay rather than a grade then this counts as ordinal data. Ordinal is a higher, more informative, level of data.

Ordinal data

Any **numerical score** will be at least ordinal data, and may even be interval data – a higher level of data again. For example, if people were ranked from tallest to shortest (rather than simply categorised as 'tall' or 'short') then this would give ordinal data. This is because each person would now have a number to represent their rank. So the person ranked 1 would be identified as the tallest individual rather than just being classed as tall along with other tall people. Knowing where a person ranks in terms of height gives more information.

Other examples of ordinal data would include: ranking people in terms of attractiveness; rating a child's drawing for aggressive content; scoring a person for their leadership ability. As can be seen, ordinal data does not just rely on ranks. It can be represented on any scale that provides a score of some sort. For example, a mark scheme provides a 'scale' for scoring essays.

Interval data

Like ordinal data, interval data also comprise scores. However, the scores come from a scale with equal intervals between units. Ordinal data come from a scale that does not necessarily have equal intervals.

It has already been stated that categorising someone as tall or short gives nominal data, and ranking their height gives ordinal data. Measuring their actual height would give interval data. This is not only because height gives a score (e.g. 175 cm) but also that score comes from an interval scale (e.g. the distance between centimetres on a ruler is always the same). It also shows that interval data are a higher level of data because they give more information about the person. For example, in Figure 1, if James is ranked 1 for his height, Kiran is ranked 2 and Lee is ranked 3, then we know James is taller than Kiran and Kiran is taller than Lee. However, we don't know whether James is much taller than Kiran or only slightly taller. The same applies to Kiran and Lee – what is the difference in their heights? Ranking heights 'hides' the actual difference.However, the actual height (the interval data) tells us how much taller James is and so on.

Hint

You might find it useful to remember the levels of data (from most informative to least) by association with the 'king of the jungle'.

- Levels of data
- Interval
- Ordinal
- Nominal

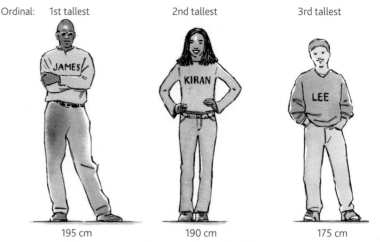

Ordinal: 1st tallest 2nd tallest 3rd tallest

JAMES KIRAN LEE

195 cm 190 cm 175 cm

Fig. 1 *Interval data are more informative than ordinal data*

Other examples of interval data would include the distance of participants' personal space; measurements of brain wave patterns; the length of time it takes for participants to complete a task. If we take the last example, this might be measured in seconds or minutes and so would follow a standard interval scale.

And what about essays? Grades can be classed as nominal data and scores are ordinal data, but is it possible to assess student performance using interval data? The answer is probably not. Interval scores require standardised scales, and it is hard to imagine a scale which 'measures' an essay using equal intervals in the same way that a ruler measures distance or a stopwatch measures time. Indeed, most of the variables measured in psychology rely on ordinal (non-standard) scales. It is difficult to construct reliable and objective tools for measuring concepts such as personality, intelligence or memory. This is discussed further below.

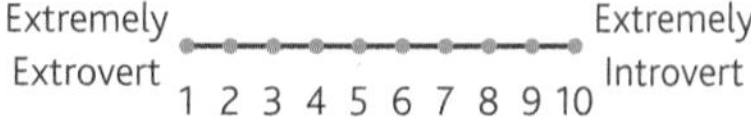

Fig. 2 *It looks like an interval scale!*

Ordinal data or interval data?

The scale depicted in Figure 2 looks like an interval scale.

However, there is no way of guaranteeing that the intervals are equal. In reality, people may perceive the gap between 4 and 5 as being quite large but the gap from 9 to 10 may be perceived as smaller. Just because intervals are drawn equal does not mean they are equal in people's minds. The problem is that such scales are essentially subjective. People read them differently, unlike true interval scales, which are objective and universal. For example, it doesn't matter who picks up a stopwatch, or what stopwatch is used, or where it is used: two minutes is always two minutes and the interval between seconds is always the same.

Some psychologists are keen to show that their data are interval as it allows them to use the most powerful inferential tests. On this basis, psychologists will argue that they have constructed an interval scale to measure a psychological phenomenon. For example, supporters of IQ tests argue that they can measure intelligence as reliably as a foot measure measures shoe size. In memory experiments, for example, some psychologists argue that the number of words recalled by a participant should be classed as interval data. This would only be the case if each word was as easy (or hard) to remember as the next. This can be controlled by choosing words of similar familiarity or length, for instance.

Take it further

See if you can find a means of measuring face recognition in such a way that you can argue that you have collected interval data. For example, imagine you show 10 faces. How do you guarantee that two participants, who recognise five different faces each, actually have equivalent scores?

A good way of testing for interval data is to use multiplication. If a score is from an interval scale, then researchers should generally be able to double it and get exactly twice the measure. For example, time provides interval data because two minutes of time is exactly double one minute of time. However, if someone is rated 8/10 for their attractiveness, are they exactly twice as attractive as a person rated 4/10? Probably not, as this is more subjective. In which case, scores for attractiveness must be classed as ordinal. Take again the example of words recalled in a memory test. If the words are equally difficult to remember, then a researcher could say that someone who has recalled 12 words has done three times better than someone who has recalled four words. This would suggest that the scores are interval. However, if some words are easier to remember than others (which could differ depending on the individual) then the scores are in fact ordinal. Indeed, if someone recalls four easy words and someone recalls four difficult words, they do not have the same score really. However, with interval data, two scores of four would always be the same (e.g. if two people ran a race in 4 minutes, or ran 4 metres, etc.).

If a researcher is not sure whether their data should be classed as ordinal or interval, there is a safe option – call it ordinal. All interval data are **at least** ordinal, but it would be a mistake to analyse data that are only ordinal as interval. It would make any findings unreliable.

Fig. 3 *A ruler measures data on an interval scale. That's why a 15 cm ruler is exactly half the length of a 30 cm ruler*

Link

Inferential tests are discussed in detail on pp314–322.

AQA Examiner's tip

It is very common to be asked why a certain test should be used. Look at the marks available and this will tell you how many reasons should be given. For example, if it is three marks then focus on hypothesis, design **and** level of data in your answer. In addition, don't just state the criteria: briefly explain why they apply (e.g. the data are nominal because yes/no are categories; the design is unrelated because different participants were allocated to each condition).

Choice of test

To summarise, the type of inferential test used to analyse data depends on:

- the hypothesis
- the experimental design
- the level of data.

The table below shows the test that should be used for each combination of prediction, design and data.

Table 10 *Choosing an appropriate test*

What does the hypothesis predict?	What type of design is used?	What level of data is measured?	Name of test
Difference	Related	Interval	Related t test
Difference	Unrelated	Interval	Independent (unrelated) t test
Difference	Related	At least ordinal	Wilcoxon signed ranks test
Difference	Unrelated	At least ordinal	Mann-Whitney U test
Difference	Related	At least nominal	Sign test
Association/ Difference	Unrelated	At least nominal	Chi-square test
Association/ Correlation	Related	At least ordinal	Spearman's rank order test
Association/ Correlation	Related	Interval	Pearson's product moment correlation

Hint

You don't have any choice but to learn this table of tests but do look for patterns to help you do this. For example, all of the Unrelated tests for difference have the letter 'U' in them but the related tests do not. Both the ordinal tests of difference are named after people but the nominal tests of difference are not. Interval data are the only data with 't' in its name, which you could associate with the 't' tests. You may be able to see other (better!) patterns.

NB It may be confusing to see that the chi-square test looks for an association between unrelated data. However, the chi-square is also the test used to see if there is a **difference** between two sets of unrelated data. In the case of nominal data, if there is not a difference then there is an association. For example, if there is no difference between the percentage of males and females that stopped at a traffic light, then there must be an association.

Parametric assumptions

The related t test, the independent t test and Pearson's product moment correlation are collectively known as parametric tests. This is because three parametric assumptions have to apply if these tests are to be used to produce reliable findings. One of these assumptions is obvious from the previous table: the tests should only be used on interval data.

The other two assumptions are:

- that the data come from a sample drawn from a **normally distributed** population
- that there is **homogeneity of variance** between conditions.

If parametric assumptions are not met, then an ordinal test has to be used instead.

Normal distribution

If a variable is normally distributed, it means that, when the variable is measured, there are a few extreme scores and the average score is most common. Many human characteristics are normally distributed, including both physical (e.g. height, weight, shoe size) and psychological (e.g. intelligence, extroversion, aggression). On this basis, there is a good chance that a behaviour under investigation in psychology is normally distributed. For example, people's ability to recall items would be normally distributed: a few people have very poor recall or very good recall and most people are somewhere in between. Therefore, if interval data were collected for a memory experiment, it would be fair to assume that memory ability would be normally distributed in the population. Please note, the sample used for the investigation does not need to show a normal distribution for the variable, but if it is a representative sample then there is a good chance that it will do anyway.

In Figure 4, graph 1 shows a normal distribution whereas graph 2 shows a skewed distribution.

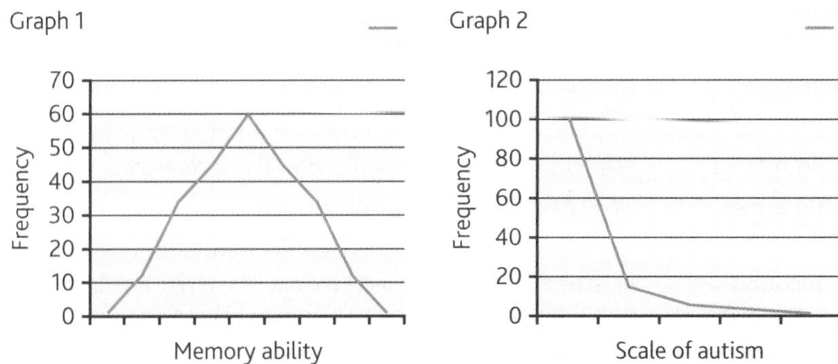

Fig. 4 *Graphs showing (1) a normal distribution; (2) a skewed distribution*

If a variable is not normally distributed (e.g. autism, where most people are at one end of the scale and few are at the other), it is not appropriate to analyse the data using a parametric test.

AQA Examiner's tip

If you are justifying the use of an ordinal test, it is worth covering yourself by saying that the data are **at least** ordinal just in case they are interval. Remember interval data can be analysed using an ordinal test (but ordinal data should not be analysed using an interval test).

Key terms

Normally distributed: a set of data distributed so that middle scores are most frequent and extreme scores are least frequent.

Homogeneity of variance: the deviation of scores (measured by a range or standard deviation, for example) is similar between populations.

Take it further

Identify three behaviours that you think are normally distributed. Decide on a way of measuring each and then test a sample of 20 people on each behaviour. Plot the results from your investigations to see if each behaviour is normally distributed.

Homogeneity of variance

Homogeneity of variance suggests that the deviation of scores (measured by a range or standard deviation (σ), for example) is similar between conditions. If a related design is used, there should be homogeneity of variance as the same or similar people are tested. For example, imagine a group of people whose eye-witness testimonies are scored with two different types of interviews. Even if all the scores improve on the second interview, we would expect a similar range of scores (the person who did best first time should be one of the best next time around). Researchers need to be more careful when an unrelated design is used, as the spread of scores may be quite different because each condition contains different people. If there is not homogeneity of variance, it would not be fair to compare the groups and a parametric test should not be used.

In Figure 5, graph 1 shows homogeneity of variance between conditions A and B whereas graph 2 shows a difference in variance between conditions A and B.

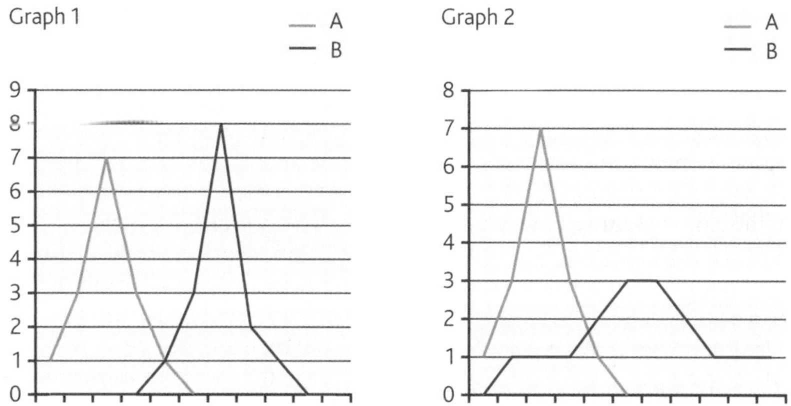

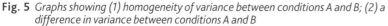

Fig. 5 *Graphs showing (1) homogeneity of variance between conditions A and B; (2) a difference in variance between conditions A and B*

Key points:

- The main criteria for selecting an inferential test are the nature of a hypothesis, the type of experimental design and the level of data.
- Hypotheses can predict differences or correlations; designs can be related or unrelated; level of data can be nominal, ordinal or interval.
- There are tests of difference: sign test (related design, nominal data); Wilcoxon signed ranks (related, ordinal); Mann-Whitney U test (unrelated, ordinal); related and independent t tests (both interval). There are also tests of association: chi-square test (unrelated, nominal), Spearman's rank order correlation (related, ordinal) and Pearson's product moment correlation (related, interval).
- To use a t test or Pearson's product moment correlation, parametric assumptions must be met: as well as interval data, the sample should be drawn from a normally distributed population and there should be homogeneity of variance between conditions.

Take it further

Test whether it is valid to suggest that repeated measures designs offer homogeneity of variance. Choose a sample of participants and test them twice under two different conditions. You may want to do this for three different types of variables. Using a measure such as range or standard deviation, investigate whether there is homogeneity of variance.

Link

For more detailed coverage of standard deviation, see *AQA Psychology B AS*, Chapter 4, Research methods.

Methods

Summary questions

11 Give two reasons why a psychologist would choose to use a Mann-Whitney U test.

12 Explain the similarity and difference between ordinal and interval data.

13 Explain how visual-spatial ability could be measured using a nominal, ordinal and interval scale.

14 A psychologist decided to investigate whether men are faster drivers than women. What inferential test should she choose to analyse her data, and why?

Identifying a critical value

Learning objectives:

- understand the role of a critical value in inferential tests
- understand what criteria are used to identify a critical value
- understand the use of significance levels.

Key terms

Observed value: a value achieved by carrying out an inferential test; a value that represents the data set from an investigation.

Critical value: a value taken from a statistical table which, when compared with an observed value, shows whether results are significant or not.

Significance level: a level of probability that defines the reliability of a set of results.

Two-tailed hypothesis: a hypothesis predicting a difference/correlation but not its direction.

Link

For tables, see pp331–340.

When data are analysed using an inferential test it involves 'plugging' data into a formula. This produces one figure – known as the **observed value**, or the calculated value. This figure basically represents the researcher's data set. In this sense, it is similar to a measure such as central tendency because it 'sums up' the pattern of data. The difference is that an observed value tells us whether there is a **significant** pattern or not. However, an observed value is meaningless by itself; it needs to be compared with a **critical value**. Critical values can be found in statistical tables (one for each test), which have been constructed by statisticians. They have worked out the level at which a difference or correlation is statistically significant i.e. the probability or chance that a result is reliable. Depending on the test, the observed value needs to be greater or less than the critical value to achieve a significant result. Table 11 shows whether each inferential test requires a higher or lower observed value.

Table 11 *The conditions for achieving a significant result for each inferential test*

Tests where observed value ≥ critical value	Tests where observed value ≤ critical value
Related t test Independent t test Chi-square test Spearman's rank order correlation Pearson's product moment correlation	Wilcoxon signed ranks test Mann-Whitney U test Sign test

Statistical tables contain many critical values, so how do researchers know which one they should be comparing their observed value with?

The critical value is identified using three criteria:

- the **direction** of a research hypothesis
- the amount of data collected in an investigation
- the **significance level** chosen by the researcher.

The direction of a hypothesis

Research hypotheses do more than just predict a difference or a correlation. They can also predict the direction of that difference or correlation. Rather than just saying that there is a difference between A and B, they can state whether or not the difference 'favours' A. Similarly, rather than just saying that there is a relationship between X and Y, they can say whether X and Y move in the same or in opposite directions.

It is useful to look at some actual hypotheses to illustrate this.

> H_1: There is a significant difference between the number of faces identified when presented in two dimensions and in three dimensions.

The above hypothesis is non-directional because it predicts a difference but does not give the direction. We do not know which set of faces are better identified. In such a case, the hypothesis is known as a **two-tailed hypothesis** because the prediction can go either way, i.e. two-dimensional or three-dimensional faces can be recognised better and the hypothesis will still be right.

Methods

However, the same hypothesis can be written as a directional or **one-tailed hypothesis** so that we know the expected direction of the outcome.

> H_1: Significantly more faces are identified when shown in three dimensions than when shown in two dimensions.

The same principles apply to hypotheses predicting a correlation:

> H_1: There will be a significant correlation between age of participant and the number of items recalled in a memory test.

The above hypothesis is non-directional because it predicts a relationship but does not give the direction. We do not know whether memory recall improves or worsens with age. This is a two-tailed hypothesis because the prediction can go either way: there could be a positive correlation (where age and memory recall increase/decrease together) or a negative correlation (where memory recall decreases as age increases or vice versa).

However, the same hypothesis can be written as a directional or one-tailed hypothesis:

> H_1: There will be a significant positive correlation between age of participant and the number of items recalled in a memory test.

This hypothesis only allows for the results to go one way, i.e. the variables have to 'travel' in the same direction rather than the opposite direction.

There is a good reason why the direction of a hypothesis has an impact on the critical value. If researchers 'hedge their bets' and predict a difference but not its direction (e.g. there is a difference in men and women's IQ), then they are saying that they are not exactly sure what the outcome of the investigation will be. The statistical analysis needs to take into account that the researchers are 'doubling their chances' of getting a significant result and make it more difficult to achieve. If the researchers 'stick their necks out' and predict the direction of difference (e.g. women have higher IQs), the statistical analysis makes it easier to achieve a significant result. Of course, the downside is that, if a difference is achieved in the opposite direction (e.g. men have higher IQs), it is not recognised as it was not predicted. With a two-tailed hypothesis, it would have counted as a significant result. This demonstrates that a researcher needs to be confident about an outcome to make a one-tailed prediction; their confidence, and prediction, would normally be based on previous research. What a researcher should **not** do is make their prediction after the results have been collected!

Amount of data

The amount of data is an obvious factor that affects the critical value. With most tests, there is a calculation based on the number of participants or scores, sometimes known as the **degrees of freedom (df)**. There is a good reason why the amount of data has an impact on the critical value. The significance of a difference or correlation is clearly related to the number of people or scores that it applies to. For example, researchers predicting a significant relationship between two variables would probably expect a perfect correlation between the scores of four people. However, they would expect a much weaker correlation between the scores of 40 people where they could not reasonably expect a perfect match between variables. Similarly, a difference of 20 per cent may suggest a significant difference between two large groups of people (e.g. if 80 per cent of 1,000 respondents said they had been a victim of crime in a British survey compared with 60 per cent of 1,000 respondents in a Swiss survey, this is a difference of 200 people). However, a 20 per cent difference would probably not be

Key terms

One-tailed hypothesis: a hypothesis predicting a difference/correlation and stating its direction.

Degrees of freedom (df): a measure based on the size of a sample; a measure of the number of pieces of data that have not been 'used up' in a calculation.

Fig. 6 *Like the two-tailed hypothesis, a two-tailed pantomime horse can travel in either direction! However, a one-tailed hypothesis (like a one-tailed pantomime horse) only has the option of going in one direction*

Methods

Hint

It is worth pointing out that null hypotheses do not have direction. If we think about it logically, this makes sense. If null hypotheses predict **no** difference or **no** correlation, then of course they are not going to be predicting a direction either!

AQA Examiner's tip

It is easy to make a mistake with the direction of hypotheses. Candidates sometimes offer a two-tailed hypothesis when they mean for it to be one-tailed. For example, the hypothesis 'Revision has an effect on exam performance' is actually two-tailed. Even though it is common sense that revision should **improve** performance, this hypothesis could imply that revision could have a negative effect.

significant if the numbers were small (e.g. if 20 per cent of 10 participants obeyed a command from an older person and 0 per cent obeyed a command from a younger person, this is a difference of only two people).

Level of significance

Let us look at a null hypothesis from earlier.

> H_0: There is no significant difference in the percentage of men and the percentage of women who have knowingly broken the law: any difference is due to chance.

Note how a null hypothesis ends by recognising that there may be a significant difference (or correlation) but essentially dismisses this and says that it would be due to chance: i.e. a researcher looking for a significant result may think that he has achieved one, but it may just be a fluke. In the above example, it means that if significantly more men did knowingly break the law it would be valid for the sample in the study. However, it would not be a reliable finding (would not apply more widely).

In fairness, whenever a significant result is achieved, there is always a probability that it may not be reliable. Psychologists can never be 100 per cent certain about a set of results unless they have tested all the people to whom it applies in all possible circumstances. On this basis, psychologists need to decide – before an investigation takes place – what level of probability they are prepared to accept that the set of results has occurred by chance. In other words, if a result is significant, then what is the chance that it is due to the variables under investigation and what is the corresponding chance that it has occurred because of other factors?

To show the level of probability that they are accepting, researchers state a significance level. The most conventional level in psychology is $p = 0.05$. This tells us that the researcher is accepting that there is a 5 per cent (0.05) chance that, if the results achieved are significant, they are due to fluke or to an extraneous variable. In other words, if the investigation was repeated 100 times, the researcher would expect genuine results 95 of those times. For most researchers, this would be a reliable finding. There is a 95 per cent chance that the independent variable (IV) has affected the dependent variable (DV). In other words, the H_1 should be retained. Strictly speaking, the researcher would have a significance level of $p \leq 0.05$, meaning that there is a 5 per cent chance **or less** of a significant result being a fluke.

Psychologists sometimes choose a significance level of $p \leq 0.01$. This is because they only want to accept a 1 per cent probability (or less) of a significant result occurring by chance. This is unusual in psychology, where researchers do not have to be as certain as, say, someone working in medical research. When $p \leq 0.01$ is selected, it is often because a researcher seeks to disprove a well-established theory. The logic here is that a researcher wants to demonstrate that they are more certain about their theory (i.e. it is more reliable) than theories tested at the 0.05 level.

However, researchers do have to be careful. If their significance levels are too stringent, they may make a **Type II error**. If they require too much certainty, they may end up rejecting their research hypothesis when they should have retained it.

In contrast, researchers can also choose a significance level which is too lenient (e.g. $p < 0.1$). Now, the probability of a significant result being a fluke is too great (e.g. 10 per cent). In these cases, the researchers may mistakenly claim to have a significant difference

Hint

The effect of choosing a one-tailed or two-tailed hypothesis can be understood in betting terms. If you placed a bet on a horse coming first, second or third in a race, you would not expect odds that are as good as someone who only bets on the horse coming first. Having a one-tailed hypothesis is like betting on a horse coming first rather than hedging your bets and considering other possibilities.

Hint

The effect of numbers on significance can be understood in terms of everyday situations. For example, if a football team goes down to 10 players this can make a significant difference. However, if a choir of 100 people have to perform without one of their group this absence will be much less significant.

AQA Examiner's tip

Candidates sometimes misinterpret what a significance level shows by assuming that it describes the probability of obtaining significant results. In theoretical terms, the probability of achieving a significant result would be 50:50. Level of significance only applies **if** a researcher achieves significant results (as it tells us the chance that those results are a fluke). On this basis, if asked about what a particular significance level shows, it is worth starting your answer with the phrase 'If the researcher achieves significant results ...'

Key terms

Type II error: a researcher wrongly retains H_0 rather than rejecting it, owing to the stringency of a significance level.

(or correlation). Consequently, they reject the null hypothesis instead of rejecting their research hypothesis. In these circumstances, they have made a **Type I error**.

There is a good reason why significance levels impact on the level of the critical value. If a researcher wants to be only 90 per cent certain in their results, a critical value is chosen that makes it easier to achieve significant results. The downside is that these results may not be that reliable. In contrast, if a researcher wants to be more certain in their results (e.g. 99.9 per cent), the corresponding critical value will make it more difficult to achieve significant results. However, if significant results **are** achieved, they will be highly reliable: the researcher would expect them to be valid 999 times out of 1,000.

Key points:

- Critical values are necessary in inferential statistics as they are compared with observed values to see whether a set of results are significant or not.
- Critical values are determined by the direction of a hypothesis, the amount of data and the accepted level of significance.
- Significance levels apply if significant results are achieved. They indicate the probability that researchers' results represent what is happening in the population as opposed to occuring by chance.

Summary questions

15 'A Type I error is more likely to occur with a significance level of $p = 0.5$ than $p = 0.1$.' True or false?

16 Decide whether the following hypotheses are one-tailed or two-tailed.

a Infants over nine months spend significantly more time searching for a hidden object than infants under nine months.

b There is a significant positive correlation between levels of dopamine and severity of schizophrenic symptoms.

c There is a significant difference between the number of suspects identified using photographs compared with the number of suspects identified using identity parades.

17 Explain the difference between a researcher using a significance level of $p = 0.05$ and using $p = 0.01$.

Key terms

Type I error: a researcher wrongly rejects H_0 rather than retaining it, owing to the leniency of a significance level.

AQA Examiner's tip

It is not uncommon for candidates to confuse Type I and II errors so find a way of clearly distinguishing between them (e.g. type one = one is lenient; type two = too strict).

Take it further

Imagine a drugs trial that is testing the effect of antidepressants against a placebo (dummy drug). Let's say that very early on it is obvious that the antidepressants are having an effect and relieving people of their depressive symptoms. Ethically speaking, it would be wrong to continue the trial and keep administering the placebo. At which level of significance would it be safe to abandon the trial? Make a choice and justify your answer.

Hint

The effect of significance levels is easier to understand if you think about how probability may occur in everyday life. For example, a plane that has a 1 per cent chance of crashing is more reliable (you would trust it more) than a plane that has a 5 per cent chance of crashing. Similarly, you would probably want to use a driving school where you have a 95 per cent chance of passing your driving test first time rather than one where there is only a 75 per cent chance, and so on.

Analysing data using inferential statistics

Learning objectives:

- understand how different inferential tests are applied to data to produce an observed value
- understand the use of critical tables in identifying a critical value
- understand how an observed value and critical value are compared to test the significance of a set of results.

Link

When observed values are compared with critical values in a test, they sometimes need to be larger or smaller than that value for a significant result. To remind yourself what is required with each test, see Table 11 on p310.

AQA Examiner's tip

You may be given an extract from a table of critical values, for a particular test, to use in the exam. Remember, if the critical values increase as the significance level gets more stringent, the test requires the observed value to be higher than the critical value. If the critical values decrease as the significance level gets more stringent, the test requires the observed value to be lower than the critical value.

$$t = \sqrt{\frac{\sum d}{(N\sum d^2 - (\sum d)^2)/(N-1)}}$$

t = observed value $\sum$ = sum of
d = difference between each pair of participant scores
N = number of participants

Fig. 7 *The formula for the related t test*

Each inferential test calculates an observed value that is then compared with a critical value. Each test has its own formula for calculating the observed value, as demonstrated in the examples below.

Using the related t test

A psychology student investigated whether noise was a cause of stress. He did this by measuring his participants' heart rates while they completed a complex task under two conditions: one where loud noises were played in the background and one where there was silence.

As shown below, he analysed his data using the related t test. This was because he was investigating a **difference** (in stress levels), using a **related design** (participants were tested under both conditions) with **interval data** (heart rate was measured by beats per minute – bpm).

Parametric assumptions also applied as there is evidence that heart rate is **normally distributed** in the population (with the majority of people having an average heart rate) and the data in Figure 8 show **homogeneity of variance** between conditions, as the standard deviations (14.63 and 10.26) are similar.

Participant	Mean bpm in noisy condition	Mean bpm in silent condition	d	d^2
1	110	92	18	324
2	85	72	13	169
3	67	68	−1	1
4	80	75	5	25
5	105	99	6	36
6	68	75	−7	49
7	101	84	17	289
8	88	84	4	16
9	80	90	−10	100
10	91	72	−19	361
	$\bar{X} = 87.5$	$\bar{X} = 81.1$	$\sum d = 26$	$\sum d^2 = 1370$
	$\sigma = 14.63$	$\sigma = 10.26$	$(\sum d)^2 = 676$	

$$t_{(obs)} = \sqrt{\frac{26}{((10 \times 1370) - 676)/9}} = 0.683$$

$t_{(crit)}$ = **1.833**, where H_1 is one-tailed (as noise was predicted to **increase** stress), df = (N − 1) = 9, and p = 0.05 (see Table 5 on p338)

observed value (0.683) > critical value (1.833) therefore H_1 is rejected

Fig. 8 *Working for the related t test*

The result of the t test shows that, in this investigation, there is no evidence that noise causes a significant increase in stress levels.

Using the independent t test

A psychology student wanted to see if there really was a difference in females' and males' visual spatial skills. She did this by timing how long it took a group of female and male students to complete a visual spatial task.

As shown below, she analysed her data using the independent t test. This was because she was investigating a **difference** (in visual spatial skills), using an **unrelated design** (she had males in one condition and females in the other) with **interval data** (she timed how long it took to complete a task).

Parametric assumptions also applied as there is evidence that visual spatial ability is **normally distributed** in the population (with the majority of people showing average ability) and the data in Figure 10 show **homogeneity of variance** between conditions, as the standard deviations (30.04 and 23.60) are similar.

$$\frac{[\bar{X}_A - \bar{X}_B]}{\sqrt{\left[\frac{S_A - S_B}{N_A + N_B - 2} \times \frac{N_A + N_B}{N_A N_B}\right]}}$$

Where $S_A = \Sigma X_A^2 - \frac{(\Sigma X_A)^2}{N_A}$

$S_B = \Sigma X_B^2 - \frac{(\Sigma X_B)^2}{N_B}$

$\bar{X}_A$ = mean of scores in Condition A
N_A = number of scores in Condition A
ΣX_A = sum of all the scores in Condition A
ΣX_A^2 = sum of all the scores in Condition A after being squared

$\bar{X}_B$ = mean of scores in Condition B
N_B = number of scores in Condition B
ΣX_B = sum of all the scores in Condition B
ΣX_B^2 = sum of all the scores in Condition B after being squared

Fig. 9 *Formula for independent t test*

Female participants		Male participants	
Timings (sec) X_A	X_A^2	Timings (sec) X_B	X_B^2
212	44 944	191	36 481
243	59 049	210	44 100
290	84 100	174	30 276
280	78 400	233	54 289
275	75 625	189	35 721
270	72 900	170	28 900
212	44 944		
253	64 009		
$\Sigma X_A = 2035$	$\Sigma X_A^2 = 523971$	$\Sigma X_B = 1167$	$\Sigma X_B^2 = 229767$

$\bar{X}_A = 254.375$ $\quad$ $\bar{X}_B = 194.5$

$(\Sigma X_A)^2 = 4141225$ $\quad$ $(\Sigma X_B)^2 = 1361889$

$\sigma_A = 30.04$ $\quad$ $\sigma_B = 23.60$

$S_A = 523971 - \frac{4141225}{8} = 6317.875$

$S_B = 229767 - \frac{1361889}{6} = 2785.5$

$$t_{(obs)} = \frac{254.375 - 194.5}{\sqrt{\left[\frac{6317.875 - 2785.5}{8 + 6 - 2} \times \frac{8 + 6}{(8 \times 6)}\right]}}$$

$= \mathbf{6.462}$

$t_{(crit)} = \mathbf{3.055}$ where H_1 is two-tailed (as the hypothesis did not predict that one sex would do better in the visual spatial task), df = $(N_A + N_B - 2) = 12$ and $p = 0.01$ (as the student was questioning the well-established finding that males have superior visual spatial skills). See Table 5 on p338.

observed value (6.462) > critical value (3.055) therefore H_0 is rejected

Fig. 10 *Working for the independent t test*

Hint

A number of psychology students often get anxious when they see the formulae used by different tests. You don't need to worry about why they work just how you use them. Having said this, there is often a logic to formulae. Look at the formula for the related t test; it mainly contains the measure 'd'. This makes sense since d is the measure of the difference between participants' scores, which is what we are interested in.

Links

Refer back to *AQA Psychology B AS*, Chapter 4, Research methods, to remind yourself how the mean and standard deviation are used to describe data.

See Table 5, on p338, for critical values for t.

Hint

The independent t test works on the assumption that participants have been randomly allocated to the two conditions. Obviously, because an individual's sex is pre-determined, it was not possible to do this in the experiment. The student should be aware that the results from the test are not as reliable as they would be when participants are randomly allocated.

Hint

Interval data are normally summarised in terms of means and standard deviations. These are the most powerful forms of descriptive data because they use all of the data in a set. Similarly, t tests are among the most robust of inferential tests.

Link

See Table 5, on p338, for critical values for t.

Hint

When ranking scores, watch out when there are two or more scores the same. When this happens, they share the same rank. You calculate this by working out how many rank places the scores 'take up' between them (e.g. two identical scores would take up the next two rank places, three identical scores would take up the next three rank places, etc.). You then add together these rank places and divide by the number of identical scores – this gives their shared rank. You then need to remember that the next score takes the rank position which comes next after the ones you have just used in the calculation.

The result of the t test shows that, in this investigation, there is evidence for a significant difference in the sexes' ability to complete the visual spatial task in favour of males.

Using the Wilcoxon signed ranks test

A psychology student wanted to show that people remember more words when they process words for meaning than when they process words phonetically. She presented participants with a list of 20 words: for 10 they had to give a synonym; and for 10 they had to give a rhyming word. She then tested their recall for the words using a surprise test immediately after the trial. She compared the recall for words processed for meaning (associated with synonyms) with recall for words processed phonetically (associated with rhyming).

As shown in Figure 11, she analysed her data using the Wilcoxon signed ranks test. This was because she was investigating a **difference** (in recall of two sets of words), using a **related design** (each participant was tested on both sets of words) with **ordinal data** (she counted the number of words recalled but could not guarantee that each word presented was as equally easy to remember as the next, regardless of type of processing).

Table 12 *Process and formula for the Wilcoxon signed ranks test*

Stage 1	Work out the difference between each pair of scores (always subtracting in the same direction) to give plus and minus differences.
Stage 2	Rank the differences (from highest to lowest) ignoring the sign of the differences. **Do not rank any differences of zero.**
Stage 3	Find the sum of the rank of the positive differences and find the sum of the rank of the negative differences. The smaller of the two sums is the observed value (T) for this test.

Hint

This example of the memory experiment demonstrates the importance of inferential tests. If we just look at the medians for these data sets, a difference of 1 may suggest that there is little difference in the recall of the two sets of words. However, a statistical test shows us that (given the size of the sample and the potential score) a difference of 1 is significant enough.

Take it further

Look at the critical table for the Wilcoxon signed ranks test. How would it have affected the results if the psychology student had started with a two-tailed hypothesis? Explain your findings. What would have happened if the student had chosen a significance level of p = 0.01? Explain your findings again.

Participant	No. of words recalled when processed for meaning	No. of words recalled when processed phonetically	Difference	Rank of difference
1	9	7	+2	6
2	7	7	0	
3	8	7	+1	8
4	8	6	+2	6
5	10	7	+3	3.5
6	9	5	+4	2
7	6	9	−3	3.5
8	5	5	0	
9	2	7	−5	1
10	10	8	+2	6
	Median 8	Median 7		

Sum of ranks of positive differences = 6 + 8 + 6 + 3.5 + 2 + 6 = 31.5

Sum of ranks of negative differences = 3.5 + 1 = 4.5

Therefore $T_{(obs)}$ = **4.5** (the smaller of the two sums)

$T_{(crit)}$ = **5** where H_1 is one-tailed (as the hypothesis predicted that more words would be recalled if processed for meaning), N = 8 (the number of participants minus the number of participants showing no difference in scores) and p = 0.05 (See Table 4 on p337).

observed value (4.5) < critical value (5) therefore H_1 is retained

Fig. 11 *Working for the Wilcoxon signed ranks test*

The results show that recall of words is significantly better if they are processed for meaning rather than processed phonetically.

Using the Mann-Whitney U test

A psychology student wanted to investigate whether it is easier to recognise a set of faces when they are presented in their normal configuration rather than upside down. To do this, he randomly divided 16 of his fellow students into two groups of eight. The first eight participants were presented with 25 teachers' faces the right way up and had to name as many as they could in one minute. The second eight participants were presented with the same 25 faces but this time upside down. They too had to name as many as they could in one minute.

As shown in Figure 12, the student analysed his data using the Mann-Whitney U test. This was because he was investigating a **difference**

Table 13 *Process and formula for the Mann-Whitney U test*

Stage 1	Label the two conditions A and B. If one has fewer scores/participants call it A.
Stage 2	Rank all of the scores as one set, from highest to lowest.
Stage 3	Find the sum of ranks for the scores in condition A and call this R_A. Find the sum of ranks for the scores in condition B and call this R_B.
Stage 4	Calculate U_A using $N_AN_B + \frac{N_A(N_A+1)}{2} - R_A$
Stage 5	Calculate U_B using $N_BN_A + \frac{N_B(N_B+1)}{2} - R_B$
Stage 6	Find the smaller of U_A and U_B. This is the observed value (U) for this test.

Participant (P_p)	Number of faces recognised when presented normally	Rank	Pp	Number of faces recognised when presented upside down	Rank
1	22	3.5	9	12	14
2	18	8	10	15	11
3	14	12	11	20	5
4	24	1	12	17	9
5	19	6.5	13	10	16
6	19	6.5	14	13	13
7	16	10	15	11	15
8	23	2	16	22	3.5
Median = 19		$R_A = 49.5$		Median = 14	$R_B = 86.5$

$$U_A = (8 \times 8) + \frac{8(8+1)}{2} - 49.5 = 50.5$$

$$U_B = (8 \times 8) + \frac{8(8+1)}{2} - 86.5 = 13.5$$

Therefore $U_{(obs)}$ = **13.5** (the smaller of the two calculations)

$U_{(crit)}$ = **15** where H_1 is one-tailed (as the hypothesis predicted that more faces would be identified if presented in their normal configuration), $N_A = 8$ and $N_B = 8$ (the number of participants in each condition) and $p = 0.05$ (See Table 3d on p336).

observed value (13.5) < critical value (15) therefore H_1 is retained

Fig. 12 *Working for the Mann-Whitney U test*

Hint

The Mann-Whitney formula is designed to account for the fact that there may be unequal numbers of scores in each condition (as could be the case with an unrelated design). However, it should still be used when there are equal numbers of scores in each condition. The Wilcoxon signed ranks test would not be appropriate as it compares 'pairs of scores', assuming they have come from the same person or similar people. This is not the case when participants have been randomly assigned to conditions.

Hint

Remember most inferential tests are quite logical. This one compares the ranks in each condition. If one condition has many high-ranked scores while the other has many low-ranked scores, this suggests that there is a difference between the conditions.

Hint

You may have noticed that the data are summarised using medians. This is because the data are ordinal. Ordinal data should not be summarised using means, as the calculation for the mean 'divides out' scores assuming that intervals between them are equal. This is clearly not a fair assumption to make with ordinal data.

(in the recognition of two sets of faces presented differently), using an **unrelated design** (each set of faces was seen by a different group of participants) with **ordinal data** (he counted the number of faces correctly named but could not guarantee that each face presented was equally as easy to recognise as the next, regardless of how it was presented).

The results show that significantly more faces were identified (in the time limit) when presented in their normal configuration as opposed to when presented upside down.

Using the sign test

A psychology student wanted to see whether employers would be less likely to give an interview to a job applicant who had been diagnosed with depression in their past than one who had not. To test this, he constructed two identical application forms apart from one difference: one application reported a history of depression in the section on health and the other did not. One application form was given to a group of 12 managers; the other was given to another 12 managers who had been matched to the first group in terms of occupation, age, sex, ethnicity and qualifications. Each participant in the experiment was simply asked whether or not they would give the applicant an interview.

As shown in Figure 13, the student analysed his data using the sign test. This was because he was investigating a **difference** (in judgements of the application), using a **related design** (because, although there were different participants in each group, they were matched pairs) with **nominal data** (as the data were in categories – either the applicant would be given an interview or not).

Participant	Applicant with history of depression	Participant	Applicant without history of depression	Difference
1	Yes	13	Yes	
2	No	14	Yes	+
3	No	15	Yes	+
4	Yes	16	Yes	
5	Yes	17	No	–
6	No	18	Yes	+
7	No	19	No	
8	Yes	20	Yes	
9	No	21	Yes	+
10	Yes	22	Yes	
11	Yes	23	No	–
12	No	24	Yes	+

Number of '+' signs = 5

Number of '–' signs = 2

Therefore $s_{(obs)} = \mathbf{2}$ (the smaller of the two)

$s_{(crit)} = \mathbf{0}$ where H_1 is one-tailed (as the hypothesis predicted that applicants with a history of depression would be less likely to get an interview), N = 7 (the number of differences excluding zero differences) and p = 0.05 (See Table 1 on p331).

observed value (2) > critical value (0) therefore H_1 is rejected

Fig. 13 *Working for the sign test*

Hint

The sign test is a really straightforward test. It simply measures whether more differences occur one way than the other way.

Take it further

The sign test could be used on any level of data as data only need to be **at least** nominal. The issue is that it is not a very powerful test and would not necessarily give reliable results. You can put this to the test by using the sign test to analyse the data provided for the related t test (p314) and for the Wilcoxon signed ranks test (p316) to investigate whether the analyses give the same findings, i.e. is the same hypothesis rejected/retained?

Methods

Hint

The sign test is often used with repeated measures designs. However, in the example, there are different participants but they are seen as 'related' because similar pairs of people are compared on this judgement. Obviously, the student could not compare the same people's judgements in this case as the application was essentially the same and the participants would have guessed the aim of the study.

Link

See Table 1, on p331, for critical values for s.

Hint

Note that for the result to be significant, in this case, the observed value would have to be zero. In other words, all the differences should go in one direction and **none** should go in the opposite direction. With so few pairs of scores, it is not enough that most go the way expected – all of them have to for the findings to be significant.

Table 14 *Process and formula for the sign test*

Stage 1	Identify the change/difference between the two conditions. No change is recorded as zero. Other changes are recorded as '+' or '−'. Where there are categories rather than scores, decide what constitutes a positive change and what constitutes a negative change. It does not matter what you decide, as long as you are consistent.
Stage 2	Count the number of '+' signs and the number of '−' signs. The smaller of these two numbers is the observed value (s) for the test.

The results show that there is not a significant difference in people's judgements of an applicant with a history of depression when compared with an applicant without.

Using the chi-square test

A psychology student wanted to investigate whether there really was a difference between four- and six-year-old children's ability to conserve number. She predicted that there was no difference and devised her own task to demonstrate this using rows of sweets, which children were asked to choose from. At the end of the task, she simply recorded whether or not each child had demonstrated conservation.

As shown below, the student analysed her data using the chi-square test. This was because she was investigating an **association** (between age and ability to conserve), using an **unrelated design** (the four-year-olds were obviously a different group from the six-year-olds) with **nominal data** (as the data were in categories – either the child could conserve or the child could not).

Table 15 *Formula for chi-square test for data from two groups of participants*

Stage 1	Put data into a 2 × 2 table. Label each cell of the table: a, b, c and d.
Stage 2	Calculate the total for each row (R) and column (C) in the table, and calculate the grand total of scores (T).
Stage 3	Construct an expected table of values, using the same 2 × 2 table. For each cell, the expected value is given by $E = \frac{R \times C}{T}$ (using the corresponding R and C for that cell).
Stage 4	For each cell, calculate $(O - E)^2/E$ where O is the score from the original table.
Stage 5	Calculate the sum of the calculations from Stage 4 and this gives the observed value (χ^2) for this test.

Table 16 *Table of observed values*

	Four-year-olds		**Six-year-olds**		**Total**	
Conserved	8	(a)	20	(b)	28	(R)
Did not conserve	12	(c)	10	(d)	22	(R)
Total	20	(C)	30	(C)	50	(T)

Methods

Hint

The table of expected values is what you would expect if there was absolutely no difference between conditions, given the same number of participants. For example, in the table of expected values in the example, 56 per cent of both age groups are expected to conserve – giving no difference. The test then simply compares the table of expected values with the table of observed values to see if there is a close match between them. If the observed values closely match the expected values, the observed values show no significant difference (like the expected values).

$$r_s = 1 - \frac{6\sum d^2}{N(N^2 - 1)}$$

where $\sum$ = sum of

d^2 = difference between ranks of scores squared

N = number of pairs of scores

Fig. 15 *The formula for Spearman's rank order correlation*

Table 17 *Table of expected values*

	Four-year-olds		Six-year-olds		Total	
Conserved	11.2 (28 × 20)/50	(a)	16.8 (28 × 30)/50	(b)	28	(R)
Did not conserve	8.8 (20 × 22)/50	(c)	13.2 (22 × 30)/50	(d)	22	(R)
Total	20	(C)	30	(C)	50	(T)

Cell a: $(O - E)^2/E = (8 - 11.2)^2/11.2 = 0.91$ Cell b: $(O - E)^2/E = (20 - 16.8)^2/16.8 = 0.61$

Cell c: $(O - E)^2/E = (12 - 8.8)^2/8.8 = 1.16$ Cell a: $(O - E)^2/E = (10 - 13.2)^2/13.2 = 0.78$

Therefore $\chi^2(\text{obs}) = 3.46$ (0.91 + 0.61 + 1.16 + 0.78)

$\chi^2_{(crit)}$ = **6.64** where H_1 is two-tailed (the hypothesis predicted no difference; the alternative is a difference), df = 1 ([no. of rows of data −1] × [no. of columns of data −1]) and p = 0.01 (as the student was questioning a well-established theory). See Table 2 on p332.

observed value (3.46) < critical value (6.64) therefore H_0 is retained

Fig. 14 *Working for the chi-square test*

The findings therefore show that there is no association between age and ability to conserve. In other words, there is no significant difference between the frequency of conservation between the four-year-olds and the six-year-olds in the investigation.

Using the Spearman's rank order correlation

A psychology student predicted that there would be a positive relationship between the age of a child and their level of morality. She measured morality using a questionnaire. The higher the score on the questionnaire, the more morally developed the individual was.

Age of child	Rank	Morality score	Rank	Difference between ranks (d)	D^2
5	12	9	11	1	1
7	9.5	11	10	−0.5	0.25
12	2	24	2	0	0
7	9.5	15	8	1.5	2.25
9	6	16	7	−1	1
6	11	8	12	−1	1
9	6	17	6	0	0
8	8	14	9	−1	1
11	3	22	3	0	0
9	6	18	5	1	1
10	4	20	4	0	0
13	1	27	1	0	0
					$\sum d^2 = 7.5$

Therefore $r_{s(obs)} = 1 - \frac{6 \times 7.5}{12(12^2 - 1)} = 1 - 0.026 = 0.974$

$r_{s(crit)}$ = **0.503** where H_1 is one-tailed (as the hypothesis predicted a positive correlation), N = 12 (the number of participants/pairs of scores) and p = 0.05 (See Table 6 on p339)

observed value (0.974) > critical value (0.503) therefore H_1 is retained

Fig. 16 *Working for Spearman's rank order correlation*

As shown in Figure 16, the student analysed her data using the Spearman's rank order correlation. This was because she was investigating a **correlation** (between age and morality), using a **related design** (as both measures came from the same individual) with **ordinal data** (age follows an interval scale but the student could not guarantee that the scores on the morality test had equal intervals).

The results show that there is evidence of a significant positive relationship between age and morality. In fact, the observed value is so much greater than the critical value that the relationship would even be significant when $p = 0.005$ (see Table 6, on p339). This indicates that the correlation is a strong and reliable one.

Figure 17 displays the data from the student's analysis of age and morality scores. It clearly shows a very strong, positive correlation as indicated by the observed value (correlation coefficient) of +0.974.

Using the Pearson's product moment correlation

A psychology student wanted to investigate whether there was a relationship between familiarity of a face and the ability to recognise a face. He predicted that the longer a member of staff had spent working at a school, the quicker they would be able to identify their current colleagues' faces from a larger set of faces.

As shown in Figure 19, he analysed his data using the Pearson's product moment correlation. This was because he was investigating a **correlation** (between familiarity and recognition of a face), using a **related design** (as each participant provided both measures) with **interval data** (as both measures used time and time occurs in equal intervals).

Participant	Length of time at school in months (x)	x^2	Time taken to identify faces in sec (y)	y^2	xy
1	192	36 864	23	529	4416
2	120	14 400	35	1225	4200
3	100	10 000	27	729	2700
4	88	7744	24	576	2112
5	75	5625	36	1296	2700
6	64	4096	40	1600	2560
7	36	1296	44	1936	1584
8	6	36	72	5184	432
9	2	4	30	900	60
	$\sum x = 683$	$\sum x^2 = 80065$	$\sum y = 331$	$\sum y^2 = 13975$	$\sum(xy) = 20764$

Therefore $r_{(obs)} = \dfrac{(9 \times 20764) - (683 \times 331)}{\sqrt{([(9 \times 80065) - 683^2] \times [(9 \times 13975) - 331^2])}}$

$= \dfrac{186876 - 226073}{\sqrt{(254096 \times 16214)}}$

$= (-)\ 0.611$

$r_{(crit)} = \mathbf{0.582}$ where H_1 is one-tailed (as the hypothesis predicted a negative correlation, i.e. more time at work, less time needed to identify faces), $df = N - 2 = 7$ and $p = 0.05$ (See Table 7 on p340)

observed value (0.611) > critical value (0.584) therefore H_1 is retained

Fig. 19 *Working for Pearson's product moment correlation*

Hint

The Spearman's rank order correlation is relatively straightforward when you think about it. Each set of scores is ranked separately and then the test simply compares those ranks to look for a relationship (e.g. does the participant who ranks high on one score also rank high on the other score?).

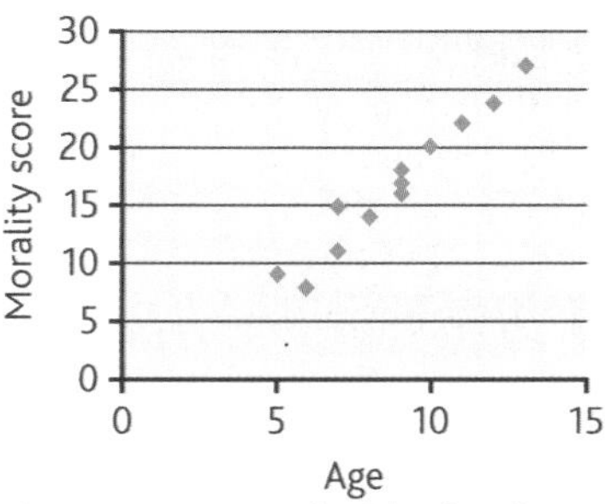

Fig. 17 *Scattergraph of the data from the student's analysis of age and morality scores*

Link

For more information on the use of scattergraphs (also known as scattergrams) and correlation coefficients, see *AQA Psychology B AS*, Chapter 4, Research methods.

$$r = \frac{N\sum(xy) - \sum x \sum y}{\sqrt{[N\sum x^2 - (\sum x)^2]\,[N\sum y^2 - (\sum y)^2]}}$$

where $\sum$ = sum of

x = scores from first variable

y = scores from second variable

N = no. of pairs of scores

Fig. 18 *The formula for Pearson's product moment correlation*

Hint

It is easy to make errors with long calculations such as this one. With correlation tests, the observed (calculated) value should always be between −1 and +1 (as this is the range for correlation coefficients). So, if your observed value is outside this range, you know that you have gone wrong somewhere!

Methods

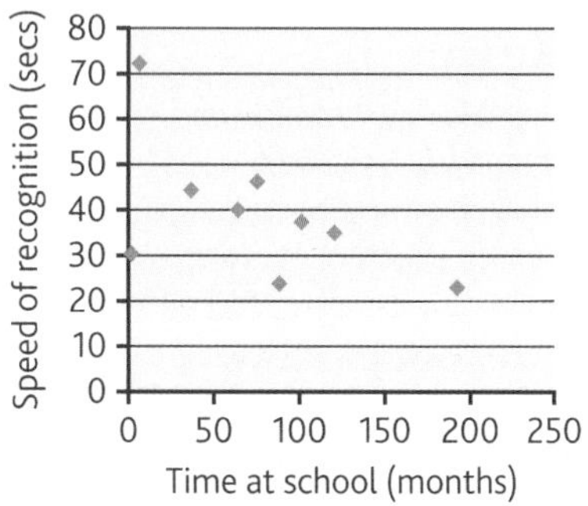

Fig. 20 *Scattergraph of the data from the student's analysis of time worked at school and speed of recognition of colleagues' faces*

The observed value is, strictly speaking, negative, giving evidence of a significant negative correlation in this investigation. In other words, staff that have worked at the school longer (and are more familiar with their colleagues' faces) need less time to identify these faces.

Figure 20 displays the data from the student's analysis of time worked at school and speed of recognition of colleagues' faces. It clearly shows a negative correlation as indicated by the observed value (correlation coefficient) of –0.611

Key points:

- Each inferential test uses data to calculate an observed value: a value that represents the data set.
- Each test also has an associated table of critical values, which vary depending on the direction of a hypothesis, the selected significance level and the amount of data.
- An observed value is compared with a critical value to establish whether or not results are significant – whether the observed value should be greater or less than the critical value depends on the test used.

Hint

It is easier to apply the test to positive values. In the above example, the observed value is negative (as predicted by the negative correlation) but critical values in the table are positive. In other words, if the observed value is more positive than the critical value it is like saying the negative value is more negative.

AQA Examiner's tip

Do not waste your time learning the formulae for the tests, as you will not be required to use them in the exam. Indeed, there is not the time for you to carry out a calculation in the exam. However, you may be required to compare an observed value with a critical value in order to decide whether to reject or accept an hypothesis, so make sure that you know how to do this (bearing in mind that it is different for different tests). You will always be given the observed value but you may have to extract the appropriate critical value from a table.

Summary questions

18 State whether for the following tests, observed values should be greater or less than the critical value in order to indicate significance:

a chi-square test

b Pearson's product moment correlation

c Wilcoxon signed ranks test.

19 Identify $r_{s(crit)}$ for a two-tailed hypothesis, where N = 17 and p = 0.01.

20 Look at the extract from the table of critical values for the sign test.

	Level of significance for a one-tailed test				
	0.05	0.025	0.01	0.005	0.0005
N = 30	10	9	8	7	5

A researcher has carried out an experiment (where N = 30) and used the sign test to analyse her data. Her observed value is 9. Explain whether she has a significant result or not.

21 A teacher wanted to investigate whether there was a significant difference between the scores of his two psychology classes. He did not predict which group would do better before the test and wanted to investigate the difference where p = 0.05.

The data are shown below:

Class A 55 45 33 32 58 12 23 33 33 30 37 40 38 Median = 33

Class B 45 56 40 37 25 40 41 33 35 49 29 Median = 40

Use the Mann-Whitney U test to analyse the data to investigate whether there is a significant difference between the classes.

Methods

Ethical considerations in investigating psychology

Learning objectives:

- be aware of the ethical issues associated with designing and conducting an investigation
- be aware of the ethical issues within the social and cultural environment.

Key terms

Respect: valuing the dignity and worth of all individuals.

Competence: working within the limits of one's knowledge, skill, training, education and experience.

Responsibility: an obligation to protect participants.

Integrity: valuing honesty, accuracy, clarity and fairness.

Link

For more detailed coverage of ethics see *AQA Psychology B AS*, Chapter 4, Research methods.

In this chapter, we have mainly focused on the mechanics of carrying out investigations. However, it is important to remember that, as psychologists, we study people. Investigating people is not like investigating particles and chemicals because people are conscious beings who experience emotions. For this reason, we should be mindful that there is a code of ethics when studying people. It is there to protect them from the potentially negative consequences of being a research participant.

The British Psychological Society's code of ethics and conduct (available on the Society's website, see end of chapter, p324) covers four main categories: **respect**, **competence**, **responsibility** and **integrity**.

Ethical issues within design and conduct

These ethical issues relate to the setting up and carrying out of research:

- respecting participants' confidentiality by protecting their identity and other details
- gaining participants' informed consent wherever appropriate
- avoiding deception of participants
- ensuring participants have the right to withdraw
- protecting participants from physical and mental harm, misuse and abuse.

Ethical issues within the social and cultural environment

Other ethical issues focus more on the consequences of research for the wider community or society, rather than just focusing on the individual participant. These may include:

- avoiding cultural bias – for example, by only studying certain cultures and ignoring others, or by implying that the behaviour of one culture is inferior to another's
- responsibility to act on results – for example, if a set of findings could benefit a group or community, there is a moral obligation to use them for this purpose
- respecting the confidentiality of a community or society – for example, if a whole culture is studied there is no need to name them or provide details that identify them.

Unethical research

Research that breaches ethical guidelines may still be carried out. For example, deception is relatively common in investigations where participants would behave differently if they had knowledge of the aim. However, such deception may cause distress, discomfort or embarrassment for the participant.

Unethical research may be carried out if the psychologist can show that the ends justify the means. For example, a researcher may argue that a small number of participants could be treated unethically if the results of the study would actually benefit the wider population. This may become even less of a problem if the participants are treated ethically after the event: for example, if they are counselled, ensured privacy, and given the right to withdraw their data.

Key points:

- Ethical considerations in investigating psychology occur at an individual level when participants take part in research.
- Ethical considerations should also apply to the wider social and cultural environment.

Summary questions

22 Give one way of protecting confidentiality.

23 Outline why participants should have the right to withdraw.

24 Distinguish between 'consent' and 'informed consent'.

25 Explain why it is not always possible to respect the rights of the individual participant and demonstrate responsibility to a social or cultural group.

End-of-chapter activity 1

Is psychology a science? Your task is to investigate whether psychology students answer this question differently from non-psychology students. But keep it simple. Your participants can only answer 'yes' or 'no', giving you nominal data.

You will need to compare the responses of your two sets of students to see if there is a significant difference in responses. In order to do this, you will need to analyse your data using an inferential test.

Use the examples in the chapter to help you to analyse and write up your results in the appropriate way.

Remember, you are looking for a difference in responses between two sets of students using nominal data.

Think carefully about your critical value. What are you predicting before you start your research and what would be an appropriate level of significance?

Further reading

For the British Psychological Society's code of ethics and conduct, see the 'Code of conduct and ethical guidelines' section of the Society's website: www.bps.org.uk

End-of-chapter activity 2

You are to devise and construct your own 20-item questionnaire to assess a behaviour/variable that you have studied at A2. Make sure that each question rates or scores this behaviour in some way using the same scale each time. Examples of behaviours might include morality, sociability, criminal tendencies, addictive personality, depressive tendencies and stress levels.

When you have finished constructing your questionnaire, your task is to test it in three ways:

- Assess its internal reliability by carrying out the split half method. You only need to find one person to complete your questionnaire. When you have calculated their overall score, split the test into two sets of 10 questions and compare their scores on these. Repeat this again twice, splitting the questions differently each time. Overall, would the findings suggest that you have an internally reliable questionnaire or not? Justify your answer.
- Test its external reliability by carrying out a test–retest. You will need to ask at least five people to complete your questionnaire now. They should do this on two separate occasions, some time apart. The aim is to compare their scores on each occasion to investigate whether there is consistency between scores or not. You should do this statistically using Spearman's rank order correlation. Overall, would you conclude that you have an externally reliable questionnaire or not? Justify your answer.
- Test the validity of your questionnaire – in other words, does it measure what it is supposed to? For this test, use qualitative analysis rather than quantitative analysis. Interview your previous participants about their own opinions of the behaviour you are measuring (e.g. how moral do they think they are? to what extent would they say their personality was addictive? how would they describe their own stress levels?). Using the information from the interviews, decide how well individuals' assessments of their own behaviour matched your scoring of it. Overall, would you conclude that you have a valid questionnaire or not? Justify your answer.

AQA Examination-style questions

Chapter 1

1 (a) Suggest three behavioural categories that could be used by researchers in an observational study of attachment of infants aged 12 months. *(3 marks)*

(b) (i) Ainsworth's strange situation is a widely used method for assessing attachment. Describe three features of the strange situation. *(3 marks)*

(ii) Explain one weakness of the strange situation as a means of assessing attachment. *(2 marks)*

(c) Describe and evaluate research into the causes and consequences of rejection in children. *(12 marks)*

2 (a) Suggest three methods that could be used to identify which children in a primary school class are friends. *(3 marks)*

(b) (i) Psychologists have studied the behaviours of popular children. Describe three of these behaviours. *(3 marks)*

(ii) Explain why it is difficult to be sure that the behaviours you have identified in 2 (b)(i) are the cause of children's popularity. *(2 marks)*

(c) Discuss the consequences of privation and deprivation. *(12 marks)*

Chapter 2

1 (a) Piaget carried out research which involved young children carrying out conservation tasks. Explain one methodological criticism of the way in which piaget conducted conservation studies. *(3 marks)*

(b) (i) What is meant by the *zone of proximal development* (ZPD)? *(3 marks)*

(ii) Briefly evaluate one way in which the zone of proximal development has been studied. *(2 marks)*

(c) Describe and evaluate the information processing approach to cognitive development. *(12 marks)*

2 (a) Suggest three behaviour categories produced by a supervising adult that could be used by researchers in an observational study of scaffolding with children aged four years. *(3 marks)*

(b) Describe and evaluate one method used by the information processing approach to study children's problem solving and thinking. *(5 marks)*

(c) Describe and evaluate Piaget's theory of cognitive development. *(12 marks)*

Chapter 3

1 (a) Eisenberg used stories to investigate pro-social reasoning in children. A child would listen to a story and then be asked a question. The answer to the question was taken as an indication of the child's level of pro-social reasoning. Create your own brief pro-social reasoning story and a question suitable for studying pro-social reasoning of eight-year-old children. *(3 marks)*

(b) (i) What did Gilligan mean by the term *ethic of care*? *(2 marks)*

(ii) Identify the three levels of moral development that were described by Gilligan. *(3 marks)*

(c) Describe and evaluate a psychodynamic theory of moral development. *(12 marks)*

2 (a) Piaget used stories involving moral comparisons in his investigation of moral development. Outline problems associated with the use of moral comparisons to investigate moral development. *(3 marks)*

(b) Briefly discuss one or more criticisms of Kohlberg's theory of moral development. *(5 marks)*

(c) Describe and evaluate Gilligan's model of moral development. *(12 marks)*

Chapter 4

1 (a) (i) Explain what is meant by 'repression'. *(2 marks)*

(ii) Explain what is meant by 'recovered memory'. *(2 marks)*

(b) Karen bumped into an old friend from school. Karen remembered her from her form but could not recall her name. 'It's Sue,' the friend said. 'Of course, I remember now. You were friends with Julie. said Karen' 'I can't remember Julie,' Sue replied. 'What did she look like?' 'She had very blue eyes and long dark hair,' said Karen.

With reference to the conversation above, identify and outline two processes involved in face recognition. *(4 marks)*

(c) Discuss at least two factors that have been found to affect the reliability of eye-witness accounts. Refer to empirical evidence in your answer. *(12 marks)*

2 (a) Outline what is meant by 'flashbulb memory'. *(4 marks)*

(b) Briefly discuss two limitations of a feature analysis theory of face recognition. *(4 marks)*

(c) At 4 a.m. Bob saw two youths smashing the cars parked on the street. He shouted at them and they looked at him before running off.

Discuss the use of eye-witness identification procedures to aid Bob's identification of the two youths. Refer to both simultaneous and sequential line-ups in your answer. *(12 marks)*

Chapter 5

1 (a) Identify two differences between unipolar and bipolar depression. *(2 marks)*

(b) Phil feels very miserable and lethargic and cannot bring himself to participate in any activities that he previously enjoyed. Phil thinks he may be suffering from seasonal affective disorder (SAD) because he felt like this last year in October but felt much better by May.

(i) Explain why Phil's condition might be diagnosed as SAD. *(2 marks)*

(ii) Briefly discuss one treatment for SAD. *(4 marks)*

(c) Discuss at least one treatment for schizophrenia. Refer to evidence in your answer. *(12 marks)*

2 Chris was diagnosed with schizophrenia in his early twenties. For the past five years he has been in and out of hospital and for the last 12 months he has been in a psychiatric unit. His doctors are concerned that he is becoming institutionalised. As Chris is now responding well to his medication, his doctors have decided that he should try community care.

(a) Briefly describe what community care might entail for Chris. *(4 marks)*

(b) Briefly evaluate the role of community care in the treatment of schizophrenia. *(4 marks)*

(c) Describe and evaluate at least one biological explanation for mood disorders. Refer to empirical evidence in your answer. *(12 marks)*

Chapter 6

1 Carol is a young newly qualified teacher who has recently begun to suffer from chronic and intense headaches. She is unhappy at work because she finds the work very demanding and believes that other newly qualified teachers are better able to cope with the job. Her doctor has referred her to a health psychologist who specialises in stress management.

(a) Identify and outline one method the psychologist might use to measure Carol's stress. *(3 marks)*

(b) Identify and explain the role of one personal variable in mediating responses to stress. Refer to Carol in your answer. *(5 marks)*

(c) Compare two techniques of stress management that the health psychologist might choose to use with Carol. *(12 marks)*

2 (a) (i) Outline one defence mechanism. *(2 marks)*

(ii) Explain how it might be used by an individual to cope with stress. *(2 marks)*

(b) John feels very stressed. His exams are only two months away but he has not started revising.

What is meant by a 'problem-focused' strategy for coping with stress? Explain how this strategy might be used by John. *(4 marks)*

(c) Discuss the role played by the autonomic nervous system in mediating and/or responding to stress. *(12 marks)*

Chapter 7

1 (a) 'Heroin is a depressant; cocaine is a stimulant.'

(i) Explain the meaning of the term 'depressant' and describe one short-term psychological effect that might result from using heroin. *(2 marks)*

(ii) Explain the meaning of the term stimulant and describe one short-term psychological effect that might result from using cocaine. *(2 marks)*

(b) Programmes to treat and prevent substance abuse may be aimed at at-risk groups.

(i) Identify an at-risk group for starting smoking and explain why this group is more likely to be involved in smoking than other groups. *(2 marks)*

(ii) Identify a different at-risk group for heavy drinking and explain why this group is more likely to be involved in heavy drinking than other groups. *(2 marks)*

(c) Discuss the effectiveness of fear-arousal techniques in preventing substance abuse. Refer to psychological evidence in your answer. *(12 marks)*

2 (a) Emma had been using heroin for several years. She was showing tolerance to it. Recently she entered a detoxification programme which caused withdrawal symptoms.

(i) Explain what is meant by 'tolerance' and explain why it has happened. *(2 marks)*

(ii) Explain what is meant by 'withdrawal symptoms' and describe one symptom that Emma would experience when she stopped using heroin. *(2 marks)*

(b) The staff of a secondary school has decided to use a social inoculation programme to try to prevent the students in Year 9 (13 to 14 year olds) from starting smoking. Outline two features of an inoculation programme that would be likely to be effective. *(4 marks)*

(c) Discuss the effectiveness of aversion therapy and/or self-management therapies in the treatment of substance abuse. Refer to evidence in your answer. *(12 marks)*

Chapter 8

1 (a) Outline and explain one problem of using victim surveys to measure crime. *(4 marks)*
(b) Outline two characteristics of the criminal personality. *(4 marks)*
(c) Discuss behaviour modification and anger management as treatments for offending. *(12 marks)*

2 (a) Briefly discuss the role of custodial sentencing in the treatment of offenders. *(3 marks)*
(b) What is meant by 'offender profiling'? Explain one limitation of offender profiling. *(5 marks)*
(c) Ricky has been caught stealing from a shop. This is not the first time that he has been caught by the police. Last year, Ricky spent three months in jail for robbery. At the police station, he tells the police officer, 'It's not my fault I steal from people. My father did loads of robberies when I was a boy.'

Discuss biological and social learning theory explanations of offending. Refer to Ricky in your answer. *(12 marks)*

Chapter 9

1 (a) Identify and briefly describe two features of psychodynamics. *(4 marks)*
(b) Briefly discuss why behaviourist psychologists justify the use of animals in research. *(4 marks)*
(c) Discuss the biological approach in psychology.
Refer to at least one example of behaviour in your answer. *(12 marks)*

2 (a) Use an example of behaviour to explain how social learning theorists might investigate 'imitation of a role model'. *(4 marks)*
(b) What is meant by 'the eclectic approach in psychology'?
Outline one weakness of adopting such an approach in psychology. *(4 marks)*
(c) Peter is driving fast to get to his sales conference. The car in front of him is slowing him down. At the next set of traffic lights, Peter gets out of his car and approaches the other driver. There is an argument and then a fight. Later Peter regrets what has happened.

Discuss how psychologists from the cognitive and the humanistic approaches might explain Peter's behaviour. *(12 marks)*

Chapter 10

1 A psychology teacher was giving a presentation to some students who were considering studying psychology. She was asked by one of the students if psychology is a science and replied, 'Yes. There are many reasons why I would argue that psychology is a science. One reason is that experiments and observations are carried out objectively and reported in detail so that other investigators can replicate the work.'

(a) Outline what is meant by 'replication' and explain the role of replication in scientific research. *(4 marks)*
(b) In the context of the free will and determinism debate, suggest why psychological explanations are usually deterministic. *(4 marks)*
(c) Discuss the role of heredity in explaining behaviour. In your answer, refer to at least two topics that you have studied in psychology. *(12 marks)*

2 (a) Using an example from psychology, explain what is meant by 'holism'. *(4 marks)*
(b) Briefly explain one limitation of the nomothetic approach in psychology. *(4 marks)*
(c) 'Psychology is a science'. Discuss this statement. Refer to the psychoanalytic and cognitive approaches in your answer. *(12 marks)*

Chapter 11

1 A psychologist decided to investigate helping behaviour using a field experiment. Her hypothesis was that an individual will receive help more quickly in a situation where there is one other person present rather than a group of people. Her theory was that when people are in groups, responsibility is shared, and so people are less quick to act.

The participants were agency staff who had been sent for a job interview at the university where the psychologist worked. There was actually no job available, but the participants did not know this. Neither did they know that they were really taking part in an experiment.

Participants arrived for the interview at different times across a week. Each participant was either taken to a room where five applicants who were confederates of the psychologist were waiting or to a room where one applicant who was a confederate of the psychologist was waiting. After the participant had been in the room for two minutes, the assistant, who was in both conditions, fell off her chair, slumped on the floor and appeared unconscious. She carried out the same action each time.

In the first condition, the other assistants had been told not to move so that the participant had to make a decision to help. In the second condition, the participant was the only person who could help.

In both conditions, the psychologist timed how long it took for the participant to help. The stopwatch was started when the assistant hit the floor and stopped when the participant made physical contact with the assistant. Chairs were always arranged in the room so that the participant had to sit the same distance from the assistant in need of help.

The table below shows the mean response time for each condition.

Table 1 *The mean response times and standard deviations for participants in the 'group' condition and the 'alone' condition*

	Group condition	Alone condition
Mean response time (sec)	19.5	16.6
Standard deviation	5.75	5.15

(a) The psychologist used a field experiment in her study. Give one strength and one limitation of using a field experiment. *(2 marks)*

(b) Identify one variable that the psychologist controlled in this study and explain why it was important to control it. *(3 marks)*

(c) Briefly explain one ethical issue raised by this study. *(2 marks)*

(d) (i) Name an appropriate inferential test that the psychologist could have used to analyse the differences in participants' response times. *(1 mark)*

(ii) State two factors which justify the use of the test that you have given in (i). *(2 marks)*

(e) The psychologist used a significance level of 5 per cent ($p = 0.05$). Outline what is meant by a significance level of 5 per cent. *(2 marks)*

(f) After analysing her results, the psychologist found no significant difference in response times between the conditions in her study. However, from her observations, she did hypothesise that outgoing people are quicker to help than shy people. She decided to test this, but first had to establish a way of distinguishing between shy and outgoing people.

Design a study to test the hypothesis that shy people take longer to respond in a situation involving a decision than outgoing people. Include in your answer sufficient detail to allow reasonable replication of the study.

In your answer, refer to:

- an appropriate but different task to the one described
- an appropriate method of investigation
- how you will operationalise shy and outgoing
- sampling technique
- materials/apparatus and procedure.

Justify your design decisions. *(8 marks)*

2 Whilst driving through her local area, a psychologist noticed that boys seemed to play on the road more than girls. She decided to carry out an observational study to test the hypothesis that boys aged 7 to 11 differ from girls aged 7 to 11 in their use of the street for play.

A category system was used for classifying use of the street. There were two categories:

- Playing on the road: this was considered to occur when a child was playing and had at least one foot on the road.
- Playing on the pavement: this was considered to be when a child was playing and had both feet on the pavement. This category also included playing on grass verges and entrances to driveways.

The psychologist conducted observations over a six-week period for a total of 20 hours.

Observations always took place on dry afternoons, when children were outside after returning home from school. The observations were carried out at different locations. For each child observed playing, and estimated to be within the required age range, the psychologist noted the sex of the child and whether the child was on the road or on the pavement. Each child was placed in one category only.

The data obtained are shown in Table 1 below.

Table 1: The number of girls and boys aged 7–11 playing 'on the road' and 'on the pavement'

	Number playing on the road	**Number playing on the pavement**
Boys	132	68
Girls	40	46

(a) Write a suitable hypothesis for this study. *(2 marks)*

(b) (i) A chi-test was used to analyse the data. The calculated value of chi-square (χ^2) was 8.7. Using Table 2 below, explain whether or not the result was significant. *(2 marks)*

χ^2 must be equal to or more than the stated value to be significant.

Table 2: Critical values of *chi*-square (χ^2)

Level of significance for two-tailed test				
df	0.1	0.05	0.01	0.001
1	2.706	3.841	6.635	10.831

(ii) Identify one factor that the psychologist had to take into account when deciding whether or not to use the chi-square (χ^2) test. *(1 mark)*

(c) The psychologist carried out observations on her own.

(i) Identify one methodological problem of her working on her own. *(1 mark)*

(ii) Explain how the problem you have identified in your answer to 2(c)(i) might have been addressed if another observer had been involved. *(2 marks)*

(d) The method used by the psychologist was naturalistic observation. Identify and discuss one limitation of this method of research. *(4 marks)*

(e) Having established the pattern of play for boys and girls, the psychologist wanted to explore differences between boys' and girls' understanding of the risks associated with playing in the road.

Design a study to investigate gender differences in children's understanding of risks associated with playing in the road. Include in your answer sufficient detail to allow for reasonable replication of the study. In your answer, refer to:

- an appropriate method of investigation
- materials/apparatus and procedure.

Justify your design decisions. *(8 marks)*

AQA specimen question

Statistical tables

Table 1 *Critical values in the sign test*

	Level of significance for a one-tailed test			
	0.05	0.025	0.01	0.005
	Level of significance for a two-tailed test			
	0.10	0.005	0.02	0.01
N				
5	0	–	–	–
6	0	0	–	–
7	0	0	0	–
8	1	0	0	0
9	1	1	0	0
10	1	1	0	0
11	2	1	1	0
12	2	2	1	1
13	3	2	1	1
14	3	2	2	1
15	3	3	2	2
16	4	3	2	2
17	4	4	3	2
18	5	4	3	3
19	5	4	4	3
20	5	5	4	3
25	7	7	6	5
30	10	9	8	7
35	12	11	10	9

Calculated S must be EQUAL TO *or* LESS THAN *the table (critical) value for significance at the level shown.*

SOURCE: F. **Clegg** *(1982)* Simple Statistics, *Cambridge University Press. With the kind permission of the author and publishers.*

Table 2 *Critical values of χ^2*

	Level of significance for a one-tailed test					
	0.10	0.05	0.025	0.01	0.005	0.005
	Level of significance for a two-tailed test					
	0.20	0.10	0.05	0.02	0.01	0.001
df						
1	1.64	2.71	3.84	5.41	6.64	10.83
2	3.22	4.60	5.99	7.82	9.21	13.82
3	4.64	6.25	7.82	9.84	11.34	16.27
4	5.99	7.78	9.49	11.67	13.28	18.46
5	7.29	9.24	11.07	13.39	15.09	20.52
6	8.56	10.64	12.59	15.03	16.81	22.46
7	9.80	12.02	14.07	16.62	18.48	24.32
8	11.03	13.36	15.51	18.17	20.09	26.12
9	12.24	14.68	16.92	19.68	21.67	27.88
10	13.44	15.99	18.31	21.16	23.21	29.59
11	14.63	17.28	19.68	22.62	24.72	31.26
12	15.81	18.55	21.03	24.05	26.22	32.91
13	16.98	19.81	22.36	25.47	27.69	34.53
14	18.15	21.06	23.68	26.87	29.14	36.12
15	19.31	22.31	25.00	28.26	30.58	37.70
16	20.46	23.54	26.30	29.63	32.00	39.29
17	21.62	24.77	27.59	31.00	33.41	40.75
18	22.76	25.99	28.87	32.35	34.80	42.31
19	23.90	27.20	30.14	33.69	36.19	43.82
20	25.04	28.41	31.41	35.02	37.57	45.32
21	26.17	29.62	32.67	36.34	38.93	46.80
22	27.30	30.81	33.92	37.66	40.29	48.27
23	28.43	32.01	35.17	38.97	41.64	49.73
24	29.55	33.20	36.42	40.27	42.98	51.18
25	30.68	34.38	37.65	41.57	44.31	52.62
26	31.80	35.56	38.88	42.86	45.64	54.05
27	32.91	36.74	40.11	44.14	46.96	55.48
28	34.03	37.92	41.34	45.42	48.28	56.89
29	35.14	39.09	42.69	49.69	49.59	58.30
30	36.25	40.26	43.77	47.96	50.89	59.70
32	38.47	42.59	46.19	50.49	53.49	62.49
34	40.68	44.90	48.60	53.00	56.06	65.25
36	42.88	47.21	51.00	55.49	58.62	67.99
38	45.08	49.51	53.38	57.97	61.16	70.70
40	47.27	51.81	55.76	60.44	63.69	73.40
44	51.64	56.37	60.48	65.34	68.71	78.75
48	55.99	60.91	65.17	70.20	73.68	84.04
52	60.33	65.42	69.83	75.02	78.62	89.27
56	64.66	69.92	74.47	79.82	83.51	94.46
60	68.97	74.40	79.08	84.58	88.38	99.61

Calculated value of χ^2 must be EQUAL *or* EXCEED *the table (critical) values for significance at the level shown. Abridged from* **R.A. Fisher and F. Yates** *(1974)* Statistical Tables for Biological, Agricultural and Medical Research, *(6th edn) Longman Group UK Ltd.*

Table 3a *Critical values of U for a one-tailed test at 0.005; two-tailed test at 0.01* (Mann-Whitney)*

n_2 \ n_1	1	2	3	4	5	6	7	8	9	10	11	12	13	14	15	16	17	18	19	20
1	–	–	–	–	–	–	–	–	–	–	–	–	–	–	–	–	–	–	–	–
2	–	–	–	–	–	–	–	–	–	–	–	–	–	–	–	–	–	–	0	0
3	–	–	–	–	–	–	–	–	0	0	0	1	1	1	2	2	2	2	3	3
4	–	–	–	–	–	0	0	1	1	2	2	3	3	4	5	5	6	6	7	8
5	–	–	–	–	0	1	1	2	3	4	5	6	7	7	8	9	10	11	12	13
6	–	–	–	0	1	2	3	4	5	6	7	9	10	11	12	13	15	16	17	18
7	–	–	–	0	1	3	4	6	7	9	10	12	13	15	16	18	19	21	22	24
8	–	–	–	1	2	4	6	7	9	11	13	15	17	18	20	22	24	26	28	30
9	–	–	0	1	3	5	7	9	11	13	16	18	20	22	24	27	29	31	33	36
10	–	–	0	2	4	6	9	11	13	16	18	21	24	26	29	31	34	37	39	42
11	–	–	0	2	5	7	10	13	16	18	21	24	27	30	33	36	39	42	45	48
12	–	–	1	3	6	9	12	15	18	21	24	27	31	34	37	41	44	47	51	54
13	–	–	1	3	7	10	13	17	20	24	27	31	34	38	42	45	49	53	56	60
14	–	–	1	4	7	11	15	18	22	26	30	34	38	42	46	50	54	58	63	67
15	–	–	2	5	8	12	16	20	24	29	33	37	42	46	51	55	60	64	69	73
16	–	–	2	5	9	13	18	22	27	31	36	41	45	50	55	60	65	70	74	79
17	–	–	2	6	10	15	19	24	29	34	39	44	49	54	60	65	70	75	81	86
18	–	–	2	6	11	16	21	26	31	37	42	47	53	58	64	70	75	81	87	92
19	–	0	3	7	12	17	22	28	33	39	45	51	56	63	69	74	81	87	93	99
20	–	0	3	8	13	18	24	30	36	42	48	54	60	67	73	79	86	92	99	105

**Dashes in the body of the table indicate that no decision is possible at the stated level of significance.*

For any n_1 and n_2 the observed value of U is significant at a given level of significance if it is EQUAL TO *or* LESS THAN *the critical values shown.*

SOURCE: ***R. Runyon and A. Haber*** *(1976)* Fundamentals of Behavioural Statistics *(3rd edn) Reading, Mass.: McGraw Hill, Inc. with kind permission of the publisher.*

Table 3b *Critical values of U for a one-tailed test at 0.01; two-tailed test at 0.02* (Mann-Whitney)*

n_2 \ n_1	1	2	3	4	5	6	7	8	9	10	11	12	13	14	15	16	17	18	19	20
1	–	–	–	–	–	–	–	–	–	–	–	–	–	–	–	–	–	–	–	–
2	–	–	–	–	–	–	–	–	–	–	–	–	0	0	0	0	0	0	1	1
3	–	–	–	–	–	–	0	0	1	1	1	2	2	2	3	3	4	4	4	5
4	–	–	–	–	0	1	1	2	3	3	4	5	5	6	7	7	8	9	9	10
5	–	–	–	0	1	2	3	4	5	6	7	8	9	10	11	12	13	14	15	16
6	–	–	–	1	2	3	4	6	7	8	9	11	12	13	15	16	18	19	20	22
7	–	–	0	1	3	4	6	7	9	11	12	14	16	17	19	21	23	24	26	28
8	–	–	0	2	4	6	7	9	11	13	15	17	20	22	24	26	28	30	32	34
9	–	–	1	3	5	7	9	11	14	16	18	21	23	26	28	31	33	36	38	40
10	–	–	1	3	6	8	11	13	16	19	22	24	27	30	33	36	38	41	44	47
11	–	–	1	4	7	9	12	15	18	22	25	28	31	34	37	41	44	47	50	53
12	–	–	2	5	8	11	14	17	21	24	28	31	35	38	42	46	49	53	56	60
13	–	0	2	5	9	12	16	20	23	27	31	35	39	43	47	51	55	59	63	67
14	–	0	2	6	10	13	17	22	26	30	34	38	43	47	51	56	60	65	69	73
15	–	0	3	7	11	15	19	24	28	33	37	42	47	51	56	61	66	70	75	80
16	–	0	3	7	12	16	21	26	31	36	41	46	51	56	61	66	71	76	82	87
17	–	0	4	8	13	18	23	28	33	38	44	49	55	60	66	71	77	82	88	93
18	–	0	4	9	14	19	24	30	36	41	47	53	59	65	70	76	82	88	94	100
19	–	1	4	9	15	20	26	32	38	44	50	56	63	69	75	82	88	94	101	107
20	–	1	5	10	16	22	28	34	40	47	53	60	67	73	80	87	93	100	107	114

**Dashes in the body of the table indicate that no decision is possible at the stated level of significance.*

For any n_1 and n_2 the observed value of U is significant at a given level of significance if it is EQUAL TO or LESS THAN the critical values shown.

SOURCE: **R. Runyon and A. Haber** (1976) Fundamentals of Behavioural Statistics (3rd edn) Reading, Mass.: McGraw Hill, Inc. with kind permission of the publisher.

Table 3c *Critical values of U for a one-tailed test at 0.025; two-tailed test at 0.05* (Mann-Whitney)*

	n_1																			
	1	2	3	4	5	6	7	8	9	10	11	12	13	14	15	16	17	18	19	20
n_2																				
1	–	–	–	–	–	–	–	–	–	–	–	–	–	–	–	–	–	–	–	–
2	–	–	–	–	–	–	–	0	0	0	0	1	1	1	1	1	2	2	2	2
3	–	–	–	–	0	1	1	2	2	3	3	4	4	5	5	6	6	7	7	8
4	–	–	–	0	1	2	3	4	4	5	6	7	8	9	10	11	11	12	13	13
5	–	–	0	1	2	3	5	6	7	8	9	11	12	13	14	15	17	18	19	20
6	–	–	1	2	3	5	6	8	10	11	13	14	16	17	19	21	22	24	25	27
7	–	–	1	3	5	6	8	10	12	14	16	18	20	22	24	26	28	30	32	34
8	–	0	2	4	6	8	10	13	15	17	19	22	24	26	29	31	34	36	38	41
9	–	0	2	4	7	10	12	15	17	20	23	26	28	31	34	37	39	42	45	48
10	–	0	3	5	8	11	14	17	20	23	26	29	33	36	39	42	45	48	52	55
11	–	0	3	6	9	13	16	19	23	26	30	33	37	40	44	47	51	55	58	62
12	–	1	4	7	11	14	18	22	26	29	33	37	41	45	49	53	57	61	65	69
13	–	1	4	8	12	16	20	24	28	33	37	41	45	50	54	59	63	67	72	76
14	–	1	5	9	13	17	22	26	31	36	40	45	50	55	59	64	67	74	78	83
15	–	1	5	10	14	19	24	29	34	39	44	49	54	59	64	70	75	80	85	90
16	–	1	6	11	15	21	26	31	37	42	47	53	59	64	70	75	81	86	92	98
17	–	2	6	11	17	22	28	34	39	45	51	57	63	67	75	81	87	93	99	105
18	–	2	7	12	18	24	30	36	42	48	55	61	67	74	80	86	93	99	106	112
19	–	2	7	13	19	25	32	38	45	52	58	65	72	78	85	92	99	106	113	119
20	–	2	8	13	20	27	34	41	48	55	62	69	76	83	90	98	105	112	119	127

*Dashes in the body of the table indicate that no decision is possible at the stated level of significance.

For any n_1 and n_2 the observed value of U is significant at a given level of significance if it is EQUAL TO or LESS THAN the critical values shown.

SOURCE: **R. Runyon and A. Haber** (1976) Fundamentals of Behavioural Statistics (3rd edn) Reading, Mass.: McGraw Hill, Inc. with kind permission of the publisher.

Table 3d *Critical values of U for a one-tailed test at 0.05; two-tailed test at 0.10* (Mann-Whitney)*

n_2 \ n_1	1	2	3	4	5	6	7	8	9	10	11	12	13	14	15	16	17	18	19	20
1	–	–	–	–	–	–	–	–	–	–	–	–	–	–	–	–	–	–	0	0
2	–	–	–	–	0	0	0	1	1	1	1	2	2	2	3	3	3	4	4	4
3	–	–	0	0	1	2	2	3	3	4	5	5	6	7	7	8	9	9	10	11
4	–	–	0	1	2	3	4	5	6	7	8	9	10	11	12	14	15	16	17	18
5	–	0	1	2	4	5	6	8	9	11	12	13	15	16	18	19	20	22	23	25
6	–	0	2	3	5	7	8	10	12	14	16	17	19	21	23	25	26	28	30	32
7	–	0	2	4	6	8	11	13	15	17	19	21	24	26	28	30	33	35	37	39
8	–	1	3	5	8	10	13	15	18	20	23	26	28	31	33	36	39	41	44	47
9	–	1	3	6	9	12	15	18	21	24	27	30	33	36	39	42	45	48	51	54
10	–	1	4	7	11	14	17	20	24	27	31	34	37	41	44	48	51	55	58	62
11	–	1	5	8	12	16	19	23	27	31	34	38	42	46	50	54	57	61	65	69
12	–	2	5	9	13	17	21	26	30	34	38	42	47	51	55	60	64	68	72	77
13	–	2	6	10	15	19	24	28	33	37	42	47	51	56	61	65	70	75	80	84
14	–	2	7	11	16	21	26	31	36	41	46	51	56	61	66	71	77	82	87	92
15	–	3	7	12	18	23	28	33	39	44	50	55	61	66	72	77	83	88	94	100
16	–	3	8	14	19	25	30	36	42	48	54	60	65	71	77	83	89	95	101	107
17	–	3	9	15	20	26	33	39	45	51	57	64	70	77	83	89	96	102	109	115
18	–	4	9	16	22	28	35	41	48	55	61	68	75	82	88	95	102	109	116	123
19	0	4	10	17	23	30	37	44	51	58	65	72	80	87	94	101	109	116	123	130
20	0	4	11	18	25	32	39	47	54	62	69	77	84	92	100	107	115	123	130	138

**Dashes in the body of the table indicate that no decision is possible at the stated level of significance.*

For any n_1 and n_2 the observed value of U is significant at a given level of significance if it is EQUAL TO or LESS THAN the critical values shown.

SOURCE: ***R. Runyon and A. Haber*** (1976) Fundamentals of Behavioural Statistics (3rd edn) Reading, Mass.: McGraw Hill, Inc. with kind permission of the publisher.

Table 4 *Critical values of T in the Wilcoxon signed ranks test*

	Levels of significance for a one-tailed test			
	0.05	0.025	0.01	0.001
	Levels of significance for a two-tailed test			
	0.1	0.05	0.02	0.002
Sample size				
$N = 5$	$T \leq 0$			
6	2	0		
7	3	2	0	
8	5	3	1	
9	8	5	3	
10	11	8	5	0
11	13	10	7	1
12	17	13	9	2
13	21	17	12	4
14	25	21	15	6
15	30	25	19	8
16	35	29	23	11
17	41	34	27	14
18	47	40	32	18
19	53	46	37	21
20	60	52	43	26
21	67	58	49	30
22	75	65	55	35
23	83	73	62	40
24	91	81	69	45
25	100	89	76	51
26	110	98	84	58
27	119	107	92	64
28	130	116	101	71
30	151	137	120	86
31	163	147	130	94
32	175	159	140	103
33	187	170	151	112

Calculated t must be EQUAL TO *or* LESS THAN *the table (critical) value for significance at the level shown.*
Source: Adapted from ***R. Meddis****, (1975)* Statistical Handbook for Non-Statisticians, *London: McGraw-Hill with the kind permission of the author and publishers.*

Table 5 *Critical values of T in the Wilcoxon sign ranks test*

	Level of significance for a one-tailed test			
	0.05	0.025	0.01	0.005
	Level of significance for a two-tailed test			
	0.10	0.05	0.02	0.01
Degrees of freedom				
1	6.314	12.706	31.821	63.657
2	2.920	4.303	6.965	9.925
3	2.353	3.182	4.541	5.841
4	2.132	2.776	3.747	4.604
5	2.015	2.571	3.365	4.032
6	1.943	2.447	3.143	3.707
7	1.895	2.365	2.998	3.499
8	1.860	2.306	2.896	3.355
9	1.833	2.262	2.821	3.250
10	1.812	2.228	2.764	3.169
11	1.796	2.201	2.718	3.106
12	1.782	2.179	2.681	3.055
13	1.771	2.160	2.650	3.012
14	1.761	2.145	2.624	2.977
15	1.753	2.131	2.602	2.947
16	1.746	2.120	2.583	2.921
17	1.740	2.110	2.567	2.898
18	1.734	2.101	2.552	2.878
19	1.729	2.093	2.539	2.861
20	1.725	2.086	2.528	2.845
21	1.721	2.080	2.518	2.831
22	1.717	2.074	2.508	2.819
23	1.714	2.069	2.500	2.807
24	1.711	2.064	2.492	2.797
25	1.708	2.060	2.485	2.787
26	1.706	2.056	2.479	2.779
27	1.703	2.052	2.473	2.771
28	1.701	2.048	2.467	2.763
29	1.699	2.045	2.462	2.756
30	1.697	2.042	2.457	2.750
40	1.684	2.021	2.423	2.704
60	1.671	2.000	2.390	2.660
120	1.658	1.980	2.358	2.617
∞	1.645	1.960	2.326	2.576

Calculated T must be EQUAL *or* EXCEED *the table (critical) value for significance at the level shown.*

SOURCE: *Abridged from* **R.A. Fisher and F. Yates** *(1974)* Statistical Tables for Biological, Agricultural and Medical Research, *(6th edn) Longman Group UK Ltd.*

Table 6 *Critical values of Spearman's r_s*

	Level of significance for a one-tailed test			
	0.05	0.025	0.01	0.005
	Level of significance for a two-tailed test			
	0.10	0.05	0.02	0.01
$N = 4$	1.000			
5	0.900	1.000	1.000	
6	0.829	0.886	0.943	1.000
7	0.714	0.786	0.893	0.929
8	0.643	0.738	0.833	0.881
9	0.600	0.700	0.783	0.833
10	0.564	0.648	0.745	0.794
11	0.536	0.618	0.709	0.755
12	0.503	0.587	0.671	0.727
13	0.484	0.560	0.648	0.703
14	0.464	0.538	0.622	0.675
15	0.443	0.521	0.604	0.654
16	0.429	0.503	0.582	0.635
17	0.414	0.485	0.566	0.615
18	0.401	0.472	0.550	0.600
19	0.391	0.460	0.535	0.584
20	0.380	0.447	0.520	0.570
21	0.370	0.435	0.508	0.556
22	0.361	0.425	0.496	0.544
23	0.353	0.415	0.486	0.532
24	0.344	0.406	0.476	0.521
25	0.337	0.398	0.466	0.511
26	0.331	0.390	0.457	0.501
27	0.324	0.382	0.448	0.491
28	0.317	0.375	0.440	0.483
29	0.312	0.368	0.433	0.475
30	0.306	0.362	0.425	0.467

For $n > 30$, the significance of r_s can be tested by using the formula:

$$t = r_s\sqrt{\frac{n-2}{1-r_s^2}} \qquad df = n - 2$$

and checking the value of t in Table 8.

Calculated r_s must EQUAL, *or* EXCEED *the table (critical) value for significance at the level shown.*
*SOURCE: **J.H. Zhar**, Significance testing of the Spearman Rank Correlation Coefficient,* Journal of the American Statistical Association, *67, 578–80. With the kind permission of the publishers.*

Table 7 *Critical values of Pearson's r*

	Level of significance for a one-tailed test		
	0.05	0.025	0.005
	Level of significance for a two-tailed test		
	0.10	0.05	0.01
df (N − 2)			
2	0.9000	0.9500	0.9900
3	0.805	0.878	0.9587
4	0.729	0.811	0.9172
5	0.669	0.754	0.875
6	0.621	0.707	[illegible]
7	0.582	0.666	0.798
8	0.549	0.632	0.765
9	0.521	0.602	0.735
10	0.497	0.576	0.708
11	0.476	0.553	0.684
12	0.475	0.532	0.661
13	0.441	0.514	0.641
14	0.426	0.497	0.623
15	0.412	0.482	0.606
16	0.400	0.468	0.590
17	0.389	0.456	0.575
18	0.378	0.444	0.561
19	0.369	0.433	0.549
20	0.360	0.423	0.537
25	0.323	0.381	0.487
30	0.296	0.349	0.449
35	0.275	0.325	0.418
40	0.257	0.304	0.393
45	0.243	0.288	0.372
50	0.231	0.273	0.354
60	0.211	0.250	0.325
70	0.195	0.232	0.302
80	0.183	0.217	0.283
90	0.173	0.205	0.267
100	0.164	0.195	0.254

Calculated r must EQUAL *or* EXCEED *the table (critical) value for significance at the level shown.*
*Source: **F.C. Powell** (1976)* Cambridge Mathematical and Statistical Tables, *Cambridge University Press.*
With kind permission of the author and publishers.

References

Child development (Chapters 1, 2 and 3)

Ainsworth, M. and Bell, S. (1970) Attachment, exploration and separation: Illustrated by the behavior of one-year-olds in a strange situation. *Child Development*, 41(1), 49–67.

Ainsworth, M.D.S., Blehar, M.C., Waters, E. and Wall, S. (1978) *Patterns of Attachment: A Psychological Study of the Strange Situation*. Hillsdale, NJ: Erlbaum.

Atkinson, R. and Shiffrin, R. (1968) Human memory: A proposed system and its control processes. In K.W. Spence and J.T. Spence (eds), *The Psychology of Learning ad Motivation*, Vol. 2. London: Academic Press.

Baddeley, A. (1966) The influence of acoustic and semantic similarity on long-term memory for word sequences. *The Quarterly Journal of Experimental Psychology*, 18(4), 302–9.

Baillargeon, R. (1987) Object permanence in 3.5 and 4.5 month-old infants. *Developmental Psychology*, 23, 655–64.

Baillargeon, R., Needham, A. and DeVos, J. (1985) Object permanence in 5-month-old infants. *Cognition*, 20, 191–208.

Bandura, A., Ross, S.A. and Ross, D. (1963) Imitation of film-mediated aggressive models. *Journal of Abnormal Psychology*, 66(1), 3–11.

Bar-On, D., Eland, J., Kleber, R. *et al.* (1998) Multigenerational perspectives on coping with the Holocaust experience: An attachment perspective for understanding the developmental sequelae of trauma across generations. *International Journal of Behavioral Development*, 22(2), 315–38.

Belsky, J., Steinberg, L. and Draper, P. (1991) Childhood experience, interpersonal development, and reproductive strategy: An evolutionary theory of socialization. *Child Development*, 62, 647–70.

Bigelow, B.J. and La Gaipa, J. (1980) The development of friendship values and choices. In H.C. Foot, A.J. Chapman and J.R. Smith (eds), *Friendship and Social Relations in Children*. New York: J. Wiley.

Boehnke, K., Silbereisen, R.K., Eisenberg, N., Reykowski, J. and Palmonari, A. (1989) Developmental pattern of pro-social motivation: A cross-national study. *Journal of Cross-Cultural Psychology*, 20(3), 219–43.

Bonn, M. and Kruger, P. (1996) Popularity and rejection in children's peer groups: A South African perspective. *Early Child Development and Care*, 125, 1–14.

Bower, T.G. and Wishart, J.G. (1972) The effects of motor skill on object permanence. *Cognition*, 1, 165–72.

Bowlby, J. (1946) Psychology in the child's education. *British Medical Journal*, 2 (4465), 175.

Bowlby, J. (1953) *Child Care and the Growth of Love*. Harmondsworth: Penguin.

Bowlby, J. (1969) Attachment and Loss, Vol. 1: *Attachment*. London: Hogarth Press.

Bowlby, J. (1971) *Attachment*, Vol. 1. Pelican: London.

Brainerd, C. (1983) Young children's mental arithmetic errors: A working-memory analysis. *Child Development*, 54(4), 813–30.

Bruner, J. (1966) *Toward a Theory of Instruction*. Cambridge, MA; England: Belknap Press.

Butterworth, G. (1974) The development of the object concept in human infants. Unpublished DPhil thesis, University Press.

Case, D.A., Fantino, E. and Wixted, J. (1985) Human observing – maintained by the negative information stimuli only if correlated with improvement in response efficiency. *Journal of the Experimental Analysis of Behavior*, 43(3), 289–300.

Chandler, M.J., Greenspan, S. and Barenboim, C. (1973) Judgements of intentionality in response to videotaped and verbally presented moral dilemmas: The medium is the message. *Child Development*, 44(2), 315–20.

Chodorow, N.J. (1978) *The Reproduction of Mothering: Psychoanalysis and the Sociology of Gender*. Berkeley, CA: University of California Press.

Coie, J.D. and Dodge, K.A. (1983) Continuities and changes in children's social status: A 5 year longitudinal study. *Quarterly Journal of Developmental Psychology*, 29(3), 261–82.

Coie, J., Dodge, K. and Coppotelli, H. (1982) Dimensions and types of social status: a cross-age perspective: Correction. *Developmental Psychology*, 19(2), 224.

Coie, J., Dodge, K. and Kupersmidt, J. (1990) Peer group behavior and social status. In S.R. Asher and J.D. Coie (eds), *Peer Rejection in Childhood*, pp17–59. New York: Cambridge University Press.

Coie, J.D., Lochamn, J.E., Terry, R. *et al.* (1992) Predicting early adolescent disorder from childhood aggression and peer rejection. *Journal of Consulting and Clinical Psychology*, 60(5), 783–92.

Coie, J., Terry, R., Leno, K. *et al.* (1995) Childhood peer rejection and aggression as predictors of stable patterns of adolescent disorder. *Development and Psychopathology*, 7(4), 697–713.

Colby, A. and Kohlberg, L. (1987) The Measurement of Moral Judgment, Vol. 1: *Theoretical Foundations and Research Validation*; Vol. 2: *Standard Issue Scoring Manual*. New York: Cambridge University Press.

Colby, A., Kohlberg, L., Gibbs, J. and Lieberman, M. (1983) A longitudinal study of moral judgement. *Monographs of the Society for Research in Child Development*, 48, 157–66.

Curtiss, S. (1977) *Genie: A Psycholinguistic Study of a Modern-day 'Wild Child'*. New York: Academic Press.

Damon, W. (1975) Early conceptions of positive justice as related to the development of logical operations. *Child Development*, 46(2), 301–12.

Damon, W. (1977) *The Social World of the Child*. San Francisco, CA: Jossey-Bass.

Damon, W. (1980) Patterns of change in children's social reasoning: A 2 year longitudinal study. *Child Development*, 51(4), 1010–17.

DeCasper, A.J. and Spence, M.J. (1986) Prenatal maternal speech influences newborns' perception of speech sounds. *Infant Behavior and Development*, 9(2), 133–50.

de Guzman, M., Carlo, G., Ontai, L. *et al*. (2004) Gender and age differences in Brazilian children's friendship nominations and peer sociometric ratings. *Sex Roles*, 51(3), 217–25.

De Wolff, M. and van IJzendoorn, M.H. (1997) Sensitivity and attachment: A meta-analysis on parental antecedents of infant attachment. *Child Development*, 68(4), 571–91.

Dien, D.S.F. (1982) A Chinese perspective on Kohlberg's theory of moral development. *Developmental Review*, 2(4), 331–41.

Dodge, K.A. (1983) Behavioural antecedents of peer social status. *Child Development*, 54, 1386–99.

Dodge, K.A., Coie, J.D., Pettit, G.S. *et al*. (1990) Peer status and aggression in boys' groups: Developmental and contextual analyses. *Child Development*, 61(5), 1289–309.

Dodge, K.A., Lansford, J.E., Salzer Burks, V. *et al*. (2003) Peer rejection and social information-processing factors in the development of aggressive behaviour problems in children. *Child Development*, 74(2), 374–93.

Donaldson, M. (1978) *Children's Minds*. London: Fontana.

Eisenberg, N. and Hand, M. (1979) The relationship of pre-schoolers' reasoning about pro-social moral conflicts to pro-social behaviour. *Child Development*, 50, 356–63.

Eisenberg, N. and Roth, K. (1980) Development of young children's pro-social moral judgement: A longitudinal follow-up. *Developmental Psychology*, 16(4), 375–6.

Eisenberg, N., Lennon, R. and Roth, K. (1983) Pro-social development: A longitudinal study. *Developmental Psychology*, 19(6), 846–55.

Eisenberg, N., Fabes, R.A., Nyman, M. *et al*. (1994) The relations of emotionality and regulation to children's anger-related reactions. *Child Development*, 65(1), 109–28.

Eisenberg, N., Carlo, G., Murphy, B. *et al*. (1995) Pro-social development in late adolescence: A longitudinal study. *Child Development*, 66(4), 1179–97.

Eisenberg, N., Cumberland, A., Spinrad, T.L. *et al*. (2001) The relations of regulation and emotionality to children's externalizing and internalizing problem behavior. *Child Development*, 72(4), 1112–34.

Elicker, J., Englund, M. and Sroufe, L. (1992) Predicting peer competence and peer relationships in childhood from early parent-child relationships. *Family-peer relationships: Modes of Linkage*. Hillsdale, NJ: Lawrence Erlbaum Associates, Inc.

Enright, R.D., Franklin, C.C. and Manheim, L.A. (1980) Children's distributive justice reasoning: A standardized and objective scale. *Developmental Psychology*, 16(3), 193–202.

Enright, R.D., Lapsley, D.K., Franklin, C.C., Steuck, K. (1984) Longitudinal and cross-cultural validation of the belief-discrepancy reasoning construct. Developmental Psychology, 20 (1) 143–149.

Feldman, N.S, Chereskin Klosson, E., Parsons, J.E. *et al*. (1976) Order of information presentation and children's moral judgments. *Child Development*, 47(2), 556–9.

Flavell, J. (1963) *The Developmental Psychology of Jean Piaget*. Princeton, NJ: D. Van Nostrand.

Fonagy, P., Steele, M., Steele, H. *et al*. (1991) The capacity for understanding mental states: The reflective self in parent and child and its significance for security of attachment. *Infant Mental Health Journal*, 12(3), 201–18.

Freud, Sigmund (1923), Das Ich und das Es, *Internationaler Psycho-analytischer Verlag*. Leipzig, Vienna and Zurich. English translation, *The Ego and the Id*, J. Riviere (trans.) Hogarth Press and Institute of Psycho-analysis, London, 1927. Revised (1961) for *The Standard Edition of the Complete Psychological Works of Sigmund Freud*, J. Strachey (ed.). New York: W.W. Norton and Company.

Gibson, R.M. (1966) Intellectual assessment of children. *University of Michigan Medical Centre*, 32(5), 235–7.

Gilligan, C. (1977) In a different voice: Women's conception of self and morality. *Harvard Educational Review*, 47, 481–517.

Gilligan, C. (1982) *In a Different Voice: Psychological Theory and Women's Development*. Cambridge, MA: Harvard University Press.

Gilligan, C. (1990) Joining the resistance: Psychology, politics, girls and women. *Michigan Quarterly Review*, 29(4), 501–36.

Gilligan, C. and Attanucci, J. (1988) Two moral orientations: Gender differences and similarities. *Quarterly Journal of Developmental Psychology*, 34(3), 223–37.

Goodnow, J.J. (1969) Effects of active handling illustrated by uses for objects. *Child Development*, 40(1), 201–12.

Gratch, G., Appel, K.J., Evans, W.F. *et al*. (1974) Piaget's stage IV object concept error: Evidence of forgetting or object conception. *Child Development*, 45, 71–7.

Grossman, K.E., Grossman, K., Huber, F. and Wartner, U. (1981) German children's behaviour towards their mothers at 12 months and their fathers at 18 months in Ainsworth's 'strange situation'. *International Journal of Behavioural Development*, 4, 157–81.

Halle, T. (1999, July) Implicit theories of social interactions: Children's reasoning about the relative importance of gender and friendship in social partner choices. *Merrill-Palmer Quarterly*, 45(3), 445–67.

Harlow, H.F. (1958) The nature of love. *American Psychologist*, 13(12), 673–85.

Haselager, G., Hartup, W., van Lieshout, C. and Riksen-Walraven, J. (1998) Similarities between friends and nonfriends in middle childhood. *Child Development*, 69(4), 1198–208.

Hodges, J. and Tizard, B. (1989) Social and family relationships of ex-institutional adolescents. *Journal of*

Child Psychology and Psychiatry and Allied Disciplines, 30(1), 77–98.

Hoffman, M.L. (1975) Altruistic behaviour and the parent-child relationship. *Journal of Personality and Social Psychology*, 31, 937–43.

Hood, B. and Williats, P. (1986) Reaching in the dark to an object's remembered position: Evidence for object permanence in 5-month-old infants. *British Journal of Developmental Psychology*, 4, 57–65.

Howes, C. (1996) The earliest friendships. In W.M. Bukowski, A.F. Newcomb and W.W. Hartup (eds), *The Company They Keep: Friendship in Childhood and Adolescence*, pp66–86. New York: Cambridge University Press.

Hughes, M. and Donaldson, M. (1979) Use of hiding games for studying the coordination of viewpoints. *Educational Review*, 31(11), 133–40.

Hymel, S., Rubin, K.H., Rowden, L. *et al*. (1990) Children's peer relationships: Longitudinal prediction of internalizing and externalizing problems from middle to late childhood. *Child Development*, 61(6), 2004–21.

Isabella, R.A., Belsky, J. and von Eye, A. (1989) Origins of infant-mother attachment: An examination of interactional synchrony during the infant's first year. *Developmental Psychology*, 25, 12–21.

Jaffee, S. and Shibley Hyde, J. (2000) Gender differences in moral orientation: A meta-analysis. *Psychological Bulletin*, 126(5), 703–26.

Kagan, C. (1984) Social problem solving and social skills training. *British Journal of Clinical Psychology*, 23, 161–73.

Kail, R. and Park, Y.S. (1990) Impact of practice on speed of mental rotation. *Journal of Experimental Psychology*, 49(2), 227–44.

Karmiloff-Smith, A. (1992), Beyond Modularity: A Developmental Perspective on Cognitive Science. Cambridge, MA: MIT Press.

Kohlberg, L. (1975) The cognitive-development approach to moral education. *Phi Delta Kappa*, 56, 670–7.

Kohlberg, L. (1981) Moral objection. *Psychology Today*, 15(11), 12.

Kohlberg, L., Levine, C. and Hewer, A. (1983) *Moral Stages: A Current Formulation and Response to Critics*. Basel: Karger.

Koluchova, J. (1976) Further development of twins after severe and prolonged deprivation: Second report. *Journal of Child Psychology and Psychiatry and Allied Disciplines*, 17(3), 181–8.

Kupersmidt, J.B. and Coie, J.D. (1990) Aggression and school adjustment: Preadolescent peer status, aggression and school adjustment as predictors of externalizing problems in adolescence. *Child Development*, 61, 1350–62.

Kupersmidt, J., Coie, J.D. and Dodge, K. (1990) The role of peer relationships in the development of disorder. In S.R. Asher and J.D. Coie (eds), *Peer Rejection in Childhood*, pp274–305. Cambridge: Cambridge University Press.

Laupa, M. and Turiel, E. (1986) Children's conceptions of adult and peer authority. *Child Development*, 57(2), 405–12.

Laursen, B., Bukowski, W.M., Aunola, K. and Nurmi, J.E. (2007) Friendship moderates prospective associations between social isolation and adjustment problems in young children. *Child Development*, 78(4), 1395–404.

Lease, A.M., Kennedy, C.A. and Axelrod, J.L. (2002) Children's social constructions of popularity. *Social Development*, 11(1), 87–109.

Lewis, M., Feiring, C. and Rosenthal, S. (2000) Attachment over time. *Child Development*, 71(3), 707–20.

Lollis, S., Ross, H. and Leroux, L. (1996) An observational study of parents' socialization of moral orientation during sibling conflicts. *Quarterly Journal of Developmental Psychology*, 42(4), 475–94.

Main, M. and Cassidy, J. (1988) Categories of response to reunion with parent at age six. Predictable from infant attachment classifications and stable over a one month period. *Developmental Psychology*, 24, 415–26.

Main, M., Kaplan, N. and Cassidy, J. (1985) Security in infancy, childhood and adulthood: A move to the level of representation. In I. Bretherton and E. Waters (eds), Growing Points of Attachment Theory and Research *Monographs of the Society for Research in Child Development*, 50(1–2).

Matas, L., Arend, R. and Sroufe, L. (1978) Continuity of adaptation in the second year: The relationship between quality of attachment and later competence. *Child Development*, 49(3), 547–56.

McDougall, P., Hymel, S., Vaillancourt, T. and Mercer, L. (2001) The consequences of childhood peer rejection. In M.R. Leary (ed.), *Interpersonal Rejection*, pp213–47. Oxford: Oxford University Press.

McGarrigle, J. and Donaldson, M. (1974, 1974–1975) Conservation accidents. *Cognition: International Journal of Cognitive Psychology*, 3(4), 341–50.

McGillicuddy-De Lisa, A.V., Watkins, C. and Vinchur, A.J. (1994) The effect of relationship on children's distributive justice reasoning. *Child Development*, 65(6), 1694–700.

McGillicuddy-De Lisa, A.V., Daly, M. and Neal, A. (2006) Children's distributive justice judgments: Aversive racism in Euro-American children? *Child Development*, 77(4), 1063–80.

Meins, E., Fernyhough, C., Fradley, E. *et al*. (2001) Rethinking maternal sensitivity: Mothers' comments on infants' mental processes predict security of attachment at 12 months. *Journal of Child Psychology and Psychiatry and Allied Disciplines*, 42(5), 637–48.

Meltzoff, A.N. and Borton, R.W. (1979) Intermodal matching by human neonates. *Nature*, 282, 403–4.

Meltzoff, A.N. and Moore, M.K. (1977) Imitation of facial and manual gestures by human neonates. *Science*, 198, 75–8.

Miyake, K., Chen, S.J. and Campos, J.J. (1985) Infant temperament, mother's mode of interaction and attachment in Japan: An interim report. In I. Bretherton and E. Waters (eds), Growing points of attachment theory and research. *Monographs of the Society for Research in Child Development*, 50, 276–97.

O'Connor, T.G. and Croft, C.M. (2001) A twin study of attachment in preschool children. *Child Development*, 72, 1501–11.

O'Connor, T.G., Rutter, M., Beckett, C. *et al.* and the Romanian Adoptees Study Team (2000) The effects of global severe privation on cognitive competence: Extension and longitudinal follow-up. *Child Development*, 71, 376–90.

Okin, S. (1996) The gendered family and the development of a sense of justice. In E.S. Read, E. Turiel and T. Brown (eds), *Values and Knowledge*, pp61–74. Hillsdale, NJ; England: Lawrence Erlbaum Associates, Inc.

Parker, J.G. and Asher, S.R. (1987) Peer relations and later personal adjustment: Are low-accepted children at risk? *Psychological Bulletin*, 102(3), 357–89.

Patterson, C.J., Kupersmidt, J.B. and Griesler, P.C. (1990) Children's perceptions of self and of relationships with others as a function of sociometric status. *Child Development*, 61(5), 1335–49.

Piaget, J. (1932) *The Moral Judgment of the Child*. New York: Free Press.

Piaget, J. (1951) *Psychology of Intelligence*. London: Routledge and Kegan Paul.

Piaget, J. (1952) *The Origins of Intelligence in Children*. New York: W.W. Norton and Co.

Piaget, J. and Inhelder, B. (1956) *The Child's Conception of Space*. London: Routledge and Kegan Paul.

Quinton, D. and Rutter, M. (1976) Early hospital admissions and later disturbances of behaviour: Attempted replication of Douglas findings. *Developmental Medicine and Child Neurology*, 18(4), 447–59.

Reisman, J.M. and Shorr, S.I. (1978) Friendship claims and expectations among children and adults. *Child Development*, 49(3), 913–16.

Robertson, J. and Bowlby, J. (1952) Responses of young children to separation from their mothers. *Courier of the International Children's Centre*, Paris, II, 131–40.

Robertson, J. and Robertson, J. (1971) Young children in brief separation: A fresh look. *The Psychoanalytic Study of the Child*, 26, 264–315.

Rogoff, B. (1990) *Apprenticeship in Thinking*. New York: Oxford University Press.

Rogoff, B., Baker-Sennett, J., Lacasa, P. and Goldsmith, D. (1995) Development through participation in sociocultural activity. *New Directions for Child Development*, 67. Jossey-Bass Inc., Publishers.

Rose, A.J. and Rudolph, K.D. (2006) A review of sex differences in peer relationship processes: Potential trade-offs for the emotional and behavioural development of girls and boys. *Psychological Bulletin*, 132(1), 98–131.

Rose, S.A. and Blank, M. (1974) The potency of context in children's cognition: An illustration through conservation. *Child Development*, 45, 499–502.

Rothbaum, F., Pott, M., Azuma, H. *et al.* (2000) The development of close relationships in Japan and the United States: Paths of symbiotic harmony and generative tension. *Child Development*, 71, 1121–42.

Rutter, M. (1972) Maternal deprivation reconsidered. *Journal of Psychosomatic Research*, 16(4), 241–50.

Rutter, M. (1981) *Maternal Deprivation Reassessed*. Harmondsworth: Penguin.

Rutter, M. (1987) Temperament, personality and personality disorder. *British Journal of Psychiatry*, 150, 443–58.

Rutter, M. and the English and Romanian Adoptees Study Team (1998) Developmental catch-up and deficit, following adoption after severe global early privation. *Journal of Child Psychology and Psychiatry*, 39, 465–76.

Schaffer, H.R. (1971) *The Growth of Sociability*. Harmondsworth: Penguin.

Schaffer, H.R. (1996) *Social Development*. Oxford: Blackwell.

Schaffer, H.R. (2003) Social interaction and the beginnings of communication. In A. Slater and G. Bremner (eds), *An Introduction to Developmental Psychology*. Oxford: Blackwell.

Schaffer, H. (2004) *Introducing Child Psychology*. Malden, MA: Blackwell Publishing.

Schaffer, H.R. and Emerson, P.E. (1964) The development of social attachments in infancy. *Monographs of the Society for Research in Child Development*, 28(3), serial no 4.

Selman, R. and Jaquette, D. (1977) Stability and oscillation in interpersonal awareness: A clinical-developmental analysis. *Nebraska Symposium on Motivation*, 25, 261–304.

Siegler, R.S. (1976) Three aspects of cognitive development. *Cognitive Psychology*, 8(4), 481–520.

Siegler, R.S. (1996) *Emerging Minds: The Process of Change in Children's Thinking*. New York: Oxford University Press.

Siegler, R. and Jenkins, E. (1989) *How Children Discover New Strategies*. Hillsdale, NJ, England: Lawrence Erlbaum Associates, Inc.

Siegler, R., DeLoache, J. and Eisenberg, N. (2003) *How Children Develop*. New York: Worth Publishers.

Smetana, J.G. (1981) Preschool children's conceptions of moral and social rules. *Child Development*, 52(4), 1333–6.

Smith, P. (2003) *Play and Peer Relations. An Introduction to Developmental Psychology*, pp311–13. Malden, MA: Blackwell Publishing.

Snarey, J.R. (1985) Cross-cultural universality of socio-moral development: A critical review of Kohlbergian review. *Psychological Bulletin*, 97, 202–32.

Sroufe, L., Fox, N. and Pancake, V. (1983) Attachment and dependency in developmental perspective. *Child Development*, 54(6), 1615–27.

Suomi, S.J. and Harlow, H.F. (1972) Social rehabilitation of isolate-reared monkeys. *Developmental Psychology*, 6(3), 487–96.

Takahashi, K. (1990) Are the key assumptions of the 'Strange Situation' procedure universal? A view from Japanese research. *Human Development*, 33, 23–30.

Thompson, R. (2000) The legacy of early attachments. *Child Development*, 71(1), 145–52.

Turiel, E. (1978) Social regulations and domains of social concepts. In W. Damon (ed.), New Directions for Child Development. Vol. 1. *Social Cognition*. San Francisco, CA: Jossey-Bass.

Turiel, E. (1983) *The Development of Social Knowledge: Morality and Convention*. Cambridge: Cambridge University Press.

Turiel, E. (1998) The development of morality. In W. Damon (series ed.) and N. Eisenberg (vol. ed.), Handbook of Child Psychology. Vol. 3. *Social, Emotional and Personality Development*, pp863–932. New York: Wiley.

van IJzendoorn, M.H. (1995) Adult attachment representations, parental responsiveness and infant attachment: A meta-analysis on the predictive validity of the Adult Attachment Interview. *Psychological Bulletin*, 117, 387–403.

van IJzendoorn, M.H., Schuengel, C. and Bakermans-Kranenburg, M.J. (1999) Disorganised attachment in early childhood: Meta-analysis of precursors, concomitants and sequelae. *Development and Psychopathology*, 11, 225–49.

Waldrop, M.F. and Halverson, C.F. (1975) Intensive and extensive peer behaviour: Longitudinal and cross-sectional analyses. *Child Development*, 46(1), 19–26.

Walker, L.J., de Vries, B. and Trevethan, S.D. (1987) Moral stages and moral orientations in real life and hypothetical dilemmas. *Child Development*, 58, 842–58.

Walker, W.J. (1984) Sex differences in moral reasoning: A critical review. *Child Development*, 55, 677–91.

Walker, W.J. (1989) A longitudinal study of moral reasoning. *Child Development*, 60, 157–66.

Waters, E., Merrick, S., Treboux, D. *et al.* (2000) Attachment security in infancy and early adulthood: A twenty-year longitudinal study. *Child Development*, 71(3), 684–9.

Wilcox, T., Nadel, L. and Rosser, R. (1996) Location memory in healthy preterm and full-term infants. *Infant Behaviour and Development*, 19, 309–24.

Wood, D. and Middleton, D. (1975) A study of assisted problem solving. *British Journal of Developmental Psychology*, 66, 181–91.

Wood, D.J., Bruner, J.S. and Ross, G. (1976) The role of tutoring in problem-solving. *Journal of Child Psychology and Psychiatry*, 17, 89–100.

Xie, H.L., Li, Y., Boucher, S.M. *et al.* (2006) What makes a girl (or boy) popular (or unpopular)? African American children's perceptions and developmental differences. *Developmental Psychology*, 42(4), 599–612.

Chapter 4 Cognition and law

Bohannon, J.N. (1988) Flashbulb memories for the space shuttle disaster: A tale of two theories. *Cognition*, 29, 179–96.

Bradshaw, J.L. and Wallace, G. (1971) Models for the processing and identification of faces. *Perception and Psychophysics*, 9, 443–8.

Brandon, S., Boakes, J., Glaser, D. and Green, R. (1998) Recovered memories of childhood sexual abuse: Implications for clinical practice. *British Journal of Psychiatry*, 172, 293–307.

Brigham, J., van Verst, M. and Bothwell, R.K. (1986) Accuracy of children's eyewitness identifications in a field setting. *Basic and Applied Social Psychology*, 7(4), 295–306.

Brown, R. and Kulik, J. (1977) Flashbulb memories. *Cognition*, 5, 73–99.

Bruce, V. and Valentine, T. (1986) Semantic priming of familiar faces. *Quarterly Journal of Experimental Psychology*, 38A, 125–50.

Bruce, V. and Young, A. (1986) Understanding face recognition. *British Journal of Psychology*, 77, 305–27.

Ceci, S.J., Huffman, M.L., Smith, E. and Loftus, E.F. (1994) Repeatedly thinking about a non-event. *Consciousness and Cognition*, 2.

Cohen, G. (1989) *Memory in the Real World*. Hove: Lawrence Erlbaum Associates.

Cohen, G. (1993) Everyday memory and memory systems: The experimental approach. In G. Cohen, G. Kiss and M. Levoi (eds), *Memory: Current Issues*, 2nd edn. Buckingham: Open University Press.

Conway, M.A., Anderson, S.J., Larsen, S.F. *et al.* (1994) The function of flashbulb memories. *Memory and Cognition*, 22, 326–43.

Davies, G.M., van der Willik, P. and Morrison, L.J. (2000) Facial composite production: A comparison of mechanical and computer-driven systems. *Journal of Applied Psychology*, 85(1), 119–24.

Deese, J. (1959) On the prediction of occurrence of particular verbal intrusions in immediate recall. *Journal of Experimental Psychology*, 58, 17–22.

Devlin, P. (1976) *Report of the Secretary of State for the Home Department Committee on Evidence of Identification in Criminal Cases*. HMSO: London.

Dunning, D. and Perretta, C. (2002) Automaticity and eyewitness accuracy: A 10- to 12-second rule for distinguishing accurate from inaccurate positive identifications. *Journal of Applied Psychology*, 87(5), 951–62.

Dunning, D. and Stem, L.B. (1994) Cited in A. Heaton-Armstrong, E. Shepherd and D. Wolchover (1999) *Analysing Witness Testimony*. Oxford: Oxford University Press.

Eakin, D.K., Schreiber, T.A. and Sergent-Marshall, S. (2003) Misinformation effects in eyewitness memory: The presence and absence of memory impairment as a function of warning and misinformation accessibility. *Journal of Experimental Psychology: Learning, Memory and Cognition*, 29, 813–25.

Ellis, H.D., Shepherd, J.W. and Davies, G.M. (1979) Identification of familiar and unfamiliar faces from internal and external features: Some implications for theories of face recognition. *Perception*, 8, 431–9.

Eysenck, M.W. (1982) *Attention and Arousal: Cognition and Performance*. Berlin: Springer.

Finkenauer, C., Luminet, O., Gisle, L. *et al.* (1998) Flashbulb memories and the underlying mechanisms of their formation: Toward an emotional-integrative model. *Memory and Cognition*, 26, 516–31.

Fisher, R.P., Geiselman, R.E., Raymond, D.S. *et al.* (1987) Enhancing enhanced eyewitness memory: Refining the cognitive interview. *Journal of Police Science and Administration*, 15, 291–7.

Flude, B.M., Ellis, A.W. and Kay, J. (1989) Face processing and name retrieval in an anomic aphasia: Names are stored separately from semantic information about people. *Brain and Cognition*, 11, 60–72.

Frankland, A. and Cohen, L. (1999) Working with recovered memories. *The Psychologist*, 12(2), 82–3.

Frowd, C.D., Carson, D., Ness, H. *et al.* (2005) A forensically valid comparison of facial composite systems. *Psychology, Crime and Law*, 11, 33–52.

Geiselman, R.E. and Fisher, R.P. (1997) Ten years of cognitive interviewing. In D.G. Payne and F.G. Conrad (eds), *Intersections in Basic and Applied Memory Research*. Mahwah, NJ: Lawrence Erlbaum Associates.

Geiselman, R.E., Fisher, R.P., MacKinnon, D.P. and Hooland, H.L. (1985) Eyewitness memory enhancement in the police interview: Cognitive retrieval mnemonics versus hypnosis. *Journal of Applied Psychology*, 70, 401–10.

Goodman, G.S. and Schaaf, J.M. (1997) Over a decade of research on children's eyewitness testimony: What have we learned? Where do we go from here? *Applied Cognitive Psychology*, 11, S5–S20.

Holliday, R.E. (2003) The effect of a prior cognitive interview on children's acceptance of misinformation. *Applied Cognitive Psychology*, 17, 443–57.

Holmes, D.S. (1990) The evidence for repression: An examination of sixty years of research. In J.L. Singer (ed.), *Repression and Dissociation: Implications for Personality Theory, Psychopathology and Health*. Chicago, IL: University of Chicago Press.

Howitt, D. (1991) *Concerning Psychology: Psychology Applied to Social Issues*. Milton Keynes: Open University Press.

Levinger, G. and Clark, J. (1961) Emotional factors in the forgetting of word association. *Journal of Abnormal and Social Psychology*, 62, 99–105.

Lindsay, R.C.L. and Wells, G.L. (1985) Improving eyewitness identifications from lineups: Simultaneous versus sequential lineup presentation. *Journal of Applied Psychology*, 70, 556–64.

Loftus, E.F. and Burns, H.J. (1982) Mental shock can produce retrograde amnesia. *Memory and Cognition*, 10, 318–23.

Loftus, E.F. and Palmer, J.C. (1974) Reconstruction of automobile destruction: An example of the interaction between language and memory. *Journal of Verbal Learning and Verbal Behaviour*, 13, 585–9.

Loftus, E.F. and Zanni, G. (1975) Eyewitness testimony: The influence of the wording of a question. *Bulletin of the Psychonomic Society*, 5, 86–8.

Loftus, E.F., Loftus, G.R. and Messo, J. (1987) Some facts about 'weapon focus'. *Law and Human Behaviour*, 11, 55–62.

Loftus, E.F., Feldman, J. and Dashiell, R. (1995) The reality of illusory memories. In D.L. Schachter (ed.), *Memory Distortion*. Cambridge, MA: Harvard University Press.

Malmquist, C.P. (1986) Children who witness parental murder: Posttraumatic aspects. *Journal of the American Academy of Child Psychiatry*, 25, 320–5.

Malone, D.R., Morris, H.H., Kay, M.C. and Levin, H.S. (1982) Prosopagnosia: A double dissociation between the recognition of familiar and unfamiliar faces. *Journal of Neurology, Neurosurgery and Psychiatry*, 45, 820–2.

Malpass, R.S. and Devine, P.G. (1981) Guided Memory in eyewitness identification. *Journal of Applied Psychology*, 66, 343–50.

Mazzoni, G.A., Loftus, E.L., Seitz, A. and Lynn, S.J. (1999) Changing beliefs and memories through dream interpretation. *Applied Cognitive Psychology*, 13, 125–44.

Pezdek, K., Finger, C. and Hodge, C. (1997) The suggestibility of children's memory for being touched: Planting, erasing and changing memories. *Law and Human Behaviour*, 21(1), 95–106.

Pike, G., Kemp, R., Brace, N. *et al.* (2000) The effectiveness of video identification parades. *Proceedings of the British Psychological Society*, 8(1), 44.

Sadr, J., Jasudi, I. and Sincha, P. (2003) The role of eyebrows in face recognition. *Perception*, 32(3), 285–93.

Sergent, J. (1984) An investigation into component and configurational processes underlying face recognition. *British Journal of Psychology*, 75, 221–42.

Shepherd, J.W., Davies, G.M. and Ellis, H.D. (1981) Studies of cue saliency. In G. Davies, H. Ellis and J. Shepherd (eds), *Perceiving and Remembering Faces*. London: Academic Press.

Steblay, N.M. (1997) Social influence in eyewitness recall: A meta-analysis review of line-up instruction effects. *Law and Human Behaviour*, 21, 283–98.

Steblay, N.M., Dysart, J., Fulero, S. and Lindsay, R.C.L. (2001) Eyewitness accuracy rates in sequential and simultaneous line-up presentations: A meta-analytic comparison. *Law and Human Behaviour*, 25, 459–74.

Talarico, J.M. and Rubin, D.C. (2003) Confidence not consistency, characterizes flashbulb memories. *Psychological Science*, 14, 455–61.

Valentine, T., Pickering, A. and Darling, S. (2003) Characteristics of eyewitness identification that predict the outcome of real line-ups. *Applied Cognitive Psychology*, 17, 969–93.

Wells, G.L. and Olson, E.A. (2003) Eyewitness testimony. *Annual Review of Psychology*, 54, 277–95.

Williams, L.M. (1994) Recall of childhood trauma: a prospective study of women's memories of child sexual abuse. *Journal of Consulting and Clinical Psychology*, 62, 1167–76.

Winningham, R.G., Hyman, I.E. and Dinnel, D.L. (2000) Flashbulb memories? The effects of when the initial memory report was obtained. *Memory*, 8, 209–16.

Yin, R.K. (1969) Looking at upside-down faces. *Journal of Experimental Psychology*, 81, 141–5.

Young, A. and Hay, D. (1986) Configural information in face perception. In V. Bruce (1988) *Recognising Faces*. London: Lawrence Erlbaum Associates.

Young, A., Hay, D. and Ellis, A.W. (1985) The faces that launched a thousand slips: Everyday difficulties and errors in recognising people. *British Journal of Psychology*, 76, 495–523.

Yuille, J.C. and Cutshall, J.L. (1986) A case-study of eye-witness memory of a crime. *Journal of Applied Psychology*, 71, 291–301.

Yuillc, J.C. and Tollestrup, P.A. (1990) A model of the diverse effects of emotion on eyewitness memory. In S.A. Christianson (ed.), *The Handbook of Emotion and Memory: Research and Theory*. Hillsdale, NJ: Lawrence Erlbaum Associates.

Chapter 5 Schizophrenia and mood disorders

Abramson, L.Y., Seligman, M.E.P. and Teasdale, J.D. (1978) Learned helplessness in humans: Critique and reformulation. *Journal of Abnormal Psychology*, 87, 49–74.

Abramson, L.Y., Alloy, L.B. and Metalsky, G.I. (1989) Hopelessness depression: A theory-based sub-type of depression. *Psychological Review*, 96, 358–72.

Alloy, L.B. and Abramson, L.Y. (1979) Judgement of contingency in depressed and non-depressed students: Sadder but wiser? *Journal of Experimental Psychology: General*, 108, 441–85.

American Psychiatric Association (1994) *Diagnostic and Statistical Manual of Mental Disorders*, 4th edn. Washington, DC: American Psychiatric Association.

Andreasen, N.C., Arndt, S., Alliger, R. *et al.* (1995) Symptoms of schizophrenia: Methods, meanings and mechanisms. *Archives of General Psychiatry*, 5(2), 341–51.

Bateson, G., Jackson, D.D., Haley, J. and Weakland, J. (1956) Toward a history of schizophrenia. *Behavioural Science*, 1, 251–64.

Bebbington, P. and Kuipers, L. (1994) The predictive utility of expressed emotion in schizophrenia: An aggregate analysis. *Psychological Medicine*, 24, 707–18.

Beck, A.T. (1967) *Depression: Clinical, Experimental and Theoretical Aspects*. New York: Harper & Row.

Beck, A.T. (1976) *Cognitive Therapy and the Emotional Disorders*. New York: International University Press.

Bentall, R.P. (1990) The syndromes and symptoms of psychosis: Or why you can't play 'twenty questions' with the concept of schizophrenia and hope to win. In R.P. Bentall (ed.), *Reconstructing Schizophrenia*. London: Routledge.

Bentall, R.P., Kaney, S. and Dewey, M.E. (1991) Persecutory delusions: An attribution theory analysis. *British Journal of Clinical Psychology*, 30, 13–23.

Birchwood, M.Y. and Spencer, E. (1999) Psychotherapies for schizophrenia: A review. In M. Maj and N. Sartorious (eds), *Schizophrenia*. Chichester: Wiley.

Bleuler, E. (1911) *Dementia Praecox or the Group of Schizophrenias* (J. Avikin, trans.). New York: International University Press.

Brown, G.W., Carstairs, G.M. and Topping, G.C. (1958) The post hospital adjustment of chronic mental patients. *Lancet*, ii, 685–9.

Chadwick, P., Birchwood, M. and Trower, P. (1996) *Cognitive Therapy for Delusions, Voices and Paranoia*. Chichester: John Wiley and Sons.

Close, H. and Garety, P.A. (1998) Cognitive assessment of voices: Further developments in understanding the emotional impact of voices. *British Journal of Clinical Psychology*, 37, 173–88.

Coffey, C.E., Wildinson, W.E., Weiner, R.D. *et al.* (1993) Quantitative cerebral anatomy in depression: A controlled magnetic resonance imaging study. *Archives of General Psychiatry*, 50, 7–16.

Cole, D.A., Martin, J.M., Powers, B. and Truglio, R. (1990) Modeling causal relations between academic and social competence and depression. A multi-trait multimethod longitudinal study of children. *Journal of Abnormal Psychology*, 105, 258–70.

Damasio, A.R. (2000) A neural basis for sociopathy. *Archives of General Psychiatry*, 57, 128–9.

Devanand, D.P., Dwork, A.J., Hutchinson, E.R. *et al.* (1994) Does ECT alter brain structure? *American Journal of Psychiatry*, 151, 957–70.

Drury, V., Birchwood, M.J., Cochrane, R. *et al.* (1996) Cognitive therapy and recovery from acute psychosis: A controlled trial II. Impact on recovery time. *British Journal of Psychiatry*, 169, 602–7.

Egeland, J.A., Gerhard, D.S., Pauls, D.L. *et al.* (1987) Bipolar affective disorders linked to DNA markers on chromosome 11. *Nature*, 325, 783–7.

Elkin, I., Parloff, M.B., Hadley, S.W. and Autry, J.H. (1985) National Institute of Mental Health treatment of depression collaborative research program. *Archives of General Psychiatry*, 42, 305–16.

Eysenck, M.W. and Keene, M.T. (2000) *Cognitive Psychology: A Student's Handbook*. Hove: Psychology Press.

Ferster, C.B. (1974) Behavioural approaches to depression. In R.J. Friedman and M.M. Katz (eds), *The Psychology of Depression: Contemporary Theory and Research*. Washington, DC: Hemisphere.

Frank, E., Kupfer, D.J., Perel, J.M. *et al.* (1990) Three-year outcomes for maintenance therapies in recurrent depression. *Archives of General Psychiatry*, 47, 1093–9.

Gottesman, I.I. and Shields, J. (1982) *Schizophrenia: The Epigenetic Puzzle*. Cambridge: Cambridge University Press.

Halford, W.K. and Hayes, R.L. (1992) Social skills training with schizophrenic patients. In D.J. Kavanagh (ed.), *Schizophrenia: An Overview and Practical Handbook*. London: Chapman Hall.

Henrique, J.B. and Davidson, R.J. (1990) Regional brain electrical asymmetries discriminate between previously depressed and healthy control subjects. *Journal of Abnormal Psychology*, 99, 22–31.

Heston, L.L. (1966) Psychiatric disorders in foster home reared children of schizophrenic mothers. *British Journal of Psychiatry*, 1(22), 819–25.

Jernigan, T.L., Zisook, S., Heaton, R.K. *et al.* (1991) Magnetic resonance imaging abnormalities in lenticular nuclei and cerebral cortex in schizophrenia. *Archives of General Psychiatry*, 48, 881–90.

Kanter, J., Lamb, H.R. and Loeper, C. (1987) Expressed emotion in families: A critical review. *Hospital Community Psychiatry*, 38, 374–80.

Kavanagh, D.J. (1992) *Schizophrenia: An Overview and Practical Handbook*. London: Chapman and Hall.

Kelsoe, J.R., Ginns, E.I., Egeland, J.A. and Gerhard, D.S. (1989) Re-evaluation of the linkage relationship between chromosome 11 loci and the gene for bipolar disorder in the Old Order Amish. *Nature*, 342, 238–43.

Klerman, G.L. (1990) The psychiatric patient's right to effective treatment: Implications of Osheroff v. Chestnut Lodge. *American Journal of Psychiatry*, 147, 409–18.

Klerman, G.L., Weissman, M.M., Rounsaville, B.J. and Chevron, E. (1984) *Interpersonal Psychotherapy of Depression*. New York: Basic Books.

Kuipers, E., Garety, P., Fowler, D. *et al.* (1997) London East Anglia randomised controlled trial of cognitive-behavioural therapy for psychosis – 1. Effects of the treatment phase. *British Journal of Psychiatry*, 171, 319–27.

Leff, J., Wig, N.N., Ghosh, A. *et al.* (1990) Influence of relatives' expressed emotion on the course of schizophrenia in Chandigarh. *British Journal of Psychiatry*, 156, 166–73.

Lerer, B., Shapira, B., Calev, A. *et al.* (1995) Antidepressant and cognitive effects of twice-versus three-times weekly ECT. *American Journal of Psychiatry*, 152, 564–70.

Lewinsohn, P.M. and Gotlib, I.H. (1995) Behavioural theory and treatment of depression. In E.E. Beckham and W.R. Leber (eds), *Handbook of Depression*, 2nd edn, pp352–750. New York: Guilford.

Lewis, S.W. (1990) Computed tomography in schizophrenia fifteen years on. *British Journal of Psychiatry*, 157, (Suppl.9), 16–24.

Liddle, P.F. (1996) Functional imaging: Schizophrenia. *British Medical Bulletin*, 52, 486–94.

Lidz, T., Hotchkiss, G. and Greenblatt, M. (1957) Patient-family hospital interrelationships: Some general considerations. In M. Greenblatt, D.J. Levinson and R.H. Williams (eds), *The Patient and the Mental Hospital*. Glencoe, IL: Free Press.

Loebel, A.D., Lieberman, J.A., Alvir, J.M.J. *et al.* (1992) Duration of psychosis and outcome in first-episode schizophrenia. *American Journal of Psychiatry*, 149, 1183–8.

Lytton, H. (1977) Do parents create, or respond to, differences in twins? *Developmental Psychology*, 13, 456–9.

Maher, B.A. (1974) Delusional thinking and perceptual disorder. *Journal of Individual Psychology*, 30, 98–113.

Manschreck, T.C. (1979) The assessment of paranoid features. *Comprehensive Psychiatry*, 20, 370–7.

McGuffin, P., Katz, R., Watkins, S. and Rutherford, J. (1996) A hospital-based twin register of the heritability of DSM-IV unipolar depression. *Archives of General Psychiatry*, 53, 129–36.

Meltzer, H.Y. (1999) Risperidone and clozapine for treatment resistant schizophrenia. *American Journal of Psychiatry*, 156, 1126–7.

Nasrallah, H.A., Olson, S.C., McCalley-Whittlers, M. *et al.* (1986) Cerebral ventricular enlargement in schizophrenia: A preliminary follow-up study. *Archives of General Psychiatry*, 43, 157–9.

Nietzel, M.T. and Harris, M.J. (1990) Relationship of dependency and achievement/autonomy to depression. *Clinical Psychology Review*, 10, 279–97.

Nobler, M.S., Sackeim, H.A., Prohovnik, I. *et al.* (1994) Regional cerebral blood flow in mood disorders, III. *Archives of General Psychiatry*, 51, 884–97.

Onyett, S. (1992) *Case Management in Mental Health*. London: Chapman and Hall.

Paul, G.L. and Lentz, R.J. (1977) *Psychosocial Treatment of Chronic Mental Patients: Milieu versus Social Learning Programs*. Cambridge, MA: Harvard University Press.

Pearlson, G.D., Tune, L.E., Wong, D.F. *et al.* (1993) Quantitative D2 dopamine receptor PET and structural MRI changes in late onset schizophrenia. *Schizophrenia Bulletin*, 19, 783–95.

Raz, S. and Raz, N. (1990) Structural brain abnormalities in the major psychoses: A quantitative review of the evidence from computerised imagery. *Psychological Bulletin*, 108, 93–108.

Robinson, L., Berman, J. and Neimeyer, R. (1990) Psychotherapy for the treatment of depression: A comprehensive review of controlled outcome research. *Psychological Bulletin*, 108, 30–49.

Rosenhan, D.L. (1973) On being sane in insane places. *Science*, 179, 250–8.

Scheff, T.J. (1966) *Being Mentally Ill: A Sociological Theory*. Chicago, IL: Aldine Press.

Seeman, P., Hong-Chang, G. and Van Tol, H.H.M. (1993) Dopamine D4 receptors elevated in schizophrenia. *Nature*, 365, 441–5.

Seligman, M.E.P. (1974) Depression and learned helplessness. In R.J. Friedman and M.M. Katz (eds), *The Psychology of Depression: Contemporary Theory and Research*. Washington, DC: Hemisphere.

Shepherd, G. (1977) Social skills training: The generalization problem. *Behaviour Therapy*, 8, 1008–9.

Slade, P.D. and Bentall, R.P. (1988) *Sensory Deceptions: A Scientific Analysis of Hallucination*. Baltimore, MD: Johns Hopkins University Press.

Stein, C.J. and Test, M.A. (1980) Alternative to mental hospital treatment: A conceptual model treatment program and clinical evaluation. *Archives of General Psychiatry*, 37, 392–7.

Strauss, J.S. (1969) Hallucinations and delusions as points on continuum functions. *Archives of General Psychiatry*, 21, 581–6.

Suddath, R.L., Christison, G.W., Torrey, E.F. *et al.* (1990) Anatomical abnormalities in the brains of monozygotic twins discordant for schizophrenia. *New England Journal of Medicine*, 322, 789–94.

Suppes, T., Baldessarini, R.J., Faedda, G.L. and Tohen, M. (1991) Risk of recurrence following discontinuation of lithium treatment in bipolar disorder. *Archives of General Psychiatry*, 48, 1082–7.

Syal, R. (1997) Doctors find pick-me-up for SAD people. *Sunday Times*, 19 January, 4.

Szasz, T. (1979) *Schizophrenia: The Sacred Symbol of Psychiatry*. Oxford: Oxford University Press.

Tarrier, N. (1987) An investigation of residual psychotic symptoms in discharged schizophrenic patients. *British Journal of Clinical Psychology*, 26, 141–3.

Tarrier, N., Beckett, R., Harwood, S. *et al*. (1993) A trial of two cognitive behavioural methods of treating drug-resistant residual psychotic symptoms in schizophrenic patients: 1. Outcome. *British Journal of Psychiatry*, 162, 524–32.

Thase, M.E. and Kupfer, D.J. (1996) Recent developments in the pharmacotherapy of mood disorders. *Journal of Consulting and Clinical Psychology*, 64, 646–59.

Wakefield, J.C. (1992) The concept of mental disorder. *American Psychologist*, 47, 373–88.

Warner, R. (1994) *Recovery from Schizophrenia: Psychiatry and Political Economy*. London: Routledge.

Watts, F.N., Powell, E.G. and Austin, S.V. (1973) The modification of abnormal beliefs. *British Journal of Medical Psychology*, 46, 359–63.

Weiner, R.D. and Coffey, C.E. (1988) Indications for use of electroconvulsive therapy. In A. Frances and R. Hales (eds), *Review of Psychiatry*, Vol. 7, 458–81.

Weissman, M.M. and Klerman, G.L. (1990) Interpersonal psychotherapy for depression. In B.B. Wolman and G. Stricker (eds), *Depressive Disorders: Facts, Theories and Treatment Methods*, pp379–95. New York: Wiley.

Weissman, M.M., Leaf, P. and Bruce, M.L. (1987) Single parent women: A community study. *Social Psychiatry*, 22, 29–36.

Whittell, G. (1995) Spectacular northern lights linked to suicidal depression. *The Times*, 15 April, 9.

Wing, J.K. (1992) Differential diagnosis of schizophrenia. In L.D. Kavanagh (ed.), *Schizophrenia: An Overview and Practical Handbook*. London: Chapman & Hall.

Wing, J.K. and Brown, G.W. (1970) *Institutionalism and Schizophrenia: A Comparative Study of Mental Hospitals, 1960–68*. Cambridge: Cambridge University Press.

Winokur, G., Coryell, W., Keller, M.B. *et al*. (1995) A family study of manic-depressive (bipolar 1) disease: Is it a distinct illness separable from primary unipolar depression? *Archives of General Psychiatry*, 52, 367–73.

Wirz-Justice, A., Graw, P., Krauchi, K. *et al*. (1993) Light therapy in seasonal affective disorder is independent of time of day or circadian phase. *Archives of General Psychiatry*, 50, 929–37.

World Health Organization (1973) *The International Pilot Study of Schizophrenia*. Geneva. WHO.

World Health Organization (1992) *The ICD-10 Classification of Mental and Behavioural Disorders: Clinical Descriptors and Diagnosis Guidelines*. Geneva: WHO.

Zimbardo, P.G., Anderson, S.M. and Kabat, L.G. (1981) Induced hearing deficit generates experimental paranoia. *Science*, 212, 1529–31.

Chapter 6 Stress and stress management

Antoni, H.M. (1987) Neuroendocrine influences in psychoimmunology and neoplasia. A review. *Psychology and Health*, 1, 3–24.

Arnkoff, D.B. and Glass, C.R. (1982) Cited in D. Dwyer and J. Scampion (1995) *Work Out Psychology*. Hants: MacMillan Press Ltd.

Atkinson, R.L., Atkinson, R.C., Smith, E.E. and Bem, D.J. (1993) *Introduction to Psychology*, 11th edn. Orlando, FL: Harcourt Brace.

Banyard, P. (1996) *Applying Psychology to Health*. London: Hodder and Stoughton.

Baum, A. (1990) Stress, intrusive imagery, and chronic distress. *Health Psychology*, 9, 653–75.

Baum, A., Grunberg, N.E. and Singer, J.E. (1982) The use of physiological and neuroendocrinological measurements in the study of stress. *Health Psychology*, 1, 217–36.

Billings, A.G. and Moos, R.H. (1981) The role of coping responses and social resources in attenuating the stress of life events. *Journal of Behavioural Medicine*, 4, 139–57.

Billings, A.G. and Moos, R.H. (1984) Coping, stress and social resources among adults with unipolar depression. *Journal of Personality and Social Psychology*, 46, 887–91.

Blaney, P.H. and Ganellen, R.J. (1990) Hardiness and social support. In B.R. Sarason, I.G. Sarason and G.R. Pierce (eds), *Social Support: An Interactional View*. New York: Wiley.

Brown, G.W. (1974) Meaning, measurement and stress of life events. In B.S. Dohrenwend and B.P. Dohrenwend (eds), *Stressful Life Events: Their Nature and Effects*. London: John Wiley.

Brown, J. (1991) Staying fit and staying well: Physical fitness as a moderator of life stress. *Journal of Personality and Social Psychology*, 60, 555–61.

Budzynski, T.H., Stoyva, J.M., Adler, C.S. and Mulanney, D.J. (1973) EMG biofeedback and tension headache: A controlled outcome study. *Psychosomatic Medicine*, 35, 484–96.

Byrne, D. (1961) The repression–sensitization scale: Rationale, reliability and validity. *Journal of Personality*, 29, 334–49.

Byrne, D. (1964) Repression–sensitization as a dimension of personality. In B.A. Maher (ed.), *Progress in Experimental Personality Research*. San Diego, CA: Academic Press.

Cannon, W.B. (1929) *Bodily Changes in Pain, Hunger, Fear and Rage*, 2nd edn. New York: Appleton.

Carver, C.S., Diamond, E.L. and Humphries, C. (1985) Coronary prone behaviour. In N. Schneiderman and J.T. Tapp (eds), *Behavioural Medicine: The Biopsychosocial Approach*. Hillsdale, NJ: Erlbaum.

Ciaranello, R.D. (1983) Neurochemical aspects of stress. In N. Garmezy and M. Rutter (eds), *Stress, Coping and Development in Children*. New York: McGraw-Hill.

Cohen, F. and Lazarus, R.S. (1979) Coping with the stresses of illness. In G.C. Stone, F. Cohen and N.E. Adler (eds), *Health Psychology: A Handbook*. San Francisco, CA: Jossey-Bass.

Cohen, S., Tyrrell, D.A.J. and Smith, A.P. (1991) Psychological stress and susceptibility to the common cold. *New England Journal of Medicine*, 325, 606–12.

Constable, J.F. and Russell, E.W. (1986) The effect of social support and the work environment upon burnout among nurses. *Journal of Human Stress*, 12, 20–6.

Cooper, C. and Faragher, B. (1993) Psychological stress and breast cancer: The interrelationship between stress events, coping strategies and personality. *Psychological Medicine*, 3, 653–62.

Cottington, E.M. and House, J.S. (1987) Occupational stress and health: A multivariate relationship. In A. Baum and J.E. Singer (eds), *Handbook of Psychology and Health*, Vol. 5. Hillsdale, NJ: Erlbaum.

Cutrona, C.E. and Russell, D.W. (1990) Type of social support and specific stress: Toward a theory of optimal matching. In B.A. Sarason, I.G. Sarason and G.R. Pierce (eds), *Social Support: An Interactional View*. New York: Wiley.

DeLongis, A., Coyne, J.C., Dakof, G. *et al.* (1982) Relationship of daily hassles, uplifts, and major life events to health status. *Health Psychology*, 1, 119–36.

DiGuiseppe, R.A. and Miller, N.J. (1977) A review of outcome studies on rational-emotive therapy. In A. Ellis and R. Grieger (eds), *Handbook of Rational-Emotive Therapy*. New York: Springer.

Ellis, A. (1962) *Reason and Emotion in Psychotherapy*. New York: Lyle Stuart.

Field, T., Alpert, B., Vega-Lahr, N. *et al.* (1988) Hospitalisation stress in children: Sensitizer and repressor coping styles. *Health Psychology*, 7, 433–45.

Fleming, R., Baum, A., Gisriel, M.M. and Gatchel, R.J. (1982) Mediating influences of social support on stress at Three Mile Island. *Journal of Human Stress*, 8, 14–22.

Folkman, S., Lazarus, R.S., Dunkel-Schetter, C. *et al.* (1986) Dynamics of a stressful encounter: cognitive appraisal, coping, and encounter outcomes. *Journal of Personality and Social Psychology*, 50, 992–1003.

Forshaw, M. (2003) *Advanced Psychology: Health Psychology*. Abingdon: Hodder & Stoughton.

Frankenhaeuser, M. (1975) Sympathetic adrenomedullary activity behaviour and the psychosocial environment. In P.H. Venables and M.J. Christie (eds), *Research in Psychophysiology*. New York: Wiley.

Friedman, M. and Rosenman, R.H. (1974) *Type A Behaviour and Your Heart*. New York: Knopf.

Gatchel, R.J. (1980) Effectiveness of two procedures for reducing dental fear: Group-administered desensitisation and group education and discussion. *Journal of the American Dental Association*, 101, 634–8.

Gentry, W.D. and Kobasa, S.C.O. (1984) Social and psychological resources mediating stress–illness relationships in humans. In W.D. Gentry (ed.), *Handbook of Behavioural Medicine*. New York: Guildford.

Glass, D.C. and Singer, J.E. (1972) *Urban Stress: Experiments on Noise and Social Stressors*. New York: Academic Press.

Goldstein, I.B., Jamner, L.D. and Shapiro, D. (1992) Ambulatory blood pressure and heart rate in healthy male paramedics during a workday and a nonworkday. *Health Psychology*, 11, 48–54.

Greer, S. and Morris, T. (1975) Psychological attributes of women who develop breast cancer: A controlled study. *Journal of Psychosomatic Research*, 19, 147–53.

Hatch, J.P., Gatchel, R.J. and Harrington, R. (1982) Biofeedback: Clinical applications in medicine. In R.J. Gatchel, A. Baum and J.E. Singer (eds), *Handbook of Psychology and Health*, Vol. 1. Hillsdale, NJ: Erlbaum.

Hobfoll, S.E. (1989) Conservation of resources: A new attempt at conceptualizing stress. *American Psychologist*, 44, 513–24.

Holahan, C.J. and Moos, R.H. (1986) Personality, coping, and family resources in stress resistance: A longitudinal analysis. *Journal of Personality and Social Psychology*, 51, 389–95.

Holmes, T.H. and Rahe, R.H. (1967) The Social Readjustment Rating Scale. *Journal of Psychosomatic Research*, 11, 213–18.

Jensen, M.R. (1987) Psychobiological factors predicting the course of breast cancer. *Journal of Personality*, 55, 317–42.

Jex, S.M. and Beehr, T.A. (1991) Emerging theoretical and methodological issues in the study of work-related stress. In G.R. Ferris and K.W. Rowland (eds), *Research in Personnel and Human Resources Management*, Vol. 9. Greenwich, CT: JAI Press.

Johnson, J.H. (1986) *Life Events as Stressors in Childhood and Adolescence*. Newbury Park, CA: Sage.

Kanner, A.D., Coynes, J.C., Schaefer, C. and Lazarus, R.S. (1981) Comparison of two modes of stress measurement: Daily hassles and uplifts versus major life events. *Journal of Behavioural Medicine*, 4, 1–39.

Kessler, R.C., Kendler, K.S., Heath A.C. *et al.* (1992) Social support, depressed mood, and adjustment to stress: A genetic epidemiological investigation. *Journal of Personality and Social Psychology*, 62, 257–72.

Kiecolt-Glaser, J.K., Fisher, L.D., Ogrocki, P. *et al.* (1987) Marital quality, marital disruption and immune function. *Psychosomatic Medicine*, 49, 13–34.

Kiecolt-Glaser, J.K., Marucha, P.T., Malarkey, W.B. *et al.* (1995) Slowing of wound healing by psychological stress. *The Lancet*, 346, 1194–6.

Kobasa, S.C. (1979) Stressful life events, personality and health: An inquiry into hardiness. *Journal of Personality and Social Psychology*, 37, 1–11.

Krantz, D.S., Durel, L.A., Davia, J.E. *et al.* (1982) Propranolol medication among coronary patients: relationship to Type A behaviour and cardiovascular response. *Journal of Human Stress*, 8, 4–12.

La Rocco, J.M., House, J.S. and French, J.R.P. (1980) Social support, occupational stress, and health. *Journal of Health and Social Behaviour*, 21, 202–18.

Lazarus, A.A. (1971) *Behaviour Therapy and Beyond*. New York: McGraw-Hill.

Lazarus, R.S. (1990) Theory-based stress measurement. *Psychological Inquiry*, 1, 3–13.

Lazarus, R.S. and Folkman, S. (1984) *Stress, Appraisal and Coping*. New York: Springer.

Levy, S.M. (1985) Behaviour and Cancer. San Francisco, CA: Jossey-Bass.

Lovallo, W.R. (1997) *Stress and Health: Biological and Psychological Interactions*. Thousand Oaks, CA: London; New Delhi: Sage Publications.

Lynch, J.J. (1990) The broken heart: The psychobiology of human contact. In R. Ornstein and C. Swencionis (eds), *The Healing Brain: A Scientific Reader*. New York: Guilford.

Maddi, S.R. and Khoshaba, D.M. (2005) Resilience at Work: How to Succeed No Matter What Life Throws at You. Amacom.

Marmot, M., Bosma, H., Hemingway, H., Brunner, E. and Stansfield, S. (1997) Contribution of job control and other risk factors to social variation in health disease incidence. *The Lancet*, 350, 235–9.

Mason, J.W. (1975) A historical view of the stress field. *Journal of Human Stress*, 1, 22–36.

McCann, I.L. and Holmes, D.S. (1984) Influence of aerobic exercise on depression. *Journal of Personality and Social Psychology*, 46, 1142–7.

McGrath, J.E. and Beehr, T.A. (1990) Time and the stress process: Some temporal issues in the conceptualization and measurement of stress. *Stress Medicine*, 6, 93–104.

Meichenbaum, D. (1977) *Cognitive-behaviour Modification: An Integrative Approach*. New York: Plenum Press.

Melamed, B.G., Dearborn, M. and Hermecz, D.A. (1983) Necessary conditions for surgery preparation: Age and previous experience. *Psychosomatic Medicine*, 45, 517–25.

Meyerowitz, B.E. (1983) Postmastectomy coping strategies and quality of life. *Health Psychology*, 2, 117–32.

Miller, N.E. and DiCara, L.V. (1968) Instrumental learning of systolic blood pressure responses by curarized rats. *Psychosomatic Medicine*, 39, 489–94.

Myers, D.G. (1998) *Psychology*. 5th edn. New York: Worth.

Myers, L.B. (2000) Identifying repressors: A methodological issue for health psychology. *Psychology and Health*, 5, 205–14.

Nezu, A.M., Nezu, C.M. and Perri, M.G. (1989) *Problem-solving Therapy for Depression: Theory, Research, and Clinical Guidelines*. New York: Wiley.

Niaura, R., Herbert, P.N., McMahon, N. and Sommerville, L. (1992) Repressive coping and blood lipids in men and women. *Psychosomatic Medicine*, 54, 698–706.

O'Leary, A. (1990) Stress, emotion and human immune function. *Psychological Bulletin*, 108, 363–82.

Patterson, C.H. (1986) *Theories of Counseling and Psychotherapy*, 4th edn. New York: Harper and Row.

Polani, P.E., Briggs, J.N., Ford, C.E. *et al.* (1960) A mongol girl with 46 chromosomes. *The Lancet*, 1, 721–4.

Ragland, D.R. and Brand, R.J. (1988) Type A behaviour and mortality from coronary heart disease. *New England Journal of Medicine*, 318, 65–9.

Rahe, R.H. (1974) The pathway between subjects' recent life changes and their near-future illness reports: Representative results and methodological issues. In B.S. Dohrenwend and B.P. Dohrenwend (eds.), *Stressful Life Events: Their Nature and Effects*. New York: Wiley.

Rahe, R.H. and Arthur, R.J. (1978) Life change and illness studies: Past history and future directions. *Journal of Human Stress*, 4, 3–15.

Roberts, L. (1988) Beyond Noah's ark: What do we need to know? *Science*, 242, 1247.

Rodin, J. (1986) Aging and health: Effects of the sense of control. *Science*, 233, 1271–6.

Roth, S. and Cohen, L.J. (1986) Approach, avoidance, and coping with stress. *American Psychologist*, 41, 813–19.

Rotter, J.B. (1966) Generalised expectancies for the internal versus external control of reinforcement. *Psychological Monographs*, 90(1), 1–28.

Sarafino, E.P. (1994) *Health Psychology*, 2nd edn. New York: John Wiley and Sons.

Sarason, I.G., Sarason, B.R., Potter, E.H. and Antoni, M.H. (1985) Life events, social support, and illness. *Psychosomatic Medicine*, 47, 156–63.

Savickas, M.L. (1995) Work and adjustment. In D. Wedding (ed.), *Behaviour and Medicine*, 2nd edn. St Louis, MO: Mosby-Year Book.

Schaubroeck (2001) In *AS-Level Psychology: The Revision Guide*. (AQA A, 2003). CGP Ltd.

Selye, H. (1956) *The Stress of Life*. New York: McGraw-Hill.

Selye, H. (1974) *Stress without Distress*. Philadelphia: Lippincott.

Stone, G.C., Cohen, F. and Adler, N.E. (eds) (1979) *Health Psychology – A Handbook: Theories, Applications and Challenges of a Psychological Approach to the Health Care System*. San Francisco, CA: Jossey-Bass.

Stroebe, W. (2000) *Social Psychology and Health*, 2nd edn. Buckingham: Open University Press.

Suls, J. and Fletcher, B. (1985) The relative efficacy of avoidant and nonavoidant coping strategies: A meta-analysis. *Health Psychology*, 4, 249–88.

Suls, J. and Mullen, B. (1981) Life change and psychological distress. The role of perceived control and desirability. *Journal of Applied Social Psychology*, 11, 379–89.

Sweeney, K. (1995) Stay calm and heal better. *The Times*, 21 December.

Tarler-Benlolo, L. (1978) The role of relaxation in biofeedback training. *Psychological Bulletin*, 85, 727–55.

Temoshok, L. (1987) Personality, coping style, emotions and cancer: Towards an integrative model. *Cancer Surveys*, 6, 545–67 (supplement).

Thayer, R.E. (1987) Energy, tiredness, and tension effects of a sugar snack versus moderate exercise. *Journal of Personality and Social Psychology*, 52, 119–25.

Thayer, R.E. (1993) Mood and behaviour (smoking and sugar snacking) following moderate exercise: A partial test of self-regulation theory. *Personality and Individual Differences*, 14, 97–104.

Uchino, B.N., Cacioppo, J.T. and Kielcolt-Glaser, J.K. (1996) The relationship between social support and physiological processes. A review with emphasis on underlying mechanisms and implications for health. *Psychological Bulletin*, 119, 488–531.

Waxler-Morrison, N., Hislop, T.G., Mears, B. and Can, I. (1991) The effects of social relationships on survival for women with breast cancer: A prospective study. *Social Science and Medicine*, 3, 177–83.

Weinberger, D.A., Schwartz, G.E. and Davidson, R.J. (1979) Low anxious, high anxious and repressive coping styles: Psychometric patterns and behavioural responses to stress. *Journal of Abnormal Psychology*, 88, 369–80.

Weinman, J. (1995) Health psychology. In A.M. Colman (ed.), *Controversies in Psychology*. London: Longman.

Weiss, J.M. (1972) Psychological factors in stress and disease. *Scientific American*, 226, 104–13.

Zeigler, S.G., Klinzing, J. and Williamson, K. (1982) The effects of two stress management programs on cardiorespiratory efficiency. *Journal of Sport Psychology*, 4, 280–9.

Chapter 7 Substance abuse

Abraham, C., Southby, L., Quandte, S., Krahe, B. and Van Der Sluijs, W. (2007) What's in a leaflet? Identifying research-based persuasive messages in European alcohol-education leaflets. *Psychology and Health*, 22, 31–60.

Ajzen, I. and Fishbein, M. (1980) *Understanding Attitudes and Predicting Social Behavior*. Englewood Cliffs, NJ: Prentice-Hall.

Asch, S.E. (1951) Effects of group pressure upon the modification and distortion of judgment. In H. Guetzkow (ed.), *Groups, Leadership and Men*. Pittsburgh, PA: Carnegie Press.

Bandura, A. (1994) Self-efficacy. In V.S. Ramachaudran (ed.), *Encyclopedia of Human Behavior*, Vol. 4, 71–81. New York: Academic Press.

Bandura, A. and Walters, R.H. (1963) *Social Learning and Personality Development*. New York: Holt, Rinehart, and Winston.

Barrett, R.J. and Sachs, L.B. (1974) Treatment of smoking by covert sensitization. *Psychological Reports*, 26, 415–20.

Berzins, J.I., Ross, W.F., English, G.E. and Haley, J.V. (1974) Subgroups among opiate addicts: A typological investigation. *Journal of Abnormal Psychology*, 83, 65–73.

Brandsma, J.M., Maultsby, M.C. Jr and Welsh, R.J. (1980) *Outpatient Treatment of Alcoholism: A Review and Comparative Study*. Baltimore, MD: University Park Press.

Bricker, J.B., Peterson, A.V. Jr, Sarason, I.G. *et al.* (2006) Prospective prediction of children's smoking transitions: Role of parents' and older siblings' smoking. *Addiction*, 101(1), 128–36.

Brook, J.S., Kessler, R.C. and Cohen, C. (1999) The onset of marijuana use from preadolescence and early adolescence to young adulthood. *Development and Psychopathology*, 11, 901–14.

Brown, A. (2006) Smoking, drinking and drug use among young people in England in 2006. *Drug Education Forum*, UK: NHS.

Cautela, J.R. (1970) Cited in Cautela, J.R. and Baron, M.G. (1977) Covert conditioning: A theoretical analysis. *Behaviour Modification*, 1, 351–68.

Cautela, J.R. and Baron, M.G. (1977) Covert conditioning: A theoretical analysis. *Behaviour Modification*, 1, 351–68.

Cloninger, C.R. (1987) Neurogenetic adaptive mechanisms in alcoholism. *Science*, 236, 410–16.

Coggans, N., Shewan, D., Henderson, M. and Davies, J.B. (1991) *National Evaluation of Drug Education in Scotland: ISDD Research Monograph Four*. UK: Institute for the Study of Drug Dependence.

Cuijpers, P., Jonkers, R., de Weerdt, I. and de Jong, A. (2002) The effects of drug abuse prevention at school: the 'Healthy School and Drugs' project. *Addiction*, 97, 67–73.

Cuijpers, P., Scholten, M. and Conijn, B. (2006) *Addiction: An Overview*. Den Haag: ZonMw.

Elkins, R.L. (1991) An appraisal of chemical aversion (emetic therapy) approaches to alcoholism treatment. *Behaviour Research and Therapy*, 29(5), 387–413.

Ennett, S.T., Tobler, N.S., Ringwalt, C.L. and Flewelling, R.L. (1994) How effective is drug abuse resistance education? A meta-analysis of Project DARE outcome evaluations. *American Journal of Public Health*, 84, 1394–401.

Fabrega, H., Ulich, R., Pilkonis, P. and Mezzich, J. (1991) On the homogeneity of personality disorder clusters. *Comprehensive Psychiatry*, 32(5), 373–86.

Festinger, L. (1957) *A Theory of Cognitive Dissonance*. Stanford, CA: Stanford University Press.

Fielding, J.E. (1990) The challenges of work-place health promotion. In S.Weiss, J.E. Fielding and A. Baum (eds), *Perspectives in Behavioural Medicine: Health at Work*. Hillsdale, NJ: Erlbaum.

Flay, B. (1985) Psychosocial approaches to smoking prevention: a review of findings. *Health Psychology*, 4(5), 449–88.

Garnier, H.E. and Stein, J.A. (2002) An 18-year model of family and peer effects on adolescent drug use and delinquency. *Journal of Youth and Adolescence*, 31(1), 45–56.

Gordon, R. (1987) An operational classification of disease prevention. In J. Steinberg and M. Silverman (eds), *Preventing Mental Disorders: A Research Perspective*, pp20–26. (DHHS Publication no. ADM 87-1492) Rockville, MD: Alcohol, Drug Abuse and Mental Health Administration.

Heather, N., Raistrick, D. and Godfrey, C. (2007) *A Summary of the Review of the Effectiveness of Treatment for Alcohol Problems*. UK: National Treatment Agency for Substance Misuse.

Helzer, J.E., Canino, G.J., Yeh, E.K. *et al*. (1990) Alcoholism–North America and Asia. *Archives of General Psychiatry*, 47, 313–19.

Hovland, C.I., Janis, I.L. and Kelley, H.H. (1953) *Communications and Persuasion: Psychological Studies in Opinion Change*. New Haven, CT: Yale University Press.

Hser, Y.-I., Grella, C.E., Hubbard, R.L. *et al*. (2002) An evaluation of drug treatment for adolescents in four U.S. cities. *Archives of General Psychiatry* 58(7), 689–95.

Insko, C.A., Arkoff, A. and Insko, V. (1965) Effects of high and low fear-arousing communications upon opinions towards smoking. *Journal of Experimental Social Psychology*, 1, 256–66.

Janis, I. and Feshbach, S. (1953) Effects of fear-arousing communications. *Journal of Abnormal and Social Psychology*, 48, 78–92.

Janis, I.L. and Terwilliger, R.F. (1962) An experimental study of psychological resistance to fear-arousing communications. *Journal of Abnormal Social Psychology*, 65, 403–10.

Kuhn, M.H. (1960) Self attitudes by age, sex, and professional training. *Sociological Quarterly*, 1, 39–55.

Kumpfer, K.L., Williams, M.K. and Baxley, G. (1997) *Selective Prevention for Children of Substance Abusing Parents: The Strengthening Families Program, Resource Manual*. Silver Spring, MD: National Institute on Drug Abuse, Technology Transfer Program.

McGue, M., Pickens, R.W. and Svikis, D.S. (1992) Sex and age effects on the inheritance of alcohol problems: A twin study. *Journal of Abnormal Psychology*, 101(1), 3–17.

McGuire, W.J. (1968) The nature of attitudes and attitude change. In G. Lindzey, and E. Aronson, (eds), *Handbook of Social Psychology*, Vol. 1, pp136–314. Reading, MA: Addison-Wesley.

Merikangas, K.R. and Avenevoli, S. (2000) Implications of genetic epidemiology for the prevention of substance use disorders. *Addictive Behaviour*, 25: 807–20.

Meyer, V. and Chesser, E.S. (1970) *Behaviour Therapy in Clinical Psychiatry*. Oxford: Penguin.

Morgenstern, J., Langenbucher, J., Labouvie, E. and Miller, K.J. (1997) The comorbidity of alcoholism and personality disorders in a clinical population: Prevalence and relation to alcohol typology variables. *Journal of Abnormal Psychology*, 106(1), 74–84.

National Treatment Agency for Substance Misuse (2002) *Models of Care for Treatment of Adult Drug Misusers*, Part 2. NTA: London.

Olsen *et al*. (1981) Cited in www.psychpage.com/problems/library/alcohol.html.

Perkins, H.W., Haines, M. and Rice, R. (2005) Misperceiving the college drinking norm and related problems: A nationwide study of exposure to prevention information, perceived norms and student alcohol misuse. *Journal of Studies on Alcohol*, 66, 470–8.

Prochaska, J.O., DiClemente, C.C. and Norcross, J.C. (1992) In search of how people change: Applications to addictive behaviours. *American Psychologist*, 47, 1102–14.

Reed, M.D. and Rountree, P.W. (1997) Peer pressure and adolescent substance abuse. *Journal of Quantitative Criminology*, 13(2), 143–80.

Robson, P. (1994) *Forbidden Drugs*. Oxford: Oxford University Press.

Rosenstock, I.M. (1966) Why people use health services. *Millbank Memorial Fund Quarterly*, 44, 94–124.

Schuckit, M.A. (1985) Genetics and the risk for alcoholism. *Journal of the American Medical Association*, 254, 2614–17.

Schuckit, M.A. (1998) *Educating Yourself about Alcohol and Drugs. A People's Primer*. Reading, MA: Perseus Books.

Siegel, S. (1988) Drug anticipation and drug tolerance. In M. Lader (ed.), *The Psychopharmacology of Addiction*. Oxford: Oxford University Press.

Siegel, S., Hinson, R.E., Krank, M.D. and McCully, J. (1982) Heroin 'overdose' death: Contribution of drug associated environmental cues. *Science*, 216, 436–7.

Smith, J.W. (1988) Long-term outcome of clients treated in a commercial stop smoking program. *Journal of Substance Abuse Treatment*, 5, 33–6.

Smith, J.W. and Frawley, P.J. (1993) Treatment outcome of 600 chemically dependent patients treated in a multimodal inpatient program including aversion therapy and pentothal interviews. *Journal of Substance Abuse Treatment*, 10, 359–69.

Sutton, S.R. (1982) Fear-arousing communications: A critical examination of theory and research. In J.R. Eiser (ed.), *Social Psychology and Behavioural Medicine*, pp303–37. Chichester: John Wiley.

Telch, M.J., Hannon, R. and Telch, C.F. (1984) A comparison of cessation strategies for the outpatient alcoholic. *Addictive Behaviour*, 9, 103–9.

Tobler, N.S., Lessard, T., Marshall, D. *et al*. (1999) Effectiveness of school-based drug prevention programs for marijuana use. *School Psychology International*, 20(1), 105–37.

White, H.R., Johnson, V. and Buyske, S. (2000) Parental modeling and parenting behavior effects on offspring alcohol and cigarette use. A growth curve analysis. *Journal of Substance Abuse*, 12(3), 287–310.

Witte, K. (1992) Putting the fear back into fear appeals: The extended parallel process model. *Communication Monographs*, 59, 329–49.

Chapter 8 Forensic psychology

Aiken, T.W., Stumphauzer, J.S. and Veloz, E.V. (1977) Behavioural analysis of non-delinquent brothers in a high juvenile crime community. *Behavioural Disorders*, 2, 221–2.

Ainsworth, P.B. (2000) *Psychology and Crime: Myths and Reality*. Harlow: Longman.

Alison, L.J. and Barrett, E.C. (2004) The interpretation and utilisation of offender profiles: A critical review of 'traditional' approaches to profiling. In J. Adler (ed.), *Forensic Psychology: Concepts, Debates and Practice*. Cullompton: Willan Publishing.

Alison, L.J., West, A. and Morgan, K. (2003) Interpreting the accuracy of offender profiles. *Psychology, Crime and Law*, 9(2), 185–95.

Ayllon, T. and Azrin, N.H. (1968) Reinforcer sampling: A technique for increasing the behaviour of mental patients. *Journal of Applied Behavioural Analysis*, 1(1), 13–20.

Ayllon, T. and Millan, M.A. (1979) *Correctional Rehabilitation and Management: A Psychological Approach*. New York: Wiley.

Bandura, A. (1986) *Social Foundations of Thought and Action*. Englewood Cliffs, NJ: Prentice-Hall.

Bandura, A., Ross, S.A. and Ross, D. (1963) Imitation of film-mediated aggressive models. *Journal of Abnormal Psychology*, 66(1), 3–11.

Bartol, C.R. (1995) *Criminal Behaviour: A Psychosocial Approach*, 4th edn. London: Prentice-Hall International (UK) Ltd.

Bowlby, J. (1946) *Forty-Four Juvenile Thieves*. London: Bailliere, Tindall and Cox.

Bukshel, L.H. and Kilmann, P.R. (1980) Psychological effects of imprisonment on confined individuals. *Psychological Bulletin*, 88, 469–93.

Campbell, C. (1976) Portrait of a mass killer. *Psychology Today*, 9, 110–19.

Canter, D. (1994) *Criminal Shadows*. London: HarperCollins.

Canter, D. (2004) *Mapping Murder: The Secrets of Geographical Profiling*. London: Virgin Books.

Christiansen, K.O. (1977) *A Review of Criminality among Twins. Biosocial Bases of Criminal Behaviour*. New York: Gardner Press.

Copson, G. (1995) Coals to Newcastle? *Police Research Group Special Interest Papers*: Paper 7. London: Home Office.

Cortes, J.B. and Gatti, F.M. (1972) *Delinquency and Crime: A Biopsychosocial Approach*. New York: Seminal Press.

Crowe, R.R. (1972) The adopted offspring of women criminal offenders. *Archives of General Psychiatry*, 27, 600–3.

Dalgaard, O.S. and Kringlen, E. (1976) A Norwegian twin study of criminality. *British Journal of Clinical Psychology*, 16, 213–32.

Davies, G.L. and Raymond, K.M. (2000) Do current sentencing practices work? *Criminal Law Journal*, 24, 236–47.

Eysenck, H.J. (1977) *Crime and Personality*, 2nd edn. London: Routledge and Kegan Paul.

Farrington, D.P., Biron, L. and LeBlanc, M. (1982) Personality and delinquency in London and Montreal. In J. Gunn and D.P. Farrington (eds), *Abnormal Offenders, Delinquency and the Criminal Justice System*. Chichester: Wiley.

Feindler, E.L., Marriott, S.A. and Iweta, M. (1984) Group anger control training for junior high school delinquents. *Cognitive Therapy and Research*, 8, 299–311.

Glaser, D. (1983) Supervising offenders outside of prison. In J.Q. Wilson (ed.), *Crime and Public Policy*. San Francisco, CA: ICS Press.

Goldstein, J.H. (1986) *Aggression and Crimes of Violence*, 2nd edn. Oxford: Oxford University Press.

Goring, C. (1913/1972) *The English Convict: A Statistical Study*. Montclaire, NJ: Patterson Smith.

Hazelwood, R.R. (1987) Analysing the rape and profiling of the offender. In R.R. Hazelwood and A.W. Burgess (eds), *Practical Aspects of Rape Investigation: A Multidisciplinary Approach*. New York: Elsevier.

Hobbs, T.R. and Holt, M.M. (1976) The effects of token reinforcement on the behaviour of delinquents in cottage settings. *Journal of Applied Behaviour Analysis*, 9, 189–98.

Hoffman, M.L. (1977) Moral internalisation: Current theory and research. In L. Berkowitz (ed.), *Advances in Experimental Social Psychology*, Vol.10. New York: Academic Press.

Hollin, C. (1989) *Psychology and Crime: An Introduction to Criminological Psychology*. London and New York: Routledge.

Hollin, C. (1999) Crime and Crime Prevention. In D. Messer and F. Jones (eds), *Psychology and Social Care*. London: Jessica Kingsley.

Hutchings, B. and Mednick, S.A. (1975) Registered criminality in the adoptive and biological parents of registered male criminal adoptees. In R.R. Fieve, D. Rosenthal and H. Brill (eds), *Genetic Research in Psychiatry*. Baltimore, MD: Johns Hopkins University Press.

Lange, J. (1929) Verbrechen als Schicksal: Studien an Kriminallen Zwillingen. Leipzig: Georg Thieme Verlag, p96. English translation by C. Haldane in Lange, J. (1931) *Crime as Destiny: A Study of Criminal Twins*, pp143–5, 154–60. London: Allen and Unwin.

Law, K. (1997) Further evaluation of anger management courses at HMP Wakefield: An examination of behavioural change. *Inside Psychology: The Journal of Prison Service Psychology*, 3(1), 91–5.

Lombroso, C. (1876) *L'Uomo delinquent*. Milan, Italy: Torin.

Piliavin, I. and Briar, S. (1964) Police encounters with juveniles. *American Journal of Sociology*, 70, 206–14.

Rice, M.E., Quinsey, V.L. and Houghton, R. (1990) Predicting treatment outcome and recidivism among patients in a maximum security token economy. *Behavioural Sciences and the Law*, 8, 313–26.

Rose, D. (2006) Crime rates soar as criminals walk free. *The Observer*, 28 May.

Schafer, S. (1976) *An Introduction to Criminology*. New York: McGraw-Hill.

Sheldon, W.H., Hart, E.M. and McDermott, E. (1949) *Varieties of Delinquent Youth: An Introduction to Constitutional Psychiatry*. New York: Harper.

Statistics Commission (2006) *Crime Statistics: User Perspectives*. Report no.30 (available at www.statscom.org.uk).

Stott, D. (1982) *Delinquency: The Problem and its Prevention*. London: Batsford.

Sutherland, E.H. (1939) *Principles of Criminology*. Philadelphia: Lippincott.

Sutherland, E.H. (1951) Critique of Sheldon's varieties of delinquent youth. *American Sociological Review*, 16, 10–13.

Walker, N. and Farrington, D.P. (1981) Reconviction rates of adult males after different sentences. *British Journal of Criminology*, 21, 357–60.

Zimbardo, P.G. (1971) The power and pathology of imprisonment. *Congressional Record*. (Serial No. 15, 1971-10-25). Hearings before Subcommittee No 3 of the Committee on the Judiciary, House of Representatives, Ninety-second Congress, First session on Corrections, Part II, Prisons, Prison Reform and Prisoner's Rights: California. Washington, DC: US Government Printing Office.

Zuckerman, M. (1969) Variables affecting deprivation results. In J.P. Zubek (ed.), *Sensory Deprivation: Fifteen Years of Research*. New York: Appleton-Century-Crofts.

Chapter 9 Approaches in psychology

Allyon, J. and Azrin, N. (1968) *The Token Economy*. New York: Appleton-Century-Crofts.

Ashfield, L. (2000) Psychoanalysis: Unscientific and outdated or misunderstood? *Psychology Review*, February, 20–2.

Bandura, A. (1965) Influence of model's reinforcement contingencies on the acquisition of imitation responses. *Journal of Personality and Social Psychology*, 1, 589–95.

Bandura, A. (1973) *Aggression: A Social Learning Analysis*. Englewood Cliffs, NJ: Prentice Hall.

Bandura, A. (1977a) Self-efficacy: Toward a unifying theory of behavioural change. *Psychological Review*, 84, 191–215.

Bandura, A. (1977b) *Social Learning Theory*. New York: General Learning Press.

Bandura, A., Ross, D. and Ross, S.A. (1961) Transmission of aggression through imitation of aggressive models. *Journal of Abnormal and Social Psychology*, 63, 575–82.

Bandura, A., Ross, D. and Ross, S.A. (1963) Imitation of film-mediated aggressive models. *Journal of Abnormal and Social Psychology*, 66, 3–11.

Billig, M. (1999) *Freudian Repression: Conversation Creating the Unconscious*. Cambridge: Cambridge University Press.

Clark, D.M. (1989) Anxiety states: Panic and generalized anxiety. In K. Hawton *et al*. (eds), *Cognitive Behavioural Therapy for Psychiatric Problems: A Practical Guide*. Oxford: Oxford University Press.

Clark, D.M., Salkovskis, P.M., Hackmann, A. *et al*. (1994) A comparison of cognitive therapy, applied relaxation and imipramine in the treatment of panic disorder. *British Journal of Psychiatry*, 164, 759–69.

Colsey, J. and Hatton, A. (1994) Changing behaviours. *Nursing Times*, 28 September, 64–5.

Crick, F. (1994) *The Astonishing Hypothesis: The Scientific Search for the Soul*. London: Simon and Schuster.

Cumberbatch, W.G. (1992) Is television violence harmful? In D. Carroll and R. Cochrane (eds), *Psychology and Social Issues*. London: Falmer Press.

Dawkins, R. (1976) *The Selfish Gene*. Oxford: Oxford University Press.

Denno, D. (2006) Revisiting the legal link between genetics and crime. *Law and Contemporary Problems*, 69, 209–57.

Dodge, K. (1986) A social information processing model of social competence in children. In M. Perlmutter (ed.), *The Minnesota Symposium of Child Psychology*, Vol. 18. Hillsdale, NJ: Erlbaum.

Dowling, H. (1994) *Horizon: The Man Who Made Up His Mind*. London: BBC/Broadcasting Support Services.

Erikson, J.M. (1997) *The Life Cycle Completed: A Review*. New York: Norton.

Eysenck, H.J. (1985) *Decline and Fall of the Freudian Empire*. Harmondsworth: Viking.

Eysenck, M.W. and Flanagan, C. (2001) *Psychology for A2 Level*. Hove: Psychology Press.

Heather, N. (1976) *Radical Perspectives in Psychology*. London: Methuen.

James, A. (2000) Behaviour therapy from hell. *Asylum*, 12(2), 8–9.

Kandel, E.R. and Squire, L.R. (2000) Neuroscience: Breaking down scientific barriers to the study of brain and mind. *Science*, 10/11, 1113–19.

Laland, K. and Brown, G. (2002) *Sense and Nonsense*. Oxford: Oxford University Press.

Littleton, K., Toates, F. and Braisby, N. (2002) Three approaches to learning. In D. Miell, A. Phoenix and K. Thomas (eds), *Mapping Psychology 1*. Milton Keynes: Open University.

Maslow, A.H. (1973) *The Farther Reaches of Human Nature*. Harmondsworth: Penguin.

Maslow, A.H. (1987) *Motivation and Personality*, 3rd edn. New York: Harper and Row.

Medin, D.L., Ross, B.H. and Markman, A.D. (2001) *Cognitive Psychology*, 3rd edn. Fort Worth, TX: Harcourt.

Mischel, W. (1973) Toward a cognitive social learning reconceptualization of personality. *Psychological Review*, 80, 253–83.

Overmeier, J.B. and Seligman, M.E.P. (1967) Effects of inescapable shock upon subsequent escape and avoidance responding. *Journal of Comparative Physiology and Psychology*, 63, 28–33.

Pavlov, I. (1927) *Conditioned Reflexes: An Investigation of the Physiological Activity of the Cerebral Cortex*. London: Oxford University Press.

Phoenix, A. and Thomas, K. (2002) Psychology in the 21st century. In D. Miell, A. Phoenix and K. Thomas (eds), *Mapping Psychology 1*. Milton Keynes: Open University.

Popper, K. (1959) *The Logic of Scientific Discovery*. London: Hutchinson.

Reason, J. (2000) The Freudian slip revisited. *Psychologist*, 13(12), 610–11.

Reicher, S. and Taylor, S. (2005) Similarities and differences between tradition. *Psychologist*, 18(9), 547–9.

Rogers, C.R. and Skinner, B.F. (1956) Some issues concerning the control of human behaviour: A symposium. *Science*, 30/11, 1057–66.

Rose, H. and Rose, S. (eds) (2000) *Alas Poor Darwin: Arguments Against Evolutionary Psychology*. London: Jonathan Cape.

Skinner, B.F. (1953) *Science and Human Behaviour*. New York: Macmillan.

Skinner, B.F. (1966) *Walden Two*. New York: Macmillan.

Skinner, B.F. (1971) *Beyond Freedom and Dignity*. New York: Knopf.

Stevens, R. (1996a) Trimodal theory as a model for interrelating perspectives in psychology. In R. Sapsford (ed.), *Issues for Social Psychology*. Milton Keynes: Open University.

Stevens, R. (1996b) Ten ways of distinguishing between theories in social psychology. In R. Sapsford (ed.), *Issues for Social Psychology*. Milton Keynes: Open University.

Stevens, R. (2002) Person psychology: Psychoanalytic and humanistic perspectives. In D. Miell, A. Phoenix and K. Thomas (eds), *Mapping Psychology 2*. Milton Keynes: Open University.

Thomas, K. (1996) The defensive self: A psychodynamic perspective. In R. Stevens (ed.), *Understanding the Self*. London: Sage.

Thorndike, E. (1898) Animal intelligence. An experimental study of the associative processes in animals. *Psychological Review Monograph Supplement*, 2, 1–109.

Toates, F. (1996) The embodied self: a biological perspective. In R. Stevens (ed.), *Understanding the Self*. London: Sage.

Tolman, E.C. (1932) *Purposive Behaviour in Animals and Men*. New York: The Century Co.

Watson, J.B. (1913) Psychology as the behaviourist views it. *Psychological Review*, 20, 158–77.

Watson, J.B. (1924) *Behaviourism*. New York: Norton.

Watson, J.B. and Rayner, R. (1920) Conditioned emotional reactions. *Journal of Experimental Psychology*, 3(1), 1–14.

Winnicott, D.W. (1947) Further thoughts on babies as persons. In D.W. Winnicott (ed.) (1964), *The Child, The Family and The Outside World*. Harmondsworth: Penguin.

Wood, J. (1990) Good Freud guide. *Guardian Weekend*, 25 August, 4–6, 41.

Chapter 10 Debates in psychology

Alexander, B.K., Coambs, R.B. and Hadaway, P.F. (1978) The effect of housing and gender on morphine self–administration in rats. *Psychopharmacology*, 58, 175–9.

Allport, G.W. (1937) *Personality: A Psychological Interpretation*. New York: Holt.

Anastasi, A. (1958) In R.M. Lerner (1986) *Concepts and Theories of Human Development*, 2nd edn. New York: Random House.

Asch, S. (1955) Opinions and social pressure. *Scientific American*, 193(5), 31–5.

Bell, A. (2002) *Debates in Psychology*. Hove: Routledge.

Belsky, J. and Rovine, M. (1987) Temperament and attachment security in the Strange Situation: A rapprochement. *Child Development*, 58, 787–95.

Blakemore, C. (1988) *The Mind Machine*. London: BBC Publications.

Blakemore, C. and Cooper, C.R. (1970) The development of the brain depends on the visual environment. *Nature*, 228, 477–8.

Bouchard, T.J. and McGue, M. (1981) Familial studies of intelligence: A review. *Science*, 212, 1055–9.

Brehm, J.W. (1966) *A Theory of Psychological Reactance*. New York: Academic Press.

Cohen, G. (1977) *The Psychology of Cognition*. London: Academic Press.

Dukes, W.F. (1965) 'N=1'. *Psychological Bulletin*, 64(1), 74–9.

Elder, G.H. Jr (1974) *Children of the Great Depression*. Chicago, IL: University of Chicago Press.

Erlenmeyer-Kimling, L. and Jarvik, L.F. (1963) Genetics and intelligence: A Review. *Science*, 142, 1477–9.

Eysenck, H.J. (1951) The organisation of personality. *Journal of Personality*, 20, 101–17.

Flanagan, C. (2002) Nature and Nurture: Why are siblings so different? *Psychology Review*, Feb. Philip Allan Updates.

Freud, S. (1900/1976) *The Interpretation of Dreams*, Pelican Freud Library (5). Harmondsworth: Penguin.

Freud, S. (1909/1977) *Analysis of a Phobia in a Five-year-old Boy*, Pelican Freud Library (8). Harmondsworth; Penguin.

Fromm, E. (1942) *The Fear of Freedom*. London: RKP.

Gale, A. (1979) *Psychophysiology: A Bridge between Disciplines*. Inaugural Lecture, University of Southampton.

Heisenberg, W. (1927) Uber den anschaulichen Inhalt der quantentheoretischen Kinematik und Mechanik.

Zeitschrift fur Physik, 43, 172–98. English translation: J.A. Wheeler and W.H. Zurek, (1983) *Quantum Theory and Measurement*, pp62–84. Princeton, NJ: Princeton University Press.

James, W. (1890) *The Principles of Psychology*. New York: Henry Holt and Company.

Jones, K.L., Smith, D.W., Ulleland, C.N. and Streissguth, A. (1973) Pattern of malformation in offspring of chronic alcoholic mothers. *Lancet*, 1, 1267–71.

Kluckhohn, C. and Murray, H.A. (1953) Personality formation: the determinants. In C. Kluckhohn, H.A. Murray and D.M. Schneider (eds), *Personality in Nature, Society, and Culture*, 2nd edn. New York: Knopf.

Kohler, W. (1925) *The Mentality of Apes*. New York: Harcourt Brace.

Koluchova, J. (1972) Severe deprivation in twins: A case study. *Journal of Child Psychology and Psychiatry*, 13, 107–14.

Kuhn, T.S. (1962) *The Structure of Scientific Revolutions*. Chicago, IL: University of Chicago Press.

Kuhn, T.S. (1970) *The Structure of Scientific Revolutions*, 2nd edn. Chicago, IL: Chicago University Press.

Laing, R.D. and Esterton, A. (1970 edition) *Sanity, Madness and the Family*. London: Penguin [1990].

Lerner, R.M. (1986) *Concepts and Theories of Human Development*, 2nd edn. New York: Random House.

Libet, B. (1985) Unconscious cerebral initiative and the role of conscious will in voluntary action. *Behavioural and Brain Sciences*, 8, 529–66.

Loftus, E.F. and Palmer, J.C. (1974) Reconstruction of automobile destruction: An example of the interaction between language and memory. *Journal of Verbal Learning and Verbal Behaviour*, 13, 585–9.

Matson (1971) Cited in D. Dwyer and J. Scampion (1995) *A level Psychology*. Basingstoke; London: MacMillan.

Meyer-Bahlburg, H.F.L., Ehrhardt, A.A., Rosen, L.R. and Gruen, R.S. (1995) Prenatal estrogens and the development of homosexual orientation. *Development Psychology*, 31(1), 12–21.

Milgram, S. (1963) Behavioural study of obedience. *Journal of Abnormal and Social Psychology*, 67, 371–8.

Morea, P. (1990) *Personality: An Introduction to the Theories of Psychology.* Harmondsworth: Penguin.

Ora, J.P. (1965) Characteristics of the volunteer for psychological investigation. Office of Naval Research, Contract 2149(03), *Technical Report 27*.

Orne, M.T. and Evans, F.J. (1965) Social control in the psychological experiment: Anti social behaviour and hypnosis. *Journal of Personality and Social Psychology*, 51, 189–200.

Palermo, D.S. (1971) Is scientific revolution taking place in psychology? *Psychological Review*, 241–63.

Piaget, J. (1953) *The Origin of Intelligence in the Child*. London: Routledge and Kegan Paul.

Plomin, R. (1988) The nature and nurture of cognitive abilities. In R.J. Sternberg (ed.), *Advances in the Psychology of Human Intelligence*, Vol. 4. Hillsdale, NJ: Erlbaum.

Plomin, R. (1994) *Genetics and Experience: The Interplay between Nature and Nurture*. Thousand Oaks, CA: Sage.

Plomin, R. and Bergman, C.S. (1991) The nature of nurture: genetic influence on 'environmental' measures. *Behavioural and Brain Sciences*, 14, 373–427.

Plomin, R., DeFries, J.C. and Loehlin, J.C. (1977) Genotype-environment interaction and correlation in the analysis of human behaviour. *Psychological Bulletin*, 84, 309–22.

Popper, K.R. (1959) *The Logic of Scientific Discovery*. London: Hutchinson.

Popper, K.R. (1972) *Objective Knowledge: An Evolutionary Approach*. Oxford: Oxford University Press.

Radford, J. and Kirby, R. (1975) *The Person in Psychology*. London: Methuen.

Reber, A.S. and Reber, E.S. (2001) *The Penguin Dictionary of Psychology*, 3rd edn. London; New York: Penguin.

Rose, S. (1976) *The Conscious Brain*. Harmondsworth: Penguin.

Rosenthal, R. (1969) Interpersonal expectations: Effects of experimenter's hypothesis. In R. Rosenthal and R.L. Rosnow (eds), *Artefacts in Behavioural Research*. New York: Academic Press.

Rosenthal, R. and Jacobson, I. (1968) *Pygmalion in the Classroom: Teacher Expectations and Pupils' Intellectual Development*. New York: Holt, Rinehart, and Winston.

Rotter, J. (1966) Generalised expectancies for internal versus external control of reinforcement. *Psychological Monographs*, 30(1), 1–26.

Sachs, D. (1991) In fairness to Freud: A critical notice of the foundations of psychoanalysis, by Adolf Grunbaum. In J. Neu (ed.), *The Cambridge Companion to Freud*. Cambridge: Cambridge University Press.

Schuckit, M.A. (1985) Genetics and the risk for alcoholism. *Journal of the American Medical Association*, 254, 2614–17.

Seligman, M.E. (1974) Depression and learned helplessness. In R.J. Freedom and M.M. Katz (eds), *The Psychology of Depression*. Washington, DC: V.H.Winston.

Shields, J. (1978) Genetics. In J.K. Wing (ed.), *Schizophrenia–Towards a New Synthesis*. London: Academic Press.

Smith, S.M., Brown, H.O., Toman, J.E.P. and Goodman, L.S. (1947) Lack of cerebral effects of D–tubocurarine. *Anaesthesiology*, 8, 1–14.

Tavris, C. and Wade, C. (1995) *Psychology in Perspective*. New York: Harper Collins.

Watson, J.B. (1913) Psychology as the Behaviorist views it. *Psychological Review*, 20, 158–77.

Werner, E.E. (1979) *Cross-cultural Child Development: A View from Planet Earth*. Monterey, CA: Brooks/Cole.

Index

Entries in **bold** are key terms